Foreign Relations

of the

United States

Diplomatic Papers

1938

(In Five Volumes)

Volume III

The Far East

United States
Government Printing Office
Washington : 1954

DEPARTMENT OF STATE PUBLICATION 5672

———

For sale by the
Superintendent of Documents, U.S. Government Printing Office
Washington 25, D.C. - Price $3.50 (Buckram)

CONTENTS

CONTENTS

UNDECLARED WAR BETWEEN JAPAN AND CHINA [1]

POLITICAL AND MILITARY DEVELOPMENTS

CHAPTER I: JANUARY 1–31, 1938

Japanese terms in China presented through German channels; occupation of Tsingtao by Japanese (January 10); Ambassador Grew's decision against delivery of proposed warning to Japan at time of Imperial Conference in Tokyo (January 14); importance of foreign military supplies in prolonging Chinese resistance; Japanese rupture of exchange of tentative terms with China (January 16); President Roosevelt's reply to General Chiang Kai-shek (January 19); reduction of American and British military establishments in China

793.94/11936 : Telegram

The Ambassador in China (Johnson) to the Secretary of State

HANKOW, January 1, 1938—10 p. m.
[Received January 1—9 : 15 p. m.]

1. My 128, December 31, 4 [2] p. m.[2]

1. Following is text of terms which Dr. Hsu Mo [3] handed me in confidence this morning stating that they were communicated to the Chinese Government by the German Ambassador [4] under instructions from his Government. Dr. Hsu Mo [said?] these terms were handed to the German Ambassador at Tokyo on December 23 by the Japanese Minister for Foreign Affairs.[5]

2. "Basic Conditions.

1st. China to abandon her pro-communist policy as well as her anti-Japanese and anti-Manchukuo policy and to cooperate with Japan and Manchukuo in the execution of their anti-communist policies.

2d. Demilitarized zones to be established and special regimes set up in necessary areas.

3d. Agreements for close economic cooperation to be concluded between Japan, Manchukuo and China.

4th. China to make necessary indemnification to Japan".

3. Dr. Hsu Mo stated that instructions had been cabled to Chinese Ambassadors at Paris, Washington, London and Moscow to communicate these terms to those Governments. He stated he had not yet heard whether C. T. Wang [6] had acted. He volunteered informa-

---

[1] Continued from *Foreign Relations*, 1937, vols. III and IV; for additional correspondence, see *Foreign Relations, Japan*, 1931–1941, vol. I, pp. 429 ff.
[2] *Foreign Relations*, 1937, vol. III, p. 847.
[3] Chinese Vice Minister for Foreign Affairs.
[4] Oskar Trautmann.
[5] Koki Hirota.
[6] Chinese Ambassador in the United States.

tion that Chinese Ambassador had an appointment with the President but he did not know whether it was for purpose of showing him these terms. He said he understood Secretary of State was ill.

4. He made the comment that terms were so general in scope that although they looked innocent, Japan, if China accepted, would be free to claim that most any demand it made was within the meaning of these terms and that China could not accept these terms as a basis of negotiation. He said that any person who had watched the actions of Japanese military leaders in China during the last few months would understand the purposes hidden behind the terms.

5. I made no comment other than to say that the wording of the terms looked to me as though it had been chosen for consumption in Europe and America to persuade the public as stated therein of the innocence of Japanese intention.

Sent to Shanghai [to] inform Commander-in-Chief;[7] Peiping transmit to Tokyo.

JOHNSON

793.94/11935 : Telegram

The Ambassador in China (Johnson) to the Secretary of State

HANKOW, January 2, 1938—10 a. m.
[Received January 2—4:10 a. m.]

2. My 1, January 1, 10 p. m. While Hsu Mo was with me, Gage, representative of British Embassy, came in and in my presence Hsu Mo handed to him copy of terms which he had given me. He said to Gage that he understood that Chinese Ambassador had seen Cadogan[8] who had remarked that China could of course not accept these terms. Hsu made same comments about terms to Gage that he had made to me.

In general conversation which followed, Gage remarked to Hsu Mo that this explained why German Ambassador had been depressed during the past few days. He said that German Ambassador had said to him yesterday "Why do you continue to encourage the Chinese to fight the Japanese" and Gage commented that of course no nation was encouraging the Chinese to fight the Japanese. Hsu said "The German Ambassador should urge the Japanese not to fight the Chinese".

After the departure of Hsu, Gage said to me that he had met German Ambassador at the house of the principal German military adviser Falkenhausen yesterday at which time question was asked. Gage stated that apparently the German Government was recalling

---

[7] Admiral Harry E. Yarnell of the United States Asiatic Fleet.
[8] Sir Alexander M. G. Cadogan, British Permanent Under Secretary of State for Foreign Affairs.

all of the German advisers. He said that adviser Krummacher said to him that he and Falkenhausen were remaining with the Chinese no matter what the German Government thought or did about it.

I dined at the house of a German friend last evening and found him much wrought up over a German illustrated paper which he had just received indicating that the press in Germany was propagating the thought that the Japanese were indeed fighting communism in China, using as evidence of this illustrations from Associated Press taken in Communist areas of northwest China by Edgar Snow. He stated to me that German Chamber of Commerce here in China had telegraphed home trying to counteract this propaganda by pointing out that Japan was driving the Chinese into the arms of Russia but without avail.

Shanghai inform Commander-in-Chief. Peiping repeat to Tokyo.

JOHNSON

793.94/11922 : Telegram

The Secretary of State to the Ambassador in China (Johnson)

WASHINGTON, January 3, 1938—7 p. m.

3. Your 128, December 31, 2 p. m.,[9] and your 1, January 1, 10 p. m. The Chinese Ambassador volunteered to me today statement that in his interview with the President, the President made no comment upon the Japanese peace terms.[10]

HULL

893.01 Provisional/18

The Department of State to the British Embassy

AIDE-MÉMOIRE

The Government of the United States appreciates the action of the British Embassy in communicating in its *aide-mémoire* of December 27, 1937,[11] the views of the French Government in regard to the desirability of maintaining diplomatic representation in Peiping and the decision of the British Government not to withdraw for the present their diplomatic staffs and Embassy guards from north China.

The Government of the United States has given attentive consideration to the importance attached by the British and French Governments to prior consultation before taking such a step and to the hope that the United States Government will agree that all three governments should concert together before any action is taken affecting their Embassies and Embassy guards in the event that this may be called

---

[9] *Foreign Relations*, 1937, vol. III, p. 847.
[10] See memorandum of January 3 by the Secretary of State, p. 519.
[11] *Foreign Relations*, 1937, vol. III, p. 839.

for by subsequent developments in north China. The Government of the United States in its *aide-mémoire* of December 18, 1937,[12] has already expressed its desire to continue to keep in close touch with the British Government in regard to these matters and is pleased to inform the British Embassy that this Government is likewise prepared to maintain close touch with the French Government. It is this Government's belief, however, that this expression of attitude and desire should be regarded as relating to exchange of information and consultation rather than as constituting an agreement to act or to refrain from action in concert.

WASHINGTON, January 4, 1938.

793.94/11969 : Telegram

The Chargé in Germany (Gilbert) to the Secretary of State

BERLIN, January 5, 1938—5 p. m.
[Received January 5—1 : 35 p. m.]

3. In a conversation today with the Chief of the Far Eastern Section of the Foreign Office respecting the recently announced changes in the Chinese Government, particularly as affecting Chiang Kai Shek,[13] he commented that Chinese internal affairs were most difficult of interpretation but that he felt that this change might have as a purpose the facilitating, with regard to the personalities involved, direct relations with Japan.

With reference to press accounts that Germany through the German Ambassador at Tokyo had made moves looking to act as mediator between the two parties, von Schmieden denied that any such action had been taken. He said that the German diplomatic representatives in China and Japan were naturally discussing with their colleagues and others the problem of the restoration of peace for which Germany was most anxious. It was evident, however, that for Germany to attempt to play the role of mediator before the time was auspicious for a successful issue would not only serve no useful purpose but would probably place Germany in a most difficult position vis-à-vis both parties.

GILBERT

---

[12] *Foreign Relations*, 1937, vol. III, p. 816.
[13] Generalissimo Chiang retired in favor of Dr. H. H. Kung as President of the Chinese Executive Yuan (Premier).

793.94/11975 : Telegram

The Ambassador in France (Bullitt) to the Secretary of State

PARIS, January 5, 1938—8 p. m.
[Received January 5—6 : 40 p. m.]

20. Leger [14] who in the absence of Delbos [15] is in charge of the Foreign Office stated to me today that it was the most ardent hope of the French Government that our Government might not become involved in war in the Far East. He added that he made this statement not for humanitarian reasons but because he felt certain that if we should become involved in war against Japan the British would be compelled to follow us and would be unable to act in Europe. This would mean that the position of France in Europe would be so greatly weakened that Germany and Italy would strike immediately. France would be left to defend her frontiers and her allies against the combined forces of Germany and Italy. That would be beyond her strength. He felt certain therefore that the involvement of the United States in war in the Far East would mean catastrophe for France and for Europe.

Leger added that he knew there were various forces in England which were doing their utmost by methods open and secret to persuade the United States to act against Japan. He said that he had discussed the possibilities of British action in the Far East at great length with various English statesmen and diplomats recently. He could assure me that there was not the slightest chance that England would go to war with Japan no matter what insults she might receive from Japan and no matter how serious might be Japanese aggression against her interests and possessions in the Far East. The British Government had no illusion that it could carry on a war successfully in Chinese and Japanese waters. A joint action in which the United States would carry the major portion of the burden would be quite another matter.

His latest information from Russia was that the Russian Government would continue supplying arms and munitions to Chiang Kai Shek but positively would not become involved in the war.

He believed that Chiang Kai Shek probably would retire into Szechuan and continue to fight but he was not sure that this was so. Chiang Kai Shek unquestionably desired to continue the war and to avoid negotiations but there were many other leaders in China who desired to enter into negotiations. The Chinese had consented to receive terms of peace from the hands of the German Ambassador in spite of the advanced warnings of the French Foreign Office as to the

---

[14] Secretary General of the French Foreign Office.
[15] French Minister for Foreign Affairs.

nature of the terms. This seemed to him to indicate that the will to continue fighting was not so strong in China as he would like to see it.

Leger was less pessimistic than Chautemps [16] with regard to the ultimate effects of Goga's appointment as Prime Minister of Rumania. He said that the King had said to the French Minister in Bucharest that the Prime Minister would have nothing to do either with foreign affairs or with military affairs. He, the King, would control Rumanian policy in both these fields and he would be entirely faithful to his friendship with France. Leger stated that General Avarescu, the new Rumanian Minister for War, had accepted the office only after pledges from the Prime Minister and the King that the policy of friendship with France should not be abandoned.

Finally, Leger stated that Goga himself had said to the French Minister that both foreign affairs and military affairs were not under his control but under the control of the King. Leger added that the military supplies which France had promised to Rumania would continue to be sent to Rumania; but would be delivered with an eye-dropper, very little at a time in return for good behavior.

Leger insisted that accord was now perfect between France and England with regard to the policies to be pursued vis-à-vis Germany and Italy. Chamberlain [17] was as convinced as the French Government that no acceptable agreement could be made with Mussolini [18] unless an agreement should have been made previously with Germany. The French and British Governments while continuing to rearm as fast as possible would therefore speak softly and amiably to Germany and ignore Italy.

BULLITT

793.94/11983 : Telegram

The Ambassador in France (Bullitt) to the Secretary of State

PARIS, January 6, 1938—6 p. m.
[Received January 6—3 : 15 p. m.]

25. In the course of conversation today Blum [19] said to me that he had authoritative information on the present point of view of the Soviet Government with regard to the Chinese-Japanese conflict. The Soviet Union would continue to assist China with supplies but would not enter the war unless either the United States or Great Britain should be drawn into war with Japan. He was certain that if Great Britain should be compelled to fight Japan the Soviet Union would make war on Japan at once.

---

[16] Camille Chautemps, President of the French Council of Ministers (Premier).
[17] Neville Chamberlain, British Prime Minister.
[18] Italian Prime Minister.
[19] Leon Blum, Vice President of the French Council of Ministers.

Blum said that he had read only a *précis* of Van Zeeland's report [20] but that there was enough in the *précis* to convince him that no progress could be made along the lines suggested by Van Zeeland. He felt certain that neither Germany nor Italy would stop its movement toward autarchy and he believed that any proposal which involved negotiations between England, France, Germany and Italy, even with the addition of the United States, smacked too much of the old Four Power Treaty to be acceptable to democratic opinion anywhere in Europe. He said that he would expect great opposition to this in Europe to say nothing of the opposition from Poland, the Soviet Union and Czechoslovakia.

BULLITT

893.102S/1595½

Memorandum by the Under Secretary of State (Welles) of a Conversation With the British Ambassador (Lindsay)

[WASHINGTON,] January 8, 1938.

The British Ambassador called to see me this morning. The Ambassador gave me first copies of some confidential information transmitted to him by his Government with regard to recent developments within Russia. I told the Ambassador I was most grateful for the information he thus gave me, although he said that he was afraid there was not much that we would find of value in it.

The Ambassador then said that he had just received a cable from his Foreign Office stating that the incident which occurred yesterday, involving the beating of four British police officers within the International Concession by Japanese soldiers, was regarded as extremely grave by the British Government. The Foreign Office had as yet received only preliminary information. If this preliminary information was confirmed, the British Government would probably find it necessary to do more than merely accept an apology from the Japanese Government. The British Government was considering "an announcement of the completion of naval preparations". I asked the Ambassador what interpretation was to be given to this phrase. He said that it was to be regarded as a step prior to mobilization and as implying that the British Navy was on a war-footing, save for the completion of naval complements, which latter was a step that would be undertaken solely as a result of mobilization. The British Ambassador desired to know whether in the event that such an announcement was made by the British Government, the Government of the United States would be prepared to make some similar gesture, which

---

[20] For correspondence concerning this subject, see *Foreign Relations*, 1937, vol. I, pp. 671 ff.

might, the Ambassador said, in the opinion of his Government be some move such as the announcement that certain units of the United States Navy were proceeding towards Hawaii in the course of naval maneuvers, or that certain units of the United States Navy were being moved from the Atlantic to the Pacific.

I replied to the Ambassador that the inquiry was one which could necessarily only be answered after the Secretary of State or I had consulted the President in the matter. The Ambassador said that he fully understood, but hoped that we could give him a reply the first days of next week.[21] He emphasized that the inquiry was, of course, a hypothetical question, contingent upon whether the British Government considered the incident in Shanghai as sufficiently serious to warrant such a move.

The Ambassador spoke in a general way about recent developments in Italy and said that he had learned from his Government that an agreement in principle had been reached between Count Ciano [22] and Lord Perth, the British Ambassador in Rome, whereby the broadcasting to the Near Eastern countries now being pursued both by the British and Italian Governments would be restricted solely to the announcement of factual news items with the elimination of inflammatory propaganda. The Ambassador said his Government felt that if this agreement was adhered to, the tension between Italy and Great Britain would be relieved to a very considerable extent.

S[UMNER] W[ELLES]

793.94/12027 : Telegram

The Ambassador in China (Johnson) to the Secretary of State

HANKOW, January 10, 1938—10 a. m.
[Received January 10—9 : 30 a. m.]

17. Following for War Department from Colonel Stilwell.[23]

"I returned Hankow January 9 from Changsha, Nanchang, Kiukiang. No peace talk anywhere in the area. Hunan Governor talks of 3 years' resistance, Kiangsi Governor same opinion. Training programs under way in Hunan and Kiangsi for roughly 1 million men in each province. Munitions and equipment admitted serious matter. Practically every Chinese soldier on guerilla warfare. Many units withdrawn to Nanchang, Hankow area for replacement. I believe there is little contact between opposing sides southwest of Nanking and that the front there has practically melted away".

Repeated to Peiping.

JOHNSON

---

[21] See memorandum of January 13, p. 19.
[22] Italian Minister for Foreign Affairs.
[23] Col. Joseph W. Stilwell, Military Attaché in China.

793.94/12030 : Telegram

The Consul at Tsingtao (Sokobin) to the Secretary of State

TSINGTAO, January 10, 1938—11 a. m.
[Received 11 : 10 a. m.]

The following memorandum was handed to the senior American naval officer this morning at 10 : 30 :

"Vice Admiral Soyemu Toyoda, the highest commanding officer of His Imperial Majesty's forces in Tsingtao District, has the honor of informing hereby the Senior Commanding Officer of the United States Navy in Tsingtao that Japanese naval landing forces are expected to enter the city today, January 10, and the public peace and order of the city will be wielded by Japanese forces thenceforth.

Regarding the protection of the third nation's lives and properties, he also has the honor of announcing herewith that he has fully instructed the forces under his command, as shown in the leaflets strewn from our airplanes this morning".

The Japanese boarding officer also verbally added that there would be no bombardment of the city, no shelling, no bombing, and no rifle fire unless provoked. He also added that 3,000 men would be landed tomorrow morning. Leaflet in Chinese language distributed from Japanese airplane reads as follows in translation:

"Urgent. Military Command.
1. The forces of the Japanese Empire have not [*now?*] come to take over Tsingtao. All principal organizations and institutions in the civic and rural districts of Tsingtao should as quickly as possible hoist white flags to indicate their willingness to submit. The hostile and the antagonistic will be subjected to attack.
2. As regards Chinese troops, police forces and other armed bodies, they shall make haste to assemble in the great harbor area and send delegates to the [local?] Japanese shrine for negotiations. Those who submit will be spared from attack while those who do not submit shall be exterminated.
3. Those of the general public who wish to cooperate with the Imperial Forces should send their district leaders or street elders to the Tsingtao Japanese shrine to indicate their sincerity in the matter".

White flags have already been hoisted on all Government buildings, Chinese now arranging delegation to meet Japanese.

All Americans are being asked to remain indoors for the time being and we are completely satisfied that no danger whatsoever exists for American persons or property. [24]

Sent to Peiping, Hankow.

SOKOBIN

---

[24] The Consul at 3 p. m. reported that the Japanese occupation of Tsingtao was proceeding without incident (793.94/12019).

893.51/6569 : Telegram

The Ambassador in Japan (Grew) to the Secretary of State

Токуо, January 10, 1938—2 p. m.
[Received January 10—8 : 45 a. m.]

17. In the course of my conversation on various subjects with the Minister for Foreign Affairs this morning he said that I might like to know of certain rumors and reports which had reached him.

1. He said that reports were circulating in Japan to the effect that certain American bankers, unspecified, are considering or have decided to advance credits to the Chinese Government to the extent of 150,000,000 gold dollars to help China pay her debts and to stabilize the Chinese currency and at the same time certain English bankers were considering similar action to the extent of 30,000,000 pounds. The Minister did not say whether he had definite confirmation of the accuracy of these rumors.

2. Hirota then turned to the question of peace negotiations with China and said that before the Brussels Conference he had suggested to the American, British, German and Italian Ambassadors that Chiang Kai Shek should take the initiative in approaching the Japanese Government for peace negotiations. About December 27 the German Ambassador in Tokyo had asked Hirota if he would state the Japanese peace terms which could be conveyed to Chiang Kai Shek through Ambassador Trautmann and that Hirota had then stated the Japanese terms as follows:

(1) Abandonment by China of all anti-Japan and anti-Manchukuo activities and cooperation with Japan for combating communism.
(2) The establishment of certain demilitarized zones.
(3) The settlement of Sino-Japanese economic relations.
(4) Indemnification for the results of the hostilities.

I asked the Minister if he would care to elaborate on these various points. He said that the demilitarized zones should be created in Inner Mongolia, North China and the district now occupied by Japanese forces south of the Yangtze River between Shanghai and Nanking. Inner Mongolia was to have an autonomous government under sovereignty of the Chinese Central Government. The regimes in the other demilitarized zones were to have a considerable degree of autonomous power but they also would be under Chinese sovereignty. As for an economic settlement this would include the development of China's natural resources and also a tariff agreement with Japan.

3. Hirota said he was aware that Kung had approached the American Government through Ambassador Wang to ask the American Government's advice with regard to the acceptance of these terms and also to request the mediation of President Roosevelt. Hirota

said that the Japanese Government had asked the Chinese Government for its reply to these terms about January 10th and that they were now awaiting a reply at any moment. Hirota said that he was telling me this merely because he thought I would like to be informed with regard to the situation.

4. The foregoing probably indicates the significance to be attached to reports published this morning in the papers that the Cabinet yesterday agreed on the principle that so long as "China manifests no desire to seek a settlement on a basis which will safeguard the peace of East Asia, Japan has no alternative but to resolve to face a war of endurance". It is reported also that various measures such as declaration of war and withdrawal of recognition of the Chinese Government were discussed but not agreed upon. The Cabinet will reportedly decide today whether the Emperor will be requested to call a special conference to consider what measures should be taken to implement the principle above described.

Repeated to Shanghai for Hankow.

GREW

793.94119/381

Memorandum of Conversation, by the Chief of the Division of Far Eastern Affairs (Hamilton)

[WASHINGTON,] January 10, 1938.

Participants: Mr. V. A. L. Mallet, Counselor of the British Embassy;
Mr. Hamilton;
Mr. Ballantine.[25]

Mr. Mallet, Counselor of the British Embassy, called at his request. He stated that according to a cable from the British Foreign Office the Japanese Minister for Foreign Affairs told Craigie [26] on January 6 that Chiang Kai-shek made an approach to the American Government in regard to the Japanese peace terms which had been communicated to the Chinese Government through the German Ambassador in China. Mr. Mallet inquired whether we could inform him of the facts.

Mr. Mallet was informed that this probably had reference to peace terms which had been communicated in confidence to our Ambassador at Hankow by the Chinese Vice Minister for Foreign Affairs, as reported in the Embassy's 1, January 1, 10 p. m. Mr. Mallet was also informed that on December 31 the Chinese Ambassador at Washington had informed the President of the Japanese peace terms and that the President had made no comment thereon. As the Chinese

[25] Joseph Ballantine, Assistant Chief, Division of Far Eastern Affairs.
[26] Sir Robert L. Craigie, British Ambassador in Japan.

had informed Ambassador Johnson that they considered the Japanese peace terms unacceptable this would appear to have ruled out any occasion for comment by our Ambassador on those terms.

Mr. Ballantine called up Mr. Mallet by telephone and stated that subsequent to Mr. Mallet's visit to the Department this morning a telegram had been received from our Embassy at Tokyo stating that the Ambassador had been informed by the Japanese Minister for Foreign Affairs that about December 27 the German Ambassador had asked Hirota if he would state the Japanese peace terms which could be conveyed to Chiang Kai-shek through Ambassador Trautmann, and that Hirota had then stated the Japanese peace terms which Hirota had repeated to our Ambassador and which were the same as those communicated to Ambassador Johnson by the Chinese Vice Minister for Foreign Affairs.

Mr. Ballantine also told Mr. Mallet the contents of the first paragraph of Hankow's 2, January 2, 10 a. m., regarding the communication of the Japanese peace terms by the Chinese Vice Minister for Foreign Affairs to Gage, the representative at Hankow of the British Embassy.

Mr. Mallet did not ask for and was not given the text of the Japanese terms.

M[AXWELL] M. H[AMILTON]

793.94/12049 : Telegram

The Ambassador in China (Johnson) to the Secretary of State

HANKOW, January 11, 1938—2 p. m.
[Received January 11—12:10 p. m.]

23. My 1, January 1, 10 p. m. In a conversation which Peck [27] had with Hsu Mo recently, latter stated that a reply might be communicated to the Japanese Government through the German Ambassador within 2 or 3 days. So far as I know this has not been done. Vice Minister stated that it would be impossible for the Chinese Government to accept these terms or to surrender to the Japanese Government in any way; that Generalissimo was firm in his determination that China should continue resistance; that if Chinese Government were to consent to terms dictated by Japan chaos would result as country would not support the Government. Vice Minister stated that all important persons and sections of Chinese Government were firm in their belief that China had no choice but to resist Japan as long as possible. They believed that the farther that the Japanese forces advanced into the interior of China the more effective would

---

[27] Willys R. Peck, Counselor of Embassy in China.

China's resistance become. He stated that Chinese Government still cherished expectation that if resistance was continued long enough and if Japanese disruption of American and British interests extended to all parts of the country, the United States and Great Britain would finally take joint action to restrain Japan's lawless acts. Peck endeavored to disabuse Hsu Mo of any such expectation as regards future policy of the United States, but although Hsu Mo stated that he personally realized this, it is doubtful whether he really has given up any such hopes.

2. In a personal message to me Admiral Yarnell has suggested that the time may be ripe, in view of the terms reported in my telegram above mentioned, for the principally interested powers, taking note of the published accounts of such terms, to issue to the Japanese a warning that they would not recognize a settlement in violation of the provisions of the Nine Power Treaty,[28] thus establishing a basis for concerted action if that were later considered necessary. I desire to pass this suggestion on thus confidentially as one in which I would be inclined to concur.

3. Entire situation is complicated for me, however, by the fact that I cannot escape the conviction that, whatever statements may emanate from official Tokyo as to Japanese intentions on the mainland, the Japanese military represented by General Matsui and his young officers at Shanghai, and Admiral Suetsugu, newly appointed Japanese Home Minister at Tokyo, intend to pursue in China, as evidenced by ultimatum served upon the Municipal Council of the International Settlement of Shanghai (reported in Shanghai's 15, January 5, 9 a. m.[29]) and the Admiral's recently published explanation of reasons for anti-British feeling in Japan, a policy aimed at eliminating occidental influence and interests from China. I am even convinced that the action of Japanese soldiers at Nanking who carried out mass executions of Chinese soldiers that had given up their arms to certain foreigners of the committee which organized the safety zone for noncombatants, was partly motivated by a desire to convince the Chinese that they must not depend upon white intervention in their opinions. We appear to face a group of young Japanese *ronin* who tolerate no control from Tokyo and who will be found to be recklessly contemptuous of any adverse effect which their actions in China may have upon Japan's relations with Western Powers, in the belief that the rest of the world is not prepared to do more than register a protest against violation of treaties relating to the Far East and to the rights and interests of third powers.

JOHNSON

---

[28] Signed at Washington, February 6, 1922, *Foreign Relations*, 1922, vol. I, p. 276.
[29] Vol. IV, p. 116.

793.94/12046 : Telegram

The Ambassador in Japan (Grew) to the Secretary of State

Tokyo, January 11, 1938—7 p. m.
[Received January 11—9 : 50 a. m.]

20. My 17, January 10, 2 p. m.

1. The Imperial Conference met at 2 o'clock this afternoon and adjourned after 1 hour's deliberation. A bulletin issued to the press stated briefly that the conference approved the principle adopted by the Cabinet (see paragraph 4 of telegram above cited). An official in the Foreign Office informed us in reply to request for amplification of the bulletin that contrary to a rumor now current that a full statement would be given to the press of today's proceedings nothing would be given out "for the time being".

2. We have been unable to get any reliable information on even the trend of the discussion at the conference. As relatively full accounts have been given out of recent Cabinet meetings, in which it was made clear that there was a division of opinion on the question of a declaration of war, but that full agreement prevails on the basic policy of carrying on the hostilities to a successful conclusion, the brevity of today's proceedings does not suggest that decision was taken to declare war. If a decision was reached to take any action of a concrete nature the probabilities are that it would involve *de jure* recognition of the "Provisional Government of China" and as a necessary preliminary act withdrawal of recognition of the Chinese Government.

Repeated to Peiping for relay to Johnson.

GREW

893.51/6569 : Telegram

The Secretary of State to the Ambassador in Japan (Grew)

Washington, January 11, 1938—6 p. m.

5. Your 17, January 10, 2 p. m.

1. Recently the British Embassy here brought to the attention of the Department information which had been communicated to the British Government to the effect that an agreement had allegedly been signed at Washington for a loan to China of 150 million dollars. The Department informed the British Embassy that there is no foundation whatsoever for such a report in so far as the United States Government is concerned. The Department is not aware that any negotiations for a Chinese loan are taking place in this country.

2. It is the Department's understanding that during a recent call of the Chinese Ambassador on the President the President made no observations on the Japanese peace terms.

HULL

793.94/12074 : Telegram

The Consul at Tsingtao (Sokobin) to the Secretary of State

TSINGTAO, January 12, 1938—5 p. m.
[Received January 13—1 : 20 p. m.]

Complete peace and order naturally prevail. Japanese authorities have informed Commissioner of Customs there will be no interference with operation of Maritime Customs but naturally he must recognize that new regime exists and that further examination will be worked out. Chinese post office also operating normally with the exception of Japanese censors.

Proclamation issued by Japanese Commander-in-Chief of naval landing forces advised international populace to continue their peaceful pursuits but they must strictly observe and obey Japanese military orders and proclamations.

Sent to Peiping, Hankow.

SOKOBIN

793.94119/378 : Telegram

The Ambassador in Japan (Grew) to the Secretary of State

TOKYO, January 12, 1938—11 p. m.
[Received January 12—1 : 15 p. m.]

23. Our 20, January 11, 7 p. m. I am told by Fleisher [30] who believes that he is quoting an absolutely reliable source that the purpose of the recent Imperial Conference was to approve revised and final peace terms to China and that these terms involving various unspecified concessions on the part of Japan were approved by the Emperor and would therefore become "immutable". It was not expected that China would accept the original terms but if these revised terms are now rejected the campaign will then be pursued to a finish. Informant stated that the emphasis of the conference was therefore on peace rather than on war and that peace is greatly desired.

Informant stated that Admiral Suetsugu was alone in the Cabinet in favoring a declaration of war and that such a proposal therefore did not come before the Emperor. The Cabinet wishes at almost any cost to avoid involving the United States, a risk which a blockade of China would entail through the possible sinking of American merchant ships. The *Lusitania* [31] was quoted as an example.

We are unable as yet to confirm the foregoing report but believe it to be plausible and it checks with the statement of the spokesman of the Foreign Office today that the "negotiations" with China are not

---

[30] Tokyo correspondent of the New York *Herald Tribune*.
[31] See *Foreign Relations*, 1915, Supplement, pp. 384 ff.

finished. Fleisher received it from a close friend of Suetsugu who has previously advised him accurately on other confidential matters and who appears to be indebted to Fleisher for past favors. Fleisher expects to telephone the story to the *Herald Tribune* tomorrow. He is convinced that the story was not "planted".

Repeated to Peiping for relay to Johnson.

GREW

793.94119/378 : Telegram

The Secretary of State to the Ambassador in Japan (Grew)

WASHINGTON, January 12, 1938—7 p. m.

10. Reference general considerations and your 23, January 12, 11 p. m. It has occurred to the Department that possibly a useful purpose might be served if there could be conveyed to the Japanese Government at this time when the Imperial Conference has under consideration matters of the gravest import, mention of points as follows: that the eyes of the world are on Japan; that the nature of the decisions reached by the Conference may have a profound effect upon the welfare and the prosperity of the whole world; that the fighting which has been going on in China for the past 6 months has seriously disturbed all normal and mutually beneficial activities in and with regard to China; that the fighting is producing political and economic and social dislocations and tensions which affect adversely not only China and Japan but other countries as well; that there is no way by which the other countries of the world or even Japan can escape various adverse effects of and from the present conflict, and that prolongation and further extension and intensification of the hostilities will inevitably increase the concern of other nations which suffer from these adverse effects and add to the chance of unfortunate international complications; that we are convinced that practical application of the principles of policy set forth in my statement of July 16 [32] would be in the best interests of Japan as well as of other countries; and that we earnestly hope that the decisions of the Japanese Government will be fully in keeping with the best traditions of wise, high-minded and farseeing Japanese statesmanship.

I realize that the question of making such an approach to the Japanese Government at this time is a delicate one and that it is highly desirable that there be avoided an appearance of foreign intrusion into questions of internal Japanese political deliberations. It is possible, however, that a friendly talk by you with the Minister for Foreign Affairs along the lines indicated might be fruitful of more of good than of harm.

---

[32] *Foreign Relations*, 1937, vol. I, p. 699.

I wish you to use your own discretion both as to whether such an approach as I have outlined should be made and, if your decision be in the affirmative, as to whether you should speak on your own initiative or as under instruction from your Government.

No mediation by us is contemplated or implied by the foregoing.

HULL

793.94/12070 : Telegram

The Chargé in Germany (Gilbert) to the Secretary of State

BERLIN, January 13, 1938—10 a. m.
[Received January 13—9 a. m.]

11. A Chief of Mission here of a State having interests in the Far East showed me last evening a copy of a despatch which the diplomatic representative of his country at London had addressed to his Government which recounted the following: Eden[33] before leaving for the Riviera had asked him to come to see him and had stated that he believed it to be highly possible that the Japanese would attack Hong Kong and that in such a case Great Britain would certainly declare war on Japan. Eden had added that London was in daily touch with Washington and that he entertained hopes that in such an eventuality Great Britain could count on the military support of the United States.

My informant said that he had shown me the despatch in strict confidence as he wanted to obtain my views on possible American action in the circumstances envisaged.

I told him in reply that as far as American public opinion was concerned, in view of the strained relations in the Far East, the course that the United States might pursue under various conditions was from time to time the subject of speculation in the American press but that in so far as I could observe from that source there was nothing approaching a definite crystallization of a common view. Respecting what official attitude my Government might adopt in the specific expectations mentioned I could throw no light whatsoever.

GILBERT

793.94/12080 : Telegram

The Consul at Tsingtao (Sokobin) to the Secretary of State

TSINGTAO, January 13, 1938—11 a. m.
[Received 3 : 33 p. m.]

Japanese Consul General called on me yesterday. He indicated plainly that the Japanese would immediately and energetically com-

---

[33] Anthony Eden, British Secretary of State for Foreign Affairs.

mence the task of economic reconstruction. One hundred and fifty leading Japanese industrialists and engineers have already landed to restore public services. The general Japanese community will commence returning about January 20.

The Consul General gave the impression that the Japanese, while desiring peace, were puzzled as to how to achieve it. He stated that the Generalissimo was surrounded by Communists who would prevent him from making peace.

The Consul General seemed apprehensive about the possible presence of "plain clothes armed men" in the city.

Sent to Hankow, Peiping.

SOKOBIN

793.94119/380 : Telegram

The Ambassador in Japan (Grew) to the Secretary of State

TOKYO, January 13, 1938—6 p. m.
[Received January 13—9 : 15 a. m.]

25. Our 23, January 12, 11 p. m. We obtained today in strict confidence from the Foreign Office certain information which may be helpful in putting into some intelligible relationship the discussions with China of terms of peace and the holding of the Imperial Conference.

1. The agenda of the Imperial Conference was prepared after several weeks of intensive discussion between the Government and the Imperial Headquarters. The underlying purpose in holding the Imperial Conference was, by obtaining the approval of the Emperor for the basis on which peace could be reestablished, to make impossible further disputation over what these terms should be and thus to consolidate national thought and sentiment.

2. The holding of the Imperial Conference on the day following the call by the German Ambassador on the Minister for Foreign Affairs reportedly to communicate the Chinese reply to the Japanese peace terms was purely accidental. Have assurances the message which the German Ambassador delivered can not be regarded as a "Chinese reply". That reply is still being awaited.

3. The Imperial Conference did not so far as our informant (who is a highly responsible official) is aware discuss any matter relating to future procedure or action. He said "I hope the Embassy is not making the mistake of emphasizing the possibility of war being declared".

Repeated to Peiping for relay to Johnson.

GREW

893.102S/1604½

Memorandum of Conversation, by the Under Secretary of State (Welles)

[WASHINGTON,] January 13, 1938.

The British Ambassador called to see me this morning. He said first that the British Government desired to express their very deep gratitude for the message from the President which I had transmitted to the Ambassador on January 10 [34] in reply to the inquiry which he had made of me on January 8. Sir Ronald Lindsay said that the British Government had determined for the time being to postpone making the statement which they had had under consideration that "naval preparations had now been completed" and had determined upon a prior step, namely, further representations to the Japanese Foreign Office through the British Ambassador in Tokyo. The Ambassador then handed me an *aide-mémoire* which summarized the instructions which had been sent by the British Foreign Office to the Ambassador in Tokyo.[35] The Ambassador remarked that this was an extremely stiff note and that he trusted that the reply to be made by the Japanese Government would be satisfactory.

[Here follow comments on various other matters.]

S[UMNER] W[ELLES]

793.94/12082 : Telegram

The Ambassador in France (Bullitt) to the Secretary of State

PARIS, January 13, 1938—6 p. m.
[Received January 13—3 : 50 p. m.]

63. Dr. Tingfu Tsiang [who] recently resigned as Chinese Ambassador in Moscow and will return to China next week via Singapore to become Secretary to the Cabinet called on me this morning and made a number of statements which seemed to me important.

He said that he was convinced that the Soviet Union would refuse to enter the Sino-Japanese conflict under any and all conditions. He believed that internal difficulties in the Soviet Union were such at the present time that the Russians would be afraid to attack the Japanese even if the Japanese Army should be greatly weakened by a prolonged Chinese resistance.

He said that Litvinov [36] had stated to him repeatedly that the Soviet Union would declare war at once on Japan if England, France and the United States should declare war on Japan. He said that he did not

[34] Not found in Department files.
[35] Not printed; it concerned Japanese assaults on British officers at Shanghai (893.102S/1600).
[36] Maxim Litvinov, Soviet Commissar for Foreign Affairs.

believe that this was true and that in his final conversation with Litvinov he had pinned down Litvinov and compelled a reply. He stated that he had asked Litvinov if he meant the Soviet Union would enter war against Japan if any one of the three nations named above should go to war with Japan or only if all three together should go to war with Japan. Litvinov had become completely evasive and finally had made it clear that the Soviet Union had no intention whatsoever of going to war with Japan under any circumstances.

Dr. Tsiang stated that on the other hand the Soviet Union was being much more generous in its support of China by munitions and supplies than he had expected. Russia had at first demanded gold from China in payment for supplies, but when the Chinese had insisted that they were unable to pay gold the Russians had agreed to supply them with everything possible on credit. The only payments that the Russians were receiving from China were in the form of antimony and other minerals which the trucks carrying war supplies to China brought back with them on their return journey.

Dr. Tsiang stated to me that most of the Russian supplies to China were not going overland but by sea, especially by way of Hong Kong and Canton, although the French railroad from Indo-China was carrying to full capacity.

The overland route from Alma Ata in Russian Turkestan to Urumchi in Sinkiang and thence to Lanchow, Sian and Chungking was now a thoroughly passable motor road but it took the best trucks under the best conditions, with no delays or accidents, at least 18 days from the Russian border to Chungking. This made the problem of supplying gasoline almost insuperable and the Chinese had now organized camel caravans to carry supplies of gasoline for the trucks.

Dr. Tsiang stated that the whole problem of Chinese resistance was one of obtaining military supplies. He believed that the Soviet Union would continue to furnish all the supplies possible on credit. It was, however, clear that the Japanese might soon blockade the main route of supply by way of Hong Kong, Canton, and Hankow. They might also be able to frighten the French into closing the route of supply by way of French Indo-China. This would leave open only the extremely difficult overland route from Alma Ata to Chungking. It would be impossible to install even a field railway on this route and as a result it might become a matter of life and death for the Chinese to find some other route to supply Chiang Kai Shek's armies if he should be compelled to repeat [retreat?] to Szechuan.

Dr. Tsiang stated that there was another excellent route which it might be possible to use: The route by way of Burma. The British railroad from Rangoon to Mandalay and thence to the border of Yunnan had been completed to within 2 miles of the Chinese frontier.

The road from that point to Yunnanfu was an old one but could be put in order comparatively easy for the transit of modern trucks. Dr. Tsiang stated that he was on his way to London this evening to attempt to make arrangements for the supplying of Chiang Kai Shek's armies by this route. He stated that the roads from Yunnanfu to Chungking were thoroughly passable. He considered that this route by way of Burma might become China's life line and hoped that the British Government would do everything possible to assist in the supplying of China through Burma.

In the course of our conversation Dr. Tsiang said that China was still receiving large quantities of military supplies from Germany and Italy and added that the German military mission in China so far as the Chinese could discover was still working loyally and efficiently in assisting Chiang Kai Shek to direct the Chinese armies.

BULLITT

793.94/12081 : Telegram

The Consul General at Shanghai (Gauss) to the Secretary of State

SHANGHAI, January 13, 1938—7 p. m.
[Received January 13—6 : 39 p. m.]

73. Following from American Embassy at Tokyo:

"January 13, 4 p. m. Your 57, January 7, 11 p. m., and previous. Area free from attack at Hankow.

Japanese Foreign Office has informed this Embassy as follows:

'Japanese forces will not attack the said area if no Chinese forces are within it, if Chinese forces make no military use whatever of it and if the movements of Japanese forces outside the area are not hindered from within it.

It is to be noted that by the riverfront of the area is understood only the river bank itself, not extending either to the line in the middle of the river or to the opposite shore.'

Please repeat Peiping, Hankow, and Department. Grew.["]

GAUSS

793.94111/111 : Telegram

The Chargé in Germany (Gilbert) to the Secretary of State

BERLIN, January 14, 1938—noon.
[Received January 14—11 : 30 a. m.]

14. The Chinese Ambassador called on me today and in the course of conversation brought out the following:

Von Neurath [37] had again yesterday assured him of German neutrality. The only feature to his knowledge in which Germany was

---

[37] Baron Constantin H. K. von Neurath, German Minister for Foreign Affairs.

not entirely neutral lay in the tone of the press which undoubtedly somewhat favored Japan. His Government was "satisfied" however that the German Government was maintaining its neutral position: while Germany was selling arms to Japan it was likewise selling to China and moreover the German Military Mission, despite repeated Japanese protests, remained in China.

While one could not tell what "irresponsible" Japanese military elements might do, the Ambassador did not believe that Japan would attack Hong Kong. Even in such a case, however, he did not believe that Great Britain would take any military steps in the Far East until some understandings had been reached with Germany. Thus from a purely Chinese point of view he hoped for a British-German *rapprochement* and was anxious over apparent delays.

GILBERT

793.94/12089 : Telegram

The Ambassador in France (Bullitt) to the Secretary of State

PARIS, January 14, 1938—1 p. m.
[Received January 14—11 : 55 a. m.]

74. Blum remarked to me last night that Litvinov had said to Delbos, and Souritz, Soviet Ambassador in Paris, had repeated to Delbos, that Litvinov had stated definitely to Norman Davis [38] in Brussels that if the United States should become involved in war with Japan, the Soviet Union would declare war on Japan at once. I replied that I felt certain that Litvinov had never made such a statement to Norman Davis.

I should be obliged if the Department would let me know if Litvinov ever made such a statement to Davis.

BULLITT

793.94119/382 : Telegram

The Ambassador in Japan (Grew) to the Secretary of State

TOKYO, January 14, 1938—5 p. m.
[Received January 14—10 : 25 a. m.]

28. Department's 10, January 12, 7 p. m. The Imperial Conference was held only for the purpose of giving the Emperor's sanction to decisions, whatever they were, already formulated and approved by the Government. It ended after a brief session and in the eyes of the Japanese the decisions previously taken are "immutable".

---

[38] American delegate to the Brussels Conference, November 1937.

Even a friendly talk with the Minister for Foreign Affairs on this subject would have to be reported to the Cabinet and in the present tense atmosphere I have little doubt that the proposed representations by the American Ambassador seeking to influence or to modify the decisions of the Imperial Conference as contrasted with the protection of specific American interests would be interpreted at this moment as an effort to interfere with the prerogative of the Emperor and would entail reaction the reverse of that desired.

Fully realizing the fundamental importance of the facts and views set forth in your telegram, I shall have them constantly in mind for expression when a favorable occasion offers. We are aware, however, that the substance of the points outlined by the Department as well as the ramifications, effects and hazards involved in Japanese policy was very carefully weighed by the Japanese Government before the proposals implementing that policy were presented to the Emperor.

I fully appreciate your wish that I should use my own discretion in this matter and I trust that the foregoing views when given consideration will prove not to run counter to your own opinion.

GREW

793.94119/384 : Telegram

The Ambassador in Japan (Grew) to the Secretary of State

TOKYO, January 14, 1938—7 p. m.
[Received January 14—2 : 05 p. m.]

29. Department's 10, January 12, 7 p. m.; and my 28, January 14, 5 p. m.

1. The situation which has faced all of us here, whether representatives of foreign governments or foreign press correspondents, has been one of extraordinary obscurity. I have endeavored in my recent telegrams on the Imperial Conference to indicate trends and to resist the temptation to associate myself with various theses with regard to what further action might be taken by Japan such as declaration of war, withdrawal of recognition of the Chinese Government, et cetera. However, some of the correspondents, in order to cover themselves and from a desire to avoid being scooped, have played up the imminent likelihood of various drastic measures being taken by Japan and I understand that their despatches have been so recast by news editors as to give the American public the impression that the Imperial Conference was called primarily to adopt measures to prolong, extend and intensify the hostilities. There has been available no authoritative information with regard to the agenda and the decision of the conference which would warrant any such conclusion. During the last 2

days we have been sifting out various rumors and reports and we present the following as our estimate of recent developments.

2. Ever since it became apparent that Nanking was about to fall, consideration has been given by the Japanese Government to the question of Japan's future procedure and among the measures which have been studied was that of a declaration of war. The *Panay* and the *Ladybird* incidents [39] occurred and brought about in the highest Japanese quarter a realization of the danger of involvement with the United States and Great Britain. The series of discussions between the Government and Imperial Headquarters which began at about that time then sought to formulate principles of a basic policy toward China that might be acceptable to all influential elements in Japan. Although it was not expected that these principles would be such as to modify objectives in China there was reason to believe that the methods to implement these principles would be such as to reduce to a minimum consistent with successful conclusion of the hostilities the possibilities of becoming involved with the United States and Great Britain. It now appears that the question of resorting to a declaration of war was at that time thoroughly discussed and was then tabled until dragged out again by Suyetsugu at the Cabinet meeting on January 9. Confirming the statement quoted in paragraph 3 of our 25, January 13, 6 p. m., the Vice Minister for Foreign Affairs [40] informed me at luncheon today that this question neither was considered by the Imperial Conference nor is it an active one at the present time.[41]

3. The conferences between the Government and Imperial Headquarters were progressing toward a final conference in the presence of the Emperor at which time the principles of a basic policy toward China were to be adopted when the Germans offered to act as a channel of communications between the Chinese and Japanese Governments. This move by the Germans was entirely fortuitous and was not a link in the chain of events which led to the conference on January 12. That conference would have taken place in any event as soon as the necessary agreement of views between the Government and Imperial Headquarters was reached.

4. The principal purpose of the conference, as pointed out in our number 25, was to expose any further agitation and argumentation with regard to the basis of a peace which would be acceptable to

---

[39] See *Foreign Relations*, 1937, vol. IV, pp. 485 ff.; and *Foreign Relations*, Japan, 1931–1941, vol. I, pp. 517 ff.

[40] Kensuke Horinouchi.

[41] In reviewing the formulating of Japanese policy, Ambassador Grew, in despatch No. 2746, January 22, stressed the importance of civilian leaders checking military action which tended toward war, not only with China and the United Kingdom, but also with the United States. "This trend toward declaring war passed," he concluded. "The change would appear to have been brought about through a disposition on the part of the Throne to avert such risks." (793.94119/397)

Japan: it was not to formulate or to adopt measures to prolong or intensify the hostilities. The basis of peace which was adopted will determine the Japanese terms whether negotiations for peace should eventuate now from the German good offices or at any time in the future. In this sense the statement in my 23, January 12, 9 [*11*] p. m., that the conference was on "peace rather than on war" is substantially correct.

5. It is in the field of future developments that the principles of policy decided upon by the conference, whatever they may be, offer grounds for apprehension. We believe that the primary principle is that China shall cooperate with Japan to combat communism; but we take it that this does not mean any association of China with Japan to combat the mere propagation of a doctrine but that it will entail some form of political and military coordination between the two countries which will permit Japan to eliminate China as a hostile factor in the event of a war between Japan and Russia. If the reply which is shortly expected of the Chinese Government should be—as is probable—such as to eliminate any chance of a peace conformable to the principles of Japan's basic policy and if China should manifest beyond all possibility of doubt its determination to continue the struggle the way has now been left open for the Japanese Government, in the exercise of its prerogatives, to consider whether it should not withdraw its recognition of the Chinese Government and to support and perhaps eventually grant *de jure* recognition to some régime which is prepared to accept the Japanese terms.

6. You may wish to review my strictly confidential telegram 634 of December 15, noon.[42]

GREW

793.94/12089 : Telegram

The Secretary of State to the Ambassador in France (Bullitt)

WASHINGTON, January 14, 1938—8 p. m.

20. Your 74, January 14, 1 p. m. Litvinov at no time made a statement, such as you describe, to Mr. Davis at Brussels. Litvinov, after asking Mr. Davis during a luncheon conversation on November 4, 1937, how far the United States would be willing to go in coercive action and after having been told by Mr. Davis that we were not considering coercive action at this time, indicated that "Russia would be quite prepared to act with England and the United States, but that she would want to feel certain that she would not be left with the bag to hold."

---

[42] *Foreign Relations*, 1937, vol. III, p. 809.

There was no other reference in Mr. Davis' conversations with Litvinov to coercive action and none to a declaration of war.

Mr. Davis, who has been consulted, confirms that the question of a declaration of war was at no time mentioned in his conversations with Litvinov, even indirectly.

HULL

793.94119/386 : Telegram

The Counselor of Embassy in China (Lockhart) to the Secretary of State

PEIPING, January 15, 1938—4 p. m.
[Received 6 : 12 p. m.]

33. Tokyo's 23, January 12, 2 [*11*] p. m., and 25, January 13, 6 p. m. If the Japanese are in earnest in wishing an early termination of hostilities, I am disposed to believe, without having any tangible evidence to support the belief, and in the knowledge that it may be too optimistic, that they will probably propose, and insist upon, a 5-province autonomous, or semi-autonomous, government in North China, fashioned on the plan of the present Provisional Government, as the minimum basis of negotiations, plus some arrangement for a demilitarized zone within a radius of 20 or 30 miles of Shanghai, plus an indemnity for property losses and an agreement regarding the suppression of communism. An area composed of Shansi, Chahar, Suiyuan, Hopei and Shantung would be about all that Japan, in addition to Manchukuo, could at this time safely undertake to control and even that would be likely to tax the resourcefulness of the Japanese selected to guide its destiny. Certainly the Japanese in Peiping are not finding it easy to discover the right type of Chinese willing to assume responsible positions in the government. To undertake such a task in wide areas in the Yangtze Valley and in the South, which areas are less responsive to control than the North, would be an undertaking from which they might well shrink. The reestablishment of a government at Nanking, with or without Chiang Kai Shek at its head, and one which would undertake to keep the peace with Japan, would seem to be within the realm of possibilities, if the Japanese desire for peace envisages moderation and some sense of the national pride and the rights of the Chinese. The Japanese would probably be reluctant permanently to occupy provinces south of Hopei and Shantung unless all hope of coming to terms with Chiang Kai Shek must be given up, in which case all of Kiangsu and Anhui, and perhaps even Honan and Hupeh, would come under Japanese domination. The persistent resistance of the Chinese and the prospect of a continuance of that attitude, coupled with what is be-

lieved to be differences of opinion among the Japanese military with regard to political aspects of the situation in China, are calculated to make it impossible for the Japanese to dictate terms which would embrace all that they would wish to exact from China as compensation for Japan's unexpectedly large losses and the tremendous expense of the campaign.

As harsh as the possible basic terms suggested above may seem, it is doubtful whether the Chinese could obtain more favorable ones 3 or 6 months hence or even a year hence. I say this because I believe, without any tangible evidence to support the belief, that the Japanese are in a position financially, economically, and militarily, to continue the conflict as a cohesive military organization for a much longer time than can the Chinese, and because I do not feel that there is a likelihood of changes taking place in the near future in Japan, or of the intervention of any third power, which would make it impossible for Japan to continue to prosecute the war. Unless both sides can be brought to realization of the urgent need for an early and just conclusion of the conflict, the war will go on to add to the misery of many more millions of Chinese and to even more widespread economic dislocation, to say nothing of the tremendous loss of life and property which will ensue—and perhaps to no benefit—and ultimately lead to more serious disorder in the Far East and further international complications, a situation which might well add also to the confusion in other parts of the world.

Repeated to the Ambassador and Tokyo.

LOCKHART

793.94119/385 : Telegram

The Ambassador in Japan (Grew) to the Secretary of State

TOKYO, January 15, 1938—6 p. m.
[Received January 15—8 : 50 a. m.]

31. Our 29, January 14, 7 p. m. At a conference today of the Government and Imperial Headquarters a draft statement on Japan's policy toward China to be issued shortly by the Government was examined. According to unconfirmed reports the draft was approved.

The German Ambassador called yesterday on the Minister for Foreign Affairs. The press states that he communicated the views of the Chinese Government on the Japanese peace terms and that these views were in the nature of a refusal to discuss the terms. Several papers forecast that the official statement on policy will:

(*a*) Stress China's persistent refusal to negotiate for peace;
(*b*) Express Japan's determination to crush the Chinese Government and other Chinese elements hostile to Japan;

(*c*) Express hope that there may develop a government in China prepared to cooperate with Japan;

(*d*) Indicate Japan's intention to support such friendly government.

Repeated to Peiping for relay to Johnson.

GREW

711.008 North Pacific/273

Memorandum of Conversation, by the Chief of the Division of Far Eastern Affairs (Hamilton)

[WASHINGTON,] January 15, 1938.

Participants: Mr. Suma, Counselor of the Japanese Embassy,
 Mr. Hamilton,
 Mr. Ballantine.

Mr. Suma called by appointment at his own request and inquired whether there were any new developments in the Alaska fisheries question. I said that the matter was still being considered by this Government and that no instructions had yet been sent to our Embassy at Tokyo. Mr. Suma asked whether it was expected that a decision on this matter would be reached next week. I said that I hoped it would be but that I could give him no definite assurances of this.

Mr. Suma stated that it had been reported to the Embassy that on January 4 a Chinese plane had been shot down on which they found the body of an American aviator who was buried in the international burying ground on January 8, 1938, and that the name of this aviator was Frank Kruezberg. Mr. Suma did not know the spelling of the name but this was as near as he could approximate it from the Japanese letters. (Note: Hankow telegraphed on January 7 that Frederick Kruezberg's body was brought to Hankow for interment in International Cemetery, Hankow, that information from Chinese aviation circles was that he was killed in an air crash on January 4 about twelve miles from Hankow.) He said that service by American aviators in Chinese air forces was likely to cause anti-American feeling in Japan. I told him that we could not prevent Americans from taking service with foreign military forces, and that we are discouraging such activities by Americans by placing on passports the statement that the passports are not valid for travel to foreign countries for the purpose of entering the military service of foreign governments. Mr. Suma said that some months ago he had spoken to Mr. Hornbeck[44] of this general matter; that Mr. Hornbeck had said that the matter (the reported recruiting on the West Coast of Americans for military

---

[44] Stanley K. Hornbeck, Adviser on Political Relations.

aviation service with the Chinese Government) was one for our judicial authorities, and that his Government appreciated our attitude but that he merely brought this matter to our attention.

At this point I was obliged to leave and Mr. Ballantine continued the conversation with Mr. Suma. Mr. Suma dwelt at some length upon the friendly feelings toward the United States which had been developed by our restrained attitude in regard to the *Panay* incident, and upon the shock which this incident had caused Japan. With this introduction he brought up, as off the record, the matter of the visit of our three cruisers to Singapore and said that as the Japanese Navy had not been invited to participate in the opening of the naval base at Singapore, or any other navy except the American, this matter was arousing considerable notice in Japan. He also referred to reports regarding a joint Anglo-American naval demonstration. Mr. Ballantine made no comment other than to say that so far as we were concerned, the visit of our vessels to Singapore was a normal matter, we having received an invitation which we had accepted.

Mr. Ballantine then inquired of Mr. Suma what the general prospects in the Far Eastern situation were and Mr. Suma said that as the Chinese Government had not accepted the peace terms which had been presented to Chiang Kai-shek by the German Ambassador, he believed that the hostilities would continue. He said that the Japanese terms were, of course, quite vague but that they were in general in line with the cardinal policies which Japan had sought to carry out even before the outbreak of hostilities. He added that, of course, the condition regarding indemnities was new. He thought Chiang Kai-shek, owing to his previous declarations, would find it difficult to accept such terms without losing face. Mr. Suma expressed in a round-about way the view that Chiang might be willing to negotiate on the basis of such terms if he could indicate that he had been advised to do so by some strong and friendly power such as the United States. Mr. Suma asked Mr. Ballantine, off the record, what his reaction would be to the United States assuming such a role. Mr. Ballantine said that in his personal opinion our Government would be unwilling to assume such a role.

M[AXWELL] M. H[AMILTON]

793.94119/387 : Telegram

The Ambassador in Japan (Grew) to the Secretary of State

ToKYO, January 16, 1938—3 p. m.
[Received January 16—7 : 20 a. m.]

32. My German colleague was this morning informed by the Minister for Foreign Affairs that the Japanese Government declines to

accede to the request of the Chinese Government for further definition and elucidation of its proposed peace terms and that the peace overtures are therefore finished. The German Embassy informs me that the tentative peace exchanges have been going on for some time and that this final break is due to the unwillingness of the Japanese to commit themselves further by making more specific their terms, particularly their military terms, as requested by the Chinese Government.

As a result of this rupture of the tentative peace exchanges the Japanese Government at noon today issued the following statement. (See our 31, January 15, 6 p. m.).

[Here follows text of statement printed in *Foreign Relations, Japan, 1931–1941*, volume I, page 437.]

Repeated to Peiping for relay to Johnson.

GREW

793.94119/389 : Telegram

The Ambassador in Japan (Grew) to the Secretary of State

Tokyo, January 17, 1938—2 p. m.
[Received January 17—6 : 55 a. m.]

35. At the end of my conversation this morning with the Minister for Foreign Affairs he said that he would like to explain to me the background of the announcement made by the Japanese Government yesterday (Embassy's 32, January 16, 3 p. m.). He said that through the good offices of the German Ambassador certain peace proposals were made to the Chinese Government in December and that an answer was expected during the early part of January. On January 14th the Chinese Government returned a "perfunctory" reply merely asking for further information concerning the proposed terms. The Japanese Government then became convinced of the futility of further negotiations and decided to have no further dealings with the Government now located in Hankow. The Minister said that this did not involve a specific act effecting a breach of diplomatic relations but simply meant a cessation of dealing with Hankow on the ground that the government in Hankow no longer represents China. The Minister said that there would be no immediate recognition of any regime but that the Japanese Government would await development. The regime in North China would constitute the "basic power" of whatever government should eventually be recognized and that that government would include such regimes as were friendly to Japan. It was not possible as yet to foresee whether such a regime would develop in Nanking.

Repeated to Peiping for relay to Johnson.

GREW

893.01 Provisional/32 : Telegram

The Counselor of Embassy in China (Lockhart) to the Secretary of State

PEIPING, January 17, 1938—4 p. m.
[Received January 17—7 : 30 a. m.]

35. Caldwell [45] inquires whether the Department's policy as stated in paragraph 2 of your 400, December 15, 7 p. m.,[46] applies with the same force to consular officers as it does to diplomatic officers, his feelings, in which I concur, being that the calls of consular officers do not convey quite the same implication as calls of diplomatic officers, and that in the ordinary course of business there is perhaps more necessity for consular officers to have contact with officials of Provisional Government than for members of the staff of the Embassy. Please clarify the point raised by Caldwell.

I received recently a call from Pan Yu Kwei, then Chief of Police under the Provisional Government, but did not return the call (with personal card) as Pan intimated that it was not necessary. I have been informed that further calls are to be made on me shortly by other municipal officials under the Provisional Government.

LOCKHART

124.9318/221

Memorandum of Conversation, by the Secretary of State

[WASHINGTON,] January 17, 1938.

After talking with the British Ambassador on another phase of the Far Eastern situation, I said that I desired to speak to him very specially regarding the question of bringing our guards and troops out of Tientsin and Peiping; that some three weeks ago the British Government inquired [47] whether we were ready to bring them out from those two places and we had indicated that the time was just a little premature in our opinion, etc., etc.,[48] the French expressing a similar view and the British later arriving at a similar conclusion; that, in great confidence, it was my understanding the British now are concerned to get their troops out of these two cities and probably to reduce the number at Shanghai down to the level existing before the Japanese invasion; that the question arises as to just how and when the evacuation of these guards and troops can and should be made to avoid the appearance of scuttling on the one hand and at

---

[45] John K. Caldwell, Consul General at Tientsin.
[46] *Foreign Relations*, 1937, vol. III, p. 811.
[47] See *aide-mémoire* of December 16, 1937, *ibid.*, p. 814.
[48] See *aide-mémoire* of December 18, 1937, *ibid.*, p. 816.

the same time possibly to permit synchronization with any naval movements which might occur on the part of our two countries. I expressed a desire that the Ambassador, in any event, should ascertain from his Government all phases of its views and suggestions by which these evacuations could take place somewhat in accordance with the views of the different governments interested, after consultation with each other. I said that the question of removing embassies from Peiping is one in which we raise the suggestion as to whether the American Embassy, for instance, should not be retained although closed, with most of the embassy personnel and some of the movable property taken away; and a Consul General retained at Tientsin; that the guards left at Peiping would make possible the continued operation of the radio station; that we had considered withdrawing a portion of our guards and troops at first but having in mind the possibility of withdrawing the remainder at any time circumstances might suggest; that in the event Japan should install a puppet government in North China we could upon the announcement of such, however, withdraw our embassy establishment at Peiping, leaving possibly a chargé, et cetera.

C[ORDELL] H[ULL]

704.9394/2

Memorandum of Conversation, by the Secretary of State

[WASHINGTON,] January 18, 1938.

The Chinese Ambassador called at his own request. He referred to his conversation of some three weeks ago [49] with Mr. Hugh Wilson [50] in regard to the matter of this Government taking over the Chinese Embassy in Tokyo and representing China's interests there after the contemplated departure within another day or two of the Chinese Ambassador from Tokyo.

I requested the Ambassador to state just what his proposal was, although I had talked the matter over somewhat with Mr. Wilson several days ago. The Ambassador replied that in the event of the contemplated departure of the Chinese Ambassador from Tokyo this week he would like to renew his request, made to Mr. Hugh Wilson, that this Government take charge of China's interests there. He then added that Mr. Wilson brought up a question to the effect that if Japan should organize a puppet government in North China and should authorize representatives of that puppet government to take charge of the Chinese Embassy and its properties and files at Tokyo, the Government of the United States might have an embarrassing

---

[49] See memorandum of December 13, 1937, *Foreign Relations*, 1937, vol. III, p. 803.
[50] Then Assistant Secretary of State.

situation presented to it with respect to whether it would or would not surrender its possession of the Chinese interests and properties. I referred more in detail to this situation and emphasized the view that since the Japanese are apparently in the act of establishing a puppet government in North China, if they have not already done so, the question of turning over possession of the Chinese Embassy and its properties at Tokyo might be brought up right away. I then inquired of the Ambassador what he would do in those circumstances if he were in our place. He was a little reserved but expressed the view that he knew we would not like to turn over properties to such puppet government agencies. I explained that that was not conclusive, however, of the question presented. He had no further comment, except that they would be desirous of calling on us to take charge of China's interests at Tokyo. I said to him that naturally this Government is always desirous of rendering any reasonable and practical service to his Government; that it would be necessary, in my opinion, for me to investigate this question which might possibly arise, and I would undertake to do so and notify him of any new or further impressions I might have as soon as was practicable.

C[ORDELL] H[ULL]

893.0146/618

The British Embassy to the Department of State

[WASHINGTON,] January 18, 1938.

It is the intention of the British Government to withdraw one British battalion from Shanghai at the end of January and the British military authorities there consider that the two remaining battalions will be enough to man those portions of the defense perimeter allotted to the British.

The British Government understands that the U. S. Marines of emergency reenforcements are likely to leave on or about the 15th of February. The British Government would be glad to know whether the United States Government have any objection to their not replacing the one British battalion which is to be withdrawn and what are the intentions of the United States Government as regards the reduction of their own military forces at Shanghai.

A similar inquiry is being made of the French Government.

893.0146/618

The Department of State to the British Embassy

[WASHINGTON,] January 18, 1938.

The American Government has for some time had in contemplation possible withdrawal from Shanghai of the regiment of marines sent to Shanghai as reenforcements last fall. The American Government has already informed the British Government of this. The American Government perceives no reason why the contemplated withdrawal by the British Government of one battalion of the British landed armed force, at about the end of January, should not be carried out. The withdrawal of the American regiment would probably take place before the middle of February. According to our understanding, if and when these contemplated withdrawals are effected, there would remain of the British force at Shanghai two battalions; and there would remain of the American force one regiment.

893.0146/618½

The Department of State to the British Embassy

[WASHINGTON,] January 18, 1938.

Several weeks ago the British Government suggested the possible desirability of withdrawing the Embassy establishments and the Boxer Protocol forces from north China and asked for this Government's opinion. Reply was made that in our opinion a withdrawal at that time would be premature. The British Government later informed us that it had conferred with the French Government, that the French Government shared substantially the opinion expressed by the American Government, and that the British Government had decided to let the matter rest.

The American Government has kept this question in mind and now believes that action toward making withdrawals would be advisable. It is our understanding that the British Government leans toward that view.

It is our opinion that withdrawals, if and as made, should be made in such manner as to avoid giving any impression of a political retreat, to cause a minimum of psychological disturbance, to afford a maximum of service of the objectives for which these establishments have existed, and to synchronize with possible other steps and developments.

We feel that most of the armed forces might in the near future be withdrawn; that the consulates general at Tientsin should remain; that small armed guards might be maintained at Tientsin and at Peiping; that at some given moment the Embassy establishments might be withdrawn from Peiping; and that then a complete withdrawal of the armed guards might be considered.

We offer this line of thought tentatively.

An indication of the present views of the British Government, as regards principle and as regards details, would be welcomed.

893.01 Provisional/32 : Telegram

The Secretary of State to the Counselor of Embassy in China (Lockhart), at Peiping

WASHINGTON, January 18, 1938—6 p. m.

18. Reference your 35, January 17, 4 p. m. The Department desires that Caldwell be guided by the principles set forth in instruction No. 400, December 15, 7 p. m.,[51] to you in his relations with the officials of the "Provisional Government". Some latitude, however, is possible in his relations with local authorities as distinguished from the central authorities of the new regime.

It is not practicable to give Caldwell instructions which would apply to every contingency that might arise in his relations with officials of the new regime but the Department relies upon his resourcefulness and discretion to meet the requirements of instruction No. 400 and at the same time to avoid undue emphasis upon matters of form. The Department desires that he keep his relations with the new officials on an informal basis.

HULL

793.94/12138 : Telegram

The Ambassador in China (Johnson) to the Secretary of State

HANKOW, January 19, 1938—9 a. m.
[Received January 19—8 a. m.]

39. Following is Central News Agency's translation of a statement issued by the National Government last evening:

"Since the outbreak of the Lukouchiao incident in July last year[52] the Chinese Government has repeatedly declared its readiness to seek an amicable settlement by any of the pacific means known to international law. But Japan regardless of all consequences embarked upon a large scale invasion of China and a wanton massacre of her people by land, naval and air forces. China was thus forced to act in self defence against violence and aggression.

During the last few months a large number of Chinese cities and towns have been illegally occupied by the Japanese Army whereas not a single Chinese soldier has set foot on Japanese territory. Lives and property have been ruthlessly destroyed by the invaders. Soldiers who had given up arms and helpless noncombatants including women and children were murdered in cold blood while untold damage was done to industrial and cultural enterprises.

---

[51] Foreign Relations, 1937, vol. III, p. 811.
[52] For correspondence, see ibid., pp. 128 ff.; see also Foreign Relations, Japan, 1931–1941, vol. I, pp. 313–334, passim.

That the action of Japan violates international law and the Anti-War Pact [53] and the Nine Power Treaty has in unmistakable terms been pronounced by the nations of the world. The responsibility for disturbing international peace clearly rests with Japan and not with China.

In spite of such well known facts Japan has now declared that she respects the territory and sovereign rights of China as well as the rights and interests of foreign powers in this country. It should be observed, however, that by respect for China's territory and sovereignty Japan means the dismembering of China through the creation by force of various unlawful organizations within Chinese territory and the making use of such organizations to usurp the sovereign rights of China. Likewise by respect for the rights and interests of foreign powers Japan means the securing of monopolistic rights through her predominant position in China.

The object of China's armed resistance is to safeguard her national existence and to maintain the sanctity of international treaties. Though her desire for peace remains unchanged, China cannot tolerate any encroachment by any foreign country upon her sovereign rights and territorial and administrative integrity which are the essential attributes of her independent status and which all interested powers by a solemn treaty have pledged themselves to respect.

Under whatever circumstances the Chinese Government will exert its utmost to maintain the sovereign rights and territorial and administrative integrity of China. Any terms for the restoration of peace, if they do not conform to this fundamental principle, are necessarily unacceptable to China.

In the meantime all acts on [of] such unlawful organizations as may be set up in areas under Japanese military occupation will be considered null and void both internally and externally by the Chinese Government. ["]

Repeated to Peiping. Please mail to Tokyo.

JOHNSON

793.94/12039 : Telegram

The Secretary of State to the Ambassador in China (Johnson)

WASHINGTON, January 19, 1938—11 a. m.

27. Please deliver the following message to General Chiang Kai-Shek:

"January 11, 1938. Dear General Chiang:—

I am glad to have Your Excellency's letter of December 24, 1937,[54] which was delivered to me personally by His Excellency the Chinese Ambassador here on December 31st.

In this letter you have been so good as to give me your appraisal of various features of the very unfortunate situation in the Far East and your views in relation to the problem of world peace.

---

[53] Signed at Paris, August 27, 1928, *Foreign Relations*, 1928, vol. I, p. 153.
[54] *Ibid.*, 1937, vol. III, p. 832.

Needless to say, I have been giving much attention to the situation and the problem to which you refer. The tragic conflict in China is of concern not only to the two countries most directly involved but to the whole world. Both the people and the Government of the United States view with anxious solicitude and profound regret the destruction which is being wrought. The cause of peace is one which we have very much at heart. We are giving constant study and thought to the problem of ways and means which may contribute most effectively toward promoting peace and facilitating international cooperation. Our efforts toward those ends will not be relaxed. It is our earnest hope that out of the present conflict in the Far East, and in place of it, there will come a settlement which, by virtue of reasonable provisions adequately considerate of the rights, legitimate interests and national integrity of all concerned, will provide a basis for amicable relationships and an enduring peace. Very sincerely yours, Franklin D. Roosevelt."

The original letter signed by the President is being forwarded to you by pouch for delivery to General Chiang Kai-Shek.[55]

HULL

793.94/12134 : Telegram

The Ambassador in Japan (Grew) to the Secretary of State

TOKYO, January 19, 1938—noon.
[Received January 19—7 a. m.]

39. My British colleague has given me for my confidential information a paraphrase of a telegram dated January 15, from the British Embassy at Shanghai reporting actions of Japanese troops at Nanking. As we have had no detailed reports on this subject from Shanghai or elsewhere I am cabling the text which was furnished to me as follows:

"I have been supplied confidentially with two separate and completely reliable reports, from an American missionary at Nanking and a missionary doctor at Wuhu who remained at their posts when the Japanese entered these cities, regarding the atrocities committed by the Japanese Army. Reports quote approximately 100 authenticated cases of rape in the American University Buildings in Nanking in the first few days of the occupation.

The Reverend Boynton of the National Christian Council who brought me these reports stated that the Japanese Embassy officials who reached Nanking shortly after the entry of the Japanese troops were horrified when they saw the orgy of drunkenness, murder, rape and robbery, which was going on openly in and around the refugee zone. Failing to make any impression on the military commander, whose attitude of callous indifference makes it probable that the army was deliberately turned loose on the cit yas a punitive measure,

---

[55] A copy was also transmitted by letter to the Chinese Ambassador on January 25.

and despairing of getting cable through to Tokyo owing to military control, Embassy officials had even suggested to the missionaries that the latter should try and get publicity for the facts in Japan so that the Japanese Government would be forced by public opinion to curb the army.

I have been promised eye witness reports from Soochow and Hang-chow where the behavior of the Japanese troops was equally bad and stories, apparently authenticated, regarding their behavior, in the neighborhood of Shanghai are now coming in".

Repeated to Peiping for relay to Hankow.

GREW

893.01 Provisional/41

The British Embassy to the Department of State

AIDE-MÉMOIRE

The representative of His Majesty's Embassy at Peking was faced some days ago with the question whether to receive a visit from the Mayor of Tientsin who has been newly appointed by the Provisional Government. In the end His Majesty's Consul and the Chinese Secretary received the Mayor at the former's house. A similar procedure was followed by the French representatives but it is understood that the United States Counsellor received the Mayor on a "personal basis" on general authority from the United States Government "to receive and return calls of officials of the present régime provided this was done in a personal manner".

His Majesty's Embassy have now asked for authority to follow in future a similar procedure to that of the United States Embassy, and His Majesty's Government agree that the closer the procedures of the two Embassies can conform the better. They would therefore be grateful if they might receive as early information as possible as to what precise procedure the United States Government would prescribe for the treatment by their diplomatic representatives, so long as these remain within the territory of the Provisional Government, both of actual members of the Provisional Government and of territorial officials such as the Mayor of Tientsin. On receipt of this information instructions will be issued to His Majesty's Representatives to ensure as far as possible the adoption of a common attitude.

WASHINGTON, January 19, 1938.

793.94/12211

Memorandum of Conversation, by the Secretary of State

[WASHINGTON,] January 20, 1938.

The British Ambassador called at my request. I said to him that, as he was aware, the situation in the Far East was becoming increasingly dangerous and desperate, calling for the closest observation and analysis and the most careful planning; that these conditions in the Pacific area were closely tied in, especially with the German and Italian situation in Europe; that any improvement in the European situation would correspondingly affect the Far Eastern situation; that naturally we here feel the vital importance of the closest possible observation of every fact, circumstance and development which might be useful and important, especially to countries like Great Britain and the United States in dealing with the situation to the best advantage and without the risk of unfortunate delay.

I then asked the Ambassador a number of confidential questions not for the record. The Ambassador concurred in the observations I offered and indicated a disposition to collaborate and cooperate at all times to the fullest extent. He did not know anything about any plans of his Government with respect to the removal of their troops out of China or any movements of their Navy.

The Ambassador thought that the bad economic and other domestic repercussions in Rumania, following the change of government, might mean an early solution of acute conditions. He thought there was no danger whatever in any dissolution or weakening of the Franco-Russian Alliance. I urged his Government to give every consistent attention to the question of how the reciprocal trade program and the kindred policies such as further exchange stabilization and others might be carried forward by any possible means, including definite steps to loosen up exchange conditions here and there and otherwise to urge and encourage other nations to proceed to take an affirmative interest in this general movement which has for its chief purpose peace by economic appeasement. He agreed to this view and added that he would be glad to keep in touch with his Government in this connection. I further remarked that, if and when he or his Government had any special or important facts pertaining to Germany or Italy in particular in relation to the proposed program which our two Governments are sponsoring, including that of general rehabilitation in Europe, we here would be most interested to have the benefit of them. He said he would be glad to bring this matter to the attention of his Government.

C[ORDELL] H[ULL]

793.94/12155 : Telegram

The Chargé in Germany (Gilbert) to the Secretary of State

BERLIN, January 20, 1938—5 p. m.
[Received January 20—3 : 03 p. m.]

22. With reference to a report from Tokyo that the Japanese Government had thanked Germany for its attempt at an adjustment in the

Far Eastern conflict, the Deutsches Nachrichten Buro last evening carried the following announcement:

"It is learned from official quarters that in the course of conversations which took place at the end of October 1937 between the German Ambassadors in Nanking and Tokyo and the Governments there, the wish was expressed by the Governments of the two countries in conflict for the assistance of Germany in the attempt to find an adjustment. In order to serve the interests of peace in the reestablishment of which Germany is as interested as the rest of the world, the German Government believed it should place itself at the disposal of the two countries with which it was on friendly terms for the proposed purpose. Hereby Germany from the beginning stressed that its attitude in the conflict was neutral and that therefore its cooperation could not transcend the simple transmission of communications which one of the two Governments might wish to transmit to the other. This principle has been observed.

"With the publication on January 16 of the manifesto of the Japanese Government the conflict between Japan and China has entered a new stage".

Referring to a report in the Paris *Temps* concerning the possibility of a joint German, French, English, American mediation in the conflict, this morning's DAZ [56] points out that the last three countries had so far shown very little understanding for Japan's action, that they had not like Germany observed a neutral attitude and that the proposed *démarche* is apparently primarily to be directed against Japan. It is intimated finally that the step would probably be of little use in view of the Japanese manifesto on January 16.

I inquired as to the basis of this announcement of Bismarck [57] at the Foreign Office this morning who informed me in substance as follows. The German Ambassadors at Nanking and Tokyo had facilitated the transmissions of two series of communications between the Chinese and Japanese Governments, one of which commencing in October last had extended into November and the other beginning at the end of December had continued for a time in January. Germany had not, however, acted in any capacity other than as a forwarding agent and had added nothing whatsoever to the communications except to express the wish to both parties that a settlement might be achieved. Germany had undertaken this in response to the request of the parties both of which had expressed the view that Germany afforded a suitable agency inasmuch as she was the only great power which through the Brussels Conference [58] or otherwise had not taken a position in the matter. Both parties had requested at the time that

---

[56] *Deutsche Allgemeine Zeitung.*
[57] Acting Chief of the Political Bureau, German Foreign Office.
[58] November 3–24, 1937; see *Foreign Relations, 1937*, vol. IV, pp. 155 ff.

Germany not make her action public. He was aware that this had been the cause of "misunderstandings" in the press (Department's 115, November 5, 1 p. m.[59]) and that Germany was thus pleased that on the initiative of Japan the matter was being cleared up. The fact that the announcement came at this time had no special meaning except that Germany's action having come to an end rendered it opportune.

Respecting the general situation in the Far East, Bismarck expressed the view that the breaking of relations between Japan and China would not affect the status of affairs unless Japan should declare war. He believed that the conflict had now entered on a phase which meant that it would be long protracted. He could see no hope for success of mediatory efforts at this time.

He said that Germany was maintaining her attitude of complete neutrality and had informed the Chinese Government that it intended to continue that course unless Russia should enter the conflict in which case Germany would have to reconsider her position. He said, however, that the Foreign Office did not perceive any indication of Russia's taking such a step.

Regarding the item in the *Temps* cited above, Bismarck said that he was not aware of its having any official basis.

GILBERT

893.00/14200 : Telegram

The Consul General at Canton (Linnell) to the Secretary of State

CANTON, January 20, 1938—5 p. m.
[Received January 21—8 : 05 p. m.]

Following fall of Nanking and Central Government's instructions respecting guerrilla warfare plan, Kwangtung military, civil and Kuomintang authorities have been making great efforts in an ambitious program best describable as martialization both military and mental of the masses. Apparent objects are:

(1) Arouse in the people and particularly peasant laborers and students an aggressive fighting spirit and conception of the war as continuation of Sun Yat Sen's popular revolution against foreign imperialist invaders and traitorous northern militarists who would sell country for degrading peace and pecuniary profit;

(2) Impress people with sense of responsibility to actively share the Government's military defence of Kwangsi, "cradle of revolution," and combating of Japanese agents and peace advocates;

(3) Raise huge armed citizen forces for garrison duty, pioneer service, and guerrilla warfare.

[59] Not printed.

Authorities have issued manifestoes: Exhorting popular support of program; inviting complete freedom in volunteer self-defense corps organization and political activities within framework of Sun's doctrine; encouraging populace in hitherto forbidden private possession of arms (said to include 400,000 rifles) and their dedication to patriotic usage.

Movement has been boosted by tremendous press publicity and by officially encouraged student activity in leading popular demonstrations and organizing young men's militant associations and propaganda campaigns, and authorities have decreed that certain students be sent to popularize it throughout interior. Revolutionary aspect of movement is being capitalized to encourage its backing by labor groups.

Several hundred thousand new rifles reliably reported being distributed to interior farmers.

A commission including highest military, civil and party authorities has been appointed to supervise program, active direction to be entrusted to nine regional leaders apparently responsible for all measures, militia organization, training, coordination of volunteer self-defense corps and emergency defense of their regions in cooperation with regular army. These leaders thus far announced are all colorful military and party figures and pro-war popular front enthusiasts reportedly including Chen Ming Shu, Tsai Ting Kai and Li Fu Lin.

While program is not yet in full operation it is reported reliably that organized armed militia under training already number about 200,000 with several hundred thousand more enrolled.

Definitely Leftist in appearance, the movement emphasizes special concern for popular, especially farm labor, welfare and apparently supports closer relations with Russia and democratic countries and the policy of destruction of Japanese and surrendered Chinese properties.

Identic coordinated movements are reported in Kwangsi and Hunan though the program is less significant in Kwangsi due to the province's already highly developed militia and police training systems.

While it is too early to estimate the movement's full significance and possible consequences, there appears no doubt of its present support by national and provincial governments and its proof of South China's determination to see the war through.

Mailed Hong Kong, Swatow.

LINNELL

793.94/12162 : Telegram

The Counselor of Embassy in China (Lockhart) to the
Secretary of State

PEIPING, January 21, 1938—3 p. m.
[Received January 21—8 : 05 a. m.]

45. Embassy's 36, January 18, 4 p. m.[60]

1. The headquarters of the Japanese forces in North China have been transferred from Tientsin to Peiping. General Terauchi arrived yesterday, stating that the primary reason for the transfer is military, that he may be able to render personal assistance to the new Government and to cooperate in the execution of administrative policies, that due to the absence of sincerity on the part of the National Government, the Japanese Government has been compelled to take steps to cease dealing with the National Government, and that his entire efforts will be directed toward complete extermination of the Kuomintang Army and the construction and consolidation of "the new and rising China".

2. The transfer of the headquarters has been under consideration for some time. Presumably the delay in transfer was due to a decision not to take a step which might create an additional hindrance to Sino-Japanese negotiations, a reason which however ceased to exist with Japan's decision not to deal without [*with the?*] National Government. The primary reason for the transfer seems to be, as Terauchi said, military, as Peiping is from the viewpoint of strategic communications more important than Tientsin. The new Chinese régime can scarcely welcome the change as its puppet character will thus be emphasized. Japanese claim that the transfer is not related to Japanese dissatisfaction with Wang Keh Min.[61]

Repeated to the Ambassador by mail to Tokyo.

LOCKHART

893.01 Provisional/41

Memorandum of Conversation, by the Chief of the Division of Far
Eastern Affairs (Hamilton)

[WASHINGTON,] January 21, 1938.

Mr. Mallet, Counselor of the British Embassy, called at his request and left with me the attached *aide-mémoire*, dated January 19,[62] in regard to questions relating to the calls upon diplomatic representatives at Peiping of officials of the new "Provisional Government".

I informed Mr. Mallet of the telegraphic instructions No. 400, December 15, 7 p. m.,[63] and No. 18, January 18, 6 p. m., sent by the

---

[60] Not printed.
[61] Head of the Japanese-sponsored regime at Peiping.
[62] *Ante*, p. 38.
[63] *Foreign Relations*, 1937, vol. III, p. 811.

Department to the American Embassy at Peiping. Mr. Mallet made note of the substance of these telegraphic instructions.

I told Mr. Mallet that if the British Government, after being informed by the British Embassy here of the substance of the instructions which the Department had sent to Peiping in this matter, wished to make any comments or suggestions, we would be very glad to consider them.

Mr. Mallet said that the information I had given, as indicated in the second paragraph of this memorandum, would constitute a reply to the *aide-mémoire*.

M[AXWELL] M. H[AMILTON]

793.94/12370

Memorandum of Conversation, by the Adviser on Political Relations (Hornbeck)

[WASHINGTON,] January 21, 1938.

Participants: Mr. Welles
                        Mr. Kojiro Matsukata (President, Matsukata Japan-
                              Soviet Oil Company, Limited)
                        Mr. Hornbeck

Mr. Matsukata's call on Mr. Welles followed upon a request by Mr. L. J. Hunt of New York City, by letter, and a request made by the Japanese Embassy here that Mr. Welles receive Mr. Matsukata.

Mr. Welles had not been informed that Mr. Matsukata would raise the question which Mr. Matsukata did raise.

Mr. Welles had in advance asked Mr. Hornbeck to be present at the interview.

When Mr. Matsukata entered Mr. Welles' office, Mr. Welles said to Mr. Matsukata that he had known and had considered it a privilege to know, when he was in Japan in the years at the beginning of the World War, Mr. Matsukata's father,[64] and that he was very glad to meet that father's son.

Mr. Matsukata appropriately acknowledged this friendly overture, remarked that Mr. Welles had mentioned meeting his father during the World War, and made the observation that he, Matsukata, had now come here at a time when Japan was "at war." He then referred to some features of the present situation and led up to and made an inquiry whether the American Government might not tender to Japan and China the good offices of this country. He developed his statement and inquiry in a manner which implied or warranted

---

[64] Former Japanese Prime Minister and "Elder Statesman" (Genro) who died in 1923.

inference that he felt that the existing situation is one of disadvantage and hazard to Japan, and he stressed the possibility of its leading to serious controversy or conflict between Japan and other countries, with the implication that it therefore makes the position of other countries hazardous.

Mr. Welles said that he wished to be perfectly frank and wished to make the attitude and position of this Government clear beyond the possibility of any misunderstanding. He would ask Mr. Hornbeck to state on what occasions this Government had already proffered its good offices. Mr. Hornbeck said that, on July 12, five days after the first armed clash between the Japanese and the Chinese near Peiping, the Secretary of State, in conversation with the Japanese Ambassador,[65] had stated that this Government regretted the outbreak of these hostilities, hoped that they would not spread, and would be prepared to be of assistance to the Japanese and the Chinese Governments, if they were willing, toward composing their differences; that the Secretary had said the same thing to the Chinese Ambassador at that time; and that, thereafter, on the occasion of almost every interview which he had had with the Japanese and the Chinese Ambassadors respectively, the Secretary had reiterated those points. Mr. Welles raised question of the position taken by this Government at the Brussels Conference, and Mr. Hornbeck went on to say that at the Brussels Conference this Government and the other Conference powers, taking note of the Japanese Government's reply to the Belgian Government's invitation in terms indicating that the Japanese Government was not prepared to attend the Conference, had suggested to and requested of the Japanese Government that that Government appoint a representative to confer with representatives of a few or a small number of the powers; and that the Japanese Government had replied that it was not prepared to do that.

Mr. Welles then referred to Mr. Matsukata's inquiry and stated that he, Mr. Welles, having lived three years in Japan, had long had a most friendly feeling toward the Japanese people and a great admiration of their many splendid qualities and outstanding achievements; that he shared Mr. Matsukata's view that the present situation is deplorable and fraught with hazards; that the Government of the United States has from the outset been desirous of contributing toward ameliorating the situation in the Far East and toward composing the conflict which is going on there. We have repeatedly proferred our good offices. The Japanese Government has at no time responded favorably. It is our understanding that the German Government a few weeks ago took steps toward mediation, that the Jap-

[65] See memorandum of July 12, 1937, *Foreign Relations*, Japan, 1931–1941, vol. I, p. 316.

256941—54——4

anese Government informed the German Ambassador in China of the Japanese Government's peace proposals, that the German Ambassador laid these before the Chinese Government, and that the Chinese Government did not find the proposals acceptable. The American Government could not take at this time an initiative; it could act only if it were informed officially by the Japanese Government and by the Chinese Government respectively that those Governments desire an exercise of good offices by it; and that, if we were to embark upon exercise of good offices, our action would have to be on the basis of terms consistent with the Nine Power Treaty.

Mr. Matsukata appeared disconcerted. He said that if the American Government felt that it must fall back on "historical" ground and insist on applying the Nine Power Treaty the whole problem was made very difficult.

Mr. Welles commented on that statement, to the effect that the American Government did not regard the Nine Power Treaty as being merely an "historical" instrument; that this Government regards that treaty as an agreement still in effect between and among the powers parties to it, among which are both Japan and the United States, and that, as we have on several occasions stated, such an agreement is binding until it has been made not so by the common assent of the parties to it, a procedure quite different from a unilateral disregard of it by some one of the parties. Mr. Welles asked whether Mr. Hornbeck would care to make any comment.

Mr. Hornbeck referred to the fact that in 1933 or 1934 this Government, in a communication to the Japanese Government through Mr. Grew,[66] had expressly and formally stated that in our view the provisions of treaties can be altered, but only by recognized processes. He continued, with the raising of an hypothetical question: Suppose that the question of the Nine Power Treaty could be left out of consideration, suppose there were no such treaty; could Mr. Matsukata expect the American Government, in view of the facts that the Germans have been endeavoring to bring about a mediation and that Japan's terms have been communicated to the Chinese and that those terms are what they are and that the Chinese have rejected them,—could the American Government at this moment step in and proffer its good offices? Mr. Matsukata replied that the United States was very different from Germany; that the Japanese had confidence in the United States; that the United States is a great and powerful and friendly power; and that he thought that a proffer on our part would be listened to. He said that the Japanese felt kindly toward the United States but were now not well disposed toward Great Britain; that Americans treated the Japanese with an attitude of understand-

---

[66] See Department's telegram No. 59, April 28, 1934, 7 p. m., *Foreign Relations, Japan, 1931–1941*, vol. I, p. 231.

ing and consideration but that the British did not; that the Japanese would be receptive toward any efforts which the United States might make in the direction of and in connection with mediation; but that if the British were included in the making of such an effort the Japanese would react unfavorably.

Mr. Welles said that he wanted to make one point perfectly clear; that Mr. Matsukata must not infer from what Mr. Hornbeck had said that the facts of the existence of the Nine Power Treaty and of matters appertaining thereto could be set aside or left out of consideration. He pointed out that Mr. Hornbeck simply asked a hypothetical question. Mr. Hornbeck said that he too felt it important that Mr. Matsukata should not infer from what he had said that the Nine Power Treaty could be left out of consideration.

Mr. Matsukata again indicated that he felt that this view on the part of the American Government made the question of bringing the hostilities to an end very difficult; and he made a plea for our sweeping all such considerations aside and concentrating entirely on the fact that there exists in the Far East a tragic situation potential of producing even worse situations. He again urged that the United States should take an initiative.

Mr. Welles stated that our position was as follows:

First, That action in the direction of mediation could be taken by this Government only if there came to it an official indication from the Japanese Government and a similar indication from the Chinese Government that good offices or mediation by this Government are desired by those Governments respectively; Second, That this Government could act only on the basis of and in the light of its being understood that the settlement must be consistent with both the principles and the provisions of the Nine Power Treaty; and Third, That it is the position of this Government that the provisions of the Nine Power Treaty are susceptible of modification, amendment and alteration, but only by recognized processes of negotiation and agreement, not by unilateral action on the part of any one power.

Mr. Matsukata arose to take leave. He thanked Mr. Welles for having received him and given him so much time. Mr. Welles again expressed his admiration of Mr. Matsukata's father and his pleasure at having met Mr. Matsukata. Mr. Matsukata, in saying good-bye to Mr. Hornbeck, remarked, "Do not be too hard on us." Mr. Hornbeck, surprised at this remark, replied that none of us has any desire to be "hard on" Japan; that we are animated by no feeling of hostility; and that we are all intent on and hopeful of doing something constructively helpful in our relations with countries of the Far East. Mr. Matsukata said, "In that case it will be all right."

The interview there ended.

ADDENDA.

1. At an early point in this conversation Mr. Welles took occasion to speak of the adverse effect on public opinion in this country which had been produced by the *Panay* incident and other unwarranted acts by the Japanese armed forces.

2. At a late point in the conversation Mr. Matsukata asked expressly whether Mr. Welles had been informed by Mr. Grew of Japan's peace proposals. Mr. Welles said that he had been informed. Mr. Matsukata asked whether the American Government could not look with approval upon those proposals. Mr. Welles said that before it would be possible for him to come to any conclusion in that connection it would be necessary for him to have more precise knowledge of the implications of the proposals; the proposals were in general and broad terms.

S[TANLEY] K. H[ORNBECK]

704.9394/3 : Telegram

The Ambassador in Japan (Grew) to the Secretary of State

TOKYO, January 22, 1938—11 a. m.
[Received January 22—1 : 30 a. m.]

48. I have today addressed to the Consul General the following instruction :

The Consulate at Nagoya has referred to me the hypothetical question whether it might take over the archives and property of the Chinese Consulate in the event that the latter office were to be closed.

I would appreciate your informing the officers in your supervisory district that if they are requested by their Chinese colleagues to assume charge of archives and effects they should take the position that they would be prepared to lend their good offices in any emergency that might occur but that in the absence of authorization from the Department they are not in a position to assume responsibility for the archives and property of Chinese Consulates.

GREW

793.94/12176 : Telegram

The Third Secretary of Embassy in China (Allison) to the Secretary of State

NANKING, January 22, 1938—noon.
[Received 8 : 56 p. m.]

32. Embassy's January 21, noon [67] and Tokyo's 39, January 19, noon. In my January 8 [5], 4 p. m.[68] from Wuhu it was reported

---

[67] Not found in Department files.
[68] Vol. IV, p. 219.

that during the first week of occupation Japanese soldiers engaged in "ruthless treatment and slaughter of civilians and wanton looting and destruction of private property". In a later report January 9, 1938, a copy of which was addressed to Tokyo, left Nanking for Shanghai on January 10, a detailed report was given of conditions in Wuhu, including as an enclosure a copy of an account prepared by an American missionary concerning Japanese actions in that city.[69]

In my January 6, 5 p. m.[70] I reported that local American residents had told "an appalling story of wanton killing of civilian Chinese and violation of women, some taking place in American property" and in my 27, January 18, 4 p. m.[71] further instances were given of the taking by force of women from American property. I have not deemed it advisable to send full details of such atrocities by telegraph but a detailed report is being prepared which will shortly be forwarded by safe means to Shanghai.[72] It can be said, however, that such facts as reported in Tokyo's telegram under reference have been fully authenticated here and that this office has on file written statements from responsible American citizens testifying to the absolutely barbarous action of Japanese troops, whose officers made no apparent effort to control them, after the occupation of Nanking.

While conditions have improved, discipline has not yet been completely restored and we continue to receive from American residents a daily average of three or four reports of rape or attempted rape within the refugee zone. How many cases take place without commanding the attention of these Americans it is impossible to say. The Japanese are now making an attempt to get Chinese refugees to return to their homes outside the refugee zone but there is considerable reluctance to do so inasmuch as many of those who have returned have been robbed, raped and in several cases bayoneted to death by Japanese soldiers. Records of such cases are on file at this office.

Sent to Embassy [at] Hankow, Peiping, Shanghai. Shanghai please repeat to Tokyo. ALLISON

893.48/1406 : Telegram

The Third Secretary of Embassy in China (Allison) to the Secretary of State

NANKING, January 22, 1938—4 p. m.
[Received 10 : 22 p. m.]

33. In common with British and German colleagues I have received the Chairman of the International Committee for the Nanking safety

---

[69] Neither printed.
[70] Vol. IV, p. 221.
[71] *Foreign Relations*, Japan, 1931–1941, vol. I, p. 567.
[72] Not printed.

zone, a German subject, outlining difficulties which the Japanese Army has raised with regard to the feeding of approximately 250,000 Chinese refugees now in Nanking.

The International Committee has been distributing rice and flour free to those who could not pay for it and selling it at a low price to those who could. Since the morning of January 10th the Japanese Army has forced them to stop sales and has said that all distribution of rice and flour must be made through local Chinese Autonomous Committee in cooperation with the Japanese Army. Between December 13th, when the Japanese occupied the city, and January 19th, the army had only assigned 2,200 bags of rice and 1,000 bags of flour for sale to the civilian population. Permission has been refused the International Committee by the army, either to bring in rice and wheat previously purchased and now outside the city walls, or to have foodstuffs shipped up from Shanghai.

It is estimated by responsible American members of the International Committee that a regular supply of 1,600 bags of rice a day is needed adequately to feed the Chinese population. At present the Japanese authorities are allowing only approximately 1,000 bags a week to be distributed. A supply of at least 40 tons of coal a day is also said to be needed and at present none whatever is being sold commercially. It is understood that adequate supplies of foodstuffs and coal are available and the action of the Japanese is therefore difficult to understand.

While the situation has not yet become serious, due to stocks already on hand in private families, it may easily become so at any moment. The International Committee is feeding, without charge, 50,000 persons a day but its stocks are running low. If sufficient food and fuel is not provided for these Chinese refugees it is quite possible that riots may occur with consequent danger to foreign lives and property.

Quite apart from the humanitarian aspect of the matter it would appear that the possible danger to American interests ensuing as a result of this slow starvation of thousands of Chinese might be sufficient grounds for this Office to take up the question with the Japanese authorities. My British colleague states that he does not wish to take precipitate action, while my German colleague, who has been taking an extremely strong stand with the Japanese regarding the inhuman activities of their troops, is willing to approach them at once. The opinion of the Ambassador in this regard would be appreciated.

Sent to Embassy, Hankow. Repeated to Peiping, Shanghai; Shanghai please repeat to Tokyo.

ALLISON

704.9394/3 : Telegram

The Secretary of State to the Ambassador in Japan (Grew)

WASHINGTON, January 23, 1938—2 p. m.

21. Your 48, January 22, 11 a. m. The Department suggests that, in order to avoid misunderstanding, you substitute for the phrase, "that they would be prepared to lend their good offices in any emergency", the following phrase: "that, without assuming representative functions, they would be prepared to render all appropriate assistance, temporarily, in any emergency".

HULL

701.9394/16 : Telegram

The Secretary of State to the Ambassador in Japan (Grew)

WASHINGTON, January 23, 1938—3 p. m.

22. Your 42, January 20, 2 p. m.[73] Under date January 21, Ambassador Johnson telegraphed from Hankow in part as follows:

"Minister for Foreign Affairs last evening told me that he had instructed Chinese Ambassador to Japan to leave Tokyo and return to China. Chinese Ambassador to Japan was not handed his credentials by the Japanese Government. Minister for Foreign Affairs commented somewhat sarcastically upon statement reported by press as emanating from spokesman of Japanese Foreign Office that members of Chinese Embassy remaining in Tokyo would not retain diplomatic status but would be treated like ordinary citizens, whereas Japanese Foreign Office apparently considers that Japanese Counselor remaining in China will be Chargé d'Affaires with all diplomatic prerogatives intact."

The Department desires to have by urgent telegram such information as you may have or may be in position discreetly to obtain in regard to the statement reported as emanating from spokesman of Japanese Foreign Office that members of Chinese Embassy remaining in Tokyo would not retain diplomatic status but would be treated like ordinary citizens.

HULL

701.9394/18 : Telegram

The Ambassador in Japan (Grew) to the Secretary of State

TOKYO, January 24, 1938—1 p. m.
[Received January 24—7 : 05 a. m.]

49. Department's 22, January 23, 3 p. m. The Foreign Office spokesman on January 21 made the following statement which appeared in the local press.

[73] Not printed.

"Although it has ceased to deal with General Chiang Kai Shek's regime, the Japanese Government will continue to accord diplomatic and consular privileges to Chinese diplomatic and consular officials representing the National Government." [74]

The Foreign Office this morning upon discreet approach confirmed the foregoing and stated categorically that the status of the Chinese Chargé d'Affaires would remain unchanged.

In other words it is the view of the Japanese Government that the *de jure* status of the Japanese and Chinese diplomatic and consular officials respectively remains unchanged.

Repeated to Shanghai for Nanking and Johnson.

GREW

893.48/1410 : Telegram

The Ambassador in China (Johnson) to the Secretary of State

HANKOW, January 24, 1938—7 p. m.
[Received January 24—12 : 54 p. m.]

54. Allison's 33, January 22, 4 p. m. I have replied as follows.

"January 24, 5 p. m. Your 33, January 22, 4 p. m. I see no reason why you should not approach Japanese military with a view to urging that International Committee be permitted to import supplies. I have repeated this telegram to Washington and Tokyo".

Repeated to Shanghai, Shanghai please repeat to Tokyo.

JOHNSON

793.94119/394

Memorandum by the Chief of the Division of Far Eastern Affairs (Hamilton) of a Conversation With the Second Secretary of the Chinese Embassy (Tsui)

[WASHINGTON,] January 24, 1938.

Mr. Tsui called at his request. He said that on Saturday the Chinese Ambassador had received a cable from the Chinese Foreign Office asking the Ambassador to inform the Department that the Chinese Government had informed the German Ambassador to China that the Japanese peace terms, as communicated to the Chinese Government through the German Ambassador, were so vague that the Chinese Government desired that the Japanese Government clarify and elucidate the terms; that the Japanese Foreign Minister, upon receipt of this information from the Chinese Government, said that because of the delay the Japanese Government had abandoned peace

---

[74] The Secretary of State informed the Chinese Ambassador to this effect on January 24 and added "that this would seem to dispose of his request, to which he assented." For the request of December 13, 1937, see *Foreign Relations*, 1937, vol. III, p. 803.

negotiations and that in the future the Japanese Government would proceed on the basis of new developments. Mr. Tsui said that according to the Chinese Foreign Office cablegram, the Chinese Government wished to inform us of the foregoing and that peace movements had ended.

I thanked Mr. Tsui for communicating this information to us and said that I would bring it to the attention of the Secretary.

M[AXWELL] M. H[AMILTON]

894.032/181

Memorandum by the Assistant Chief of the Division of Far Eastern Affairs (Ballantine)

[WASHINGTON,] January 25, 1938.

The speech made by Mr. Hirota, Minister for Foreign Affairs, before the Imperial Diet on January 22, 1938,[75] consists for the most part of stereotyped generalities on Japan's foreign policy. He deals in turn with Japan's objectives in China, Japan's relations with "Manchukuo", the Soviet Union, the United States, Great Britain, Germany and Italy, foreign trade and trade relations, and Japan's "cultural work" abroad.

[Here follows summary of address.]

Comment. Mr. Hirota's announcement regarding Japan's intentions in relation to China appears to strengthen the view that the pledge regarding China's territorial integrity will be meaningless in view of the indication contained in the announcement that Japan will proceed with the dismemberment of China under similar fictions to that employed when Manchuria was occupied. With regard to the assurances concerning the intention of Japan to respect the principle of the "open door", there are already indications from reports regarding the economic program in North China that this principle will be subordinated, as it was in Manchuria, to the exigencies of a policy of economic nationalism.

The most hopeful feature of Mr. Hirota's address does not therefore appear to lie in his pronouncements with regard to China's territorial integrity or the "open door" but in his statement that "The importance to the conduct of our foreign affairs of American understanding needs scarcely to be mentioned. We shall continue to do our best toward the furtherance of Japanese-American amity and good will". This statement serves to indicate that the United States is still in position to exercise a certain degree of moral influence upon Japan although not to the extent of causing Japan to desist from its present aggressive course in and with regard to China.

[75] *Foreign Relations,* Japan, 1931–1941, vol. I, p. 438.

893.48/1410 : Telegram

The Secretary of State to the Ambassador in China (Johnson)

WASHINGTON, January 25, 1938—2 p. m.

35. Nanking's 33, January 22, 4 p. m., and your 54, January 24, 7 p. m. The Department approves your instruction to Allison and suggests that Allison be advised to stress the humanitarian aspect of the matter.

The Department feels that the situation is one which might warrant action in Tokyo should action in Nanking fail to accomplish the ends desired.

Repeated to Tokyo.

HULL

———————

893.48/1420 : Telegram

The Consul General at Shanghai (Gauss) to the Secretary of State

SHANGHAI, January 26, 1938—11 a. m.
[Received January 26—8 : 50 a. m.]

138. Following from Tokyo:

"January 25, 8 p. m.   For relay to Nanking:
'Your 33, January 22, 4 p m.

1. The Foreign Office informed us today that Okazaki, who is now temporarily in Tokyo, reported that an arrangement had been made by which the International Committee could bring into the safety zone whatever supplies it might have owned prior to the Japanese occupation of Nanking and is authorized to purchase supplies up to Mexican dollars 100,000 granted to the Committee by the Nanking municipality.

2. The Foreign Office also stated that it has instructed the Japanese Consul General at Shanghai to submit a full report on the situation at Nanking and to extend in the meantime full cooperation to the International Committee with respect to caring for Chinese refugees.

3. The impression given us at the Foreign Office is that the military authorities at Nanking who have not "recognized" the International Committee feel that conditions at Nanking do not warrant this Committee assuming continued responsibilities of the care of the Chinese refugees and are anxious to have this work turned over to the local Chinese Autonomous Committee'.

Please repeat to Hankow".

GAUSS

———————

693.002/470

Memorandum of Conversation, by the Secretary of State

[WASHINGTON,] January 26, 1938.

The Chinese Ambassador called on his own request. He referred to my recent telephone message to him regarding the Chinese proposal that this Government take over their interests in Tokyo and the lack of occasion for our doing so now. He remarked that he had sent this information on to his Government and had since heard nothing to the contrary. I expressed the view that probably this settled the matter for an indefinite period, in which he acquiesced.

The Ambassador then stated that a rather serious development seems to be in prospect in connection with the understanding that the Japanese puppet government located at Peiping is undertaking to lower or abolish certain tariffs; that this would probably be chiefly or entirely for the benefit of Japan; that up until last year China had been meeting her debt service, both internal and external; that I, of course, would understand the large factor these Chinese customs receipts constitute, and that therefore such action will play havoc with their continued meeting of debt service. I first inquired as to which port or ports these customs reductions would probably be applied, and the Ambassador expressed the view that Tientsin would be at least the chief place of entry of goods. I then remarked that this Government for some time has made known its position of standing for the integrity of customs organization in China, as well as its reasons therefor; that naturally it has also expressed its frank view when any entry of goods for the Japanese Government or groups of Japanese individuals was being undertaken or so reported.

The Ambassador then said that he thought a declaration of war by Japan was less remote now than heretofore, and he would be interested to know what our policy would be in that event. I replied that that was a matter I would be obliged to discuss with him if and when such development actually took place; that I would not be in a position to do so earlier. He at least seemed to understand the situation.

The Ambassador then stated that there was a report to the effect the British and the Japanese have some sort of agreement whereby the Japanese are to deal gently with Canton and the British are to be less disposed to allow arms, ammunition, and implements of war to enter China through Hong Kong. He asked if I knew anything about this report, to which I replied in the negative.

He said the fighting was fairly brisk at this time.

C[ORDELL] H[ULL]

893.0146/625

The British Embassy to the Department of State

AIDE-MÉMOIRE

His Majesty's Government in the United Kingdom are not opposed in principle to a gradual withdrawal of their military establishment in North China in the manner indicated in the communication made by the State Department on the 18th January, but they have to consider a danger which does not face the United States Government since there is no United States concession at Tientsin.

The Japanese military authorities in Tientsin recently demanded the surrender of a Chinese in the British concession on the ground of his anti-Japanese activities. They offered no evidence in support of their charge and the demand was refused. They then gave a time limit within which the man was to be surrendered and failing compliance they threatened to enter the concession and take him by force. On learning however that such action would be forcibly resisted the higher Japanese authorities explained that a misunderstanding had occurred.

In the light of this experience it is clear that a withdrawal or even a reduction of the British garrison would encourage further attempts of the same kind and possibly inflict the humiliation of violation or seizure of the concession. This being so, it is suggested that, unless the situation in North China deteriorates dangerously in the meantime, the question of withdrawal might be left for a general settlement which His Majesty's Government hope that it may be possible to initiate at a later stage.

His Majesty's Government's views as regards the diplomatic establishments in North China are that these would constitute a useful bargaining counter and that their withdrawal might also await a general settlement if such a settlement is not forestalled by Japanese recognition of the new provisional government or by other decided action.

Should the United States Government nevertheless be in favour of an early withdrawal of diplomatic and military establishments in North China it is hoped that they may agree to discuss the matter further with His Majesty's Government and the French Government to whom no further communication is being made by His Majesty's Government at present.

WASHINGTON, January 26, 1938.

793.94/12231 : Telegram

The Ambassador in China (Johnson) to the Secretary of State

HANKOW, January 27, 1938—2 p.m.
[Received January 27—1:25 p.m.]

61. It is learned from unofficial but apparently reliable source that during Chinese air raid on Nanking January 26 one plane was shot down and one made forced landing and was captured by the Japanese. Aviators in both were Russians and since this is the first time the

Japanese have obtained positive proof of Chinese employment of Russian personnel there is some speculation here whether relations between Japan and the Soviet Union will be affected. Report believed reliable is that in a Japanese plane shot down by Chinese at Nanchang recently the aviator who was killed was found to be Italian. This information has been released by the Chinese.

Repeated to Peiping.

JOHNSON

793.94 Conference/362

Memorandum of Conversation, by the Secretary of State

[WASHINGTON,] January 29, 1938.

The Chinese Ambassador called on his own request. He said that his Government had instructed him to inquire what the attitude of this Government would be with respect to functioning in the event there should be a reconvening of the Nine-Power Treaty signatories. I replied that that question should really answer itself; with respect to a duly called meeting of the signatories of the Nine-Power Treaty, that this Government would, of course, promptly accept and attend such meeting; that this was logically its situation as a signatory and as a member of the Brussels Conference. I added that we would likewise continue to function in connection with any duly called meetings of the Advisory Committee,[76] if I might further illustrate the situation of this Government. I then said that in my opinion there was an important preliminary question about which we have heard no expression from those who may be suggesting a reconvening of the Nine-Power signatories, and that question was whether there had been made any attempt whatsoever to forecast the opportunities for substantial accomplishment by such meeting of the Nine-Power Treaty signatories. I said that a meeting called haphazardly, without any preliminary preparations or plans to reasonably insure at least its substantial success in behalf of peace, would probably be doomed to failure and this would simply give a black eye to peace and to the Ambassador's country and my own; that I mentioned my own for the reason that whenever any meeting or conference is in prospect, one or more important governments, or those assuming to speak for them, immediately begin to circulate reports and rumors which get into the press that they will go as far as the United States, that they will first call upon the United States to know if it will do such and such, as in case of the despatch this morning that three governments are calling upon the United States to join them in furnishing arms, ammunition and implements of war to China, although they

---

[76] For League of Nations activities, see pp. 488 ff.

fully know our situation and should know that such questions and statements are more harmful than helpful. I concluded by suggesting to the Ambassador, in addition to my answer to his inquiry, that I would like finally to emphasize again the question of whether those at Geneva who convened as the members of the Council, having seemingly failed to do anything themselves, are merely seeking to shift the situation to another meeting of the Nine-Power Treaty signatories without any thought or preparation, as stated. I said that I was not making this observation from the standpoint of either encouraging or discouraging a meeting of the Nine-Power Treaty signatories, but for the reason that ought to be manifest to every practical statesman having anything to do with the matter.

C[ORDELL] H[ULL]

893.0146/621a

The Department of State to the British Embassy

AIDE-MÉMOIRE

Acknowledgment is made of receipt of the British Embassy's *aide-mémoire* of January 26 on the subject of withdrawal of establishments in north China.

The Government of the United States would welcome exposition of the British Government's references to "a general settlement."

In the interval, the Department requests that the British Ambassador inform the British Government that the Government of the United States is making plans to withdraw its present armed force at Tientsin, two battalions of the 15th Regiment U. S. A., on or about March 4, and simultaneously to send from Peiping to Tientsin, to be stationed temporarily at Tientsin, two companies from the marine guard which this Government now has stationed at Peiping, leaving at Peiping two companies of that guard.

WASHINGTON, January 29, 1938.

893.0146/621b

Oral Statement by the Adviser on Political Relations (Hornbeck) to the Counselor of the British Embassy (Mallet) [77]

The making of arrangements for these changes necessarily involves issuance of orders and beginning of execution of orders well in advance of the date on which withdrawals and transfers are to become

---

[77] Statement made at the time of handling to the Counselor of the British Embassy the Department's *aide-mémoire, supra.*

Similar oral statement, but including also information as to plans for withdrawal of troops, was made to the Third Secretary of the French Embassy, January 31 (893.0146/646a).

effective. In order to give the British Government time to consider what changes, if any, it may desire to make, effort will be made by the American Government to avoid, for a period of at least one week, publicity with regard to the changes which it is preparing to make. We cannot undertake, however, absolutely to guarantee that this effort will be successful.

[WASHINGTON,] January 29, 1938.

893.01 Provisional/43 : Telegram

The Counselor of Embassy in China (Lockhart) to the Secretary of State

PEIPING, January 30, 1938—10 p. m.
[Received January 30—11:43 a. m.]

75. Representatives of the Provincial [*Provisional*] Government and the East Hopei Anti-Communist Government signed an agreement here this afternoon by which the latter will be merged with the former on February 1. All agreements entered into by the East Hopei Government will be recognized by the Provisional Government. More details will be telegraphed tomorrow.[79]

Repeated to Ambassador.

LOCKHART

793.94/12353

Generalissimo Chiang Kai-shek to President Roosevelt [80]

HANKOW, January 30, 1938.

DEAR PRESIDENT ROOSEVELT: I was greatly pleased to receive on January 24 through His Excellency the American Ambassador here a telegraphic copy of Your Excellency's letter of January 11 [81] in reply to my message of December 24, 1937.[82]

I have been deeply moved by the warm tone in which you have responded to my appeal. Your earnest hope for a settlement of the present conflict with such reasonable provisions as you have indicated coincides with the very object of our sanguinary struggle against Japan's aggression and vandalism. We are not only defending our own rights and our own national integrity, but also striving for the preservation of the rights and interests of all powers concerned. In

---

[79] Not printed.
[80] Copy handed to the Secretary of State on February 7 by the Chinese Ambassador. Acknowledgment was made by the Secretary on February 16 at President Roosevelt's request (793.94/12440).
[81] See telegram No. 27, January 19, 11 a. m., to the Ambassador in China, p. 36.
[82] *Foreign Relations*, 1937, vol. III, p. 832.

a settlement you have visualized, we will show due regard even for Japan's rights and legitimate interests in China.

I am happy to learn that you are giving constant study and thought to the problem of the ways and means which may contribute most effectively toward promoting peace and facilitating international cooperation. The United States has always played a leading role in the promotion of international peace and order in general and justice and harmony in the Far East in particular. We recall with gratification the historical instances in which the United States endeavored to meet the disturbing conditions in this part of the world with timely and helpful intervention. At the end of the last century when China was going through the most trying period of her diplomatic relations, it was the American Government which initiated (and has ever since upheld) the principle of equal opportunity for the commerce and industry of all nations. It was again through the effort of the President of the United States of America as mediator that a Far Eastern conflict in the beginning of this century was brought to an end.[83] That the Washington Conference [84] at which the Pacific questions were discussed and settled owed its origin and success to the United States of America is a fact which is still fresh in our memory.

Your great country has not only significantly contributed toward the general cause of peace and concord in the Far East, but has from time to time given exemplary assistance of one kind or another to the Government and the people of China. The United States was the first country which remitted to China the American portion of the indemnity of 1901. The American universities and colleges have imparted useful knowledge to countless Chinese youth who, imbued with American ideals, have returned to render valuable service in the development of this country. The American generous public has given us inestimable aid and relief in time of dire need. American financial help such as the Cotton and Wheat Loan has contributed in no small measure to China's success in carrying out her plan of national rehabilitation and reconstruction. The American Government was the first to conclude with the Chinese Government a treaty restoring to China the right to tariff autonomy.[85] All these and other instances testify to the traditional friendship which exists between the United States and China.

It is the acknowledged leadership of the American Government in the common task for seeking international peace and security that has led all other powers to look to the United States for co-operation in

---

[83] President Theodore Roosevelt's mediation in the Russo–Japanese War, 1905; see *Foreign Relations*, 1905, pp. 807 ff.

[84] 1921–1922; see *Foreign Relations*, 1921, vol. I, pp. 18 ff., and *ibid.*, 1922, vol. I, pp. 1 ff.

[85] Signed at Peking, July 25, 1928, *ibid.*, 1928, vol. II, p. 475.

dealing with the present catastrophe in the Far East. It is on the strength of the unexcelled Sino-American friendship that China naturally looks to the United States for assistance during our momentous struggle for national existence. Permit me, Mr. President, to appeal to you once more to do everything possible to help hasten the end of Japan's aggression and the realization of the ideal for which both China and the United States of America firmly stand. It is our urgent wish that the United States will enable us to continue our resistance. I leave it to Your Excellency to decide what further measures may be adopted by the United States to bring about the final settlement you have in mind. I am as confident as ever that our common cause for peace and justice for the sanctity of treaties and for orderly and amicable relationship among nations is destined to win.

Very sincerely yours, CHIANG KAI-SHEK

893.0146/625

The Department of State to the British Embassy

AIDE-MÉMOIRE

The Department refers to the last paragraph of the British Embassy's *aide-mémoire* of January 26 on the subject of withdrawal of diplomatic and military establishments in north China, to the Department's *aide-mémoire* of January 29 on the same subject, and to previous recent exchanges of communications on the same subject.

The Department requests that the British Embassy ask the British Foreign Office to be so good as to inform the French Government of the contents of the Department's *aide-mémoire* of January 29 and to discuss with the French Government questions of reciprocal interest to the British and the French Governments in the light of that communication from the American Government to the British Government.

WASHINGTON, January 31, 1938.

893.0146/598 : Telegram

The Secretary of State to the Chargé in the United Kingdom (Johnson)

WASHINGTON, January 31, 1938—8 p. m.

41. Department's 498, December 19, 3 p. m.[86] The Brigade Headquarters of the Second Marine Brigade and the Sixth Regiment of United States Marines which were sent from San Diego to Shanghai in August last for temporary duty as a reenforcement to the Fourth

---

[86] *Foreign Relations*, 1937, vol. III, p. 822.

Marine Regiment already there, are to be withdrawn and are due to sail from Shanghai on board the Navy transport *Chaumont* on February 18.

Please informally inform the Foreign Office of the foregoing.

HULL

CHAPTER II: FEBRUARY 1–MARCH 14, 1938

Nature of American-British cooperation in Far East; Chinese mission to Moscow in search of further aid; exacerbation of Anglo-Japanese relations over China; British memorandum on possible peace terms for Japan and China (February 14); Ambassador Grew's review of Japanese naval building (February 18); Ambassador Johnson's opinion of German recognition of "Manchoukuo" (February 24); Soviet view of situation in Far East and Europe (March 4); Japanese plans for reorganization of China (March 14)

793.94/12271 : Telegram

The Ambassador in Japan (Grew) to the Secretary of State

TOKYO, February 1, 1938—1 p. m.
[Received February 1—9 : 10 a. m.]

63. My unnumbered telegram January 31, 5 p. m., via Shanghai.[87]

1. The period of military and political quiet in China which has existed since the Japanese Government's announcement of policy on January 14 [*16*] [88] has begun to raise in the Japanese popular mind some perplexity and doubt as to future developments. The official announcements had been preceded by several weeks of mysterious discussions within the Government and had a somewhat theatrical setting. For a short time it was believed that the ground was being prepared for some powerful blow which was to be dealt to China either in a political sense or in a military sense or both. Continued inactivity is therefore tending to become anticlimatic and is having adverse effect on public morale.

2. It is therefore in an atmosphere tinctured with some degree of pessimism and perplexity that reports were received of discussions between Great Britain, France and Soviet Russia with regard to some form of systematic aid to China. If such an arrangement were reached it is obvious that it could not be ignored by Japan without risking a collapse of public confidence in Japan's ability to meet any challenge from European quarters. The logical step for Japan to take to support that confidence would be to declare war. It is realized by the Japanese that such measure would not facilitate the prevention of the entry of arms from Indochina and Soviet Russia and that the closing of the Hong Kong route would merely divert the traffic to the

---

[87] See telegram No. 177, February 1, 11 a. m., *Foreign Relations*, Japan, 1931–1941, vol. I, p. 446.
[88] *Ibid.*, p. 437.

other routes. The practical results would be small but the belief prevails amongst many Japanese that if Japan were not to take formal cognizance of any such arrangement if made the moral consequences in Japan itself would be extremely serious.

3. We have no information with regard to the degree to which the building up of a consensus of opinion within the Government has developed and we would be inclined to advise the Department to discount reports from correspondents affecting to know that a decision to declare war has been reached if a specified condition of affairs should occur. Certainly the statement of the Prime Minister[89] reported to the Department might warrant such a conclusion but we do not believe that "inside" information will be permitted to leak out.

Repeated to Shanghai for Hankow.

GREW

711.41/377a : Telegram

The Secretary of State to the Chargé in the United Kingdom (Johnson)

WASHINGTON, February 2, 1938—7 p. m.

50. In the course of a speech in the Senate yesterday Senator Borah[90] made the following statement:

"But we are being placed in an attitude toward the other nations of the world which seems to me to need clarification. We are being charged throughout the world with having formed an alliance or alliances. The Secretary for Foreign Affairs for Great Britain,[91] speaking in the House of Commons a short time ago, and discussing the relationship of Great Britain to the United States, stated, in substance, that we—that is, Great Britain—have no actual treaty with the United States, but we have an understanding or relationship, and daily we are in consultation with reference to our foreign policy; and when asked what was that relationship, he stated that he could not reveal it. I do not quote his exact language, but I quote it in substance sufficiently to be entirely correct as to its import. Mr. President, I regard that statement as most unfortunate. It gave the world to understand that the United States and Great Britain had a working alliance or working relationship with reference to the eastern question particularly, and that it was of such nature that it must be kept a secret."

We are unable to identify any such statement by Eden and suggest that you might discuss the matter in the Foreign Office and say how helpful it would be if Mr. Eden would give me, for discreet use, any clarifying comment.

HULL

---

[89] For Prince Fumimaro Konoye's address of January 22, see *Foreign Relations, Japan, 1931–1941*, vol. I, p. 438.
[90] William E. Borah of Idaho, ranking Republican member of the Senate Committee on Foreign Relations.
[91] Anthony Eden.

793.94/12301 : Telegram

The Ambassador in China (Johnson) to the Secretary of State

HANKOW, February 3, 1938—2 p. m.
[Received 6 : 50 p. m.]

76. Tokyo's 63, February 1, 1 p. m.   Seven months have elapsed since the incident at the Marco Polo bridge precipitated the present invasion of China by Japan.   Japanese armies have succeeded during this time, at enormous cost in lives, material and treasure, in driving the Nationalist Government of China and its armies away from the coast, from Shanghai to Shanhaikwan, and have occupied the ruined and depopulated cities of Hangchow, Shanghai, Soochow, Wusih, Nanking, and Wuhu.   They hold Tsingtao, Tsinan, Taiyuan, Tientsin and Peiping.   They have systematically destroyed Chinese industry in these areas.   They control the railways between Shanghai and Suiyuan, and a good part of the Peiping–Hankow Railway.   Japanese bombing planes based within this area are able at will to bomb practically all of the other commercial centers of China.   It is believed that Japanese military forces, if disposed to do so, and at further considerable expense of lives, material and treasure, can in time occupy the Lunghai Railway, Hankow and the rest of the railway between Peiping and Hankow.   If this happens Japanese military forces will then have occupied practically the whole of the Yangtze and Yellow River valleys where the bulk of China's population lives and from which it draws the bulk of its food supply.   But the Japanese military will still be a long way from conquering or occupying the whole of China.

The intellectual life which has dominated the areas thus occupied and which has given character to modern Nationalist China will then have been driven into the western, more mountainous and less fertile areas.   There is no apparent evidence that this intellectual leadership and what is left of its armed forces are prepared to capitulate and make peace.   It is true that what is left of China's armed forces will be without equipment necessary to enable it to wage effective offensive war on the plains, but it will still have access to sufficient quantities of small arms and ammunition to enable it to equip mobile units which will roam the country attacking trains, destroying crops and supplies, attacking Japanese and those working with them.   The Japanese military will therefore have to garrison its holdings and police every mile of the lines of communications along which supplies for its forces must be carried.   The future prospect for the plains occupied by the Japanese during the next 3 or 4 years promises little in the way of peaceful development.   I believe that conditions throughout those areas will be chaotic in the extreme, with robberies, assassinations, and kidnappings.

The prospect for the immediate future is hopeless unless Japan is prepared to send far greater forces into China to enable her to garrison and police the occupied areas. Trade is and will continue to be completely disrupted. Chinese industry no longer exists. Travel in the interior is already well nigh impossible.

The situation as between China and Japan at the present time is therefore at a stalemate, with Japan's armies carrying destruction into the very areas from whose population she apparently expected to receive cooperation and where she expected to market her goods.

A declaration of war will not in my opinion materially affect this situation. It will have its effect upon trade through Hong Kong and possibly Hanoi, but it will not lessen the necessity for Japan to continue the present heavy expense and future military operations. It will not close China's back doors through India, Burma and Turkestan. Japanese hostilities have entered the stage of long time operations to pacify immense areas where the populations have been impoverished and terrorized. Japan must soon come to a realization that up to the present time all that her efforts have netted her has been hostility abroad and expense in China. Japan can hardly expect to recoup this expense from Chinese trade in another 20 or 30 years.

Repeated to Peiping and Shanghai. Shanghai please relay to Tokyo and show to Commander-in-Chief.

JOHNSON

793.94/12371a : Telegram

The Secretary of State to the Ambassador in Japan (Grew)

WASHINGTON, February 3, 1938—5 p. m.

34. Your 41, January 19, 8 p. m.[93] The Department has not observed any recent press reports of or editorial comment relating exclusively to incidents involving the mutilation of the flag. On January 25 the *New York Times* published an account of continued Japanese excesses at Nanking, referring to them as "indescribable". Japanese lawlessness as described in this report and in our note of January 17 to the Japanese Government,[94] together with the assault on Allison,[95] the stiffening resistance of the Chinese forces, and the attitude of the Japanese Government toward rights of others in China have formed the chief subjects of recent editorial comment on the Far Eastern conflict, which continues to hold public interest.

---

[93] Not printed.
[94] *Foreign Relations*, Japan, 1931–1941, vol. I, p. 565.
[95] See press release issued by the Department of State, January 28, 1938, *ibid.*, p. 570.

Discussing the lawlessness in Nanking, the *New York Times* on January 26 stated "Now triumphant soldiers in occupied Nanking are enjoying the fruits of military victory by looting and ravaging of helpless Chinese. It is thus Japan is bringing order into China". The *Philadelphia Inquirer* asserts "Although there may be grounds for charging the Nanking lawlessness to mutinous troops, the fact remains that Japan's whole program of aggression in China has been such as to incite its soldiery to brutal acts". The *Baltimore Sun* refers to the behavior of Japanese soldiery as "shocking". The stiffening Chinese resistance is epitomized in such expressions as "Japan is in trouble up to her neck", and "War Not Over Yet", some even predicting Japan's ultimate ruin. Skepticism of recent declarations in the Diet that foreign rights would be respected is expressed in such editorial titles as "Deceptive Diplomacy", "Meaningless Words", "Fair Words from Japan", "Open Door But How Open?".

There is considerable editorial sentiment in favor of depriving Japan of materials and resources with which to consolidate her aggression. On January 28 in Washington a league of women shoppers held a "Life Without Silk" fashion show to dramatize and encourage individual boycotting of Japanese silk. Evidently alarmed by actual and prospective boycotting, a delegation of hosiery workers on the same day held a parade in Washington to advertise the extent to which American labor would be penalized by a boycott of silk.

The President's message to Congress on January 28 asking supplementary appropriations for national defense [96] was well received by Congress and public.

The press is showing a growing tendency to discount the sincerity of recent official Japanese apologies for disregard of American rights and for the Allison outrage, as well as of popular Japanese expressions of regret for injuries done to us. The *Baltimore Sun* asks how much weight can be attached to Japanese assurances if the Japanese Government is unable to control its soldiers. The *Washington Times* alluding to the Allison slapping advises its readers as follows: "Let's keep our shirts on as we managed to do when the *Panay* was sunk" and explains that "the invading Japanese soldiers . . ."[97] seem to be paying no more attention to the home authorities' ideas on proper war conduct than a band of Iroquois raiders in the old days would have paid to the ideas of the medicine men mumbling among the tepees back home". A Washington *Star* columnist facetiously remarks "Foreign Secretary Hirota has ordered his clerks to have an abundant supply of Form No. 2247 'Apologies to the United States' so as to save time whenever the United States protests", and the same idea is

---

[96] *Congressional Record*, vol. 83, pt. 2, p. 1187.
[97] Omission indicated in the original telegram.

expressed in the New York *Herald Tribune's* leading cartoon of January 31.

You may consider it desirable when a suitable opportunity presents itself in conversations with officials of the Foreign Office to call their attention to the growing and widespread skepticism in the United States, as illustrated by the foregoing comments, as to the worth of Japanese official assurances.

HULL

793.94/12306 : Telegram

The Ambassador in China (Johnson) to the Secretary of State

HANKOW, February 4, 1938—9 a. m.
[Received February 4—7 a. m.]

79. In recent conversation with Vice Minister Hsu Mo latter informed Peck [98] that the Secretary of State had said to the Chinese Ambassador in regard to reports that Great Britain, France and the Soviet Union were discussing plan for assisting China to resist Japan, that the United States would go as far as other powers in aiding China but declined to commit itself in regard to any plan still in stage of discussion. The remark of the Vice Minister was made casually in a general conversation but may be of interest.

JOHNSON

893.0146/632

Memorandum by the Adviser on Political Relations (Hornbeck) of a Conversation With the First Secretary of the British Embassy (Broadmead)

[WASHINGTON,] February 4, 1938.

Reference, the Department's *aide-mémoire* of January 29 and January 31 to the British Embassy.

Mr. Broadmead called me on the 'phone and, referring to the Department's *aide-mémoire* of January 31, said that the British Embassy had a message from the Foreign Office stating that the Foreign Office had complied with our request that they communicate with the French Government. Also, that the British Government does not intend at this time to reduce its armed forces in north China.

Further, with regard to the request in the Department's *aide-mémoire* of January 29 for information regarding the British Government's reference to a "general settlement," Mr. Broadmead said that the Foreign Office said that it was hoping to give us something on that subject shortly.

---

[98] Willys R. Peck, Counselor of Embassy in China.

793.94/12314a : Telegram

The Secretary of State to the Ambassador in Japan (*Grew*)

WASHINGTON, February 4, 1938—5 p. m.

38. An Associated Press report from Tokyo under date February 2 states that the Minister for Foreign Affairs,[99] in reply to a question, made a statement in the Diet on February 2 as follows: "There is no Chinese Central Government recognized by Japan. A state of war exists between the two countries". A further press report from Tokyo under date February 3 states that Prince Konoye, in reply to a question in the Diet, "indicated that Japan did not intend to declare war on China formally at present, but said it was reasonable to expect that under conditions which might arise in the future, a declaration might be issued".

The Department has found most helpful your telegrams 63, February 1, 1 p. m., and your unnumbered telegram January 31, 5 p. m., via Shanghai,[1] as well as previous telegrams in regard to developments relating to a possible declaration of war by Japan, and the Department desires that you continue to keep it currently informed of any significant developments, adding such comments of appraisal and interpretation as may be helpful.

HULL

793.94 Conference/362 : Telegram

The Secretary of State to the Ambassador in China (*Johnson*)

WASHINGTON, February 4, 1938—9 p. m.

54. Your 72 [*79*], February 4, 9 a. m. On January 29 the Chinese Ambassador [2] called on me at his request. During the course of the ensuing conversation I referred by way of illustration to a press report from Geneva that various foreign governments contemplated approaching the American Government in regard to a proposal to extend credits to China for the purchase of arms and munitions. I said to the Ambassador that he knew the situation in this country in regard to a question of that sort and that I of course assumed that the representatives of any governments which might have presented to them for consideration any such plan would have knowledge and understanding of the situation here in this regard. I made no statement of the nature mentioned in your telegram under reference.

HULL

---

[99] Koki Hirota.
[1] See telegram No. 177, February 1, 11 a. m., *Foreign Relations*, Japan, 1931–1941, vol. I, p. 446.
[2] C. T. Wang.

793.94/12313 : Telegram

The Chargé in the United Kingdom (Johnson) to the Secretary of State

LONDON, February 4, 1938—11 p. m.
[Received February 4—6 : 47 p. m.]

99. Mr. Hugh Wilson [3] informs me that, when talking privately with Mr. Eden for a moment this afternoon, Mr. Eden told him that if the Japanese attacked Hong Kong they would act at once in its defense; that this might mean the withdrawal of substantial forces from the Mediterranean but that the British could not do otherwise. He further said that the British would act to defend Hong Kong if attacked regardless of what American action might be.

JOHNSON

711.41/378 : Telegram

The Chargé in the United Kingdom (Johnson) to the Secretary of State

LONDON, February 5, 1938—2 p. m.
[Received February 5—9 : 28 a. m.]

101. Your 50, February 2, 7 p. m., was taken up informally and confidentially with an appropriate official of the Foreign Office on February 3. When I saw Mr. Eden yesterday I mentioned the matter to him and he said that he would have a message to send to you today. This morning I was requested to call at the Foreign Office and an official gave me the following message:

"I am authorized by the Secretary of State to ask you to convey to Mr. Hull his personal assurance that neither in Parliament nor elsewhere has he made any statement that could lead any one to understand that the United States and Great Britain had a working alliance or working relationship with reference to the Far Eastern question and that it was of such nature that it must be kept a secret.

"On the other hand, the fact that Mr. Borah's allegation is unfounded does not mean, as the Secretary of State pointed out in the course of his speech in the House of Commons on the 21st December last, to which the Senator perhaps alludes, that the existing situation in the Far East has not necessitated constant and close consultation between the Governments of the United States and Great Britain. Such consultation, which is natural in view of the similarity of the interests of the two countries in that part of the world, is of course perfectly consistent with the pursuit of an independent policy by the two governments, but Mr. Eden, as he endeavored to make plain in his above mentioned speech, rejoices, like all men of good will of both sides of the Atlantic, at the fact that during a period of international anxiety our two countries are moving on parallel lines".

---

[3] Newly appointed Ambassador to Germany.

The following paragraph appears in the *Times* this morning in a despatch from its correspondent in Washington:

"It is upon the revelation some time ago that Captain Ingersoll [4] had been despatched to London, and that President Roosevelt's rearmament programme had not been sent to Congress until he had returned and made his report, that the opposition bases its allegation that what Senator Borah calls 'a tacit alliance' exists between the United States and Britain".[5]

JOHNSON

793.94/12357 : Telegram

The Chargé in the Soviet Union (Henderson) to the Secretary of State

Moscow, February 5, 1938—5 p. m.
[Received 5 : 44 p. m.]

35. Reference to my telegram No. 5, January 8, 7 p. m.[6] Yui Ming, Chinese Chargé d'Affaires, told me the following yesterday in strict confidence.

1. (*a*) The mission of Sun Fo [7] has obtained its first objective, namely, the creation of an atmosphere of mutual confidence which permits a friendly exchange of views (whether or not he meant by this statement that contact had been established with Stalin [8] is not clear).

(*b*) The negotiations are considered to be of so delicate a nature that the members of the mission avoid seeing any persons except the highest Soviet officials for fear their statements or actions may be given a false interpretation; they are not even telegraphing their home government since they do not trust their own codes. Telegraphing is unnecessary, however, since the mission has full powers to negotiate and sign without reference to the Chinese Government.

(*c*) Most members have an American education and are carrying on negotiations with best Western traditions; they will give no promise which China will not keep, which it may regret in happier years or which may prejudice the position in China of other friendly powers.

(*d*) Rumors that the Soviet Government is agreeing to recognize full Chinese sovereignty over Outer Mongolia in return for certain concessions or that the Kremlin is intriguing with the purpose of having Chiang Kai Shek replaced by more liberal Chinese leaders are Japanese inspired.

---

[4] Royal E. Ingersoll, U. S. N., director of War Plans Division, Naval Operations, Navy Department; technical assistant to the American delegation at the London Naval Conference, 1935.
[5] For a letter from the Secretary of State in reply to the Chairman of the Senate Committee on Foreign Relations on February 8, see *Foreign Relations, Japan, 1931–1941*, vol. I, p. 449.
[6] Not printed.
[7] President of the Chinese Legislative Yuan.
[8] Secretary General of the Communist Party of the Soviet Union.

2. Although I elaborated somewhat on the various rumors relating to Mongolia, he did not deny that Mongolia figures in the negotiations. It has not been possible as yet to obtain through any authoritative source in this particular the concrete points under discussion.

3. (a) Japan estimates the present strength of the Trans-Baikal Army at about 20 divisions totalling slightly more than 350,000 men. Our Military Attaché considers this figure as excessive.

(b) During recent weeks there has been a tendency to move those divisions hitherto stationed in the neighborhood of Baikal towards the east and to replace them with fresh troops from Central Siberia.

(c) His Government is somewhat concerned at unconfirmed rumors that troops are being concentrated in rather large numbers in Central Siberia in localities which would permit their rapid transfer into the Trans-Baikal region.

(d) There are two fully equipped Soviet divisions in Outer Mongolia.

(e) In his opinion the Soviet Union does not desire to enter into an armed conflict with Japan at present although during recent weeks it has been following a policy only short thereof.

4. There is little doubt that shipments of supplies and equipment which could be devoted to military purposes have been going to the Far East in larger volume than usual during the last 6 weeks. The supplies apparently include both clothing and foodstuffs; nevertheless the foreign observers in whom I have most confidence still feel that these measures are of precautionary measures only and that the Soviet Union is not seriously preparing to make an attack on Japan.

5. The Soviet press although continuing to carry on an anti-Japanese campaign nevertheless from time to time displays resentment at rumors that the Soviet Union is preparing to enter the war in the Far East. An article in yesterday's *Pravda* for instance denounces the authors of slanderous rumors who are seeking to excite Japan against the Soviet Union by intimating "that the Soviet Union is preparing to make an attack on Japan". The article continues: "they are trying to frighten the Japanese to persuade them that it is necessary to hurry and beat the Soviet Union to it. On the other hand they are endeavoring to provoke the Soviet Union by trying to prove the necessity of a preventive move against Japan. In vain are the reactionary English circles secretly nourishing the hope that they will be able to turn the wave of aggression away from the British Empire."

HENDERSON

793.94/12316 : Telegram

The Ambassador in Japan (Grew) to the Secretary of State

TOKYO, February 5, 1938—7 p. m.
[Received February 5—8:27 a. m.]

79. My unnumbered January 31, 5 p. m. via Shanghai.[9] We were told at the Foreign Office that the Minister for Foreign Affairs, replying to a request for clarification of his statement in the Diet of January 25 that "both internally and externally the present struggle is in fact a war", stated at a meeting this afternoon of the Budget Committee of the Lower House that: Japan has not claimed the rights of a belligerent and this position was not in any way changed by the Government's statement of January 16 [10] (see our 32, January 16, 3 p. m.).

Repeated to Shanghai for relay to Hankow.

GREW

793.94/12326 : Telegram

The Ambassador in Japan (Grew) to the Secretary of State

TOKYO, February 6, 1938—3 p. m.
[Received February 6—7:15 a. m.]

80. Department's 38, February 4, 5 p. m. There was no session on February 2nd of either House of the Diet. There was a meeting on that day of the Budget Committee but we find no record of any statement made on that occasion by the Minister for Foreign Affairs even remotely resembling that quoted in the Associated Press report. The statement quoted together with that attributed to the Prime Minister are probably excerpts from the addresses reported in our unnumbered telegram January 31, 5 p. m. via Shanghai.

GREW

793.94/12336 : Telegram

*The Third Secretary of Embassy in China (Allison) to the
Secretary of State*

NANKING, February 6, 1938—5 p. m.
[Received 9:58 p. m.]

49. Yesterday afternoon Major General Amaya, the new garrison commander, gave a welcoming tea at the Japanese Embassy for the foreign diplomatic representatives in Nanking during the course of

[9] See telegram No. 177, February 1, 11 a. m., *Foreign Relations*, Japan, 1931–1941, vol. I, p. 446.
[10] *Ibid.*, p. 437.

which he made a long statement outlining his opinion on the local situation and in which he criticised the attitude of the foreigners who had been sending abroad reports of Japanese atrocities and encouraging the Chinese in their anti-Japanese feeling. The gist of the statement is given below. Because of the importance and length of the statement an opportunity was taken of checking this morning with my British and German colleagues for possible errors or omissions and it is therefore believed that the following summary is substantially complete.

The General regretted the prominence which had been given abroad to reports of atrocities committed in Nanking by Japanese troops and in extenuation pointed out the long and strenuous fighting and the unexpected strong resistance of the Chinese. The rapid advance had caused the failure of food supplies and the exhaustion of the troops had led to a lack of discipline and hence looting and violence. However, he added that the Japanese troops were the best disciplined in the world and that in the Russo-Japanese War and in the Manchurian incident which had been comparatively mild there had been no atrocities. He hoped Europeans and Americans would refrain from criticism and remain onlookers and to respect the great Japanese nation. Endeavors were now being made to restore discipline. The Japanese troops were not hostile to Chinese citizens but they were angry at the existence of snipers and spies among the latter resulting from the anti-Japanese spirit which Chiang Kai Shek had instilled among the people as well as among the Chinese soldiers.

It was stated to be the desire of the Japanese military to restore order and normal conditions in Nanking as soon as possible. In Yangchow, from which place the General has just come, relations between Chinese and Japanese were good but in Nanking interference by foreigners which encouraged continuance of anti-Japanese feeling amongst the local Chinese population had hindered a return to normal and large numbers of Chinese continued to live in the so-called "safety zone." He referred to particularly reports and activities of nationals of a "certain country" which was damaging relations between Japanese and that country (this obviously refers to the United States). The General expressed dislike of the attitude of a judge in a law court taken by the foreigners and warned them that their criticisms and interference between the Chinese and Japanese would anger the Japanese troops and might lead to some unpleasant incident. He asked to be trusted and gave assurances that he would do his best to restore order and normal life in the country and that foreign lives and property would be protected. He requested foreign representatives to discuss their difficulties with him as far as they concerned protection against foreign property but to refrain from interference with matters which concerned the Chinese.

After conclusion of the statement he asked for criticisms and comments from the foreigners present but none of them spoke. When asked if it would be possible to have a copy of the remarks, Counselor Hidaka of the Japanese Embassy stated that it was not an official announcement.

He denied statement was obviously directed mainly against the International Relief Committee, composed mostly of Americans but with a German chairman. This commission has been feeding 50,000 Chinese refugees daily and has been extremely active in attempting to prevent and in reporting Japanese atrocities. In view of his [the?] strong opposition on the part of the local military authorities to the International Committee, instructions are requested as to how far this Office should go in assisting Committee in its humanitarian activities.

Sent to Embassy, Hankow. Repeated to Peiping and Shanghai. Shanghai please repeat to Tokyo.

ALLISON

793.94/12353

Memorandum of Conversation, by the Secretary of State

[WASHINGTON,] February 7, 1938.

The Chinese Ambassador called at his own request, primarily, he said, to inform me of his call on the President to present to him a letter from Chiang Kai-shek, and also to hand me a copy of the same letter.[11]

I inquired what news he had from China. He said that the fighting was stiff and that his people were making a good showing. I further inquired what he knew about the reports in the press today to the effect that a large amount of war supplies had gone into China through Hong Kong. He promptly replied that the reports were true and that such supplies should be helpful for some time.

The Ambassador then said that what his country needed was credit, and since they were making extensive purchases of goods in this country, his Government was very anxious for all possible cooperation here in the establishment of credits. I replied that, of course, his Government had considerable available liquid credits here in this country now. He agreed that this was true and that the credits were very substantial. I then commented further that thus far China had only purchased six or seven million dollars of arms and implements of war from this country. He did not press the matter further except to say that they were looking ahead in thus requesting credits.

I went on to say that at present we were interested almost entirely in the passage of the increased armament measure and in getting before the country more clearly our situation and our policies.

---

[11] Dated January 30, p. 59.

The Ambassador then inquired as to the significance of the withdrawal of the United States armed forces from Tientsin. I replied that sometime before the fighting broke out in July last, my associates in the Department were collaborating in the plan relative to the withdrawal of these troops; that the War Department had wanted them returned, for one reason, among others, that it was not considered a wholesome policy to keep these troops in one place and away from this country for an indefinite period of time; that, therefore, what is taking place in connection with their evacuation is just about what would have occurred at this time had no fighting arisen between China and Japan, and, therefore, there is no significance to the withdrawal of these troops from the standpoint of China or any other government; that they are no longer of any great use where they are now located and this is a further reason for their evacuation. I said I might go further and say that if trouble had not arisen between China and Japan, the Chinese Government and my Government equally would have agreed in the desire for these troops to come out not later than this date; and that the policy of the Chinese Government relative to the discontinuance of extraterritoriality at Shanghai and elsewhere would have been carried out by this time, including the removal of all remaining guards of foreign governments. The Ambassador did not take issue with this view.

I finally remarked that from every viewpoint, therefore, it must be apparent to him and his Government that there is no significance in the evacuation of this regiment from Tientsin. I said further that the British had recalled their troops temporarily sent to Shanghai just as we had recalled ours temporarily sent to that city; and that we took this action in sending the Marines and returning them upon the recommendation of Admiral Yarnell in charge of the Asiatic squadron.

C[ORDELL] H[ULL]

893.0146/633

Memorandum of Conversation, by the Under Secretary of State (Welles)

[WASHINGTON,] February 8, 1938.

The French Chargé d'Affaires called to see me this morning to take up with me various matters by instruction of his Government.

The French Government was concerned because of the receipt of information that the Government of the United States intended to withdraw a portion of its armed forces from China in the near future. Mr. Henry explained the point of view of his Government in this regard as contained in a memorandum [12] which he left with me and

---

[12] *Infra.*

which he asked me to regard as entirely personal and informal. I told him that I would reply in the same manner within the next few days.

He then referred to an instruction which he had received from his Government requesting him to inform the Department of State of the reasons which had caused the French Government to modify in two regards the note which the French Government transmitted to the Japanese Government at the same time as those sent by the United States [13] and Great Britain. As reported in a recent cable from London, the point of view of the French Government in this regard was that inasmuch as the French Government did not have the same budgetary complications as those confronting the United States and Great Britain, there was no need for it to fix February 20 as the date before which it desired to have a reply from Japan with regard to the construction of naval units. Furthermore, the increase in the navies of the United States and of Great Britain was in large part contingent, according to the French Government, upon the rumored increase in the Japanese navy, whereas the French navy was not in the same situation and if the French Government had adopted the same language as that utilized by the United States and Great Britain in their notes to Japan, the French Government believed that it would immediately have incurred the suspicions of Italy and Germany. It was for these reasons the French Government desired us to know that they had decided to modify the language of the suggested note to the Japanese Government.

Finally, the French Government had been informed through its Embassy in China of the negotiations which had been taking place between the American Consul General and the British representatives in Shanghai and the Japanese authorities with regard to the question of Chinese customs.[14] The French Government desired to know if any final conclusions had been reached by the United States Government with regard to this matter. I replied to Mr. Henry by saying that the matter of Chinese customs was one which was so complicated and concerning which there had been so much correspondence that I was unable, unfortunately, to answer his query immediately but that I would be glad to look into the matter and advise him of our present position within the next few days.

S[UMNER] W[ELLES]

---

[13] Note dated February 5, *Foreign Relations*, Japan, 1931–1941, vol. I, p. 303. For additional correspondence, see *Foreign Relations*, 1938, vol. I, pp. 891 ff.
[14] See pp. 626 ff.

893.0146/633

The French Embassy to the Department of State [15]

On the occasion of the partial withdrawal of American troops from Northern China, it is recalled that last December, the British Government had approached the French Government requesting for an expression of opinion concerning a project attributed to the Japanese Government to recognize the new Peiping administration.

The French Foreign Office called the attention of the British Embassy in Paris to the fact that the Protocol of 1901 [16] (Diplomatic Missions, military protection and liberty of communication between Peiping and the sea) is a collective pact signed by China on one side and the Representatives of other Governments on the other side, and that, should modifications be found necessary in that pact, they should be brought about only after an exchange of views between the interested Governments. The French Government added that it did not think the time had come when such a change could take place. It pointed out the necessity of avoiding to give the Chinese Government the impression that Peiping was no longer under Chinese Sovereignty. Furthermore, it might encourage Japanese ambitions. The French Foreign Office also pointed out that any decision concerning the Peiping area might affect the security and the future of foreign concessions in Tientsin. Of course, the French Government clearly realized that the development of events in the Far East would necessitate the revision some time of the position of the different Powers in the regions of Peiping and Tientsin, but such a revision should, in its opinion, be carefully prepared by conversations between the United States, Great Britain and France.

After the British Government had been informed of the position of the French Government, the matter brought up in the British Embassy's note to the French Foreign Office was set aside.

Today, on the occasion of the American decision, the French Government still feels that any important changes made by the United States, Great Britain or France, in their military and diplomatic position in Northern China, will give China and Japan the impression that those countries are more or less indifferent to the future of that region. The Protocol of 1901 constitutes a sort of limitation to Japanese action in Northern China and protects Chinese as well as foreign interests, and it is recalled that last December, the Chinese Ambassador in London emphasized the importance of that particular point before the British Government.

---

[15] Handed to the Under Secretary of State by the French Chargé, February 8.
[16] Signed at Peking, September 7, 1901, *Foreign Relations*, 1901, Appendix (Affairs in China), p. 312.

The French Government feels that the decision of the American Government may strengthen the position of the Japanese. Furthermore, any restriction of the rights presently enjoyed by the Powers in Northern China may weaken their diplomatic position when the time comes for negotiating changes in the provisions of the Protocol of 1901.

As stated above, in the opinion of the French Government, it would be advisable that any changes which might be contemplated in the present *status quo*, take place after consultation between the interested Powers.

793.94/12384 : Telegram

The Third Secretary of Embassy in China (Allison) to the Secretary of State

NANKING, February 10, 1938—3 p. m.
[Received February 10—1 : 44 p. m.]

53. I have just been informed by Bos, of the Netherlands Legation, who has come to Nanking for a few days, that in a conversation this morning with Fukui [17] the actions and reports of the foreigners in Nanking were severely criticized. According to Bos, Fukui tried to impress upon him that conditions here were improving daily, that the Japanese soldiers were well under control and that any reports to the contrary made by foreigners were just "anti-Japanese propaganda".

While it is true that conditions have improved to some extent there are still numerous reports of disorder and violence committed by Japanese soldiers. A similar attempt has been made to impress upon the Japanese authorities that complaints made to them of the actions of Japanese troops are not the result of anti-Japanese feeling but are made in an effort to assist the responsible people to know what is going on and thus put a stop to it. However, with the Acting Japanese Consul General adopting the attitude shown above, constructive work is almost impossible.

Sent to Embassy, Hankow, Peiping and Shanghai. Shanghai please repeat to Tokyo.   ALLISON

893.00/14207b

The Secretary of State to the Consul General at Hankow (Josselyn)

WASHINGTON, February 10, 1938.

SIR: With reference to the Department's telegram of February 9, 1938,[18] requesting that you subscribe to the *Hsin Hu Shih Pao*, official

[17] Japanese Consul General at Nanking.
[18] Not printed.

communist daily newspaper, beginning with its first issue on January 11, 1938, it is desired that you follow carefully editorials and leading articles in this publication which may be helpful to you in your evaluations of the political situation in China. It is realized that your office is confronted at the present time with an unusual amount of work incidental to disturbed conditions in your district and that this circumstance may for the time being make it impossible for you to examine closely the material in question. It is hoped, however, that you will later be able to give careful attention to the contents of this communist daily.

The Department is especially interested in obtaining information with regard to important developments in the communist movement in China, such as, for example, the inspiration, aims, and policies of the Communist Party of China; the present influence of the communist movement upon Chinese political or social conditions, and the reaction of high government officials to the movement. It is believed that the material in the *Hsin Hu Shih Pao*, supplemented by that obtainable through other channels, will prove of value in the preparation of political reports pertaining to this subject and that it also will prove of assistance to the Embassy in estimating the influence of the Communist Party of China in national developments.

China has long been regarded by the Communist International as the leading example of a colonial country exploited by "imperialist" countries. The solution formerly advanced by the Communist International for the correction of this alleged situation was the overthrow of the Central Government in China by force and violence, the setting up of a soviet form of government, the abolition of extraterritorial privileges enjoyed by foreigners, and a close alliance between a contemplated new Chinese Government and the Soviet Union.

At the Seventh World Congress of the Communist International in the summer of 1935 Communists made substantial modification of their program of world revolution. With regard to China it appears that preparations were made for the abandonment of several points in the program of the Communist Party of China to which prominent noncommunist Chinese had taken exception. The more important of these points which subsequently were abandoned were the advocacy of violence for the overthrow of the Kuomintang, and agitation for the forcible confiscation of property to be followed by the introduction of a soviet form of government. These modifications were made for the purpose of bringing about a united front in China in opposition to Japan. The Communists hope that because of these modifications they will be accepted by the Kuomintang as participants in the present Chinese Government. Communists frankly admit that a united front government will not provide a solution for the internal difficulties of China. They look upon it as merely a step in the direction of their ultimate goal: a Soviet Government of China.

As of possible assistance in your study of this subject there is enclosed the December 15, 1937, issue of *International Press Correspondence*,[19] an official organ of the Communist International. This issue is a special edition devoted entirely to matters pertaining to China. In it are presented the views of leading Communists of many countries with regard to present political conditions in China and their implications.

Very truly yours,   For the Secretary of State:
                                     SUMNER WELLES

793.94 Conference/367 : Telegram

The Chargé in the United Kingdom (Johnson) to the Secretary of State

LONDON, February 11, 1938—5 p. m.
[Received February 11—1:22 p. m.]

121. Department's 6, January 29, 1 p. m., to Geneva.[20] Lord Cranborne[21] sent for me this morning and said that before he left Geneva Wellington Koo[22] had pressed upon him a reconvening of the parties to the Nine Power Treaty[23] and had earnestly requested that he convey this desire to the United States Government. Cranborne had no comment to make and said that he was merely passing the Chinese request on as he had promised. I asked him what reply he had made to Wellington Koo and he said that he did "not give him any encouragement".

JOHNSON

761.94/1017 : Telegram

The Chargé in the Soviet Union (Henderson) to the Secretary of State

MOSCOW, February 11, 1938—7 p. m.
[Received February 11—3:52 p. m.]

43. 1. Today's *Pravda* carries a long unsigned front page article entitled "Instigators of War" in which it attacks authors of "provocative rumors" appearing in the foreign press in regard to a possibility of a Soviet-Japanese war and takes particular exception to reports of an increase in Soviet military preparations in the Far East. The American correspondent Knickerbocker and several British papers are made the particular target for attack.

[19] Not attached to file copy of instruction.
[20] *Post*, p. 495.
[21] British Parliamentary Under Secretary of State for Foreign Affairs.
[22] Chinese Ambassador to France.
[23] *Foreign Relations*, 1922, vol. I, p. 276.

2. After stating that instigators of war "whether English or others" will not succeed in seeing the Soviet Union follow "a policy on orders from anyone, or as a result of pressure from anyone, or on account of anyone's promises", the article continues:

"The Soviet Government, unwaveringly adhering to a policy of peace, will wage war only with aggressors, only with violators of peace, with the violators of Soviet frontiers. No stormy international orchestra of slander and excitement can shake the iron Soviet resolution and calmness."

3. The article in question has been given so prominent a place in the newspaper and [that it?] is intended to represent a statement of Soviet foreign policy particularly with regard to the Far East.

4. The above passage is so worded as to make it subject to two different interpretations. Examined from a strictly grammatical point of view it would appear to mean that the Soviet Union will go to war only in the event of an invasion of Soviet territory by an aggressor. Since the article appears to be devoted almost entirely to the denial of Soviet intentions to attack Japan, it is believed that the passage above quoted is intended to relate only to the conditions under which the Soviet Government would go to war in the Far East. It contains no geographic reservations and taken literally may be construed to apply to Soviet foreign policy in general.

5. The article also contains an attack upon "a certain important personage from the Afghan Embassy", apparently the Afghan Ambassador, whom it accuses of spreading "inciting rumors in regard to preparation by the Soviet Union for war with Japan". The writer asks "was it for this reason that this personage was sent here by the Afghan Government."

I doubt if this charge has any foundation. I have had numerous conversations with the Afghan Ambassador and have never heard him even mention the Far Eastern situation. It is my belief as well as that of other members of the Diplomatic Corps that this attack is motivated by Soviet displeasure with the attitude taken by him with regard to the Soviet request that Afghan Consulates in the Soviet Union be closed (see my despatch No. 899 of January 31, 1938 [24]) and can be partially attributed to the fact that he is the first dean of the Diplomatic Corps for many years who has made any real effort to prevail upon the Soviet authorities to grant to the Diplomatic Corps privileges and courtesies customarily extended by other governments to members of foreign diplomatic missions. It is believed also from the wording of the attack that it represents an effort on the part of the Soviet authorities to bring pressure upon the members of the Diplomatic Corps to prevent them from exchanging with one another their views regarding Soviet policies.

HENDERSON

[24] Not printed.

793.94/12412 : Telegram

The Ambassador in Japan (Grew) to the Secretary of State

TOKYO, February 12, 1938—noon.
[Received 3 : 20 p. m.]

100. 1. My British colleague,[25] who talks to me freely and so far as I can judge frankly, has told me of the following conversation with the Minister for Foreign Affairs on February 9 which would appear to be significant owing to the marked change in the Minister's usually placid, courteous and friendly bearing. The fact that for the first time in our respective dealings with him Hirota twice lost his temper with Craigie might be due to nervousness engendered by the strain of the current sessions of the Diet or the mounting irritation at the tone, insistence and volume of Craigie's continual representations both oral and written in connection with British interests in China or perhaps to both. The Minister's demeanor tends to confirm reports which have come to both Craigie and myself that Hirota is steadily becoming harder and more intransigent as regards foreign interests in the Far East and that it is Hirota rather than Suetsugu[26] who leads the ultra-chauvinistic element in the Government. I myself have as yet seen no outward demonstration of any change of attitude on Hirota's part as regards American interests.

2. The conversation referred to arose when Craigie informed the Minister that he is in possession of evidence indicating that Japanese forces have occupied several of the smaller Chinese islands in the general vicinity of Hong Kong and again asked for specific assurances that the statements of the Japanese Government that it has no territorial designs in China apply as well to the islands as to the mainland. According to Craigie, the Minister in some instances in their intercourse became very angry, inveighed against the continual British demands for renewed assurances, said that under present war conditions Japan had given all the assurances that can reasonably be expected, and asserted that if the warfare is prolonged Japan may be forced to occupy more territory whether insular or on the mainland. If the warfare becomes permanent, said Hirota, the occupation will also be permanent. Referring specifically to Hainan, Hirota said that the Japanese could not possibly give a permanent pledge not to occupy. Craigie pointed out that whereas Hong Kong cannot be regarded as a threat to Japan, the occupation of these islands by Japanese forces does constitute a very real threat to Hong Kong. The general tone of this conversation appears to have been acrimonious.

---

[25] Sir Robert L. Craigie, British Ambassador in Japan.
[26] Admiral Nobumasa Suetsugu, Japanese Minister for Home Affairs.

3. Craigie is aware that there are large concentration[s] of Japanese troops in Formosa (see our 61, January 31 [*30*], 6 p. m.[27]) and of Japanese ships in the port of Takao and he believes that an attack on Canton or some other point in South China is impending.

4. Craigie's general reaction to this conversation with Hirota is that the longer the warfare is prolonged the greater will be the likelihood of permanent occupation by Japan not only of the islands but of territory on the mainland. He believes that Japanese assurances of "no territorial designs" are likely to be withdrawn at short notice. These prospects so seriously concern British interests that he contemplates recommending or has already recommended to his Government (*a*) that continued support of Chiang Kai Shek, whether by furnishing war supplies and funds or otherwise, is detrimental to British interests and (*b*) that the British Government should be alert to foster any outlook for peace negotiations which might leave to China any hope of eventual resurrection.

5. Craigie is informed and believes that it was the Japanese industrialists and politicians and not the military who favored and brought about the withdrawal of recognition from the Central Government.

6. I think that the nature of the conversation reported above indicates that our own practice of concentrating our representations to the Minister on important issues and with discreet timing is likely to prove more effective than the British practice of constant hammering by almost daily notes, letters, and other communications with continual personal visits to the Minister or the Vice Minister both on important and routine issues. The British procedure appears to be based on the theory that constant hammering will wear away a stone but in the present temper of the Japanese Government and military this practice is liable to defeat its own object through the irritation which it inevitably engenders, clearly demonstrated in Craigie's last interview with the Minister. The representations of the American Government are at least listened to with respect and an evident inclination on the part of the Foreign Office to meet our wishes so far as the military can be influenced in that direction.

7. About 2 weeks ago Craigie told me that he had heard from a trustworthy source that there was to be a change for the better in the Japanese attitude toward Great Britain and that press and other agitation against the British was to be discontinued. I did not put much stock in Craigie's information. Since then General Matsui [28] in the interview which he gave to Woodhead [29] sharply criticised the British for trying to create political issues out of the problem of pre-

---

[27] Not printed.
[28] Japanese military commander in the Yangtze area.
[29] British journalist at Shanghai.

serving British economic and commercial interests in China while the Japanese press has expressed the conviction that it was Great Britain which initiated the three-power *démarche* with regard to naval construction. The feeling in Japan against the British is not in our opinion altogether artificially created as Craigie believes it to be but flows from the conviction that the British are constantly endeavoring to establish a common front against Japan in order to preserve British political and economic interests in the Far East.

Repeated to Hankow.

GREW

793.94/12417 : Telegram

The Consul General at Shanghai (Gauss) to the Secretary of State

SHANGHAI, February 14, 1938—noon.
[Received February 14—noon.]

255. A number of acts of terrorism were committed last week. Four severed heads of Chinese were discovered in the French Concession, the first being that of the editor of an anti-Japanese vernacular paper, the other three not having been identified. To two of the heads were attached warnings in Chinese against carrying on anti-Japanese activities. Bombs were also detonated without injuring any one, on the premises of the *Shanghai Evening Post and Mercury*, the *Hwa Mei Wan Pao* which is allegedly partially owned by an American citizen and a vernacular paper being operated by British subject. It is understood that Chinese employed by these papers received threatening letters before the bombings occurred warning them not to publish further anti-Japanese items. In the case of the bombing of the *Evening Post and Mercury*, the police arrested two Chinese who have confessed the crime but from whom no information appears to have been elicited thus far regarding the identity of the party or parties who instigated the bombings. It is believed in some circles, however, that both the bombings and beheadings were committed by a terrorist organization working directly or indirectly under Japanese direction.

Repeated to Peiping and Hankow.

GAUSS

793.94/12393

The Secretary of State to the Chairman of the House Committee on Foreign Affairs (McReynolds)

WASHINGTON, February 14, 1938.

MY DEAR MR. McREYNOLDS: The receipt is acknowledged of a letter of February 9, 1938, from Mr. I. R. Barnes, Clerk of the Committee on Foreign Affairs,[30] asking the Department to furnish the Committee on Foreign Affairs a report, in duplicate, on H. Res. 418, "Requesting the President of the United States to furnish certain information pertaining to the diplomatic relationship between Japan and China".[31]

With regard to the inquiry contained in section (1) of the Resolution, the Department has information to the effect that, although the Japanese Ambassador to China has returned to Japan, the Counselor of the Embassy has remained in China as Chargé d'Affaires.

With regard to the inquiry contained in section (2) of the Resolution, the Department has been informed that the Chinese Ambassador to Japan returned to China under instruction from his Government but that he was not handed his credentials by the Japanese Government, and that the Counselor of the Chinese Embassy has remained in Japan as Chargé d'Affaires. On January 21 the spokesman of the Japanese Foreign Office made a statement to the press as follows: "Although it has ceased to deal with General Chiang Kai-Shek's regime, the Japanese Government will continue to accord diplomatic and consular privileges to Chinese diplomatic and consular officials representing the National Government." It appears to be the view of the Japanese Government that the *de jure* status of the Japanese and Chinese diplomatic and consular officials in China and Japan, respectively, remains unchanged.

With regard to the inquiry in section (3) of the Resolution, it is believed that the remark attributed to Mr. Hirota as quoted in the Resolution is based upon a press report from Tokyo under date February 2 which refers to a statement made in the Diet on February 2. The Department has been officially informed that there was no session of the Diet on February 2 and that the press report probably has reference to Mr. Hirota's statement in the Diet under date January 25. There is enclosed a translation of the pertinent portion of that statement as telegraphed to the Department.[32] It will be observed that the remark quoted in the Resolution does not occur in the statement and the Department has no information indicating that Mr. Hirota made such a remark. The comment may be made in this connection that replies to interpellations in the Diet generally consist of impromptu remarks which are at times characterized by ambiguity which while often passing unnoticed in a language as vague and impersonal as the Japanese language may be lacking in clarity and be subject to misconstruction when translated into English. However, it would appear to be clear from the statement of Mr. Hirota that Japan has not declared war upon China and that Mr. Hirota does not consider that a *de jure* state of war exists between the two countries. In this connec-

---

[30] Not printed.
[31] *Congressional Record*, vol. 83, pt. 2, p. 1679.
[32] See telegram No. 80, February 6, 3 p. m., p. 72.

tion attention is invited to his statement that "In the light of the situation in China and in international relations we have not yet taken the step of declaring war".

With regard to section (4) of H. Res. 418, there must be taken into account, in deciding whether the President should be advised in regard to the invocation of the Joint Resolution approved May 1, 1937,[33] commonly referred to as the Neutrality Act, various factors—and especially the broad, general interest of this country and its nationals. In the present situation in the Far East, the President has been of the opinion that, in the light of all of the facts and circumstances, and with due and conscientious consideration of both the letter and the spirit of the neutrality legislation, the intent of that legislation and the general interests of this country and its nationals are best served by not invoking the provisions of the Joint Resolution.

Sincerely yours,   CORDELL HULL

893.0146/633

The Under Secretary of State (Welles) to the French Chargé (Henry)

WASHINGTON, February 14, 1938.

MY DEAR MR. CHARGÉ D'AFFAIRES: In the course of our conversation on February 8, I stated that I would furnish you with information within a few days in response to your inquiries with regard to the reduction and redistribution of American armed forces in north China and with regard to the Chinese customs question.

On January 31 Mr. Hornbeck made an oral statement to Mr. Lucet of your Embassy in regard to our decision to withdraw the Fifteenth Regiment, United States Army, from Tientsin, and to transfer to Tientsin a portion of the American marines now stationed at Peiping.

The matter of effecting a reduction and redistribution of American armed forces in north China is one to which we had been giving consideration for some time before the fighting broke out in north China last July. The change that is now about to take place is what might have occurred earlier had not the conflict arisen between China and Japan. Our decision now to reduce and redistribute our troops in north China does not involve modification of our treaty position in north China. We are continuing to maintain armed forces in both Peiping and Tientsin in accordance with our rights and responsibilities under the Boxer Protocol of 1901.[34]

The question of the withdrawal of diplomatic representatives and armed forces from north China was raised by the British Government

---

[33] 50 Stat. 121.
[34] *Foreign Relations*, 1901, Appendix (Affairs in China), p. 312.

in an *aide-mémoire* handed to us on December 16 by the British Embassy.[35] We replied that we felt that it would be premature to take action in the immediate future but stated that the matter should be kept constantly in mind and expressed the desire to continue to keep in close touch with the British Government. In an *aide-mémoire* of December 27,[36] the British Embassy informed us of the views of the French Government in regard to the desirability of maintaining diplomatic representation and embassy guards in north China and of the decision of the British Government not to withdraw for the present its diplomatic staff and guards from Peiping and Tientsin. The British Government expressed the hope that the French, British, and American Governments would concert together before taking any action in the matter. We replied that we would be pleased to maintain close touch with the French Government, as well as with the British Government, but that we felt that this expression of attitude should be regarded as relating to exchange of information and consultation rather than as constituting an agreement to act or to refrain from action in concert.

With regard to the Chinese customs issue our Ambassador in Tokyo, on February 3, was authorized [37] to consult with his French and British colleagues with a view to taking action along parallel lines to obtain certain assurances from the Japanese Government with regard to the preservation of the integrity of the Chinese customs service. We have now under consideration certain questions raised in an *aide-mémoire* received from the British Embassy and upon completion of that consideration I shall expect to communicate with you further.

I am [etc.] SUMNER WELLES

893.01 Provisional/70

The British Embassy to the Department of State

AIDE-MÉMOIRE

In an interview with the Counsellor of His Majesty's Embassy on the 21st January Mr. Hamilton expressed the readiness of the Department of State to receive any suggestions which His Majesty's Government in the United Kingdom might have to offer with regard to the question of calls to be paid on the representatives of the Provisional Government at Peking and on territorial officials. The following information on this subject has now been received from the Foreign Office.

---

[35] *Foreign Relations*, 1937, vol. III, p. 814.
[36] *Ibid.*, p. 839.
[37] Telegram No. 34, February 3, 5 p. m., p. 65.

As regards diplomatic representatives His Majesty's Government feel that, even if visitors are received on a personal footing, more formal arrangements may be made to receive return visits; while for them to receive territorial appointees such as the Mayor of Tientsin and not to receive actual members of the new Provisional Government at Peking might cause extreme ill-feeling. Moreover the expedient of returning calls by sending a card even by the hand of a personal representative would seem rude if done more than once or twice and is therefore, in the opinion of His Majesty's Government, undesirable as a general procedure.

In view of these objections His Majesty's Chargé d'Affaires is being instructed to the effect that the exchange of visits on a personal and informal basis should be restricted to consular officers; as, in any case, representations to the Provisional Government would have to be conducted through a consular officer in view of the nonrecognition of that Government, this procedure would not seem likely to affect the protection of British interests all the more because these representations would in most cases be addressed through the Japanese Embassy. In point of fact there is reason to believe that members of the Provisional Government are aware of the awkwardness of the situation and that the likelihood of their wishing to exchange calls with foreign missions is at present remote.

As regards invitations to functions, His Majesty's Government consider they should as a general rule be refused; but in special circumstances and where other missions favour similar action there might be no objection to consular officers attending.

In this connection His Majesty's Government appreciate that the United States Embassy staff at Peking are all Foreign Service officers holding diplomatic rank, so that it would no doubt in practice be impossible for the United States Government to draw the same distinction as they do. His Majesty's Government however venture to hope that the United States Government will see their way to instruct their diplomatic representative at Peking to adopt a more or less identical procedure, for example on the lines that calls limited as above should be received and returned by subordinate officers and not by the diplomatic representative in charge of the mission.

His Majesty's Government are approaching the French Government in a similar sense.

WASHINGTON, February 14, 1938.

793.94/12855½

The British Permanent Under Secretary of State for Foreign Affairs (Cadogan) to the Adviser on Political Relations (Hornbeck)[38]

[LONDON,] 14 February, 1938.

MY DEAR HORNBECK: In Brussels, you and Norman Davis suggested that we should try to work out an outline of a decent settlement of the Far Eastern situation. At the time, I was inclined to think that this was a work of supererogation. But we have been thinking it over, and have now produced an essay on the subject, which I should like you to see. I therefore enclose it, for your personal information, and in the hope that, on the same purely personal basis, you may give us your perfectly frank opinion and any suggestions that you can think of.

I should explain that this memorandum sets out the kind of settlement which we in the Foreign Office would consider reasonable, and which we should like to bring about if we had a perfectly free hand to lay down the lines of a settlement. Which we have not—as yet! It has not been considered by the Government and must not be taken as committing them. The Japanese will of course want far more, and unless a great and unforeseen change of mood occurs in Japan, we cannot expect to see a settlement on the lines sketched, unless our two Governments were able to exercise effective pressure to secure it. On the other hand, if the Japanese were once brought to accept it, the advantages it would offer them might be sufficient to produce a stable situation not requiring to be maintained by sustained pressure of a kind beyond our ordinary capacity.

Yours sincerely,   ALEXANDER CADOGAN

[Enclosure]

Memorandum on Possible Peace Terms for Communication to the United States Government

His Majesty's Government in the United Kingdom have given consideration to the question of the possible terms of settlement that might be brought about through the influence of the United States Government and of His Majesty's Government acting on parallel lines. Action for the restoration of peace through the established peace machinery of the League of Nations or through any *ad hoc* machinery that may be set up for the purpose under the Pact of Paris [39] or the Nine Power Treaty must, under present world conditions, prove ineffective. The only way, therefore, in which the influence of His

---

[38] Forwarded to the Adviser on Political Relations by the Counselor of the British Embassy in his letter of February 23.
[39] Signed at Paris, August 27, 1928, *Foreign Relations*, 1928, vol. I, p. 153.

Majesty's Government could effectively be brought to bear in the direction of restoring peace would be by action taken in defence of purely British interests. So far such action has been limited to representations to the Japanese Government and to various Japanese military and civil officials in China. These representations have not been entirely ineffective but action on these lines seems unlikely to cause Japan to abandon her present intention of destroying the Chinese Government and setting up in place thereof one or more puppet Governments or Administrations that would be completely subservient to the will of Japan. Under such a settlement it seems clear that all foreign interests would suffer serious injury and might indeed in the course of time find themselves excluded from China, as they have already to a large extent been excluded from Korea and Manchuria. If, however, representations were backed by naval forces adequate to defend any vital British interest that might be threatened it seems probable that the attitude of the Japanese Government towards China would be considerably modified. The question of possible peace terms has therefore been considered from this angle: on the assumption that His Majesty's Government are in a position to enforce respect for vital British interests and thus dictate terms of peace, what should these terms be?

2. Vital British interests in the Far East are: (1) peace and stable political conditions, (2) the open door and equality of opportunity, (3) the security of Hong Kong. No. (3) might conceivably be obtained independently of Nos. (1) and (2), but it is clear that if Nos. (1) and (2) were obtained it would not be necessary for His Majesty's Government to take any special measures to ensure the security of Hong Kong. Consequently, if His Majesty's Government were able to secure a peace of a stable nature and based upon the principles of the open door and equality of opportunity every vital British interest would thereby be fully safeguarded and they might hope to secure the co-operation of other Powers having substantial interests in the Far East in the attempt to secure such a settlement. In particular they hope that the United States Government will also find that all that is necessary for the protection of American interests in the Orient is the due observance by all parties of the Nine Power Treaty, and would therefore be disposed to take action parallel to that of His Majesty's Government. Such action might consist in representing to Japan that American (British) interests are suffering damage through the failure of Japan to observe the terms of Article 1 of the Nine Power Treaty and in taking such measures as will make it evident that the United States (United Kingdom) Government does not intend to acquiesce in any further or continuing breach of the terms of the Treaty. At the same time, each Government might make

it clear that in their view the terms of peace, besides being fair to China, should be fair and even generous to Japan.

3. The arrangements for the future administration of Shanghai would seem to be the crux of the whole problem. The obvious solution would be to restore as far as possible the administration as it existed prior to July 1937 with possibly some improvements on the lines suggested in the Feetham Report.[40]   Japan, however, has 20,000 nationals residing in Shanghai and a considerable share in the vested interests and foreign trade.   As it is essential to avoid arrangements that would be either unfair or humiliating to Japan it would be necessary to allow Japan to take measures for the protection of her nationals and her interests, and to accord her a share in the control of the foreign administered area corresponding to the numbers of the Japanese population and the importance of Japanese trade and vested interests.   The administration, and more particularly the police force, would thus become to a large and increasing extent, Japanese in character.   This would lead to friction with the Chinese, and eventually almost certainly armed clashes and a recurrence of the disastrous events of 1932 and 1937.

4. It is moreover difficult to reconcile the foreign administration of Shanghai with the provisions of the Nine Power Treaty. Shanghai is the sixth largest city in the world.   In finance, commerce, shipping and industry it is the heart of China and it may be argued with some force that China can hardly develop the effective and suitable Government contemplated in the Nine Power Treaty so long as Chinese authority is in any degree excluded from Shanghai.   Company legislation, insurance laws, control of education and relations between employers and employees, protection of labour, housing, protection and development of manufactures, control of key industries, economic planning generally—all these are essential elements in the social and economic structure of a modern state.   But in the case of China that structure is distorted because nearly one half the population of Shanghai resides in areas from which Chinese authority is excluded. The traditional aim of American and British policy, enshrined in the Nine Power Treaty, has been to encourage China to develop into a modern state.   But this aim has been to a large extent frustrated by inability to break away from the older tradition of imposing tutelage and protecting foreign interests by armed force.   Important as the foreign interests concentrated in Shanghai may be, it is doubtful whether security can in fact be obtained for them in future by the old methods of foreign administered areas and foreign garrisons.   It is improbable that the Chinese will accept a situation in which one half the population of their greatest city is withdrawn from Chinese con-

---

[40] Printed by the North-China Daily News & Herald, Ltd., at Shanghai, 1931.

trol and the Governments of, at any rate, the United States of America and the United Kingdom will be reluctant in future to use force for the protection of vested interests, or for the maintenance of foreign municipal institutions either against Chinese nationalism on the one hand or Japanese aggression on the other.

5. For two reasons therefore, viz. the uneasy situation which will persist if Japanese control is not eliminated from Shanghai and the impediment to the normal development of China which foreign control generally in Shanghai will constitute, there would seem to be much to be said for a radical change in the existing conditions in Shanghai. A solution that would be both in harmony with the Nine Power Treaty and not humiliating to Japan can only be found by means of a self-denying ordinance under which whatever Japan is asked to surrender other Powers would also surrender, even though this might involve abandoning safeguards which have hitherto been regarded as indispensable for the protection of foreign interests at Shanghai. The only alternative to maintaining the International Settlement by force is to surrender all foreign control and restore complete Chinese control. The rendition of the International Settlement need not mean the end of foreign participation in local municipal government. It is suggested that on the withdrawal of the Japanese troops from Shanghai the Governments of the United States of America and the United Kingdom should each use their influence to secure that one municipal authority should be set up by the Chinese Government for the whole of Greater Shanghai, including Pootung, the International Settlement, the external Roads area, and, if possible, the French Concession. The existing municipal administration of the Settlement would be merged in the larger body which, while remaining a Chinese authority, would contain a foreign element with full representation of Japanese, British and other foreign interests. There would be one police force—also containing a foreign element—and Chinese laws would be applied and the Chinese writ would run throughout Shanghai. No troops, Chinese or foreign, would be stationed within a radius of, say, 30 miles round Shanghai, thus giving effect to one of the desiderata to which the Japanese have always attached great importance.

6. A solution of the Shanghai problem on these lines would facilitate a settlement on the other points at issue on the basis of the open door and equality of opportunity, and in the spirit of the Nine Power Treaty which should obviously connote the withdrawal of Japanese armed forces from China and probably the withdrawal of all foreign garrisons. The Chinese would doubtless be willing to give assurances that the Maritime Customs Administration would be maintained on a basis of international co-operation fair to all powers trad-

ing in the Far East. She might also be pressed to give satisfaction to Japan on a number of points to which the Japanese Government legitimately attach great importance, such as anti-Japanese teaching in school text books, the suppression of anti-Japanese propaganda, the tariff rates to be applied to Japanese trade, etc. Japan attaches very great importance to her special position in North China. The terms of peace might therefore also include the recognition of Manchukuo by China—a measure which would remove one of the irritants that tend to disturb international relations generally—and the grant of special facilities for economic co-operation and the investment of Japanese capital in North China. This might include mining and industrial concessions for Japanese corporations, and some measure of Japanese participation in the management of the Northern Railways. Finally if, in the course of the general settlement, an opportunity should occur for dealing with the question of extraterritoriality, His Majesty's Government would favour a solution on the lines of the draft agreement of 1931 [41] which of course would be considerably modified—in the direction desired by China—by the rendition of the International Settlement as proposed above.

793.94/12426 : Telegram

The Consul General at Shanghai (Gauss) to the Secretary of State

SHANGHAI, February 15, 1938—5 p. m.
[Received February 15—12: 47 p. m.]

259. Since February 12 the Japanese each day have been despatching small patrols consisting of from 2 to 12 soldiers in charge of a junior or noncommissioned officer into the International Settlement area south of Soochow Creek. These patrols march up Nanking Road, circumvent Thibet Road, and by Peiping Road to the Bund and back to Hongkew.

I am informed by the intelligence officer of the 4th Marines that according to the Shanghai municipal police the Japanese did not notify them of their intention to despatch such patrols into the Settlement and that upon bringing the matter to the attention of the Japanese military authorities the police were informed that the Japanese were merely exercising the same right as is enjoyed by the other foreign defense forces of sending out patrols to protect their respective military details. In the area south of Soochow Creek Japanese details consist of an occasional Japanese military truck, despatch rider or staff car.

---

[41] For negotiations, see *Foreign Relations*, 1931, vol. III, pp. 716 ff.; see also telegram of June 8, 1931, 1 p. m., *ibid.*, p. 874.

On three occasions these patrols upon reaching the junction of Bubbling Well Road and Thibet Road have sought to march up Bubbling Well Road which is within the American defense sector. In each instance they have been courteously turned back by the United States Marines on duty at this point.

No serious incidents have occurred thus far but it would not be surprising if Chinese special service agents or terrorists attempted to bomb these patrols whose presence south of Soochow Creek is extremely provocative.

Repeated to Hankow and Peiping.

GAUSS

793.94/12859

The Consul at Harbin (Merrell) to the Ambassador in China (Johnson)[42]

No. 35   HARBIN, February 16, 1938.

SIR: I have the honor to report that Mr. A. T. Steele, representative in North China of the *Chicago Daily News*, recently called at the Consulate General and reported an interesting conversation he had had the previous day in Hsinking with Major General Kanji Ishihara, Vice Chief of Staff of the Kwantung Army. In commenting upon the reports of the looting by Japanese troops in Nanking after the taking of the capital, General Ishihara stated emphatically that if the reports were true, General Matsui was completely responsible for the troops' behavior. He said that the morale of the Japanese Army had never been at a lower level than it was at the present time. He deprecated the current lack of discipline among Japanese troops.

In the course of their conversation he also informed Mr. Steele that the Japanese would not open hostilities against Soviet Russia and that he believed Russia would not make the first attack against Japan unless it was assured of Great Britain's support. He said that it therefore meant that Japan would not fight Russia unless it had to fight Great Britain as well.

In this connection it seems worth mentioning that Mr. Richard T. Evans, a prominent American attorney from Tientsin who called this morning on Major General Sueichiro Higuchi, chief of the Japanese Military Mission in Harbin, was likewise informed by General Higuchi that Japan would not take the initiative in bringing about a conflict with Soviet Russia. When Mr. Evans remarked to the General that he had been under the impression that, whereas the responsible authorities in Japan and perhaps the highest officers in command

[42] Copy transmitted to the Department by the Consul at Harbin in his covering despatch No. 38, February 16; received April 18.

of the Japanese Army, were opposed to opening hostilities with Soviet Russia, such was not the case with a comprehensive group of younger officers who advocated attacking Russia at this time while there was an enthusiasm for military conquest among the public in Japan which it would be difficult to rouse again when it had once been allowed to subside. General Higuchi agreed that there had been such a conviction on the part of the younger officers, that he had been one of them, and had shared their conviction, but that he had now changed his mind and was firm in the belief that it was wiser for Japan to show restraint vis-à-vis Soviet Russia.

The *Harbin Nichi Nichi* of February 16 published a report that Manchurian troops guarding the third tunnel of the railroad near Pogranichnaya were attacked on February 14 by 15 Soviet soldiers with scouting dogs who had invaded "Manchukuo" territory by about 150 meters. The invaders were repulsed immediately with fire, and it was considered unlikely that the incident would lead to further trouble; the government at Hsinking had, however, considered it serious enough to make a strong protest to the Soviet Consulate General in Harbin.

From Harbin Mr. Steele, armed with proper Japanese credentials, went by rail to the strongly fortified town of Taheiho directly across the Amur River from Blagoveshchensk. Upon his return he informed the Consulate General that he had seen nothing of particular interest either from a military or a political standpoint, and that he did not believe the 2½ days' journey had been worth making.

Respectfully yours, GEORGE R. MERRELL

793.94/12449 : Telegram

The Consul General at Shanghai (Gauss) to the Secretary of State

SHANGHAI, February 17, 1938—2 p. m.
[Received 5 : 16 p. m.]

272. Reference penultimate paragraph my 259, February 15, 5 p. m. I am informed by intelligence officer of the 4th Marines that Lieutenant Colonel Oka of the Japanese Military Attaché's office called this morning at Marine Headquarters and apologized for attempts made by Japanese patrols to enter the American defense sector. He said that these attempts had been made due to ignorance and added that instructions had now been issued to all patrols to refrain from entering the defense sector. Colonel Oka inquired regarding the possibility of Japanese patrols entering some sections of the American sector by mutual arrangement but was informed by Colonel Price [43]

---

[43] Col. Charles F. B. Price, commanding U. S. 4th Marines Regiment at Shanghai.

that he was not in favor of such arrangement, that such patrols were unnecessary and would merely cause friction and provocation whereupon Colonel Oka dropped the matter.

Japanese patrols twice a day continue to march through the downtown area of the International Settlement. No incidents have occurred thus far.

Repeated to Hankow and Peiping.

GAUSS

793.94/12460 : Telegram

The Third Secretary of Embassy in China (Allison) to the Secretary of State

NANKING, February 18, 1938—4 p. m.
[Received 6 : 39 p. m.]

61. I am pleased to be able to report that within the past 10 days there have been a noticeable improvement in conditions in Nanking. Most of the Chinese are returning from the so-called "safety zone" to former homes in other parts of the city. While reports still come in from time to time of disorder and unlawful acts of Japanese soldiers, the number of such reports has materially decreased and there is definite evidence that the Japanese authorities are making efforts to better the present living conditions of the local population. Restrictions on movements of foreigners are gradually being loosened, and permission has recently been obtained for the return to Nanking of an American doctor whose presence is urgently needed at the Nanking University Hospital, an American institution.

Sent to Embassy [at] Hankow, repeated to Department, Peiping and Shanghai. Shanghai please repeat to Tokyo.

ALLISON

500.A15A5 Construction/131

The Ambassador in Japan (Grew) to the Secretary of State

No. 2779   TOKYO, February 18, 1938.
[Received March 9.]

SIR: The recent refusal of the Japanese Government to reply affirmatively* to the inquiry addressed to it by the British, French, and American Governments [44] as to whether the Japanese Government

---

*Embassy's telegram No. 101, February 12, 7 p. m. [Footnote in the original telegram not printed; for text of Japanese note of February 12, see *Foreign Relations*, Japan, 1931–1941, vol. I, p. 304.]

[44] For note dated February 5 from the Ambassador in Japan to the Japanese Minister for Foreign Affairs, see *ibid.*, p. 303. For further correspondence on naval construction, see *Foreign Relations*, 1938, vol. I, pp. 891 ff.

has undertaken or intends to undertake the construction of capital ships and cruisers of a tonnage greater than that allowed under the London Naval Treaty of 1936,[45] must be regarded as a logical action, consistent with the repeated expressions of Japanese naval policy. This action on the part of the Japanese Government is, of course, apart from such questions as the reasons underlying that policy or the effect upon the Japanese Government and public opinion of the inquiry itself.

I. Beginning with the return to Japan of the delegates to the London Conference of 1930 [46] when the Japanese nation became more and more convinced that the country had been sold out to the other naval powers, the Japanese Navy has laid down a policy which has been consistently followed and which *nolens volens* must be recognized by the Powers as the basis for any Japanese approach to the question of naval disarmament. This policy is one of independent naval construction of a nature designed to meet what the Japanese Navy considers to be its needs: (1) to provide impregnable defense for the Empire and (2) to implement its policy of dominating East Asia and of the "southward advance". This is described by the Japanese as defensive and, if we exclude the "southward advance" and admit the preponderance of Japanese interests on the mainland of East Asia, it can be accepted as such. There is no evidence that their present Navy or their future building program are of such a nature as to constitute a threat to any country beyond the sphere roughly known as East Asia. This policy of independent naval construction has found expression in three phrases well-known to the Powers which have had dealings with Japan in naval matters for the past few years. These phrases, which first appeared early in 1935, some six or eight months prior to Japan's abrogation of the Washington and London Naval Treaties, have been used on every outstanding occasion; upon their notice of abrogation,[47] upon their departure from the second London Conference in January, 1936,[48] in their rejection of the proposal to the limitation of the caliber of guns for capital ships to fourteen inches in June, 1937,[49] and now in their refusal to give information concerning naval construction. These phrases are (1) "common upper limit" (2) "no qualitative without quantitative limitation" and (3) "non-menace and non-aggression".

It may be observed in this connection that on no occasion has the Japanese Government closed the door to participation in any future

---

[45] Signed March 25, 1936 ; 50 Stat. 1363.
[46] See *Foreign Relations*, 1930, vol. I, pp. 1 ff.
[47] Note dated December 29, 1934, *Foreign Relations*, Japan, 1931–1941, vol. I, p. 274.
[48] Note dated January 15, 1936, *ibid.*, p. 297.
[49] See telegram No. 161, June 18, 1937, 4 p. m., from the Ambassador in Japan, *ibid.*, p. 301.

disarmament conference provided only that the foregoing principles be accepted beforehand by the other Powers.

Of these three phrases the first is self-explanatory, but may be expressed in another form as an insistence upon parity in tonnage in principle; the second merely means that without quantitative limitation, i. e., acceptance by all of a common upper limit, qualitative limitation will not, in Japanese eyes, serve the purposes of realistic disarmament; the third is an expression of the defensive policy of construction which the Japanese maintain they are pursuing. And they are so convinced of their inherent right to the domination of the territory adjacent to their Empire that they are sincere in their characterization of their naval policy as defensive.

There immediately comes to mind the question as to whether it is possible to reconcile the Japanese views of defensive naval construction and of non-menace and non-aggression with the fact, if true, of their building battleships and cruisers of a tonnage in excess of those now possessed by Great Britain and the United States. This question is capable of being approached along the following lines: In the first place the construction by Japan of vessels in excess of 40,000 tons would immediately stimulate the United States and Great Britain to respond in kind which, in fact, it appears that they are about to do; therefore the possibility of aggressive action by Japan against a country as far distant as, say, the United States, would in no way be increased. In the second place it is generally believed by technical observers that the new vessels, while more heavily armed than their present ships, will probably have little increased cruising radius and that, therefore, they can be regarded as defensive in character, at least in the view of the Japanese.

As to the policy of "southward advance", it is generally conceded that mere ship construction cannot further the pursuit of this policy—which it is admitted must be regarded as aggressive—unless and until the Japanese construct new naval bases further southward than Formosa, and there is no evidence as yet that they intend to do so.

To sum up the foregoing, therefore, it can be stated that the present Japanese naval policy is one which actually does and will continue to constitute a threat to the interests of the western Powers in East Asia, but which does not, and probably will not in the immediate future, constitute a threat to the territory of the western Powers themselves. This, we repeat, is what the Japanese believe to be the pursuit of a defensive policy.

II. The reasons underlying this policy have been frequently touched upon in despatches from this Embassy. They can be summed up as follows: (1) It has been abundantly clear to the Japanese that with the relatively meagre resources at their command they could never hope to compete successfully in a ship-for-ship construction race with greater and richer Powers; this is both obvious and axiomatic but nevertheless it should not be left unstated. (2) Japan feels that she can neither feed her population nor continue to exist in the industrial world without gaining access to such raw materials as may be within her grasp or without stabilizing and increasing her markets in China; consequently the control of China and the approaches to it render domination of East Asia, in the minds of the Japanese, an absolute necessity. (3) The existence of the League of Nations with its constant threat of the use of economic sanctions brings unceasing pressure to bear upon Japan to take such steps as she deems necessary to defend herself against the possible consequences of the application of such sanctions. (4) Her geographical location makes it possible for her to make her defense, from a naval point of view, nearly impregnable provided that she be free to build unrestrictedly the types of ships which suit her needs. (5) Her passionate desire for equality in the eyes of the world and for the preservation of her *amour propre*, as well as her necessity for maintaining "face" in the eyes of the Chinese, has led her to hold out for parity in principle even at the cost of stimulating further construction on the part of the other naval Powers. For example, if Japan's policy results in the building by the United States of a navy so large that the ratio between it and that of Japan is increased to an extent even beyond the present ratio, Japan's defensive position, i. e., not only as regards the Empire itself but as regards its domination of East Asia, will be scarcely affected—a fact which concerns Japan greatly—whereas Japan's offensive position, i. e., her ability to attack the United States will be, of course, greatly reduced—a fact which concerns Japan virtually not at all.

Without intending to make an exhaustive study of the motives behind Japanese naval policy, the foregoing are among the outstanding factors which must be taken into consideration in evaluating that policy. It may well be argued from the above that the Japanese have much to gain and little to lose by pursuing a policy of independent naval construction and permitting the other nations to do what they like. Japan has no present intention of carrying the battle to the western Powers; but if the western Powers wish to carry the battle to Japan, the Japanese navy is and can be prepared.

III. The effect upon the Japanese Government and public opinion of the recent inquiry addressed to Japan by the three Powers, in which information was requested as to whether Japan were building ships in excess of the treaty tonnage, has been, to judge by the tone of the Government's reply, and the press comment, to arouse a feeling of resentment that the treaty Powers should call upon Japan to furnish information not required by any obligation incumbent upon her. At the same time, however, the Japanese Government placed itself on record once more as being willing to enter upon discussions on the matter of disarmament "which give primary importance to a fair quantitative limitation".

From the point of view of the press here the action of the three Powers was designed to throw the burden of naval armament expansion upon Japan in the eyes of the world and for no other reason. The press argues that as common sense will show that Japan's budget will not permit the building of a fleet large enough to menace the United States, why, then, does the American press maintain that the Japanese reply will make Japan responsible for beginning a naval armament race? "The real intention of Great Britain, France and the United States," says the *Nichi Nichi Shimbun*, "is to shift to Japan the burden of responsibility for their respective armament expansion. The primary intention of Great Britain is to protect its rights and interests in China by indirect means." And so on; there is no need to quote further from the press. The fact remains that the action of the three Powers was resented and that the Japanese are apparently indifferent to the prospect that a naval race may be started by their refusal to furnish information concerning their naval construction.

IV. It may at this point be desirable to speculate upon the reasons underlying the refusal of Japan to furnish information regarding her naval building in order to prevent the Powers from exercising their rights under the "escalator" clause of the 1936 Treaty and so stimulating a naval armament race. The reasons which come to mind are three:

(1) The Japanese are convinced that, due to world conditions elsewhere than in the Far East, Great Britain (followed by the United States) would in any case greatly increase her strength in categories of vessels which, even though they might remain within treaty limits, as to tonnage, would make it necessary for Japan to build further for defense; hence Japan would rather be left free to construct as she pleases; and not to tie herself down to ships of a specified tonnage.

(2) Japan is fully aware of her "nuisance value" and she is hopeful that, with her ability to maintain secrecy regarding her naval construction to a far greater degree than any other nation, she is in a position—by creating fear that she is building new types of vessels which would render obsolete existing types—to be such a constant menace to the Powers that she may force them eventually to accept the principle of parity in exchange for information regarding her naval construction.

(3) And lastly, the Japanese feel that they can afford to be more or less indifferent to the expansion of naval armaments by the Powers for the reasons given under II above; namely, that Japan is confident of her ability to take care of her security in East Asia irrespective of what the Powers may do.

There are enclosed herewith copies of the American, British and French notes of February 5, 1938, and of the Japanese replies thereto as supplied by the Japanese Foreign Office in English and French translation. It may be added in this connection that while we are transmitting to the Department our reply in English translation exactly as it was received from the Foreign Office, the British Embassy chose to "polish up" the translation which they received before transmitting it to London. A comparison of the two texts will reveal that the British Embassy version of the translation conveys a rather more brusque tone than does the original as received by this Embassy.

Respectfully yours, JOSEPH C. GREW

793.94/12463 : Telegram

The Ambassador in Japan (Grew) to the Secretary of State

TOKYO, February 19, 1938—noon.
[Received February 19—9 : 35 a. m.]

117. The following memorandum was submitted to me today by the Military Attaché: [50]

"With reference to the statement by the War Minister in this morning's papers concerning the 'replacement' of units in China, the 'strengthening of the fighting power of the Japanese Expeditionary Army' et cetera, a visit to the War Office for the purpose of clarifying the above statement has brought forth the following information:

That the moves contemplated do not necessarily mean either a strengthening or a weakening of the forces in China from a numerical standpoint but rather a reorganization and redistribution with a view to a strengthening of the Japanese forces organically and strategically for the more or less prolonged condition of hostilities which the Japanese High Command now feel lies before them, and that while the moves to this end may well involve the replacement of certain units, it is likely that the units replaced will be those not necessary in the type of operation which they visualize for the future.

When questioned as to whether this statement by the War Minister implied any change in the objectives of the Japanese Army, the officer to whom I spoke stated with considerable emphasis that their objectives remained the same, i. e., the destruction of the Chinese forces opposing them and the anti-Japanese communistic influences in China and he added that the big question at present lies in the decision as to the manner by which these ends may best be achieved".

Repeated to Shanghai for Hankow.

GREW

---

[50] Col. Joseph W. Stilwell.

893.01 Provisional/32 : Telegram

The Acting Secretary of State to the Counselor of Embassy in China (Lockhart), at Peiping

WASHINGTON, February 19, 1938—1 p. m.

51. Reference Department's 400, December 15, 7 p. m.[51] The Department has received an *aide-mémoire* from the British Embassy [52] transmitting information from the British Foreign Office on the subject of calls on representatives of the provisional government at Peiping and on territorial officials. In summary, it is stated that the British Embassy, Peiping, is being instructed to the effect that the exchange of visits on a personal and informal basis should be restricted to consular officers; that as representations to the provisional government would in view of the non-recognition of that government have to be conducted through a consular officer, this procedure would not seem likely to affect the protection of British interests more particularly because representations would in most cases be made through the Japanese Embassy.

With regard to invitations to functions, the British Government considers that they should as a general rule be refused, but in special circumstances and where other missions favor similar action, there might be no objection to consular officers attending. In conclusion, it is stated that the British Government appreciates that as all the officers of our Embassy staff hold diplomatic rank it would not be practicable to draw the same distinction as the British do, but the hope is expressed that this Government will see its way to instruct its Embassy to adopt a procedure more or less identical, e. g., that calls limited as above be received and returned by subordinate officers and not by the senior diplomatic officer. A similar approach, it is added, is also being made to the French Government.

Keeping in mind the basic principle involved, as set forth in the Department's instruction under reference, to the effect that there should be avoided action or attitude that might be construed as carrying any degree of official recognition of the new régime, and in view of the desirability of the principally interested Governments following procedures more or less identical in regard to matters of protocol, the Department suggests that you consult with your British and French colleagues with regard to the British proposal outlined above and give the Department the benefit of your views and suggestions.

WELLES

---

[51] *Foreign Relations*, 1937, vol. III, p. 811.
[52] Dated February 14, p. 87.

893.01 Provisional/56 : Telegram

The Counselor of Embassy in China (Lockhart) to the Secretary of State

PEIPING, February 23, 1938—noon.
[Received February 23—4 : 48 a. m.]

125. Your 51, February 19, 1 p. m.

1. I believe that a distinction should be drawn between officials of the "Provisional Government" and municipal officials serving thereunder. It seems to me that the proposal made by the British Government could probably be applied to municipal officers as distinguished from Provisional Government officials with the exception that in the case of this Embassy it might be necessary on occasions to substitute a subordinate diplomatic officer for a consular officer, depending somewhat on the circumstances of the call from the local official. There is one career consular officer attached to the Embassy at present. As regards officials of the so-called "Provisional Government" it would seem to be preferable to adhere to the procedure defined in the Department's 400, December 15, 7 p. m.,[53] that is to say, calls received from such officials should be acknowledged by sending, or if deemed definitely expedient, taking in return the personal card of the officer in charge with the personal name of the official called upon written thereon. I received a call from the Mayor recently and returned it on this basis.

2. The question of attending functions would present a more difficult problem, but there is reason to believe that this question will not arise at least until after the appointment of a chairman of the "Provisional Government."

3. It will be difficult for the Embassy to escape the necessity of informal representations to the local authorities, (generally to the municipal authorities by subordinate officers) from time to time, on subjects such as local taxes, municipal regulations, and protection. So far there has been no occasion to approach the "Provisional Government" on any subject.

4. The substance of the above has been discussed with my British and French colleagues.

The latter has referred matter to his Ambassador and the former will inform his Government of the views herein expressed.

LOCKHART

---

[53] *Foreign Relations*, 1937, vol. III, p. 811.

793.94/12496 : Telegram

The Ambassador in Japan (Grew) to the Secretary of State

TOKYO, February 23, 1938—5 p. m.
[Received February 23—11 : 40 a. m.]

125. Reference Shanghai's 280, February 19, 10 [*11*] a. m.[54]

1. The replacement of General Matsui by General Hata has just been announced.

2. The Vice Minister for Foreign Affairs [55] yesterday stated to my British colleague who inquired with regard to the reasons for the then impending change that: "Hata is a good soldier and is less interested in politics than Matsui."

3. The Military Attaché of the Embassy [56] has just presented me with his estimate of the considerations entering into the decision to replace General Matsui, as follows:

"(1) (*a*) The widespread feeling in Japanese Army circles that operations in China are likely to be more or less protracted and that the army forces in China are being reorganized accordingly.

(*b*) That General Matsui is about 60 years old and was on the retired list before being called to active service in the Shanghai area.

(*c*) That General Matsui is a man of strong political ideas and less amenable to control by a central authority than would be an officer of a more conservative type.

(2) To what extent each of the above considerations entered into the decision is impossible to determine though it is felt that the one relating to politics has played a greater part than the Japanese with whom this matter was discussed were willing to admit. However, the operations in China are now in course of transition from a very active military phase to a phase in which, while military operations will still be carried out, more politico-military in character, and in which the Japanese efforts in China are directed toward a political as well as a military stabilization. Under such circumstances and with the above mentioned reorganization for a long haul in view it appears quite natural that central authority both in and out of the army should lean toward a commander whose actions may be expected to be in greater harmony with both a political and a military stabilization policy.

(3) The relief does not imply any censure of General Matsui in the military or popular mind. After all he is a commander who has succeeded and it is not unlikely that his return to Japan will be accompanied by acclaim for a work well done.

(4) In the sense that the change of command may indicate a change of policy in China the following remarks concerning the two men will indicate their respective backgrounds.

(*a*) General Matsui: an officer of undoubted ability and known throughout the service as an authority on China. Recognized as

---

[54] Not printed.
[55] Kensuke Horinouchi.
[56] Maj. Harry I. T. Creswell.

the mainspring of the 'Continental Policy' and since going to the reserve list at the time of the February 26th incident [57] he has been head of the Pan Asiatic Society. He is reported as having not much use for the West or its institutions except insofar as they may be beneficial to Japan.

(b) General Hata: at present Director General of Military Training, one of the important positions in the army. Has had a distinguished career and is known as a 'non-party' man with no political enthusiasms or inclinations. He is also known as a strict disciplinarian in the sense of order and subordination in the army and with men like General Terauchi [58] strongly deplored the trends indicated by the February 26th incident."

Repeated to Shanghai for Hankow and Peiping.

GREW

793.94/12695

The Consul General at Hong Kong (Southard) to the Secretary of State

No. 115 HONG KONG, February 23, 1938.
[Received March 21.]

SIR: I have the honor to report that Mr. G. Cora, Italian Ambassador to China, is at present spending a few days in Hong Kong. His arrival here coincided with that of Sir Archibald Clark Kerr, the new British Ambassador to China, who stopped in Hong Kong three days en route from Europe to Shanghai.

Mr. Cora was my colleague in Addis Ababa and we are somewhat intimately acquainted. In the course of a general conversation which I had today with him he remarked that he had in effect advised General Chiang Kai-shek, on the occasion of their last meeting, to get together with the Japanese and thus save what he could for China; that the battle was inevitably a losing one (just as was that of Haile Selassie against the Italians in Ethiopia!) and the longer it went on the less China would have at the end. Cora further remarked to me that he couldn't see why the Chinese continued to resist; that they must have some one to help develop their country, and why not have the Japanese who were so well situated and equipped for the purpose.

These particular comments of Mr. Cora are repeated because I am impressed that they represent, although he did not specifically so state, thoughts inspired by his official instructions from Rome. The Italian Ambassador is leaving Hong Kong on February 25th, 1938, to return to Shanghai.

Very respectfully, ADDISON E. SOUTHARD

---

[57] See *Foreign Relations*, 1936, vol. IV, pp. 706 ff.
[58] Japanese military commander in North China.

793.94/12507 : Telegram

The Ambassador in Japan (Grew) to the Secretary of State

TOKYO, February 24, 1938—4 p. m.
[Received February 24—10 a. m.]

129. Shanghai's 39, January 7, 11 p. m.[59] and our January 13, 4 p. m. to Shanghai,[60] reference Hankow safety zone.

1. Craigie has recommended to his Government that the terms of the Japanese undertaking to refrain from attacking the safety zone be communicated to the Chinese Government. He believes that "if we fail to pass on to the Chinese authorities the Japanese proposals in respect of a safety zone, we not only discourage the Japanese from making conciliatory suggestions in future but give them a pretext for maintaining the powers have failed to cooperate in their humanitarian efforts."

2. In his letter to me Craigie refers to the Japanese undertaking as an "offer" and apparently assumes that an explicit engagement by the Chinese Government to fulfill the Japanese conditions is necessary before the Japanese undertaking become binding on the Japanese Government. The Japanese note to us of January 11 reported in our January 13, 4 p. m. via Shanghai does not so indicate. The question whether or not our Government should make representations to the Chinese Government in the matter is one which the Department may wish to decide in consultation with Johnson.

Repeated to Shanghai for Hankow.

GREW

893.01 Manchuria/1501 : Telegram

The Ambassador in China (Johnson) to the Secretary of State

HANKOW, February 24, 1938—4 p. m.
[Received 6:50 p. m.]

120. My 104, February 15, 3 p. m.[61] While there have been a few comments in the local Chinese press indicating Chinese disappointment with German recognition of Manchukuo,[62] Chinese authorities appear to accept situation calmly. They are probably more interested in continued purchase of German military supplies and service of military advisers. I think German attitude was expected. It is my opinion that it does not change materially Far Eastern situation.

---

[59] Not printed.
[60] See telegram No. 73, January 13, 7 p. m., from the Consul General at Shanghai, p. 21.
[61] Vol. IV, p. 267.
[62] See pp. 441 ff.

It gives a certain amount of encouragement in regard to Japanese who were already embarked upon military conquest of China for the purpose of destroying the Chinese nationalism founded on occidental democratic and capitalistic rather than communistic lines. Soviet Russia will not attack Japan but may be expected to aid China to prolong campaign, content with the hope that Japan will exhaust itself in China. A Germany involved with Soviet Russia can hope for little assistance from a Japan preoccupied with China.

Far more serious consideration will doubtless be given by the Chinese to future attitude of England. Resignation of Eden is feared as possibly portending a shift in British policy to one that will be more acceptable to Japan. T. V. Soong [63] arrived at Hankow yesterday. Since despatch of Leith-Ross [64] to China in 1935, the Chinese adoption of his advice in reform of Central Bank and linking of Chinese currency with that of Great Britain, Soong's chief interests there [*in relation?*] to Chinese Government lay in his possible usefulness in bolstering Government's credit abroad because he enjoyed confidence of British finance. Soong may now find that he has lost that support. In this connection please see reports forwarded to Office of Naval Intelligence by McHugh [65] from Hong Kong by Clipper February 9 and 17, dated January 20 and February 8 respectively,[66] especially with reference to part played by Rogers of Bank of England in career and prospect of Soong. Advice understood to have been conveyed to London by Craigie, mentioned in Tokyo's telegram No. 100 of February 12, noon, may find Chamberlain [67] readier to listen than Eden might have been. I learned last evening from British Embassy that Kung [68] has held up instructions to Commissioner of Customs mentioned in my 102 of February 14, 11 a. m.,[69] after receiving British advice mentioned in my 117, February 21, 3 p. m.,[70] waiting to see what better method of preserving customs to Chinese British may have to offer. Furthermore Chinese under present conditions do not desire to go against wishes of British Government. A cynical interpretation of British advice to Kung would be that British Government desires door left open for Maze [71] and his commissioners to take service with a Japanese fostered Chinese Government, thus maintaining formal customs and integrity in the interest of British loans secured on customs.

---

[63] Former Chinese Minister of Finance.
[64] Sir Frederick Leith-Ross, Chief Economic Adviser to the British Government.
[65] Capt. James M. McHugh, U. S. M. C., Assistant Naval Attaché in China.
[66] Neither found in Department files.
[67] Neville Chamberlain, British Prime Minister.
[68] H. H. Kung, Chinese Minister of Finance and President of the Executive Yuan (Premier).
[69] *Post*, p. 656.
[70] *Post*, p. 659.
[71] Sir Frederick Maze, British Inspector General of the Chinese Maritime Customs Administration.

Sent to Peiping, Shanghai. Shanghai please repeat to Tokyo and show to Commander-in-Chief.

JOHNSON

793.94/12518 : Telegram

The Ambassador in China (Johnson) to the Secretary of State

HANKOW, February 25, 1938—1 p. m.
[Received February 25—10:45 a. m.]

123. Tokyo's 129, February 25 [*24*], 1 a. m. [*4 p. m.*]. I have read back over my 33, December 13, 4 p. m.,[72] and subsequent exchange of telegrams with Department, Embassy [at] Tokyo, and Consulate General [at] Shanghai, and I find that throughout we have refrained from any action which would imply obligation on our part to communicate Japanese assurances to Chinese authorities, thereby becoming responsible to one for the conduct of the other. Throughout I have endeavored to limit action to notifying Japanese military of foreign property, shippers and nationals, and asking for assurances against attack. Craigie's point of view would appear to be based upon attitude set forth in British note to Japanese Ambassador, Shanghai, reported in Shanghai's 1243 of December 28, 10 p. m.[73] I at all times kept my colleagues here informed of my attitude, but British went beyond us in apparently promising to obtain an undertaking from the Chinese.

Consular body at Hankow under date of January 12 made representations to Chinese authorities locally stating that Japanese had given assurances not to attack such places as were not utilized by Chinese troops for military purposes, and requesting Chinese to remove from area any military works or any troops that might be stationed therein. Chinese replied stating that no anti-aircraft batteries had been placed within municipal area. It is obviously impossible for us to obtain from Chinese any undertaking upon which we can depend as to what situation may be should fighting actually occur in the vicinity of Hankow. Craigie's note to Grew may arise from the fact that British are now trying to return to basis upon which my original proposal was made and to line which I have consistently followed, and from the feeling that original British communication does not permit this.

Repeated to Shanghai. Shanghai please repeat to Tokyo.

JOHNSON

[72] *Foreign Relations*, 1937, vol. IV, p. 401.
[73] Not printed.

793.94119/400 : Telegram

The Counselor of Embassy in China (Lockhart) to the Secretary of State

PEIPING, February 27, 1938—10 a. m.
[Received February 27—7 a. m.]

136. At the instance of Wang Keh Min [74] and with the knowledge and acquiescence of the military authorities, Dr. Leighton Stuart [75] left Peiping yesterday via Shanghai for Hankow for the express purpose of seeking audience of Chiang Kai Shek on the subject of possible peace negotiations. On asking Dr. Stuart on what basis the Japanese would be willing to negotiate he said: (1) Suppression of anti-Japanese movements; (2) establishment of a good administrative area in North China (which I interpret to mean an independent government in the north such as now exists); (3) economic cooperation and (4) reparation. I remarked that this seemed to be substantially the basis submitted to the Chinese several weeks ago by the Japanese and which the Chinese rejected. Dr. Stuart said that Japanese military hope to be in occupation of the Lunghai Railway shortly and that after that occurs the Japanese will be willing to enter into a truce with Chiang Kai Shek not exceeding 4 weeks to allow time for preliminary peace negotiations to take form; that the Japanese would be willing to discuss peace terms with Chiang Kai Shek himself (which is contrary to repeated announcements from Tokyo) or a responsible representative or representatives. Dr. Stuart who is very close to some of the leaders in the Provisional Government stated also that the Japanese favor some sort of a plan for "internationalizing the Yangtze valley." The term is vague but I believe it means the return of the Yangtze River (and perhaps the adjacent cities and countryside) to the *status quo* prevailing before the trouble began. Dr. Stuart further stated that the Japanese will not insist upon the withdrawal of Chiang Kai Shek from the present Government and that they would recognize that the British Government has a special sphere of influence in Kwangtung and Kwangsi and that similarly it would recognize that the Soviet Republic has a special sphere of influence in Kansu, Sinkiang and Ninghsia. I told Stuart that the Chinese would undoubtedly have some very pronounced views on these two points as well as on the others.

Dr. Stuart hopes at least to obtain from Chiang a statement of the basis on which Chiang would be willing to negotiate and having obtained such a statement it will be taken or communicated at once

---

[74] Head of the Japanese-sponsored regime in Peiping.
[75] American, president of Yenching University, Peiping.

256941—54——8

to Tokyo.   I do not know whether the Japanese authorities at Tokyo
have knowledge of Dr. Stuart's mission.

Sent to Ambassador.   Repeated to Tokyo.

LOCKHART

793.94119/401 : Telegram

The Ambassador in China (Johnson) to the Secretary of State

HANKOW, February 27, 1938—11 a. m.

[Received 4: 05 p. m.]

129. T. V. Soong arrived in Hankow about February 23.   On
February 26 he talked with McHugh and sent me confidentially a
message which he thought would interest our Government.   Following is synopsis of this information: Cora, the Italian Ambassador,
accompanied by Ito the "unofficial Japanese Ambassador" arrived in
Hong Kong just before Soong left and brought greetings and presents
to him from Ciano [76] which led Soong to think that Mussolini and
Ciano sanctioned the visit.   The Ambassador said he had come to talk
about peace terms and that his position was different from that taken
by the German Ambassador in December because he would convey only
such terms as he personally believed to be a reasonable basis for
negotiation.   The terms outlined by Cora were described by him as
"very lenient" and were roughly as follows: (1) China shall recognize Manchukuo; (2) Japan shall station garrisons in North China;
(3) Japan shall have economic privileges in the same area; (4) a
neutral zone shall be established in the Shanghai area but Japan shall
not demand a Japanese concession; (5) an indemnity shall be paid.
Soong inquired of Cora which nation should receive the indemnity
and whether the intention was for Japan to indemnify China for the
destruction of Nanking and the bombing of Shanghai.   Cora answered
that after every war an indemnity always had to be paid and that
naturally Japan expected something.   Soong said he tried to be tactful with the Italian Ambassador because he hoped that friendly relations might be restored eventually and also was very careful with Ito
"because unofficial representatives are always the most dangerous".
Soong commented to McHugh that the terms described above were
more moderate than earlier ones and he felt they showed that Japan
wished to end the hostilities as soon as possible but that China would
go on fighting because there was no possible solution of the present
crisis.

Soong said that shortly before Cora's visit a representative of
Matsui had called on him and had promised "very easy terms" if he

---

[76] Count Galeazzo Ciano di Cortellazzo, Italian Minister for Foreign Affairs.

would discuss peace. Soong thought the approach had been made to him because the Japanese thought him trustworthy and possessed of enough influence both within and outside of China to enable him to speak authoritatively. This was the end of the message.

In informal conversation Soong expressed doubt whether the Chamberlain Government in Great Britain as reorganized would last long and said that any close association between Great Britain and Germany and Italy was "unnatural"; that a durable policy could be based only on complete understanding with the United States and that as long as the present British Government remains in power this would be impossible. McHugh inquired whether it was possible that Great Britain might veer toward Japan in the present struggle in order, for example, to preserve the integrity of the customs. Soong thought this possible and that the Japanese had ceased to await friendly overtures from the British and were taking the initiative in cultivating the British.

Repeated to Peiping. Peiping please repeat to Tokyo.

JOHNSON

793.94119/400 : Telegram

The Secretary of State to the Ambassador in China (Johnson)

WASHINGTON, February 28, 1938—6 p. m.

87. Peiping's 136, February 27, 10 a. m. In proceeding as indicated in the telegram under reference Dr. Leighton Stuart is of course not acting on behalf of or with the approval of this Government. I desire that, upon the arrival of Stuart at Hankow, you ask him to make abundantly clear to such officials of the Chinese Government as he may approach that this Government is in no way associated with his action. Please ask him also to make this clear to Wang Ke-ming and to the Japanese military authorities with whose knowledge and acquiescence he left Peiping for Hankow, as well as to any other Japanese authorities with whom he may have discussion of this matter. You should also point out to him in tactful language that assumption by an American private citizen of the role of an intermediary between authorities of foreign countries in relation to a question of major international import, or participation by such citizens in deliberation by such authorities with regard to high governmental policies are forms of activities which create and entail tremendous personal responsibilities and have been shown by experience to have more often unfortunate than beneficial consequences. I desire further that as suitable opportunity presents itself you discreetly inform the appropriate authorities of the Chinese Government of the fact that Stuart is not acting on behalf of or with the approval of this Government.

In view of the fact that Stuart has presumably not as yet reached Shanghai en route to Hankow, I suggest that you repeat Peiping's telegram under reference and this telegram to Gauss at Shanghai with request that Gauss communicate to Stuart upon his arrival at Shanghai the views which you also will later communicate to him.

Please repeat this telegram to Peiping and request that Peiping repeat it to Tokyo.

HULL

793.94119/402 : Telegram

The Ambassador in China (Johnson) to the Secretary of State

HANKOW, March 1, 1938—10 a. m.
[Received March 1—8 : 45 a. m.]

137.   Peiping's 136, February 27, 10 a. m. to the Department.   I feel fairly sure that it would be possible for me to discourage Stuart's mission by informally conveying knowledge thereof to Chinese authorities.   I feel however that it would be most unwise to do this, and unless instructed otherwise I propose to ignore Stuart's mission entirely. I also propose to refuse to be the channel for communicating any messages which he may desire transmitted in connection therewith, as I do not feel that conditions warrant our becoming sponsor for such discussions at this time even by implication.

Repeated to Peiping.   Peiping please repeat to Tokyo.

JOHNSON

793.94119/403 : Telegram

The Ambassador in China (Johnson) to the Secretary of State

HANKOW, March 2, 1938—3 p. m.
[Received March 3—10 : 35 a. m.]

140.   Am repeating to you Peiping's 136, February 27, 10 a. m., and Department's 87, February 28, 6 p. m.   Please attempt to see Leighton Stuart if you can when he passes through Shanghai and communicate to him as from me views expressed by the Department regarding assumption by an American private citizen of role [of] intermediary. You may inform Stuart that I shall take advantage of a suitable opportunity to make it known to the appropriate authorities of the Chinese Government that he is not acting on the behalf of or with the approval of the American Government.

Sent to Shanghai, repeated to Peiping.   Peiping please repeat to Tokyo.

JOHNSON

793.94119/402 : Telegram

The Secretary of State to the Ambassador in China (Johnson)

WASHINGTON, March 2, 1938—5 p. m.

89. Your 137, March 1, 10 a. m. The Department concurs in the view expressed in the last substantive sentence of your telegram under reference.

With regard to the first and second sentences of your telegram under reference, Department desires that you follow the procedure outlined in its 87, February 28, 6 p. m., which you will note gives you discretion as to the manner and time of informing the appropriate authorities of the Chinese Government that Stuart is not acting on behalf of or with the approval of this Government.

HULL

793.94/12565 : Telegram

The Chargé in France (Wilson) to the Secretary of State

PARIS, March 2, 1938—5 p. m.
[Received March 2—4 : 57 p. m.]

324. The Chief of the Far Eastern Division of the Foreign Office [77] said to me today that affairs in China have reached a relatively "static" stage. The immediate preoccupation of the French is the question of the Chinese customs.[78] The British Ambassador in Tokyo presented yesterday or will present today a request that customs revenues pledged for the service of foreign loans be deposited in a British bank at Shanghai or if the Japanese insist upon the deposit in the Yokohama Specie Bank of the revenues pledged for Japanese loans, then at least the revenues earmarked for other foreign loans should be placed in the British bank. The Foreign Office here feels that the Japanese will insist upon the deposit of all customs receipts in the Japanese bank but is hopeful that an arrangement can be worked out to control satisfactorily the disbursement of these funds.

The Chinese are still getting a few airplanes from France via the Indo-China route in fulfillment of orders "placed before the outbreak of hostilities". (I have the impression that this phrase is interpreted with some elasticity.) In this connection the Naval Attaché [79] is confidentially informed that an order was recently placed for China for 30 *Potez–63* planes, a latest type French light bomber-pursuit plane.

---

[77] Henri Hoppenot.
[78] See pp. 626 ff.
[79] Capt. Francis Cogswell, U. S. N.

Hoppenot said that the Russians are steadily increasing their shipments of airplanes and war material to China. How this is being financed is a puzzle to the French. Sun Fo, the son of Sun Yat-sen and President of the Chinese Legislative Yuan, has been in Russia for 2 months arranging it. It is believed that his visit has had to do with financing and accelerating Russian shipments of war supplies to China.

Sun Fo is due in Paris next week but the only information the French Government has received regarding his visit here is that it is of a personal nature to get in touch with old friends, et cetera.

Apart from shipments of supplies to China the Foreign Office is convinced that the Soviet Government will continue to refrain from taking any more direct or aggressive interest in the Chino-Japanese conflict. On the other hand, the French Ambassador in Tokyo has reported that without any tangible proof he nevertheless has the "feeling" that the Japanese may be preparing for a move against the Russian maritime provinces. My informant said that although he did not himself share this feeling he knew that it existed on the part of other competent observers of the Far East who reason as follows: The Japanese Army chiefs realize that today the Japanese people are worked up to a pitch where they will accept any sacrifice in prosecution of war; that if this patriotic fervor is allowed to subside it will be extremely difficult to whip it up again; and that therefore advantage should be taken of this situation to strike against Russia. Furthermore these military chiefs are convinced that they will be able to wage a successful war against Russia while holding the Chinese in check on their flank with little difficulty. My informant added that this was also the view of many French military officers.

Referring to the recall [of] General Matsui, my informant said that it was possible that the real reason for his return to Japan was to be prepared to head a military coup in case the national mobilization bill should be defeated by the civilian opposition of the army. Matsui is just the person he said to head a movement of this sort.

WILSON

793.94119/404 : Telegram

The Counselor of Embassy in China (Lockhart) to the Secretary of State

PEIPING, March 4, 1938—11 a. m.
[Received March 4—6 a. m.]

149. Your March 2, 2 p. m.,[80] and your 140, March 2, 2 [3] p. m. Stuart gave me no hint that he desired, or expected to seek, the as-

---

[80] Not found in Department files.

sistance of anyone in connection with his mission to Hankow. He did not ask me to transmit the information contained in my 136, February 27, 10 a. m. I transmitted it as information which I believed the Ambassador and the Department should have notwithstanding it was given to me confidentially. To avoid violating a confidence, however, I asked Dr. Stuart if he had any objection to my informing the Ambassador and the Department of the object of his trip to Hankow and he said he had no objection. Heretofore, Stuart has made it a point to call on me just before leaving Peiping on his periodical trips to inform me of his destination, object of his trip, length of his stay and of conditions at Yenching. He volunteered the information contained in my 136, February 27, 10 a. m., and stated that he was undoubtedly asked to proceed to Hankow for the purpose named because of the long standing friendship between himself and Chiang Kai Shek. I made no comment other than that contained in my 136, February 27, 10 a. m.

Sent to the Ambassador. Repeated to Shanghai, Tokyo.

LOCKHART

793.94/12583 : Telegram

The Ambassador in China (Johnson) to the Secretary of State

HANKOW, March 4, 1938—3 p. m.
[Received March 5—8 : 40 a. m.]

143. Following for War Department from Colonel Stilwell :

"Estimate of general situation as of March 1st. Factors favorable to Chinese : General determination to resist to bitter end, educated and moneyed classes gradually taking part, more students in ranks, enormous man power, military training of reserves going on everywhere, more favorable outlook for munitions supply, good financial position according to foreign financial advisers, losses in men fully replaced, gradual improvement in the command, experience in fighting being acquired, increased foreign support in aviation, communication by motor roads being greatly improved (road open to Sinkiang, work started on outlet to Burmah, outlet to Indo-China nearly ready), another instance of Japanese air threat rapidly decreasing, more spirit visible in the ranks and among wounded, many new divisions nearly ready, loyal cooperation by the Reds, good example of execution of Han Fu Chu,[81] no apparent depression due to loss of men and territory, guerrilla war in Shansi growing serious, Japanese let down since capture of Nanking, Japanese failure to press to an objective, Japanese failure to get Chinese help politically, time working for Chinese and against Japanese, China's basic industry, agriculture, cannot be destroyed, moral backing of the democratic states, no serious dissension in China's Government.

Factors unfavorable to Chinese : no sign as yet of the offensive spirit, continued dependence on passive defense, continued excuses about

---

[81] Chairman of the Shantung Provincial Government.

insufficient artillery and aviation, retention of many incompetent commanders, many desertions, many self-inflicted wounds, danger of spread of guerrilla idea to regular units (they will withdraw as soon as the pressure hurts), loss of revenue.

Conclusion: Since Japan cannot pull out and China refuses to quit, the prospect of a long drawn out struggle increases. It is possible for China to win. Japan, to get a decision, must make a greatly increased effort. I still believe she must occupy all China east of the 110th meridian, and that even that may not be enough."

Repeated to Peiping.

JOHNSON

793.94/12578 : Telegram

The Ambassador in the Soviet Union (Davies) to the Secretary of State

Moscow, March 4, 1938—8 p. m.
[Received March 4—4 : 43 p. m.]

59. In a conference which I had with Litvinov [82] yesterday, he described a meeting of Eden, Delbos,[83] Wellington Koo and himself held in Geneva last month in which the Japanese situation was discussed. He said that the discussion had to do with renewed efforts along the lines of the Brussels Conference;[84] that Delbos would take no definite stand without England's express backing on account of the fear for Indo-China; that Eden would take no stand without assurance of parallel action by the United States; that the situation was left with the understanding that Eden would explore the situation with Washington; that it was recognized that the United States Government would participate in no alliance but hope was had that something might be accomplished through parallel action; that what specifically was considered was not military or naval action but the imposing of sanctions that would prevent Japanese banking institutions from selling securities in enterprises in China and Manchuria among nationals of these countries and, second, the possibility of imposing sanctions on supplies, particularly oil. Litvinov was pessimistic as to outcome of any such plan. As illustrative, he pointed out that an embargo on oil would require not only action by the United States but also action by Holland and that in all probability Holland would not participate except under guaranties of military and naval defense by the other powers.

I gathered that the Soviet attitude, similar to French and English, was that it will take no action except with the assured support of France or England or both.

---

[82] Soviet Commissar for Foreign Affairs.
[83] French Minister for Foreign Affairs.
[84] See *Foreign Relations, 1937,* vol. IV, pp. 155 ff.

With reference to the European situation, Litvinov's opinion was that Hitler and Mussolini had Chamberlain on the spot; that Chamberlain had to make good with his public by effecting some arrangement; that the dictators would either drive so hard a bargain as to make that impossible or that Chamberlain would secure a paper peace that really amounted to nothing except as a sham for home consumption.

DAVIES

793.94119/404 : Telegram

The Secretary of State to the Ambassador in China (Johnson)

WASHINGTON, March 5, 1938—1 p. m.

93. Peiping's 149, March 4, 11 a. m. After careful consideration of the additional information communicated in Peiping's telegram under reference, which the Department welcomes, the Department is of the opinion that the instructions sent you in the Department's telegrams Nos. 87, February 28, 6 p. m., and 89, March 2, 5 p. m., need no modification.

Please repeat to Peiping.

HULL

793.94119/405 : Telegram

The Consul General at Shanghai (Gauss) to the Secretary of State

SHANGHAI, March 7, 1938—7 p. m.
[Received March 7—11:25 a. m.]

367. I have today carried out the instructions contained in the penultimate paragraph of the Department's 87, February 28, 6 p. m. to the Ambassador. The person concerned states that he is fully aware that he is acting in a purely private capacity, that he is in no sense an intermediary between any governments, that he is simply trying to maintain the personal relations between Chinese friends of his who are in responsible positions in Hankow and Peiping and Shanghai, that he will try to see that we are in no way embarrassed in the matter and that he agrees in general with the views expressed by the Department. For the rest, his trip is simply an attempt to understand the outlook better in its practical bearing on his University affairs.

Sent to Hankow, repeated to Peiping.

GAUSS

893.01 Provisional/70

The Department of State to the British Embassy

AIDE-MÉMOIRE

Reference is made to the *aide-mémoire* of the British Embassy of February 14, 1938, in regard to the matter of calls to be paid on the representatives of the Provisional Government at Peiping and on territorial officials. In the *aide-mémoire* there was given the substance of instructions which were being sent by the British Government to the British Embassy in China on that subject, and the hope was expressed that this Government might see its way clear to adopting a similar procedure.

It will be recalled that on January 21, 1938, during a call at the Department of Mr. Mallet, Counselor of the British Embassy, Mr. Hamilton informed Mr. Mallet of the substance of the Department's instructions to the American Embassy at Peiping in regard to the question of calls on representatives of the new régime. This Government has given further consideration to this matter, and as a result it has issued to the American Embassy in Peiping supplementary instructions to the effect that informal relations, including exchange of calls, with representatives of the new régime should, so far as is practicable, be restricted to officers acting in their consular capacity. It may be mentioned that three members of the staff of the American Embassy at Peiping have the dual status of diplomatic officer and consular officer.

WASHINGTON, March 10, 1938.

793.94/12630 : Telegram

The Consul General at Shanghai (Gauss) to the Secretary of State

SHANGHAI, March 11, 1938—11 a. m.
[Received March 11—8 a. m.]

378. My 365, March 5, 2 [5?] p. m.[85] Fairly heavy fighting is reported in the immediate vicinity of Linyi, southeastern Shantung. Little activity on the Tsining or southern Tsinpu fronts. Military observers estimate Japanese reenforcements totaling approximately 70,000 men with considerable quantities of heavy artillery have been landed at Woosung during the past 2 weeks. Over 50 percent of these reenforcements are believed to be destined for the southern Tsinpu front, the balance being distributed between Wuhu, Hangchow and along lines of communication.

---

[85] Not printed.

Mr. M. Tani, Japanese Minister at Large who recently arrived in Shanghai, informed Japanese press representatives that he had been placed in charge of all Japanese diplomatic organs in Central and North China and would commute frequently between Shanghai and Peiping. He is also reported to have stated that Japanese intend to respect fully foreign rights and interests in China and with reference to Anglo-Japanese relations that "there can be no friction between Japan and Britain unless Japan infringes British trade interests and vested rights in the Orient. This has especially been made true by the replacement of Eden diplomacy by Chamberlain diplomacy or in other words the replacement of idealism by realism. Japan must pay careful attention to this point so as not to violate Britain's rights and interests".

General Chou Feng Chi, formerly acting Provincial Chairman of Chekiang, was assassinated here on March 7th. His assassination is reported to have been connected with overtures made to him by the Japanese to become Minister of War in the Central China Government which the Japanese are seeking to establish.

Repeated to Hankow and Peiping.

GAUSS

793.94119/416

The Ambassador in China (Johnson) to the Secretary of State

No. 16   HANKOW, March 11, 1938.
                                              [Received May 2.]

SIR: I have the honor to refer to recent telegraphic correspondence with the Department in regard to a journey now being made by Dr. J. Leighton Stuart from Peiping to Hankow, which has for its apparent object suggestions to General Chiang Kai-shek for a possible compromise between the Chinese and Japanese Governments.

The idea that such a compromise might be possible seems to have occurred to a number of persons, and there have reached me intimations that various persons would be willing to take steps to promote a settling of the present conflict.

In this connection I have the honor to enclose memoranda [86] of conversations with a Mr. Cressey,[87] of the National Christian Council, on March 5, 1938, and with Mr. John Foster Dulles, well-known writer and lawyer, on the subject of mediation.

It will be noted that Mr. Cressey was actuated by a desire to bring Chinese and Japanese Christians together in the interest of peace,

---

[86] Not printed.
[87] Earl H. Cressy, of the Associated Boards for Christian Colleges in China, New York.

and that I informed him that I thought it would be unwise for American citizens at this time to attempt to become channels for attempts at mediation.

It will be observed that Mr. Dulles and I agreed that there was no basis upon which either the Government or the citizens of the United States could attempt to act as mediators between China and Japan, and that I expressed the view that the present Chinese Government would be forced to continue resistance against Japan until it should be wiped out, or until the Japanese Government should be prepared to consider a settlement on some precisely defined basis, in distinction to earlier so-called "terms," which have been so general in scope as to permit the interpretation that Japan intends to reduce China to a condition of vassalage.

The attention of the Department is invited to the view expressed by Mr. Dulles that, since the British Government is on its way to a settlement of its differences with the Italian Government over Mediterranean problems,[88] it would soon be in position to exert a firmer influence in the Far East and might even attempt to compel the Chinese to accept some kind of settlement at the hands of the Japanese.

On the afternoon of March 9, the day following my conversation with Mr. Dulles, Dr. Hsu Mo, Vice Minister for Foreign Affairs, informed Mr. Peck, Counselor of the Embassy, in the course of a general conversation, that the Chinese Government was somewhat puzzled over the failure of the American and British Governments to adopt stronger measures than had been taken by them to protect their treaty and other rights in China from infringement by Japan; in the case of Great Britain the Chinese Government was inclined to attribute this failure to the preoccupation of the British Government with the Italian threat to British interests in the Mediterranean. Assuming this reasoning to be well-founded, officials in the Chinese Government were speculating on the course which Great Britain might follow in the Far East in the face of Japanese encroachments if, as seems probable, the present Italian-British discussions result in a friendly understanding between the two countries in reference to various points at issue between them. Dr. Hsu Mo said that one view was that Great Britain was showing a clear tendency to deal realistically with Germany, Italy and Japan, members of the Anti-Comintern group, and that when its hands were comparatively free in Europe Great Britain would come to an understanding with Japan over British interests in the Far East, more or less ignoring China; while another view was that Great Britain would, when the time arrived, take a strong attitude toward Japan in defense of British rights in the Orient.

---

[88] For correspondence on the Anglo-Italian agreement of April 16, see vol. I, pp. 133 ff.

Mr. Dulles had conversations with General Chiang Kai-shek and other Chinese leaders on March 6–8, inclusive, and it is possible that these speculations regarding probable British action were suggested by him to the Chinese, or vice versa, but I am unable to hazard any opinion regarding this.

Yours respectfully, NELSON TRUSLER JOHNSON

793.94/12642 : Telegram

The Consul General at Shanghai (Gauss) to the Secretary of State

SHANGHAI, March 12, 1938—9 p. m.
[Received March 12—1 : 40 p. m.]

386. Following a military review held at the former civic center of the municipality of Greater Shanghai and at which high Japanese military, diplomatic and consular officials were present, General Hata, the new Commander-in-Chief of the Japanese Expeditionary Forces in Central China, made a statement to Japanese press representatives. *Inter alia*, he is reported to have stated that the Japanese Army is ready to cooperate with a new regime in Central China if its basic policies are friendship with Japan and war on the Kuomintang and the Communist Party; that in dealing with third powers "we shall follow the honorable path of justice in accordance with the Government's foreign policy"; that friction with third powers will arise only should they attempt to interfere with army operations; and that he would exercise caution in dealing with the problem of the International Settlement in view of the complex inter-relationships of foreign interests within it.

Repeated to Hankow and Peiping.

GAUSS

893.01 Provisional/72 : Telegram

The Third Secretary of Embassy in China (Allison) to the Secretary of State

NANKING, March 14, 1938—2 p. m.
[Received 2 : 10 p. m.]

75. My 56, February 14, 6 p. m.[89] I was told yesterday evening by the same information [90] mentioned in my No. 56, that the new government for Central China would be set up within the very near future but that the actual date could not yet be announced. There is still said to be some difference of opinion as to whether Shanghai or

[89] Not printed.
[90] An "official of the Japanese Embassy at Nanking."

Nanking will be the seat of the new government though Nanking is believed to be the more likely site.

Upon being asked what connection this new government would have with the regime now functioning in Peiping, my informant stated that this was perhaps the most delicate matter to be solved but that it was probable the two governments would be independent of each other. The reasons for this were said to be that Japan feels more confident of her ability to control as well as develop economically the region now under the Peiping regime but that in South and Central China it would be much more difficult directly to control the government and it will be impossible fully to develop economically Central and South China without foreign assistance. It is believed that foreign governments or private business interests will not give the desired cooperation to a regime in Central China which is so obviously and directly controlled by Japan as the Peiping Government.

My informant then stated that Japan fully realizes the difficulties facing her in Central China and that she is hopeful that some Western nation will come to understand Japan's true aims in this region and come forward with an offer to cooperate in its economic exploits. He stated that one foreign government was rumored to be making tentative suggestion along this line but that Japan wanted more than anything else to have real friendship and cooperation with the United States and it hoped that America would be the country which would cooperate with Japan in an economic and commercial way. I stated that America's only interest was to see peace and order restored as quickly as possible and to see that the interests and rights of its citizens were respected. I added that at the present time there could be no question of cooperating with Japan inasmuch as the American attitude was one of strict neutrality. I was then told it was hoped that this new government of Central China would be the medium through which foreign nations might work with Japan in the economic development of the country. However, this could only be done if the Western nations ceased their policy of giving encouragement to the government of Chiang Kai Shek. In this connection I was told that the Japanese had been greatly disappointed at the announced decision of the new British Ambassador to fly to Chungking to present his credentials to the Chinese Government. With the exception of stating that the ideas advanced by my informant were interesting, I made noncommittal rejoinders and the subject was then changed.

I was told that a new China Affairs Bureau was shortly to be set up in Tokyo headed by Mr. Toshio Shiratori, former Japanese Minister to Sweden, and at present on a special mission in Peiping. This bureau will report directly to the Cabinet rather than to the Foreign Minister and will have among its personnel representatives of the army and navy, though the majority will probably be taken from the present China Bureau of the Foreign Office. It will be the function of this bureau to coordinate the viewpoints regarding China of the military and civilian elements in Japan and then to make concrete plans for the carrying out of Japanese policy towards this country. It is interesting to note that Mr. Shiratori, who will seemingly occupy a leading position in the formulation and carrying out of Japan's continental policy, has made the following statement in a recent issue of the magazine *Chuokoron*, published in translation in the *Japan Advertiser* of February 4th "Japan may send her immigrants to the continent or undertake to develop natural resources there, but over and above such materialistic considerations she takes it as part of her cultural mission to enlighten the various Asiatic races on the continent and relieve them from their present miserable condition. For the realization of this national ideal she is determined to have her own way and will combat any influence attempting to thwart her course of advance."

Sent to Embassy, Hankow. Repeated to Peiping and Shanghai. Shanghai please repeat to Tokyo.

ALLISON

CHAPTER III: MARCH 15–MAY 31, 1938

Creation of special bureau by Japan to control Chinese affairs (March 19); establishment at Nanking of puppet government for Central China (March 28); Soviet denial of Japanese claim that Soviet citizens fight for China (April 5); British inquiry regarding possibility of mediation (April 11); American memorandum concerning basis for peace (April 13); Sun Fo's report on mission to Europe (May 9); British readiness to consult United States on economic reprisals against Japan (May 23); Ambassador Johnson's review of events in China since beginning of 1937 (May 23); German withdrawal of aid to China in military advisers and supplies (May 26)

793.94/12658 : Telegram

The Third Secretary of Embassy in China (Allison) to the Secretary of State

NANKING, March 16, 1938—11 a. m.
[Received March 16—7 : 44 a. m.]

78. During an informal conversation yesterday evening with a Japanese official the question of foreign rights and interests in China came up for discussion and I was given the following information said to be typical of the viewpoint of high ranking army officers in China on this question. My informant said that at a dinner he attended given on March 13, by Lieutenant General Fukita, the new Commander-in-Chief in this area, General Fukita had stated it was his opinion that there was no reason why the Japanese Army should give any consideration to foreign rights and interests as long as the foreign

governments continued to give encouragement and assistance to Japan's enemy, namely, the government of Chiang Kai Shek. He is said to have added that it might be necessary to respect foreign rights already established but that in the future foreign interests should be disregarded unless the various nations changed their present attitude towards Japan's activities in China. Reference was made to the displeasure of the army at Western nations providing China with military supplies and I pointed out that while it is true that military supplies are being sold to China, they are also being sold to Japan and that any attempt to govern the sales of munitions to but one party to a dispute would be equivalent to taking sides, which was not the desire of the United States.

It is perhaps interesting to note that during the course of this conversation my informant referred on several occasions to the action of Hitler in Austria [91] and stated that this action had been a great encouragement to the Japanese in carrying on their activities in China.

Sent to Embassy, Hankow. Repeated to Peiping and Shanghai. Shanghai please repeat to Tokyo.

ALLISON

793.94119/406 : Telegram

The Ambassador in China (Johnson) to the Secretary of State

HANKOW, March 16, 1938—11 a. m.
[Received March 16—10 : 10 a. m.]

163. Department's 87, February 28, 6 p. m. Doctor J. Leighton Stuart [92] arrived in Hankow on March 11. I saw Minister for Foreign Affairs [93] afternoon March 12 and communicated to him Department's message. Minister for Foreign Affairs stated that he thoroughly understood and said that he would convey information to members of Government who might be approached by Stuart. I saw Stuart on March 15. He stated that he had had an interview with the Generalissimo but had not communicated Wang Keh Min's [94] message as he discovered very quickly that there was no basis for any hope of mediation. Stuart said that his visit to Hankow had convinced him that peace between China and Japan was not yet possible.

Repeated to Peiping and Shanghai. Shanghai please repeat to Tokyo.

JOHNSON

---

[91] See vol. I, pp. 384 ff.
[92] American, president of Yenching University, near Peiping.
[93] Wang Chung-hui.
[94] Head of Japanese-sponsored regime at Peiping.

893.01 Provisional/77 : Telegram

The Consul General at Shanghai (Gauss) to the Secretary of State

SHANGHAI, March 16, 1938—5 p. m.
[Received March 16—1:36 p. m.]

403. Reference Nanking's numbers 75 and 77 of March 14, 2 p. m., and March 15, 6 p. m.,[95] regarding establishment of new government for Central China. It is reported in well-informed circles hereabouts that personnel will probably include: Liang Hung-chih as Minister of Communications (formerly Secretary General under Tuan Chi-jui[96]), Chen Chung-fu as Minister of Justice (former President of Foreign Affairs Commission, Hopei–Chahar Political Council), Wen Tsung-yao as President of Legislative Yuan (many years ago Commissioner Foreign Affairs at Nanking and Shanghai), Chen Lu as Minister for Foreign Affairs (formerly Minister to France), Chen Chun as Minister of Interior (Japanese returned student), Dr. Chen Chin-tao as Minister of Finance (former Minister of Finance in Peiping in 1926), Chao Tse-yu as Minister of Industries (at one time Mayor of Hangchow), Chen Tse-min as Minister of Education (a Shanghai lawyer). Whether Tang Shao-yi[97] will consent to head this government is still uncertain.

With reference to Nanking's No. 75 of March 14, 2 p. m., in which reference was made to the establishment of a China Affairs Bureau at Tokyo to be headed by Shiratori,[98] it is learned from a reliable Japanese official that Shiratori is a strong rightest, a close friend of the Japanese Prime Minister[99] and the man largely responsible for Japan's policy in Manchuria.

Italian good will mission to Japan headed by Marquis Paulucci di Calboli Barone arrived here yesterday morning and was given an impressive welcome by prominent Japanese and Italian officials. Last night General Hata, Admiral Hasegawa, and prominent Japanese diplomatic and consular officials gave a reception and dinner in honor of the mission which leaves for Japan today.

Repeated to Embassy at Hankow and Peiping.

GAUSS

---

[95] Telegram No. 77 not printed.
[96] Chinese Privisional Chief Executive at Peking, 1924–26.
[97] Chinese Prime Minister, 1912.
[98] Toshio Shiratori, formerly Japanese Minister in Sweden.
[99] Prince Fumimaro Konoye.

256941—54——9

893.01 Provisional/72 : Telegram

The Secretary of State to the Ambassador in China (Johnson),
at Hankow

WASHINGTON, March 16, 1938—6 p. m.

105. Nanking's 75, March 14, 2 p. m.

1. The Department is telegraphing Nanking as follows:

"The information conveyed in your telegram under reference has been noted with interest.

With regard to the comment made by you to your informant that America's only interest was to see peace and order restored as quickly as possible, etc., the Department is confident that you are keeping in mind the fact that a fundamental interest of this Government is not only that peace be restored as soon as possible but that the settlement by which peace is restored shall be on lines consistent with the provisions of existing international commitments and with principles of equity and justice in relation to all concerned".

2. You will realize, of course, that, in the existing circumstances of tension and conflict in various parts of the world, all officers of the American Government who have occasion to make statements relating to American national interest or policy should be extraordinarily careful in their phrasing of such statements.

3. Please repeat to Shanghai and Peiping and ask Peiping to repeat to Tokyo.

HULL

793.94/12675 : Telegram

The Ambassador in Japan (Grew) to the Secretary of State

TOKYO, March 18, 1938—4 p. m.
[Received March 18—8 : 55 a. m.]

180. Department's 77, March 5, 2 p. m.[1]

1. There exists no consensus of opinion among foreign observers here on the question whether Japan is preparing to move in the near future against the Soviet Union. European opinion is that no such military action is being planned. All shades of opinion agree that there are no evidences of such action.

2. Our estimate of the situation is:

(*a*) The Japanese public is not especially aroused at this time against Russia and it does not appear that any effort is being made to mobilize public opinion as might be expected if military action were imminent.

(*b*) Japanese forces in Manchuria are estimated to be smaller than Soviet forces in Eastern Siberia.

[1] Not printed.

(*c*) Economic issues and frontier and other disputes will probably aggravate ill-feeling especially if both countries resort to reprisals and counter-reprisals as seems likely but these disputes have been occurring more or less continually during the past several years.

(*d*) The irresponsible young officer element in the Japanese Army which is capable of precipitating a conflict introduces a strong element of uncertainty into any estimate.

A despatch will go forward in tomorrow's pouch.[2]

GREW

894.032/187 : Telegram

The Ambassador in Japan (Grew) to the Secretary of State

TOKYO, March 19, 1938—6 p. m.
[Received March 19—8 : 08 a. m.]

186. This morning's press reports that the following views were expressed by the Foreign Minister [3] yesterday at a session of the Lower House Budget Committee:

(1) The Nine Power Treaty [4] is of only nominal existence inasmuch as many of its provisions have never been fulfilled. Abrogation of the treaty is to be expected at an appropriate time.

(2) Japan has no territorial designs in China. This however is not a consequence of the treaty; it is based upon the functioning of Japan-China relations.

(3) In time the Provisional Government of China will come to be recognized by the powers. Japan is doing all it can to assist the regime but recognition by Japan now would be premature.

(4) Japan's withdrawal from the International Labor Office will perhaps come about.

(5) With the Permanent Court of International Justice the Foreign Minister intends to maintain the relations now existing.

GREW

894.02/19

The Ambassador in Japan (Grew) to the Secretary of State

No. 2827
TOKYO, March 19, 1938.
[Received April 5.]

SIR: Compromising on the divergent plans submitted by the Legislative Bureau and the Foreign Office for the establishment of machinery to govern China affairs, the Japanese Government decided on March 15 to create the China Economic Affairs Bureau under the direction of the Cabinet.

[2] Not printed.
[3] Koki Hirota.
[4] *Foreign Relations*, 1922, vol. I, p. 276.

Originally, the Legislative Bureau proposed the establishment of an organ under the Premier to be called the Cabinet China Affairs Board and to be entrusted with political, economic, and cultural matters relating to China, independently of the Foreign Office. Opposing this plan, Mr. Hirota and the Foreign Office stood out for the establishment of a bureau under the direction of the Minister for Foreign Affairs but not necessarily an integral part of the Foreign Office, to handle economic exploitation of China but without any authority to deal with political or cultural matters, which would be controlled as hitherto by the Foreign Office. According to the Japanese press, the Minister for Foreign Affairs insisted that Japan's policy toward China was entirely different from that toward Manchuria, that the political, economic, and cultural body projected by the Legislative Bureau would possibly be accused of infringing upon China's sovereignty and would hence be displeasing to third countries, and that, aside from relations with the Powers, for technical reasons alone administrative affairs relating to China should be left to the Foreign Office.

Apparently unable to reconcile the conflicting points of view between the Legislative Bureau and the Ministry for Foreign Affairs, the Cabinet arrived at the compromise plan mentioned above, namely, to create the China Economic Affairs Bureau which would have no voice in diplomatic matters and whose principal duty would be to supervise the North China Development Company and the Central China Rehabilitation Company. It is understood that there will also be set up a provisional body to be called the China Economic Inquiry Commission, headed by the Premier, composed of members chosen from the Cabinet, the Cabinet's Advisory Counsel, and financial circles, and entrusted with examination of matters relating to economic exploitation of China.

There may be a substantial amount of truth in the report that Mr. Hirota opposed the establishment of a political, economic, and cultural board to control China affairs on the ground that such a step would unnecessarily antagonize countries possessed of treaty rights with China and would lay Japan open to the accusation that it contemplated a definite infringement of China's sovereignty and administrative integrity. While the respect by Japan of China's sovereignty and administrative integrity is only a fiction advanced by the Japanese Government, the placing of China affairs under an organization akin to the Manchurian Affairs Bureau would undoubtedly hamper Japan's well-known dialectics on its actions in China.

It has been remarked by observers in Tokyo that Mr. Hirota's antagonism toward the setting up of a body, distinct from the Foreign Office, to deal with Chinese matters was due to a desire to check the ambitions of the militarists and of the more nationalistic members of the Cabinet. However, it is more likely that the Minister for Foreign Affairs is loath to relinquish a power which he has wielded firmly and is unwilling to turn over the direction of China affairs to a group of men who might take a more moderate view toward the Chinese than that assumed by the Foreign Office itself.

In this connection the Department's attention is invited to my telegram No. 100 of February 12, 1938, in which it was stated that reports had come both to the British Ambassador and to me that it was Mr. Hirota rather than Admiral Suetsugu, the Home Minister, who led the ultra-chauvinistic element in the Government. Likewise pertinent is a despatch to me from Mr. William T. Turner, Consul at Dairen, a copy of which he sent to the Department,[5] in which is reported a conversation between Mr. Turner and a Japanese official (presumably Mr. Okazaki, Japanese Consul-General-at-large for China). The Japanese official in question said that the Japanese military were taking a more moderate position toward China than the Cabinet, that Admiral Suetsugu was about the most moderate man in the Cabinet as regards China policies, that Mr. Hirota and Prince Konoye were the leaders of those advocating a strong hand in China, and that it was the civilians who were "pressing hard for a fundamental solution of the issue with Chiang Kai-shek."

Respectfully yours, JOSEPH C. GREW

893.01 Provisional/88 : Telegram

The Ambassador in Japan (Grew) to the Secretary of State

TOKYO, March 25, 1938—9 a. m.
[Received 10 : 55 a. m.]

205. Nanking's 82, March 23, 5 p. m.,[5] Nanking Provisional Government. In reference to reports of impending inauguration at Nanking of a provisional government, Foreign Minister Hirota has stated in the House of Representatives that Japan's relations with the existing Peiping regime will not thereby be changed; that Japan expects that the Peiping regime will in time develop into a unified administration for both North and Central China; but that in the meantime commercial interests contemplating activities in Central China must deal with the impending Nanking regime.

Repeated to Shanghai for Hankow.

GREW

---

[5] Not printed.

893.01 Provisional/95 : Telegram

The Consul General at Shanghai (Gauss) to the Secretary of State

SHANGHAI, March 28, 1938—1 p. m.

[Received March 28—12: 03 p. m.]

465. My 403, March 16, 5 p. m. The "Reformed Government of the Republic of China" was formally inaugurated at Nanking at 10 a. m. this morning. Representatives of General Hata and Admiral Hasegawa were present and in addition to felicitating the new Government upon its inauguration indicated that they would give it strong support.

A long manifesto issued by the "Reformed Government of the Republic of China" was distributed in Shanghai this morning. The manifesto takes the National Government severely to task for driving "an untrained populace to fight in an unequal combat" and charges that the policy of "scorched earth spells national suicide and in affiliating with the Communists they have invited robbers into our home". The manifesto continues: "though still keeping up the pretense of a government in their refuge in Szechuan, Hupeh and Hunan, they have forfeited their authority and virtually lost their power of control. The record of the misdeeds perpetrated by this defunct administration is indeed unequalled in the long annals of the history of China. Impelled by feelings of righteous indignation in consideration of the urgency of saving the country from ruin, in view of the necessity of discarding the old regime and starting anew with the citizens of the Republic, the undersigned and their associates do hereby proclaim on this the 28th day of March the Reformed Government of the Republic of China in Nanking and that its primary duty is to restore the territorial sovereignty of the Republic as it existed prior to the outbreak of hostilities. In pursuing this aim negotiations will be started to restore the ties of amity and to end the deplorable strife between neighboring states whose peoples are of the same race. On the other hand the friendly relations happily existing between this country and the European and American powers will be maintained and upheld."

The manifesto states further that inasmuch as the "Reformed Government is founded on the realities of the prevailing situation in the provinces of Kiangsu, Chekiang and others it is therefore temporary in nature and is established without any intention of contending with the administration of the Provisional Government. Functions pertaining to a central government which cannot be delegated will continue to be performed by the Provisional Government in consultation with the Reformed Government. As soon as communications are restored on the Tsinpu and Lunghai railways the Reformed Government will amalgamate itself with the Provisional Government. It is not our desire to have two rival governments functioning within the country."

The manifesto is signed by Liang Hung Chih, Wen Tsung Yao and others mentioned in my 403, March 16, 5 p. m. The new Government is to be headed by Liang Hung Chih at least for the time being, it is reported locally. The inauguration of the new regime at Nanking has thus far created little stir locally. Two small demonstrations organized by the so-called "Great Way Government" took place this morning in the extra-Settlement roads area and West Hongkew respectively while a Japanese plane scattered leaflets.

Repeated to Hankow and Peiping.

GAUSS

793.94/12726 : Telegram

The First Secretary of Embassy in China (Salisbury) to the Secretary of State

PEIPING, March 28, 1938—4 p. m.
[Received March 28—7 : 30 a. m.]

191. Embassy's 184, March 23, 4 p. m.[7]

1. An agreement was signed March 26 inaugurating a "Sino-Japanese Economic Council" (paragraph 4 of Embassy's 178, March 19, 11 a. m.[7]) with Wang Keh Min as Chairman and Hachisaburo Hirao as Vice Chairman. According to the Japanese press, this organ will be the highest organ for directing economic activities in North China (including finance, commerce, industry, mining and agriculture) and a special "Ministry" will be established for the carrying out of its decisions. It is reported, however, that a similar organ is to be set up in the Japanese North China Army with Hirao as its head, and it seems probable that this organ will give instructions to the new organ of the Provisional Government.

2. The local Japanese military spokesman outlined this morning alleged Japanese successes in southern Shantung, northern Honan, and Shansi. None of them appears to alter the military situation significantly. Chinese reports indicate some successes in counter attacks by Chinese forces. From the reports of both sides it would appear that Japanese advances in southern Shantung and Shansi have been checked, at least temporarily, and that severe engagements are in progress in which Japanese as well as Chinese forces are suffering heavy losses.

3. A strike began March 24 among Chinese workers of the Kailan Mining Company in eastern Hopei and has affected several mines of

---

[7] Not printed.

the company. At one mine 15 strikers were reportedly killed March 25 and 40 wounded while 7 or 8 Chinese of a "self protection" corps were also killed. Strikers are understood to have occupied on March 27 the compound and offices of the company of Tangshan. The strikers have not yet damaged company property. The origin of the strike is obscure but there is evidence which indicated that, if Japanese interests did not instigate the trouble, they may now be making use of it in the hope of obtaining control of the company's interests. The local British Embassy is understood to have requested the assistance of the Japanese authorities in settling the strike.[8]

Repeated to Hankow, by courier to Tokyo.

SALISBURY

793.94/12956

The Consul General at Hong Kong (Southard) to the Secretary of State

No. 149

HONG KONG, April 1, 1938.
[Received May 3.]

SIR: I have the honor to report that a couple of days ago, during one of the calls he makes occasionally on me, the Japanese Consul General in Hong Kong asked the definite question of what I thought would be the effect on American interests and public opinion of the severing by Japanese forces of communication between Hong Kong and Canton. As he arrived at the posing of this question by even more than his usual circumlocution I suspect that it may have been an inspired one.

My reply was, of course, noncommittal. I then casually asked if he thought a campaign to that end was about to begin. He said that he didn't know definitely about that but was sure that "something must be done" soon to interrupt the flow of war supplies from Hong Kong into Kwangtung. Mr. Nakamura, who was Japanese Consul General at Canton until the present hostilities began, then went on to say that the Kwangtung authorities were becoming definitely "fed-up with Chiang Kai-shek" and were, he thought, progressively weakening in their support of the so-called National Government. Kwangtung, he said, had in the beginning sent many troops to fight under Chiang Kai-shek's command but these troops had persistently been placed in the front firing line and killed to such an extent that no more considerable bodies of them would be sent from Kwangtung Province. He cited the thousands of Kwangtung soldiers betrayed by Chiang Kai-shek's troops at Nanking. According to information which he claimed to have, Kwangtung troops would now be kept at home and,

---

[8] The mines were again normal by April 29.

furthermore, a goodly proportion of the war materials passing through Hong Kong for the Chinese National Government would be kept in Canton for the use of Kwangtung troops. In brief, my Japanese colleague expressed the firm opinion that both Canton and Yunnanfu (Kunming) were becoming less and less inclined to support Hankow and were, of course, beginning to see more and more the light of reason and their own best interests.

Undoubtedly my Japanese colleague's thoughts have been fathered by his wishes. On the other hand expression of many similar thoughts is heard in Hong Kong from sources which are neither Japanese nor biassed by any national or selfish motives, and that is why my Japanese colleague's conversation has seemed to be of more than average interest. We have undertaken no special investigation to endeavor to verify the alleged state of affairs in Kwangtung and Yunnan, as such would not seem to be within the jurisdiction of this office, but copies of this despatch are being referred to the appropriate offices in China proper.

As to the intention of the Japanese soon to make an effort to cut communication between Hong Kong and Canton the only information of direct relation, which is available here, is that from usually reliable sources to the effect that there have recently been a noticeably greater number of Japanese naval units in the waters near Hong Kong. There is no reasonable confirmation that troop transports have increased in number.

Very respectfully, ADDISON E. SOUTHARD

793.00/299

The Chinese Ministry for Foreign Affairs to the Chinese Embassy [9]

[HANKOW,] April 2, 1938.

At the conclusion of the emergency session of the Kuomintang (National Party) National Congress today there was issued a manifesto defining China's foreign and domestic policies.

In regard to the hostilities with Japan the Manifesto says that the security of the northern Provinces means the security of China as a whole. If they cannot be preserved, not only the hope of a reasonable settlement of the question of the four north-eastern Provinces will be forever lost, but the whole territory of China will virtually be gone. "Our final object is peace, which has been the basis of our policy. But the peace we value is the peace founded upon justice. The peace patched up at the expense of justice is no peace at all. It is mere surrender." The hope for peaceful co-existence between

---

[9] Copy of telegram transmitted to the Secretary of State by the Chinese Ambassador under covering letter of April 4.

China and Japan cannot be fulfilled until Japan has courageously forsaken her misguided plans and abandoned her policy of aggression, and cooperates with China for the re-establishment of peace on the basis of righteousness and justice. Meanwhile, the struggle must be continued. China is determined not to stop at any sacrifice that may be necessary.

China's foreign relations are governed by two principles: firstly, China will scrupulously respect all the treaties for the maintenance of peace whereto she is a party and unflinchingly defend their sanctity and inviolability; and secondly, China will seek not only to preserve but further promote the friendly relations with other Powers. "At this time of unprecedented national calamity we realise all the more that we should not entertain any false hopes of miraculous happenings, nor entirely count upon foreign assistance, but instead we should rescue ourselves and carry on our struggle by dint of our own efforts amidst whatever difficulties and privations."

Turning to internal problems, the Manifesto says that the guiding principles for building up new China are the San Min Chu I (the Three People's Principles). China must proceed with the struggle of self-defence simultaneously with the task of national reconstruction. Prior to the promulgation of the permanent Constitution, the Government should set up the organs of participation by the people in public affairs. Efforts should be directed not only towards the maintenance of rural economy but towards its active improvement. Three points are of great importance: first, the entire nation must practice the greatest of economy in accumulating the capital, secondly, all industrial plans must be directed toward one goal, namely, China's victory, and thirdly, the Government should carry out the planned economy in accordance with the San Min Chu I. The task of carrying on the hostilities and national reconstruction simultaneously seems difficult, but its final achievement is sure if we preserve our internal solidarity and oneness of purpose.

Among the important resolutions the Congress adopted were the one calling for the creation of the People's Political Council to enable the people to participate in public affairs, and another setting up Tsung Chai (Director-General) and Fu Tsung Chai (Deputy Director-General) within the Kuomintang and General Chiang Kai-shek and Mr. Wang Ching-wei were elected thereto respectively. The Congress also adopted a political platform for the Government's guidance during the period of armed resistance. The platform stipulates that the San Min Chu I shall be the guiding principles of the national thought and re-affirms the freedom of speech, publication and assembly within the bounds of law.

893.01 Provisional/100 : Telegram

The Third Secretary of Embassy in China (Allison) to the Secretary of State

NANKING, April 3, 1938—4 p. m.
[Received April 3—11 : 45 a. m.]

91. According to an announcement in this morning's Nanking *Min Pao*, a spokesman for the Reformed Government of China stated yesterday that the new government will respect the property rights and interests of foreign nations in China in accordance with the principles of international law but that agreements made with the National Government of China (Chiang Kai Shek's government) by foreign nations will not be recognized and the new government will assume no responsibility nor any obligations towards such agreements.

It has not yet been possible to confirm that statement nor to obtain any amplification of it. However, according to the Chinese member of Embassy staff who translated the article today, it is believed the meaning is that all treaties made with foreign nations prior to formation of the National Government in 1927 will be honored as will any which might be made in future with the new government, but all those made between 1927 and 1938 will be disregarded.

Sent to Embassy [at] Hankow, Peiping and Shanghai; Shanghai repeat to Tokyo.

ALLISON

793.94/12764 : Telegram

The Chargé in France (Wilson) to the Secretary of State

PARIS, April 5, 1938—11 a. m.
[Received April 5—10 a. m.]

532. The Chinese Ambassador [10] told me yesterday that he was greatly encouraged by Chinese successes in recent military operations, particularly in southern Shantung. He said that the intense fighting which began in this area on March 24 and has been going on continuously since then constitutes one of the major engagements of the war. He said that there are nearly 200,000 Japanese troops in this region including 50,000 who have been brought secretly from Manchuria since the first of the year; opposing them are over 300,000 Chinese.

I said that I had noticed an article in the London *Times* from its Shanghai correspondent reporting the appearance north of Suchow of new Chinese tanks, artillery and anti-tank guns. Wellington Koo said that this was true and that all this material had come from Rus-

---

[10] V. K. Wellington Koo.

sia. He said that the Russians had been "very generous" in furnishing war material, particularly since January 1st. The Chinese have been acquiring very little war material from England; some artillery and rifles but no airplanes. From France they have been receiving but little war material since the French had little to spare, but since the coming into office of the present Blum government on March 13 several military planes of the latest type have been shipped to China.

I asked what routes these shipments have followed. Wellington Koo said that part of the material from Russia came in via Hong Kong, part through Indo-China and many shipments of light material take the Alma Ata route. About two-thirds of the new tanks and artillery which have appeared recently north of Suchow came in via Hong Kong and about one-third via Indo-China. French planes were shipped via French Indo-China. The French Government had not raised difficulties about shipment of planes via Indo-China although they had limited the passage of other war material on the Yunnanfu Railway. At one time facilities had been provided in Bordeaux for assembling planes destined for China. When the last Chautemps government came in power the middle of January, however, these facilities had been withdrawn, and increased difficulties had been placed in the way of shipment of war material through Indo-China.

The Ambassador said that he had always had trouble with the Foreign Office here in obtaining permission for shipments to pass through Indo-China but since the formation of the second Blum government with Paul Boncour at the Foreign Office his task had been made much easier. He said that the French Government was still apprehensive about permitting shipments to go over the railway but that he had recently been given permission to have important shipments of war material which had been held up in Indo-China transshipped and transported through territorial waters of Indo-China to Southern China.

I said that I had been interested to meet Sun Fo not long ago in Paris and asked the Ambassador if he could tell me anything of Sun Fo's mission to Russia. The Ambassador said that Sun Fo had been most successful in arranging for the supply of Russian airplanes and war material. Sun Fo had not been so pleased however with the outcome of his talks concerning "political arrangements". The Soviet Government had indicated that they could not be expected to enter the conflict in the Far East unless they were assured that in case they did so and Germany should then attack Russia they would receive military support from other countries in Europe.

With regard to rumors concerning Outer Mongolia the Ambassador said that it was not true that the Soviet authorities had asked Sun Fo for certain concessions in return for recognition of full Chinese sovereignty over Outer Mongolia. He said that both sides continued to maintain their respective positions regarding the status of Outer Mongolia and that this situation caused no difficulties for either China or Russia.

WILSON

761.94/1032 : Telegram

The Ambassador in the Soviet Union (Davies) to the Secretary of State

Moscow, April 5, 1938—1 p. m.
[Received April 5—9 : 15 a. m.]

94. A Tass communiqué published in today's *Pravda* states that the Japanese Ambassador protested yesterday to Litvinov [11] against evidence of Soviet planes and pilots fighting for the Chinese, saying that on account of the peculiar structure of the Soviet Government special responsibility lay upon it.

Litvinov rejected the protest; said that his Government had sent no military forces or individuals to take part in the war; that other foreign volunteers are serving with Chinese forces and that "the numerous military groups from certain countries (fighting for China) were not only not considered an unfriendly act by the Japanese Government but did not even prevent it from establishing with these countries the closest treaty relations".

The communiqué further brought out the fact that the Soviet Union a few days ago proposed to the Japanese Government a general settlement of many concrete incidents which have arisen between the two Governments, including the detention of the Soviet mail plane and of two Soviet schooners by the Japanese authorities, the failure to make payments for the Chinese Eastern Railway and Japanese claims regarding alleged oppression of Japanese citizens in the Soviet Union.

A new incident between the two countries indignantly publicised in the Moscow press of April 3 was the alleged endeavor of the Japanese Chargé d'Affaires at Kabul in the course of a "courtesy call" upon a new Soviet Ambassador to enlist him as a spy in the service of the Japanese.

DAVIES

---

[11] Soviet Commissar for Foreign Affairs.

793.94/12811 : Telegram

The Consul General at Shanghai (Gauss) to the Secretary of State

SHANGHAI, April 11, 1938—5 p. m.
[Received April 11—11 a. m.]

531. My 514, April 8, 1 p. m.[12] Foreign military observers state that the Chinese launched a new and well coordinated counteroffensive against the Japanese at Taierchwang on April 8th and succeeded in driving the Japanese northward toward Yihsien. The Japanese 10th Division which has borne the brunt of the fighting in the Taierchwang sector for the past 2 weeks is reported to have suffered heavy casualties and to have been disorganized. The Japanese military authorities here continue to deny reports of Chinese victories.

Liang Hung Chih, Acting Head of the so-called "Reformed Government", returned recently from Peiping where he conferred with Wang Keh Min regarding the merging of the two governments. Liang informed Japanese press reporters that the amalgamation will take place as soon as possible and that the two governments will appoint commissioners to work out the details. The more important members of the "Reformed Government" continue to spend most of their time in Shanghai.

Repeated to Hankow and Peiping.

GAUSS

894.00/784 : Telegram

The Ambassador in Japan (Grew) to the Secretary of State

TOKYO, April 11, 1938—6 p. m.
[Received April 11—10 : 50 a. m.]

239. There is much discussion in the press of a possible change of Government in the near future. Press accounts of the situation within the Cabinet and evidence presented to support forecasts of political changes are obscure, contradictory and I believe largely speculative. The only statement of fact which I am now prepared to make is that the Cabinet is apparently not united in matters of important policy and that its reorganization is under consideration. Our analysis of the situation made in the light of discussions in the press and orally by well informed Japanese is presented hereunder.

2. The most important element in the situation is a difference of opinion that has developed within the Cabinet as to the courses, military and political, which should be pursued by Japan in dealing with the conflict with China. Our best information is that Konoye heads a group which believes that it is not enough for Japan to cease "dealing

---

[12] Not printed.

with" the Chinese Government (as expressed in the declaration of January 16 [13]) and that that Government can be destroyed only by the most drastic and positive measures; and that the Minister of War heads an opposition group, which believes that the same results can be more economically obtained by continuation of the "long duration war" policy through inevitably causing the economic and financial collapse of China. Our information as to the respective positions of the two leaders may be incorrect, but there appears to be little doubt but that the issue has arisen.

3. The political parties have repeatedly expressed to the Prime Minister desire for greater representation in the Cabinet. This is believed to be a matter which can be adjusted with not too great difficulty as the Ministry of Health is vacant and the Overseas Minister and the Minister of Agriculture, both close personal friends of the Prime Minister, are said to be willing to give way.

4. We understand that the present situation was precipitated by the Prime Minister expressing a desire to resign because of ill-health and other personal reasons (he has not been well for several years). He has apparently been persuaded to exclude such personal reasons in deciding his future course.

5. As the position taken by the Minister of War with regard to the China conflict is presumably the considered position of the army, no improvement in the situation in the Cabinet can be expected were Sugiyama to be replaced by another general. It is our view, therefore, that the problem which Konoye must solve is whether (a) he should continue in office with the present Cabinet (not importantly reconstituted to include a few more representatives of the political parties) or (b) resign and thus make possible the organizing of a new and more united Cabinet. It is reported that on April 17 Konoye will send a messenger to Prince Saionji [14] to obtain his "advice". Probably no important development will occur before that date.

Repeated to Shanghai for Hankow.

GREW

793.94119/411

The British Embassy to the Department of State

AIDE-MÉMOIRE

His Majesty's Ambassador [15] recently had occasion to inform the Department of State of an approach made early in February by the Japanese Ambassador in London [16] to Mr. Eden,[17] in which Mr. Yoshida suggested on his own personal initiative and without instruc-

---

[13] *Foreign Relations*, Japan, 1931–1941, vol. I, p. 437.
[14] Surviving "Elder Statesman".
[15] Sir Ronald Lindsay, British Ambassador in the United States.
[16] Shigeru Yoshida.
[17] Then British Secretary of State for Foreign Affairs.

tions from his Government that an opportunity might shortly occur for an offer of good offices by His Majesty's Government in the United Kingdom in order to bring the hostilities in the Far East to a close. Mr. Eden explained to Mr. Yoshida that it would be possible for His Majesty's Government to use their good offices except in conjunction with the Government of the United States, and that in the light of the similarity of their positions in the Far East, and the parallel action which they had been taking, it would be only natural that His Majesty's Government should wish to approach the United States Government if any such step were contemplated.

Commenting on Mr. Yoshida's suggestion, His Majesty's Ambassador at Tokyo [18] has expressed the opinion that if ever the time arrives to offer good offices in the Sino-Japanese dispute there is no doubt that combined Anglo-American action would be the best course from every point of view. Sir Robert Craigie reports, however, that he has recently received indications from one or two well-informed quarters that public opinion in Japan is not likely to welcome or even accept joint action by the United Kingdom and the United States owing to the implications of pressure in so powerful a combination. On the other hand he is told that influential opinion is coming more and more to the view that when the right time comes good offices by either the United States or Great Britain would be the best and surest method of settling the dispute. But Sir Robert Craigie does not at the present moment see any prospect of useful intermediary action except in the improbable event of Marshal Chiang Kai Shek being willing to retire in order to bring peace to his country. He admits at the same time that the situation may change at any moment.

As at present advised the feeling of His Majesty's Government in the United Kingdom is that although they would much prefer joint mediation they should not definitely exclude the possibility of mediation by one government, and that it is not of any great importance whether that government be His Majesty's Government or the United States Government if the Japanese set any store by one mediating rather than the other. They do, however, think that whichever Government mediates should keep the other neutral governments, including the German Government, reasonably well informed of the progress of negotiations.

Sir Ronald Lindsay is instructed to invite the views of the United States Government on this question, pending the receipt of which His Majesty's Government prefer not to form any final opinion of their own. [19]

WASHINGTON, April 11, 1938.

---

[18] Sir Robert L. Craigie.
[19] For the Department's reply, see *Foreign Relations*, Japan, 1931–1941, vol. I, p. 463.

793.94/12855⅔

The Adviser on Political Relations (Hornbeck) to the British Permanent Under Secretary of State for Foreign Affairs (Cadogan) [20]

WASHINGTON, April 13, 1938.

MY DEAR SIR ALEXANDER: It was very gratifying to me to have, through the British Embassy here, your letter of February 14 and the memorandum enclosed therewith.

I had long been intending to write you, but, in the press of many matters which have kept me more than busy since my return from Brussels, I have failed thus far to carry out that good intention— along with many other failures to perform.

Turning to the memorandum, I have noted carefully what you say in explanation of the conception which it represents and I fully understand that it does not commit your Government. I note especially your expression of the view that a settlement on the lines sketched cannot be expected unless our two Governments should be able to exercise effective pressure to bring it about. With all of that in mind, I have discussed the memorandum with some of my closest associates, and, in the light of our discussion, we have put on paper a record of discussion in the form of a memorandum which I enclose herewith. As is the case with your memorandum, this memorandum has not been seen by the highest policy-making officials of my Government and does not commit them. It should in fact be regarded as committing no one. However, it accurately reflects, its authors believe, the spirit and the manner in which, in the light of prevailing public opinion in this country, approach is made here to the difficult problems inherent in and presented by current developments in the situation under consideration. Much of what is said is tentative, and all of it is unofficial. I realize, as will you, that it does not offer much on the constructive side. More will be possible, we hope, on that side, later.

I enclose, also, for your convenience of reference, the full text of the most recent extended utterance of the Secretary of State on the subject of this country's foreign policy.[21]

Assuring you again of my appreciation of your letter, and hoping that I may be able better in the future than during the past four months to make good on the promise which I made early in December last that I would keep in touch with you.

I am [etc.]   [STANLEY K. HORNBECK]

---

[20] Transmitted to the Counselor of the British Embassy by the Adviser on Political Relations in letter dated April 13.

[21] Address of March 17, *Foreign Relations*, Japan, 1931–1941, vol. I, p. 452.

[Enclosure]

"Memorandum on Possible Peace Terms for Communication to the United States Government"

Analysis and Comment

(Note: The memorandum gives a tentative indication of the kind of settlement between Japan and China which its Foreign Office authors believe the British Government might consider reasonable. It has not been considered by the British Government and is not to be regarded as committing the British Government. Its authors are of the opinion that a settlement on the lines sketched in its paragraphs should be expected only in case the British and American Governments should be in position to exercise effective pressure toward bringing it about.)

1. The Foreign Office authors envisage action on parallel lines by the American Government and by the British Government. They are of the opinion that action toward restoration of peace in the Far East through machinery which might be set up *ad hoc* under the Pact of Paris or the Nine Power Treaty would, under present world conditions, prove ineffective.

Comment: The two Governments have been pursuing in regard to many matters in the Far East courses of action which run parallel. They have been doing this without mutual or reciprocal commitments and (when and where so doing) because their views, interests and objectives have been similar. The view now expressed by the Foreign Office authors that *ad hoc* machinery would under present conditions prove ineffective is shared by the authors of these comments.

The Foreign Office authors feel that action along the lines thus far employed is not likely to cause Japan to abandon her present intention of destroying the Chinese Government and setting up in place thereof puppet régimes subservient to the will of Japan.

Comment: We concur.

The Foreign Office authors feel that under such an arrangement all foreign interests would suffer serious injury and might in course of time find themselves excluded from China.

Comment: We concur, but with emphasis on the word "might."

The Foreign Office authors reason that if representations were backed by naval forces adequate to defend any vital British interest that might be affected, the attitude of the Japanese Government toward China would probably be considerably modified. They therefore approach the question of possible peace terms from this angle: assuming that the British Government should be in a position to enforce respect for vital British interests and thus dictate terms of peace, what should those terms be.

Comment: We are not in position to make an assumption that the American Government would be in a position (that the United States would be willing) to make a disposal of naval forces for the purpose of defending and enforcing respect for American interests or of dictating terms of peace. Therefore, our approach to the question what the terms of peace should be (in fact, to the whole situation and its problems) is and must be from an angle different from that from which the Foreign Office authors have in this memorandum considered that question.

2. The Foreign Office authors envisage vital British interests in the Far East as being: (1) peace and stable political conditions, (2) the open door and equality of opportunity, and (3) the security of Hong Kong. They consider that if the first two of these were assured the third would be thereby taken care of. Hence, if the British Government were able to secure a peace on the basis of the first two, "every vital British interest would thereby be fully safeguarded and they might hope to secure the cooperation of other powers having substantial interests in the Far East in the attempt to secure such a settlement." They hope that the United States Government would also be of the view that all that is necessary for the protection of American interests in the Far East is the due observance by all parties of the Nine Power Treaty, and that this Government would therefore be disposed to take action parallel to that of the British Government. They suggest that such action might take the form of making representations to Japan that American (British) interests are being damaged through the failure of Japan to live up to the provisions of Article 1 of the Nine Power Treaty, and of taking such measures as will indicate clearly that the United States (United Kingdom) Government does not intend to acquiesce in further breaching of the provisions of the treaty and making it clear that in the view of the United States (United Kingdom) Government the terms of settlement should be on the one hand fair to China and on the other hand fair and even generous to Japan.

Comment: Without attempting to distinguish between interests and vital interests, it is a well-known fact that this country is deeply concerned in regard and in relation to the questions of peace, stable political condition, open door and equality of opportunity, the world over; and that it is opposed to aggression and conquest and procedures of violence in international relations—everywhere, and therefore in the Far East. Hence, its objectives in regard to points 1 and 2 are similar to the British objectives; and, it would have an indirect concern in regard to point 3. This country of course desires that there be peace, stable conditions, an open door and equality of opportunity in China (and elsewhere) and that there be no aggression against the sovereignty or the territory of any power in the Far East (or elsewhere). The Government of the United States has repeatedly given indication of the importance which it attaches to and the value which it places upon the provisions of the Nine Power Treaty. However, the action which the British authors suggest toward obtaining respect by Japan for the provisions of that treaty calls for a disposal of naval forces, and, as stated above, it cannot be assumed that the United States is or will be willing to employ that method. Moreover, there is room for doubt whether an approach—to the problem of satisfactory terms of settlement—within the limits of the Nine Power Treaty alone would be sufficiently broad to cover the needs of the situation.

In the two declarations of the Brussels Conference [22] the delegations present, with some exceptions, reaffirmed the principles of the Nine Power Treaty and gave notice that the settlement ultimately made between Japan and China must be acceptable to the parties to that treaty. That action should ultimately have substantial influence upon the course of events in the Far East. But, both the Japanese and the Chinese realize that the fundamental issue in the present conflict is whether China (or large parts of China) is to be ruled by Chinese or by Japanese. It apparently is, as stated by the Foreign Office authors, the present intention of the Japanese to destroy the Chinese Government and to set up in place thereof puppet régimes "that would be completely subservient to the will of Japan." There is warrant for believing that an objective of the Japanese is to gain complete control of China. In the light of those considerations, the Japanese insistence on their contention that the issues concern Japan and China exclusively and, also, their persistent refusal to give countenance to any intrusion by other powers are intelligible.

As matters stand, would a peace settlement brought about now by pressure from foreign governments with a threat of use of force be anything other than an uneasy, not-to-be-relied-upon, and short-lived truce?

With regard to the menace to the interests of foreign powers, while it is true that Japan is, in those areas which have been occupied by the Japanese Army, steadily undermining and whittling down the rights and interests of other powers, and while there is at all times an incidental menace to the lives and property of foreign nationals, does it not appear that both the Japanese and the Chinese are, and for some time to come will be, so completely occupied with problems of their military operations against each other as to render it unlikely that either power will go out of its way to add to its troubles by an officially planned armed assault upon the territorial or physical pos-

[22] November 15 and 24, 1937, *Foreign Relations, Japan, 1931–1941*, vol. I, pp. 410 and 421.

sessions of a third power? If, however, one or more third powers were at the present time to dispose naval forces in a manner threatening to Japan, would not the likelihood of substantial assault by some Japanese armed forces upon territories or property of such power or powers be greatly increased? If such an assault were made, would not such power or powers at once—or soon—suffer injuries and incur losses greater in extent and in amount than would otherwise be those which they had sought—by making such a threat—to obviate? Suppose also that third powers were to bring to bear upon China a pressure directed toward causing China to compromise (at China's expense) with Japan. Would not such a course be inconsistent with the treaty pledges of the powers? Leaving aside considerations of justice and of international morality, would a peace (?) agreement brought about now by such pressure in any way produce conditions of security, more than perhaps momentarily, for anything belonging to or appertaining to the powers and their interests?

Would any effort by third powers directed toward helping Japan to acquire control of any portion of Chinese territory bring any permanent advantage to any of such powers?

The situation and its potentialities being what they are, is not the policy which has thus far been pursued and which is now being pursued by the United States as sound a policy as can be pursued? In the course which it has followed, the Government of the United States at the outset urged upon both the Japanese and the Chinese Governments that hostilities be not entered upon; it thereafter urged upon both Governments that resort be had to processes of conciliation, and it assured both that it would be glad to be of assistance toward resort to such processes; it has throughout preserved an attitude of impartiality ("neutrality") as between the parties; it has refrained from any action of interference or intervention; it has in effect taken note of impairments of American rights and injuries done to American interests by processes and instrumentalities of *force majeure*, in some cases by Japanese and in some cases by Chinese agents; it has, however, refused to give any assent or countenance to such acts by either or both of the parties; it has made appropriate protests and entered appropriate reservations; it has notified both parties that it will hold them responsible for results of their unlawful acts; and it has taken steps toward strengthening and augmenting the armed forces of the United States, without adopting a menacing attitude or suggesting that it might use force for purposes of coercion. The Government of the United States took a definite stand in 1932 when it addressed to the Japanese and Chinese Governments its declaration [23] that it

---

[23] The nonrecognition doctrine of January 7, 1932; see *Foreign Relations, Japan, 1931–1941*, vol. I, p. 76; also see *Foreign Relations, 1932*, vol. III, p. 7.

could not admit the legality of any situation *de facto* and it did not intend to recognize any treaty or agreement entered into between those Governments which might impair the treaty rights of the United States or its citizens in China or to recognize any situation, treaty or agreement which might be brought about by means contrary to the provisions of the Pact of Paris. This Government has during the current hostilities given no assent to violations of international law or of treaty provisions by either the Japanese or the Chinese. This Government and the American people perceive today no useful purpose that could be served, no lasting advantage that might be gained by facilitating or giving countenance to any acquisition by Japan of new rights, titles or privileges on the basis of armed conquest in China.

There would seem to be little warrant for an expectation that Japan can gain a clear military victory over China in the near future. Meanwhile, armament programs are being pushed both in the United States and in Great Britain, and in course of time it should become evident to Japan that she cannot both have her way in China and keep up in an armament race—if either—and that, because of relative changes in strength and of other developments in the general situation, her self-interest will be best served by her showing reasonable regard for the rights, the interests and the opinions of Great Britain and the United States and other concerned powers.

On the basis of these various considerations, it is believed that the most feasible course for the United States—and, if we may venture to suggest, for Great Britain—would be to persevere along these lines and await the coming of a time when it may appear that the Japanese and the Chinese have reached states of mind in the presence of which assistance toward the making by them of a reasonable settlement may to advantage be offered—and be given—from without.

Sections 3, 4, 5 and 6 of the Foreign Office memorandum contain suggestions regarding possible terms of a peace settlement. (It was stated in section 2 that the terms "besides being fair to China, should be fair and even generous to Japan.")

3, 4 and 5. The Foreign Office authors express the view that arrangements for the future administration of Shanghai would seem to be the crux of the whole problem. They state that restoration as far as possible of the administration as it existed prior to July 1937 with possibly some improvements on the lines suggested in the Feetham Report would meet with certain difficulties because of the large number of Japanese nationals residing at Shanghai and the large amount of the Japanese share in the vested interests and foreign trade there. They speak of an inconsistency between certain provisions of the Nine Power Treaty and exclusion of Chinese authority from Shanghai.

They mention a traditional aim of American and British policy, that of encouraging China to develop into a modern state. They affirm that the United States and the United Kingdom will be reluctant in future to use force for protection of vested interests or maintenance of foreign municipal institutions there, whether against Chinese nationalism or against Japanese aggression. They feel that—in view of the uneasy situation which will persist if Japanese control is not eliminated from Shanghai and if foreign control should continue to impede the normal development of Shanghai—there are strong arguments in favor of making a radical change in the existing conditions at Shanghai. They suggest that a self-denying ordinance is called for, under which both Japan and other powers would abandon certain safeguards which have hitherto been regarded as indispensable for the protection of foreign interests there. They express the view that the alternative to maintaining the International Settlement by force is to restore complete Chinese control and that this need not mean the end of foreign participation in local municipal government. They suggest that on the withdrawal of the Japanese troops from Shanghai the Governments of the United States and the United Kingdom should use their influence to bring about the setting up by the Chinese Government of a single municipal authority for the whole of greater Shanghai; the municipal administration to contain a foreign element, with full representation of Japanese, British and other foreign interests; the police force to be unified, containing a foreign element; Chinese laws to be applied and the Chinese writ to run throughout; and no troops, Chinese or foreign, to be stationed, within a radius of, say, 30 miles, around Shanghai.

Comment: These views and suggestions with regard to Shanghai have a strong appeal. Our thoughts have been running along substantially those lines. It is believed that official opinion here would be favorably disposed in principle toward them. We feel, however, that the time has not yet arrived for a commitment—such as would be involved in the launching of any particular "plan"—regarding the future of Shanghai.

6. The Foreign Office authors suggest that a solution of the Shanghai problem along the lines indicated above would facilitate a settlement of other points and should connote withdrawal of Japanese armed forces from China and probably withdrawal of all foreign garrisons; that the Chinese would doubtless be willing to give assurances that the Maritime Customs Administration would be maintained on a basis of international cooperation fair to all powers trading in the Far East; and that China might be pressed to give satisfaction to Japan on a number of points such as anti-Japanese teaching in school textbooks, the suppression of anti-Japanese propaganda, and the tariff rates to be applied to Japanese trade.

Comment: With most of this, it is believed that official opinion here would be in accord, in principle.

The Foreign Office authors state that Japan attaches very great importance to her position in north China and suggest that the terms of peace might include the recognition of "Manchukuo" by China and the granting of special facilities for economic cooperation and for the investment of Japanese capital in north China, including perhaps mining and industrial concessions for Japanese corporations, and some measure of Japanese participation in the management of railways in north China. They indicate, also, that if opportunity should occur for dealing with the question of extraterritoriality, British officialdom would favor a solution on the lines of the draft agreement of 1931 modified by the rendition of the International Settlement at Shanghai.

Comment: With regard to the suggestion that the terms of peace might "include the recognition of Manchukuo by China—a measure which would remove one of the irritants that tend to disturb international relations generally—. . .," [24] there is room for doubt whether recognition of "Manchukuo" by China really would "remove one of the irritants that tend to disturb international relations generally." Such recognition (followed by recognition of "Manchukuo" by other countries) might conceivably operate as a palliative, but would it in any way go to the root of any of the causes of conflict which disturb the relations of Japan, China and the Soviet Union? Its one assured effect would be to confirm the confidence of the Japanese in the efficacy of the method which they have been following, that of using armed force, in pursuance of objectives of policy. And this development in the Far East would inevitably encourage other powers which have the inclination to employ or to persevere in employment of that method in other parts of the world. It is not believed in the United States that "Manchukuo" possesses the characteristics of a sovereign and independent state. It must be assumed that this country would not wish to take, to participate in or to be associated with any initiative toward persuading the Chinese to accord the recognition under reference.

With regard to the suggestion that the terms of peace might include the granting of "special facilities for economic cooperation and the investment of Japanese capital in North China," it is, of course, highly desirable that there be economic cooperation between the Chinese and the Japanese. By virtue of her geographic position and of the fact that she has become highly industrialized earlier than have other Far Eastern countries, Japan enjoys in China and in other Far Eastern markets certain definite "natural" advantages. Measures should

[24] Omission indicated in the original.

be devised whereby the Japanese may reside in, do business in, and trade with China under conditions of safety and of non-discrimination. But, is there reason why the Japanese should be accorded (by any political action) a preferred position there? Would it not seem that only when and as Chinese nationals and Japanese nationals arrive at a common conception that mutual and reciprocal advantages are to be had through amicable economic cooperation between them will there exist a basis for successful carrying out of joint or cooperative Chinese-Japanese undertakings? Can any agreements toward that end to which Chinese authorities might commit China under conditions of duress, if giving the Japanese any "special" position, have beneficial effects of any long duration? In the past, the Chinese authorities have on many occasions found it expedient under conditions of duress to enter into agreements according special rights ("privileges") to foreign countries and their nationals. However, the circumstances antecedent and the situations prevailing when such agreements were concluded have never been, generally speaking, such as those which prevail in connection with the present Japanese-Chinese conflict. Never have the issues been such as are the issues, between Japan and China, today. The questions of Japanese penetration and of Japanese influence in and over China are questions of vital concern to the Chinese. The question whether foreign governments should bring to bear any substantial measure of influence or pressure toward bringing about the conclusion of an agreement which would accord to the Japanese special rights, privileges, or advantages in north China differing in any way from those accorded to China (and others) in Japanese territories or from those enjoyed by other powers in north China, is a question answer to which can be given to advantage only in the light of most serious and extensive consideration of the many implications and the various possible consequences of such a procedure.

The suggestion that there should be mining and industrial concessions for Japanese corporations seems on its face reasonable and meritorious. However, there at once arise the questions: Circumstances being what they are, would Japan enter into any such agreements on a reciprocal basis; would China derive any real benefit therefrom; and what would be the results in terms of harmony or of friction?

The suggestion that there should be some measure of Japanese participation in and management of the northern railways raises the questions: What, in the event of such a development, would become of the already established interests of other countries, conspicuously those of Great Britain, France, and Belgium, in the northern railways; and would such a measure be consistent with certain provisions of existing treaties and contracts, and with certain features of China's national policy?

With regard to the broad general subject of Chinese-Japanese cooperation, the question arises: Does the evidence afforded by observation of what has taken place in the areas in which conditions have been theoretically favorable to Chinese-Japanese cooperation (the Kwantung Leased Territory, south Manchuria, and since 1931 all of Manchuria) give warrant for an expectation that such cooperation would be attainable in fact in north China? Over the period of the past thirty-three years the Kwantung Leased Territory might with warrant be viewed as having afforded a laboratory for testing the practicability of Chinese-Japanese cooperation, and, viewed in this light, the results of the test would seem to afford little basis for an answer in the affirmative. With the factors of a Japanese administration, an industrious Chinese population, abundant natural resources, and an adequacy of available capital, there has not been produced any real economic cooperation or any substantial collaboration of any kind. Much the same may be said also regarding south Manchuria, where Japanese influence has been predominant for twenty-three years, and regarding "Manchukuo," where the Japanese have been in control since 1931. In "Manchukuo" not only has there been little or no genuine Chinese-Japanese economic cooperation but economic developments have been kept subservient to political and military objectives, and there has been afforded little or no opportunity for private Chinese participation (as distinguished from "Manchukuo" government participation) or for foreign participation. In the light of these facts, can it be assumed that Chinese-Japanese economic cooperation in north China would be realizable—or would eventuate? Might it not more warrantably be expected that facilities extended for economic cooperation and Japanese investment in north China, if and when, would contribute toward creating in north China a situation in all essential respects similar to the situation in Manchuria? The difficulty which the Chinese find in cooperating, even among themselves, is well known. Also well known are the rigidity of form, of national consciousness, and of political influences which characterize and accompany Japanese official and economic activities. To these factors, there has been added during recent years the factor of intense reciprocal distrust and antipathy. These observations and queries need not imply criticism either of the Japanese or of the Chinese. They do, however, give rise to a further question: Is effective Chinese-Japanese cooperation possible?

In general, does not observation of Japanese penetration into areas populated by Chinese lead to the conclusions: (1) that, where there is close contact between Japanese and Chinese, conflict rather than cooperation develops; (2) that Japanese economic effort in China relies heavily upon Japanese official support; (3) that such effort when and where engaged in tends toward subordination or exclusion of the Chinese interests; and (4) that in areas in which such effort is successful, American and European interests also are gradually and effectively excluded?

Are not these outstanding among the actualities and the possible consequences to which serious consideration must be given in connection with the question whether third powers should or should not urge that special facilities be accorded to Japan for economic cooperation and Japanese investment in north China?

The suggestion that if in the course of a settlement an opportunity should occur for dealing with the question of extraterritoriality a solution might be sought on the lines of the draft agreement of 1931, with modification in the direction desired by China in regard especially to the rendition of the International Settlement as discussed in an earlier section of these authors' memorandum, is altogether in line with views which have for some time past been those in principle of the American Government.

Additional Comment: The contention is often made that the United States maintains an attitude and follows courses in regard to Far Eastern problems which are unduly "idealistic" and not closely enough responsive to "realities." Without going into a discussion of the question: What constitutes realism in relation to the situation in and the problems of the Far East?—it is our belief that the approach which the Government of the United States makes to the problems involved is in fact definitely and conspicuously realistic.

During the century of increasingly close contact between the occidental powers and China which preceded the Washington Conference, the occidental powers made trial of and had experience of a great variety of methods of approach. Against the background of experience, and in the light of serious and careful consideration of existing situations and existing trends of thought in various parts of the world, the powers concluded, at Washington, under the leadership of the American and the British Governments, a collection of agreements which were intended to diminish frictions, regulate contacts, and eliminate some at least of the factors which were making for international conflict—especially in the Far East and the Pacific. Whatever may have been the inadequacies and the deficiencies of those agreements, the provisions of one of them, the Nine Power Treaty, constitute, in our opinion, a sound basis for the regulation of the activities of the powers, including Japan, in China and in relations with China. Although there has been during recent years much criticism of that treaty and much contention from some quarters that the treaty either is defunct or is obsolete, from no source has there come any proffer of a better set of principles and provisions which might be agreed upon by the powers for the furthering of the objectives which were sought to be attained by commitment of the powers to (and respect—were it given—by the powers for) the provisions of that treaty. The treaty was based on the assumption that the Chinese people would be capable, if not subjected to unwarranted molestation, of working out by their own methods and their own efforts a new political organization and an economic reorganization which would contribute toward conditions of stability and peace within their country and in the Far East. The American people still feel that the assumption under reference was (and is) sound. The Government of the United States believes that, generally speaking, the provisions of the Nine Power Treaty are fair and susceptible of practical application. It therefore seems to us that the fundamental problem in connection with China and Japan (and the relations of the powers with and in China) is that of bringing about a realization by Japan that relations between Japan and China must conform to the general principles which have been evolved in world experience for the regulation of relations between sovereign and independent states; realization by Japan that neither the Chinese people nor the peoples of other countries which have interests in the Far East are capable of becoming reconciled to a domination by Japan of China; realization by the Japanese that other powers not only have rights in and with regard to China but are incapable of relinquishing some of those rights; realization by Japan that conquest of China by force of arms is expressly forbidden by international legislation, in the form of multilateral treaties, enacted during recent decades; realization by Japan that, whatever may be her immediate success in use of armed force, several other nations, including the Chinese, have greater resources and power of endurance than has Japan; realization, in short, by the Japanese that principles, interests, law, treaty provisions, and the public opinion of many countries too powerful to be disregarded in the long run are opposed to Japan's present policies and methods in regard to China, and that it therefore is advisable that the Japanese themselves revise both of these.

Such evidence as we have gives no indication that there is imminent a breakdown either of China or of Japan. Nor have we any indication that the Chinese are at this time eager to enter upon any negotiation the objective of which would be a settlement favorable to Japan at the expense of China. Attempts at mediation have already been made by an official representative of at least one power. Suggestions which that representative made to the Chinese apparently with the approval of the Japanese, have been rejected by the Chinese. The efforts of the Brussels Conference to bring about a negotiation were rejected by the Japanese. The Conference is on record in reaffirmation of the principles of the Nine Power Treaty and in affirmation that the settlement between Japan and China when made must be acceptable to the powers party to the Nine Power Treaty which they represented. At the present moment no settlement acceptable to the Chinese would be likely to be acceptable to the Japanese—and vice versa.

In the light of the above, we feel that the time has not yet come when it would be opportune for the American Government or for the British Government or for these two Governments or for any group of governments to put forward a suggested plan of settlement. It seems to us advisable to withhold such a step until both the Japanese and the Chinese shall have reached a state of mind more favorable to a disposition on their part to take into consideration what we believe to be the realities which underlie the whole situation and which sooner or later must be faced. Is there not warrant for an expectation that, as the situation in China further develops, the Japanese will come to a realization that the cost of a perseverance by them in their effort to conquer China will be greater than such a conquest, if achievable at all, could possibly be worth to them; and that in the interval they will, as a result of representations made by other governments and in the light of developments in the fields of public opinion and of military preparedness in other countries, tend to show increasingly greater respect for the rights and interests of third powers?

(Note: Certain officers here are examining, with a view to possible future action at some opportune moment, the question of the practicability (possible methods and calculable effects) of taking action in the nature of "reprisals" in the commercial field against Japan or China or both in connection with disregard, growing out of the present hostilities, for the rights, the interests and the diplomatic representations of the United States and other countries. We would be interested to know whether officers of the British Government have made or are making studies of this question and, if so, to what conclusions.)

[WASHINGTON,] April 13, 1938.

793.94/12863 : Telegram

The Ambassador in China (Johnson) to the Secretary of State

HANKOW, April 19, 1938—2 p. m.
[Received April 19—10 : 40 a. m.]

207. I have examined again my 76 of February 3, 2 p. m., [25] and I find little to add to the estimate of the situation then attempted. During interval since then Captain Carlson [26] returned from a trip in Shansi

---

[25] *Ante,* p. 64.
[26] Capt. Evans F. Carlson, U. S. M. C., Navy Department language officer in China.

which took him throughout area occupied by so-called Communists and partisans. He brought eloquent testimony of the thoroughness with which the country people throughout all that area are being aroused and trained in guerrilla tactics which have prevented the Japanese Armed Forces making their hold effective beyond lines of railway communication. Commander Overesch [27] has been down from Peiping and says that areas south of and to within sight of walls of Peiping are roused in opposition. Colonel Stilwell has returned from a trip to the northwest which took him to Sining in Chinghai, and tells me that throughout area which he traveled the people are being drilled and aroused. More recently Captain Carlson has returned from a trip which enabled him to watch 3 days of the fighting at Taierchuang, and tells me that Chinese troops in the field there won a well deserved victory over Japanese troops, administering the first defeat that Japanese troops have suffered in the field in modern times. All of this confirms my belief that Japan will have to use a great deal more force than it now has in the field if it hopes to pacify and begin reconstruction operations even in those areas close to Shanghai and Tientsin.

2. Conditions here at Hankow have changed from an atmosphere of pessimism to one of dogged optimism. The Government is more united under Chiang and there is a feeling that the future is not entirely hopeless due to recent failure of Japanese arms at Hsuchow. This optimism is based more upon the hope of wearing out the Japanese than any expectation of being able by force to drive out Japanese forces now on Chinese soil. Realization of this hope is dependent upon the Japanese economic factor which is a highly speculative quantity. Chinese ability to maintain a stubborn long time resistance is fairly good, as the Chinese can feed themselves indefinitely while Japanese forces in China will have to be supplied continually at colossal expense.

3. I find no evidence of a desire for a peace by compromise among Chinese, and doubt whether the Government could persuade its army or its people to accept such a peace. The spirit of resistance is slowly spreading among the people, who are awakening to a feeling that this is their war. Japanese air raids in the interior and atrocities by Japanese soldiers upon civilian population are responsible for this stiffening of the people.

Repeated to Peiping and Shanghai. Shanghai please relay to Tokyo and show Commander-in-Chief.[28]

JOHNSON

---

[27] Commander Harvey E. Overesch, Naval Attaché in China.
[28] Admiral Harry E. Yarnell, United States Asiatic Fleet.

793.94119/414 : Telegram

The Ambassador in Japan (Grew) to the Secretary of State

TOKYO, April 21, 1938—4 p. m.
[Received April 21—6:40 a. m.]

260. My British colleague has consulted me with regard to certain alleged recent conversations between Lindsay and the Department concerning the hypothetical question eventual peace mediation. I have had to plead ignorance.

GREW

793.94119/414 : Telegram

The Acting Secretary of State to the Ambassador in Japan (Grew)

WASHINGTON, April 21, 1938—6 p. m.

141. Your 260, April 21, 4 p. m.

1. Texts of an *aide-mémoire* of April 11 from British Embassy and an *aide-mémoire* in reply of April 14 by the Department [29] are in pouch which leaves tomorrow for Tokyo, Department having preferred mail instruction to telegraphic instruction for informing you of the subject matter.

Department assumes that your British colleague has informed you of substance of the British Government's inquiry. Department has stated in reply that in our opinion the circumstances which now prevail are not propitious for action and that it seems to us advisable to defer reaching a decision with regard to procedure until a moment when circumstances make it appear that action would be opportune. We have added that we hope that our two Governments will keep each other informed of any views and any developments which seem significant in regard to the matter under reference.

WELLES

793.94/12905 : Telegram

The First Secretary of Embassy in China (Salisbury) to the Secretary of State

PEIPING, April 25, 1938—noon.
[Received April 25—7 a. m.]

254. Embassy's 232, April 14, noon.[30]

1. The Japanese controlled press continues to give considerable space to plans for economic exploitation of North China. Concrete and significant steps are not apparent except (*a*) the taking over of

[29] For latter, see *Foreign Relations, Japan, 1931–1941*, vol. I, p. 463.
[30] Not printed.

certain industrial installations in the occupied areas, (*b*) the creating of organs intended for the carrying out of exploitations, and (*c*) the making of plans for creating still more such organs.

2. A Japanese Embassy official concerned with economic development states that:

(*a*) the purely Japanese North China Development Company, capitalized at yen 500,000,000 will be the chief organ of exploitation;

(*b*) five or six Sino-Japanese companies of a smaller scale will be formed to develop industries which have an "unavoidably monopolistic character" such as railways, salt, iron, electric power, and certain Shansi coal;

(*c*) half the capital of each of the Sino-Japanese companies will be supplied by the North China Development Company, the remainder to be supplied by interested Japanese and Chinese concerns;

(*d*) a representative of the North China Development Company will participate in the direction of each of the Sino-Japanese companies;

(*e*) the company controlling railways will receive part of its capital from the South Manchuria Railway Company and will be run by personnel formerly serving in that company;

(*f*) the above-mentioned Company will form the skeleton of economic exploitation around which lesser industries will develop;

(*g*) it will take a year for the skeleton organization to be put into working order; and

(*h*) meanwhile little is being accomplished economically in a concrete way.

3. He further stated that the Sino-Japanese Economic Council (reference Embassy's 191, March 28, 4 p. m.) will begin to function after return in May of Hirao, Vice Chairman of the Council, from Japan to Peiping, will formulate the policies of the Provisional Government and will give advice to the North China Development Company and to all lesser companies as necessary. Presumably as an aid to the Economic Council in its duties a "Ministry of Industries" is shortly to be inaugurated by the Provisional Government. According to the press Renzo Sawada, recently Counselor of Embassy at Hsinking, will arrive shortly to assist the Economic Council.

3 [4?]. Matsuoka of the South Manchuria Railway Company is reported in the press as stating that some delay may occur in establishing the projected North China Communications Company as the primary problem is to prevent the organizing of the North China Development Company which is "to supervise all enterprises in North China" and that the South Manchuria Railway Company may be able to invest yen 500,000,000 in North China during the next 5 years.

Repeated to Ambassador at Hankow.

SALISBURY

893.00/14226 : Telegram

The Ambassador in China (Johnson) to the Secretary of State

HANKOW, April 26, 1938—2 p. m.
[Received April 26—12 : 35 p. m.]

218. McHugh [31] had an informal conversation with British Ambassador on April 24 in the course of which latter expressed admiration for spirit of resistance which Chinese are showing and hope for their eventual success. He commented upon difference in viewpoint in this respect which he had achieved since coming to Hankow and stated that he expected to make this place his headquarters. He stated that he had arranged with the Chinese and hoped to make similar arrangements with Japanese for use of a British plane to enable him to travel between Shanghai and Hankow. British Ambassador said he had informed Donald [32] that financial circles in London (by which he doubtless meant Rogers, representative of Bank of England, who came to China with Leith-Ross [33] and has since been working with Soong [34] and Bank of China) had confidence in Soong and did not have confidence in Kung.[35] He permitted McHugh to infer that such financial circles might find it possible to extend additional credits to China provided that Soong is disposed to assume office as Financial Minister, but stated that he would not intervene actively with Chinese in behalf of Soong.

Later on same day McHugh had lunch with Soong who informed him that British Ambassador had urged him quite frankly to iron out his difficulties with Generalissimo and resume office. Soong was apparently pleased with what he described as British Sahib's amazing directness on short acquaintance and stated that he had seen the Generalissimo and had informed him of his willingness to assist in any way possible. He told McHugh that he would not ask for any office and would return only if invited.

The morning of April 25 Donald told McHugh that Kung had submitted his resignation to the Generalissimo.

This morning Donald informed McHugh that Soong offered to return to Ministry of Finance on conditions which were unacceptable to the Generalissimo who has now refused to accept the resignation of Kung. Chiang was quoted as saying that he could not possibly work with Soong and that if his failure to do so meant the forfeiture of foreign assistance he would accept this fact and continue to fight the enemy without such assistance.

JOHNSON

---

[31] Capt. James M. McHugh, U. S. M. C., Assistant Naval Attaché in China.
[32] W. H. Donald, Australian adviser to Generalissimo Chiang Kai-shek.
[33] Sir Frederick Leith-Ross, chief economic adviser to the British Government.
[34] T. V. Soong, former Chinese Minister of Finance.
[35] H. H. Kung, Chinese Minister of Finance and President of the Executive Yuan (Premier).

893.00/14232

The Ambassador in China (Johnson) to the Secretary of State

No. 32   HANKOW, April 26, 1938.
                                               [Received June 13.]

SIR: I have the honor to submit the following summary of the activities of the Extraordinary National Congress of the Kuomintang which was held in Hankow March 29 to April 1, 1938.

The Congress was according to announcements called to deal with the many important questions arising out of the Sino-Japanese hostilities. Since the beginning of the hostilities the powers of government have been intrusted to a supreme war council which has been superimposed upon the regular governmental departments. This organization with General Chiang Kai-shek at its head did not derive its power directly from the Kuomintang but was born of necessity, and created by strong-arm methods without the sanction of any recognized responsible representative body. It is dictatorial and military in character and derives its justification for existence solely from the force of circumstances. The creation of this supreme war council has, of course, robbed the Kuomintang of much of its power over the National Government, which prior to the formation of the council was the tool of the Party.

Prior to the convocation of the Extraordinary Congress there was considerable speculation as to how the Party would take this curtailment of its powers. It was therefore gratifying to many to find that the Congress was prepared to accept in good spirit the Party's loss of prestige and to swim with the tide of popular opinion in its will to unite all factions within the country in the primary objective of continuing and strengthening resistance to Japanese aggression.

Probably the most important action of the Congress was its unanimous election of General Chiang Kai-shek to the post of Tsungtai (Director General). By this action the Kuomintang in effect gave public legal sanction to the dictatorship of General Chiang. Dr. Wang Ching-wei was simultaneously given the post of Deputy Tsungtai.

Among the numerous resolutions adopted by the Congress were resolutions to further the cause of resistance by means of a foreign policy designed to strengthen the friendly relations of China with those powers seeking international peace and standing for the sanctity of international agreements. Other resolutions dealt with the furthering of mass military training, the improvement and simplification of political administration within the nation, the realigning of the nation's economic and financial structure in order to make possible the exertion of all energies in the cause of resistance, and the mobilization of the masses through education into a united front against Japan.

As an indication of the Party's willingness to forego its dictatorial powers over the Central Government, the Congress adopted a resolution calling for the creation of a Peoples' Political Council which apparently is intended to extend beyond the bounds of the Kuomintang and which will be vested with considerable power. This council will, it is presumed, serve as the forum for the so-called united front.

At its final meeting on April 1 the Congress adopted a long manifesto which appeared in translation in the English language press. A copy of the press translation is enclosed [36] with this despatch. Following is a brief summary of the manifesto which sums up the attitude of the Congress.

The manifesto points out that China has consistently striven for peace with honor; the maintenance of its territorial integrity and sovereign rights. When Japanese aggression became unbearable, however, China was forced to fight and it must now continue the struggle to the bitter end. Victory, when it is won, will mean not only the preservation of China's territorial integrity, but also gain for it equality and freedom in the family of nations. The manifesto points out that the only peace which China can accept is a peace based upon justice. Any peace resulting from a compromise will be tantamount to complete surrender to Japan, therefore, the struggle must be carried through to the very end.

With reference to foreign policy the manifesto reiterates China's determination to respect its international agreements and to continue and increase its efforts to maintain friendly relations with other powers. It points to the fact that China is fighting for world peace and the sanctity of international agreements. This fact it maintains must be impressed upon the world. It bemoans the fact that while China has the sympathy of the world it has failed to receive any active support from the powers.

With respect to domestic policy the manifesto stresses the point that the task of national reconstruction undertaken by the Central Government must not be side-tracked or permitted to lag because of the present hostilities. It maintains that the task of national reconstruction and the stemming of Japanese aggression are synonymous; that only through the revitalization and solidification of the nation can the aggressors be repelled; and that, therefore, it is imperative that all energies be directed simultaneously to the resistance of aggression by military force and the reconstruction, unification and strengthening of the nation.

---

[36] Not printed; see communication of April 2 from the Chinese Ministry for Foreign Affairs to the Chinese Embassy, p. 133.

The manifesto stresses the necessity for the fostering of a spirit of nationalism in China. It points out that the Japanese have used as a slogan in their propaganda campaign in China the catch phrase "self determination" meaning that the various racial groups within China should have the right of self government. This the manifesto says is a hoax. It asserts that all groups in China are equally threatened by the Japanese and that only by uniting and fighting together can these various groups within the nation insure their freedom and make possible the enjoyment of that freedom within the Republic of China which the Kuomintang has guaranteed to all races.

While granting that political freedom is indeed a valuable possession, the manifesto goes on to demonstrate that only through wholehearted cooperation and through the subordination of the will and desires of individuals to the will of the state can China hope to achieve sufficient unity and strength to resist the aggressors. It maintains that political freedom must, therefore, for the time being be limited and that all political factions must work together under a centralized control in order to present a united front against the enemy.

The manifesto draws attention to the path that Japanese activities have followed within the areas that have been occupied by the Japanese military. It asserts that Japan's primary objective is to destroy China's rapidly growing industries; that Japan seeks to conquer China in order to be able to force it into a position where it will function as a perpetual supplier of raw materials for Japan's industries while serving at the same time as an ever growing market for Japan's manufactured goods.

The manifesto states that while every effort must be made to improve the lot of China's vast agrarian population, at the same time no effort should be spared in the endeavor to foster, protect and promote those very industries which Japan is endeavoring to destroy. Upon them to a large extent depends the success with which China will be able to meet Japan's onslaught. In this connection the manifesto lays down three cardinal principles which should serve as the guide posts of the nation in its efforts to promote industrialization.

1. The entire nation must practice the greatest economy in order to store up working capital.
2. The interests of the state should always be made paramount to those of the individual, and all efforts at reconstruction should follow this line.
3. The government should take over those industries which are essential to the welfare of the state and operate them for the common good.

In its final paragraphs the manifesto exhorts all members of the Kuomintang to realize their responsibility as leaders of the nation and to put forth every effort in the struggle for national salvation. It goes on to point out that all patriotic citizens of China have, despite widely divergent political views, rallied behind the Government in resisting Japan, and it maintains that if, and only if, the people continue to work together in a spirit of self-sacrifice, China will win.

The Kuomintang Congress only echoed the general trend which is being displayed throughout China to forget internal difficulties and dissension in an effort to cope with the paramount issue, Japanese aggression. Japan by its military invasion of China has succeeded in accomplishing in China that which no Chinese leader has been able to accomplish; stir the people up to a fighting pitch, instil in them the idea of China as a united nation, and give them a rallying point which has universal appeal and is strong enough to force them to abandon their factional differences and personal animosities. The struggle against Japan is no longer the struggle of the Government leaders— it is the people's struggle. The Japanese military by their brutal actions in the areas which have been occupied by Japanese troops and by their air bombing of cities far in the interior have worked up in the Chinese common people a hatred against Japan which will be slow indeed in burning out. Should China succeed in its present struggle against Japan it must certainly emerge a much stronger and more unified nation.

Moreover the tone of hopefulness expressed in the manifesto is not mere bravado. The Chinese are coming to feel that their troops, though not as well equipped as the Japanese, are a fair match for the aggressors, and they are sanguine of being able, by forcing Japan to drive deeper and deeper into China, finally to cause the collapse of Japan.

Respectfully yours,

NELSON TRUSLER JOHNSON

761.94/1040 : Telegram

The Ambassador in the Soviet Union (Davies) to the Secretary of State

Moscow, April 28, 1938—5 p. m.
[Received April 28—1 : 15 p. m.]

107. 1. The following is a summary of a Tass communiqué published by *Izvestiya* today:

(a) On April 4 the Soviet Government proposed to Tokyo the settlement of the list of problems outstanding between the two Governments including: the immediate return of a Soviet mail plane, four Soviet citizens and a cutter held in Manchuria and the release of two Soviet ships held in Japan; the immediate payment of the last installment on the Chinese Eastern Railway due March 23 last; the freeing and return to Japan of eight Japanese arrested by the Soviet authorities "in retaliation" for the Japanese detention of a Soviet schooner; the release of several Japanese vessels and their crews held by the Soviet authorities; the favorable consideration of Japanese petitions concerning Sakhalin concession; the reestablishment of parcel post service with Japan suspended on account of the detention of the above mentioned mail plane; and the continuance of the Japanese Consulate at Okha on Sakhalin Island.

(*b*) The Japanese reply referred the Soviet Government to Hsinking for the settlement of certain of the issues relating to Manchuria and requested as additional *quid pro quo* the immediate signature of the Fisheries Convention and the retention of the Japanese Consulates at Khabarovsk and Blagoveshchensk.

(*c*) The Soviet Government on April 25 stated in reply that it had not included among its proposals any relating to basic policy but only such especially annoying ones as were susceptible of immediate solution; that the fisheries matter was not urgent and that the closing of the two Japanese Consulates above referred to was a matter of policy. While holding Japan ultimately responsible for the matters relating to Manchuria the Soviet Government then took them up at Hsinking and is now awaiting a definite reply from the Japanese Government before defining its views concerning Japanese requests relating to Sakhalin concessions.

2. It is apparent that the number of annoying incidents which have arisen between the two Governments during the last 3 months have been due in a large measure to retaliation, counter retaliation, and jockeying for position. None seems to be more grave than numerous incidents which have taken place in the past.

DAVIES

894.00/786 : Telegram

The Ambassador in Japan (Grew) to the Secretary of State

TOKYO, April 28, 1938—7 p. m.
[Received April 28—11 a. m.]

282. Our 239, April 11, 6 p. m.

1. Last week the Prime Minister issued a public statement announcing his intention to assume again his official duties. This statement was generally construed as an announcement that the differences of opinion within the Cabinet have been in some way adjusted.

2. In view of the recent brief inspection by the Minister of War of conditions in China we attach some significance to indications in the press that the military operations in China will be prosecuted hereafter more vigorously than they have in the past.

3. The Prime Minister is reported to be of the opinion that there is no urgent need for changes in the personnel in the Cabinet.

4. Our opinion is that Cabinet differences have been tided over. It is our estimate that the army has made substantial concessions to

those who advocate the resort to more vigorous and more intensive military operations. The opinion is now more frequently and widely heard among Japanese that a drive to Hankow is inevitable.

Repeated to Shanghai for Hankow.

GREW

893.01 Provisional/115 : Telegram

The Consul General at Shanghai (Lockhart) to the Secretary of State

SHANGHAI, May 2, 1938—4 p. m.
[Received May 2—12 : 16 p. m.]

602. Wang Keh Min, who has been in Shanghai for several days, flew to Tokyo yesterday morning accompanied by Major General Kita. Wang was shown every courtesy by high Japanese military and civil officials here who took extraordinary precautions for his safety. The Japanese Embassy spokesman denied the report that Wang's position is insecure. While here Wang saw Liang Hung Chih of the so-called "Reformed Government" and according to Japanese press reports reached a complete understanding regarding the merger of the two puppet governments. It is also reported to have been agreed to equally divide the customs revenues. A further Japanese report states that Li Chao Nan has been appointed Superintendent of Customs at Shanghai by the so-called "Reformed Government".

Repeated to Hankow and Peiping.

LOCKHART

793.94119/418 : Telegram

The Ambassador in China (Johnson) to the Secretary of State

HANKOW, May 3, 1938—noon.
[Received May 3—8 : 20 a. m.]

232. Department's 124, April 13, 7 p. m.[37] Counselor [of] British Embassy informed me today in the course of a conversation that question of mediation had been recently canvassed by the British Government, but that conclusion had been reached that mediation was out of the question as there was no basis upon which mediation could be profitably offered to either side.

JOHNSON

---

[37] Not printed.

851.50/164 : Telegram

The Ambassador in France (Bullitt) to the Secretary of State

[Extract [38]]

PARIS, May 9, 1938—7 p. m.
[Received May 10—12: 40 p. m.]

739. . . .

. . . .

5. China.

Daladier [39] said that he felt the resistance of the Chinese to the Japanese was a magnificent and heartening example of courage and patriotism. As soon as he had become Prime Minister he had given orders to the French authorities in Indo-China to open the railroad completely to all shipments of planes and munitions to China. The Japanese had protested frequently and vigorously, and a Japanese Consul in Indo-China had gone so far as to say to the French General there that if the shipment of munitions through Indo-China should not be stopped Japan might have to make war. The French General had replied: "Come on and see what happens to you!" This had produced a very salutary effect. The Japanese Consul had left at once for Japan and had not returned.

BULLITT

793.94/12985 : Telegram

The Ambassador in France (Bullitt) to the Secretary of State

PARIS, May 9, 1938—8 p. m.
[Received May 10—7: 45 a. m.]

740. Sun Fo, President of the Legislative Yuan, lunched with me alone yesterday and in the course of a long conversation made the following statements:

He was confident that China could continue to resist Japan for another year at least. In England there had been talk of mediation. He believed that no offer of mediation at the present time could have any chance of success but thought that by the end of another 12 months the Japanese would find themselves in such difficulties that they would be seeking mediation by England and the United States.

As a result of his lengthy visit to England he had the impression that while the British did not desire to see Japan overwhelm China, they also did not desire to see Japan defeated because they feared that the defeat of Japan would mean the domination of China by the

---

[38] For text of sections 2 and 3 of this telegram, see vol. I, pp. 493 and 192.
[39] Edouard Daladier, President of the French Council of Ministers.

Soviet Union. He asserted that the Chinese Communist leaders were now cooperating in full loyalty with Chiang Kai Shek and expressed the opinion that the Chinese Communists were Chinese patriots first and Communists second. There was no danger of communism in China.

He said that the Russians had furnished China with munitions to date costing approximately 150,000,000 Chinese dollars. They had not asked China for any payments on these purchases and indeed had shipped some of the munitions even before China had promised to pay for them. The road across Sinkiang had been kept open all winter by an army of snow shovelers. There were 175,000 coolies working now on the road from Burma into the interior of China and he could assure me that within 2 months this road would be capable of bearing not merely light supplies but also trucks carrying planes and the heaviest cannon.

Sun Fo said that the chief worry of his Government at the moment was the position of the currency. China did not need money for the purchase of war supplies but a currency stabilization loan or some other form of assistance for the stabilization of Chinese currency would be of immense help. He asked me if I thought there was any possibility of the Chinese Government obtaining assistance from the Government of the United States or from private American financial interests for this purpose. I said that I could not pretend to be sufficiently conversant with the subject to give him an authoritative answer but that it was my decided impression that the Government of the United States had no funds which could be used for this purpose and that it seemed unlikely that private bankers would be interested.

Sun Fo is leaving tomorrow for China via Moscow. He described to me in detail the 6-hour conversation he had with Stalin on his recent visit to Moscow. He said that Stalin had assured him that he knew that China was fighting Russia's battle as well as her own; that it was the ultimate objective of the Japanese to capture the whole of Siberia as far as Lake Baikal; that China would continue to receive all possible assistance from Russia in the form of munitions, airplanes and other supplies; that the Soviet Union would not, however, intervene militarily in the war. Stalin was apprehensive that Germany might attack the Soviet Union if the Soviet Union should make war on Japan. Stalin also felt that neither Great Britain nor the United States would permit Japan to be crushed by the Soviet Union.

BULLITT

793.94119/422

Memorandum by the Chief of the Division of Far Eastern Affairs (Hamilton) of a Conversation With Mr. Earl H. Cressy, of the Associated Boards for Christian Colleges in China, New York

[WASHINGTON,] May 11, 1938.

During the course of a call Mr. Cressy outlined to me some of the difficulties with which American mission and educational institutions were confronted as a result of the present situation in China.

Mr. Cressy said that while in Tokyo en route to the United States he had talked with Mr. Horinouchi, Vice Minister for Foreign Affairs, and that during the conversation Mr. Horinouchi had intimated that the time might be ripe for mediation in the Sino-Japanese conflict by a friendly power. Mr. Cressy said that he had reported this remark to Ambassador Grew and that Ambassador Grew had asked Mr. Cressy to communicate the remark to the Department. Mr. Cressy said that he was now doing that.

At an earlier point in the conversation Mr. Cressy had remarked that as the situation now stood there was no course open to China but to continue to fight. I referred to that remark and said that it was very difficult for me to conceive of any terms of peace which would be mutually acceptable to both China and Japan. Mr. Cressy stated that he concurred and that in his opinion, much as he deplored the fighting, the fighting must continue for a further period before there would be any practical basis for peace.

Mr. Cressy said that the suggestion had been made to him by Japanese in Japan that it might be useful for a small representative group of Japanese Christians to meet with a similar group of Chinese to see whether they could bring about a better understanding of their respective positions to the end that they might possibly formulate a program for bringing about peace between the two countries. Mr. Cressy said that he realized that there was only one chance in a thousand of such a meeting bringing about the desired end but that he was inclined to favor the bringing together of such a Chinese-Japanese group. He said that the Chinese and Japanese chosen would be responsible individuals who, although private citizens, had ready access to governmental persons. Mr. Cressy asked me what I thought of this project. I inquired whether the meeting would be attended solely by Chinese and Japanese or whether Americans would be involved. He said that possibly one American, perhaps himself, might undertake the arrangement of such a meeting but that the meeting as such would be essentially between the Chinese and Japanese. I said that in regard to an American private citizen becoming involved in any matter which might smack of mediation, the Department had of course very definite views to the general effect that such activity on the part of an American citizen was inappropriate and the question of mediation could best be handled through normal diplomatic channels. I said that from Mr. Cressy's description of the project I judged that it was essentially a meeting between Japanese and Chinese private citizens and that I could see no objection to such a meeting. I added that, speaking personally, I agreed with a previous remark made by him that meetings between such Chinese and Japanese groups might possibly tend to bring about better understanding and appreciation on the part of each of the other's point of view and might therefore be constructive in results.

M[AXWELL] M. H[AMILTON]

893.01 Provisional/119 : Telegram

The Consul General at Shanghai (Lockhart) to the Secretary of State

SHANGHAI, May 13, 1938—4 p. m.
[Received 4 : 50 p. m.]

655. My 624, May 6, 4 p. m.[40]

1. A letter has been received from Li Chien-nan, who signs himself "Superintendent of Customs" announcing that he has been appointed to that position by the Reformed Government and that he assumed his duties on April 28. It is known, however, that he is not yet occupying his offices in the customs building. No acknowledgment is being made of the letter.

2. It is reported in the press that Ling Chi-hung has been appointed by the Reformed Government Judge of the First Special District Court, but has made no effort thus far to assume his duties.

Repeated to Hankow and Peiping.

LOCKHART

793.94/13028 : Telegram

The Consul at Canton (Fletcher) to the Secretary of State

CANTON, May 13, 1938—5 p. m.
[Received May 16—7 a. m.]

Reported number of Chinese planes arriving Canton on 10th is 70 including 12 Russian bombers, 32 Russian pursuits and 17 Siberian Russian pilots. In organizing two raids on Japanese on 11th one Japanese destroyer set on fire, one Japanese plane shot down, fuel tanks on Japanese occupied island airfield set on fire. No Chinese

[40] *Post*, p. 703.

planes lost. Most Chinese planes left Canton early on 12th to avoid danger to city from aerial combats.

Canton airfield bombed on night of 11th without damage. Both Canton airfields on 12th.

Bocca Tigris forts shelled by Japanese warships afternoon 12th without reported damage and forts not replying.

Sent to Peiping, Hankow, Shanghai.

FLETCHER

894.02/63

The Ambassador in Japan (Grew) to the Secretary of State

No. 2938

TOKYO, May 16, 1938.
[Received June 3.]

SIR: I have the honor to report that, according to the local papers of May 9, a committee which has been studying the problem of coordination within the Government of conduct of foreign relations, has recommended a drastic reorganization of the Foreign Office. As the recommendations of the committee have not as yet been made public, a discussion of the changes proposed in detailed terms would be premature, but it is understood that the present East Asia Bureau and the Intelligence (Press) Section will be converted into quasi-independent agencies of the Government, but placed under the direction of the Minister for Foreign Affairs. The present business of the Foreign Office, other than that now handled by the above-mentioned offices, is to be redistributed between four geographical bureaus (Eastern European, Western European, American and South Seas) and the Treaty Bureau and the Commercial Bureau. The Ministry is to be redesignated as the Ministry of Foreign Policy.

The proposed changes do not reflect merely the desire to improve the efficiency and effectiveness of the Foreign Office. The tide of nationalism, which is being manifested toward government by a directive organization instead of by personal leadership, has now caught the Foreign Office. There is growing opposition to the conduct of foreign relations by a small group of professional diplomats, whose training and experiences tend to develop an attitude of liberalism, and growing insistence that foreign intercourse be based on that "immutable policy toward China" which is now being implemented by the armed services.

Criticism of the "weak-kneed diplomacy" of the Japanese Foreign Office has been the stock in trade of the reactionaries ever since the Foreign Office was instituted, but such criticism has been especially vehement since the outbreak of the Manchurian conflict in 1931. There has been a prevailing belief for some time that the professional diplomats have not shown a disposition to make a positive contribution toward setting up a foreign policy program unfettered by international commitments calculated largely to preserve the rights in the Far East of Occidental powers. This feeling bore fruit during the last session of the Diet in a plan put forward by the Bureau of Legislation, one of the offices placed under the Prime Minister, to set up an independent agency of the Japanese Government where there would be centralized control over all Japan's interests in China, including the conduct of relations with China and the development of economic interests in that country. The Foreign Office took strong exception to this plan, on the ground that relations with China needed to be conducted with reference to Japan's relations with other countries and in the light of conditions existing in other parts of the world—that to isolate China relations would lead to complete confusion. It seemed as if the matter had there ended, especially when provision was made for the establishment of two organizations for the economic development of North China and Central China, respectively. However, whether the Foreign Office promised to make a counter proposal to the Bureau of Legislation, or realized that danger lay in letting matters rest merely with rejecting the plan of that Bureau, a committee of the Foreign Office began a study of the organization of their Department and after 2 months' work brought forth the plan above-outlined.

We are informed by officials in the Foreign Office that this plan is a compromise. The senior officers in the department—the Vice Minister, Mr. Horinouchi, and the bureau directors—apparently favor the making of modifications in organization with a view to the elimination of friction with other departments on matters relating to China, but without structurally changing the department. The section chiefs and the younger men, however, are agitating for drastic changes—for the centralization of power in matters relating to China, now distributed among the Finance, Overseas Affairs, and Commerce and Industry Ministries, along with the Foreign Office.

We understand that the latter group first proposed the setting up of a Board of East Asian Affairs, to embrace the Manchuria Bureau of the Ministry of Overseas Affairs, and the East Asia Bureau and the Intelligence Section of the Foreign Office. This was to be an agency independent of the Foreign Office, but to be under the direction of the Minister for Foreign Affairs. The group of senior men criticized the plan as unworkable, in which position the Minister agreed, but it appears also that Mr. Hirota did not think too well of the counterplan of the senior group, which is, in short, an enlargement of the present East Asia Bureau and the Press Section and their assimilation into a Political Affairs Bureau of which the director would be the

Vice Minister. The plan adopted by the Foreign Office committee obviously contains certain features of both plans.

Whether the plan of reorganization has been formally adopted by the Foreign Minister and will be presented to the Prime Minister is not yet known. The important fact is that publication of the plan was followed by a chorus of derision from those quarters whose views on public matters now carry weight. The substance of their observations was that the entire nation had made sacrifice of "blood and treasure" to implement Japanese policy on the Continent, and that the time had come when the exploitation of the fruits of their sacrifices was a matter in which all elements of the community must share, and not be left as a special prerogative of the professional diplomatists or any other special group. The Prime Minister has promised to look into the entire question of the administration of Japanese interests in China, and one can expect to see in due course some interesting developments which will leave some substantial mark on the Foreign Office.

There has been taking place for some years a gradual change in the type of men comprising the more successful group of the Japanese Foreign Service. Such men as Baron Hayashi, Viscount Ishii, and Mr. Matsudaira, who typify the Japanese diplomatist of an epoch now past, are, by their personality, character and enlightened ideals, qualified to take a high place in any society. The standard which formerly prevailed is being gradually and steadily lowered by process of dilution, the men entering the service for the past 15 years being progressively more parochial in their outlook and nationalistic in their attitude. When the process of making the Foreign Office an instrument of reactionary forces will have been completed, one will be able to make the comment that it will then be more truly reflective of national aspirations than it has been in recent years.

Respectfully yours,   JOSEPH C. GREW

794.00/129

The Ambassador in Japan (Grew) to the Secretary of State

No. 2941   TOKYO, May 17, 1938.
[Received June 3.]

SIR: As of possible interest in so far as it may shed further light upon the somewhat vague and ill-defined recent Japanese policy known as the "Southward Advance", I have the honor to transmit herewith a translation [41] of an interpellation on this subject in the Lower House of the Diet during the hearings on March 16, 1938, on the Navy

---

[41] Not printed.

Budget, and of the Navy Minister's reply thereto. A translation of the hearings in full on the Navy Budget were transmitted by the Naval Attaché [42] to the Navy Department in his confidential report No. 71, dated March 30, 1938.[43]

Although this Southward Advance policy was developed, probably at the instigation of the navy, some two years ago, references to it have been relatively infrequent and not of such a nature as to clarify it; and although the present question and reply leave much to be desired in respect of precision and clarity, nevertheless they do reveal that the present intention of the naval authorities is that such a policy should be pursued by means of peaceful economic penetration rather than by force. In bringing up the subject the interpellator opened by stating that the present "Continental Policy", (by which it may be presumed he refers to the policy of expansion on the Asiatic mainland), is by itself insufficient to meet the needs of Japan's growing population which increases by one million per annum. He points out, significantly, that the various agrarian reform laws which have been and are constantly being tried have proven to be powerless to remedy the situation and that, therefore, thought must be given toward the question of "Southward Advance." It is stated that "Manchukuo" has failed to prove an outlet for the surplus population as not more than 200,000 Japanese have been induced to emigrate there since 1931, but that the South Pacific offers room.

The interpellator is not specific as to the areas he has in mind although he makes reference to the desirability of obtaining the "understanding" of the United States for a peaceful exploitation of islands "in the vicinity" of the Japanese Mandated Islands and he remarks that Japan's policy of expansion in this area need never menace the United States. There are also mentioned as possibilities for Japanese peaceful exploitation the Malay Peninsula and North Africa and there is an oblique reference to the fact that Holland is holding colonies in area eighty times as large as the motherland. The interpellator closes by saying that industrialization alone will not save the situation because the markets of the world are closed to Japan's surplus goods by tariff barriers; that there are many peaceful means of pursuing the "Southward Advance"; and that it is foolish to antagonize the United States and Great Britain and be drawn into a naval race in spite of Japan's policy of non-menace and non-aggression.

The Navy Minister replied briefly, refusing to comment upon the Continental Policy but agreeing that the "Southward Advance" was worth thinking about. He emphasized, however, that this policy

---

[42] Capt. Harold M. Bemis.
[43] Not found in Department files.

should be pursued by peaceful and economic means only and he regards the Japanese Mandated Islands as furnishing the first step in this direction. "It would be better for people to go there first", he says, "and thence to the south or southwestward."

This last phrase falls somewhat short of furnishing a definite description of Japan's objectives and embraces a substantial amount of territory.

Respectfully yours,   JOSEPH C. GREW

793.94/13054 : Telegram

The Ambassador in Japan (Grew) to the Secretary of State

TOKYO, May 21, 1938—11 a. m.
[Received May 21—2: 14 a. m.]

322. 1. The Japanese Government is discouraging through the press and radio any disposition on the part of the public to assume that the capture of Hsuchow will directly lead to the collapse of Chinese military resistance. Such indication of the Government's views has had a sobering effect, and there is general realization that the end is still far off.

2. Among informed Japanese, both official and private, emphasis is being placed on the fact that since classic times Hsuchow, by reason of its strategic position, has been the goal of those who sought to conquer China, and that its occupation by Japanese forces will have profound immediate effects, both strategic and psychological, on the Chinese. They admit, however, that the secondary effects are as likely to be the passing of control from Chiang Kai Shek to the Communist element, with intensified Chinese resistance and increased possibility of Soviet involvement, as the development of Chinese internal dissension.

3. Belief that the drive on Hankow will occur (see my 282, April 28, 7 p. m.) is becoming more pronounced.

Repeated to Shanghai for Hankow.

GREW

793.94/12855⅜

The British Permanent Under Secretary of State for Foreign Affairs (Cadogan) to the Adviser on Political Relations (Hornbeck)

[LONDON,] 23 May, 1938.

MY DEAR HORNBECK: I must thank you for your letter and enclosure of April 13th, and for the care with which you and your colleagues have considered and replied to the points contained in our statement.

As you say, the two documents were written from different stand-points, which accounts largely for such differences of opinion as they contain.

Ours contemplated the protection of our interests in the Far East and the restoration of peace by some form of armed intervention, while you have considered the problem in an attitude of greater detachment. I can only hope your expectations may be justified and that Japan will in course of time be brought to see the error of her ways by reason only of the moral indignation of other nations and her own economic difficulties.

I note with interest the statement that certain of your officers are examining the possibility of commercial reprisals in connection with the disregard of your interests and representations by the parties to the present hostilities. Hitherto our consideration of this question has been with a view to cooperation with other Powers in applying economic sanctions against Japan with the object of forcing her to cease hostilities. Like you, however, we are now turning our attention to the possibility of economic retaliation against the many insults and injuries to which our nationals and interests are being subjected and for which we have failed so far to obtain any reasonable satisfaction.

As soon as we have come to any definite conclusions on the subject we shall be glad to inform you of them. Needless to say, we should be extremely interested to learn on what lines you have been working and what conclusions seem to be indicated by your enquiry so far; and we shall be happy to exchange information on Japan's economic position if that would be considered helpful.

Yours sincerely,
ALEXANDER CADOGAN

893.00/14242

The Ambassador in China (Johnson) to the Secretary of State

No. 37
HANKOW, May 23, 1938.
[Received July 5.]

SIR: I have the honor to submit the following, which is intended somewhat briefly to review events in China since the beginning of 1937.

The year opened with a domestic political situation upset by the kidnapping of Chiang Kai-shek during the closing days of 1936. There was a definite impression that the Generalissimo's release from his captors, who comprised a group made up of Chinese communists, officers of the northeastern army under Chang Hsueh-liang, and officers of the Shensi provincial forces under Yang Hu-cheng, had been effected as the result of an understanding between the Generalissimo and those forces calling for a more active policy of opposition to Japanese encroachments on China.

Up to this time China's policy vis-à-vis Japan had been one of conciliation tempered by passive resistance. The Generalissimo and those who immediately surrounded him, feverishly working on plans of national reconstruction and dominated by business interests in Shanghai, feared a policy of active opposition to the Japanese lest it bring war, for which they felt the country was unprepared and which would bring reconstruction plans to a halt. The Government was in no position to make a formal settlement of outstanding issues with Japan, however, because it was too weak to accept a settlement along the very onerous lines laid down by the Japanese Government— amounting almost to complete capitulation—and to lead the rest of the country into accepting such a settlement. Its policy was one of weakness and depended for its success upon domestic developments in Japan: there was always the hope that in Japan the advocates of a strong policy in China would lose, in the conflict which it was known was going on between them and those who advocated a more liberal China policy.

Since Japanese occupation of Manchuria in 1931 and the advance of the Japanese southward into eastern Hopei, there had arisen among the Chinese a longing for a cessation of the domestic strife which had racked the country since the Revolution of 1911. People high and low realized that domestic disunity made China an easy prey for the kind of aggression which Japan seemed prepared to wage. The kidnapping of the Generalissimo at Sian in December, 1936, did more than anything else to crystallize public attention upon this main weakness in China's domestic politics, and centered all eyes upon the Generalissimo as a symbol of Chinese unity,—as opposed to Chang Hsueh-liang, the Young Marshal, who became overnight the symbol of that disunity which the people hated and were ashamed of. It was not so much the popularity which the Generalissimo as an individual may have enjoyed that brought the country as a whole suddenly to his support, but the feeling that the forces in favor of unity had won a victory. The people began to feel that the Generalissimo and those who stood with him at the head of Government had done more for Chinese unity in the past ten years than any other group which had come forward to leadership.

But this victory for unity had not been achieved without a price. The price paid was the terms which apparently were made at Sian before the Generalissimo was freed. It was believed then—and I know no reason to change that opinion now—that, as the result of conferences which the Generalissimo had with communist leaders at Sian, he agreed that there would be no further active hostilities against the communists, who would be allowed to remain in peace where they then were in northern China; that the communist forces would be given financial assistance by the Central Government; and that by gradual stages officials sympathetic to the communists would be introduced into the Central Government. More important and more fateful for the Government's course of action, though, was the understanding that the Government's policy vis-à-vis Japan would stiffen. A stiffening of the Government's policy vis-à-vis Japan was acceptable not only to the communist groups concentrated in northern Shensi, but also to the Kwangsi group led by Li Tsung-jen and Pai Chung-hsi. Put in another way, the settlement at Sian was understood to mean a shift in policy away from conciliation of Japan to conciliation of Russia, although there is no evidence to indicate that Soviet Russia at that time had anything to do with the settlement. The shift was due to fear of Japan rather than love of Russia.

The Chinese people and their leaders were not interested then, nor are they interested now, in seeking the alliance of any foreign country. There are plenty of Chinese, prominent political leaders among them, whose training was received in Japan and whose tendency was in the direction of closer and friendly relations with the Japanese, a people whose culture and civilization they understood and were in sympathy with. But they feared Japan. They feared the loss of independence which closer relations with Japan threaten, not only because of Japan's actions in Manchuria and North China, but because such advances as Japan had made indicated a Japanese ambition completely to dominate China politically and economically. To this the Chinese were opposed, and if compromise with the so-called communist group in China meant a drift in the direction of Russia, the Chinese preferred that course with its uncertainties to what they considered to be a certain future with the Japanese. Thus it was that the Sian incident which occurred at the end of 1936 left the Chinese Government and its leadership definitely pledged to a policy of resistance by force to further Japanese encroachment.

[Here follows review of foreign and domestic developments since early 1937.]

In so far as this Embassy has been able to observe, responsible leaders of the Chinese National Government had, by July, 1937, reached the determination that, at the next indication of Japanese encroachment upon China, China would have to throw its entire strength into resistance. They were forced to this decision by two considerations: (1) a review of Sino-Japanese relations during the past thirty odd years revealed a never-ending series of Japanese encroachments upon China's sovereignty and territorial integrity, which the Chinese leaders believed must lead ultimately to the subjecting of China to a domination by Japan not unlike that which Great Britain exercises in India; and (2) the commitments which the National Government had been forced to make to the communists and other dissatisfied groups as a result of the Sian incident. These commitments, although they were wrested from the Central Government by a small group of dissatisfied leaders, carried the popular support of the nation; and political and intellectual leaders who have guided the destinies of the Chinese people on the road toward national, political, economic and intellectual unity during recent years realized that they could not survive if they permitted the continuation of the gradual process of Japanese aggression without resistance.

From this determination it logically followed that, with the outbreak of hostilities in North China between the Japanese forces and the troops of General Sung Che-yuan—who were reported as being none too determined and not to be counted upon, but who at the same time stood between the popularly-termed Central Government forces and the Japanese—the Chinese should, if possible, do what they could to shape the course of events so as to extend as much as possible the Japanese lines and at the same time make it possible for China's best troops to grapple with the Japanese forces at a point most advantageous to the Chinese. Therefore, the Chinese were prepared, willing and anxious to see the hostilities extended even to the Shanghai area where foreign interests were concentrated and where China's cause might be expected to receive the widest publicity in the West. The Chinese were naturally not unmindful of the effect this would have upon Western interests which would be affected.

Whatever the situation might have been before hostilities began as regards the ability of Chinese leadership to unite the common people of the country in a war of armed resistance to Japanese invasion, the methods used by the Japanese military forces since the beginning of hostilities certainly have resulted in bringing home to the common people of China the realities of what the hostilities mean. The result is that a spirit of resistance has steadily spread throughout the country, uniting the people to their political, military and intellectual leaders as they have never been united before. The country people, in a resistance born of despair, are arming themselves everywhere. It becomes increasingly doubtful whether Japan can by mere force of arms conquer the country except by completely ruining it. From Suiyuan in the North to Hangchow in the South, armed bands of Chinese peasants are attacking Japanese wherever they find them. It is, I think, a fair assumption that when hostilities commenced the Japanese military leaders expected that with the capture of Nanking they would be able to obtain from a defeated Chinese Government a dictated peace which would be along the lines of Hirota's three points. The Japanese Army lost the war when they took Nanking and failed to obtain such a peace, and when they allowed their soldiers to wage pitiless war upon the civilian population of the country between Shanghai and Nanking, and in the city of Nanking.

This result left the Japanese to face two alternatives: they could either consolidate their positions already achieved and bide their time, or proceed to the conquest of China. It would appear that Japan chose the latter alternative. Indeed, it would have been difficult for them to do otherwise, for an armed China would have remained as a constant threat to the position which they had achieved. An Imperial Conference was held in Tokyo, and it was solemnly announced that the Japanese Government would no longer recognize the Government headed by Chiang Kai-shek. The Japanese Ambassador was called home, and the Chinese Ambassador to Japan was withdrawn.

ATTEMPTS AT CONCILIATION WITH JAPAN

Throughout all of these difficulties between China and Japan there has existed in China a peace party interested in reaching some peaceful settlement with Japan. The idea of Sino-Japanese cooperation, economic or otherwise, has a certain appeal to Chinese. There is a large group of Chinese who were trained in Japan and who have friends there. This is especially true in army circles. General Chiang Kai-shek who got his early education in Japan has always been considered as one of those; while Chang Chun, who was Minister for Foreign Affairs for a time and who had been a fellow student with the Generalissimo in Japan, was also considered as one of those who were inclined to be conciliatory toward Japan. Wang Ching-wei was another, and, as political heir to Sun Yat-sen, he wielded an influence in politics which should have been available to the Japanese. Dr. H. H. Kung and the War Minister General Ho Ying-chin were also numbered among this group. All of these were men of influence in the Government, and it is believed that if the Japanese had chosen to play their cards differently it should have been possible to have utilized the cooperation of these men to a better advantage.

Chiang Kai-shek has at all times been deeply conscious of the weakness and lack of unity in China. His public utterances at all times indicated a desire to meet the Japanese half way; the sincerity of these public utterances was borne out by statements which he made in private. But the conditions under which the Japanese publicly and privately announced their readiness to cooperate with the Chinese were such that none of these Chinese leaders, no matter how influential they might have been in Chinese circles, could have accepted them or hoped to induce their own people to accept them.

The Chinese were never able to obtain a clarification of Hirota's three points, which may be set down roughly as follows:

1) Alienation of China from foreign powers other than Japan.
2) Sino-Japanese economic cooperation.
3) Suppression of anti-Japanese activities.

It was generally believed that under these terms the Japanese expected a Japanese Inspector General of Customs with Japanese appointees to dominate the Customs at the several ports; a Sino-Japanese military alliance directed against Russia; Japanese rights to station troops at interior points. The Chinese had always contended that communism is a domestic matter; and they wanted to live at peace with both Russia and Japan, their nearest neighbors. Sino-Japanese cooperation was believed to include an economic bloc, consisting of Japan, "Manchukuo" and the Chinese republic; and a revision of the tariff to permit exchange of products of Japanese industry against Chinese raw materials,—a tariff which in Chinese eyes would have resulted in the complete destruction of nascent Chinese industry which was beginning to parallel Japanese industry. By suppression of anti-Japanese activities the Chinese understood the Japanese to mean the complete revision of Chinese text books of history and the use of Japanese teachers in the schools, with the adoption of an educational policy that would look to a complete denationalization of the Chinese. Thus interpreted—and there was no reason for a different interpretation—no Chinese leader could hope to work out any scheme of cooperation with Japan for which they could win the support of the people of the country.

The Japanese Government apparently expected to dictate peace along these lines with the fall of Nanking. There is no reason why they should have been surprised at their failure, for it has been clear enough to those who have continued among the Chinese that such a peace would be impossible as long as the Chinese Government and its people could resist.

Communism

There has been a good deal said about the existence of communism in China. There has been much said about the Chinese drift in the direction of Soviet Russia. Chinese leadership was no more interested in entering into an alliance with Soviet Russia, with all that that might imply, than it was interested in entering into an alliance with Japan. Soviet Russia and Japan are China's nearest neighbors. Soviet Russia has been instrumental in depriving China of Outer Mongolia, and is at the present time strongly entrenched in Sinkiang. Chinese leadership had its fill of Soviet interference in Chinese politics in 1926, and does not wish to repeat that experience. China has fought communism on its own soil for ten years.

Chinese communism was a communism which grew out of agrarian discontent. It was essentially an agrarian movement, and in no sense an industrial proletarian movement such as that which took over the cities and established communism in Russia. This agrarian movement in China used the slogans and the catch phrases, and some of the philosophy of Marxian socialism borrowed from Soviet Russian advisers, but it never achieved any position of importance in Government or in the industrial centers. There existed plenty of domestic reason for a spirit of revolt in the rural communities in the provinces of Kiangsi, Hunan, Honan and Hupeh, where there was much discontent among the predominant tenant farmer class and where agriculture was bankrupt.

In 1923 and 1924, when Sun Yat-sen was organizing the Kuomintang with Russian assistance along the totalitarian lines of the communist party in Russia, he permitted Chinese communists to become members of the Kuomintang. These were days of active intervention in Chinese domestic affairs by agents of Soviet Russia who were being used as advisers. But a break came in 1927 between the communist and the nationalist elements in the Kuomintang. Perhaps, to use a popular conception, one might refer to it as a break between the communist and fascist elements in the Kuomintang.

After the break and the departure of the Russian advisers, the communist element in China took to the mountains of Kiangsi and there began a conflict which ended only in the winter of 1936, when the remnants of the determined bands of rural revolutionaries, still burning with the fires of Marxian socialism, were finally permitted by the Government to settle down in peace in the arid and inhospitable regions of northern Shensi. Their leaders who had brought them through the difficulties of the ten years' war were still with them. Recent visitors to that area tell of meeting men who joined the movement as children and have followed it through all its long struggle, and who still burn with enthusiasm for the cause. It is the only element in China indicating that the Revolution of 1911 has touched and moved the peasant population.

By January, 1937, Soviet Russia was solidly installed in Sinkiang, with advisers employed in the Government at Urumchi. That some intercourse was possible between Soviet Russia and the Chinese communists in northern Shensi there can be no doubt; but that this intercourse went far is doubtful. By January, 1937, Soviet Russia was in the midst of a domestic political purge which indicated the existence of a domestic struggle, with a drift toward nationalism and isolationism.

By August, 1937, an arrangement had been entered into between the Central Government and Chinese communist leaders which brought the communists into Shansi and allied them definitely with the Central Government in the struggle of resistance against Japanese invasion. The function of these communist forces has been to pursue against Japanese invaders the same guerrilla tactics which they had used so successfully in resisting Chinese Government forces during ten years of warfare, and to train the country people of Shansi and Hopei for guerrilla warfare behind the Japanese lines. There is reason to believe that the Kwangsi leader, Pai Chung-hsi, participated in bringing about this arrangement.

It is true that the Soviet Ambassador signed with the Chinese Government, after the beginning of the Sino-Japanese conflict, a non-aggression treaty. It is true also that the Chinese have been able to obtain military equipment from Soviet Russia, and Soviet Russian volunteer aviators, but it is believed that all of this equipment and service is being paid for. The former Soviet Ambassador complained to me of the difficulty which he had had in persuading the Chinese to sign a non-aggression pact, and further, of his failure to negotiate a commercial treaty. The Soviet Ambassador was recalled to Russia with his Military Attaché at the end of September, and was replaced by a new Ambassador who is only thirty-eight years of age, whose entire adult life has been spent in Russia or in Turkestan, and who evidently definitely belongs to the group of young Russians whose experience has been Russia, who are followers and supporters of Stalin and the group of Bolshevist leaders whose services as revolutionaries were rendered entirely within the Government and who never lived abroad as exiles.

The path of Soviet Russia has been a wary one. The Chinese have leaned over backwards trying to avoid an arrangement which might lend color to Japanese accusations of an alliance. One may say the same of the conduct of Soviet Russia throughout these hostilities,—although it is apparent that Soviet Russia has been guided in its relations with China by a hope that the Chinese would continue resistance to Japan to the point where Japan would be exhausted, believing that a Japan exhausted and occupied in China would not be a menace to Soviet Russia.

As this is being written, ten months after the first shot was fired at Lukouchiao, the Japanese, at an enormous expenditure of blood and treasure, are battling determined Chinese troops for the possession of Hsuchow. Japan has withdrawn recognition from Nationalist China, although diplomatic relations have not been broken off and no war has been declared. It is expected shortly that Japan will extend *de jure* recognition to the puppet régime which is being established in Peiping and Nanking under the protection of Japanese military force. This régime is helpless except in areas immediately occupied by Japanese troops who hold a number of cities and patrol constantly the connecting lines of communication. All of the interior area is controlled by Chinese forces who carry on guerrilla tactics against the Japanese and the forces of the Japanese-fostered régime. This chaos will spread, the farther Japanese forces penetrate into the country. Japan will make a treaty along the lines of Hirota's three points with the régime which it has fostered at such expense. Japanese advisers will be appointed to aid in the processes of government,—civil, judicial and military. A tariff bloc will be established with tariffs favoring Japanese goods. Extraterritoriality will be abolished as was done in Manchuria. But the time is yet distant when Japan will have succeeded in establishing peace throughout China. The struggle will go bitterly and stubbornly on, and it is doubtful whether Japan, single-handed, can muster enough men or money to complete the task. The East is apparently doomed to a period of warfare and turmoil which will last for years.

Respectfully yours, NELSON TRUSLER JOHNSON

893.01 Provisional/119 : Telegram

The Secretary of State to the Consul General at Shanghai (Lockhart)

WASHINGTON, May 24, 1938—4 p. m.

337. Your 655, May 13, 4 p. m., paragraph 2, Appointment by "Reformed Government" of Judges of the First Special District Court.

1. The Chinese Ambassador called at the Department on May 19 and stated that the Chinese Government had knowledge of an intention on the part of the Japanese Government to replace the members of the judiciary in Shanghai with new appointees to be appointed by the Japanese sponsored authorities at Nanking. The Ambassador expressed the very earnest hope that the Department would instruct its Consular representative at Shanghai to refuse to recognize any new judges who might be appointed by Japan. The Chinese Ambassador was informed that the question raised by him would receive immediate consideration by the Department.

2. Please refer to Shanghai's despatch No. 1283, March 16, 1938,[44] entitled "Chinese Courts at Shanghai", particularly comment on page 7 thereof, and telegraph what action, if any, has been taken by the Consular Body and the Municipal Council to deal with the question under reference.

HULL

---

[44] Not printed.

893.20/671 : Telegram

The Ambassador in China (Johnson) to the Secretary of State

HANKOW, May 26, 1938—11 a. m.
[Received May 26—7 : 50 a. m.]

265. Department's 157, May 25, 3 p. m.[45] Rumors regarding possible recall of the German advisers have been current in Hankow for some time and finally culminated in the reported reason for the visit of the German Ambassador [46] to Hong Kong covered by my 244, May 10, 4 p. m. [47] The German Ambassador has returned to Hankow and yesterday gave to the press a statement to the effect that the German Government had expressed a desire to the Chinese Government that the advisers should be allowed to cancel their contracts with the Chinese Government and return to Germany. German Ambassador is credited with having stated that this request was motivated by the consideration of neutrality. I have not asked German Ambassador for any explanation, but I believe move at this late date is result of pressure from Japan.

What action advisers will take remains to be seen. It is reported that General Von Falkenhausen, chief adviser, may seek to remain as guest of Generalissimo. I understand that German Ambassador opposed recall. Departure of advisers will have a depressing effect upon Chinese whom they have served well and loyally. I understand that Germany has also put a stop to sale of munitions. This may have greater effect than departure of advisers as I understand Japanese forces are evidently now making a determined effort to obtain control of Lunghai Railway and appear to be having considerable success. Chinese forces in retreat will break up into small guerrilla bands. Loss of Hankow seems only a question of time. Perhaps these developments involving failure of Chinese armies have helped to bring German Government to this action.

JOHNSON

793.94/13089 : Telegram

The First Secretary of Embassy in China (Salisbury) to the Secretary of State

PEIPING, May 26, 1938—1 p. m.
[Received May 26—6 a. m.]

323. 1. The Counselor of the local German Embassy who has many years of service in China has just returned from 4 weeks in Chahar

---

[45] Similar to telegram No. 77, May 26, 7 p. m., to the Ambassador in Germany, p. 183.
[46] Oskar Trautmann.
[47] Not printed.

and Suiyuan where he traveled as far as Outer Mongolia border. He has given the Embassy the information contained in the next paragraph.

2. The Japanese military hold no places off the Peiping–Suiyuan Railway. The Chinese and Mongol population along the railway is bitterly anti-Japanese. Chinese irregulars approach close to cities along the railway and frequently cause traffic to be suspended. They occupy such points as Changpei 25 miles north of Kalgan and Anpei northwest Paotou. The Japanese have given up all pretense of developing a puppet Mongol régime and direction of affairs along the railway is for the time being in the hands of Japanese military. Prince Teh no longer has significance. The Japanese are obtaining little raw material because Chinese and Mongols, having received inadequate compensation, now do not bring their produce to market.

3. Informant stated that the number of Japanese troops along the railway is small. However, reports current in Peiping indicate that some reenforcements have been sent to the area during the past few days, presumably some of those troops mentioned in the Embassy's 307, May 18, 6 p. m.[48]

Repeated to Embassy Hankow, by mail to Tokyo.

SALISBURY

893.20/667 : Telegram

The Secretary of State to the Ambassador in Germany (Wilson)

WASHINGTON, May 26, 1938—7 p. m.

77. In the past few days the American press has carried reports to the effect that the German Government has ordered the withdrawal of the German military mission from China and the stoppage of the shipment of German military supplies to China. The Department would welcome such information in regard to these reported developments as you may be able discreetly to obtain, together with your comment.

HULL

893.01 Provisional/123 : Telegram

The Consul General at Shanghai (Lockhart) to the Secretary of State

SHANGHAI, May 26, 1938—10 p. m.
[Received May 26—7 : 25 p. m.]

722. Your 337, May 24, 4 p. m.

1. At an informal meeting on May 17 attended only by the Senior Consul and the British, French and American Consuls General and

---

[48] Not printed.

the Chairman and Secretary General of the Shanghai Municipal Council, the question of the status of the First Special District Court was discussed as a preliminary to possible consideration later at a full meeting of the consular body, which body has not yet considered the question. Prior to meeting it had been rumored that the Japanese might attempt to seize the court on May 16 but no such attempt was made. As a precautionary measure, however, added police protection had been thrown around the court building on that day, augmented by a guard from the Seaforth Highlanders and a small detail from the Fourth Marines which afforded additional protection to one of the court buildings in the American sector. These measures were taken as a precaution against any possible attempt to use force to acquire possession of the court or against possible kidnapping or other incident. The day passed quietly and there was no threat of intrusion. It is possible that the above mentioned rumor may have been based on the fact that a small group Japanese judges, who were visiting in Shanghai at the time, desired to visit the court. This visit was made without incident or undue commotion.

2. On May 18 Jermyn Lynn, who has been appointed president of the First Special District Court by the new Reform Government at Nanking, visited the British Consul General apparently with a view to ascertaining the attitude of the British authorities toward his assuming office. The British Consul General promptly informed him that he was speaking purely in his private capacity and that the caller was being received in the same capacity. Lynn, who is an American returned student, is the person referred to in paragraph 2 of my 655, May 13, 4 p. m. Apparently his reputation is not good and there is reason to believe that he is an active participant in the effort to impair the position of the First Special District Court. He informed the British Consul General that he had been selected because of his knowledge both of Japanese and foreign "ideas" and that he had accepted the appointment because some one else might have been appointed who might not have been so reasonable in the matter of taking over the court. He asked for sympathetic consideration and cooperation and stated that he intended to make no changes in the staff; and [sic] if they were willing to remain and cooperate with him, and that, if they did not cooperate, he had a staff he could install. The British Consul General pointed out that the Special Court was not an ordinary Chinese court but a special organ devised as a result of an experience of many years to meet the peculiar needs of Shanghai and that it was inadvisable that any change should be made at this time inasmuch as the court was working satisfactorily. Lynn was asked what laws

it was proposed to enforce and he stated it would be the existing laws of the Chinese Government. He also stated that it was necessary for the Reform Government to have control of the courts just as it did of all other functions of the Government in this area. At the close of the interview Lynn stated that all rumors that the courts would be taken over by force were without foundation.

3. Lynn called on the Senior Consul, Mr. Aall,[49] on May 25 and the discussion which took place was along the lines of that between Lynn and the British Consul General on May 18. Lynn has made no effort to see me on the subject. If he does approach me I shall receive him only in my private capacity and will let him know that he is being received in the same manner.

4. At the conference on May 17, Mr. Fessenden [50] stated that he could assure the consular representatives present that he would know at least 48 hours in advance of any serious effort to take possession of the court.

5. I believe that the views set forth on page 7 of Shanghai despatch No. 1283, March 16, 1938,[51] are substantially correct and that the despatch in its entirety presents a clear picture of the court situation as it exists now, with the exception that a president of the court has since been appointed by the Reform Government and that we are now much nearer to a crisis in the court question, as the movement to take over the court has gained some momentum since the appointment of Lynn. I personally doubt if any attempt will be made to take over the court by force, but other means, among which may be found intimidation and political chicanery, to accomplish this end will probably be employed.

Code text by mail to Hankow, Peiping, and Tokyo.

LOCKHART

741.94/187

The Consul General at Shanghai (Lockhart) to the Secretary of State

No. 1454   SHANGHAI, May 26, 1938.
                                                [Received June 20.]

SIR: I have the honor to report that there has been a perceptible stiffening of the attitude of the British authorities in Shanghai vis-à-vis the Japanese during the past month in connection with various incidents which have arisen involving Japanese military or naval units and British subjects or interests.

---

[49] Norwegian Consul General at Shanghai.
[50] American, Secretary General of the Municipal Council.
[51] Not printed.

On April 26, the British merchant vessel S. S. *Tungwo* was boarded by the Japanese military and compelled to proceed to Tsungming Island, at the mouth of the Yangtze River. The vessel was held there for twenty-four hours, notwithstanding immediate and repeated protests made by the British consular authorities. The vessel was finally released following very strong representations to the Japanese authorities and the dispatch of H. M. S. *Cricket* to Tsungming Island with orders to stand by until the S. S. *Tungwo* was released.

On May 2, the British merchant vessel S. S. *Kingyuan* was stopped while proceeding down river from Shanghai and boarded by a party of Japanese gendarmes who detained the vessel for two hours and thoroughly searched her before permitting her to proceed. The local British authorities are understood to have made strong representations concerning this further instance of the unauthorized boarding and search of a British merchant vessel and to have pointed out that such action was in complete disregard of British rights and the "Gentlemen's Agreement" reached between the British and Japanese Governments at the commencement of the Japanese blockade whereby it was agreed that Japanese naval vessels should be permitted to ascertain the right of a vessel to fly the British flag provided that no British naval vessel was in the vicinity at the time.

On May 13, Mr. E. S. Wilkinson, a well known British resident and local naturalist who was out walking in the early morning in the Hungjao district and observing bird life, was not only arrested by Japanese soldiers but was also assaulted and stabbed in the back. He was held for twelve hours by the Japanese military authorities and all attempts to see him and effect his release, including an attempt made in person by General Telfer Smollett, Commandant of the British Defense Forces, were ineffectual. British consular and diplomatic authorities made repeated representations throughout the day and eventually brought about his release. The local British authorities, including the British Ambassador who had just returned to Shanghai, took a serious view of this incident in which a British subject was without apparent reason or provocation set upon and stabbed by Japanese soldiers and held incommunicado for twelve hours. A strong formal protest was lodged with the Japanese authorities here by the British Consul General and the British Ambassador is understood to have made use of strong and forthright language in writing informally to Mr. Tani, the senior Japanese diplomatic officer in China. Strong representations were understood to have been made also in Tokyo by the British Ambassador. The British are understood to have demanded a formal apology, compensation for the injuries sustained by Mr. Wilkinson and specific information regarding the disciplinary action taken against the soldiers responsible for the assault.

In discussing these cases with the British consular authorities in Shanghai the definite impression has been gained that both the oral and written representations concerning these incidents have been couched in much stronger language than has been the case heretofore and that in general the attitude of the British authorities has stiffened.

Another instance of the stronger policy apparently being followed by the British authorities in local affairs is to be found in the action of the British military authorities in suddenly commencing to patrol Nanking Road and the Louza district of the central area. The first occasion on which British military patrols appeared was May 1 when a bomb exploded on Nanking Road just after a Japanese naval truck had passed. About an hour later Japanese soldiers and gendarmes commenced patrolling Nanking Road in considerable force. British troops were thereupon also dispatched to the scene of the incident and remained on patrol "to protect the Japanese patrols" it was explained by British military headquarters, until the Japanese troops and gendarmes had been withdrawn. Since then British troops have regularly patrolled Nanking Road and the Louza district. In this connection it is of interest to note that this sector was taken over from the Shanghai Volunteer Corps by the British Defense Forces following the demobilization of the former last year and that theoretically the latter are responsible for the defense of this area and to some extent responsible also for the maintenance of peace and good order. However, heretofore the British have made no effort to patrol this area and have in fact studiously avoided assuming any responsibility for this area notwithstanding the fact that a considerable number of incidents occurred therein in which the Japanese military acted with little regard for the rights of the International Settlement or the peace and security of its residents.

It is felt, therefore, that the dispatch of British patrols into this area since the first of May is of considerable significance and is a further indication that the British authorities here propose to show a firmer attitude in dealing with the Japanese authorities concerning matters affecting British interests in the Shanghai area. Some observers connect this firming of the British attitude with the conclusion of the accord between the British and Italian Governments on April sixteenth.[52]

Respectfully yours,

FRANK P. LOCKHART

---

[52] See vol. I, pp. 133 ff.

793.94/13495

The Consul General at Shanghai (Lockhart) to the Secretary of State

No. 1493   SHANGHAI, May 27, 1938.
                                                [Received July 19.]

SIR: I have the honor to transmit herewith, as of probable interest to the Department, copies of an exchange of correspondence [53] between the Commanding Officer of the United States Fourth Marines [54] and the Japanese military and naval authorities concerning the entry of armed Japanese units into the American defense sector and the passage of Japanese military and naval trucks through that sector.

It will be noted that definite understandings were reached both with the Japanese naval and military authorities on these matters. The agreement with the Headquarters of the Japanese Naval Landing Party is set forth in the memorandum dated March 17 attached to Admiral Yarnell's letter to Mr. Gauss dated March 18. It indicates clearly that when the American naval authorities decided to permit the billeting of a small number of naval units in Japanese mills located within the American sector, it was agreed by the Headquarters of the Japanese Naval Landing Party that no patrols should operate outside of these mills and that Japanese liaison and ration trucks were to move to and from these mills to Chapei only via the Ichang Road Bridge over Soochow Creek. By reference to the memorandum mentioned it will be noted that this understanding was not scrupulously observed, inasmuch as on several occasions armed Japanese naval units in considerable numbers passed through the American sector without previous notification and other than by the route agreed upon. However, the situation with respect to Japanese naval traffic has greatly improved.

The American Marine authorities experienced greater difficulties with the Japanese military. Japanese military traffic through the American sector became so heavy that Colonel Price protested repeatedly to Japanese Military Headquarters and eventually an understanding was reached regarding these matters and is set forth in Colonel Price's letters of March 22 and 24. The agreement of the Japanese Military Headquarters to Colonel Price's stipulations regarding the passage of Japanese army traffic through the American defense sector appears in Colonel Takahashi's letter of March 26. It will be noted that this agreement specifies the type of Japanese military vehicles permitted passage and refers to the arms which may be carried by the personnel riding in such vehicles. With reference

---

[53] Not printed.
[54] Col. Charles F. B. Price.

to the number of supply trucks permitted each day it will be seen by reference to the letter from Japanese Military Headquarters dated March 26 and Colonel Price's letter of March 28, that the latter acceded to the request of the Japanese military and agreed that a total of twenty supply trucks, ten east bound and ten west bound, might daily pass through the American sector. Both parties, it will be noted, reserved the right to modify, amend or suspend this understanding.

The Japanese military authorities in agreeing to Colonel Price's stipulations had requested that American Marine sentries be removed as a gesture of friendliness and goodwill. Colonel Price intimated, however, that until the volume of traffic had been definitely restricted he could not comply with the request. A gradual improvement did take place between March 26 and April 2 and on the latter date Marine sentries were removed. Almost immediately armed and unarmed Japanese soldiers in considerable numbers appeared in the American sector, while the volume of traffic increased to two hundred and sixty trucks per day carrying all types of "supplies" and running over routes not included in the original understanding. Protests made by Colonel Price to Japanese Military Headquarters brought about some improvement but from the subsequent correspondence on these matters it will be seen that many violations occurred. Such violations still continue although there has been some improvement.

It is believed this correspondence is of interest inasmuch as it upholds the principle that the armed forces of one country may not move through the defense sector at Shanghai assigned to another country without prior notice and agreement and indicates, furthermore, that this principle is recognized by the Japanese military and naval authorities. In this connection it may be noted that the British military authorities were disinclined to cooperate with the American defense forces in these matters and made no effort to prevent Japanese military traffic through their sector. It is believed that this *laissez faire* policy was followed because of the strained relations existing between the British and Japanese here and because the British did not wish to aggravate an already delicate situation.

The other point of interest brought out in this correspondence is the fact that although a definite understanding was reached between the American Marine authorities and the Headquarters of the Japanese Expeditionary Forces at Shanghai regarding these matters, and repeated written and oral assurances were received to the effect that orders implementing this understanding had been issued and that every effort was being made to carry them out, violations varying in degree and number continuously occurred. It can only be inferred either that the responsible officers attached to Japanese Military Headquarters did not sincerely attempt to carry out the terms of the understanding or that the Japanese military are extraordinarily inefficient in the matter of disseminating and executing orders.

Respectfully yours,   FRANK P. LOCKHART

793.94/13120 : Telegram

The Ambassador in Japan (Grew) to the Secretary of State

TOKYO, May 31, 1938—10 p. m.
[Received May 31—11:16 a. m.]

343. Our 100, February 12, noon.[55] My British colleague has addressed a letter to me dated May 30, stating that his Government feels that if the Japanese Government acts upon its rumored intention to make public announcement of the occupation of certain Chinese islands it might be difficult for the Japanese to relinquish control of these islands on the conclusion of hostilities. Having been instructed to express his views, after consultation with our French colleague and myself, on the desirability of renewing representations to warn the Japanese authorities against such a step before they commit themselves so far that they cannot withdraw without loss of prestige, Craigie has expressed to me the feeling that in view of Hirota's attitude at their meeting on February 9 (see our telegram under reference) any further representations would have no useful results. Craigie is furthermore of the opinion that public announcement of the occupation of the Chinese islands would not, provided it does not mention annexation, make their relinquishment more difficult than it already is; and furthermore that if public announcement is made we can seize the opportunity to reserve all our rights.

I have replied briefly stating that my feeling coincides with his but that I have not consulted my Government and that this represents only my personal attitude.

Copies of Craigie's letter and of my reply go forward by pouch today.[56]

This Embassy knows of no intended Japanese announcement concerning occupation.

GREW

---

[55] *Ante,* p. 82.
[56] Not printed.

CHAPTER IV: JUNE 1–AUGUST 31, 1938

Severe Japanese bombing of Canton from air; closing of Chinese diplomatic establishment in Japan (June 10); instructions to Ambassador Grew in disapproval of Japanese acts in China (June 25); Anglo-French warning against Japanese seizure of Hainan Island (June 29); Ambassador Grew's interview with Japanese Foreign Minister Ugaki (July 5); discussion of responsibility for maintaining Chinese resistance (July 23); Chinese Foreign Minister's plea for good offices by United States and United Kingdom (July 27); consideration of denunciation of American commercial treaty with Japan (July 30); American standing offer of good offices to both China and Japan (August 3); attitude of British Government in regard to good offices (August 11, 18); Premier Kung's letter to President Roosevelt (August 30)

893.20/674 : Telegram (part air)

The Ambassador in Germany (Wilson) to the Secretary of State

BERLIN, June 2, 1938—11 a. m.
[Received June 3—6 : 55 a. m.]

286. Department's 77, May 26, 7 p. m.

1. The Chief of the Far Eastern Section of the Foreign Office in the course of a conversation stated that the German Ambassador at Hankow [57] had informed the various German ex-army officers who have been acting as military advisers to the Chinese Government that it was "out of line with Germany's neutral position" for them to continue their service.

Von Schmieden went on to say that the German Government had taken this step with considerable reluctance and had indeed deferred doing so until the present. It had been hoped that the conflict coming to a close would render such action unnecessary but that now that hostilities had assumed proportions of large scale warfare, the problem of neutrality became more definite. In answer to an inquiry he said that he assumed that the majority of the individuals involved would withdraw but that some might continue in the service. He admitted that the reason why some might continue was that they were presumably *persona non grata* to the present German Government. He said as respecting individuals that the matter was somewhat complicated as each was under a separate contract with the Chinese Government. He added that there were numerous German nationals in civil positions under the Chinese Government including ex-officers in the police services. He said that none of these were involved but only those whose duties were distinctly and unquestionably military.

In commenting on other matters, von Schmieden said that he had noted that the United States had obtained compensation for the *Panay* affair but that Berlin had been less successful in obtaining repatriations [*reparations?*] which they had claimed from Tokyo and that

---

[57] Oskar Trautmann.

cases were still pending. Respecting the recent bombing of Canton he said that he could not understand Japanese terrors which were serving to unite all China against them. He characterized the bombing of Canton as a cheap victory and said he believed it was to place before the Chinese people as an "answer" to the flight over Japanese territory by Chinese planes which had made a marked impression on the Japanese public. He commented on the cynicism of Tokyo in declaring that the bombing of Canton was for military purposes. Although the Japanese had apparently ultimately reached certain military objectives, the loss of civilian life could have been avoided by an advance notification.

2. The Chinese Ambassador confirmed the notifications for withdrawal to German ex-officers serving with the Chinese General Staff and said that on May 29 the German Embassy at Hankow had informed the Chinese Foreign Office that such notifications had been issued. The Ambassador had been so apprised by his Government and instructed to lodge a protest with the German Government against this action. He had made such a protest but as yet had received no reply.

3. It has been characteristically impossible to obtain any satisfactory information respecting any possible stoppage in the shipment of German military supplies to China.

WILSON

793.94/13168 : Telegram

The Consul General at Canton (Linnell) to the Secretary of State

CANTON, June 5, 1938—1 p. m.
[Received June 8—6 : 45 a. m.]

Japanese air raids on Canton June 4th were probably the most destructive of civilian life and property to date. Bombs were dropped in the most thickly populated and busiest part of the city near the Honam bridge approach, the junction of Winghorny Road and Munming Road and about the civic and Government center. Officially estimated 120 bombs dropped in city limits. Many buildings, including part of Kwangtung Provincial Bank, were destroyed. It is not possible to determine the number of civilians killed as many are buried in the ruins but the official estimate is more than 1000 killed and wounded. It is possible that the objectives were the Government center, the electric light plant, water plant and perhaps the highway bridge to Honam Island.

Sent to Peiping and Shanghai.

LINNELL

793.94/13169 : Telegram

The Consul General at Canton (Linnell) to the Secretary of State

CANTON, June 6, 1938—4 p. m.
[Received June 8—6 : 45 a. m.]

Japanese air raids on Canton proper continued June 5th and 6th resulting in further great loss of life, and injury to civilians and damage to property. French hospital on bund partly destroyed by two bombs on 6th. Several buildings and market demolished in rear electric light plant but latter not hit. Bomb landing on bund in front of French hospital and Y. M. C. A. killed many persons on bund and in sampans. Tung warehouses bombed both days, several primary and middle schools struck, and many pupils killed and injured.

Canton–Hankow station again bombed with slight damage to terminal buildings but none to railway.

Canton–Kowloon Railway attacked both days but damage negligible.

I would re-emphasize that whatever the objectives Japanese claim to be aiming at the only result of bombings during past week has been killing and wounding of civilians and destruction of private property.

The Chairman Canton Red Cross has written asking me to report that on May 28th after Japanese had bombed Saikui area the planes suddenly returned and machine gunned and bombed Red Cross workers and firemen who were attempting to succor those wounded in first raid. Many firemen and Red Cross workers were killed and wounded.

I have advised Baptist mission to leave Tungshan.

Registered Americans of white race in Canton area now number 117 residing as follows : Canton proper 19, Fongchuen 3, Honan 6, Lingnan 37, Pakhoktung 18, Tungshan 11, Shameen 23. In addition about 15 temporarily in hotels in Canton and Shameen.

LINNELL

893.01 Provisional/125 : Telegram

The Third Secretary of Embassy in China (Allison) to the Secretary of State

NANKING, June 6, 1938—4 p. m.
[Received June 6—1 : 40 p. m.]

111. Bos, Chinese Secretary of the Netherlands Legation on visit to Nanking, told me in strict confidence this morning that during a recent conversation in Shanghai with Tang Shao Yi,[58] he obtained the distinct impression that Tang would become the titular head of the

---

[58] Chinese Prime Minister in 1912.

Reformed Government of Central China if the Japanese authorities should display anything like a reasonable attitude. Tang determinately holding out for assurances with regard to the extent of Japanese control over Chinese industry in the occupied areas, as well as the manner in which political control is to be exercised. Seemingly Tang believes the Japanese are so anxious to obtain a man of his prestige and experience to take the lead in the new government that they will go far towards meeting his requirements.

Tang told Bos that he believed the Japanese intend to place the major emphasis on agrarian development with a view to improving the standard of living of the Chinese farmer so that he can purchase Japanese manufactured goods. Chinese raw materials will then be exploited by the Japanese for use in Japan or by Japanese companies in China.

As a result of his conversation, Bos believes that Tang's attitude is due to a combination of two main factors; (1) a sincere belief that the good which can be accomplished for the benefit of the millions of Chinese in the occupied areas will outweigh any possible sacrifice Tang will make, and (2) a hatred of the Kuomintang and its blue shirt terrorists who Tang states are responsible for the recent murders in Shanghai of two of his close friends.

Sent to Embassy [at] Hankow, repeated to Peiping and Shanghai. Shanghai please mail to Tokyo.

ALLISON

793.94/13163 : Telegram

The First Secretary of Embassy in China (Salisbury) to the Secretary of State

PEIPING, June 7, 1938—3 p. m.
[Received June 7—10 : 40 a. m.]

342. 1. The Japanese announce the occupation yesterday noon of Kaifeng which has been seriously menaced since the close of May when Yucheng, Kweiteh and Kihsien were taken in quick succession. Lanfeng was reportedly evacuated by Chinese forces prior to the fall of Kaifeng, thus removing a serious threat to the Doihara Division, and it appears now that the second phase of the Lunghai campaign is nearing a close and that a direct campaign for the capture of Hankow will ensue. This probability becomes more and more real if Japanese reports of a Chinese retreat from Chengchow, Honan, are true and if as also claimed by the Japanese a Japanese force from east of Kaifeng has cut down to the Pinghan Railway south of Chengchow.

2. The Japanese claim further to have occupied on June 6 Chengyangkuang, Anhwei, about 60 miles northwest of Hofei (Luchowfu).

While this does not bring the Japanese column operating in northern Anhwei actually much nearer to Hankow (some 200 miles distant) than it was at Hofei, this movement may be an important step in the advance on Hankow which appears to be taking form.

3. Repeated to Hankow, Nanking, Shanghai. By mail to Tokyo.

SALISBURY

793.94/13241

Statement Issued by the Chinese Ambassador (C. T. Wang) on June 8, 1938 [59]

The report carried in some of the newspapers alleging that there is a split between Generalissimo Chiang Kai-shek, Commander-in-chief of the Chinese army, and General Li Tsung-jen is entirely groundless. It must be fabricated by an interested party with the malicious intention to discredit to the world the unity of the Chinese people.

The plan calling for withdrawal from certain cities which are strategically difficult to defend is a part of the whole plan agreed upon by all the Chinese military leaders and dovetails perfectly with the pronounced policy of the Chinese Government to fight a protracted war and to meet the Japanese army only in the places the topography of which will not give great advantage to their mechanized equipment. It has been more than once proved in the history that the deep penetration of an invaded country does not necessarily give advantage to the invading army. The Japanese may soon find out that their deep penetration into the interior of China, coupled with their employment of inhuman methods of warfare by bombing ruthlessly the open towns, will find a Chinese people increasingly united and more determined than ever to resist them.

793.94/13219

The Chinese Embassy to the Department of State

In response to the inquiries from the foreign correspondents, Generalissimo Chiang Kai-shek issued today a statement reviewing the political and military situation. The following is a gist of the statement.

In the past eleven months the armed resistance has fortified our nation's determination to fight and simultaneously augmented our faith in the final triumph. In the first place, the whole nation is solidly united as never before. The evidence of unity can be seen everywhere. Even those who were formerly dissatisfied with the Kuomintang (National Party) are one and all supporting the National Gov-

---

[59] Copy transmitted to the Department by the Chinese Embassy on June 8.

ernment and taking part in the armed resistance. Secondly, China's military strength has been considerably increased since the outbreak of hostilities. The Chinese army's fighting strength is more than doubled; its armaments are considerably improved in quality and increased in quantity. China's resistance will last as long as the Japanese continue the campaign of aggression. Thirdly, the topographical advantages henceforth will be more with China than with Japan. The crux of the military situation is not found in the success or failure of defending a particular city or area. What is vital is the ability to pick advantageous battlefields where we could reduce the enemy's main strength. Our withdrawals are dictated by the necessity to avoid unnecessary sacrifices. At the same time we have been forcing the Japanese to give battle on the fields we have chosen. This tactics is essential to the success of prolonged resistance.

The Generalissimo then stressed upon the paramount necessity for the friendly nations to fulfill their treaty obligations by giving China positive assistance. That the Japanese fighting forces have bombed non-combatants, slaughtered prisoners of war, and even employed poison are well-known facts. The treaty obligations require that the friendly Powers oppose the aggression openly and in so doing they merely exercise their treaty rights. If these nations could resort to the application of sanctions, not only would the innocent Chinese people's suffering be lessened, but the security of future peace of mankind and human justice enhanced.

WASHINGTON, June 9, 1938.

701.9394/20 : Telegram

The Ambassador in Japan (Grew) to the Secretary of State

TOKYO, June 10, 1938—11 a. m.
[Received June 10—1:43 a. m.]

370. The Chinese Chargé d'Affaires informs me by note dated June 8 that in view of the facts that all Chinese Consulates in Japan have been closed since February 8, that since the end of April the Chinese Embassy has been subjected to restrictions inconsistent with its position and to obstructions disadvantageous to its functioning, and that in spite of various representations to the Japanese Government the latter has taken no effective measures of relief, the Embassy will be temporarily closed from June 11 in conformity with instructions from the Chinese Government, the entire personnel of the Embassy to leave Japan on that day.

Repeated to Shanghai for Hankow.

GREW

793.94/13183 : Telegram

The Consul General at Canton (Linnell) to the Secretary of State

CANTON, June 10, 1938—4 p. m.
[Received June 10—9 : 25 a. m.]

Department's June 9, 6 p. m.[60]   Official estimates by 4th Route Army Headquarters of civilian casualties caused by Japanese bombing Canton: May 28th over 1500, May 29th over 500, May 30th about 1300, May 31st 234, June 1st no damage, June 2nd nearly 100, June 3rd 102, June 4th about 2000, June 5th about 100, June 6th more than 2000, June 7th approximately 100, June 8th approximately 225, June 9th approximately 104, total casualties nearly 8,685.   It is still impossible to get exact figures of killed and wounded as bodies are still being removed from ruins.   The above figures are believed perhaps somewhat exaggerated but total probably nearly figures given.

Sent to Hankow, Shanghai, Tokyo.   LINNELL

793.94/13226 : Telegram

The First Secretary of Embassy in China (Salisbury) to the Secretary of State

PEIPING, June 15, 1938—3 p. m.
[Received June 15—12 : 15 p. m.]

365. The Japanese spokesman admits that the Yellow River flood which he states has now reached the Lunghai Railway has completely checked the Japanese advance on Chengchow, Honan.   He informed me that the spreading water would probably make necessary the abandonment by forces in the Kaifeng–Chengchow area of a southward push toward Hankow down the Pinghan Railway.   This would seem to indicate that attacks on that railway south of Chengchow will come from the east and that the direction of the main Japanese attack upon Hankow will be from the east (including attack up the Yangtze and along the north shore of that river).

Repeated to Hankow, Nanking, Shanghai.   By mail to Tokyo.
                                                        SALISBURY

793.94/13238 : Telegram

The Commander in Chief, United States Asiatic Fleet (Yarnell), to the Chief of Naval Operations (Leahy)[61]

[SHANGHAI,] June 16, 1938—4 : 12 p. m.
[Received June 16—12 : 30 p. m.]

0016. Japanese source states that unless Chinese initiate peace talks soon after fall Hankow Japs intend renew drive against armies at

---

[60] Not printed.
[61] Copy of telegram transmitted to the Department by the Navy Department.

once not repeating mistake of waiting allowing Chinese to recover as after fall Nanking.

701.6193/155 : Telegram

The Ambassador in China (Johnson) to the Secretary of State

HANKOW, June 18, 1938—11 a. m.
[Received June 18—6 a. m.]

302. Soviet Ambassador left secretly on the 16th for Moscow being sent as far as Urumchi in Generalissimo's private plane.

Chiang has informed German Ambassador that German advisers could not leave because they possess his military secrets.

For Shanghai. McHugh [63] requests above information be given to Overesch. [64]

Repeated to Peiping and Shanghai.

JOHNSON

793.94/13467

The Ambassador in Japan (Grew) to the Secretary of State

No. 3025   TOKYO, June 21, 1938.
[Received July 15.]

SIR: I have the honor to transmit herewith a newspaper article [65] commenting upon Foreign Minister Ugaki's meeting of June 17 with the foreign press correspondents. In answering questions the Minister made liberal use of a large sheaf of notes which had been prepared in anticipation by the press section of the Foreign Office, and most of the correspondents were annoyed by the consequent lack of spontaneity in the replies. What seems to be most noteworthy in Mr. Ugaki's statements on this occasion is his assertion that with sufficient change in the state of affairs in China the Japanese Government might come to a reconsideration of its decision not to deal with Chiang Kai-shek.

This assertion bears out statements made at somewhat greater length both by the Premier [66] and by the Foreign Minister in separate interviews with Mr. John Gunther on June 2, as recounted by him to a member of my staff on that date. Mr. Gunther, well known as a correspondent and as author of *Inside Europe*, was granted

---

[63] Capt. James M. McHugh, U. S. M. C., Assistant Naval Attaché in China.
[64] Commander Harvey E. Overesch, Naval Attaché in China.
[65] Not reprinted.
[66] **Prince Fumimaro Konoye.**

interviews with several outstanding individuals of the present cabinet, among which interviews that with Premier Konoe was particularly successful. What would be the next step, asked Mr. Gunther, after the decisive defeat of the Chiang Kai-shek regime which the Japanese say is their aim, when the Imperial conference of January 11 committed the country to a policy of no negotiating with Chiang Kai-shek? Prince Konoe's reply, according to Mr. Gunther, was that that decision was specifically necessary to counteract the effect of the Trautmann peace approach, which had proved itself a premature error; that the decision is not beyond the possibility of change; and that Japan, whose chief aim is peace, is ready to negotiate with Chiang Kai-shek whenever he shows a proper attitude.

Respectfully yours, JOSEPH C. GREW

894.00/797 : Telegram

The Ambassador in Japan (Grew) to the Secretary of State

TOKYO, June 22, 1938—noon.
[Received June 22—8 : 40 a. m.]

399. 1. Further intelligence and observations enable us reliably to extend as follows the estimate of the recent reconstruction of the Cabinet contained in our 333, May 26, midnight and 335, May 27, 6 p. m.[67]

2. The Prime Minister and certain other members of the Cabinet had long realized that if progress were to be made in bringing the China campaign to a successful conclusion and in consolidating Japan's position in China without serious friction with Great Britain and the United States, the control of all but purely military affairs must be taken out of the hands of the military and lodged in the civil part of the Government.

3. Hirota [68] fell because he was paradoxically too weak in opposing certain demands of the army while at the same time too intransigent in insisting that the Foreign Office which is unpopular with the army must control Japan's foreign relations concerning China. By way of compromise the authorities are now in process of setting up the so-called "China Organ" which is to consider political, economic and other non-military affairs relating to China.

4. Ugaki and Ikeda accepted office [69] only on condition that the control of political and economic affairs in connection with China should be taken out of the hands of the military. This coincided with the views of Prince Konoye and further explains the appointment of

[67] Vol. IV. pp. 599 and 601, respectively.
[68] Former Japanese Minister for Foreign Affairs.
[69] As Ministers of Foreign Affairs and of Finance, Commerce and Industry, respectively.

General Itagaki as Minister of War because he possesses the confidence of the younger officers in the army and at the same time believes that the army should stay out of politics and should attend exclusively to its duties as an efficient fighting machine.

5. Both Ugaki and Ikeda realize that the solution of Japan's problems in China will be difficult unless good relations are maintained with Great Britain and the United States. Ugaki therefore proposes to do all in his power to ensure the protection of the respective interests of those and other foreign countries at least to the extent of reducing friction to a minimum.

6. With regard to economic affairs the purpose of the setting up of the North China Development Company and the Central China Promotion Company is to take these matters also out of the hands of the military. It is intended that these companies shall function under the general direction of the "China Organ".

7. With reference to point 5 above we have recently seen indications of Ugaki's desire to remove causes of friction with the United States in connection with American interests in China. Having in mind the arbitrariness of the army and navy it is hardly to be expected that the Foreign Minister will be able to accomplish this desirable end rapidly or completely. Nevertheless while omitting no proper step ourselves and while continuing to make official representations as specific cases and developments arise, I have felt it desirable to avoid bringing early pressure to bear on the Minister while closely watching the working out of his efforts. I have therefore confined our recent representation to interviews with the Vice Minister and other officials of the Foreign Office with the idea of "saving ammunition" for an eventual frank discussion with Ugaki on the whole field of American interests in China along general lines.[70] I believe that this procedure will add weight to such an interview when it takes place. I see no good reason why such an interview should not take place in the near future and suggest, if the Department concurs, that an up-to-date outline of American desiderata be cabled me for use at an opportune moment. The Embassy is presumably in possession of all or most of the data which might be used for such an interview but I feel that an instruction from the Department would be helpful in indicating the specific issues which should be brought forward in such a general discussion and the relative emphasis to be placed upon them as reflecting the views of the American Government. This telegram is being repeated to Mr. Johnson who may desire to submit comments to the Department.

Repeated to Shanghai for Hankow.

GREW

[70] See also vol. IV, pp. 1 ff.

793.94/13292 : Telegram

The Ambassador in Japan (Grew) to the Secretary of State

Tokyo, June 22, 1938—9 p. m.
[Received June 22—12:10 p. m.]

401. 1. The *Nichi Nichi* states today that, in connection with criticism during a recent press interview by the Minister for Foreign Affairs of those countries supplying arms to China, Ugaki has under active consideration the possibility of a Japanese declaration of war against China. It is argued in the article that, although Ugaki has indicated that he is endeavoring to attain the desired end through diplomatic channels, it is unlikely that the countries concerned can be persuaded to refrain from exercising their right to supply arms to China unless Japan offers satisfactory *quid pro quo;* but that he could force these countries to weigh more carefully the advantages and disadvantages of this practice if war were declared. The army and navy further states that diplomatic officials in the field have been instructed to submit to Tokyo all data necessary for final decision on the matter.

2. As we have stated on several occasions, the question of a declaration of war will revolve around the effects on the military operations of imports of munitions by China. We believe that this aspect of the question has all around been kept under observation, and that, if China's imports of arms are now such as to be an important factor in the continuation by China of its resistance, declaration of war might well be under active consideration. However, it would be well to bear in mind that today's story appears in no other paper, which indicates at least that the Government is not actively interested in giving it publicity. It seems to us that the story may have some basis in fact, but that it has not been presented in accurate perspective.

3. The spokesman of the Foreign Office is reported as having characterized the *Nichi Nichi* story as groundless and false, adding that Japan could not declare war on China unless she discontinues adherence to various treaties concerned, including the Kellogg–Briand Peace Pact and the Nine Power Treaty "by which she is now bound".

4. We are, of course, endeavoring to obtain some authoritative information on the subject, which the Department will realize is no easy matter. The only suggestion which we have obtained directly from Japanese official sources thus far is that the *Nichi Nichi* story "should not be taken too seriously".

Repeated to Shanghai for Hankow.

GREW

893.20/679 : Telegram

The Ambassador in China (Johnson) to the Secretary of State

HANKOW, June 23, 1938—3 p. m.
[Received June 23—11:02 a. m.]

312. Chief of German advisers informed McHugh today that on June 22nd he had been called to the German Embassy along with Hsu Mo, Vice Minister for Foreign Affairs, and that in the presence of the Vice Minister German Ambassador had delivered to him an ultimatum to be answered within 24 hours. Ultimatum was that failure of advisers to sever connections with the Chinese Government and return to Germany at once would be regarded as high treason punishable by deprivation of citizenship and confiscation of personal property and possibly other penalties. German Government demanded that they abrogate their contracts if Chinese Government refused, promising favorable treatment and reemployment in Germany. This applied to all military advisers of whom none would be permitted to remain.

German advisers to the number of 20 expect to leave on international train on June 28th. McHugh has been informed that a farewell dinner was given to them by Dr. Kung [72] on June 22, indicating that Chinese would put no obstacles in the way of their departure. It is estimated that 5 of 11 German advisers classed as non-military will remain.

McHugh asks that this information be given to his Department.

JOHNSON

894.00/798 : Telegram

The Ambassador in China (Johnson) to the Secretary of State

HANKOW, June 25, 1938—9 a. m.
[Received 10:30 a. m.]

313. Tokyo's 399, June 22, noon. In my opinion the situation of American citizens and their interests in China will be much improved if the Japanese can be persuaded to adopt a more reasonable attitude towards civilians generally. Civilian enterprise and interests in the cities and noncombatants in the country areas appear to be specially marked for attention. This is particularly true of hospitals, schools and relief work in which American missionaries are prominently interested in Central China.

Shanghai please repeat to Tokyo.

JOHNSON

---

[72] President of the Chinese Executive Yuan (Premier).

894.00/797 : Telegram

The Secretary of State to the Ambassador in Japan (Grew)

WASHINGTON, June 25, 1938—4 p. m.

212. Your 399, June 22, noon.

1. The Department finds your estimate of Cabinet developments and attitude very helpful, approves the course which you have pursued, and favors the procedure which you have in contemplation.

2. Careful note has been made of your observations, especially those in regard to the conditions under which Ugaki and Ikeda accepted office. The Department notes with concern, however, that in the establishment of the "China Organ" and the setting up of the North China Development Company and the Central China Promotion Company, the Japanese are closely following the formula developed in Manchuria. In this connection attention is invited to pages 12, 13 and the last paragraph of page 16 of Harbin's despatch 569, October 22, 1937,[73] entitled "The Trend of Events in Manchuria since September 18, 1931". The "China Organ" appears to be patterned after the "Manchuria Affairs Board", and the account of the organization and purposes of the two special companies mentioned, as given in your despatch No. 2950, May 25, 1938,[73] indicates that these companies closely resemble the special companies in Manchuria which occupy a preferred status and which in practice operate to exclude non-Japanese enterprise from that area.

3. As general background for your proposed conversation with the Japanese Minister for Foreign Affairs the Department suggests that you re-read Department's telegram 187, September 2, 2 p. m., 1937;[74] my National Press Club address [75] (see Radio Bulletin 62, March 16, 1938); and my Nashville address [76] (see Radio Bulletin 128, June 2, 1938). As I indicated in these, public opinion in the United States deplores the fact and the circumstances of the present conflict in China and has become increasingly critical of Japan; this Government looks with disapproval upon the present manifestation of Japan's foreign policy and the methods which Japanese armed forces are employing in pursuit thereof; the widespread bombing of civilian populations in China has shocked both our people and the Government not only on grounds of humanity but also on grounds of the menace to American lives and property; and this Government is deeply desirous that the hostilities be concluded and peace be restored as soon as possible along lines consistent with the provisions of existing international

---

[73] Not printed.
[74] *Foreign Relations*, 1937, vol. III, p. 505.
[75] *Foreign Relations*, Japan, 1931–1941, vol. I, p. 452.
[76] Department of State, *Press Releases*, June 4, 1938, pp. 645, 646.

commitments and with principles of equity and justice in relation to all concerned, and with due regard for the establishment and maintenance of orderly processes in the relations of nations. The concern of this country is, as set forth in the documents cited, broad and fundamental. It transcends in importance specific desiderata which, however, have a proper place in the broad field of American interest in and concern regarding China.

4. Certain specific desiderata are outlined below:

(a) Maintenance of the personal rights of American citizens.[77] This calls for exercise of care by Japanese armed forces to avoid injury to American citizens through direct military activities; precaution by Japanese authorities against molestation and affront to American citizens by members of the Japanese armed forces; and assured enjoyment by American citizens of their right to visit and control their properties and goods and to resume their lawful occupations in Japanese-controlled areas wherein hostilities have ceased.

(b) Maintenance of equality of opportunity in Japanese-controlled areas as between Japanese and others [78] in conformity with the situation which existed prior to the occupation of those areas by Japanese armed forces. Effectuation of this desideratum calls for avoidance of such restrictions upon and obstacles to American enterprise and trade as would result from establishing of "special" companies with official support and preferred status, from granting of monopolies to officially-operated or controlled companies or others, and from establishing of exchange control with accompanying restrictions upon trade between China and the United States while at the same time permitting the free movement of goods and funds between China and Japan. In short, the restrictions upon American enterprise and trade resulting from the situation in Manchuria and from the relations between that area and Japan afford an illustration of what we desire not to have occur in other parts of China.

(c) Respect for American property rights. This desideratum includes the exercise of care by Japanese armed forces to avoid damaging American properties by direct military activities, especially through bombing by planes; restoration to American citizens of the full possession and unmolested use of their properties in Japanese-controlled areas wherein hostilities have ceased; and prompt compensation for damage and loss caused by Japanese military operations in China.

(d) Respect for legitimate American financial interests. This desideratum includes preservation of the administrative machinery of the Chinese Maritime Customs [79] and continued servicing of American-held obligations secured upon customs, salt and consolidated tax revenues.

(e) Abstention from interference with American treaty and prescriptive rights in China. This desideratum includes non-interference with American extraterritorial and other rights growing out of

[77] See also vol. IV, pp. 214 ff.
[78] See also ibid., pp. 1 ff.
[79] See also pp. 626 ff.

American-Chinese treaties; and abstention from interference with the organization and administrative functions of the International Settlement at Shanghai and with the organization and functions of the Chinese courts serving the International Settlement.

5. The foregoing is suggestive and the Department would wish you to exercise your discretion with regard to supplementing or modifying the suggestions outlined above. You may consider it advisable to mention illustrative examples such as the continued occupation by Japanese of the University of Shanghai property at Shanghai, the continued detention at Nanking of a large shipment of American wood oil, and the recent slapping by Japanese soldiers of an American citizen at Nanking and of one at Tsingtao. The Department believes it advisable that in your discussion with the Minister for Foreign Affairs you endeavor to prevent there arising an impression that this Government's concern relates only to concrete and tangible issues inherent in matters such as are mentioned among the various desiderata. It would seem desirable that you especially endeavor to cause the Minister for Foreign Affairs to appreciate and understand also the character of the interest and concern emphasized in paragraph 3 of this telegram.

6. You will, of course, use your own judgment as to the moment when it may be opportune to make the contemplated approach. The Department suggests, however, that if practicable it might be advisable for you to telegraph short advance notice of your intention to proceed, so that in the event of any development here which might make the moment inopportune, the Department could so indicate to you.

HULL

793.94/13335 : Telegram

The First Secretary of Embassy in China (Salisbury) to the Secretary of State

PEIPING, June 28, 1938—3 p. m.
[Received 7 : 42 p. m.]

392. Embassy's 382, June 20, 3 p. m.[80]

1. Japanese military plans appear to have been further altered because of (*a*) floods from the Yellow River and (*b*) flooding of the Yangtze near Taihu, 40 miles west of Anking. Following the abandoning of the attack on Chengchow preparatory to an advance down the Pinghan Railway toward Hankow, a part of the Japanese troops on the Lunghai front began moving eastward and then south to Nanking to be incorporated in the forces advancing up the Yangtze. The number of troops thus reorientated is unknown. Another part, num-

---

[80] Not printed.

ber also unknown, is now moving northward across the Yellow River, the general presumption being that a renewed attack in Shansi is foreshadowed and that an advance may be made on Sian.

2. Flood waters from the Yangtze near Taihu appear to have impelled the Japanese to direct their land advance along the southern rather than the northern bank of the river where the immediate objective is the Matang barrier and whence a drive will probably be attempted via Nanchang to Changsha and then north along Hankow–Canton Railway. Stiff Chinese resistance and some Chinese success in counter-attacks near Matang are reported and Chinese reports claim also continuing aerial success in bombing Japanese naval vessels below the Matang barrier and in bombing Wuhu and Anking air fields. The presaged land attack on Nanchang is reportedly being preceded by heavy aerial bombardments in which the Japanese claim success.

3. Repeated to Embassy at Hankow, Nanking, Consul at Shanghai to Tokyo.

SALISBURY

894.00/799 : Telegram

The Ambassador in Japan (Grew) to the Secretary of State

TOKYO, June 28, 1938—7 p. m.
[Received June 28—8:47 a. m.]

422. Department's 212, June 25, 4 p. m., paragraph 2. I learn on completely reliable authority that Ikeda is determined that the "China Organ" and the two companies mentioned shall not follow the Manchurian pattern by excluding non-Japanese enterprise from the occupied areas of North and Central China. He has stated categorically in privacy that the reconstruction of China without foreign cooperation would be impossible and that he will insist upon observance of the principle of the Open Door. It is for this very reason that the effort is being made to take these matters out of the hands of the army.

Likewise Kodama, who has been appointed to head the Central China Promotion Company, states privately but categorically that he shares Ikeda's views and that as his opinions are well known his selection would have been impossible if the Government had intended to institute a monopolistic system.

Naturally I am disinclined to accept such assurances at their face value but the wind appears at least to be blowing in the right direction. I shall discuss this subject with the Minister for Foreign Affairs.

Repeated to Shanghai for Hankow.

GREW

93.94/13328 : Telegram

The Ambassador in Japan (Grew) to the Secretary of State

TOKYO, June 28, 1938—8 p. m.
[Received June 28—9 : 45 a. m.]

423. 1. My British colleague [81] informs me that the French Ambassador in London recently told the British Foreign Office that if Japanese troops should occupy Hainan the French Government might find it necessary to take some step further than mere diplomatic representations and expressed the hope that the British Government would cooperate. When asked what sort of step his Government visualized, however, Corbin pleaded ignorance. No Anglo-French understanding on this issue appears therefore to have been reached.

2. Craigie yesterday took occasion to bring up with the Minister for Foreign Affairs the question of Hainan. Ugaki said that there is no present intention to occupy Hainan but that if in the course of the advance on Hankow or a later advance on Canton such occupation should become a strategic necessity it would take place. The Minister, however, said that such occupation would be temporary and repeated to Craigie the former categorical assurances of the Japanese Government that the territorial integrity of China will be respected both as to the mainland and the islands.

3. Craigie informs me that there can be no question but that great quantities of arms and ammunition are coming into China from French Indo-China by different routes, a considerable amount being smuggled by Chinese junks. He believes that most of this material is contraband and that a great amount of graft is involved in the process of importation. This is one of the chief problems with which the Japanese now have to cope.

Repeated to Shanghai for Hankow.

GREW

793.94119/429

Memorandum by Mr. Norman H. Davis of New York [82]

LONDON, June 28, 1938.

Mr. Yoshida, the Japanese Ambassador, who asked for an appointment to see me, came at ten o'clock this morning. He began by expressing regret that on account of my illness he had been unable to see me and have a talk with me in Paris on my return from the Brussels Conference last Fall.

---

[81] Sir Robert L. Craigie, British Ambassador in Japan.
[82] Memorandum transmitted to the Adviser on Political Relations, Hornbeck, by Mr. Davis in his covering letter of July 13 from Washington. Mr. Davis, who was the American delegate to the Brussels Conference of November 1937, was Chairman of the American Red Cross in 1938.

What he wanted to talk with me about then, he said, was to urge us and the British to persuade his and the Chinese governments to accept our mediation in the settlement of the Sino-Japanese conflict; and it seemed even more important to him now than it did then and, also, that he was satisfied that his government would be more receptive than ever to accept such mediation.

I explained to him that just now I was here on Red Cross work alone, and was not in a position to speak for our government on this subject, or to discuss any such proposed step. He said he knew I was here just on Red Cross but that he wanted to talk to me frankly, as he had always done, and he proceeded to insist that he knew now that his government would welcome mediation; that he had been talking to the British government and urging them to offer to intervene; that while the British had been willing to discuss it, they had not shown any enthusiasm and were constantly intimating that they would not take any step without the United States. He was therefore in hopes that as a result of his talk with me, he could send word to his government that the United States would be favorably inclined to make such a move.

I told him that I could give him no such word whatever and that, in fact, the last time such a matter was discussed, we had come to the conclusion that it would not be wise or practicable to inject ourselves to that extent in the situation, at least unless there were reasons to believe that Japan and China would welcome mediation and that it would be possible, as a result of mediation, to arrive at a constructive and mutually acceptable solution; that while I could only express my own personal views, it seemed to me that the issue between China and Japan was so fundamental that it was not susceptible of a compromise that would remove the issue.

I asked him if he thought the Japanese militarists had either concluded that they could not conquer China, or that they should abandon the determination to dominate China; or if the Chinese were getting in a state of mind where they would be willing, in fact, to accept Japanese control and abandon their own efforts to maintain their independence. He said the militarists were drawn into that conflict; that they had thought they could inflict enough punishment on China quickly to bring her to her senses, but that they had never contemplated getting in so deep as they had, and that while he was not sure just what their state of mind is now, he was confident that the Army was losing prestige in Japan and that through mediation by Great Britain and the United States, the people would support the government in any reasonable settlement; that while the Army had gained public support by conquering Manchuria, which had not been possible through diplomatic negotiations, the Army had overplayed its hand and public opinion was turning against them.

I asked him what kind of a settlement did he think possible. He thought that the recognition of Manchukoa and the creation of a buffer state in North China, as security to Manchukoa; and a cessation of anti-Japanese propaganda, and cooperation for the economic rehabilitation of China, with some kind of guarantee. I told him my personal reaction to that was doubt as to whether China would accept; a question as to whether a mediator would be willing to support such a program; and as to what he meant by "guarantee." He said his idea of a "guarantee" was one in which Great Britain and the United States and China all recognized the special position of Japan, and would enter into an agreement for joint efforts toward economic rehabilitation. He felt that when Japan had captured Hankow would be the psychological moment for offering mediation because China would probably then be more amenable to reason and also Japan; that while China had suffered greatly in a material way, Japan was suffering, mentally, and he was confident that the time would soon come when England and America could, if they would, successfully urge China and Japan to accept mediation. I asked him if he thought England would be willing to mediate alone and he said he did not think so.

In conclusion, I told him that I could in no way speak for the American government on this question but that, personally, I could not give him any encouragement, and the situation itself did not as yet look encouraging to me.

N[ORMAN] H. D[AVIS]

793.94/13354a : Telegram

The Secretary of State to the Consul General at Shanghai (*Lockhart*)

WASHINGTON, June 29, 1938—6 p. m.

410. Following for Tokyo:

"221, June 29, 6 p. m. According to the *New York Times* of June 28, Butler, Under Secretary for Foreign Affairs, made a statement in the House of Commons as follows:

'His Majesty's Government and the French Government, through their Ambassadors at Tokyo, have made clear to the Japanese forces and Government that they would regard any occupation of Hainan by the Japanese forces as calculated to give rise to undesirable complications.

Should any complications unfortunately arise, His Majesty's Government and the French Government would no doubt afford each other such support as appears warranted by the circumstances'."

HULL

793.94/13328 : Telegram

The Secretary of State to the Ambassador in Japan (Grew)

WASHINGTON, June 29, 1938—7 p. m.

222. Your 423, June 28, 8 p. m., first paragraph. Press despatches from London, under date June 27, indicate that the British and French have reached an understanding on the issue under reference. Quotation from the press is being sent in a separate telegram via Shanghai.[83]

HULL

793.94/13351 : Telegram

The Ambassador in France (Bullitt) to the Secretary of State

PARIS, July 1, 1938—9 a. m.
[Received July 1—7 : 50 a. m.]

1038. Sun Fo [84] who returned to Paris recently from Moscow said to me that his negotiations in Moscow had been most successful. The Soviet Government had promised to continue to supply China with arms and munitions on credit. He asserted that six Japanese divisions had lost all their heavy artillery and tanks as a result of the Yellow River inundations. He added that he believed that the Japanese offensive against Hankow would be held up for many months and reaffirmed the determination of the Chinese Government to continue to fight to the end.

BULLITT

793.94119/426 : Telegram

The First Secretary of Embassy in China (Salisbury) to the Secretary of State

PEIPING, July 1, 1938—5 p. m.
[Received July 2—7 a. m.]

407. Embassy's 377, June 20, 1 p. m.,[85] Wang Keh Min's [86] peace appeal.

1. Some kind of peace plans are now under consideration here, one being reportedly sponsored by Japanese in Peiping and possibly another by Wang Keh Min. The Japanese plan allegedly contemplates a division of China into five regimes: (a) the present Mongol border districts, (b) provisional government, (c) reformed government, (d) a national government regime, and (e) a southwest regime. No men-

---

[83] See *supra*.
[84] President of the Chinese Legislative Yuan.
[85] Not printed.
[86] Head of the Japanese-sponsored regime at Peiping.

tion of the withdrawal of Japanese forces is made. Further details are lacking.

2. The motives apparently are not [*sic*] (*a*) a genuine desire on the part of some local Japanese as well as Chinese to see the end of hostilities, (*b*) a hope of creating disunity in the National Government, and (*c*) a maneuvering for personal power. A number of reports that Generals Kita and Terauchi may go, in which case Wang's position would be weakened and political changes could be anticipated, indicate that the third motive may be important.

3. The proposal outlined above can scarcely be acceptable to the various elements composing the National Government although it may prohibit [*presage?*] the future course of events if hostilities and Japanese military successes continue.

4. The question of amalgamation of the Peiping and Nanking regimes seems to be indefinitely suspended. A new administrative plan is the proposed creation of a special military affairs organ to be in control of all such organs already existing in China.

Repeated to Embassies, Hankow, Nanking, Tokyo, Consulate General Shanghai.

SALISBURY

894.00/803 : Telegram

The Consul General at Shanghai (*Lockhart*) *to the Secretary of State*

SHANGHAI, July 5, 1938—noon.
[Received July 5—9 : 09 a. m.]

945. Following from Tokyo:

"July 4, 7 p. m. Department's 212, June 25, 4 p. m. In an interview of more than 2 hours with the Minister for Foreign Affairs this morning I covered the general field of American desiderata in connection with the Japanese hostilities in China as outlined by the Department.[87] My representations were forceful and emphatic both in matters of detail and principle. The Minister was given a perfectly clear picture of the viewpoint and attitude of the American Government and people. I left with the Minister a typewritten statement [88] of every point covered, not as a diplomatic document but as an informal aid to him in recording our conversation so that there can be no misunderstanding whatever as to what was said. Also an itemized list [89] of more than 250 specific cases of damage and other interference marked 'Partial list of incidents affecting American rights and interests as a result of activities of the Imperial Japanese forces in command since July, 1937 as known to the American Embassy Tokyo June 30, 1938'. Copies of these papers will go to the Department in the next pouch.

[87] See memorandum of July 4, *Foreign Relations*, Japan, 1931–1941, vol. I, p. 605.
[88] *Ibid.*, p. 611.
[89] Not printed.

Representations were made under the following headings:

(1) Preamble.
(2) Respect for American property rights.
(3) Maintenance of the personal rights of American citizens.
(4) Maintenance of equality of opportunity in Japanese controlled areas in China as between Japanese and others.
(5) Protection of legitimate American financial interests.
(6) Avoidance of interference with American treaty rights in China.
(7) Japanese-American relations.
(8) General principles.

The following individual cases were mentioned: [90]

(1) Thomson incident.
(2) Massie.
(3) Scovel incident.
(4) Occupation of University of Shanghai.
(5) Werner and Smith Company wood oil case.
(6) Embargo upon exportation of hides and skins in North China (Department's 329 [*229*], July 2, 7 p. m., via Peiping [91]).
(7) Statement by Japanese special representative in Shanghai regarding extraterritoriality.
(8) Salvaging of Standard Oil vessels on Yangtze without presence of representatives contrary to assurances (Department's 223, June 29, 8 p. m.[92]).

The Minister after listening to my complete representations said that he wished to express appreciation of the manner of my approach. He would take a further opportunity to discuss the points which I had raised. These points required most careful investigation, consideration and detailed examination. For the present he wished to make the following comments.

The Japanese Government is making whole-hearted efforts to settle the conflict and to secure peace in East Asia at the earliest possible moment. The Minister hopes that we understand that desire.

2. The Japanese Government is giving most careful thought to Japanese-American relations. There must be frank discussion and we must understand each other on a basis of mutual fairness and justice.

3. The Open Door in China will be maintained. We may rest assured that the Japanese Government will maintain full respect for the right of equal opportunity. In some cases there may be temporary difficulties during the period of hostilities not entirely satisfactory to the American Government. These are purely temporary.

4. Indiscriminate bombing is strictly prohibited by special instructions. In actuality a few Japanese aviators have not had long enough training and miss their marks which explains the damage of which

---

[90] See also vol. IV, pp. 214 ff.
[91] See telegram No. 176, July 2, 7 p. m., *ibid.*, p. 23.
[92] Not printed.

I complained. Every effort is to be made to avert this kind of damage.

5. Full consideration is being given to the return of American citizens to their goods and property. The Minister hopes we will understand that ordinary Japanese people are not allowed to follow the army but only contractors and purveyors. He gave the illustration of sea gulls following a ship.

6. In Shanghai and Nanking there is now peace and order but while the Japanese are pushing their drive on Hankow those places are actually bases of military activity. The Minister hopes that we will take that fact into consideration.

Certain points raised by the Minister before my representations began reported to the Department separately.

Please repeat to the Department and Hankow as our 427 [437], July 4, 7 p. m. Grew."

LOCKHART

893.20/682 : Telegram

The Ambassador in China (Johnson) to the Secretary of State

HANKOW, July 5, 1938—noon.
[Received 8 : 30 p. m.]

337. German military advisers left for Hong Kong at 9 : 00 this morning on special train provided by the Chinese Government.

It is understood that on July 2 a banquet was given in their honor by the Generalissimo and on July 4 by the Minister of War. The press reports today that the Chinese Government, appreciating the difficult position in which the advisers were placed, had voluntarily released them from their unexpired contracts.

A Chinese Government spokesman is quoted in the press today as follows:

"The German advisers are leaving with our assurance of high appreciation of their past service and also with our very best wishes."

Repeated to Peiping.

JOHNSON

793.94/13654

Memorandum on Military Supplies Entering China [93]

It is estimated that over seventy-five percent of the military supplies imported into China since the start of the hostilities have been routed through Hong Kong. The routes of entry for the remainder in order of their importance are French Indo-China, Russian Turkestan, Kwangchowan (French leased territory on the Kwangtung

---

[93] Apparently prepared in the Division of Far Eastern Affairs as part of a study, dated July 5, of the "Sino-Japanese conflict".

coast 220 miles southwest of Hong Kong), Macao, and Burma. A negligible amount of military supplies may enter China from Siberia via Urga. Small quantities may pass through the Japanese blockade into ports on the China Coast.

Extensive road and railway construction and improvement are now in progress with a view toward bettering communications with countries bordering China and so facilitate shipments of military supplies. In Yunnan, the caravan route from Talifu to Burma is being improved into a road suitable for wheeled traffic, and an extensive road net is being constructed connecting Yunnanfu, the terminus of the French railway from Hanoi, with roads leading north, east and west. In Kwangsi railroads and roads are under construction connecting the railway terminus at Langson, French Indo-China, with the Canton–Hankow railway via Nanning and Kweilin. The long route from Russian Turkestan has in large part been made suitable for heavy hauls in all weathers.

The material imported consisted primarily of the following:

(a) Aircraft and aircraft supplies.
(b) Explosives and other components for the manufacture of bombs, artillery ammunition, trench mortar ammunition, small arms ammunition and hand grenades.
(c) Small arms ammunition.
(d) Artillery ammunition.
(e) Machine guns and small arms.
(f) Antiaircraft guns and ammunition.
(g) Antitank guns and ammunition.
(h) Artillery and trench mortars.
(i) Tanks and armored cars.
(j) Aircraft bombs.

Little artillery (other than as indicated above) has been imported since the start of hostilities.

Germany, until its recent decision to cease shipping munitions to China, furnished the largest percentage as well as the largest variety of military supplies. Other countries furnishing munitions in order of their probable importance are Russia, Italy, England, France, United States, Belgium, Sweden, Austria, Switzerland, and Denmark. The heavy German participation in the munition trade to China is probably due to a barter agreement between the two countries concluded in 1935 and to the presence of the German advisers. Practically all the materials purchased from Germany can be procured elsewhere provided China can secure the necessary credit or provide foreign exchange.

Chinese claim they now have sufficient supplies on hand for one more year of warfare.

It is believed that the military supplies now being imported into China together with the reserve on hand are sufficient to maintain the Chinese forces in defensive operations on the present extensive scale. It is estimated that a minimum reserve of four months' supply of essential military supplies are now in China either in arsenals and supply dumps or en route thereto.

From the standpoint of supply, continued large scale Chinese operations are contingent upon the maintenance of China's purchasing power abroad, upon keeping the present route via Hong Kong open until efficient substitute routes can be established, and upon continued Chinese occupation of the areas containing important Government arsenals, particularly those in the Hankow area.

793.94/13408 : Telegram

The Consul General at Shanghai (Lockhart) to the Secretary of State

SHANGHAI, July 8, 1938—3 p. m.
[Received July 8—1 : 32 p. m.]

964. My 960, July 7, 3 p. m.[94] With 14 bombings, 4 killings and the employment of practically all military and police protection together with a part of the Shanghai volunteer forces including the Russian company to prevent disorder, yesterday was one of the tensest days spent in Shanghai for some time. Hundreds of suspects were arrested by the Settlement and French police authorities and close patrols were maintained throughout the day and night. The French police arrested a Chinese in whose possession was found a hand grenade. The arrested Chinese, at French police headquarters, confessed to being one of a group of Chinese terrorists sent to Shanghai from Hankow, with the necessary equipment, to create terrorism in the Settlement and French Concession. There is a common belief in the city that the organized terrorism that has prevailed in the city for the past several weeks, which was particularly flagrant yesterday, has been instigated by the Hankow authorities. This belief is so strong that the Chairman of the Shanghai Municipal Council, Mr. Cornell S. Franklin,[95] came to see me this morning and requested that this phase of the matter be brought to the attention of the Department with a view to the Department instructing the Ambassador at Hankow to bring the matter to the attention of the Chinese authorities there. Mr. Franklin emphasized the fact that, in spite of every effort of the police of the Settlement to prevent terrorism, the neutrality of the Settlement has repeatedly been violated by such acts. He further pointed out that

---

[94] Not printed.
[95] American lawyer.

the Settlement police have done their utmost to protect the vast amount of Chinese property in the Settlement as well as the property of all others. He believes that the Hankow authorities should cooperate in every possible way with the Settlement authorities in preventing acts of terrorism and he asks the help of the American authorities to that end in the manner suggested above. He has also discussed the matter with the British Consul General who is referring it as requested.

Repeated to Hankow.

LOCKHART

793.94/13408 : Telegram

The Secretary of State to the Ambassador in China (Johnson)

WASHINGTON, July 9, 1938—3 p. m.

202. Shanghai's 964, July 8, 3 p. m., in regard to terrorism in the Shanghai Settlement. The Department suggests that you consult with your British colleague in regard to this matter. If you feel that you can with propriety do so and your British colleague is prepared to take substantially similar action, you are authorized to bring to the attention of the Chinese Government informally the facts and considerations mentioned in Shanghai's telegram under reference and in your discretion to urge upon the Chinese authorities, if and in so far as the Chinese Government has any contributory responsibility in relation to these developments, that such acts and their consequences are not only harmful to other countries, including those friendly to China, but are contrary to the best interests of China herself.

Please repeat to Shanghai.

HULL

793.94/13416 : Telegram

The Consul General at Shanghai (Lockhart) to the Secretary of State

SHANGHAI, July 9, 1938—5 p. m.
[Received July 9—1: 15 p. m.]

972. Consulate's 2, January 2, 10 a. m.[95a] and 5, January 3, 3 p. m.,[95b] and my 960, July 7, 3 p. m.[96] The Shanghai Municipal Council proposes, among the measures to be adopted to suppress bombing outrages, to issue a new proclamation one paragraph of which will read as follows:

"Any person found in the International Settlement in possession of arms or explosives, without a permit from the Settlement author-

---

[95a] *Ante,* p. 2.
[95b] Vol. IV, p. 215.
[96] Not printed.

ities, or engaged or connected with terrorist activities, will be liable to be expelled from the Settlement, provided always that where such possession or such activities are found to be in no way, directly or indirectly, against the armed forces outside the Settlement, normal procedure through the courts will be followed."

The above quoted paragraph is to take the place of paragraph 1 of the proclamation issued January 1, 1938 referred to in No. 2, January 2, 10 a. m. reading as follows

"That any persons committing an offense against armed forces in the International Settlement will be liable to be handed over to the armed forces concerned."

My concurrence has been requested by the Shanghai Municipal Council but I hesitate to acquiesce in the regulation even as regards non-Americans unless instructed to do so by the Department. In the meantime I have informed the Chairman of the Shanghai Municipal Council that I am unable to accept the proclamation as applying to American nationals or American property in derogation of American extra-territorial rights or jurisdiction.

Repeated by mail to Peiping and Tokyo.

LOCKHART

793.94/13425 : Telegram

The Ambassador in China (Johnson) to the Secretary of State

HANKOW, July 11, 1938—5 p. m.
[Received July 11—1 : 02 p. m.]

348. Department's 202, July 9, 3 p. m. I saw British Ambassador [97] this afternoon in regard to this matter. He tells me that he received similar message from his Consul General yesterday just before going to keep an appointment with the Generalissimo and that he put message in pocket and read it to Chiang who stated that while he disclaimed any connection with these crimes he assured the British Ambassador that he would use all of his influence to prevent their occurrence. In view of the above it seems to us both that nothing further needed be done at this time. If Consulate at Shanghai using the above in any information conveyed to Chairman of Municipal Council he should impress upon Chairman desirability of avoiding any publicity regarding appeal to us or to representations made.

Repeated to Shanghai.

JOHNSON

---

[97] Sir Archibald Clark Kerr.

751.94/60

The Ambassador in Japan (Grew) to the Secretary of State

No. 3102   Tokyo, July 11, 1938.
                                                [Received July 29.]

Sir: Japan's relations with France, which have been unusually quiescent since the outbreak of the present Sino-Japanese hostilities, have recently come to the fore and French policies and actions in the Far East have been attacked in the local press with vehemence. In fact, the tone of bitterness and editorial vituperation suddenly directed against France, whose attitude of strict neutrality and impartiality had previously elicited approving comment, reveals a sensitiveness and a state of nerves on the part of the press somewhat out of proportion to the offenses alleged; this, in turn, may be an indication that the strain of the past year's hostilities has been greater upon the Japanese than they themselves have suspected.

In general, the criticism is based on an allegation by the Japanese that France, whose precarious position in Europe is now so greatly dependent upon the closest possible association with Great Britain, has seen fit to follow British policy in the Far East and that France has now aligned itself with Great Britain in endeavoring to obstruct the unfolding of Japan's plans in China.

Specific complaints are based upon allegations that France has agreed to extend loans to China and to send to China military officers who would take the place of the German military advisers who have been recalled by the German Government. The Japanese furthermore complain that there has been a marked increase in the shipment of arms and munitions to China through Indo-China, especially since France appears virtually to have ceased supplying the Spanish Government with war material which has now become available for sale to the Chiang Kai-shek régime. Mr. Sugimura, Japanese Ambassador at Paris, is reported to have protested to the French Foreign Minister against the use of the Yunnanfu Railway for this purpose and to have deprecated the alleged agreement concluded between the French and the Chinese governments for the construction of a new railway from Chennankwan, French Indo-China, to Nanning in Kwangsi Province, China.

In a conversation between the Counselor of the French Embassy and a member of the staff of this Embassy, Baron Fain remarked that the contract for the construction of this new railway had actually been signed prior to the outbreak of the present hostilities, that it was a purely private business enterprise in which the French Government felt it could not interfere, and that it would in any case be at least two years before the construction would be completed. Continuing the conversation the Counselor said that such arms as were at present being shipped over the railway to Yunnanfu represented the fulfillment of regular contracts for the sale of arms to China which had likewise been entered into before the outbreak of hostilities. He maintained that there was no smuggling of arms or munitions across the Indo-China frontier. (See our telegram No. 423, June 28, 8 p. m.)

Questioned concerning the reports that French military advisers would replace the departing German military advisers to Chiang Kai-shek, a further source of considerable concern to the Japanese, the Counselor said that he had no information on the matter but that, in his personal opinion, there was no truth in the report; that France's policy of strict neutrality was being adhered to and that such action as alleged above would not be consistent with this policy. He said that there were, of course, a few free-lance individuals of French nationality who, like soldiers of fortune from other countries, were serving in various capacities in the Chinese air force and armies but that they had no significance. He thought that possibly the recent arrival of one or two of these individuals from Spain may have been made the basis for the rumor that France intended to supply military advisers to the Chinese Government.

Other irritants in the question of Japanese-French relations have been the increasing French concern in the possible occupation by the Japanese of the island of Hainan (see our telegram No. 423, June 28, 8 p. m.) and the landing by the French of ten Annamite policemen and the establishment of a lighthouse and a wireless station on the Paracel Islands, a scattered group of tiny islets and reefs some 120 miles to the southeast of Hainan. The sovereignty of the Paracels is under dispute between the French and the Chinese; the French, however, maintain that title to those islands lay with the former Kingdom of Annam by virtue of a treaty between that Kingdom and China and that when France took over Annam the title to the Paracels passed to the French. The Japanese claim no title but sustain the Chinese claim that the islands are Chinese. At all events, the recent action of the French in landing policemen on the Islands was made the subject of a formal protest by the Foreign Office here through the French Ambassador on July 4, and the Vice Minister for Foreign Affairs is reported, in an official communiqué later issued by the Foreign Office, to have said that he "called attention of the French Government to the possibility that the stationing of the Annamese policemen in the (Paracel) Islands was likely to give rise to some unexpected misunderstanding between them and the Japanese engaged in the work mentioned above (collection of sea-weed and rock phosphates), and expressed the hope that the said police force would be withdrawn". The nature of the French reply to these representations is not known but the Embassy understands that the Japanese request will be rejected.

In the non-political field a further difficulty has interjected itself in the form of the imposition by the French of retaliatory measures banning further importation into France of certain Japanese commercial products hitherto admitted under quotas. In February of this year an arrangement was entered into between the two countries by which Japan undertook to import from France during 1938 goods to a value not less than the value of the import figures for the calendar year 1936. A survey of the figures for the first six months of this year shows that the Japanese have fallen considerably short of the necessary imports; consequently the foregoing measures have been taken by way of retaliation. French trade with Japan has for some years in the past shown a balance consistently adverse to France. The arrangement of last February was entered into for the purpose of restricting the amount of this adverse balance but with no thought of attempting to convert this into a favorable balance; the arrangement provided that if the Japanese imports should fall short of the specified amount the measures which have now been taken should be put into effect, pending further negotiations in an endeavor to remedy the situation. In 1936 Japan sold to France goods to the value of Yen 43,475,000 and bought goods to the amount of Yen 19,898,000. During the first four months of 1938, imports from France amounted to Yen 5,101,000 as compared with Yen 7,327,000 for the same period last year; exports to France amounted to Yen 11,221,000 as compared with Yen 15,150,000 for the same period last year. It is understood that the Japanese will seek to negotiate a new arrangement.

Respectfully yours,   JOSEPH C. GREW

_____

793.94119/428 : Telegram

The Ambassador in China (Johnson) to the Secretary of State

HANKOW, July 12, 1938—5 p. m.
[Received July 13—10 : 43 a. m.]

352. Donald [98] informed McHugh this morning that a daughter of Tang Shao Yi arrived in Hankow at about the same time as the British Ambassador and called on Generalissimo with a message from her father congratulating him upon his stiff resistance to Japanese. She then visited Wang Ching Wei [99] and proposed to him that he, Tai Chi Tao [1] and Chu Cheng [2] go to Hong Kong to confer with her father with regard to possible mediation and peace. Wang is reported

_____

[98] W. H. Donald, Australian adviser to Generalissimo Chiang Kai-shek.
[99] Deputy leader of the Kuomintang (Nationalist Party).
[1] President of the Chinese Examination Yuan.
[2] President of the Chinese Judicial Yuan.

to have declined the invitation and to have informed Generalissimo of approach. Donald stated that some time before Wang had been approached through some other and unnamed source with the suggestion that he write directly to Prince Konoye to assure him that there would be no enmity between them after hostilities were over. This Wang is said also to have refused to do and to have informed the Generalissimo of approach and of his decision. Donald interpreted the above as efforts by the Japanese to separate some of the leaders in the present Government. Donald stated that Japanese would even be willing now to permit Generalissimo to remain as a power behind the scenes as long as hostilities are over.

In recent conversations which I have had with British Ambassador who is now in Hankow, I found him interested in the question as to whether the present Chinese Government could hold together after loss of Hankow. Today I had a conversation with Blackburn [3] who arrived yesterday from Shanghai to join British Ambassador. Blackburn, who at Nanking was inclined to criticise his Ambassador for a tendency to spend too much time away from Nanking and the Central Government, seemed now to feel that it was necessary for him to keep his Ambassador from being too enthusiastic about Chinese Government's chances of success. Blackburn appeared to believe that there was likelihood that Wang Ching Wei and possibly Tai Chi Tao might leave Government to find berths for themselves with Japanese fostered regimes in occupied areas. I inferred that he was informed of Tang Shao Yi's overtures. I have observed no evidence here of any tendency or likelihood of break up among leaders of Government. I pointed out to Blackburn that I would attach much more significance to efforts to bring leaders like the Generalissimo, Chu Teh, Mao Tse Tung, Li Tsung Jen or Pai Chung Hsi [4] over to the Japanese side as the Government always had been embarrassed in its relations with these leaders because of the presence in it of leaders like Wang Ching Wei. I pointed out that while I was by no means confident of the ability of the present Chinese Government to drive the Japanese out of China or even to control the activities of the growing mass of guerrillas throughout the whole occupied areas, I was convinced that resistance would continue for a long time with the Generalissimo growing as a leader and a symbol of Chinese nationalism as opposed to a Japanese controlled China. Blackburn stated that the Chinese leaders were not [now?] much worried over the danger of the collapse of Chinese currency, saying that this was evidenced by Chinese insistence that China must have financial support through a British or other foreign loan, that the Chinese were worried lest with the col-

---

[3] Sir A. D. Blackburn, Chinese Secretary of the British Embassy in China.
[4] Two Communist and two Kwangsi leaders, all generals.

lapse of the currency the Government would not have the wherewithal to pay its troops. I pointed out that while it was natural for the Chinese Government to desire to obtain a loan to assist in maintaining its credit abroad and its currency in foreign exchange I saw less reason for the Chinese Government to be disturbed over the possible collapse of the currency than for the Japanese. I pointed out that a collapse of Chinese currency would be far more disastrous to the Japanese fostered Chinese regimes than it would be to the Central Government which would still be able to pay its soldiers with a currency usable within the areas under its control. I stated that I could not yet see any basis for peace between the Chinese Government and the Japanese, that I believed and feared that the struggle would go on for a long time with disastrous results to everyone's interests. I agreed that there was no evidence of war weariness in Japan but pointed out that the change in the Japanese Government brought about by the failure of the Hsuchow campaign (loss of advantage of dry spring weather for pushing attack on Lunghai and Hankow), the putting into operation of the mobilization law now, a law obtained by deceiving the Diet, was in my opinion a measure not so much precautionary on the part of the Japanese Government as a measure of desperation, saying that if at the end of a year the Japanese Government had been forced to mobilize its entire strength for a drive on Hankow I wondered what would be left to mobilize for the long haul that must follow the capture of Hankow, the rehabilitation in the occupied areas, et cetera. I report the above as possibly indicating not only that the Japanese are very anxious to find some way of stopping the present hostilities but also as possibly indicating a feeling in the British Embassy that Chinese resistance is about to break up, to be followed by a drift of leaders toward the Japanese controlled regimes, a feeling which I do not share.

Repeated to Shanghai. Shanghai please repeat to Tokyo.

JOHNSON

793.94/13416 : Telegram

The Secretary of State to the Consul General at Shanghai (*Lockhart*)

WASHINGTON, July 13, 1938—4 p. m.

438. Your 972, July 9, 5 p. m., in regard to proposed proclamation by the Shanghai Municipal Council aimed at suppression of terrorist activities.

1. The Department approves your refusal to accept proposed proclamation as applying to American nationals.

2. The Department perceives no objection to your acquiescence, as a member of the Shanghai Consular Body and in consultation and agreement with your interested colleagues, in the issuance of the

proposed proclamation subject to the reservation that it shall not apply to extraterritorial nationals.

HULL

793.94/13658

The Ambassador in China (Johnson) to the Secretary of State

No. 1690   PEIPING, July 13, 1938.
                                                   [Received August 12.]

SIR: I have the honor to report information, received from foreign missionaries in the provinces of Shansi, Shantung, and Hopei, which shows widespread and ruthless destruction of towns and villages and considerable killing and wounding of Chinese civilians by Japanese military. So extensive has the destruction been during recent months in some areas that it would seem that some units of the Japanese military have adopted a definite policy of destruction, the purposes being one or more of the following: retaliation against civilians who have harbored—willingly or unwillingly—Chinese irregulars, impoverishing of the countryside so that Chinese irregulars will find subsistence difficult, and terrorization of the people so that they will be frightened into refusing aid to irregulars.

Destruction in Shansi Province:

The most detailed information received by the Embassy in regard to methodical destruction relates to southeast Shansi, the informant being an American missionary stationed in that area. He stated that methodical destruction by various Japanese military units of towns, villages, and isolated houses took place in the middle of April; that the destruction was evidently a planned maneuver as several Japanese units acted simultaneously; that he personally knew of the destruction of five hsien towns (Wuhsiang, Yuhsia, Heshun, Chinchow, and Hsiangyuan) and probably a sixth (Chinhsien); that towns, villages, and isolated houses lying along the roads connecting the district towns (which are sometimes 30 miles apart) had also been largely destroyed, although sometimes the fires set by the Japanese military were not as effective as intended; that there were few Chinese in the district towns at the time of the entry of Japanese forces because the Chinese authorities, having prior information of Japanese approach, had effected evacuation of civilians; that, however, in some other towns and villages prior information was not received, as a result of which there were some civilian casualties, especially Chinese whose movements were regarded as suspicious by Japanese; that in some instances Japanese destroyed food stocks; that the Japanese forces withdrew after firing the area, allegedly for service in south Shantung; that the Chinese authorities soon returned; that the district town in which he lived (Liaochow) was not destroyed, although many villages in Liaochow district were burned; and that the Japanese also intentionally destroyed some temples. The informant took photographs of four of the destroyed hsien towns, prints of which are enclosed,[5] as well as prints indicating treatment of villages, isolated residences, and temples.

Another foreign missionary (Canadian), stationed at Luan, in southeast Shansi but further south than the area referred to in previous paragraphs, traveled this spring from Luan to Wuan, in the northern tip of Honan Province. He informed a reliable American missionary that towns and villages along the more than seventy miles of the road which he followed had been destroyed by Japanese.

Destruction in Shantung Province:

Similar destruction, although probably not so systematic, has taken place in Shantung. An American missionary, stationed at Tsinan, whose mission district extends south to Taian, has informed the Embassy that he has received too many reports from responsible Chinese not to believe that in his mission district the Japanese military have burned villages, shot down civilian men, and raped the women, sometimes bayonetting the women after rape. A European priest, stationed along the Tsinan–Tsingtao Railway, wrote recently to an American friend in Peiping that he saw from a point in his district fifteen villages burning simultaneously, fired by Japanese. The bombing by Japanese planes of towns and villages in northeastern Shantung which are still under Chinese control has already been reported by the Consulates at Chefoo and Tsingtao. It is understood that the Japanese are still pursuing this practise.

Destruction in Hopei Province:

Destruction—partial or complete—of towns and villages in Hopei Province has previously been reported by the Embassy. Destruction has reportedly been most thorough east and west of the P'inghan Railway in the general area of Paoting. However, an American missionary stationed at Shuntehfu on the P'inghan Railway in southern Hopei has informed the Embassy that similar destruction has occurred west of the railway in his area. A missionary in eastern Hopei southwest of Tientsin stated some time ago that the Japanese policy of destruction of towns and villages in his area was evidently being abandoned, a report which indicated that the policy had been in force prior to that time.

Respectfully yours,

For the Ambassador:
LAURENCE E. SALISBURY
First Secretary of Embassy

---

[5] Not reproduced.

793.94/13451 : Telegram

The Consul General at Shanghai (Lockhart) to the Secretary of State

SHANGHAI, July 14, 1938—6 p. m.
[Received July 14—1 : 36 p. m.]

992. My 972, July 9, 5 p. m. The Shanghai Municipal Council has sent me today the following draft of a revised proclamation which it has recommended for the approval of the interested members of the Consular Body.

"Whereas, despite the warnings and penalties prescribed in the emergency proclamation of January 1, 1938, a period of grave emergency still continues to exist;

Whereas, also, armed outrages continue to occur on an aggravated scale in the International Settlement;

Whereas, accordingly, it appears necessary to the Shanghai Municipal Council to accord to the Municipal police wider emergency powers, in furtherance of its firm resolve to suppress these armed outrages.

It is hereby proclaimed :—

(1) That any person committing an offense against armed forces in the International Settlement will be liable to be handed over to the armed forces concerned;

(2) That any person committing an armed crime in the International Settlement will be refused the sanctuary of the Settlement and will be liable to expulsion therefrom;

(3) That the Municipal police are authorized to search all premises, public or private, for unauthorized arms;

(4) That a reward not exceeding $5,000 will be paid to any person giving information that leads to the apprehension of terrorists;

(5) That a substantial reward will be paid to any person giving information that leads to the seizure of unauthorized arms;

(6) That any person found in the International Settlement in possession of arms or explosives without a permit from the Settlement authorities, or engaged in or connected with terrorist activities, will be liable to be expelled from the Settlement".

2. Inasmuch as it is decided to issue the proclamation on July 16, I should be glad to have the Department's immediate instructions as to whether I should acquiesce in the regulations, with a reiteration of the reservation stated in the last sentence of the penultimate paragraph of my 972, July 9, 5 p. m. My British colleague will make a similar reservation as regards British subjects. Otherwise he is disposed to give his consent to the issuance of the proclamation in the form herein quoted. I am myself disposed to make no formal acquiescence, simply leaving the matter of the issuance of the proclamation entirely to the discretion of the Shanghai Municipal Council, but keeping on record the reservation above mentioned.

Repeated to Hankow; by mail to Peiping and Tokyo.

LOCKHART

793.94/13745

The Ambassador in China (Johnson) to the Secretary of State

No. 51   HANKOW, July 14, 1938.
                                          [Received August 26.]

SIR: I have the honor to transmit herewith, for the files of the Department, a copy in translation of a message [6] addressed by General Chiang Kai-shek to all friendly nations on the first anniversary of the Lukouchiao incident.[7] The translation, made by the China Information Committee of the Central Publicity Board, appears to be satisfactory.

In expressing appreciation for the aid heretofore rendered to China, the Chinese Generalissimo reminds the signatories of the League Covenant, the Pact of Paris, and the Nine Power Treaty of their commitments thereunder and urges upon them the desirability of implementing their pledges in order "that world justice and righteousness may be firmly re-established."

General Chiang expresses the conviction that "justice will triumph in the end," and reaffirms the determination of the Chinese people to continue the war of resistance "until Japan withdraws her invading forces and until we recover our territorial and administrative rights." In closing his plea to the friendly foreign powers, General Chiang asserts that "peace is indivisible and isolation is impracticable," and that "as long as Japan's aggression is unchecked, the Far East and the world will remain in turmoil." He therefore urges the powers to discharge their responsibilities in maintaining justice in the world and the sanctity of treaties.

Respectfully yours,   NELSON TRUSLER JOHNSON

793.94/13451 : Telegram

The Secretary of State to the Consul General at Shanghai (Lockhart)

WASHINGTON, July 15, 1938—noon.

443. Your 992, July 14, 6 p. m., proposed proclamation by the Shanghai Municipal Council. Department's 438, July 13, 4 p. m. outlines Department's position in regard to this matter.

The Department perceives no objection to your acting in accordance with the last sentence of paragraph 2 of your telegram under reference.[8]

HULL

---

[6] Not printed.
[7] See *Foreign Relations, 1937*, vol. III, pp. 128 ff.; also *Foreign Relations, Japan, 1931–1941*, vol. I, pp. 313–334, *passim*.
[8] The proposed proclamation was promulgated July 18.

894.515/40 : Telegram

The Ambassador in China (Johnson) to the Secretary of State

HANKOW, July 19, 1938—9 a. m.
[Received 7 : 15 p. m.]

360. The following is the substance of views communicated to a member of my staff by Mr. Hall-Patch, Financial Adviser to the British Embassy in China, who has recently arrived in Hankow after visit to North China and Japan.

1. He reports British traders in North China have not been appreciably affected by recent financial developments in that area but is apprehensive that Japanese may endeavor to obtain control of foreign exchange derived from exports, a large portion of which remains in foreign hands and which provides bulk of cover for payment of foreign imports. He says advantages derived by Japanese importers as a result of the linking of the Federal Reserve currency and the yen are not so marked as would appear in view of shortage of commodities, transport difficulties, et cetera, but he feels foreign traders in North China ultimately may have to cooperate as best they can with the Japanese, eschewing the support of their Governments. Alternatively, the foreign powers must take steps to see that their nationals are afforded equal opportunity to trade in North China. He believes United States and Great Britain are now faced with a situation requiring a decision as to whether they will choose to cooperate with the Japanese in so far as possible in North China or whether they will choose to support China with a view to furtherance trade and position. He personally believes and has suggested to his superiors that to support China is the best policy to pursue, but is not sanguine as to London's policy.

2. With regard to the creation of the Federal Reserve Bank, Hall-Patch expresses the view that this move was a mistake and says that while informed Japanese share this opinion the extent to which the situation has developed and the question of face will preclude dissolution of the bank. He believes a similar organ will not be created in Central China.

3. He is of the opinion that the fall in the exchange value of the Chinese dollar has been as disastrous in its effects in the Japanese occupied areas as in Chinese Government controlled territory and that this fact has exerted a weakening influence on the yen. If Chinese currency should collapse completely, he thinks the Japanese would find it necessary to establish a new currency in China, an action which Japan would find difficult of accomplishment in view of her own financial troubles.

4. He considers that Japan is now beginning to feel the strain of hostilities in China. He says that if the United States and Great Britain should at this time apply a system of sanctions effectively blocking the supply of important commodities and credits to Japan, he is convinced Japan could be brought to terms within a year. He believes British Government has given consideration to this matter but would act only with full collaboration of the United States.

5. He states he learned in Japan that the Standard Vacuum Oil Company recently extended old or granted new credits to Japan for the purchase of petroleum, apparently in contravention of a tacit agreement to consult beforehand with the Asiatic Petroleum Company which seems to have received advice from London not to grant further credits to Japan. Hall-Patch deplores this split in the policy of the oil companies, as the British firm must follow suit in order to preserve its position in Japan, all of which is tantamount to affording active aid to Japan in a time of great need. He moreover believes the extension of credits to Japan at this juncture is a dangerous risk. Without foreign assistance and the continuation of hostilities, he considers that Japan's financial structure will collapse within another 12 to 18 months.

6. It would be appreciated if the Department will endeavor to confirm for my information whether the Standard Vacuum Oil Company has recently extended old or granted new credits to Japan as reported in paragraph 5 above.[9]

Repeated to Peiping. Peiping please repeat to Tokyo.

JOHNSON

793.94/13506 : Telegram

The First Secretary of Embassy in China (Salisbury) to the Secretary of State

PEIPING, July 19, 1938—2 p. m.
[Received July 20—8 a. m.]

451. This office's 436, July 12, 1 p. m., and Ambassador's 355, July 16, 10 a. m., from Hankow.[10]

1. Rumored impending Japanese military changes in North China (particularly the possible assignment here of Doihara [11] to be in charge of all special military affairs organs in China) have caused some apparently well founded speculation in regard to possible result of the changes in the Peiping and Nanking regimes. A current report

[9] The Ambassador in Japan telegraphed on July 23 the oil company's denial of this report, and the Secretary on July 25 assumed this denial would be communicated by the Ambassador in China to his British informant (894.51/584).
[10] Neither printed.
[11] Gen. Kenji Doihara.

is that Itagaki favors an immediately amalgamated regime under Chin Yun Peng,[12] that Doihara favors amalgamation under Tang Shao Yi, and that hope of Wu Pei Fu's emergence [13] has been practically abandoned.

2. A well informed official of the National Government who has close connection with Tang Shao Yi's family has informed an officer of the Embassy that: (1) Tang is distinctly a probability; (2) Tang's son-in-law, who was a schoolmate of Konoye, visited Japan and North China not long ago in connection with Tang's emergence; and (3) Tang has gone so far as to make certain stipulations to his assuming office, namely (a) pledging fall of Hankow to the Japanese, (b) establishment of amalgamated new regime at Nanking, and (c) freedom to direct the new regime along the lines in the "Three People's Principles" as laid down by Sun Yat Sen. The informant stated that stipulation (a) is based on the consideration that the National Government is not defeated so long as it retains Hankow; that meantime to further the purposes of puppet regimes would be traitorous; and that, after the expected fall of Hankow, Tang, as a leader of worth, respectability and prestige, can conscientiously take upon himself the burden of heading the regime which by the nature of things must be set up in the occupied areas. (The above outline has also been given to the Embassy by a retired official closely connected with members of the Peiping staff.)

3. The informant believes that the expected fall of Hankow will be a political turning point. He thinks that (1) the National Government will thereafter come more and more under the domination of the Communist leaders, and (2) the new regime or regimes cannot, with or without Tang, succeed because of the influence of the Communists with (a) the irregulars who will never be wiped out, and (b) the young generation in China. He adheres to the opinion that Japanese aggression is in effect creating the communism which it ostensibly seeks to destroy. He points out that a kind of communism has already spread through the occupied areas in the form of guerrilla activities and banditry. He states that the young generation has come to look to communism or some offshoot thereof as the only means of saving China from the Japanese, that the coming into influence of the young generation will be coincident with the widespread growth of a communistic or quasi-communistic movement, which will be directed irrevocably to the freeing of China from the Japanese yoke and will ultimately be successful, and that meanwhile China must go through a period of growing chaos whose effect on

---

[12] Chinese Premier in 1921.
[13] Marshal Wu had been in retirement since 1926.

Chinese and foreigners can be envisaged only in the most tragic outlines.

Repeated to the Embassy, Hankow, Nanking, Consulate General Shanghai, by mail to Tokyo.

SALISBURY

793.94/13515 : Telegram

The Ambassador in China (Johnson) to the Secretary of State

HANKOW, July 19, 1938—3 p. m.
[Received July 20—2:24 p. m.]

362. The statement in my 355, July 16, 10 a. m.[14] that the Japanese intend to use the capture of Hankow as a symbol to their people of the end of the military phase of their campaign in China calls for an estimate of the possible effect of the loss of Hankow upon the future ability of the Chinese Government to continue its resistance to the Japanese. To that end I have asked McHugh, Jenkins, Dorn [15] and the Consulate General for their opinions. The following estimate is based upon their study of the situation.

From a military point of view Hankow forms the third corner of a great triangle which to date has circumscribed the hostilities—as Peiping, Shanghai, Hankow area. Until Hankow is taken the Japanese forces are continually being stretched farther and farther from the base of this triangle—the Peiping–Shanghai line and down its hypotenuse from Peiping toward Chengchow. The strain on the Japanese lines of communication has therefore been constantly increasing. The merging of the two segments of the base with the capture of Hsuchow was an alleviating factor but was largely vitiated when the Chinese blocked the advance on Chengchow by breaching the Yellow River dykes. By holding the Hankow–[Chengchow?] segment of the hypotenuse, the Chinese have maintained contact with a vast area to the north and northwest which has been a constant menace to the whole right flank of the Japanese area, safeguarding their Sian–Lanchow route of supply from Russia.

When Hankow falls into Japanese hands a considerable part of this tension is bound to be relieved. The opening of the river will greatly simplify the question of supply for the Japanese Army. Not only will it be less susceptible to interruption by guerrilla warfare, as in the case of the railroads, but by establishing their advanced base at Hankow the Japanese will be able to support their troops on the Peiping–Hankow hypotenuse from two directions, thereby facilitating any operations to the westward.

---

[14] Not printed.
[15] Assistant Naval Attaché, Third Secretary of Embassy, and Assistant Military Attaché in China, respectively.

It is not yet clear just how the Japanese intend to proceed in their attack on Hankow, except that their original main effort from the northeast now appears definitely to have been abandoned, and that an advance up the river will figure largely in the present effort. Presumably they will first attempt to take Nanchang, thus depriving the Chinese of control of the largest air base in China and securing it for themselves from which they can conduct aerial operations against the whole of Central China. This will restore to them complete air superiority for their advance on Hankow, the lack of which seems to have handicapped them to some extent during their recent river operations around [Kiukiang?], and will be an important factor in the coming campaign.

In their advance upon Hankow the Japanese may adopt either of the following moves, and the nature of the resultant situation is largely dependent upon how they proceed. They may rely on (1) a direct thrust up the river of combined military and naval operation, or (2) they may elect to drive overland from Nanchang either to Wuchang or straight to Changsha.

There has been some speculation in fact that they might coordinate this second move with one from the north through southern Shansi and down the Han River valley in a gigantic pincers movement. It seems more likely at present however that their present operations in western Honan and southern Shansi will keep them fully occupied in those regions for some weeks to come and probably will eventually lead them against the Sian–Lanchow area rather than down the Han River valley. In fact, if they choose the latter, then a new and separate force will have to deal with the former.

The Chinese actually occupy very strong positions in the areas they are now holding and they will be further assisted during the next few weeks by the summer floods. It remains to be seen however how successful they will be in their defense, observers are now looking for the blind spots, for experience has proved that the Chinese have never been able to coordinate their defense. The efforts of the majority have consistently been nullified by the negligence, stupidity, failure to obey orders or failure to fight on the part of a few.

If the Japanese take Hankow by a direct push up the river, they obviously will still have to cope with the Nanchang–Shanghai–Wuchang area as well as some very extensive mopping up operations to the north of Hankow. Hunan is actually the strategic center of China, and the Japanese can never really control it and the continuous areas to the westward until they take Hengyang, a junction point south of Changsha on the Canton–Hankow Railway where roads and rivers connect with the west and southwest.

Three weeks ago it appeared that the Chinese High Command did not intend to make a serious effort to hold Hankow. This attitude now seems to have changed as present indications are that the Chinese intend to make the taking of Hankow as expensive as possible. To this end large numbers of troop[s] have recently been sent to the Nanchang area. Moreover, Chiang Kai Shek has been making extensive preparations for a long time to hold western Hunan. One of his most trusted lieutenants Chang Chih Chung was installed there as Governor early this year and 25 divisions of fresh troops have been in training there under younger officers who are themselves products of the Generalissimo's own schools and are intensely loyal to him. Reliable foreigners state that a large majority of the war supplies which have come up over the Canton Railway in recent months have been cached in western Hunan.

The loss of Hankow will without doubt be a serious blow to the Chinese strategically as well as politically and economically. The strategic effect has already been indicated. Politically it will separate the Government from access to the North where fighting and defense measures are now in the hands of the former Communists and the remains of the northern provincial troops. How serious this effect will be only time can tell. It is not expected that it will greatly affect the activities of the guerrillas in the northern areas as the Government has never really been in very close touch with them. And there has been no evidence yet of a tendency on the part of the forces left in these areas to desert the cause. From a political point of view the Government will be thrown into closer contact with the southern areas where a tendency toward opposition to the Government has for a long time been more than evident. The consolidation of supplies in western Hunan mentioned above has been in anticipation of this as well as of invasion by Japan of Hunan, Kweichow, Kwangsi area, backed by Szechwan and Yunnan, promises to continue perfectly active for a considerable time.[16] In some respects the Government will be strengthened politically by the loss of some of the provincial levies which will be left behind in the north to fight as guerrillas. The mere existence of this strongly nationalistic government center to the south will in itself make it difficult for the Japanese military machine to stop at Hankow.

Economically the loss of Hankow will be a much more severe blow than a military or political one. When the Government loses Hankow it will lose all of the revenue that the trade of Hankow during recent months has been able to give it. Such statistics as are available indicate that exports from Hankow during the past few months have

---

[16] Sentence apparently garbled.

averaged about Chinese currency dollars 5 million per month. It is estimated that under the present exchange control set up by the Government this trade has given the Government control over about United States dollars 1,475,000 per month of foreign exchange which has been useful in its foreign transactions. Most, if not all of this, will be lost to the Government with the loss of Hankow and the interruption of traffic on the Canton–Hankow Railway. In addition there will be the loss of revenue from customs (Hankow receipt being estimated at Chinese dollars 1,000,000 per month) salt taxes and consolidated taxes, Hankow being a manufacturing center producing large quantities of cigarettes. An indirect loss will result from the opening up of the river and the revival of trade at Shanghai for the blocking of the Yangtze has practically halted the trade of Shanghai. The loss of Hankow means the loss of the last great Chinese industrial center with its cotton mills and other factories and of the revenues which this industry has brought to the Government. It has been said that this will have its effect upon the financial stability of the Chinese Government. However, there is reason to think that a collapse of Chinese currency will have a far more serious effect in the occupied areas and the economic position of Japan than upon the Chinese, for in the areas under their control Chinese currency will continue to serve the Government and the people as a medium of exchange for domestic transactions.

It is our conclusion that serious as the loss of Hankow will be it does not mean the collapse of Chinese resistance. We find it difficult to believe that the taking of Hankow will enable the Japanese to call a halt to Japanese military campaign in China or even materially to reduce the number of Japanese troops that will be necessary to garrison and hold the areas of occupation. The task of eliminating the irregular guerrilla forces scattered all over and around the area of occupation will constitute a major command and it is believed that the Japanese military will find sufficient threat left in the Chinese Government that remains to make them feel impelled to continue the campaign westward—Hankow thus resulting in another and more expensive Nanking rather than a final victory marking the end of hostilities.

McHugh and Dorn would like substance of the above to be communicated to their Departments.

Repeated to Shanghai, Peiping. Shanghai please repeat to Tokyo.

JOHNSON

793.94/13729

Mr. John Carter Vincent of the Division of Far Eastern Affairs to the Adviser on Political Relations (Hornbeck)[17]

[WASHINGTON,] July 23, 1938.

DEAR DR. HORNBECK: Several days ago I had luncheon, at his request, with Frederick Moore, who, as you know and as he frankly admits, has been for a long period and is now employed as adviser to the Japanese Government (Foreign Office, I think).

Mr. Moore talked at considerable length and with seeming frankness about the situation in the Far East and in particular about the problems and difficulties faced by the Japanese. Although many of his observations add little to our knowledge and understanding of the situation, the following statements, I believe, will interest you, especially in view of their source:

1. The morale of Japanese civilians is at a low ebb. Mr. Moore mentioned especially the circumstance, which he said he had on very good authority, that Japanese in Tokyo are praying at temples for the withdrawal of Japanese soldiers from China.

2. The morale of Japanese troops, with the exception of those in the Kwantung Army, is bad and may be expected further to deteriorate when, as seems to be anticipated, aggressive warfare ends with the capture of Hankow and defensive operations against guerrillas ensue.

3. The Japanese are counting heavily upon a disintegration of the Chinese Government after the anticipated fall of Hankow.

4. If the Chinese can maintain resistance in a reasonable degree of effectiveness (that is, I presume, sufficient to keep an army, say, of four or five hundred thousand Japanese engaged), conditions at home will compel the Japanese military to withdraw from China within a year.

5. Even though the present venture in China should prove outwardly successful, the Japanese military are doomed to failure in their imperialistic designs upon China because of their lack of moral stability and imaginative intelligence.

6. The Chinese do not appreciate the strength of their own position in the present situation. If they, Mr. Moore professes to think, understood fully the moral and material vulnerability of the Japanese, the urgency and importance of continuing resistance would be unquestionable.

7. The best (for all concerned) outcome of the present conflict would be for the Japanese military to be discredited with the Jap-

---

[17] This memorandum was read by officers of the Department and marked with approval by the Secretary and Under Secretary of State.

anese people and lose power while it is still possible to ward off complete disaster for Japan. Mr. Moore is a proponent of the Shidehara [18] school which advocates patient endeavors at peaceful cooperation with and leadership of the Chinese.

8. Public opinion in the United States would support some form of sanctions against Japan, mild initially but more drastic in time. Mr. Moore said that rationally he did not favor such a course (a) because it might, without very careful leadership, result in war with Japan, and (b) because it would cause the Japanese military to fail in their plans without being discredited at home.

9. The Japanese Embassy and other agencies of the Japanese Government in the United States have been overwhelmed with offers from American would-be advisers and propagandists to put Japan right with the American public "for a price". Mr. Moore stated that his advice to the Japanese Embassy that it not utilize a large sum put at its disposal for propaganda purposes had not been followed. He felt that the expenditure, however, had been ineffectual.

I have been well but not intimately acquainted with Mr. Moore for about ten years. I was impressed by the earnestness and, in view of his position, critical frankness with which he spoke to me. Many of his remarks tend to strengthen and illumine conclusions I had drawn from a conversation about two weeks ago with Dr. Takeuchi (Japanese scholar and professor—author of the book entitled "War and Diplomacy in the Japanese Empire"), who cautiously intimated that Japanese civilians and soldiers were far from enthusiastic about the hostilities in China and indicated a lack of sympathy with the Japanese Army's methods of attaining objectives. He stated that the primary purpose of the Army in the present conflict was to oust foreigners and foreign influence, particularly the much-feared Soviet Russian (communist) influence, from China.

I feel, as I think you do, that the Japanese are now treading (and realize that they are) very unsafe ground. I feel that very much now depends upon the strength of the Chinese will and ability to continue effective resistance. My conversation with Mr. Moore and more recent conversations with Dr. Buck,[19] Treasury official lately returned from China, confirm these views. The position of the Chinese, should Hankow fall, would undoubtedly be critical and the matter of continued effective resistance would be in the balance. It appears easy to fall into the errors of placing too much faith in the ability of the Chinese, unassisted, to carry on the fight and of placing too much confidence in predictions that the Japanese will be unable to consolidate their gains.

---

[18] Baron Kijuro Shidehara who resigned December 11, 1931, as Japanese Minister for Foreign Affairs.

[19] Professor John Lossing Buck, of Nanking University, special agent for the Treasury Department in China.

I believe, as I think you do, that it is vitally important not only for China but for us and for other democratic nations that Chinese resistance not collapse. Believing as I do, I cannot but earnestly recommend that, within the limitations of our desire to avoid involvement (but within reasonable limitations which take into account the fact that the element of chance cannot be completely eliminated from any policy worthy of the name), we should overlook no opportunity now to bolster up Chinese will and ability to resist, and to embarrass the Japanese in their attempts to conquer China. To those ends I believe (a) that the doctrine of non-recognition should be unequivocally restated to apply in the present situation, (b) that as a corollary to non-recognition steps should be taken effectively to discourage loans or material credits to Japan or to Chinese regimes or agencies under Japanese control, (c) that the possibility of affording financial assistance to China should be thoroughly explored, (d) that our trade with Japan should be carefully examined with a view to withholding, either through export or import restrictions or both, assistance to Japan, and (e) that consultation and collaboration, if possible, with other interested governments in regard to the implementation of feasible measures should be undertaken.[20]

I realize that some of these matters can only appropriately be dealt with legislatively rather than administratively, but in so far as action may be taken administratively I feel that it should be taken, and where legislative action is required I think that the influence of the Department should be brought to bear.

During recent months I have followed editorial comment throughout the country closely, and I have also discussed the Far Eastern problems with many people not especially interested in those problems. I am willing to hazard the estimate that although a very large proportion of the people in this country continue to desire (1) that we avoid involvement in the conflict in the Far East, a very substantial and influential body of public opinion desires also (2) that American rights and interests in China be protected and preserved in so far as possible, (3) that the integrity and sovereignty of China be preserved, and (4) that for the ultimate good of all, Japanese militarism be defeated. Examining these estimated desiderata, one is tempted to observe, in the light of experience, that American rights and interests may not be preserved * unless China's sovereignty is preserved, that China's sovereignty may not be preserved unless Japanese militarism is defeated, and that from the long viewpoint our involve-

---

[20] See also pp. 519 ff.

*The evidence of the past year indicates clearly that those rights and interests are not being respected by the Japanese, and that in the absence of intention to take retaliatory or coercive measures diplomatic action is of little avail. [Footnote in the original.]

ment in the Far East may not be avoided unless Japanese militarism is defeated.

I am not one to hold up the bugaboo of Japanese attack upon the United States, but I do believe that the chance we take now of involvement by rendering assistance to China is slight in comparison with the chance we take in watching Japanese militarism succeed in China. Predictions that Japan will be fully occupied in China for many years to come if she succeeds in her present military campaign are not borne out by experience. The same comforting predictions were made when Japan took Manchuria and I believe that just such a mistaken thought was back of British and European policy at that time. I was in Manchuria in 1931–32 [21] and I do not recall that any one in a position to know, including Japanese civilian officials, actually thought that Japanese military aggression would stop in Manchuria, and it is not believed that Japanese aggression, if successful in China, will stop there. It cannot be too frequently repeated that the Japanese military is psychologically an aggressive force which should not be expected to become satiated on successful aggression or deterred from aggression by normal economic and political considerations.

I believe that, although Japanese control of China would probably result in new and increased difficulties and friction between the United States and Japan, it need not be assumed that such a situation would of itself lead to an open breach between the two countries. In this connection it is well to be mindful, of course, that for many years to come the Philippine Commonwealth may constitute a delicate problem in our relations with Japan. Furthermore, I hope that, should Japanese aggression subsequently be directed against British, Dutch, or French possessions in the Far East, or against the Soviet Union, we would be able to avoid involvement. However, I restate that in my opinion the chances of our involvement, were Japanese aggression in China to prove successful, would be measurably greater than would be the chances of our becoming involved in the present conflict were we now to render reasonable assistance to China.

I believe that we have a very great and urgent obligation of responsibility, nationally and internationally, to ourselves and to posterity, to do what we can within reason and without assuming undue risk of involvement toward influencing the course of the present conflict along lines favorable to the Chinese—toward endeavoring to forestall an outcome of the conflict that would do violence to principles which we earnestly desire to have prevail—, and that now is the psychological moment for us to take practicable steps toward discharging that obligation.

---

[21] As Consul at Mukden.

793.94119/432 : Telegram

The Ambassador in China (Johnson) to the Secretary of State

HANKOW, July 27, 1938—2 p. m.
[Received July 29—11 p. m.]

376. Minister for Foreign Affairs [22] called upon me on evening of July 24 and asked me to express to you the hope that at a favorable moment, and before Japan should recognize any puppet regime at Nanking or Peiping (thus as he said closing the back door to negotiations, the front door having been closed by the statement of the Japanese Government last January that they would refuse to recognize or treat with what they termed the Chiang Kai Shek government), the Government of the United States, taking parallel action with Great Britain (and possibly France), would extend to both Japan and to China an offer of good offices to bring both sides together to bring to an end the present hostilities without, of course, mentioning that such an offer was made at the suggestion of the Chinese. He expressed the further hope that if such an offer of good offices should fail of its purpose and Japan should proceed to set up and recognize a new regime in Nanking or elsewhere the United States Government would notify both China and Japan, as it had done in 1915 [23] in connection with the 21 demands, that it refused to recognize such a regime and reserve its position and rights under existing treaties between China and the United States.

This move should not in my opinion be interpreted as indicating a readiness on the part of the Chinese Government to make a compromise agreement with the Japanese. Chinese appear to believe that Japan is approaching a point where they might be expected to withdraw from China, citing Japanese reaction to French attitude on the subject of Hainan Island and Soviet occupation of hill overlooking strategic Rashin–Hunchun Railway [24] (which Chinese authorities insist is on the Chinese side of the boundary as contended by the Japanese) as indicating weakening of Japanese spirit.

The Minister for Foreign Affairs stated that the Chinese Government intended to make every effort to defend Hankow, making its capture expensive as possible to the Japanese. He stated that Japanese people were well aware that the Japanese were tired of the war, that they were beginning to realize that they could not make a conquest of China, that the present campaign for Hankow would either result in its capture at great expense to the Japanese or a deadlock and that therefore a moment might present itself when an offer of

---

[22] Dr. Wang Chung-hui.
[23] See telegram of May 11, 1915, 5 p. m., *Foreign Relations*, 1915, p. 146.
[24] See also pp. 441.

good offices by the United States and Great Britain would be listened to by the Japanese. China, he pointed out, could not sue for peace and Japan would not, but an offer from a friendly and disinterested outsider might make it possible for the Japanese to climb down from a difficult position.

The Department has already received my estimate of the situation here in my 362 of July 19, 3 p. m. I feel certain that the Chinese Government will not collapse and sue for peace when Hankow falls. Minister for Foreign Affairs confirms this view. I am of course not in any position to say whether the time might or may have come when an offer of good offices to Japan by the United States and Great Britain would be useful. I shall repeat this message to Tokyo in order that Grew may have an opportunity to comment upon this phase of the matter.

Foreign Minister expects that if we refuse to recognize position established by the Japanese by force in contravention of Kellogg Pact and Nine Power Treaty and made reservation of our position and rights under existing treaties between us and China we would be in a position to assert those rights if and when by conference these present hostilities may be brought to a close.

British Ambassador informs me that Minister for Foreign Affairs made a proposal similar in all respects to the above (which I have made known to him) and that he is transmitting it to his Government upon his arrival in Hong Kong about August 3.

JOHNSON

793.94/13567 : Telegram

The Ambassador in Japan (Grew) to the Secretary of State [25]

TOKYO, July 27, 1938—3 p. m.
[Received July 27—10 : 05 a. m.]

494. Following is a general digest of a long conversation with the British Ambassador yesterday.

1. The Ambassador, on returning from the mountains for 2 days in Tokyo, said that he wished to tell me of his plan for a talk with the Minister for Foreign Affairs yesterday afternoon. The British Government feels that the time has come when it must examine its future policy toward Japan in connection with the situation in China. It must ascertain whether any confidence can be placed in Japanese assurances of the intention and desire to respect British interests without discrimination in China or whether the Japanese propose progressively to crowd British interests out of China. Great Britain must reach a

---

[25] In its telegram No. 447, August 13, 2 p. m., the Department repeated the substance of this telegram to the Embassy in the United Kingdom.

decision as to whether she can in future cooperate with Japan or whether she must throw her full weight behind the Chinese Central Government. Sir Robert Craigie therefore proposed to present to General Ugaki a list of some of the principal British desiderata and to discuss the situation along general lines.

2. The Ambassador said that he proposed to tell the Foreign Minister that Japan was going to face great difficulties in the process of consolidation and reconstruction in China even after complete military victory and that at that time Japan would stand greatly in need of foreign financial cooperation.

3. There then arises the question of sanctions in case the British representations lead to no favorable results. Craigie asked me if I had been informed of a recent approach to our Government by the British Government to ascertain whether we would consider some kind of financial support of the Chinese Central Government in the form of loans or credits. I replied that I had not been informed thereof. The Ambassador said that an unfavorable reply to the British inquiry had been given by the American Government on the ground that such a sanction as the British Government proposed would not accord with American policy and that there were other methods which the American Government would prefer to follow. Craigie asked me if I knew what methods my Government had in mind to which I replied in the negative.

4. Craigie realized that the position of our Government with respect to foreign financing was somewhat different from that of the British Government but he felt strongly that if it could become known in Japan that unless the Japanese respect our respective interests in China Japan could hope for no financial support either from American or British sources during the period of reconstruction the effect would be important and salutary. (In this connection I have constantly in mind Department's 338, December 10, 7 p. m., 1943).[26]

5. Craigie informs me today that his interview with the Foreign Minister yesterday followed the lines which he had sketched to me and that nothing particularly new emerged. Sir Robert nevertheless received the impression that in spite of the difficulties and especially the opposition of the Japanese authorities in China, genuine efforts are being made in Tokyo to comply with British requirements.

6. The partial list of British desiderata as presented to the Foreign Minister follows:

["] *Northern district of Shanghai.*

(a) Modification of pass system in the northern district for employees of British firms and for removal of British owned goods. Application in all such cases to be made by His Majesty's Consulate

---

[26] *Foreign Relations*, 1937, vol. III, p. 785.

General to the Japanese Consulate General without necessity for reference to any other Japanese authorities.

(*b*) Resumption of normal municipal activities by Shanghai Municipal Council in return for which the Council will be prepared to take next step along agreed lines towards reconstitution of Japanese branch of the police force.

(*c*) Resumption of bus and tram service.

Navigation of Yangtze.

Permission for two British vessels per week to navigate the Yangtze up to Wuhu. (It would be understood that full guarantees could be given and no Chinese passengers carried.)

Removal of restrictions on the following British owned or controlled concerns:

(*a*) Immediate reopening of Zoongsing mill.
(*b*) Cessation of interference with Chunta mill.
(*c*) Evacuation of Sungsing number 7 mill and its return to control of the Hong Kong and Shanghai Bank to which it is mortgaged.

Railways.

Grant of inspection facilities for nominees of the British Chinese Corporation of those railways which are not now the scene of major military operations. (See British Embassy memorandum of 20th April, 1938 [27] regarding the Shanghai–Nanking and Shanghai–Hangchow–Nippon [*Nanchang?*] Railways.)

Whangpoo Conservancy.

Removal of all restrictions on conservancy work in the Whangpoo River under the authority of the International Consultative Board".

Paragraphs numbered 1, 2, 5 and 6 repeated to Shanghai for Hankow.

GREW

793.94119/431 : Telegram

The Ambassador in China (Johnson) to the Secretary of State

HANKOW, July 27, 1938—3 p. m.
[Received July 29—10 : 09 p. m.]

377. My 376, July 27, 2 p. m. At lunch today at which I was only guest Generalissimo inquired what I thought of suggestion which Wang Chung Hui had made. I told him that while I was sure that American Government would be willing at an appropriate time to offer its good offices to bring hostilities to an end I felt that it was an open question as to when such an appropriate time might arrive. Generalissimo stated that he felt that should Japan take Hankow a reiteration of America's often stated policy of refusing to recognize a regime set up by force and in contravention of treaty would have a beneficial effect

---

[27] Not found in Department files.

upon Japanese policy. He expressed appreciation that America had maintained its Embassy at seat of Government throughout present hostilities.

Repeated to Tokyo.

JOHNSON

793.94/13578 : Telegram

The Consul General at Shanghai (Lockhart) to the Secretary of State

SHANGHAI, July 28, 1938—10 p. m.
[Received July 28—7 : 40 p. m.]

1042. My 1011, July 19, 5 p. m.[28] and Hankow's No. 379, July 27, 5 p. m.[29]

1. The Chinese mentioned in my 964, July 8, 3 p. m., who was arrested on July 7 with a bomb in his possession and who later confessed that he was one of a group who had been sent here from Hankow for the purpose of conducting terrorism, was handed over to the Japanese authorities on July 25. This is the first, and up to date the only application of the revised proclamation of July 18. Despite apparent efforts on the part of the municipal authorities to avoid publicity, the local press is now carrying reports of the protest made by the National Government. The municipal police are still holding and questioning 29 other persons who have been arrested since July 7, most of them in connection with the two murders reported in my 1028, July 23 [22], 1 p. m.[30] It has not been learned what further evidence has been obtained from these suspects nor what final action will be taken in regard to them.

2. An attack on July 25 has been the only one since my July 23, 1 p. m. The intended victim, an official of the Salt Tax Bureau of the "Ta Tao government" escaped with slight injuries. Police inflicted serious wounds on the assassin who died soon after his capture.

Repeated to Hankow and Peiping.

LOCKHART

793.94/13580 : Telegram

The Consul General at Shanghai (Lockhart) to the Secretary of State

SHANGHAI, July 29, 1938—noon.
[Received July 29—7 a. m.]

1043. After repeated efforts on the part of the Commanding Officer of the Fourth Marines to persuade the Japanese military authorities

---

[28] For substance of telegram, see footnote 8, p. 226.
[29] Vol. IV, p. 135.
[30] Not printed.

to live up to a "gentleman's agreement" entered into some time ago by which armed men of the Japanese forces would not pass through the American defense sector, Colonel Price notified the Japanese military authorities yesterday that the Marine Corps traffic control posts would be at once reestablished in the American sector and that the passage through the sector of armed men would be stopped. There have been daily violations of the understanding by Japanese men under arms passing through the sector for some time and these have repeatedly been brought to the attention of the Japanese military authorities by Colonel Price.

Repeated to Hankow, Peiping and Tokyo.

LOCKHART

793.94/13582 : Telegram

The Consul General at Shanghai (Lockhart) to the Secretary of State

SHANGHAI, July 29, 1938—4 p. m.
[Received July 29—10:40 a. m.]

1049. My 1043, noon, today. A Japanese officer called on Colonel Price today and explained that the violations were due to a recent change in personnel. He promised that effective steps to prevent passage of Japanese men under arms through the American defense sector will be taken at once.

Repeated to Hankow, Peiping and Tokyo.

LOCKHART

793.94/13752

The Consul General at Shanghai (Lockhart) to the Secretary of State

No. 1572

SHANGHAI, July 29, 1938.
[Received August 26.]

SIR: I have the honor to enclose a brief account [31] of the activities of the Japanese Army on entering Hsuchow in May of this year, from which it will be noted that the orgy of looting, raping, drinking and murder which marked the entry of the Japanese forces into Nanking was duplicated at Hsuchow. It seems reasonable to assume, therefore, that, whatever may be the cause, such tendencies are characteristic in the Japanese Army, and become credible to foreigners only when there are foreigners present on the scene.

The account was supplied by Dr. A. A. McFadyen, who is an American medical missionary of long residence still practising in Hsuchow, and it is therefore necessary for his safety that the source be very carefully guarded.

Respectfully yours,

FRANK P. LOCKHART

[31] Not printed.

793.94/13957

The Ambassador in China (Johnson) to the Secretary of State

No. 64   HANKOW, July 29, 1938.
                                          [Received September 26.]

SIR: I have the honor to transmit, as of possible interest to the Department, a copy of a memorandum [32] prepared by Captain Frank Dorn, Assistant Naval [*Military*] Attaché to this Embassy, which incorporates a report prepared by Dr. H. Talbot, a British doctor, on the subject of his investigation at Nanchang, Kiangsi, of a number of suspected gas cases occurring among Chinese troops who participated in the hostilities at Ma Tang on the Yangtze River between Anking and Kiukiang. Captain Dorn and an American missionary accompanied Dr. Talbot on his tour of investigation.

The Embassy is of the opinion that Dr. Talbot's report of his diagnosis of the cases examined [33] can be accepted without question. Dr. Talbot's report, as quoted in Captain Dorn's memorandum, was released for publication by the Central News Agency, the Chinese official news agency, on July 19, 1938.

Respectfully yours,   NELSON TRUSLER JOHNSON

894.512/53

Memorandum by the Chief of the Division of Trade Agreements (Hawkins) to the Secretary of State [34]

[WASHINGTON,] July 30, 1938.

MR. SECRETARY: I have made a rather hasty survey of the considerations of a commercial nature which would be involved in reaching a decision as to the desirability of terminating our treaty of commerce and navigation with Japan [35] and wish to offer the following comments as my preliminary reaction.

Mr. Hornbeck's memorandum [36] refers to various violations by Japan of our rights under the treaty. So far as I am aware, there are no cases outstanding of violations of the commercial clauses of the treaty. In the course of a study recently undertaken of the possibility of suspending the generalization of trade-agreement concessions to Japan because of Japanese activities in China, it was concluded that

---

[32] Not printed.
[33] Dr. Talbot concluded that the cases "were all caused by gas poisoning, of the Mustard Gas type." Capt. Dorn suggested that some of the cases might have been caused by Chlorine Gas.
[34] See also memorandum of October 10 by the Chief of the Division of Far Eastern Affairs, vol. IV, p. 62.
[35] Signed at Washington, February 21, 1911, *Foreign Relations*, 1911, p. 315.
[36] Not found in Department files.

there was no clear evidence of discrimination against American trade in Japan. There is a possibility that the Japanese Government may be influencing Japanese spinners to divert purchases of cotton to sources other than the United States, but no evidence which would support this suspicion has been unearthed.

In connection with the study of suspending Japan to which I have referred, consideration was given to the possible effects of retaliatory action by Japan against our trade. In view of the fact that Japan has reduced its imports from this and other countries to the barest essentials, the conclusion was reached that retaliatory action by Japan would not have a significant effect upon our trade with her at the present time.

These conclusions tend to suggest that termination of the treaty would have little effect upon the present trade situation. Furthermore, it is open to question whether Japan would have anything to gain in the immediate future by pursuing an openly discriminatory trade policy in so far as the United States is concerned.

On the other hand, termination of the treaty, unless it were replaced by a new one, would remove one important barrier to the adoption of a more openly bilateralistic policy by Japan and would wipe out whatever protection the treaty offers for future trade development. Both of these possibilities would appear to warrant further consideration.

The foregoing comments relate solely to the commercial clauses of the treaty. I assume that consideration will be given in other divisions to the value to us of the provisions dealing with navigation, residence and related matters.

I should like to venture one further suggestion in the event that it is decided to terminate the treaty. It is that notice of termination not be given on the ground that Japan has violated the treaty. Japan has in many instances been excluded from the benefit of trade-agreement concessions on products in which she is interested by the establishment of subclassifications and value brackets. However justifiable this policy may be, Japan would doubtless charge that we have violated at least the spirit of the treaty ourselves.

The particular case which is dealt with in the attached file [37] involves a matter of disputed interpretation. An open charge that Japan has violated the treaty might cause the Japanese to claim that tariff specialization in our agreements has been carried to such an extent as to represent a wholesale evasion of our obligations. While we could defend our action in these instances to our own satisfaction the questions involved are highly technical ones and some doubt as to whether we are not ourselves guilty of evading the treaty might remain in the public mind if there were a controversy on the subject.

---

[37] Identity not recorded.

If an alternative reason for termination is desired, and if we would be prepared to enter into new negotiations with Japan, we might give as a reason for termination our desire to have the treaty revised in the light of modern conditions and requirements, citing the action we have already taken in the case of our treaty with Italy.[38] Both the treaty of 1911 and our earlier treaty of 1894 with Japan [39] (the provisions "relating to tariff" of which are still in force) contain the most-favored-nation clause in its conditional form.   Furthermore, any embargo upon the shipment of arms or other commodities to Japan would apparently conflict with the two treaties.   A proposal could be made to Japan that the provisions of the 1911 treaty be brought up-to-date. If negotiations for a new treaty were undertaken, it is to be assumed that this Government would insist upon the inclusion of a reservation similar to those contained in our Italian *modus vivendi* and our trade agreement with Czechoslovakia [40] permitting the application of measures "relating to neutrality".

If, however, it is desired to place our relations with Japan on a more flexible basis and the suggestion that the treaty be terminated does not envisage any new arrangement with Japan of either a temporary or a long-term character, consideration might be given to the desirability of terminating the treaty without an explanation or merely with the statement that it no longer corresponds to present-day conditions and requirements.[41]

HARRY C. HAWKINS

893.00/14260

The Consul General at Hankow (Josselyn) to the Secretary of State

No. 480   HANKOW, July 30, 1938.
                                             [Received September 12.]

SIR: With reference to the Department's instruction of February 10, 1938,[42] concerning the submittal of information relating to the Communist Party of China, I have the honor to enclose a translation of an editorial [43] on China's foreign policy, appearing in the *Hsin Hua Jih Pao*, an official daily publication of the Chinese Communist Party.

---

[38] For denunciation of the treaty, signed February 26, 1871 (Malloy, *Treaties*, 1776–1909, vol. I, p. 960), see *Foreign Relations*, 1936, vol. II, pp. 339 ff.   For text of temporary commercial arrangement of December 16, 1937, see 51 Stat. 361.
[39] Signed at Washington, November 22, 1894, Malloy, *Treaties*, 1776–1909, vol. I, p. 1028.
[40] Signed March 7, 1938; 53 Stat. 2293.
[41] Marginal comment at end of memorandum by the Adviser on Political Relations, Hornbeck: "If any reason is given it should be (only) that we wish to be free to deal as we see fit with matters now covered by the treaty."
[42] *Ante*, p. 78.
[43] Not printed.

This editorial is believed to be the outgrowth of an acrimonious dispute during the last session of the People's Political Council, which convocation met from July 5 to July 15, 1938.

The dispute arose when one of the delegates, Mr. Li Shen-wu, an editor of the *Commercial Press* and a member of the clique led by Mr. Wang Ching-wei, General Chang Chun, and General Ho Ying-ch'in, recommended that China take steps to come to an understanding with Germany and Italy. Wang Ming, formerly Chinese member of the Communist International, hotly replied that Germany and Italy were allies of Japan and that any *rapprochement* with them would lead to capitulation to the Japanese. The Soviet Union, Wang Ming declared, is the natural ally of China.

Li Shen-wu and those delegates of similar persuasion thereupon demanded of Wang Ming, "Are you a Chinese or a Russian?" A scuffle was avoided only by the intercession of more temperate elements and the appeal of the Chairman, Dr. Chang Po-ling, to remember the United Front.

The enclosed editorial carries Wang Ming's, and of course the Chinese Communist Party's, foreign policy platform to the public. The program is the alignment of China with the democracies and the Soviet Union and opposition to Japan, Germany and Italy, who are classified as "aggressors".

The alliance of Germany and Italy with Japan is motivated, the Communists contend, by (1) a desire to make use of Japanese aid in prosecuting military adventures in Europe, (2) on Germany's part, a wish to secure through joint action with Japan colonies in the South Pacific, (3) the need for assistance from the east in a combined attack on the Soviet Union, and (4) a hope that out of the Japanese invasion of China they may secure a share of the benefit. Because of the close understanding and association which Germany and Italy have with Japan, the Chinese communists consider those two European states as enemies of China. Therefore, any proposal of a *rapprochement* with Germany and Italy is viewed as a betrayal of China, through Germany and Italy, to Japan.

The ability of the democratic powers to take common action is conceded by the editorial to be weaker than that of the aggressor bloc. An advance, however, is professed to be noticeable, in joint restraint of aggression on the part of the democracies.

It is in the Soviet Union that the Chinese Communist Party places its greatest reliance for assistance to China's cause. Only through alliance with the Soviet Union and through its assistance, the editorial maintains, can China maintain its place in international affairs and continue the struggle in the war of resistance.

Respectfully yours,   P. R. JOSSELYN

893.48/1605: Telegram

The Consul General at Hankow (Josselyn) to the Secretary of State

HANKOW, August 1, 1938—3 p. m.
[Received 9 p. m.]

I have received the following communication from the Refugee Zone Committee with the request that it be transmitted to the Japanese authorities:

"A Committee composed of American, British, French, German, and Italian nationals has been working for some time on a plan for refugee zones in Hankow and Wuchang respectively. The proposed refugee zones would comprise (*a*) at Hankow the area bounded on the east by the Yangtze River, on the west by the Peiping–Hankow Railway, on the south by the Kianghan Road and on the north by the Japanese concession and a line extending westward from it to but not including the Peiping–Hankow Railway. The French Concession and special administrative district number 3 being excluded from the proposed zone, so far as administration is concerned, although geographically they are within the area. (*b*) At Wuchang the area included between the old Tsao Hu Men and the small East Gate, following the line of the City Wall; the west boundary to be Tsao Hu Men Kai, Fu Kai and Huen Kai to San Tao Kai; the south boundary to be San Tao Kai, the rear of the old Fu Tai Yamen and then extending out to Ya Li Chu Kai. Maps of Hankow and Wuchang showing the proposed refugee zones will be forwarded for transmission to the Japanese authorities.

The proposed zones consist largely and indeed predominately of foreign owned property, the inviolability of which is admitted and it is hoped that this will facilitate the present efforts. It is realized that the approval of refugee zones must be dependent upon their complete demilitarization. The Committee have received provisional assurances from the Chinese side that their approval would be accompanied by compliance with this basic condition and the Committee would naturally only put their scheme into operation if and when this compliance has been made effective.

Steps would be taken effectually to isolate the refugee zones from adjoining non-demilitarized areas, and it is likely that the administrative bodies thereof would consist of this Committee or its nominees.

The Committee understands a refugee zone to be an area which having been previously demilitarized shall prior to the occupation of the city be immune from bombing or shelling or any other form of attack; which during an entry into or assault on the city shall remain outside the scope of military operations; and which, after occupation of the city, may be entered and subsequently controlled solely by military police acting under regular authority.

The maintenance of an adequate police force being essential for the proper administration of the zones, the immunity of its members in common with that of the Chinese populace in the zones in general must be assured.

The Committee request that the Japanese Government and the Japanese military and naval authorities will be good enough to accept the scheme above outlined.

(Signed) A. A. Gilman, Chairman Refugee Zone Committee."

The members of the Committee are Bishop Gilman and Bishop Espelage, Americans; Bishop Galvin, Reverend A. J. Gedye, Mr. W. H. Dupree and Mr. R. Marker, British; Bishop Massi, Italian; Mr. E. A. Chaudoin, French; and Mr. G. Tolle, German.

Please deliver copies of this message to the diplomatic or consular representatives in Shanghai of Great Britain, France, Germany and Italy. Hankow consular representatives are telegraphing separately to their representatives in Shanghai.

Maps showing proposed zones in Hankow and Wuchang being forwarded today.

Sent to Shanghai, Shanghai please inform Tokyo.

JOSSELYN

793.94/13605 : Telegram

The Third Secretary of Embassy in China (Allison) to the Secretary of State

NANKING, August 2, 1938—10 a. m.
[Received August 2—7 a. m.]

144. With reference to Japanese reports that one of their hospital ships was bombed by Chinese near Kiukiang, the captain of the U.S.S. *Oahu* reports that a Japanese hospital ship which went up river towards Kiukiang a short time ago was filled with troops when it passed Nanking. It is not likely that all these were wounded men as there would be no point in sending a shipload of casualties towards the front.

In this connection it has been noted that during the past few days a large number of Japanese hospital corps units have been coming into Nanking. Members of the Embassy staff, as well as other foreigners who have seen these units, all testify that while each man wears a Red Cross brassard on his arm, approximately 50% of the men are armed with rifles, and the officers and noncommissioned officers wear pistols.

Sent to Shanghai. Repeated to Hankow and Peiping. Peiping please mail to Tokyo.

ALLISON

793.94119/433 : Telegram

The Ambassador in Japan (Grew) to the Secretary of State

Tokyo, August 2, 1938—10 p. m.
[Received August 2—7 p. m.]

510. Johnson's 376, July 27, 2 p. m.

1. With regard to the question presented by Johnson whether "the time might or may have come when an offer of good offices to Japan by the United States and Great Britain would be useful", I am assuming that it continues to be the position of our Government that if the tender of good offices were made by the United States to Japan and China, it would be clearly indicated that terms of settlement could not be recommended to China by us which would be inconsistent with the Nine Power Treaty (Department's 305, November 19, 2 p. m.[44]).

2. To us who are in direct touch with Japanese of all classes and who would be bound to sense a war weariness, however sedulously and effectively overt manifestations thereof were suppressed, it is surprising that there should prevail belief in despatch of responsible quarter abroad that there is "weakening of Japanese spirit". Indeed there persists especially among the urban population a noticeable attitude toward the conflict of levity and mock seriousness which the official movement for "spiritual mobilization" has not eradicated. With reference to the indications of such weakening cited in the second paragraph of Johnson's telegram, the events of the last few days on the Soviet border [45] rule out the previous negative Japanese attitude on the Changkufeng incident as evidence of Japanese weakening; of others [I?] dare say that if all the facts of the Hainan issue were known a substantially different conclusion from that apparently reached by the Chinese might reasonably be drawn. Possibly the various Japanese restrictions on commerce and on the non-military uses of essential war materials have stimulated (and perhaps not unnaturally) the belief abroad that there is growing discontent with the protracted hostilities. I refer the Department to our despatch No. 3100, June [*July*] 11 [46] in which this subject is discussed. Actually the restrictions apply in the main to commodities which are still exotic to the indigenous mode of living and thus do not work hardship on the mass of the people. While emphasizing the gravity of the problems with which Japan is confronted and our doubt whether the continental policy can ever be successfully implemented by methods which must forfeit the cooperation of the Chinese people we perceive no evi-

---

[44] *Foreign Relations*, 1937, vol. III, p. 699.
[45] See pp. 441 ff.
[46] Not printed; for enclosure to despatch, see statement by the Japanese Prime Minister on July 7, *Foreign Relations*, Japan, 1931–1941, vol. I, p. 467.

dences of any serious movement in opposition to drastic reorganization of the economic, industrial, (and possibly political) systems to meet the exigencies of a war of endurance.

3. The official Japanese declaration of January 16 [47] that Japan would no longer deal with the "Nationalist Government of China" has been reaffirmed on every conceivable opportunity by responsible Japanese. At the same time it is privately admitted that any settlement with any Chinese personage other than Chiang Kai Shek would not be worth the paper it was written on and there is cherished a lingering hope that eventually Chiang might disassociate himself from uncompromising anti-Japanese elements and come to a settlement with Japan. But that there is at present disposition on the part of Japan to entering into a settlement with the Chinese Government as now constituted, I cannot bring myself to believe. Certainly there is no manifestation of any such disposition.

4. There is finally the fundamental and irrevocable conflict between Japan's objectives in China and the determination of China that a negotiated peace shall be consistent with the Nine Power Treaty. Even before the fall of Nanking it seemed to us highly doubtful if an offer of American good office bridged the gap between Japan and China and led to a settlement consistent with the letter if not the spirit of that treaty. If any Japanese thought with regard to the conflict has subsequently been crystallizing and promise[s] soon to become dominant, it is that the eventual settlement, if and when made, shall bring to Japan material advantages commensurate with the cost of the hostilities. Far from any thought of withdrawing from China, the human and material resources of the nation are being mobilized against the time when the unfolding of the military campaign will enable Japan to maintain a permanent domicile in China. In the light of Johnson's estimates of China's position an offer at the present time of American good offices would in our opinion immediately betray any Chinese expectation that terms of peace acceptable to Japan would also be acceptable to China. We believe that such an offer if made today would (a) be abortive and (b) probably by reviving controversy over principles over which issue has long been joined between the United States and Japan render more difficult the problem of maintaining relations of peace between the two countries.

5. In view of Johnson's having scheduled departure on August 1 from Hankow,[48] I have not repeated this telegram to him.

GREW

793.94119/434

Memorandum of Conversation, by the Secretary of State

[WASHINGTON,] August 3, 1938.

After the Chinese Ambassador [49] had spoken to me on another subject, during his call, he referred to the recent *démarche* handed to Ambassador Johnson by the Chinese Foreign Office, suggesting the idea of mediation by this government between China and Japan. He stated that his government had called this to his attention and he was wondering what we might have in mind in that connection. I replied that I would be glad to propound a question to the Ambassador, and that question was—what, in the Ambassador's judgment, would be best for China? Would it be desirable on China's part for an approach to be made to Japan for mediation without the slightest knowledge as to what Japan's future plans relative to occupation and otherwise remaining in China would be in the event of mediation? The Ambassador said that if he might express his personal opinion he would readily say that this preliminary question as to Japan's future intentions in China would be absolutely necessary. I replied that of course this Government has made many offers of mediation to both governments and that we have said repeatedly to the Japanese officials that we stand ready to exercise our good offices in this respect whenever it may be desirable on the part of the governments of China and Japan. The Ambassador said that his government might desire us to feel out the situation in respect to mediation at Tokyo. I repeated what I had just said, and added that, naturally, Japan knows when she might be willing to accept mediation and she knows of our standing offer, and that she will undoubtedly determine what her future policy will be with reference to the occupation of China, its extent and nature, before she will be ready to agree to mediation. Finally, I said, "You can say to your government, if you desire, what your individual views are with respect to the preliminary question I propounded at the outset, and then you can add that this Government has been keeping in mind all phases of the mediation question since the outbreak of hostilities and that it continues to do so, but that this does not necessarily mean that there are in immediate prospect any new developments." I commented that the Ambassador could himself judge as well as we could as to this latter possibility and when same might occur.

C[ORDELL] H[ULL]

---

[49] C. T. Wang.

893.48/1609 : Telegram

The Secretary of State to the Consul General at Shanghai (Gauss)

WASHINGTON, August 4, 1938—3 p. m.

Following for Tokyo:

"268, August 4, 3 p. m.   Your 509, August 2, 9 p. m.,[50] in regard to refugee zones at Hankow and Wuchang.

1. Your action in making available to the Foreign Office the text of the communication from the Refugee Zone Committee is approved.

2. The Department desires that American officials scrupulously avoid any responsibility to the Chinese or Japanese for the observance by either of assurances given by the other in connection with the establishment of refugee zones.

3. On the other hand, the Department would not wish to take the position of discouraging any attempt by private individuals to procure the establishment of safety zones.

4. With the above considerations in mind the Department desires that American officials in China and Japan, in their discretion, extend appropriate informal and unofficial assistance to the Wuhan Refugee Zone Committee."

Repeat to Hankow.

HULL

793.94/13623 : Telegram

The Consul General at Hankow (Josselyn) to the Secretary of State

HANKOW, August 4, 1938—3 p. m.
[Received August 5—12 : 25 a. m.]

The pronounced pessimism of Chinese civil and military officials noticeable during the past weeks concerning the progress of Sino-Japanese hostilities has been modified by the recent Manchurian border disturbances.[51] The hope of third power intervention on behalf of China is now at its liveliest. The more so because a major conflict between Japan and the Soviet Union promises, with a shift of the main theater of Japanese operations to the northeast, the possibility of a relaxation in fighting Japanese, the uncompromising and exacting character of which warfare is most uncongenial to the temperament of the average high Chinese official.

A Russo-Japanese war at the present time would however tend to split the Chinese united front, a large portion of the Kuomintang being more anti-Russian than anti-Japanese. The Communists and Leftist member of the Kuomintang therefore view the split in the northeast with mixed feelings, fearing a recrudescence of domestic dissension.

---

[50] Not printed.
[51] For hostilities between Japanese and Soviet forces, see pp. 441 ff.

From the point of view of the Chinese Reds the most advantageous moment for a Russo-Japanese war would be after the Japanese capture of Wuhan when the Central Government may be expected to be critically weakened and the Communists relatively strengthened through a continuation of the process whereby the Central Government has been losing the principal lines of communications and cities to the Japanese and the remainder of the territory behind the Japanese lines to the Communists.

Repeated to the Ambassador, Peiping, Shanghai. Shanghai please repeat to Tokyo.

JOSSELYN

793.94119/441

Memorandum by the First Secretary of Embassy in the United Kingdom (Millard)[52]

In the course of a conversation today with Ronald, Assistant Chief of the Far Eastern Department, he gave me the following information concerning the steps taken by the Italian Ambassador to China towards mediation.

Ronald said the middle of July the British Ambassador to China had reported from Hankow a conversation with General Chiang Kai-shek who stated that the end of June the Italian Ambassador had sent a Secretary to see the Chinese Minister for Foreign Affairs with a message to the effect that the Italian Ambassador had the best reasons to believe that the Japanese wanted peace at once and were ready to offer terms much more favorable to China than those communicated through the German Ambassador in the spring [*winter*]. It was proposed that the Chinese Minister for Foreign Affairs write to the Japanese Prime Minister to the effect that henceforward "the policy of the Chinese Government will not be anti-Japanese." The Italian Secretary said that the Japanese attached importance to the sending of a letter from the Chinese Minister for Foreign Affairs rather than Chiang Kai-shek with whom their repeated declarations made it difficult for them to deal.

According to this account the Chinese Minister for Foreign Affairs told the Italian Secretary in reply that the proposal could not be considered in its present form excluding, as it did, Chiang Kai-shek. He said, however, the Chinese were equally anxious for peace and would accept mediation. The Chinese Foreign Minister also informed the Italian Secretary that China did not want to do anything without the approval of the British Government.

---

[52] Copy transmitted to the Department by the Chargé in the United Kingdom in his despatch No. 932, August 5; received August 16.

Ronald added that since the above nothing had occurred. Asked whether the British Ambassador made any comment to General Chiang Kai-shek, Ronald replied that he had not.

H[UGH] M[ILLARD]

[LONDON,] August 5, 1938.

793.94119/436 : Telegram

The Chargé in the United Kingdom (Johnson) to the Secretary of State

LONDON, August 11, 1938—7 p. m.
[Received August 11—2 : 45 p. m.]

748. The Foreign Office informed me this afternoon that the British Ambassador in China on a recent visit to Hankow was approached by the Chinese Government with a request for the good offices of the British Government between themselves and Japan. According to the British Ambassador, a similar approach was made by the Chinese Government at the same time to Ambassador Johnson. Last night instructions in the following tenor were telegraphed to Ambassador Craigie at Tokyo:

After consultation with Ambassador Grew and in his discretion with the German Ambassador,[53] and subject to concurrence of the British Ambassador in China who has been informed of the instructions to Tokyo, Ambassador Craigie is to approach the Japanese Foreign Minister and tell him that the British Government is prepared, either alone or acting with other neutral powers, to offer its good offices with a view to settlement of the Sino-Japanese difficulty. Ambassador Craigie is being requested to avoid the use of the word "mediation" and to confine the British offer strictly to "good offices". The Foreign Office explains that they are not willing to be anything more than a "post office" in the matter and that if their offer of good offices is accepted they do not propose to comment upon or discuss the merits of any proposals which may be made by either side to the other except to the party making the proposals, in the event that British comment or criticism is requested. In other words, they will not comment to the Chinese upon Japanese proposals nor to the Japanese upon Chinese proposals. Ambassador Craigie at the same time is to invite the attention of the Japanese Foreign Minister to the statement made in the House of Commons on July 26, as follows: "In the Far East we should be very glad to offer our services to bring about the cessation of hostilities if ever and whenever we can see an opportunity

[53] Gen. Eugen Ott.

which presents a favorable prospect of success" (see Embassy's despatch No. 862, July 28, 1938,[54] enclosure, Hansard, top of column 2972). This statement of the Prime Minister's [55] incidentally anticipated the Chinese request by 2 or 3 days.

Following the overture made by the Chinese Government to the British Ambassador, it was confirmed in London by the Chinese Ambassador acting under instructions and the Foreign Office has been informed that a similar procedure was carried out with the United States Government.

In explanation of the instruction to Ambassador Craigie authorizing him in his discretion to consult also with the German Ambassador, the Foreign Office explained that Ambassador Henderson in Berlin has repeatedly urged the advisability of associating Germany, if at all possible, in any steps which might be taken toward a settlement of the Far Eastern conflict. He urges this on the ground that it could only be interpreted as a gesture of friendliness toward Germany on the part of Great Britain and because in fact, if the German Government wished to do so, it could be of genuine help in bringing about a pacific settlement of the Sino-Japanese dispute. With this opinion the Foreign Office agrees.

JOHNSON

793.94119/437 : Telegram

The Chargé in the United Kingdom (Johnson) to the Secretary of State

LONDON, August 12, 1938—7 p. m.
[Received August 12—2:35 p. m.]

756. My 748, August 11, 7 p. m. The Foreign Office informs me that an acknowledgment has been received from Ambassador Craigie who intends to discuss the matter with Mr. Grew on Monday. The Ambassador says that he considers secrecy to be of the utmost importance if there is to be any chance of success in this endeavor and suggests that he consult with his French colleague as well as with the German Ambassador. To this the Foreign Office will make no objection. Accordingly the French Government will be informed in confidence of the Chinese proposal to the British and of the instructions to Ambassador Craigie.

JOHNSON

---

[54] Not printed.
[55] Neville Chamberlain.

793.94119/436 : Telegram

The Secretary of State to the Ambassador in Japan (Grew)

WASHINGTON, August 12, 1938—7 p. m.

285. Department's 276, August 8, 6 p. m.,[56] and Ambassador Johnson's 376, July 27, 2 p. m.

[Here follows report of contents of telegram No. 748, August 11, 7 p. m., from the Chargé in the United Kingdom, printed on page 255.]

On April 14 the Department informed the British Ambassador here,[57] in response to an approach made by the Ambassador,[58] that insofar as the information in the possession of this Government indicates, neither the Chinese Government nor the Japanese Government would be prepared at this time to agree to terms of peace which would be acceptable to the other. That view remains unchanged and in this connection the Department has taken note of the views recently expressed by you and by Ambassador Johnson. As you know, we have repeatedly offered our good offices to the Japanese; we have made it clear to both the Chinese and the Japanese Governments that whenever both those governments considered it desirable we stood ready to exercise our good offices; and the Japanese Government is aware of our standing offer. In the absence of an indication by Japan of a readiness to accept an offer of good offices and without previous knowledge concerning Japan's intentions and desires with especial reference to the extent to which Japan might wish to remain in China, we would be reluctant to associate ourselves in a procedure wherein we would function as a "post office", because the powers so functioning would probably not only be called upon to transmit terms inconsistent with the provisions of treaties to which we are committed and with principles in which we believe, but because of the implication that the powers acting in such capacity were pressing such terms. In view of these considerations we do not desire that you make an approach to the Japanese Government similar to that which Craigie has been authorized to make. You may discuss the matter fully with Craigie and inform him that we are of the opinion that an offer of good offices at the present time would have no chance of success and that in the light of considerations set forth hereinbefore we are not prepared to make a *démarche* at Tokyo similar to that which he has been authorized to make. Please inform Craigie that we hope that the British Government will continue to keep us fully and currently informed of developments in order that we may, should developments make such action on our part practicable, be afforded

---

[56] This telegram reported the Secretary's memorandum of August 3, p. 252.
[57] *Foreign Relations*, Japan, 1931–1941, vol. I, p. 463.
[58] See *aide-mémoire* of April 11, p. 139.

opportunity to make such contribution as we appropriately might toward bringing about a settlement of the conflict on terms fair and just to all concerned.

In case your present views should not coincide with those expressed in this telegram, I should welcome your further comment.

Please repeat to Hong Kong with request that Hong Kong forward code text to Ambassador Johnson at Chungking by air mail.

HULL

893.102S/1670 : Telegram

The Consul General at Shanghai (Lockhart) to the Secretary of State

SHANGHAI, August 13, 1938—11 a. m.
[Received August 13—8 a. m.]

1102.   1. At 6 : 15 this morning, passengers in a motor car, bearing a Shanghai defense force license created a disturbance in Robinson Road (American defense sector).   A marine sergeant approached the car which had three Japanese in plain clothes in the back seat, all armed with pistols, and one Chinese chauffeur in the front seat. On the approach of the marine, the Chinese chauffeur started the car.   The marine jumped on the running board and one of the Japanese in the rear of the car pointed his pistol at the marine's neck. The marine then drew his own pistol and ordered the chauffeur to halt.   At this point another marine, armed with a Thomson submachine gun, approached and the Japanese dropped their pistols. At this point Colonel Price [59] arrived and took charge.   Marine authorities escorted the three Japanese to the Pootoo Road police station.   They refused to give their names or to get out of car when asked.   They were thereupon forcibly removed from the car, searched and disarmed against resistance, one of them receiving a slight cut on the back of the head.   They had no license for carrying arms in the Settlement, nor any paper permitting them to use a Shanghai defense force license or showing that they had any connection with the Japanese Armed Forces.   They denied any such connection.   In these circumstances, the Marine authorities turned them over to the police as armed thugs caught creating a disturbance in the American sector.

2. Japanese consular police arrived, and after examination by them, the accused admitted connection with the Japanese Army, whereupon the consular police refused to take custody of them.   They are still in the hands of the Marines.

---

[59] Col. Charles F. B. Price, commanding officer of the United States Fourth Marines.

3. Marine authorities have requested Japanese Army authorities to send an officer to identify the accused. If they can identify them, they will be handed over against a receipt from the Japanese military authorities. If they cannot, Marine authorities propose handing them to the custody of Settlement police.

4. The above information was obtained from Marine Headquarters.

Repeated to Chungking, Peiping and Tokyo.

LOCKHART

893.102S/1673 : Telegram

The Consul General at Shanghai (Lockhart) to the Secretary of State

SHANGHAI, August 13, 1938—7 p. m.
[Received August 13—10 : 10 a. m.]

1110. 1. Reference my 1102, August 13, 11 a. m. Fourth Marines report that two of the Japanese taken this morning have been turned over to Japanese military for disciplinary action against receipt after identification as members of the Special Service Section of the Japanese Army. The third was permitted to go to hospital by the police while in their custody.

2. Reference my 1109, August 13, 6 p. m.[60] Fourth Marines also report that passengers in motor car referred to consisted of two Japanese of the Special Service Section and two Chinese (members of Ta Tao Government) all armed and in civilian clothes. Car had defense force license plates. They were apprehended by the municipal police after firing two shots in attempt to intimidate Chinese displaying national flags. The two Japanese were handed over to Japanese consular police but the Chinese are still being held by the municipal police.

Source also reports a similar incident, involving four persons in the French defense sector but no details yet available.

Repeated to Chungking, Peiping, Tokyo.

LOCKHART

893.102S/1677 : Telegram

The Consul General at Shanghai (Lockhart) to the Secretary of State

SHANGHAI, August 15, 1938—3 p. m.
[Received August 15—8 a. m.]

1111. My 1102, August 13, 11 a. m. and 1110, August 13, 7 p. m.

1. Events on the 12th, 13th and 14th tend to confirm that the Japanese are not as much interested in the maintenance of peace and order

[60] Not printed.

in the International Settlement as they would have the public believe. In every incident which occurred on the 13th they were directly implicated, if not the actual instigators, and the most significant fact was that those involved were members of the Special Service Section of the Japanese Army. With the active assistance of the agents of the Ta Tao Government, they were bent on creating disturbances and it was only because of the vigilance and courage of the marines in the American defense sector that serious trouble was averted in that area. Vigilance on the part of the British forces, the volunteers and municipal police in both the International Settlement and French Concession likewise prevented serious disturbances. Both the Japanese and the Ta Tao Government were greatly annoyed at the widespread display of Chinese national flags in the area south of Soochow Creek.

2. There were four arrests of members, all armed and in civilian clothes, of the Japanese Special Service Section yesterday, one each by the American, British, Italian and International Settlement authorities. One Japanese officer of the rank of major was detained but in each of the foregoing cases the Japanese were turned back to the Japanese authorities after due investigation.

3. The situation is greatly relaxed today, the volunteers having been demobilized last night and many of the barricades now having been removed.

4. The dissemination of the anti-foreign leaflets reported in my No. 1096, August 12, 2 p. m.[61] was unquestionably a part of this attempt to create ill feeling and trouble. The Japanese, however, according to press reports have denied any connection with this affair, claiming that the plane was a Japanese commercial one leased to the Ta Tao Government for the purpose of distributing pamphlets in the interior.

5. It is quite evident that the extensive preparations made to preserve order in the Settlement and French Concession were timely and in every way warranted. Otherwise it is very likely that the city would have been thrown into near chaos because of the activities of members of the Special Service Section, the agents of the Ta Tao Government and possibly also anti-Japanese organizations.

Repeated to Chungking, Peiping and Tokyo.

LOCKHART

---

[61] Not printed.

793.94119/439 : Telegram

The Chargé in the United Kingdom (Johnson) to the Secretary of State

LONDON, August 15, 1938—8 p. m.
[Received August 15—4: 10 p. m.]

770. The substance of your 443, August 12, 6 p. m.,[62] was communicated orally and informally to the Foreign Office today. A copy of the instructions to Ambassador Craigie outlined in my 748, August 11, 7 p. m., was telegraphed to the British Ambassador in China who has now replied that these instructions go beyond the Chinese request, the essence of which he says was the suggestion for a simultaneous parallel approach to the Japanese by the United States, British and possibly French Governments. I understand that Ambassador Kerr is doubtful of the advisability of the British approaching the Japanese alone and has informed the Foreign Office that he would be reluctant for this to be done until he has had time to consider the matter and to consult with the Chinese. He will then send his further recommendations. The Foreign Office is telegraphing to Ambassador Kerr tonight the substance of the American views, with which the official said he agreed. The Chinese have not been informed of the instructions sent to Ambassador Craigie.

The Foreign Office appears to understand clearly our position and, in view of our attitude and of the doubts expressed by the British Ambassador in China as to the acceptability of a British approach to the Japanese alone, it was stated by the official that they would probably decide not to take the action at this time. He thought it would be useful, however, for Ambassador Craigie to have the exchange of views with Mr. Grew and that he would inform me of further developments and of the recommendations which may be expected from the Ambassador in China.

JOHNSON

793.94119/438 : Telegram

The Ambassador in Japan (Grew) to the Secretary of State

TOKYO, August 15, 1938—9 p. m.
[Received August 15—10: 28 a. m.]

534. Department's 285, August 12, 7 p. m.

1. I believe your analysis and decision to be thoroughly sound. My views have not changed and they coincide with those expressed in your telegram.

---

[62] This telegram reported on the Chinese attitude and quoted from telegram No. 285, August 12, 7 p. m., to the Ambassador in Japan, p. 257.

2. Last week Craigie, who is in the mountains, telephoned that he must see me before his appointment with the Foreign Minister which is scheduled for Wednesday, August 17. Craigie is to return to Tokyo today and I therefore expect to see him tomorrow. In our conversation I shall be carefully guided by your instructions.

Repeated to Hong Kong with request that Hong Kong forward code text to Ambassador Johnson at Chungking by air mail.

GREW

793.94/13695 : Telegram

The Consul General at Hankow (Josselyn) to the Secretary of State

HANKOW, August 16, 1938—5 p. m.
[Received August 16—2 : 30 p. m.]

With the cessation of hostilities on the Manchurian border,[63] the pessimism referred to in my telegram August 4, 3 p. m. has returned.

Confronted with the problem of defending Wuhan the Chinese fail to show unity of purpose. The Central Government professes that a determined stand will be made but in the opinion of foreign military observers is now conserving and later will probably withdraw its best troops and equipment to ensure its transcendency in domestic politics. Central Government hope for victory in the present hostilities still rests in the economic collapse of Japan and third power economic or military intervention.

Declaring that with cooperation and determination Wuhan can be another Madrid, the Communists published 2 months ago a comprehensive plan for the defense of the Wuhan area, the salient feature of which was the mobilization, training and arming of the masses. Apprehending an increase of Communist strength if the people are mobilized, the Central Government has blocked fulfillment of the program even to the extent of preventing the Communists from organizing labor and first aid corps for work at the front.

Sent to the Ambassador, Peiping, Shanghai.

JOSSELYN

793.94119/440 : Telegram

The Ambassador in Japan (Grew) to the Secretary of State

TOKYO, August 16, 1938—8 p. m.
[Received August 16—3 : 16 p. m.]

539. My 534, August 15, 9 p. m.

1. In my talk with Craigie today the question of response to good offices was fully discussed along the lines of your 285, August 12, 7 p. m.

---

[63] See pp. 441 ff.

2. Craigie said that he fully concurs in the analysis presented in our 510, August 2, 10 p. m. He does not propose at the present time to make to the Foreign Minister an offer of good offices and I gather that he will not now approach our German colleague.

3. The Foreign Minister has twice in conversation with Craigie referred to the statement of the British Prime Minister in Parliament that Great Britain were ready to offer good offices if both sides so desire. General Ugaki said that the moment for such an offer was not opportune. He remarked that Chiang Kai Shek himself is not intensely anti-Japanese but that he must bear the responsibility for the intensive anti-Japanese propaganda in the schools and elsewhere and that until he undergoes a conversion the Japanese Government cannot deal with him. Craigie interprets this as meaning "until the Generalissimo breaks with the Communists." Nevertheless Craigie feels that Ugaki's approach to this subject twice on his own initiative emphasizes the importance of "keeping the door open" for an eventual offer of good offices when the time appears opportune. Craigie believes that such a moment may arise after the fall of Hankow because he feels that even the army, after it had achieved that outstanding victory, would welcome an opportunity to retire from that area.

4. In view of the foregoing considerations Craigie proposes in his interview with the Foreign Minister tomorrow afternoon to approach the subject by inquiring whether any importance can be attached to certain observations made by Tani [64] in Shanghai after his recent return from Tokyo. Since his return Tani has seen a number of leading British business men and has been at great pains to impress on them the Japanese desire to improve relations with the British. He has given the impression of being very frank and outspoken. Regarding the policy of the Japanese Government he has said that:

"(a) They are now ready to make peace with Chiang Kai Shek but on condition that he breaks completely with the Communists;

(b) Japan is determined to have a special area in Inner Mongolia recognized as such by the Chinese, run by Japanese military possibly on the lines of Manchukuo;

(c) Apart from Inner Mongolia Japan has no territorial ambitions: she is willing to recognize Chinese sovereignty over the whole of the rest of China, but must have a voice in the affairs of North China and for that purpose wants Japanese advisers appointed to various offices;

(d) Central China to be completely independent of Japanese or other foreign influence with all (sic) open door, equal opportunity for all. Japan has no demands to make about Central China except that she must agree to a wide demilitarized area around Shanghai;

(e) Wishes the customs and other national services to be maintained."

---

[64] Japanese Minister at Large in China.

5. It appears that Tani conveyed the impression that while Japan would demand recognition of "predominant interest" for Japan in North China and freedom from Japanese "or other foreign influence" in Central China, it would be understood that Great Britain or France (*sic*) might properly claim predominant interest in South China. Craigie observed that this plan of course visualized a return to the old system of spheres of influence. (It is to be noted that, somewhat naively, Craigie did not mention the United States in this connection.)

6. Craigie says that on Thursday morning he will tell me the result of his interview with Foreign Minister which I shall report to the Department.

Repeated to Hong Kong with request that Hong Kong forward code text to Ambassador Johnson in Chungking by air mail.

GREW

793.94119/442 : Telegram

The Ambassador in Japan (Grew) to the Secretary of State

TOKYO, August 18, 1938—1 p. m.
[Received August 18—7 : 45 a. m.]

542. My 539, August 16, 8 p. m.

1. In view of the unfavorable atmosphere of his talk which was with the Minister for Foreign Affairs (described in my 543, August 18, 2 p. m.[65]) Craigie did not approach the question of good offices and he did not inquire concerning the importance of the five points mentioned by Tani in Shanghai.

2. Craigie did, however, talk to the German Ambassador in a general way concerning the advisability of watching the situation in case an opportune moment for an offer of good offices might eventually appear. He did not inform the Ambassador of the *démarches* of the Chinese Government. Ott said that since his return from Berlin he had found the Japanese more determined than ever to proceed with the campaign and therefore he did not think the present moment opportune for an offer of good offices but he thought that such a moment might arise after the fall of Hankow which he considers inevitable and he agreed with Craigie that the door should constantly be kept open for such a step at a favorable time.

3. Craigie likewise talked with the French Ambassador who, he says, thoroughly agrees with our estimates of the situation and does not consider the present moment opportune for an offer of good offices.

Repeated to Hong Kong for Chungking.

GREW

---

[65] *Infra.*

793.94/13700 : Telegram

The Ambassador in Japan (Grew) to the Secretary of State

Tokyo, August 18, 1938—2 p. m.
[Received August 18—10 : 02 a. m.]

543. Our 494, July 27, 3 p. m.

1. My British colleague yesterday inquired of the Minister for Foreign Affairs whether he was now in a position to reply to the five points presented by the Ambassador on July 26 as the principal desiderata of the British Government relating to British interests in China.

2. The Minister for Foreign Affairs replied that owing to recent statements in Parliament by the Prime Minister,[66] Halifax [67] and Butler [68] of a nature threatening to Japan, public opinion in Japan had become greatly exacerbated and would tolerate no concessions to Great Britain at this time. Craigie asked if this reply was final. The Minister counseled patience and suggested that Craigie come to see him again at the end of August.

3. Craigie feels that the Japanese authorities are definitely determined to discriminate against Great Britain and he told Ugaki that if this were the case his own country would have no alternative but to discriminate against Japan. Craigie believes that the Japanese will try to avoid a showdown until after the fall of Hankow and that they will then openly snap their fingers in Great Britain's face.

4. Craigie says that he therefore proposes to recommend to his Government that since conciliatory efforts are proving abortive, his Government should now or soon radically alter its tactics and proceed to take all counter measures "short of a *casus belli*" against Japan. He thinks that one of the first steps should be the denunciation of their Treaty of Commerce with Japan [69] and that other measures, such for instance as action in the discount market, should follow. In other words, said Craigie, the time has come when Great Britain must "show her teeth". He added, as usual, that similar action by the United States would double the effectiveness of the measures taken but he also believes that discriminatory measures against American interests in China will be far less marked than those against Great Britain. He especially observed that Mr. Hull's recent public statements condemning military aggression had mentioned no names whereas the name of Japan had been emphatically and disparagingly mentioned by British officials in Parliament. Craigie considers those British statements as unfortunate, particularly because at the same

---

[66] Neville Chamberlain.
[67] Viscount Halifax, British Secretary of State for Foreign Affairs.
[68] British Parliamentary Under Secretary of State for Foreign Affairs.
[69] Signed April 3, 1911, *British and Foreign State Papers*, vol. CIV, p. 159.

time it was decided not to proceed with plans for a loan to China which he thinks the Japanese interpret purely as a weakening of British determination.

Repeated to Hong Kong for Chungking.

GREW

793.94119/443 : Telegram

The Chargé in the United Kingdom (Johnson) to the Secretary of State

LONDON, August 18, 1938—2 p. m.
[Received August 18—11 : 09 a. m.]

791. My 770, August 15, 8 p. m. The Chinese Ambassador was informed at the Foreign Office this morning that the British Government agrees with the Government of the United States that the present moment is not a propitious one for inviting the attention of the Japanese and Chinese Governments to their standing offer of good offices. The Chinese Ambassador at the same time had his attention again called to the Prime Minister's statement of July 26 and was informed that the British Ambassador at Tokyo will continue to sound the possibility of useful results from further suggestion of good offices to the Japanese Government; and that there is not at the moment any indication whatever that the Japanese attitude would be receptive.

The British Government has instructed Ambassador Craigie to approach the Japanese Foreign Minister regarding the most recent bombings at Canton, pointing out to him the serious effect this continued indiscriminate killing of civilians is having on the position of Japan in public opinion abroad. The Foreign Office states that numerous influential individuals, at the head of whom is the Archbishop of Canterbury, as well as British organizations, are exceedingly worked up about these last bombings and are bringing constant pressure to bear on the Government here.

JOHNSON

893.102S/1684 : Telegram

The Consul General at Shanghai (Lockhart) to the Secretary of State

SHANGHAI, August 18, 1938—2 p. m.
[Received August 18—1 : 25 p. m.]

1126. My 1102, August 13, 11 a. m., and 1110, August 13, 7 p. m. Colonel Kusomoto, Chief of the Special Service Section of the Japanese Army in this area, called on Colonel Price this morning and extended apologies for the incident described in the telegrams under reference. Colonel Kusomoto assured Colonel Price that the Japanese members of the Special Service Section involved in the incident have been disciplined and that he had taken steps to prevent a recurrence of such incidents. Colonel Kusomoto has been seeking an audience of Colonel Price for 2 days for the above purpose but the latter was not able to receive him until today because of a slightly infected foot.

Repeated to Chungking, Peiping and Tokyo.

LOCKHART

793.94/13740

Memorandum of Conversation, by Mr. Leo D. Sturgeon of the Division of Far Eastern Affairs

[WASHINGTON,] August 18, 1938.

Mr. Henry W. Kinney, with whom I have had long acquaintance and who is now attached to the Japanese Foreign Office, came to see me this morning and talked at length about Sino-Japanese relations. A number of remarks made by Mr. Kinney, some in response to my questions, contained substance of possible interest to the Department and are set forth below. Mr. Kinney has had important assignments as a publicist for the Japanese Government, enjoys acquaintance with the highest Japanese Government officials, and was called out of retirement for his present mission which is to make a survey of American opinion with respect to Far Eastern developments. Prior to making the present trip to the United States, Mr. Kinney apparently conferred with important members of the Japanese Cabinet and Government, and it is, therefore, possible that certain of his observations are entitled to more than ordinary notice.

Mr. Kinney stated in regard to the hostilities in China that the Tokyo Government was inclined to believe that the taking of Hankow by the Japanese forces would probably disorganize Chinese opposition and create dissension among its leaders, thus preparing the way for peace.

In regard to possible peace terms that the Japanese may present in the event of victory over the Chinese, Mr. Kinney observed that the reasonableness of Japanese demands might prove a surprise in many quarters; that actually it had been indicated to him by a high Japanese official that indemnity would more likely be sought in the form of economic concessions of various kinds than in money. Mr. Kinney added that the Japanese could not expect to get a large money indemnity from China when it was obvious that China was impoverished.

Mr. Kinney mentioned General Chiang Kai-shek and stated that he believed the General had at the moment greater prestige with the Chinese people than ever heretofore. This remark may represent a translation by Mr. Kinney of views of members of the Japanese Government.

With regard to the British position in China, Mr. Kinney observed that the British appeared to desire peace possibly more than the Japanese. He thought also that the British would take part in any effort to bring about a peace conference provided there should be a Chinese Government in prospect that could practically be recognized. He added that he did not believe it mattered much to the British what the composition of this Government might be so long as it would work.

Mr. Kinney stated that the object of his mission to the United States was to take a cross section of American public opinion with respect to Japanese activities in the Far East, that he had been engaged in this task for some time, and that he proposed upon his return to inform the Foreign Office that Japanese efforts to win American support for their cause through propagandist activities should cease. He thought such activities were a waste of effort in the present temper of the American people, and that for some time to come the Japanese would have to give evidence of their intentions through actions rather than words.

Mr. Kinney made some attempt to establish that relatively the Chinese had offended against American interests in China to much the same degree as had the Japanese. When I indicated that our records did not appear to bear this out, Mr. Kinney dropped the matter, and it was evident that he had merely attempted a pretense, at which he is skilful.

793.94119/443 : Telegram

The Secretary of State to the Chargé in the United Kingdom
(Johnson)

WASHINGTON, August 20, 1938—2 p. m.

466. Your 791, August 18, 2 p. m. With reference to the first sentence of your telegram under reference you will note from the Department's 443, August 12, 6 p. m.,[70] that the Secretary in his talk with the Chinese Ambassador here [71] made no categorical statement of the attitude of this Government such as appears from your telegram to have been attributed to this Government by the British Foreign Office in the information given the Chinese Ambassador at London; the Secretary merely posed a question, offered for consideration general comments and indicated that additional action on our part was not to be expected at this time. Your telegram would appear to indicate that the information conveyed by the Foreign Office to the Chinese Ambassador at London carried the implication that the

---

[70] Not printed.
[71] August 3; see memorandum by the Secretary of State, p. 252.

responsibility for a negative decision on the question of good offices rested on this Government. While we would have seen no objection to the British Foreign Office informing the Chinese Ambassador that we had been consulted and that our views were as indicated by us, we feel that the Foreign Office should not have left, if indeed they did leave, the Chinese Ambassador in any doubt that the British Government's decision was made on its own initiative.

Department desires that in your discretion you bring this point orally and informally to the attention of the Foreign Office.

HULL

793.94/13732 : Telegram

The First Secretary of Embassy in China (Salisbury) to the Secretary of State

PEIPING, August 23, 1938—4 p. m.
[Received 8 : 28 p. m.]

516. Embassy's 453 [*455*], July 20, 11 a. m.[72]

1. Reliable foreigners who have recently visited areas of Central and West Hopei and East Shansi under the control of Chinese guerrillas, associated with and now considered a part of the former Eighth Route Army of Communist troops, report that their organization is growing in efficiency and numerical strength. The headquarters of one of the four organized guerrilla districts in Hopei claims that there are 200,000 organized guerrillas in that province, that their chief lack is rifle ammunition, but that they are well supplied with hand grenades of their own manufacture and are obtaining considerable amounts of explosives. (It was reported in the second week of August that several bridges had been blown up near Techow on the Tientsin–Pukow Railway and that the line was interrupted for over 1 week. Several wrecks were also reported on the Peiping–Hankow Railway in Hopei, with at least 200 casualties in one wreck south of Paoting. At least one train was completely wrecked in July on the Shihkiachuang–Taiyuan Railway presumably with heavy casualties. Yesterday afternoon's express from Mukden was derailed between Tangku and Tientsin.)

2. According to Chinese sources, the Kuomintang Commander Lu Chung-lin who was appointed in June by the National Government to be Governor of Hopei has crossed the Japanese lines and is established near Taming, South Hopei, and is engaged in inspecting the various guerrilla organizations.

3. Guerrilla activities north and east of Peiping have continued. Within last 2 days there was a skirmish not far from one of the

---

[72] Not printed.

256941—54——18

north gates of Peiping; and for over a month the Tientsin–Peiping motor highway has been considered too dangerous for use because of guerrillas and bandit activities.

4. Notwithstanding their successes in harassing Japanese outposts and lines of communications and in killing small detachments of Japanese, observers in general express surprise at the comparative ineffectiveness of the guerrillas as a military force, especially at their failure to destroy railways under Japanese control. Many observers, however, consider that their effectiveness is being increased as their training and organization progress, and it is reliably reported that Japanese attacks upon villages by planes and troops, and the policy of fear which is also reliably reported as being carried out by the Japanese against villages thought to harbor guerrillas, has turned the countryside population into active supporters of the organized irregulars, who in general treat the people well, with one result that frequently the survivers of Japanese attacks on civilians join with the guerrillas for active service. There are many indications that the guerrilla movement will continue to grow in Hopei, Shantung, and Shansi and that irregular activities, already a formidable problem to the Japanese military, will become a menace of increasingly greater magnitude.

Repeated to Chungking, Nanking. By mail to Tokyo.

SALISBURY

793.94119/446 : Telegram

The Chargé in the United Kingdom (Johnson) to the Secretary of State

LONDON, August 23, 1938—7 p. m.
[Received August 23—2 : 38 p. m.]

810. I had no hesitancy in taking up informally with the Foreign Office the substance of your 466, August 20, 2 p. m., as in the conversation reported in my 770, August 15, 8 p. m., I had specifically said that I thought it would be most desirable to avoid giving the Chinese any impression that the British decision, whatever it might be, was not an entirely independent one. The same Foreign Office official this afternoon said that they agreed with that view and that they had had no intention of conveying any such impression to the Chinese Ambassador in the talk reported in my 791, August 18, 2 p. m., nor did he think the Chinese Ambassador had received any such impression. He produced a memorandum of the conversation with the Chinese Ambassador of that day and read me substantially as follows: The Chinese Ambassador was informed that the suggestion of his Government made through the British Ambassador in China had been

very carefully examined here and that we had consulted with the United States Government in the matter. I told him that we had come to the conclusion that on the whole we concurred with the viewpoint of the United States Government that the present was not a propitious moment for inviting the attention of the Chinese and Japanese Governments to the standing offer of good offices. The Chinese Ambassador in reply said that personally he was of the same opinion and that he thought the time for again bringing forward the offer of good offices must be very carefully chosen.

I had not been informed until this afternoon of the fact that the Chinese Ambassador had personally concurred in the decision.

The Foreign Office has perfectly understood the nature of the statement made by the Secretary in his talk with the Chinese Ambassador at Washington on August 3.

JOHNSON

793.94119/447 : Telegram

The Ambassador in China (Johnson) to the Secretary of State

CHUNGKING, August 26, 1938—noon.
[Received 12:15 p. m.]

426. The spokesman of the Chinese Foreign Office, according to the local Chinese press of August 25, denied rumors apparently emanating from London to the effect that Italy is endeavoring to mediate in the Far Eastern hostilities and that a tentative approach had been made by the latter to Wang Ching-wei in the matter. A spokesman declared that Italy had not approached China on the subject and that the rumor was probably fabricated by the Japanese for ulterior reasons.

2. In a recent conversation with H. H. Kung, the latter, in making reference to the truce reached between Russia and Japan over the Changkufeng incident, told me that he was puzzled as to why Germany had intervened in that matter to advise the Japanese that they should not so aggravate the situation as to become involved in a war with Russia. Dr. Kung is apparently convinced that Germany acted in the sense described above and that as a result he is seeking to moderate the situation on the Manchurian-Siberian border.

3. Linked with the above is a conversation which I recently had with Alessandrini, local representative of the Italian Embassy in China, who in the course of a discussion of the Sino-Japanese hostilities commented to the effect that the Japanese military were making a hopeless mess of their program and activities in China. He added that the Italian Government had informed the Japanese Government that Italy had no desire to become involved in an international war precipitated by Japan.

4. I am led by the foregoing and other observations to the conclusion that neither Germany nor Italy is pleased with the manner in which Japan has been acting in the Far East; and that these two powers have intimated to Japan that the latter cannot depend upon them for assistance in case Japan should become involved in hostilities with the Soviet Union.

Repeated to Peiping and Shanghai. Shanghai please repeat to Tokyo.

JOHNSON

793.94116/92

The Secretary of State to the Chinese Ambassador (C. T. Wang)

WASHINGTON, August 29, 1938.

MY DEAR MR. AMBASSADOR: I have read with concern your note of August 24, 1938,[73] quoting a telegram from the Chinese Ministry of Foreign Affairs in regard to a report from the Commander of Chinese forces in north Kiangsi to the effect that the Japanese forces used poison gases during a recent attack upon opposing Chinese troops.

I assure you that throughout the present conflict in the Far East this Government has exerted and continues to exert its influence through such appropriate means as are at its disposal to the end that practices of an inhumane character be abandoned.

I am [etc.]

CORDELL HULL

793.94/14212

The President of the Chinese Executive Yuan (Kung) to President Roosevelt [74]

CHUNGKING, August 30, 1938.

DEAR MR. PRESIDENT: As Mr. K. P. Chen, Adviser of the Ministry of Finance, is coming to your country, I am pleased to take this opportunity to convey to you through him my best wishes and sincere greetings. I recall the great kindness you extended to me during my sojourn in Washington last year, and enjoyed the luncheon and talk with you.

On Mr. Chen's departure for America, we recall with renewed appreciation the kind reception which you extended to him and his colleagues during their monetary mission to Washington in 1936 and particularly the friendly cooperation of your Government which made his mission a success.

Mr. Chen is now coming to America on another mission. Your friendship towards our Government justifies my hope that Mr. Chen's mission will again receive the ready assistance of your Government.[75]

[73] Not printed.
[74] For reply dated October 26, see p. 342.
[75] See pp. 519 ff.

Ever since the outbreak of the Sino-Japanese hostilities, you and your Government and people have shown unmistakable signs of friendship towards China. Your sympathy and moral support of our national cause and the humanitarian services which your nation has rendered in the relief of our war refugees have won the deep gratitude of our Government and people. The timely and courageous utterances you have made in the interest of peace and justice, particularly, not only represent America's traditional policy in the Far East but ring through the world like clarion calls warning all peace-loving and democratic peoples against the grave dangers of the forces of aggression and lawlessness. Indeed, they symbolize America's moral leadership in world affairs, so ably strengthened by your statesmanship.

Much as we regret the interruptions to our financial and economic development that have been caused by Japan's armed aggression, we are nevertheless resolutely and courageously facing the urgent problems that confront us in the present crisis. I need hardly say that the continued friendship and assistance of America will not only be helpful in the successful prosecution of our war against Japan's aggression but will be even more valuable when we come to tackle the greater problems that will arise at the end of the hostilities. I have every confidence that, under your illustrious leadership, our two nations will cooperate closer than ever in protecting our common ideals of peace and democracy in the Pacific and in promoting your noble policy of "Good Neighborhood."

I am [etc.] H. H. KUNG

CHAPTER V: SEPTEMBER 1–OCTOBER 31, 1938

Growth of Communist influence in North China; Chinese inquiry respecting reconvening of Nine-Power Treaty signatories (September 7); accountability of Japan and China for safety of Americans at Hankow (September 9); possible Japanese policy as affected by crisis in Europe; Chiang Kai-shek's appeal to President Roosevelt on behalf of peace in Far East (October 8); Chinese Communist Party's recommittal to "united front" against Japan (October 9); British warning to Japan against military alliance with Germany and Italy (October 12); Japanese occupation of Canton and Hankow (October 24, 26); Chinese appeals for American aid and President Roosevelt's replies

893.00/14258 : Telegram

The Ambassador in China (Johnson) to the Secretary of State

CHUNGKING, September 1, 1938—11 a. m.
[Received September 6—1:23 a. m.]

431. Following is a summary of data received by me from Captain Carlson [76] covering his recently completed tour of 3 months duration over a distance of 1700 miles in the northwestern provinces.

---

[76] Capt. Evans F. Carlson, U. S. M. C., Navy Department language officer in China.

1. At Yenan, center of Communist activities, he visited various leaders; though impressed with Mao Tse Tung's undoubted ability, he felt Lo Fu, Secretary General of the party and a recluse, to be the most capable official of the Communist Party. He found Shensi to be of great strategic value to the Chinese as it provides the route whereby supplies reach Suiyuan, Shansi and even Hopei; consequently Chinese defenses along the Yellow River were ascertained to be formidable, with central troops stationed in South and North Shensi and with Communist troops in the central section.

2. Conditions in Suiyuan were observed to be unfavorable to China owing to mediocre leadership and faulty coordination of military leaders (Fu Tso Yi, Teng Pao Shan, Ma Chan Shan and Ho Chu Kuo), poor discipline and lack of training among military forces, and oppression of the people by the military.

3. The Chinese were observed to control Shansi south of the Great Wall as well as South Hopei except for railway lines, some highways and a few important cities and political and military developments in these provinces were found to have undergone marked improvement since his former visit in January largely due to the success of the Communists in organizing and gaining the support of the populace under a fixed program designed, (1) to prevent Japan from gaining political control of the areas in question, (2) to prevent commercial or other intercourse with Japanese dominated areas, (3) to obstruct Japanese exploitation of the natural resources of these areas.

4. In Shantung friction was observed to exist between Shen Hung Lieh, chairman of the province, and the Soviets who have penetrated into the province and who desire to expand their system of organization of the people along the lines followed in Hopei and Shansi. Shen has not accepted the proposals and has hesitated to affiliate the people under his own supervision. He has however restored communications and has taken steps to organize a local army of about 120,000 men.

5. Carlson emphasizes that the Communist plan of organizing the people is meeting with marked success whereas similar efforts on the part of the Central Government have fallen short. He observed that the Soviets are winning the support of the people, that in consequence they now control a large section of North China extending from Kansu to the sea, and that their strength and influence are constantly on the increase. Carlson believes that the Communists intend to remain loyal to the Central Government during the course of hostilities and says they profess to hope to be able to continue the united front after the war, looking ultimately to the establishment in China of a democratic form of Government, but with official control of banks, mines, railways, public utilities, et cetera, and with cooperatives as the basis of distribution. Subject to the above mentioned limitations,

private enterprise would be permitted and the investment of foreign capital encouraged from nations treating China as an equal. He pointed out, however, that if a rift should occur, the Communists will be in a strong position vis-à-vis the Central Government.

6. I believe Carlson has made a competent and sound survey of the trend of developments in the areas in which he has traveled. If support is forthcoming from Soviet Russia, Chinese Communist influence will doubtless continue to grow in North China and Japan, which has yet to crush the Chiang regime, will find it more difficult as time passes to eradicate this growing power in the north, while the possibility of large scale Japanese exploitation of North China seems remote so long as the Communists are able to carry on their activities in that area.

Repeated to Tokyo.

JOHNSON

793.94/13792 : Telegram

The Ambassador in Japan (Grew) to the Secretary of State

TOKYO, September 2, 1938—noon.
[Received September 2—7 : 37 a. m.]

572. Our 494, July 27, 3 p. m.

1. In one of my periodic talks with the British Ambassador [77] today he reverted to the five principal points of British desiderata in China which the British Government consider as representing its minimum requirements and regard compliance therewith as a minimum criterion of Japanese sincerity. As reported in my 543, August 18, 2 p. m., the Foreign Minister [78] after having previously intimated that these points would be given favorable consideration said on August 17 that no concessions to Great Britain could be made at the present time owing to the threatening nature of statements in Parliament and suggested that Craigie come to see him again on August 31. This appointment was later canceled and the Foreign Minister now proposes to see the British Ambassador some time next week. In that interview unless the Foreign Minister is able to give satisfactory assurances for the future Craigie proposes to tell General Ugaki that his Government can believe no longer in Japan's sincerity and that since his own efforts at friendly conciliation have proved abortive the British Government will now be obliged to adopt other methods. Craigie does not yet know whether these measures would take the form of help to China or retaliation against Japan. The decision must be left to his Government which is under constant pressure to take some action of this delicate nature.

[77] Sir Robert L. Craigie.
[78] Gen. Kazushige Ugaki.

2. In trying to estimate the reasons for the postponement of his interview with the Foreign Minister, Craigie is inclined to attribute it to Ugaki's difficulties with the military or possibly to a desire to await the outcome of the present European crisis. He has been informed that the inept publicity that a series of "Ugaki-Craigie conversations["] taking place has served to antagonize the army which believes that the Foreign Office is weak and inclined to make undesirable concessions to foreign interests. Craigie is informed that Ugaki's prestige and influence have greatly weakened and that there is serious risk of some attack on him by young military officers of reactionary tendencies.

3. I am aware that such rumors are in circulation and that several of my colleagues believe that attempts on the lives of both Ugaki and Ikeda [79] are likely to occur. I do not think that we can definitely rule out the possibility of such an incident and we feel a certain tenseness in the air but I understand that the authorities have sent most of the young malcontents to the front lines in China and it seems probable that the local authorities are in a position to control those who remain in Tokyo.

GREW

893.102S/1709

The Consul General at Shanghai (Lockhart) to the Secretary of State

No. 1645   SHANGHAI, September 2, 1938.
                                            [Received September 24.]

Subject: Intrusion of Armed Japanese into American Defense Sector.

SIR: I have the honor to refer to my despatch No. 1619 of August 18, 1938 [80] on the subject mentioned above and also to my despatch No. 1493 of May 27, 1938 [81] on the subject "Exchange of Correspondence between American and Japanese Military and Naval Authorities regarding Passage of Military Trucks through American Defense Sector" and to enclose for the files of the Department copies of correspondence [82] of August 30, 1938, and September 1, 1938, between Colonel Price, Commanding the United States Fourth Marines, and officers of the Japanese Army, regarding their repeated violations of the agreement regarding passage of Japanese military trucks and armed men through the American defense sector.

Colonel Price has informed me orally that he has consistently taken an even stronger attitude in conversations with Japanese army representatives than that brought out in his letters to them.

Respectfully yours,   FRANK P. LOCKHART

[79] Seihin Ikeda, Japanese Minister of Finance, Commerce and Industry.
[80] Not printed.
[81] *Ante,* p. 187.
[82] Three letters not printed.

793.94/13816 : Telegram

The Ambassador in Japan (Grew) to the Secretary of State

Tokyo, September 5, 1938—3 p. m.
[Received September 6—8 a. m.]

577. Our January 13, 4 p. m. to Shanghai,[83] Hankow safety zone. The following is translation of a *note verbale* dated September 3, received today, from the Foreign Office:

"The Imperial Ministry of Foreign Affairs present its compliments to the American Ambassador and has the honor, in view of the attack which is soon to be made on Hankow and its environs by the Imperial Army, to convey to the American Ambassador the following communication regarding the safety of the rights and interests in Hankow of third countries.

Information concerning the safety of the rights and interests in Hankow of third powers was conveyed in a *note verbale* dated January 11 of this year. From that time up to the present the attack on Hankow has been limited to aerial bombardment.

Since the capture of Hankow is soon to be carried out by means of military force both land and water, the Imperial Government by enlarging upon and explaining the purport of the above mentioned *note verbale* is desirous of contributing toward assuring the safety of the rights and interests of third countries.

As was stated in the preceding *note verbale*, the conditions under which the Imperial Army will not attack the specified area are that Chinese forces are not present within the said area; that absolutely no military advantage of the area be taken by the Chinese Army and that the movements of Japanese forces outside the area are not hindered from within the area. In consequence of these conditions:

1, the Chinese forces are not to be allowed to pass through the said area;
2, the Chinese forces' arms, ammunition, military supplies, et cetera are not to be allowed to be stored in or to be transported thru the area;
3, the Chinese forces are not to confront the Imperial forces by taking a position in front of this area;
4, the area is not to be utilized by the Chinese military authorities for espionage, communication, or as a base of operations for creating disturbances behind Japanese lines;
5, vessels used by the Chinese forces are not to be allowed to navigate along or to anchor at the river front in the said area;
6, troops, assassins, and criminals are to be considered as elements of the Chinese Army and the foregoing conditions are properly to be applicable also to them.

The Imperial forces consider these to be especially important items in connection with the need for planning for the safety of third party interests at the time of the capture of Hankow, and accordingly they

[83] See telegram No. 73, January 13, 7 p. m., from the Consul General at Shanghai, p. 21.

urgently ask that the countries concerned will take steps to see that they are strictly carried out.

In regard to the abuse by the Chinese forces of third party rights: The experiences during the hostilities in the western part of Shanghai last year fully evidence that, in the event that the Chinese forces confront the Japanese forces in the vicinity of foreign property or use such property as cover, as an unavoidable consequence the property of third parties is unintentionally subjected to fire.

Accordingly it is particularly to be added that as long as there are Chinese military forces or military emplacements within 1,000 meters from the outer edge of the established area at Hankow herein referred to, it is exceedingly difficult for the Imperial forces to bear responsibility for unforeseen damages to the rights and interests of third parties which may occur as a result of an attack on such Chinese forces or emplacements."

GREW

793.94/13945

Memorandum by the Chief of the Division of Far Eastern Affairs (Hamilton) of a Conversation With the British Ambassador (Lindsay)

[WASHINGTON,] September 6, 1938.

The British Ambassador called at his request. He referred to statements made to him by the Secretary when the Ambassador was calling on the Secretary last Saturday to the effect that it seemed desirable that thought be given to matters as follows: the question presented by the Japanese objections to the passage of the U. S. S. *Monocacy* to Shanghai; the question whether additional representations of a broad character were called for by the continued Japanese activity in the field of commercial enterprise which resulted in impairment of our commercial rights; and the question whether approaches should be made to the Japanese Government along the lines of the approaches made to Germany during the World War in reference to Japanese pronouncements that certain areas constituted zones of hostilities within which third party interests could not operate or could operate only at their own risk. The Ambassador asked me whether I could throw any further light on these matters.

I said that with reference to the U. S. S. *Monocacy* the British also had a gunboat at Kiukiang and that there was involved in this matter the whole question of freedom of movement on the Yangtze. I said that all the treaty powers having naval vessels or commercial vessels on the Yangtze were confronted by this large problem.

With regard to our commercial interests in China and the steps being taken by the Japanese through the formation of special com-

panies, monopolies, etc., to close the open door to other foreign enterprises, I said that this Government, like the British Government, had
been making representations in regard to individual cases affecting
our respective interests as such cases arose. I said that quite recently
the British Ambassador at Tokyo had presented to the Japanese
Government a list of certain desiderata relating to British interests
in China. I said that on July 4 Mr. Grew had taken up with the
Japanese Foreign Office in a broad, comprehensive way the question
of American rights and interests in China.[84] I said that in addition
to these approaches and to the representations which were made in
individual cases, we were giving thought to the question whether it
would be advisable to approach the Japanese Government in any more
comprehensive and thoroughgoing manner than had heretofore been
the case.

With regard to the assertion by the Japanese Government from
time to time that certain areas constituted zones of military operations, I said that, as the Ambassador knew, during the World War
this Government had made representations to the German Government as well as to the British Government in regard to our inability
to recognize the right of those governments to delimit large areas as
areas within which American vessels could not operate. I said that
in reference to the situation in China this Government had made representations to the Japanese Government on the occasion of the Japanese
Government issuing certain of its notices of the character under discussion. I said that we did not admit that the Japanese Government
had belligerent rights and that we proceeded on that basis, at the
same time endeavoring to have our action conform to the rule of
reason. I said that we were giving study to the question whether it
would be advisable to make a general and comprehensive approach to
the Japanese Government on this whole question. I added that I
personally would prefer, if any such approach were to be made, to
have it rest on a case involving completely American rights and interests rather than on a case of only a partial American interest, such
as that of the China National Aviation Corporation.

Note: The conversation of which record is made hereinbefore was
carried on in very general terms and the subjects mentioned were
treated as matters to which consideration of an exploratory character
was being given.

M[AXWELL] M. H[AMILTON]

---

[84] See memorandum of July 4, *Foreign Relations*, Japan, 1931–1941, vol. I,
p. 605.

793.94 Conference/373

Memorandum by the Secretary of State of a Conversation With the Chinese Ambassador (C. T. Wang)

[WASHINGTON,] September 7, 1938.

During his call the Chinese Ambassador inquired as to the attitude of this Government towards a reconvening of the signatories of the Nine-Power Pact, to which I replied that I had not heard the matter discussed recently. The Ambassador then said that his Government would be making such a request and our Government would be expected to take the lead in the matter; that he would be glad if he could get some intimation as to what we might do. I asked him if it would not be very advisable first to consider and determine whether any accomplishment would be possible in the event of such meeting, and stated that it would be hurtful to call a meeting which would prove entirely fruitless. I said that while the delegate of this government might be chairman of the meeting (and about this I am not certain at the moment), in any event all of the signatories of the Nine-Power Pact would be consulted and all would consider the circumstances relating to the question of whether a reconvening would be advisable; that, therefore, I assumed the Chinese Government would lay its reasons before each of the signatories to the Nine-Power Pact, who in turn would among themselves give consideration to the same and the weight of opinion among them determine as to whether there should or should not be a reconvening of the Nine-Power signatories. The Ambassador then said that when the Council of the League of Nations convenes later in this month[85] his Government would seek more active aid from the League Council and also from the signatories of the Nine-Power Pact; that it would strengthen that movement if this Government in the meantime should have rendered important aid to China. I made no reply but inquired what Great Britain, France, and other countries, are doing in this respect. The Ambassador replied that he did not know.

C[ORDELL] H[ULL]

793.94/13837 : Telegram

The Ambassador in Japan (Grew) to the Secretary of State

TOKYO, September 8, 1938—11 p. m.
[Received September 8—7 : 30 p. m.]

590. Our 572, September 2, noon.

1. The Minister for Foreign Affairs received my British colleague this afternoon and in a 2-hour session did nearly all the talking, reading from copious notes with which Craigie believes he was furnished by the military authorities.

---

[85] See pp. 488 ff.

2. The Minister began with a long statement in which he charged Great Britain with aiding Chiang Kai Shek and said that until the British attitude should change, improvement in Anglo-Japanese relations could not be expected. Specifically he charged the British Navy with an attitude and actions contrary to Japanese interests while indicating that the American Navy had followed a correct course throughout the hostilities.

3. The Minister said that the fall of Hankow is imminent and that as soon as this occurs a strong Chinese central government will emerge which will cooperate with Japan and will render useless further assistance to Chiang Kai Shek.

4. The Minister then proceeded to reject scheme for the five points which Craigie had presented on July 26 (see our 494, July 27, 3 p. m.). Such reasons as the Minister advanced for this rejection centered about the requirements of the military campaign and the terrorist activities of Chinese in Shanghai. Under the heading "railways" the Minister made a single minor concession, namely, that the nominees of the British-Chinese Corporation would be permitted to inspect the North Station in Shanghai. With regard to the Whangpoo conservancy, the Minister thought that an agreement through local negotiations was impending. (Craigie at this point told me of his regret that the provisional agreement, which he considered reasonable, had failed owing to French objection.) When Craigie endeavored to discuss his five points specifically, the Minister pleaded ignorance of the details which he said were better understood by the Vice-Minister.[86] Craigie replied that affairs of such importance should properly be discussed in detail by an ambassador with the Foreign Minister himself. He feels that Ugaki has no detailed comprehension of these matters.

5. At the end of the interview Craigie conveyed to the Foreign Minister, not as formal representations but as a personal message from Lord Halifax,[87] certain proposals for the avoidance of bombing civilian populations which Craigie says he will send me later.

6. Craigie characterized the interview as completely unfavorable and discouraging. He has noted in the last few days a recrudescence of anti-British publicity in the Japanese press and has observed that this publicity so closely follows comments made to him by the Foreign Office as to render certain that this propaganda is officially inspired.

7. Craigie informs me in strict secrecy that owing to the crisis in Europe he has been directed by his Government to avoid a showdown with the Japanese Government at present and to carry on as best he can.

Repetition left to the Department's discretion.

GREW

---

[86] Kensuke Horinouchi.
[87] British Secretary of State for Foreign Affairs.

793.94/13847 : Telegram

The Ambassador in Japan (Grew) to the Secretary of State

Tokyo, September 9, 1938—11 a. m.
[Received September 9—8 : 25 a. m.]

591. Our 590, September 8, 11 p. m. Craigie informs me that in his talk yesterday with the Minister for Foreign Affairs Ugaki held up the United States as a paragon of virtue in contradistinction to Great Britain. This tends to bear out reliable reports which have come to us to the effect that there is a strong element within the Japanese Government which advocates (in the observation of one informant) "throwing Great Britain out of China and at the same time conciliating and favoring the United States". This informant added however that the predominant view in the Foreign Office is that the United States and Great Britain must be considered for all practical purposes in connection with the Far Eastern situation as one unit and that Japan cannot take aggressive measures against the interests of either nation without eventually becoming involved with the other.

I request that there be no repetition of this telegram.

GREW

———————

793.94/13846 : Telegram

The Ambassador in China (Johnson) to the Secretary of State

Chungking, September 9, 1938—11 a. m.
[Received September 9—8 : 42 a. m.]

439. Following from Shanghai:

"September 8, 4 p. m. My September 6, 11 a. m. repeating Tokyo's 577, September 5, 3 p. m. regarding Hankow safety zone.

The British and French Ambassadors are considering what action they will take with reference to this matter and the latter has expressed a desire to have your views on the subject. He desires especially to know whether you have made any representations on the subject to the Chinese authorities or whether you intend to make such representations. I have communicated orally to the French Ambassador the substance of Hankow's September 7, 3. p. m.[88]

I shall be glad to communicate to the French Ambassador any comments you may care to make on the above subject."

JOHNSON

———————

[88] Not printed.

793.94/13848 : Telegram

The Ambassador in China (Johnson) to the Secretary of State

CHUNGKING, September 9, 1938—noon.
[Received 1:50 p. m.]

440. With reference to Tokyo's 577, September 5, 3 p. m., and Hankow's September 7, 3 p. m.,[89] and Shanghai's September 8, 4 p. m., which is being separately repeated to the Department in my 439, September 9, 11 a. m. The erection of defence works in the two ex-concessions at Hankow which are under Chinese jurisdiction but which are included in the area described in the Embassy's 33, December 13, 4 p. m., 1937,[90] and the statement of the Wuhan garrison commander that these defences are being erected under orders of a higher military authority when he was approached by the senior Consul at Hankow raises the question whether I should, either as senior Ambassador or as American Ambassador with nationals residing within the two ex-concessions mentioned, protest to the higher authorities in the matter. I am diffident about approaching the Chinese authorities in this matter as it would be impossible for me to offer any guarantee whatever to the Chinese authorities as to the fate which may be meted out to Chinese citizens found within those areas by the Japanese. Similar defensive works apparently were erected within the area where foreigners were living in Kiukiang and yet it is apparent that the Japanese forces in taking Kiukiang were careful of foreign property in that area. I have hitherto taken the stand that I could not be responsible for more than informing Japanese of the location of American property and the presence of American nationals and hold them responsible for their protection. I am not disposed to go to the Chinese authorities about this matter and protest against steps which they are apparently taking for the protection of their own lives for I can offer no substitute. Unless the Department desires otherwise I propose to take no action with the Chinese, relying upon what we have already said to the Japanese about the location of American properties in those areas for their protection.

Shanghai please repeat to Tokyo, Hankow, Shanghai [*sic*].

JOHNSON

793.94/13816 : Telegram

The Secretary of State to the Consul General at Shanghai (Lockhart)

WASHINGTON, September 9, 1938—5 p. m.

The following for Tokyo and to be repeated to Hankow and Chungking:

---

[89] Telegram of September 7 not printed.
[90] *Foreign Relations*, 1937, vol. IV, p. 401.

"309. Your 577, September 5, 3 p. m., Hankow safety zone.

1. The Department desires that you consult your interested colleagues, with the thought that they may wish to take substantially similar but separate action, and reply to the Japanese Ministry for Foreign Affairs, in such manner as you may deem appropriate, in the following sense:

2. The Department has carefully studied the Japanese Foreign Office's *note verbale* of September 3.

3. Our views in regard to military operations in and against the specified area at Hankow are well known to both the Chinese and the Japanese Governments. In this connection, however, the Japanese Government will doubtless understand that the American authorities cannot assume any responsibility to either side in the present unfortunate hostilities between Chinese and Japanese forces for any actions or undertakings of the other side.

4. Attention is called to the fact that from time to time the American authorities have, with the purpose of facilitating the protection of American lives and property and without prejudice to the general rights involved, supplied the Japanese authorities with maps showing the location of American properties in areas of hostilities in China, including properties in Hankow and Wuchang. The specified area at Hankow consists very largely of foreign owned property, including a considerable amount of American property. A considerable number of American citizens are amongst the large foreign community concentrated in that area, and, as the Japanese Government is aware, there are also American citizens and American property in Wuchang.

5. Irrespective of the outcome of efforts made to separate the specified area at Hankow from all military activities, the American Government fully expects that the Japanese authorities will so conduct their military activities in China as to avoid injury to American lives and properties and makes full reservation of its rights and of the rights of its nationals in the event of the failure of the Japanese authorities so to do."

HULL

793.94/13846 : Telegram

The Secretary of State to the Ambassador in China (Johnson)

WASHINGTON, September 9, 1938—5 p. m.

245. Tokyo's 577, September 5, 3 p. m., Hankow's September 7, 3 p. m.,[91] and your 439, September 9, 11 a. m., in regard to Hankow safety zone.

1. The Department is authorizing the Embassy, Tokyo, to reply to the Japanese *note verbale* of September 3 in the sense that the American Government fully expects that the Japanese authorities will so conduct their military activities in China as to avoid injury to American life and property and that the American authorities naturally cannot assume any responsibility to either side for actions or undertakings of the other side.

---

[91] Telegram of September 7 not printed.

2. The Department believes that we should adopt the same attitude toward the Chinese authorities. Please give the Department your opinion as to whether we could with propriety specifically urge the Chinese authorities to avoid military activities in or adjacent to the specified area at Hankow that would give the Japanese authorities reason or excuse for attacking that area on the grounds outlined in the Japanese note quoted in Tokyo's 577, September 5, 3 p. m. You may care to consult the Military Attaché [92] on this point. Please also give the Department your views in regard to this whole problem, including suggestions for any feasible measures having for their object the safeguarding of Americans at Hankow.

Repeat to Hankow, Tokyo and Shanghai.

HULL

793.94/13846 : Telegram

The Secretary of State to the Ambassador in China (Johnson)

WASHINGTON, September 9, 1938—7 p. m.

246. Your 439, September 9, 11 a. m., Hankow Safety Zone. The Department authorizes you in your discretion to ask Lockhart to utilize the substance of Department's 245, September 9, 5 p. m. to you and 309, September 9, 5 p. m. to Tokyo via Shanghai [93] in discussing this whole matter with the French and British Ambassadors.

Please repeat to Tokyo this telegram and your telegram under reference.

HULL

793.94/13848 : Telegram

The Secretary of State to the Consul General at Shanghai (Lockhart)

WASHINGTON, September 10, 1938—[4 p. m. ?]

Following for Embassy, Chungking, as Department's 247, September 10, 4 p. m., and for repetition to Tokyo, as Department's 312, September 10, 4 p. m., and Hankow:

"Department's 245, September 9, 5 p. m., to you, and your 440, September 9, noon, Hankow safety zone.

1. Today's papers here carry news report dated Shanghai, September 10, that British and French Ambassadors have protested to Chiang Kai-shek against Chinese 'obstructive' attitude in regard to establishment of safety zone at Hankow and specifically against erection of fortifications in vicinity of safety zone. Department would be interested in learning whether this report is accurate.

[92] Col. Joseph W. Stilwell.
[93] See unnumbered telegram of September 9, 5 p. m., to the Consul General at Shanghai, p. 283.

256941—54——19

2. Your 440 crossed Department's 245 to you. Department would appreciate your further comment, especially in regard to an approach on general grounds to the Chinese authorities in the sense that the American Government fully expects that the Chinese authorities will so conduct their military activities as to avoid endangering American life and property.

3. Department realizes that you and the Consul General at Hankow,[94] together with the American naval authorities, are continuing to give careful thought to the whole problem of the safety of Americans at Hankow in the light of present developments. In this connection Department would welcome your comment upon the last sentence of Department's 245."

HULL

793.94/13856 : Telegram

The Ambassador in China (Johnson) to the Secretary of State

CHUNGKING, September 11, 1938—noon.
[Received 12 : 55 p. m.]

446. Department's 245, September 9, 5 p. m., paragraph 2. I do not see how we can adopt same attitude toward Chinese as towards Japanese since Chinese are attempting to defend their own nationals and their property against attack by Japanese without assuming responsibility for such protection. It devolves upon the Japanese to do everything possible to protect non-combatant Chinese and foreigners within zone of their activities. Therefore I do not see how we can ask Chinese authorities to avoid military activities adjacent to specified area at Hankow especially as Japanese advance may have the effect of driving fighting Chinese back into that adjacent area. As we are in all cases uncertain as to Japanese definition of military activities it would in any case be difficult for us to ask Chinese to avoid activities "that would give Japanese an excuse for attacking that area on the grounds" outlined in Japanese note. It seems clear to me that if we were to attempt to carry out the Japanese conditions and were to fail as would be probable the danger to our nationals would be increased because the Japanese in that event would feel themselves absolved from responsibility for the safety of American citizens. I am repeating the Department's telegram to Hankow and am requesting comments on the question of feasible measures of safeguarding lives and property of Americans through Josselyn of Military Attaché and Commander of Yangtze Patrol [95] (whose immediate problem this will be), but in my opinion Americans at Hankow will run no greater risks than they have run at Kiukiang, Hsuchow, and Kaifeng during present hostilities, provided they remain as much

---

[94] Paul R. Josselyn.
[95] Rear Adm. David McDougal LeBreton, U. S. N.

aloof from actual fighting areas as may be possible. The Consul General at Hankow and the Commander of the Yangtze Patrol have taken all of these contingencies into consideration and will I am sure have made every arrangement humanely possible to enable Americans to avail themselves of shelter away from the scene of active hostilities. Sent to Hankow, Shanghai and Shanghai repeat to Tokyo.

JOHNSON

793.94/13858 : Telegram

The Ambassador in Japan (Grew) to the Secretary of State

TOKYO, September 12, 1938—noon.
[Received September 12—8 a. m.]

594. For Hankow and Chungking. Department's 309 received undated via Shanghai,[96] Hankow safety zone.

We have today addressed a *note verbale* to the Foreign Office embodying substantially the text in paragraphs 2 to 5 inclusive of the Department's telegram under reference.

I have furnished copies of our *note verbale* to my British, French, German and Italian colleagues expressing the thought that they might wish to take substantially similar action and requesting that they inform me of such action as they may take. The Department will be informed by telegram of their action, if and when taken.

GREW

793.94/13870 : Telegram

The Ambassador in Japan (Grew) to the Secretary of State

TOKYO, September 13, 1938—1 p. m.
[Received September 13—6 : 51 a. m.]

596. I am told on fairly substantial authority[97] that the Emperor has given his approval to plans for a move on Canton after the fall of Hankow. The same source of information indicates that an attack on Soviet Russia may likewise take place after the fall of Hankow.

I do not think that these reports should be accepted as certainly reliable but feel impelled to pass them on to the Department in view of the substantial character of the informant and in order that due consideration may be given in advance to the possibility that the reported plans may materialize.

It seems logical in this connection to consider the important influence which the present crisis in Europe must exert on Japanese policy both with regard to Great Britain and Soviet Russia and the proba-

[96] See unnumbered telegram dated September 9, 5 p. m., to the Consul General at Shanghai, p. 283.
[97] Vice President of the Japanese House of Representatives.

bility that such policy and future decisions will depend in great measure on trend of European developments.

GREW

793.94/13873 : Telegram

The Ambassador in China (Johnson) to the Secretary of State

CHUNGKING, September 13, 1938—4 p. m.
[Received September 13—11 : 06 a. m.]

447. Department's 247, September 10, 4 p. m.,[98] paragraph 1 has been referred to Shanghai for verification. In regard to paragraphs 2 and 3, the Department will have noted from my 446, September 11, noon, that I feel impelled to the conclusion that in the circumstances existing at Hankow it would be useless and inappropriate to ask the Chinese to conduct their military activities in a way to avoid endangering American life and property. The Chinese are on the defensive in the area in question and, short of abandoning it to Japanese occupation, there would seem to be no way for them to comply with this request if made. I repeated Department's 245, September 9, 5 p. m. to Hankow and asked the Consul General to ascertain and submit to the Department the views of the Military Attaché and Commander of Yangtze Patrol regarding its subject matter (including of course the last sentence).[99]

Repeated to Hankow, Shanghai. Shanghai repeat to Tokyo.

JOHNSON

793.94/13878 : Telegram

The Consul General at Hankow (Josselyn) to the Secretary of State

HANKOW, September 13, 1938—7 p. m.
[Received September 13—6 : 50 p. m.]

Mayor of Hankow informed me orally this morning that due to military necessity Chinese intend to erect defenses on the various foreign properties above Seven Mile creek [which] include the installations of the Standard Oil Company and the Texas Company unless a guarantee were given that Japanese will not utilize such properties to land troops. I replied I was sure that we could give no such assurances but that such defenses would constitute grave danger to the American property and I would have to object. Colonel Stilwell who visited area this afternoon states that installations are in a place which should be defended from a military point of view. I told Mayor that the

---

[98] See unnumbered telegram of September 10, 4 p. m., to the Consul General at Shanghai, p. 285.
[99] The views of the Military Attaché and Commander of Yangtze Patrol were in accord with those expressed by the Ambassador in his telegram No. 446, September 11.

matter was being referred to Embassy and he stated that work would not start for 2 or 3 days. Please instruct.

Sent to Chungking.

JOSSELYN

793.94/13879 : Telegram

The Ambassador in China (Johnson) to the Secretary of State

CHUNGKING, September 14, 1938—10 a. m.
[Received September 14—8 : 15 a. m.]

449. Hankow's September 13, 7 p. m., offers a specific case where the responsible Chinese authorities are apparently prepared to refrain from defending a part of the river bank below Hankow which forms frontage of an American owned property whereon is stored the only oil supply available to American naval vessels remaining at Hankow to perform mission of protecting American lives provided we will guarantee that hostile Japanese forces will not use property to land troops in attack on Hankow. Attitude taken by Consul General in Consular Body [*conversation with?*] Hankow mayor seems only attitude we should take and yet Chinese willingness to refrain from erection of defense works on property mentioned provided we can prevent use by Japanese suggests possible basis for request to Japanese to refrain from using property in question. Otherwise property will be threatened with destruction. Of course it is quite possible that as in similar case at Kiukiang nothing will happen even in the absence of such an arrangement. I would like to have Department's advice in instructing Hankow.

Sent to Hankow.

JOHNSON

793.94/13881 : Telegram

The Consul General at Shanghai (Lockhart) to the Secretary of State

SHANGHAI, September 14, 1938—2 p. m.
[Received September 14—1 : 40 p. m.]

1222. [For Chungking.] Your September 12, 10 a. m., and September 12, noon and 447, September 13, 4 p. m.[1] The substance of paragraph 1 of the Department's 245, September 9, 5 p. m., was orally communicated to the French and British Ambassadors today and the Department's 309, September 9, 5 p. m.,[2] was shown to both Ambassadors pursuant to Department's 246 of September 8, 7 p. m., quoted in your September 12, 10 a. m.

[1] See last paragraph of telegram No. 447, p. 288.
[2] See unnumbered telegram of September 9, 5 p. m., to the Consul General at Shanghai, p. 283.

I have made oral inquiry of the French and British Ambassadors in connection with the Department's 247, September 10, 4 p. m.,[3] as to whether the newspaper report is true that they have protested to Chiang Kai Shek against "obstructive" attitude in regard to establishment of safety zone at Hankow, and specifically against erection of fortifications in vicinity of safety zone. The report is not correct. On September 9 the British Ambassador instructed his representative at Hankow to inquire whether the Chinese were willing to accept in principle the Japanese conditions for the establishment of a safety zone. This inquiry was made in agreement with the French Ambassador. Both Ambassadors confirmed this and the British Ambassador informed me today that a reply has been published from his representative stating that Chiang Kai Shek has categorically rejected the proposal and has let it be known in unmistakable terms that there is no chance whatsoever of acceptance of the Japanese conditions. The British Ambassador stated that Chiang Kai Shek took exception to the Japanese offer and stated *inter alia* that he was not only fighting for China but for all the democracies of the world. The British Ambassador stated that Chiang Kai Shek's attitude toward the safety zone proposal as now revealed is a complete *volte face* from his attitude as the Ambassador understood it when he last saw him in Hankow.

Sent to Chungking, repeated to Hankow and Tokyo.

LOCKHART

793.94/13884 : Telegram

The Ambassador in France (Bullitt) to the Secretary of State

PARIS, September 15, 1938—4 p. m.
[Received September 15—12 : 35 p. m.]

1471. Mandel, Minister of Colonies, said to me today that 2 days ago the Japanese had occupied a small island about 25 miles from the coast of the Island of Hainan and had bombarded Hainan. He expressed the opinion that this action of the Japanese Navy was not unrelated to the extreme tension which had arisen in Europe over the Czechoslovak crisis.

BULLITT

793.94/13879 : Telegram

The Secretary of State to the Ambassador in China (Johnson)

WASHINGTON, September 15, 1938—9 p. m.

250. Your 449, September 14, 10 a. m., and related telegrams in regard to the protection of American interests at Hankow.

---

[3] See unnumbered telegram of September 10, 4 p. m., to the Consul General at Shanghai, p. 285.

1. The Department is of the opinion that the isolated properties in question, located as they are because of their use for the storage of petroleum products, should be regarded differently from the foreign residential and business area concerning which we approached the Japanese without reference to any undertaking on the part of the Chinese. That area from its beginning has been identified with foreign interests and administration and has been a special place set aside for foreign residence and business. Our concern in regard to it derives principally from our desire for the protection of American lives.

2. The Department has noted your observation that the Chinese willingness to refrain from erection of defense works on the properties mentioned suggests a possible basis, provided we should be able to prevent use by Japanese, for a request to the Japanese to refrain from using those properties. But, if an American Government agency obtained and passed on such assurances, and if thereafter, in the stress of fighting, advantage were unfairly taken by either side of the situation thus produced, American authorities, because of their action in having partaken in the exchange of such assurances, would have the responsibility of an unfortunate association with the matter.

3. The Department therefore is regretfully of the opinion that in the circumstances appertaining to the properties in question it would not be advisable that American authorities make an approach to the Japanese on the basis indicated.

4. The Department has given careful consideration to the views expressed in your 446, September 11, noon, and 447, September 13, 4 p. m., in regard to the difference between the Japanese and Chinese positions in relation to foreign lives and property at Hankow and fully appreciates the point made by you that the Chinese are on the defensive there. The Department believes, however, that a considerable latitude of action in the formulation of defense measures is open to the Chinese and that such measures might be designed either to invite or to discourage hostilities in the neighborhood of the foreign residential area, without material sacrifice of legitimate military considerations. The Department, with the foregoing in mind, believes that it would be entirely appropriate for you and the American Consul General at Hankow to exert every effort, as occasion offers, to keep before the Chinese authorities the location of American nationals and property to the end that the Chinese take measures to avoid, within the latitude indicated above, measures that would tend to endanger American lives and property.

Repeat to Hankow.

HULL

793.94/13906 : Telegram

The Ambassador in Japan (Grew) to the Secretary of State

Tokyo, September 19, 1938—4 p. m.
[Received September 19—10 a. m.]

608. Our 590, September 8, 11 p. m.

1. Carrying on their series of conversations the Minister for Foreign Affairs received my British colleague towards the end of last week and according to Craigie reiterated his previous observation that until Great Britain should "desert Chiang Kai Shek" and should cease aiding him Japanese concessions to Great Britain in China would be impossible. Craigie pointed out that while British moral sympathy lay with Chiang Kai Shek there had been little material assistance afforded him and that Germany and other nations had supplied him with arms and ammunition far exceeding British supplies. Craigie furthermore pointed out that the Japanese grievances against the British Navy, mentioned by the Minister at their last interview, chiefly concerned individual acts by officers and men which did not necessarily represent the attitude of the British Government. He received today a more detailed list of grievances which the Minister undertook to furnish him at their next interview. Craigie's five points were again discussed without favorable result.

2. Ugaki then asked Craigie whether he was now in a position to give assurances as to Great Britain's intention to cooperate with Japan in China "in future". Craigie replied that until current difficulties were settled it was obviously impossible to give future assurances.

3. In analyzing the situation Craigie notes that a marked change in the attitude of the Japanese Government toward Great Britain took place toward the end of July at about the time of the return of the German Ambassador from Berlin, and while Craigie realizes that the adverse statements of representatives of the British Government in Parliament may have influenced the issue, he is now inclined to believe that messages from the German Government conveyed by General Ott forecasted the European crisis and tended to stiffen Japan's back towards Great Britain.

4. I called Craigie's attention to a press report to the effect that the Japanese Ambassador in Rome had recently assured the Italian Government of Japan's support of Italy and Germany in the event of war. This report, as well as a similar statement made by the spokesman of the Foreign Office in Tokyo last week, Craigie proposes to discuss with the Vice Minister for Foreign Affairs today and says he will inform me tomorrow of the result. It seems to me preferable to obtain an interpretation of those reported statements by this indirect method rather than by a direct approach to the Foreign Office myself.

5. In our ensuing conversation Craigie expatiated on the great importance both to British and American interests in China of maintaining Chiang Kai Shek in the picture, more especially in case of a European war, and expressed his belief that even a comparatively nominal "subsidy" by Great Britain and the United States would exert a perhaps decisive effect. Once again I explained to Craigie the position of the American Government in these matters.

6. These telegrams reporting my periodic talks with my British colleague appear to ring constantly the same general tune but I assume that the Department desires me to continue to report such conversations.[4]

No repetition made.   GREW

761.94/1098

The Chargé in the Soviet Union (Kirk) to the Secretary of State

No. 1667   Moscow, September 19, 1938.
                                                    [Received October 19.]

SIR: With reference to the Embassy's confidential despatch No. 1472, dated July 14, 1938,[5] regarding recent developments in relations between the Soviet Union and the Far East, I have the honor to inform the Department of subsequent developments with regard thereto.

JAPAN

General Relations.

Relations between Japan and the Soviet Union have been featured by the Changkufeng incident, recently settled, involving the most serious fighting that has taken place during the long history of frontier disputes between the two countries, which has been fully reported to the Department in separate despatches and telegrams.[6]

"Oppression" of Japanese Concessionaires in Sakhalin.

Although the importance of the Changkufeng hostilities temporarily overshadowed all the other incidents outstanding between the two Governments, foreign press reports received here indicate that just prior to the outbreak of the fighting between Japanese and Soviet troops the Japanese Government was becoming increasingly dissatisfied with the treatment accorded Japanese coal and oil concessionaires in North Sakhalin by Soviet officials and had lodged new protests with regard thereto. Soviet officials, according to the Embassy's information, were alleged to have pursued such obstructive tactics that half of the short four-months' working season was consumed in futile attempts to obtain Soviet laborers to work the concessions and in en-

---

[4] The Department replied (telegram No. 328, September 19, 8 p. m.) that it found these telegrams to be "of substantial interest and assistance."
[5] Not printed.
[6] See pp. 441 ff.

deavors to obtain the assistance of the foreign section of the Soviet Commissariat for Heavy Industry in settling other pending issues. Since the Changkufeng truce of Aug. 10th the negotiations over the composition and scope of the boundary commission and the approach of the winter season in Sakhalin have temporarily put these problems into the background.

Closure of Two Additional Japanese Consulates in the Soviet Union.

During the period immediately succeeding the truce in the Changkufeng hostilities the Soviet Government forced Japan to close two additional Japanese consulates on Soviet territory, those at Khabarovsk and Blagoveshchensk. The Embassy understands that a strong but unavailing protest was made to the Soviet authorities in this connection. At present, according to a member of the Japanese Embassy here, there remain on Soviet territory only four Japanese consulates,—those at Vladivostok, Alexandrovsk & Okha-on-Sakhalin, and Petropavlovsk-on-Kamchatka; the latter of which is a seasonal consulate established each summer to render assistance to Japanese fishing interests which operate in Soviet Far Eastern waters in accordance with a series of agreements between the two countries flowing out of the Treaty of Portsmouth.[7]

Release of Soviet Vessel Seized by Japan.

Since the settlement of the Changkufeng hostilities only one minor incident between the two countries has come to the Embassy's attention here, that of a Soviet motor boat which drifted to Ushige on the western coast of Sakhalin on June 3, was seized by the Japanese authorities and not permitted to depart for Soviet territory until the 24th of August, after a long series of examinations held by Japanese officials at Toyohara.

Soviet Protest to Japan Regarding the Alleged Torture of Soviet Citizens by Japanese Police.

As reported to the Department,[*] the Soviet Government presented a protest to the Japanese Government against the alleged torturing by Japanese officials of the captain and certain members of the crew of the Soviet refrigerator ship No. 1, which was seized by the Japanese in La Perouse Strait on May 31, 1938.[†] A full translation of this protest, taken from the Moscow *Pravda*, is attached hereto [8] for the Department's information.

CHINA

The new Chinese Ambassador to the Soviet Union,[†] General Yang

---

[7] Signed September 5, 1905, *Foreign Relations*, 1905, p. 824.
[*] Embassy's telegram No. 264, August 21, 1938. [Footnote in the original; telegram not printed.]
[†] See Embassy's despatch No. 1426, June 29, 1938. [Footnote in the original; despatch not printed.]
[8] Not printed.

Chieh, presented his credentials to Mr. Kalinin, Chairman of the Presidium of the Supreme Soviet of the U. S. S. R., on September 4, 1938. In a statement handed to the press at the time of presenting his credentials, General Yang expressed admiration for the successes of the Soviet Union and for what he characterized as the new culture and new life of the Union "under the highly gifted leadership of Lenin and Stalin". He expressed his conviction that "basing itself on what it has already attained and forging ahead, the Soviet Union, by its example and by its tremendous moral influence, will guarantee progress and happiness to the whole of humanity". The new Ambassador further referred to the developments in China under the leadership of Sun Yat-sen and Chiang Kai-shek and stated that in the circumstances "the undeniably friendly relations existing between the two great countries and gaining in strength every day are quite natural". A full translation of General Yang's statement is transmitted herewith [9] for the Department's further information. According to the Soviet press [‡] General Yang is a member of the Central Executive Committee of the Kuomintang Party, Rector of the Chinese Military Academy and Assistant Chief of the General Staff. A short biographical sketch published in the Soviet press is as follows:

During the period of the Northern Expedition, 1926–27, he commanded the 6th and 18th National Revolutionary Armies. In 1928 he was Chief of Staff to the Commander in Chief of the National Revolutionary Army. In 1930–31 he was commander of a fortress on the Yangtze River. In 1933 he commanded the 8th Corps on the front at the Great Chinese Wall against the Japanese invasion. In 1933–34 he was chairman of a Chinese military delegation visiting European countries. During the period 1933–35 he was chairman of the commission dealing with civil affairs in the provinces of Shansi and Shensi.

Soviet Assistance to China.

Although it is impossible to confirm in Moscow the nature and extent of Soviet assistance to China in its fight against Japan, press reports continue to circulate here of the actuality of such assistance, particularly in the shape of pilots and planes as well as, less insistent, reports of tanks and military instructors. Recently, in discussing present conditions in China, a member of the Chinese Embassy said that China is no longer having difficulty in obtaining military supplies and intimated that a portion of them are coming from the Soviet Union. He stated in this connection that it is an open secret that the purpose of the present Chinese Mission here is to obtain as much military assistance as possible.

Respectfully yours,   A. C. KIRK

---

[9] Not printed.
[‡] Moscow *Pravda*, September 5, 1938. [Footnote in the original.]

760F.62/924 : Telegram

The Ambassador in Japan (Grew) to the Secretary of State

Tokyo, September 20, 1938—6 p. m.
[Received September 20—10 : 45 a. m.]

609. Our 608, September 19, 4 p. m.

1. With regard to the statement given out by the Foreign Office
on September 14, which the Embassy assumes was published in the
United States, a translation prepared by the Embassy of the pertinent
passage in the Japanese text reads that in connection with the Sudeten
problem Japan "is prepared to resist the mechanisms [machinations]
of the Comintern in cooperation with Germany and Italy and in accordance with the spirit of the Anti-Comintern Pact",[10] whereas the
official English translation given out simultaneously by the Foreign
Office states that Japan "is prepared as ever to join forces with Germany and Italy for fighting against Red operations in accordance
with the spirit of the Anti-Comintern Agreement". The discrepancy
in the tone if not in the phraseology of the two versions is obvious.

2. My British colleague yesterday called the English version to
the attention of the Vice Minister for Foreign Affairs who denied
categorically that this should be interpreted as meaning that if the
Czechoslovak crisis should lead to war, Japan intended to align herself with Germany and Italy. The intention of the statement was to
show that Japan as a party to the Anti-Comintern Pact was concerned
in combating the Comintern activities which the Japanese Government believed to be largely responsible for present difficulties in
Czechoslovakia. The Vice Minister said that the statement referred
to Comintern activities only and that it would be quite wrong to give
it a wider interpretation.

3. With regard to the press report of a statement allegedly given
out by the Japanese Ambassador in Rome on September 16, the Vice
Minister said that no instruction to that effect has been sent to the
Japanese Embassy in Rome and that no report of such a step had
been received from the Embassy.

4. My British colleague has informed his Government that in the
event of war in Europe he does not believe that Japan will attack
Soviet Russia, at least not immediately, but will await developments,
meanwhile intensifying Japanese operations in China with greater
ruthlessness against foreign interests.

5. Craigie believes that in case of war in Europe, Japan will carefully watch the attitude of the United States because the development
which Japan would most fear would be combined action of the United
States, Great Britain and Soviet Russia against her which would
spell her ruin. Craigie entered a long plea during our talk today that

[10] *Foreign Relations, Japan, 1931–1941, vol. II, p. 153.*

we "keep Japan guessing" upon uncertainty as to possible action by the United States [which?] would exert a powerful restraint on Japanese depredations against foreign interests in China.

6. With regard to Japan's current interference with British interests in China, the Vice Minister acknowledged that this was due not only to the present anti-British wave of feeling in Japan but also to the intrinsic military difficulties in complying with British desiderata.

7. Craigie expects to pursue his series of interviews with the Minister for Foreign Affairs later this week.

GREW

893.01 Provisional/142 : Telegram

The First Secretary of Embassy in China (Salisbury) to the Secretary of State

PEIPING, September 21, 1938—4 p. m.
[Received September 21—1: 30 p. m.]

577. Embassy's 574, September 20, 4 p. m.[11]

1. Announcement has now been made of inauguration tomorrow of the "United Council of the Republic of China" established by the Provisional and Reformed Governments and composed of six members, each regime being represented by three, with Wang Keh Min as Chairman and the temporary seat Peiping.

2. The stated functions of the new council are "to supervise matters of common interest to the two governments and to pave the way for the establishment of a new central government of China". The Council will meet once a month and "deliberate on matters relative to communications, traffic, postal affairs, finances, customs, coordinated taxes, salt affairs, education and other matters which shall require government control". In addition to Wang the members named are: for the Provisional Government: Chu Shen (President of the Legislature Commission), Wang I-tang (Home Minister) ; for the Reformed Government: Liang Hung-chih (Chairman of the Executive Yuan), Wen Tsung Yao (President of the Legislature Yuan), and Chen Chun (Home Minister). Chen Lu (Foreign Minister of Reformed Government) is appointed Secretary General.

3. According to announcement by Wang and Liang, a new "Hankow Government, after the overthrow of the Chiang Kai Shek hegemony, and possibly a southwestern government, as well as the Mongol autonomous Mengchiang Government, shall be incorporated into the structure in the future."

Repeated to Chungking, Nanking, Hankow, Shanghai, by mail to Tokyo.

SALISBURY

---

[11] Not printed.

793.94/13948 : Telegram

The Consul General at Hankow (Josselyn) to the Secretary of State

HANKOW, September 23, 1938—2 p. m.
[Received 7 : 13 p. m.]

My September 13, 7 p. m. regarding proposed Chinese defenses on oil company installations.

Mayor informed me orally this morning that Chinese military had decided not to erect defenses on Standard Oil Company or Texas Oil Company property.

Sent to Chungking.

JOSSELYN

793.94/13962 : Telegram

The Ambassador in Japan (Grew) to the Secretary of State

TOKYO, September 27, 1938—noon.
[Received September 27—8 : 30 a. m.]

623. Our 577, September 5, 3 p. m., Hankow safety zone. The British Ambassador has informed the Foreign Office that the British Government in taking note of the conditions under which the Japanese forces will refrain from attacking the safety zone is "unable to accept any responsibility towards either party to the present hostilities in respect of any action or undertaking of the other party" and that it reserves all rights "in the event of any injury or damage being suffered by British subjects or British property in or near Hankow as the result of military operations by the Japanese armed forces".

The French Ambassador has made to the Foreign Office a substantially similar communication.

GREW

760F.62/1156 : Telegram

The Ambassador in Japan (Grew) to the Secretary of State

TOKYO, September 27, 1938—9 p. m.
[Received September 27—1 : 10 p. m.]

626. Our 609, September 20, 6 p. m., crisis in Europe.

1. Unlike Italy, which apparently is issuing repeated if equivocal expressions of intention to take the part of Germany in the event of a general war in Europe, Japan has made no public or other authoritative declaration of her position. Although there is some desire by extreme reactionary and other irresponsible popular elements for military alignment by Japan with Germany, the predominant feeling is one of strong hope that not only will Japan avoid becoming involved but that a general conflagration may be avoided. The evident anxiety of the Vice Minister for Foreign Affairs in his conversations

with my British colleague to discourage assumption of Japanese military alignment with Germany is, we believe, reflective of such hope.

2. It is impossible at this time to make any estimate of Japanese attitude in a situation which may have developed in Europe beyond the opening gambit. It is our opinion that in the circumstances predicated Japan will take no initiative toward, or alternatively will try to avoid, becoming involved. We base our conclusions on the following considerations: (*a*) As a corollary to the fundamental Japanese policy of seeking to eliminate Occidental political influence from the Far East, there has been since 1931 steady withdrawal by Japan from participation in the affairs of Europe; (*b*) with a declining export trade, Japan has thus far been able to finance purchase of munitions for the conflict with China and of other necessary primary commodities only by resort to drastic trade control. Even if Japan were to remain neutral, the worldwide economic dislocations which must inevitably follow an outbreak of a general European war would add immeasurably to her difficulties, first, in maintaining her overseas markets and second, in procuring munitions and raw materials. There is very grave doubt whether in such circumstances she could afford to lose, by joining Germany, her British, French and possibly other markets and sources of supply. There is some optimistic speculation over the possibility of Japan benefitting by decrease of European goods in world markets, but the question arises whether Japan has the resources necessary to exploit such opportunity.

3. It is reasonable to believe that Japan in her present position would prefer to a general war in Europe a continuation of the conditions of unrest which have prevailed there for some years—conditions which have prevented Great Britain especially from active intervention in the Far East.

4. In the event of war actually breaking out, I propose as on my own initiative to inquire of the Minister for Foreign Affairs with regard to the attitude and [policy?] of the Japanese Government, provided the Department does not cable disapproval of such a step.

GREW

893.00/14263 : Telegram

The Consul General at Hankow (Josselyn) to the Secretary of State

HANKOW, September 28, 1938—10 a. m.
[Received 4 p. m.]

The three outstanding Chinese Communist political leaders south of the Yellow River, Chou En Lai, Wang Ming and Chin Po Ku, departed from here about a month ago for a brief conference at Yenan. During the past 2 weeks they have repeatedly been reported as imminent[ly] returning; yet they have thus far not arrived in Hankow.

The Yenan conferees are reliably reported to be formulating party policy to be followed after the fall of Wuhan.[12]

The prolonged absence of the three leaders at the present juncture when it would be logical to expect them to be exerting every effort towards mobilization of the people for the defense of Wuhan together with their preoccupation with a policy to be followed after the fall of Wuhan suggests that the Communists have abandoned hope for mobilization of the people in accordance with their plans, Central Government obstruction having proved insurmountable.

Repeated to Chungking, Peiping, Shanghai.

JOSSELYN

760F.62/1211 : Telegram

The Ambassador in Japan (Grew) to the Secretary of State

TOKYO, September 28, 1938—3 p. m.
[Received September 28—4 : 10 a. m.]

628. Department's circular.[13] The message of the Government of the United States decoded and transcribed at 1 o'clock, and was placed in the hands of a responsible official of the Foreign Office at 1 : 05 in anticipation of my appointment with the Minister for Foreign Affairs at 2 : 50. At that hour, opening the conversation, I observed to the Minister that this is a moment of the utmost gravity in the history of civilization and a moment at which decisions and actions may fundamentally influence the future course of civilization. The message of the American Government was then presented both orally and in an informal paper so that the text would be clear on the record, accompanied by a written transcription of the text of the President's appeal to the Chancellor of the German Reich, the President of Czechoslovakia and the Prime Ministers of Great Britain and France.[14]

After listening to the interpreting of the message into Japanese, carefully followed [by] Coville[15] who was present at the interview, the Minister replied substantially as follows:

I would express on behalf of the Japanese Government full agreement with the action taken by the President of the United States in the controversy between Germany and Czechoslovakia. As you are aware, Japan is always desirous of peace and although unfortunately engaged at the present time in hostilities in China, Japan hopes to establish there conditions of peace. We also seek a peaceful settlement between Germany and Czechoslovakia, but there is a question whether action by Japan similar to that taken by the President would

---

[12] The tri-cities, Wuchang, Hankow, Hanyang.
[13] Dated September 27, 3 p. m., vol. I, p. 677.
[14] See President Roosevelt's telegram of September 26 to Chancellor Hitler, *ibid.*, p. 657.
[15] Second Secretary of Embassy in Japan.

be efficacious. We must give careful consideration to what action we, as Japan, may best take, from the point of view of our own position. At the same time we firmly share the convictions expressed by the President.

GREW

760F.62/1191 : Telegram

The Ambassador in Japan (Grew) to the Secretary of State

Токуо, September 28, 1938—6 p. m.
[Received September 28—9 : 10 a. m.]

630. Embassy's 628, September 28, 3 p. m. An hour ago I was approached by the Foreign Office as to how I would feel about the Japanese Government's giving publicity to my call this afternoon on the Foreign Minister and to his expression of appreciation for and agreement in the spirit in which the President sent his message. I stated that in my opinion any publicity to favorable reaction on the part of the Japanese Government would be all to the good. I am now given to understand that the Minister shares this view and that a release will be given out in such tone.

GREW

760F.62/1239 : Telegram

The Ambassador in Japan (Grew) to the Secretary of State

Токуо, September 28, 1938—9 p. m.
[Received September 28—1 p. m.]

631. Our 609, September 20, 6 p. m.

1. In conversation today the Vice Minister for Foreign Affairs told my British colleague that there had been no change in the attitude of the Japanese Government towards a possible conflict in Europe since their interview on September 19, but acknowledged that the Government was under great and increasing pressure from reactionary ele- ments and especially from the various patriotic societies, now being consolidated and incited under the leadership of Toyama, to join Germany and Italy actively in war, should war occur. The Vice Min- ister said that the principal basis for this movement was the strong anti-British feeling in Japan engendered by the supposition that Great Britain's support of Chiang Kai Shek is largely responsible for the latter's continued resistance to Japanese arms. The Vice Minister acknowledged that this supposition was a misconception of the facts but said that the theory generally existed none the less.

2. Craigie and Horinouchi were in agreement that some substan- tial gesture indicative of Anglo-Japanese friendship might serve to improve the atmosphere although it does not appear that any concrete proposals were discussed or advanced.

3. The proposal of the Foreign Minister, reported in our 633, September 28, midnight,[16] might however be regarded as pertinent.

4. Craigie considers that the publicity to be given by the Foreign Office expressing the full agreement of the Japanese Government with the action taken by the President in the controversy between Germany and Czechoslovakia (see our 630, September 28, 6 p. m.) will be very helpful as placing the Japanese Government's attitude squarely on record. The Vice Minister, in referring to my *démarche* to the Minister this afternoon, told Craigie that the reason for the hesitancy of the Japanese Government to accede to our Government's proposal that it take action similar to that of the President was the feeling that being engaged in hostilities itself, it might be embarrassing for Japan to issue such an appeal to other nations.

GREW

893.0146/669

Memorandum by the Adviser on Political Relations (Hornbeck)

[WASHINGTON,] September 28, 1938.

Indications have come from China that some Japanese (apparently some Army authorities and some civilian elements) are giving consideration to the possible taking of steps toward seizing areas at important ports which have been and are under the administrative jurisdiction of occidental powers, especially Great Britain and France. From time to time certain Japanese Army officers have made threats that in certain contingencies Japanese forces might occupy the International Settlement (and the French Concession?) at Shanghai. Recently, at Tientsin, there have been controversies between Japanese elements and the authorities of the British and the French Concessions; from some Japanese quarters there have emanated demands that the Japanese authorities take drastic steps; and it is reported that the Japanese military are building an encircling roadway around the boundaries of the two concessions. Today, it is reported from Shanghai that stories are current there of a recent landing at the port of 10,000 Japanese soldiers. During the past few days of anxiety with regard to developments in Europe, there has been speculation to the effect that, if war begins in Europe, the Japanese will engage in acts of aggression against British and French interests in China which may include seizure of some or all areas where those powers now exercise administrative jurisdiction. As against this, there came yesterday from the American Embassy at Tokyo a telegram [17] giving the Embassy's estimate to the effect that Japan would probably, in the event

---

[16] *Post*, p. 305.
[17] Dated September 27, 9 p. m., p. 298.

of war beginning in Europe, not precipitately embark upon activities aligning her with Germany.

It is believed desirable that consideration be given to the question of policy and action by this Government and its agencies in China, in the event of war beginning in Europe, in regard to the American landed armed forces at Tientsin and at Shanghai.

Press reports yesterday and today indicate that the British Government has issued some instructions regarding and is making some redistribution of the British armed forces, both those landed at Chinese ports and their naval vessels operating in China waters. We have no evidence of the British Government's having informed us of its intentions or consulted us in regard to these matters.

Although we have an informal understanding between the Department of State and the British Foreign Office to the effect that if and as either country is considering making alterations in the distribution of its landed armed forces in China, it shall, if circumstances permit, consult with or notify the other, it is believed that, in the light of repeated omission on the part of the British Government to consult or notify this Government, we would be warranted, if we so chose, in proceeding as we may see fit with regard to possible changes in the distribution of our landed armed forces, without consulting or notifying the British Government. However, if and as we make decisions in this matter, it will probably be possible for us without inconvenience to consult with or notify the British Government, and there might be advantage in our doing so.

It is believed that we need not concern ourselves here with the question of possible movements of American naval vessels now at Shanghai: Admiral Yarnell [18] can either make his own decisions in that connection or ask the Navy Department for instructions.

What need concern us is the matter of our Marine contingents at Tientsin and at Shanghai, and possibly those at Peiping.

We have at present landed at Shanghai about 1300 Marines, officers and men; at Tientsin about 250; and at Peiping about 250.

Since the readjustment made early in the current year in the distribution of our landed armed forces in north China, at which time we withdrew the 15th Infantry from Tientsin and transferred from Peiping to Tientsin two companies of Marines, we have proceeded on the theory that the Guard, consisting of two companies of Marines at Peiping, and the two companies of Marines at Tientsin are maintained at those points for the purpose of general policing, of maintaining communications (especially through the operation of radio stations), and to be of assistance to American nationals, in the general capacity of an armed escort, in the event of there arising a

---

[18] Commander in Chief, United States Asiatic Fleet.

situation calling for withdrawing of American nationals from those cities and bringing the said nationals to the coast or to some agreed-upon concentration point. It is believed that we should continue for the time being to maintain those forces at those points for those purposes. As the situation unfolds, there may develop reason for reconsidering this view. Any disturbance at this moment of the existing set-up as regards the disposal of those forces would be premature and gratuitously productive of alarm in the "foreign" communities at the points under reference. It is especially desirable that our bases of communication at Tientsin and Peiping continue in operation.

The Marine contingent which we now have landed at Shanghai is there for the purpose of policing and, in particular, of guarding one sector of the boundary of the International Settlement. It functions in cooperation with similar landed armed forces of other countries, especially Great Britain and Italy, and those of France, which guard the outer boundaries of the French Concession (the inner boundary of which is coincident with a part of the boundary of the International Settlement). It is believed that this American Marine contingent should be left where it is for the present, pending developments in regard to disposal of the British and the French forces (and possibly the Italian) at Shanghai. In the event of an impending withdrawal of the British and/or the French forces, renewed consideration should be immediately given by us to the question of the disposal of our forces at Shanghai.

The one point with regard to which it is highly desirable that we make a decision at this time is this: In the event of an authorized movement by the Japanese toward seizing control of the International Settlement at Shanghai, and if such movement were accompanied by threat of or use of Japanese armed force, should our Marines participate in any effort at armed resistance? It is believed that the answer to this question should be in the negative. It stands to reason that neither our landed force nor the landed forces of the other powers, either separately or collectively, could hold their positions against such armed forces as the Japanese could easily employ for seizure and occupation of the Settlement. Resistance to the point of combat could only result in a defeat, with its accompaniment of large loss of life and extensive destruction of property. If and when, in advance of a possible Japanese movement toward occupation, the British and/or the French withdraw their forces, we can then consider whether we will withdraw our force. In the meantime, leaving our force where it is, we may advisedly come to a decision that an attempt at seizure by the Japanese, if and when, is to be resisted by diplomatic processes only, and not by resort to force.

It is believed that the standing orders under which our landed armed forces in China are operating, together with instructions which have been issued, in explanation of policy, to State Department representatives in China, for communication to the officers of the armed forces, together with special instructions which have been issued by the Navy Department from time to time, cover all contingencies which are likely to arise except those referred to above, and that no special instruction or orders need be sent at this time. If we can have a meeting of the minds here to the effect that an authorized movement by Japanese armed forces with the objective of seizing control of the Settlement is not to be resisted by armed force, this Department and the Navy Department would be prepared to act instantly in the event of there arising need for instructions to be given on that point. There will be time for the issuing of such instructions after evidence reaches us of a Japanese intention so to act. To put on the cables or in the air now an instruction to the effect suggested would be to take an unnecessary chance of an interception by the Japanese the result of which, information of our intention being in their hands, would encourage them to take the step which we hope that they will refrain from taking.[19]

S[TANLEY] K. H[ORNBECK]

893.102S/1711 : Telegram

The Ambassador in Japan (Grew) to the Secretary of State

TOKYO, September 28, 1938—midnight.
[Received September 28—3 : 48 p. m.]

633. 1. My British colleague informs me that in his last conversation with the Minister for Foreign Affairs a few days ago the latter said that the Japanese Government is prepared to restore the northern Settlement area in Shanghai (Hongkew and Yangtzepoo) to the authority of the Municipal Council subject to the following conditions:[20]

(*a*) Better cooperation by the British and other municipal authorities with the Japanese authorities in maintenance of law and order (in particular transfer of the District Court to the *de facto* authorities), and

(*b*) British help in realization of Japan's proposals in regard to the reorganization of the Municipal Council's police force.

2. Craigie has communicated this proposal to his Government with a strong recommendation for acceptance. He feels that the large number of Japanese residents in the northern Settlement area justifies the Japanese conditions and believes that with regard to the transfer of the District Court some reasonable compromise might be worked

---

[19] Marginal notation to paragraph by the Chief of the Division of Far Eastern Affairs : "Approved by the Secretary, Oct. 1, 1938."

[20] See telegram No. 1300, October 6, 9 a. m., from the Consul General at Shanghai, vol. IV, p. 138.

out insuring the appointment of judges not affiliated either with Chiang Kai Shek or with the Renovation Government. He has told his Government that time is of the essence in forestalling Japan's complete tie up with Germany and believes that to carry out this proposed compromise in Shanghai would have a very favorable effect. He believes that the proposal could be worked out without sacrificing any matter of principle and certainly without involving any recognition of the Renovation Government.

3. Craigie asks me to regard the foregoing as strictly confidential and not to repeat this telegram to Shanghai because any risk of publicity at present is to be avoided. The British Ambassador in Shanghai [21] feels that the Japanese proposal should be refused but Craigie believes that Clark Kerr does not appreciate the larger issues involved. No reply has yet come from London to Craigie's recommendation.

4. I refrained from expressing an opinion as to the merits of the Japanese proposal but said that I would pass it on to Washington in strict confidence.

GREW

793.94/13999 : Telegram

The Ambassador in Japan (Grew) to the Secretary of State

TOKYO, October 4, 1938—4 p. m.
[Received October 4—9 : 20 a. m.]

643. The following reports one of my periodic talks today with my British colleague.

1. Craigie feels that Anglo-Japanese relations are steadily deteriorating and that the anti-British campaign by the reactionaries is becoming intensified.

2. The local press reports that in a press interview yesterday the Prime Minister was asked whether, as Minister for Foreign Affairs, he would continue the so-called "Ugaki–Craigie conversations" and he was quoted as replying that while the Vice Minister would normally conduct such interviews, he himself would receive the British Ambassador if the latter insisted, the press ascribing to Prince Konoye a distinctly condescending tone. Craigie has therefore asked the Foreign Office for a report as to precisely what the Minister did say.

3. The Vice Minister yesterday taxed Craigie with the alleged fact that the British delegate at Geneva had the text of the resolution applying to Japan the sanction clause of the Covenant [22] and appeared very angry at this reported action. He repeated to Craigie that

---

[21] Sir Archibald Clark Kerr.
[22] See telegram No. 260, September 30, midnight, from the Consul at Geneva, p. 518.

Great Britain should make some important gesture of friendship to Japan in order to remove the current belief that Great Britain is definitely hostile.

4. Craigie learns from two sources that plans are now afoot to take Canton prior to the final attack on Hankow and has reason to believe that the proposed move is being inspired by the Germans. The latter are reported to hold the opinion that the fall of Hankow will not in itself prove decisive in terminating the conflict; that Germany desires Japan to emerge from the conflict as still a strong power and therefore feels that every effort should be made to reach an early decision; and that the fall of Canton, by effectively cutting off Chiang Kai Shek from the outside world, would tend to hasten the successful conclusion of the conflict.

5. We have no direct evidence tending to confirm the plans reported in paragraph 4.

GREW

760F.62/1740

The Ambassador in Japan (Grew) to the Secretary of State

No. 3306   TOKYO, October 6, 1938.
                                        [Received October 21.]

SIR: In my telegram 626, September 27, 9 p. m. I had the honor to present our analysis of the attitude of Japan with regard to the war which was then apparently impending in Europe. I stated that there were reactionary elements among the Japanese populace which were actively agitating for the giving of military support by Japan to Germany, but I expressed the opinion that the predominant feeling in this country was one of hope that not only would Japan avoid becoming involved in any general conflagration in Europe but that the calamity itself could be prevented. When, as a result of the agreement reached at Munich by the heads of government of Great Britain, France, Germany and Italy,[23] the immediate likelihood of war was removed, certain of my colleagues believed that the predominant reaction of Japan to this development was one of profound disappointment. Happily, there did not eventuate that catastrophic conclusion to the prolonged efforts of the statesmen of Europe to find a peaceful settlement of the issue between Germany and Czechoslovakia which alone could have brought forth an authoritative expression of the position of the Japanese Government; and I fervently hope that there will never arise any occasion or need for clarification

---

[23] Signed September 29; *Documents on British Foreign Policy, 1919–1939*, 3d ser., vol. II, doc. No. 1224, p. 627, and *Documents on German Foreign Policy, 1918–1945*, ser. D, vol. II, doc. No. 675, p. 1014. Cf. telegram No. 262, September 30, 1 p. m., from the Minister in Czechoslovakia, *Foreign Relations*, 1938, vol. I, p. 702.

of Japan's position in this respect. However, as the alignments among the nations of Europe and the tension between the rival camps have not yet been entirely dissolved or relaxed, a discussion of the question whether a general war in Europe would be welcomed by Japan may be of something more than academic interest.

In my telegram under reference, the first consideration on which was based our conclusion that Japan desired for Europe a peaceful issue out of all its difficulties is the policy which the Japanese Government has consistently pursued since 1931, of withdrawal from participation in the affairs of Europe. This consideration was mentioned first for the reason that it has a fairly extended historical background.

The inclusion of Japan among the Principal Allied and Associated Powers in the war against the Central European Powers, which gave Japan a voice in the settlement of a number of European problems of not even the most remote concern to Japan, gratified the aspirations of the Japanese people to be numbered among the great Powers. It was flattering to be given a permanent seat in the Council of the League of Nations and to have a voice in such matters as, for example, the final disposition of Bessarabia. However, that outburst of chauvinism and nationalism—the conflict with China in Manchuria—was also a manifestation of a policy which had long been agitated in Japan, of eliminating Occidental influences from the Far East. It was obvious that practical considerations, notably the limited economic and military resources of Japan, attached to the cry of "East Asia for the Japanese" the corollary that Japan could not undertake to oust European influence from the Far East and at the same time continue to participate in the management of the affairs of Europe, with all the risks and hazards which that involved. Judgment pronounced on Japan by the League of Nations in February 1933 [24] gave further impetus to the retreat from Europe, and by 1936 Japan found itself in a state of complete political isolation. True, in 1936 she concluded an agreement with Germany ostensibly to combat the spread of communism and in the following year associated herself also with Italy by a similar instrument.[25] It is recalled that the Japanese Minister for Foreign Affairs stated, with reference to the Convention with Germany, that one of the purposes in concluding that agreement was to open a way for Japan to escape from the isolation which encompassed her and to proceed by gradual stages toward the development of more friendly relations with the other great Powers. It might therefore be reasonable to assume that Japan had found occasion to regret her

---

[24] See resolution of February 24, 1933, *Foreign Relations*, Japan, 1931–1941, vol. I, p. 113.
[25] Signed November 25, 1936, and November 6, 1937, *ibid.*, vol. II, pp. 153 and 159, respectively.

withdrawal from Europe. However, it is unlikely that such an assumption contains the whole truth or even a large portion of the truth. There exists today as there has existed for some years past, a section of the Japanese people which regrets, and even regrets bitterly, the chain of events which began with the Japanese military occupation of Manchuria in 1931, and which yearns for the "good old days" when Japan was a member in good standing of the family of nations. Nevertheless, even this element realizes that Japan will not of its own accord retrace its steps, and that the road back cannot be by way of the anti-Comintern Pact. Nor is there any warrant whatever for assuming that the Army has any intention of becoming embroiled in troubles in Europe under anything short of the most compelling reasons. The fact that the economic dislocations which would follow the outbreak of war in Europe was cited by us as one of the reasons for Japanese hope that the crisis in Europe would be successfully surmounted, may perhaps be queried by those who remember that the World War brought about a period of unprecedented prosperity in Japan. However, it must be remembered that Japan today is not in the same position that she was in 1914 and subsequent years. In 1914–18 the diversion of the industrial and economic resources of Europe to the production of munitions and the blockading of the Central European Powers resulted in a virtual vacuum in world markets for manufactured articles. Whereas a large part of the merchant marine of the combatants was either inactive or engaged in the carrying of troops and munitions, the Japanese merchant marine, which even in those days was of substantial size, was left free for the development and expansion of Japan's commerce. The war was a god-sent hope which Japan exploited to the limits of its resources, then unencumbered by the exigencies of the conduct of military operations. Today, however, Japan is engaged in China in hostilities over a front line of more than one thousand miles, she has about 1,300,000 men under arms, her financial and economic structure is being preserved only by recourse to trade, fiscal, industrial and other control measures of the most drastic character, while a substantial portion of her merchant shipping is being used to munition her forces in China. In the unfavorable circumstances existing today only an incorrigible optimist would believe that it would be possible for Japan, were a general war to break out in Europe, even to maintain her diminished export trade to a point necessary for the purchase of the most essential commodities, to say nothing of having the industrial and financial reserves essential for replacement in world markets of goods which had thus far been supplied by Europe. How, in these circumstances, it would be possible for Japan to deprive herself completely, first of British Empire markets and next of other markets beyond the effective sphere of influence of the Japanese Navy, without there resulting a collapse of her economic structure, it is difficult to see.

There is a third, and perhaps the most important, consideration of all. When our telegram under reference was being prepared it was not known that, along with ultranationalistic private organizations which placarded the streets of Tokyo with demands that Japan take advantage of war in Europe to move against Soviet Russia, a substantial feeling existed in the Army that Japan should take advantage of an opportunity which might never again occur to settle once and for all its account with that country. Several responsible Japanese officials have recently informed us in confidence that, if a general war had broken out in Europe, it would have been impossible for the Japanese Government to have continued successfully to resist such demand; that with Japan allied with Germany and possibly with Italy against Great Britain, France, and Soviet Russia, the entry into the war of the United States on the side of the democratic Powers would have been a virtual certainty; and that with the United States also in arms against Japan there could have been but one conclusion—and that a disastrous one for Japan.

There no doubt exists among uneducated Japanese, and even among some of those Japanese who are in a position to have an intelligent perception of the situation, a feeling of disappointment that the final conference at Munich did not prove abortive, and thus have made it impossible for the democratic Powers of Europe, especially Great Britain, to intervene forcibly in the Far East. Although a conflagration in Europe would have given Japan a completely free hand in China, I cannot believe that the trend of events involving Japan which would have been started with inevitable certainty by a war in Europe and which might well have ultimately concluded in the collapse of the Japanese Empire, was not clearly apparent to those elements and individuals who are now formulating the policies of this country.

There are enclosed memoranda of conversations [26] which I had with my British colleague when the subject of the Japanese attitude toward the situation in Europe was discussed. I think it will be clear from the various statements made to Sir Robert Craigie by the Vice-Minister for Foreign Affairs that it was not the desire of the Japanese Government that there should prevail the belief that Japan would necessarily give military support to Germany in the event of a war in Europe.

Respectfully yours,   JOSEPH C. GREW

---

[26] None printed; but see the Ambassador's telegrams No. 608, September 19, 4 p. m., p. 292; No. 609, September 20, 6 p. m., p. 296; and No. 631, September 28, 9 p. m., p. 301.

893.01 Provisional/150 : Telegram

The Second Secretary of Embassy in China (Smyth) to the Secretary of State

NANKING, October 7, 1938—4 p. m.
[Received 8:17 p. m.]

165. Yesterday afternoon a Chinese, whose card indicated that he was chief of the Bureau of Protocol of the Foreign Office of the "Reformed Government," called, this being the first call received by this office from any official of that government. He said that Liang Hung Chih, President of the Executive Yuan and head of the government, would give a reception on October 10 at which foreigners would be welcome. He added that he realized our Government had not recognized the "Reformed Government" and that it would therefore be difficult for me to attend in an official capacity, but he expressed the hope that I could attend as a private individual. It seemed evident from his conversation that he expected no foreign officials, except Japanese, to attend, and as no statement from me was asked for or seemed necessary I made none.

The general question of calls on and relations with officials of new regimes is dealt with in telegrams between the Department and Peiping, the most recent on record here being Peiping's 125, February 23, noon, and the Department's 74, March 10, 4 p. m.,[27] but the question of attending functions does not appear to have been definitely determined. I believe, however, that it would not be advisable or necessary for me to attend the reception on October 10, even in a private capacity, as the presence of an American official, which would no doubt be reported in the local press, would be regarded, at least by the general public, as an indication of approval if not recognition of the new regime and would be bitterly resented by Chinese here, apart from those connected with the new regime. Unless otherwise instructed, I will not attend.

The British and German Consuls, the only other foreign officials now in Nanking apart from the Japanese, received calls from the Chinese above mentioned, but they do not propose to attend the function.

I also received a call yesterday from a Chinese, representing himself to be a secretary in the new municipal government, who handed me the new Mayor's card. During the casual conversation with him I inquired whether the Mayor's office was busy, to which he made the illuminating reply "oh, no, the Japanese do everything."

Practically all officials of the "New Government" have now arrived in Nanking and are busy establishing themselves in office quarters,

---

[27] Latter not printed; see second paragraph of Department's *aide-mémoire of* March 10, p. 118.

not an easy task as many of the suitable buildings have already been taken over by various Japanese organs. Furthermore, tenure is uncertain; the Foreign Office, for example, which settled down some time ago in spacious quarters, was unceremoniously ejected a few days ago by the Japanese Special Service Section, which desired to use the premises, and has been forced to remove to less suitable offices.

Sent to Shanghai, repeated to Department, Peiping.

SMYTH

793.94/14047½

Generalissimo Chiang Kai-shek to President Roosevelt [28]

"Mr. President, you have recently told the world that 'force produces no solution for the future good of humanity'; that 'should hostilities break out, the lives of millions of men, women, and children in every country involved will be lost in circumstances of unspeakable horror'; and that 'in the event of a general war the American people face the fact that no nation can escape some measure of the consequences'.[29]

"These words of yours once more rekindle in the Chinese Government and people their faith in the love of peace and justice of the American nation.

"May I point out, Mr. President, that, while your powerful appeals have contributed so much to the appeasement of Europe, the resort to brutal force and slaughter still prevail in the Far East and world peace is still far from realization? I am confident that you, Mr. President, who have already done so much in the past for peace, surely will not ignore the problem of peace in the Far East. The American Government whose mediation decades ago brought about the termination of the Russo-Japanese War,[30] is certainly most closely concerned with the peace of the East.

"It is said that, owing to heavy human losses and economic difficulties, Japan is beginning to realize that force solves no problem. More than once she has sought mediation for peace by Germany and Italy.

"But, Mr. President, my people feel that they can only look to your Government for leadership in the active search for peace, because we have complete faith that the kind of peace the American Government is inspired to sponsor will be a just peace.

---

[28] Cabled message received by the Chinese Embassy October 8; copy handed to the Adviser on Political Relations by the appointed Chinese Ambassador on the same date. The opening paragraph reads:

"Please communicate personally and in strict confidence to the kind consideration of President Roosevelt the following message in my own name:"

[29] Quotations taken from President Roosevelt's telegram to Chancellor Hitler, September 26, vol. I, p. 657.

[30] See *Foreign Relations*, 1905, pp. 807 ff.

"Now that the European situation is settling down, may it not be possible for the American Government to initiate a move for the peace of the Far East by inviting all the Governments interested to attend a Conference, stipulating a general cessation of hostilities as a precondition and aiming at seeking a lasting settlement through calm and fair-minded deliberation? May I not venture to suggest that success in such a move would surely mean the crowning achievement of the policy in the Far East with which your Government has identified itself ever since the Washington Conference?

"I also wish to point out that the present moment seems to be the most opportune time for such a move, because the Japanese are engaged in a most difficult war for the attack and occupation of the Wu-Han cities."

CHIANG CHUNG-CHENG

OCTOBER THE EIGHTH.

793.94/14031 : Telegram

The Consul General at Hankow (Josselyn) to the Secretary of State

HANKOW, October 9, 1938—noon.
[Received 8 : 20 p. m.]

My September 28, 10 a. m. and October 3, 11 a. m.[31]

1. Conversation with Chou En-lai and a press statement by him indicate that the Chinese Communist Party as a result of the Yenan conference of September 28 to October 7 has recommitted itself to the united front.

2. At the time of the departure of the political leaders mentioned in the Consulate General's telegram of September 28, 10 a. m. there was evident resentment on the part of the Communists against the Government because of the latter's effective opposition to the Communist propaganda and mass mobilization program for Chinese held territory, especially the Wuhan area.

3. After his return here on October 1 Chou En-lai once more pledged the Chinese Communist Party to cooperation with the Kuomintang during and after the present hostilities, allegiance to the leadership of Chiang Kai Shek, recognition of the Three People's Principles as the political base of the united front and asked for obliteration of the memory of 10 years of civil strife. The Chinese Communist Party intends to continue, however, its independent existence. It calls for the establishment in each province and *hsien* a people's political council that democratic principles may thereby be put into effect.

4. Chou En-lai is now conferring with Kuomintang leaders in an effort to strengthen the united front.

---

[31] Latter not printed.

5. The zeal of the Chinese Communist Party for the United Front is real for it is by means of the United Front that the Reds hope to hold defeatist elements in the National Party to prolonged resistance against Japan. To insure continuance of the United Front it has quieted its vociferous agitation concerning the suppression of Communist China organizations and thorough mobilization of the people.

6. The Central Government so far as can be ascertained has made no concession to the Communists in Chinese held territory. So long as the ruling faction retains its present character it will hardly establish genuinely representative congresses for fear that the Communists, using democracy as a Trojan horse, will ride into power.

7. Freedom of action in Chinese held territory is at present for the Chinese Communist Party a secondary and academic issue overshadowed by the military, political and economic situation confronting it in a steadily expanding area of actual and potential Communist control behind the advancing Japanese lines.

8. Finally it is increasingly evident from its program of action for the present and any predictable future that the Chinese Communist Party is not justified in designating itself as a Communist organization. Its action for the present and any predictable future envisages little more in the way of social revolution than land reform, cooperatives, lower rents and interest and in official life plain honesty.

Repeated to Chungking, Peiping, Shanghai.

JOSSELYN

760F.62/1581 : Telegram

The Ambassador in Japan (Grew) to the Secretary of State

TOKYO, October 10, 1938—midnight.
[Received October 10—7 : 30 p. m.]

655. Our 626, September 27, 9 p. m.

1. We have substantial confirmation of the accuracy of our analysis of the official Japanese attitude toward war in Europe which seemed inevitable 2 weeks ago, and we believe that such attitude remains unchanged even though it is obvious that over the short haul such a war would give Japan freedom from European intervention in China. However, the apparent success with which Chamberlain [32] is exploiting the momentum given by the Munich Agreement to his policy of appeasement is being noted here with concern. The possibility of the Far East being brought by the European powers within the compass of a plan for assuring a general peace is under discussion, one leading paper today suggesting the likelihood that a move with such end in view may be made by Britain and France jointly with

---

[32] Neville Chamberlain, British Prime Minister.

Germany and Italy in the event of the present Anglo-Italian conversations and projected French-Italian conversations ending in friendly arrangements.

2. The Department will appreciate that the scarcity here of any but tendentious or otherwise unreliable news with regard to European developments makes it difficult for us to place in accurate perspective Japanese discussions of the nature above indicated. As stated in my previous telegram on this subject, Japan would have preferred to a European war the continuation in that area of conditions of unrest and alarm. We assume that, whereas the trend in Europe is definitely favorable, progress has not yet been made to a point where definite thought is being given to the Far East. If that assumption is correct, Japanese anticipation at this early date of possible European intervention in the Far East would appear to betray absence of confidence in continued support from Fascist countries and a state of nervousness over the future hitherto not apparent. It may be significant in this connection that much prominence is being given to reported assurances received from Poland and Peru that these countries will not apply economic sanctions against Japan.

3. The increased vigor shown in the last few days in the Japanese offensive on Hankow may be due, as is suggested by one paper today, to desire to reach that objective in anticipation of European developments referred to in paragraph 1 above.

Repeated to Canton for Chungking.

GREW

793.94/14048 : Telegram

The Ambassador in Japan (Grew) to the Secretary of State

TOKYO, October 12, 1938—3 p. m.
[Received October 12—8:20 a. m.]

660. Our 657, October 12, 10 a. m.[33]

1. My British colleague understands that all preparations for landing Japanese forces on the coast of Kwangtung Province for a drive on Canton have been made for some time past and that the Japanese were only awaiting certain circumstances to put the plan into execution. He believes that the circumstances which have brought matters to a head are: (a) information that Chiang Kai Shek when he leaves Hankow may proceed to the south instead of to the west, and (b) a desire to distract public attention in Japan from the delays and occasional defeats incidental to the drive on Hankow, or both.

2. Craigie yesterday told the Vice Minister that a drive on Canton could have a seriously adverse effect on Anglo-Japanese relations from

---

[33] *Foreign Relations,* Japan, 1931–1941, vol. I, p. 476.

the following points of view: (*a*) the danger to Japanese residents in Hong Kong from an enflamed Chinese populace; (*b*) the serious problem of Chinese refugees flocking into the colony; (*c*) the attendant problem of food supplies; and (*d*) the risk of incidents involving British shipping. The Vice Minister merely replied that such of these points as concerned the Japanese authorities on the spot would be referred to them for consideration.

Repeated to Hong Kong for Chungking.

GREW

762.94/259 : Telegram

The Ambassador in Japan (Grew) to the Secretary of State

TOKYO, October 12, 1938—4 p. m.
[Received October 12—7 : 45 a. m.]

661. My British colleague yesterday in his conversation with the Vice Minister referred to a recent press interview in which the Prime Minister had advocated the strengthening of the Anti-Comintern Pact. Craigie said he had heard from reliable sources that great pressure is being brought to bear on the Japanese Government to conclude actual alliances with Germany and Italy. If this were done, the move could only be interpreted as hostile to Great Britain and as dividing the world still further into hostile camps. So long as the pact was aimed exclusively against the Comintern, Great Britain could have no good grounds for protests, but formal alliances with the totalitarian states would be quite a different matter. Craigie elaborated on the unfortunate effect which such alliances would exert on the current efforts to ensure peace in Europe.

It was noticeable that Horinouchi made no denial of the report. Craigie believes that the German Ambassador returned from Berlin in the summer with definite instructions to strengthen the Anti-Comintern Pact and that he is bringing steady pressure to bear on the Japanese Government.

GREW

893.102S/1719 : Telegram

The Ambassador in Japan (Grew) to the Secretary of State

TOKYO, October 13, 1938—11 a. m.
[Received October 13—3 : 40 a. m.]

663. Department's 348, October 8, noon,[34] Shanghai Northern Settlement.

1. With the consent of the British Ambassador we are sending

---

[34] Not printed.

by safe hand to the American Consul General at Shanghai the substance of our 633 [35] as well as the substance of the present.

2. Craigie states that he fully appreciates the difficulty in acquiescing in judicial appointments to the courts of the Settlement by the puppet government at Shanghai but he is still exploring the possibility of some compromise. He is taking the position that the present judges in the courts of the Settlement are honest impartial men without political bias but he is at present considering the possibility of working out a return during the period of the emergency to the consular courts with Chinese assessors.

GREW

793.94/14058 : Telegram

The Ambassador in Japan (Grew) to the Secretary of State

TOKYO, October 13, 1938—5 p. m.
[Received October 13—10:15 a. m.]

665. Our 657, October 12, 11 [*10*] a. m.[36]

1. The Naval and Military Attachés,[37] in appraising the landing of Japanese forces on the South China coast, agree that: (*a*) the primary purpose is to block ingress into China of arms and munitions over the only railway leading from a port not under Japanese control. Whereas such supplies are also being received from Indo-China and Russia, the quantities are probably not large when compared with the volume received over the Hankow-Kowloon line and probably insufficient to meet Chinese needs over a long period of time; (*b*) the fact that this move was made now and not later, say after the capture of Hankow, seems to indicate that the Japanese High Command had satisfied itself that the main Chinese forces intend to retreat from Hankow to the south and southwest. This would be a rational course for the Chinese to follow, as the five southwest provinces must hereafter provide the greater part of the resources of money, personnel and material for continued resistance. In view of these considerations, an advance along the railway toward Hankow is probably contemplated.

2. Careful search of press comment this morning reveals little of Japanese objectives, military and political, not covered in the appraisal [as?] outlined. Editorials emphasize: (*a*) the importance of cutting off military supplies shipped through Hong Kong; (*b*) the importance of depriving the Chinese forces of their last substantial base of operations; (*c*) the need for "correcting the misapprehensions of the

---

[35] September 28, midnight, p. 305.
[36] *Foreign Relations,* Japan, 1931–1941, vol. I, p. 476.
[37] Capt. Harold M. Bemis, U. S. N., and Maj. Harry I. T. Creswell.

256941—54——21

Kwangsi–Kwangtung faction who have long been a thorn in the side of Sino-Japanese cooperation, concerning the strength and motives of Japan"; and (d) the importance of Japan and other concerned powers guarding against the Chinese exploiting the complicated international situation in South China to involve Japan with third powers, notably Great Britain.

3. We have been unable to obtain comment from any responsible Japanese which would offer basis for the tempting conjecture that the move in South China was made at this time to hasten settlement of the general military situation in anticipation of European developments discussed in our 655, October 10, midnight.

Repeated to Hong Kong for Chungking.

GREW

793.94/14061 : Telegram

The Chargé in France (Wilson) to the Secretary of State

PARIS, October 13, 1938—7 p. m.
[Received October 13—6 : 30 p. m.]

1751. The Chief of the Far Eastern Division at the Foreign Office [38] said to me this afternoon that the Japanese invasion of South China which has begun with the landing of troops at Bias Bay had been under consideration by the Japanese authorities for a long time. The Japanese Navy had always wanted to take this action but the Foreign Office had opposed it for fear of complications with foreign powers. With the fall of Ugaki [39] and decline of Foreign Office influence, the navy view had prevailed.

Hoppenot believed the first Japanese objective will be to cut the railway in the section north of Kowloon and that for this purpose troops will be landed on the east bank of the Canton River in addition to those landed at Bias Bay. After this has been done he expects the Japanese to attack Canton but believes that in order to avoid the difficulties of an approach overland through the mountain and lake regions the Japanese will move troops on junks up the Canton River. He said that the force of some 35,000 men already landed at Bias Bay should be sufficient to cut the railway. A considerably larger force will be needed to capture Canton although his information indicates that the Chinese military at Canton are lukewarm about putting up a strong defense and that recently the best troops which had been stationed there have been moved to the north.

He believes that the Japanese intend to set up an autonomous government in Kwangtung and that while they will be able to accomplish

---

[38] Henri Hoppenot.
[39] Foreign Minister Ugaki resigned September 30.

their objectives in this area, including cutting off of supplies going to Hankow from Hong Kong, this will have little effect upon the ultimate outcome of the conflict.

Hoppenot said that he did not like the looks of things. The Japanese are becoming "excited" and unpleasant in conversations in Tokyo between the Foreign Office and the French Embassy and between the Japanese Embassy and the Foreign Office here. The Japanese Embassy had protested because a few Chinese officers and soldiers in mufti had been allowed to cross Tonkin going from Kwangsi to Yunnan. The French Foreign Office had replied that they could not prohibit Chinese transiting Tonkin, that a few Chinese soldiers in civilian attire could not be distinguished from ordinary civilians and that in any case there was no declared war and France had no obligation to prohibit even Chinese troops from crossing Indo-China. The Japanese Embassy, however, maintained its point of view and insisted that the French should do something yeoman [*regarding?*] situation. Also the Japanese Counselor (the Ambassador is quite ill) had lately protested a decree authorizing the authorities in Indo-China to prohibit the export of iron ore and manganese. Hoppenot had explained that this decree had been issued only in order to permit the prohibition of exports if it should appear in the future that these ores were needed in Indo-China and had pointed out that the decree had not been applied and that Japan was continuing to receive shipments of these ores. Japanese Counselor nevertheless had insisted that Japan had the "right" to obtain these ores and had been unpleasant about the matter.

Hoppenot stated that there was a clear relation between recent events in Europe and the changing attitude of the Japanese. Throughout the month of September it had seemed as if the Japanese attitude in the Far East and the German attitude in Central Europe had been synchronized. The British had noted this as well as the French. Hoppenot expressed the opinion that the only hope of preventing the situation in the Far East from steadily deteriorating would be for the United States to express its views strongly to Japan on the necessity of reasonable behaviour by the latter. I asked if he felt that French interests were menaced by this new Japanese invasion. He said that he feared there would be difficulties concerning the French Concession at Canton and also that the Japanese might seize Hainan. I asked what the French would do in this latter case. He said that France would protest. France would certainly not go to war with Japan over Hainan.

Hoppenot said that the Japanese had charged that shipments of war material to China were continuing to pass over the French railway in Indo-China. The French Government had replied that for the past 2 months not a single rifle had been carried on this railroad and had asked the Japanese Government to produce facts to substantiate its charges. The Japanese had insisted that shipments were going forward all the time and that it would be beside the point to present detailed information. I asked Hoppenot if it were really true that the French were not letting any shipments of war material go over the railway to Yunnan. Hoppenot said that this was absolutely true. I remarked that this was bad luck for the Chinese. He said that it was indeed bad luck but no matter how much the French might love the Chinese they could not risk war with Japan on their account.

I asked if the Russians were increasing their shipments of war materials to China. Hoppenot replied that they were. They also were sending large numbers of aviation instructors as well as a number of military experts to take the place of the German mission. With the cutting of the Canton–Hankow Railway, the shipment of Russian war material will have to be overland via Sinkiang since the Burma route is not yet in condition.

WILSON

893.00/14267 : Telegram

The Consul General at Hankow (Josselyn) to the Secretary of State

HANKOW, October 14, 1938—2 p. m.
[Received 9 : 37 p. m.]

From a reliable source it is learned that General Chiang Kai Shek is increasingly exasperated with and contemptuous of Government and Kuomintang officials. In the October 10 memorial service he upbraided the attending dignitaries for being failures as officials and even as men and declared that they were wholly unworthy of their positions. The denunciation was unrelieved by any note of encouragement much less commendation.

A non-partisan source stated that the Generalissimo has been discovering ever since the Sian incident and especially during the present crisis that many of his former enemies are serving his and the nation's interest better than the group surrounding him. Mainly because of peculiarly Chinese ties of personal loyalty he does not disencumber himself of this group. It is generally agreed that despite Chiang's commitment to prolonged resistance, the faction desiring capitulation and peace is strong and not inarticulate. Chen Li Fu day before yesterday frankly expressed himself as being in favor of the Government coming to terms with the Japanese.

The poor showing made at Sinyang by Hu Tsung Nan and Chinese mechanized units, together with the drives on the Canton-Hankow line southwest of Yangsin and in Kwangtung, have depressed head-quarters morale. Indicative of the heavy losses of the Chinese in the northeastern defense of Wuhan, it is reported that about 12,000 wounded a week are arriving here. They are being steadily evacuated after preliminary treatment.

Repeated to Chungking, Peiping.

JOSSELYN

793.94/14335

Generalissimo Chiang Kai-shek to President Roosevelt [40]

MR. PRESIDENT: It has been eight and a half months since I wrote you my last message. During all these months Japanese aggression in China has not only not abated, but methodically increased in magnitude and intensity. From across the Great Wall, the Japanese invading forces have penetrated into the Yellow River Basin and devastated the Yangtse Valley, and have now started their campaign in South China. City after city has been attacked, ransacked and reduced to ruins. Countless men, women and children have lost their lives or become permanently disabled due to utter disregard by the invader of the elementary rules of law and humanity. Death missiles have been constantly rained from Japanese aircraft on populous towns far remote from the area of actual hostilities, even vehicles of civilian communication not being spared. Poisonous gases have been invariably used as a last resort by the Japanese forces whenever hard pressed by the Chinese defender. As the conflict drags on, it becomes as clear as daylight that Japan, though being gradually aware of her increasing difficulties, is determined to use all the means at her disposal to bring about complete conquest of China.

Despite their unprecedented suffering from Japan's mediaeval vandalism wrought with the ultra-modern weapons of war, the Chinese people have shown exemplary courage and always kept up their morale. This is attributable as much to their ever growing confidence of the ultimate triumph of right over might as to the moral support we have received from you and the people whom you represent. Your public utterances and personal assurances have convinced us that you view our momentous struggle in precisely the same light as we ourselves do. Our victory over Japan means the re-assertion of law and order among the nations. Our defeat by Japan means the complete breakdown of peace and security in the whole Pacific as well as the

---

[40] This cabled message, dated Wuchang, October 15, and sent through the Chinese Ministry for Foreign Affairs, October 16, was transmitted by the appointed Chinese Ambassador to the Secretary of State October 19, and to President Roosevelt on October 20. For previous messages, dated January 30 and October 8, see pp. 59 and 312.

negation of all the principles of international relations for which the United States and the other peace-loving countries stand. It is undoubtedly considerations like these that have led you to make repeated warnings to the aggressor and show your deep sympathy for the victims of aggression. Words of encouragement coupled with such material help as the silver purchases have produced a most soothing effect on the anguish and suffering of the Chinese people who realize that China at this trying hour has not been forsaken at least by the President of the United States.

On behalf of millions of our bleeding people I want to thank you once more for all that you have done for our cause. May I at the same time on behalf of these same people once more appeal to you to render us yet greater assistance so as to ensure China's success in repelling Japanese aggression. Being in urgent need of the sinews of resistance, we naturally look to the United States for such financial and economic help as will enable us to carry on the struggle to a successful end. A loan of a fairly large amount from American sources will at once instill more confidence into our people and make us resist Japan's onslaught with greater force and effect. I wish that the negotiations now going on in America toward this end may with your blessing be brought to a successful conclusion at an early date. I need not assure you, Mr. President, that I shall feel most grateful to you for whatever effort you may exert to increase China's strength on the one hand and to awaken Japan to the folly of her present policy on the other, thereby bringing about a speedy restoration of peace in the Far East.

CHIANG KAI-SHEK

793.94119/450

Memorandum by the Adviser on Political Relations (Hornbeck) to the Secretary of State

[WASHINGTON,] October 17, 1938.

MR. SECRETARY: The Chinese Ambassador [41] writes me under date October 16 that he has received from General Chiang Kai-shek a message as follows:

"The landing of enemy forces on the coast of Kwangtung is in reality a threat to Great Britain and indirectly a challenge to all Anglo-Saxon Powers. This seems to be the most opportune time for the American Government to give encouragement to Great Britain for a policy of co-operative intervention in the Far Eastern situation. The solution of the Far Eastern Problem must depend upon some such Anglo-American action of co-operation; but the leadership for such action must come from the American Government",

---

[41] Hu Shih.

and the Ambassador requests that I inform you of the above.

The Ambassador also requests that I inform you of comments which he has made to me upon and in explanation of the above.

S[TANLEY] K. H[ORNBECK]

793.94/14094 : Telegram

The Consul General at Hong Kong (Southard) to the Secretary of State

HONG KONG, October 17, 1938—2 p. m.
[Received October 17—7 a. m.]

I have just talked with my Japanese colleague who assures me that the Japanese forces are about to enter Pingwu on the Hong Kong–Canton Railway. He also says that he thinks there is no intention of landing strong Japanese forces from Pearl River in west Kwangtung because forces from Bias Bay will easily reach Pearl River in a day or so. He also has told me that he has by authorization of his Government offered Hong Kong Government to arrange for Japanese merchants in Formosa to supply this colony with vegetables and other foodstuffs in case of shortage but that local government has not yet accepted. He says Formosa has plenty of food supplies to spare. My colleague telegraphed his Government at the request of Bishop of Hong Kong and associated religious representatives for delimitation of neutral zone for refugees along the railway just over the Hong Kong frontier and has had "tacit consent" from Tokyo which he has communicated to the Bishop here. My colleague very confidentially says he knows that there are a number of influential Cantonese who are willing to treat with the Japanese and that some approaches have been made but certain individuals among them are not entirely trusted and that accordingly no negotiations have been definitely entered into.

Repeated to Chungking, Peiping.

SOUTHARD

793.94/14106 : Telegram

The Ambassador in Japan (Grew) to the Secretary of State

TOKYO, October 17, 1938—3 p. m.
[Received October 19—6 a. m.]

672. Our 577, September 5, 3 p. m., and 594, September 12, noon, Hankow safety zone.

Following is a translation of a *note verbale* dated October 14, received October 16, from the Foreign Office:

"The Imperial Ministry of Foreign Affairs presents its compliments to the American Embassy in Tokyo and has the honor to acknowledge the receipt of the latter's *note verbale* dated September 12, 1938, in which the views of the American Government concerning the safety of the rights and interests of third countries in a specified area at Hankow were set forth.

In the above-mentioned *note verbale*, the American Government urgently requested that the Japanese authorities so conduct their military operations in China as to avoid injury to the lives and property of American nationals. The fact that the Imperial military forces are already, to as great an extent as possible, strictly adhering to a policy of giving consideration to the safety of the lives and property of the nationals of third countries has previously been made clear by frequent communications and public statements by the Japanese Government, and has been substantiated by past examples. Accordingly, even if a lack of concurrence and cooperation on the part of the Chinese authorities should unhappily prevent the implementation of the arrangement between the Japanese Government and the powers concerned looking toward the safety of the lives and property of the nationals of third countries as a whole in a specified area in Hankow, there will be, of course, no change in the policy followed up to the present.

When the Chinese military utilize the rights and interests of third countries for military operations, that is, when they offer military resistance from points in close proximity to such interests or use such interests as cover, it becomes practically impossible to avoid the occurrence of unforeseen damage to the rights and interests of third countries. Nevertheless, according to reports from all sources, the Chinese military are utilizing the rights and interests of third countries, within and without the area in question, they are building military emplacements, and they are storing arms, ammunitions, military supplies, et cetera. It is important that the powers concerned, if they are desirous of securing the safety of those interests, should take effective and appropriate measures to prevent acts of the Chinese forces which can be anticipated to jeopardize or injure such rights and interests. If, on the contrary, measures which should appropriately be taken are not taken, and the powers concerned demand of the Japanese Government alone satisfaction in regard to the results of damages to rights and interests, such demands cannot be said to be just. For this reason the Imperial Government must continue to hold the view, as set forth in its *note verbale* dated September 3, 1938, that in such circumstances the Japanese Government cannot assume responsibility for damages to rights and interests. October 14, 1938."

Repeated to Chungking and Hankow.

GREW

893.515/1331 : Telegram

The Consul General at Shanghai (Gauss) to the Secretary of State

SHANGHAI, October 18, 1938—6 p. m.
[Received October 18—3 : 18 p. m.]

1347. The Commercial Counselor of the British Embassy informs me confidentially that there has been much difficulty and friction at

Tientsin with the Japanese over central silver to the value of about 40,000,000 Chinese dollars in a Chinese bank in the French Concession and about $14,000,000 in a Chinese bank in the British Concession. British Embassy understands that the chief concern of the Japanese is that the silver may be shipped out of the port. British Embassy is contemplating a suggestion that the silver stocks in question should be placed under seal with the concurrence of the Chinese banks and the Japanese and the matter thus disposed of for the time being. Before proposing this solution, however, the British Embassy inquires whether the American Government is perhaps interested in this silver or its possible purchase, it being indicated that such interest might affect a decision as to making the proposal above outlined. I stated that I had no information but would inquire. What reply shall I make?

GAUSS

793.94/14047½

President Roosevelt to Generalissimo Chiang Kai-shek [42]

The appointed Chinese Ambassador at this capital has communicated to me your message of October 8.

The situation in the Far East has been and continues to be a subject to which I give close attention and a great deal of thought. The need for a solution of the tragic conflict which has arisen in the Far East through pacific negotiation, on a basis of justice and neither through the exercise of force nor under the threat of the exercise of force, is daily becoming more imperative in the interest of the re-establishment of the reign of law and order in the world. I am profoundly hopeful that in this manner adjustments and settlements may be found in the Far East which will remove causes of conflict, conform to the standards of real equity, and thus contribute effectively to the cause of peace.

You may rest assured that if in my opinion an appropriate opportunity is presented for me to assist in the furtherance of these objectives, I shall gladly avail myself of the occasion.

793.94/14047½

Memorandum by the Adviser on Political Relations (Hornbeck)

[WASHINGTON,] October 19, 1938.

The ribbon copy of the paper hereunder attached [43] was handed this morning by Mr. Hornbeck to the Appointed Chinese Ambassador.

---

[42] This message was handed to the appointed Chinese Ambassador on October 19 by the Adviser on Political Relations, for transmittal to Generalissimo Chiang Kai-shek.
[43] *Supra.*

Mr. Hornbeck stated to the Ambassador that the President wished it to be understood by General Chiang that he, the President, was giving close and sympathetic attention to the situation and the problem which were the subject of General Chiang's communication and that he was observing every development with a desire so to act as to contribute, while safeguarding the interests of the United States, toward an alleviation of the distress, destruction and suffering, which are inherent in and produced by the Chinese-Japanese hostilities. The Ambassador said that he well understood that the President could not make any commitment at this time; and, in the brief conversation which ensued, the Ambassador made it clear that he entertained no thought that a mediation undertaken at this time could be conducive to any settlement other than one in which China would come off badly.

S[TANLEY] K. H[ORNBECK]

793.94/14113 : Telegram

The Chargé in France (Wilson) to the Secretary of State

PARIS, October 19, 1938—7 p. m.
[Received October 19—5 : 45 p. m.]

1786. For Ambassador Bullitt: [44] Wellington Koo[45] asked me this afternoon to transmit to you the following personal message from him.

"Japanese campaign against South China intended not only to cut communications between Canton and Hong Kong but also to establish base for threatening Hong Kong, Singapore, Indo-China, Dutch Indies and Philippines. Unless effectively checked now Japan will take advantage of next crisis in Europe when British and French hands will again be tied to press forward, without fear of intervention, her policy of southward expansion always strongly advocated by Japanese Navy. German Chancellor's Saarbrucken speech, Italian intransigence towards France, aggravation of Palestine revolt, and Japanese campaign against South China all evidence of conspiracy of Berlin–Rome–Tokyo Axis, further supported by Tokyo's appointment Jap Military Attaché in Berlin as Ambassador to Germany [46] for purpose of concluding Nippon-German military alliance.

I told Bonnet [47] above Monday and suggested to him to consult Washington and London with view to making *démarche* in Tokyo— joint or parallel—in order to persuade her discontinue adventure and concert other measures for the purpose.

After 14 months of war Japan in no position to counter Anglo-French-American opposition evidenced by Japan's retreat in regard dispute Paracels and Hainan with France and Changkufeng affair with Soviet Union in face of French and Soviet firmness.

[44] William C. Bullitt, Ambassador to France, was on leave in the United States.
[45] Chinese Ambassador in France.
[46] Maj. Gen. Hiroshi Oshima.
[47] Henri Bonnet, French Minister for Foreign Affairs.

I also asked him for assurance of complete transit facilities through Indo-China for Chinese war material so necessary to enable China continue her resistance and abstention from supplying Japan with arms and war material particularly airplanes, oil, and iron ore. I pointed out Washington's advice to American manufacturers to stop furnishing airplanes [48] to Japan has produced appreciable result. He assured me he would approach Washington at once as regards proposed *démarche* and consider other two suggestions.

Knowing the value of your personal influence and always grateful for your past collaboration, I venture to invoke your support of our appeal when you see President Roosevelt. With cordial regards."

Koo told me that the Chinese Ambassador in London saw Halifax on Monday and suggested that the British consult Washington and Paris regarding a *démarche* in Tokyo. Halifax replied that he would take the matter under consideration.

Presumably the new Chinese Ambassador in Washington has already talked with the Department along similar lines.

I asked Koo if he really believed a *démarche* such as he suggests could be effective in persuading the Japanese Navy and Military to withdraw from this South China invasion in which their prestige is engaged. He admitted that it was a bit late but asserted his belief that an unmistakable indication by the three governments that they would stop furnishing Japan military supplies and raw materials needed for her armament industry, unless the South China adventure is abandoned, would be effective.

WILSON

893.515/1334

Memorandum by the Chief of the Division of Far Eastern Affairs (Hamilton) of a Conversation With the Assistant Secretary of the Treasury (Taylor)

[WASHINGTON,] October 21, 1938.

After discussing the matter [49] with Mr. Feis, Mr. Hornbeck and Mr. Hackworth,[50] and obtaining their concurrence, and under authorization from the Secretary, I telephoned Mr. Wayne Taylor of the Treasury Department and told him that the Secretary felt that, inasmuch as we have heretofore handled this matter orally, it would be preferable to continue that procedure and to communicate to him orally a statement of our attitude which he had requested yesterday on behalf of the Secretary of the Treasury. I then said that we were of the opinion that any move by this Government toward acquiring

---

[48] Letter of July 1, *Foreign Relations*, Japan, 1931–1941, vol. II, p. 201.
[49] Possible interest of the American Government in Chinese silver stocks held in North China.
[50] Green H. Hackworth, Legal Adviser.

a property interest in the silver in question under the circumstances now pertaining thereto would be inadvisable. Mr. Taylor made note of this statement. I also said that we proposed issuing an instruction to the American Consul General at Shanghai asking the Consul General to inform the British Embassy orally and informally, in response to its inquiry, that he had no comment to make other than to say that he understood that the silver in question was not specifically included in any arrangement now in effect between the Chinese and American Governments. I asked Mr. Taylor whether that was a correct statement as to fact. He replied in the affirmative. I said that we would not send off such a telegram at once and that we would appreciate being informed that the Treasury Department had no objection to such a telegram.[51]

During the conversation I said that we of course assumed that so far as the Chinese Government was concerned, the Chinese Government was aware of the fact that if this silver should be delivered at some American port the Treasury Department in all probability would be prepared to purchase it. Mr. Taylor indicated that this assumption was correct.[52]

M[AXWELL] M. H[AMILTON]

793.94/14135 : Telegram

The Ambassador in China (Johnson) to the Secretary of State

CHUNGKING, October 21, 1938—9 a. m.
[Received 5 : 52 p. m.]

507. Minister for Foreign Affairs [53] asked me to see him yesterday the 20th and after referring to Japanese organization of South China stated that he was anxious to know reaction of United States to this new situation. I explained that I was unable to enlighten him as I had no information bearing upon this question. Foreign Minister then said that Chinese Government, when inquiring at London, Paris and Moscow, had been told by those powers that they were waiting upon initiative by the United States before giving assistance to China in the present situation. He said that the Government and people of China hoped that the United States would take the initiative in assisting the Chinese to continue resistance to the Japanese either by refusing supplies to the Japanese or by financial assistance to the Chinese or, failing such positive acts of assistance they hoped that the Ameri-

---

[51] See telegram No. 594, October 27, 6 p. m., to the Consul General at Shanghai, p. 346.
[52] See also memorandum of November 9, by the Chief of the Division of Far Eastern Affairs, p. 567.
[53] Wang Chung-hui.

can Government would take the initiative and concert with the powers to bring about peace in the Pacific. He referred with appreciation to the fact that the Government of the United States had already done something in that it had expressed its disapproval of sales of planes to Japan by American plane manufacturers, which he said had had an effect. He hoped we might go farther and similarly disapprove supplies of petroleum products and similar supplies.

I remarked that I would be happy to communicate his message to you, that I was not informed as to all measures that the American Government might be able to take within the limits of law. I expressed my conviction that these matters had been thoroughly canvassed by the leaders of the administration and my belief that when this present message came before them there would be found to exist a feeling that the American Government had perhaps done more than any other single power in giving positive assistance to the Chinese Government through its purchase of Chinese silver thereby enabling the Chinese Government to stabilize its currency and maintain it among the currencies of the world. Minister for Foreign Affairs admitted this and expressed gratitude of the Chinese Government and people. He again said that something more was needed now if China was to continue its resistance of [or] if an honorable peace was to be made. With reference to the establishment of peace I said that the American Government was anxious to see peace reestablished, that we had canvassed the subject of good offices which was previously brought up by the Minister (see my 376, July 27, 2 p. m.) and that as a result we had come to the conclusion that the leaders of the Japanese military were not ready to receive or entertain proposals which would be acceptable to the Chinese. I said, however, that I would communicate the purport of our conversation to you and that I would communicate to him any message that you might care to send.

JOHNSON

793.94/14137 : Telegram

The Consul General at Canton (Linnell) to the Secretary of State

CANTON, October 22, 1938—1 p. m.
[Received October 22—7 a. m.]

2. American observers report looting by Chinese in Canton last night and today. Destruction of utilities by the Chinese continues and last night Wongsha, the Canton terminal of the Canton–Hankow Railway, was burned with many of the buildings in the vicinity. Much of the defense apparatus, anti-aircraft guns, et cetera, have been taken out of the city by the retiring local forces and no guns are being

fired at the Japanese planes which are flying over the city observing and dropping leaflets, two of which are addressed to Commander-in-Chief Yu Han Mou, Governor Wu Te Chen and Mayor Tseng Yang Fu, one stating that the Japanese forces have complete command of the air and the eastern part of Kwangtung and urging these three as men of talents to cooperate with the Japanese to establish eternal peace in East Asia and save the people of Kwangtung from terrible sufferings. The second pamphlet says that Canton now being enveloped by a powerful Japanese Army, the entire city of Canton will be converted into scorched land within a couple of days by which time the political and economic development as well as the public buildings and frontier will with certainty be destroyed and asks, why do you gentlemen do nothing to save the innocent people.

LINNELL

793.94/14153 : Telegram

The Consul General at Hankow (Josselyn) to the Secretary of State

HANKOW, October 22, 1938—2 p. m.
[Received October 22—6 a. m.]

1. (1) Responsible military officials make in private conversation no suggestion that with the fall of Wuhan there will be on their part any thought of capitulation to Japan.

(2) They observe that the Japanese have identified the capture of Wuhan with the destruction of Chiang Kai Shek's military power, but now that the main Chinese force is being withdrawn from Wuhan area they anticipate a reorientation in Japanese campaign plans. The Japanese are not expected to repeat the Nanking error of concentrating their major effort upon the occupation of the capital and then with its seizure relax their military operations, thus giving the Chinese an opportunity to rally. It is suggested that the drive on Wuhan is now secondary to the campaign directed at the Chinese forces evading the envelopment of this center. The offensive on Sienning is expected to turn southward on the Canton–Hankow Railway, that in the Sinyang sector to proceed northward and westward.

(3) It is recognized, however, that, because the Japanese have identified the capture of Wuhan with the destruction of Chiang Kai Shek's military power, they may thereby be deflected from a determined pursuit of the retreating Chinese.

(4) Six hundred Kuomintang Youth Corps members trained to organize guerrillas have recently been sent behind the Japanese lines in the Yangtze Valley. Central Government authorities behind the Japanese lines are also training local youth for such work. Communist organizers are now active in every Japanese occupied province.

The Eighth Route Army has sent 60 of these young men to work in South Manchuria. However, the military effectiveness of partisan activities as now conducted is over-emphasized by most foreign observers.

(5) A Central Government division has been ordered to a locality north of Hopei, Anhwei; another is leaving the area east of Nanchang for northeastern Kiangsi.

Repeated to Chungking, Peiping. Peiping please mail code text to Mukden for information.

JOSSELYN

793.94/14174 : Telegram

The Consul General at Canton (Linnell) to the Secretary of State

CANTON, October 22, 1938—2 : 30 p. m.
[Received October 22—7 a. m.]

4. Two cars with Japanese officers and two lorries with Japanese troops came to British and French bridges of Shameen at 2 p. m. today. Japanese officers saluted and shook hands with the British Concession Chief of Police and then went on to the city. Planes are flying low covering the entry.

Repeated Chungking, Peiping, Hong Kong.

LINNELL

793.94/14154 : Telegram

The Consul General at Hankow (Josselyn) to the Secretary of State

HANKOW, October 24, 1938—10 a. m.
[Received October 24—5 a. m.]

4. Chu Teh [54] arrived in Hankow on October 22 and conferred with Chiang Kai Shek concerning military and communications between the Eighth Route and Central armies north and south of the Yangtze. He returned to the northwest the same day.

Pai Chung Hsi [55] has either left or is about to leave here for Changsha where he will direct, it is reliably reported, the defense of Hunan and coordinate the war activities of Kwangsi with those of Hunan.

The Kwangsi troops in the Tapieh mountains commanded by Li Tsung Jen are withdrawing westward to be based on Hsiangyang located on the Han River.

Repeated to Chungking, Peiping.

JOSSELYN

---

[54] Communist military commander.
[55] Kwangsi military commander.

793.94/14164 : Telegram

The Consul General at Canton (Linnell) to the Secretary of State

CANTON, October 24, 1938—10 a. m.
[Received October 25—6 a. m.]

12. Fires are still burning. Business section almost completely destroyed by fire and looted. Customs house was saved by work of customs staff, British naval units and others. Canton Hospital still intact but unoccupied. Fire has not gone very near Hackett Memorial Hospital and conditions there good. Buildings on bund from near French bridge almost to British bridge gutted by fire, precautions being taken continuously to prevent fire crossing to Shameen. Unless an unfavorable wind should spring up it is believed Shameen is safe.

Conditions in Tungshan reported quiet and men in Baptist Hospital and Seventh Day Adventist Hospital safe, nearly 600 Chinese refugees at Fingnam. Conditions there and at Pakhoktung reported good. Only a few Japanese soldiers have been seen in Canton as yet.

Repeated to Chungking, Peiping and Hong Kong.

LINNELL

793.94/14152 : Telegram

The Chargé in the Soviet Union (Kirk) to the Secretary of State

MOSCOW, October 24, 1938—noon.
[Received October 24—7 : 15 a. m.]

365. My 359, October 15, noon.[56] The newspaper *Red Star*, organ of the Commissariat for Defense, in commenting today on the capture of Canton repeats the previously expressed Soviet view that this new Japanese action is a direct result of the capitulation of the democratic powers to Japan's "Anti-Commintern" allies in Europe and that the resultant economic and strategic blow to Hong Kong is further proof that Chamberlain's policy is destructive to Britain's own interests since the threat to British possessions in the Far East is becoming more real.

The article also states that the capture of Canton does not mean that the war in China is any closer to a conclusion but that on the contrary the Chinese will continue to defend their territory and that widespread guerrilla warfare will prevent the Japanese from consolidating their position in southern China as has proved the case in the northern and central areas.

KIRK

---

[56] Not printed.

793.94/14156 : Telegram

The Consul General at Canton (Linnell) to the Secretary of State

CANTON, October 24, 1938—3 p. m.
[Received October 24—8 : 30 a. m.]

15. Japanese officers visited Shameen today and stated the Japanese Army would not enter in force. Only a few of the principal centers such as Civic Center, Government Headquarters, et cetera, would be occupied. They demand that the telephone system be put in operation as quickly as possible and I am endeavoring to arrange conferences between Mr. Rhame of the China Electric Company which is managing the Canton Telephone Administration and the Japanese proper authorities.

Japanese aircraft are dropping many leaflets stating that no harm will be done to innocent people, that there will be no harsh treatment, no looting and in general attempting to persuade the people to return to their homes and occupations.

There are refugees under the auspices of Americans as follows: at Pakhoktung in three groups about 1000, at Mingsum School for the Blind in Fonggett about 600, at Lingnan University about 700. Today it is intended to transfer 120 more across the river from the Baptist Hospital at Tungshan to Lingnan.

Repeated to Chungking, Peiping, Hong Kong.

LINNELL

793.94/14175a : Telegram

The Secretary of State to the Consul General at Hong Kong
(Southard)

WASHINGTON, October 24, 1938—7 p. m.

4. The Department desires to receive by telegraph from each of the three offices to which this telegram is addressed a confidential comprehensive summary report of the factors believed to be responsible for the rapidity of the Japanese invasion of South China and the comparative ease with which the Japanese have occupied Canton.

Repeated to Canton and Chungking.

HULL

793.94/14180 : Telegram

The Consul General at Hankow (Josselyn) to the Secretary of State

HANKOW, October 24, 1938—8 p. m.
[Received October 25—4 p. m.]

9. In the Communist daily *Hsin Hua Jih Pao* yesterday and today Chou En Lai editorially stated that Japan now has demonstrated it

has a new policy of expansion [of] the area of hostilities in China in an effort to cut external and internal communications, isolate and demoralize Chinese resistance and bring the conflict to an early end. He anticipates Japanese occupation of all of the Canton–Hankow and Pinghan lines and Lunghai to Sian.

The Japanese decision to extend hostilities to South China, Chou declared, came largely as a result of the exhibition of British and French attitude in the Czech crisis. He believed Japan hopes Britain and France will in an attempt to salvage their interest in Far East bring pressure on China to sacrifice herself through capitulation. The application of the Chamberlain policy was a failure in Europe, Chou maintains, and it is definitely not applicable to the Far East because, firstly, China will not compromise with Japan and, secondly, because interests are more patently affected in Far East than [they] were in Central Europe.

In the face of the expanding Japanese invasion, Chou calls for unwavering and protracted resistance, preparation for counter offensive when the Japanese are fully extended, further development of guerilla operations to rear of Japanese and organization of the people for total warfare. China must convince the world, he declared, that her defensive war is being fought with confidence in an ultimate victory and that it will not be suspended before that victory.

JOSSELYN

793.94/14172 : Telegram

The Consul General at Hankow (Josselyn) to the Secretary of State

HANKOW, October 25, 1938—10 a. m.
[Received October 25—6 : 30 a. m.]

The Mayor of Hankow is leaving today and all civil officials have left or are leaving. The police have been withdrawn except those in Special Administered District No. 3. In addition, about 100 police are remaining who will be placed under the orders of the Refugee Zone Committee. For composition of this Committee see my telegram August 1, 3 p. m. I understand that the Committee have obtained approval of the Chinese authorities for demilitarization of the refugee zone in Hankow and plan to take over control of such zone today.

The British Navy have landed approximately 100 men this morning who are being quartered in the British Consulate. They will be used to assist the police.

General Kuo Chan, garrison commander, and the Wuhan garrison troops are still here but will probably leave soon.

Sent to Chungking, Peiping.

JOSSELYN

793.94/14167 : Telegram

The Consul General at Hankow (Josselyn) to the Secretary of State

HANKOW, October 25, 1938—11 a. m.
[Received October 25—7 : 15 a. m.]

11. Commander of the Yangtze Patrol states that he plans to land 30 men and 1 officer to cooperate with the British police in Special Administrative Districts 2 and 3 during interim between evacuation of Chinese police and the establishment of Japanese authority.

Repeated to Chungking, Peiping.

JOSSELYN

793.94/14170 : Telegram

The Consul General at Canton (Linnell) to the Secretary of State

CANTON, October 25, 1938—noon.
[Received October 25—6 a. m.]

16. The transfer of refugees from Baptist Hospital, Tungshan, to Lingnan was carried out yesterday. The fires are still burning and last night buildings on Shakee Bund at the west end of the British Concession were destroyed. Undoubtedly new fires are being started as others die down and a British naval force is now attempting to clear all Chinese out of the buildings on Shakee Bund which have not yet been destroyed.

Another refuge is being started under control of the Salvation Army in the old Pui Ying School at Fati. This is American property. It is expected to have nearly 1,000 refugees in a few days.

I have today sent a letter to the Japanese colonel in charge of the forces in Canton asking him to discuss with me the questions of the safety of Pakhoktung refugee camp, the setting up of a limited telephone service and other matters. The Telephone Administration is and has been for some time under the management of the China Electric Company, Limited, an American Corporation, and Mr. Rhame, an American citizen, is in charge here.

Looting continues and much loot is being carried out of the city on sampans by people coming in from outside villages.

Repeated to Chungking, Peiping, and Hong Kong.

LINNELL

793.94/14215a : Telegram

The Secretary of State to the Ambassador in Japan (Grew)

WASHINGTON, October 25, 1938—noon.

360. I should appreciate your estimate and that of Ambassador Johnson as to the question of the bearing of the Munich agreement

and its aftermath upon the Japanese decision to invade south China and upon manifestation by the Japanese of an increasingly truculent attitude. As indicative of such attitude reference is made *inter alia* (*a*) to recent communications from the Japanese evidencing an intention to close the Yangtze and the Pearl Rivers to all shipping [57] until Japanese interests have been served and (*b*) to press reports from Tokyo that the *Yomiuri* carried in its issue of October 23 a 5-column advertisement by the Shiunso, a reactionary organization, appealing to the Japanese people to rise and "be prepared to chastise the British". Please give outline of the reasoning upon which your estimate is based.

Repeated to Chungking.

HULL

793.94/14181 : Telegram

The Consul General at Hankow (Josselyn) to the Secretary of State

HANKOW, October 25, 1938—2 p. m.
[Received 4 : 35 p. m.]

12. Spokesman of National Military Council declared this morning that Chinese have decided to withdraw from Wuhan and [*the ?*] move having been prompted by necessity of shifting Chinese forces.

This action he declared is based upon:

1. Fundamental policy of prolonged warfare and all-front resistance. "The Chinese military authorities do not attach importance to the retention or loss of any particular place but take the whole scope of military operations into consideration. They do not greatly concern themselves regarding the advance or withdrawal of the Chinese forces at one particular moment; instead, every possible effort is to be made to prolong the present war so that in the very process of wearing down the enemy's strength China's capacity for resistance may be preserved and strengthened."

2. "The real significance of defending the Wuhan area does not lie in the possession of the three cities but in the protection given to the transfer of man power and material resources from Southeast and Central China to China's northwest and southwest."

3. "The Chinese military strategy is based on the principle of retaining the initiative—in order to have freedom of action; they cannot afford to be cornered by the enemy and thus become the passive party in the conflict. After offering resistance the past 6 months on the Yangtze front, having caused the enemy great losses, slowed down the pace of the Japanese advance, and protected the transfer of man power and materials resources to the interior, it is considered unnecessary further to defend the Wuhan area. Otherwise the Chinese would fall into the enemy trap by centering the main body of their forces in the Wuhan area to be annihilated, and that would be contradictory to the policy of prolonged resistance.

---

[57] See vol. IV, pp. 143 ff.

4. "Lastly, one reason why the Chinese authorities do not wish to hold fast to the Wuhan cities is a desire to minimize the peril and suffering which confront foreign residents and women and children who cannot find means to evacuate."

JOSSELYN

793.94/14381

The Consul General at Shanghai (Gauss) to the Secretary of State

No. 1780   SHANGHAI, October 25, 1938.
                                    [Received November 21.]

SIR: I have the honor to enclose copies of two memoranda,[58] prepared by the Regimental Intelligence Officer of the Fourth U. S. Marines, dated October 18 and 24, 1938, containing observations on two recent trips he has made through Japanese occupied territory.

His summary at the end of the second report is particularly interesting as showing confirmation, by a trained observer's first-hand observations on the spot, of this office's feeling on several points, as reported from time to time.

His summing up may be condensed briefly as follows:

1. The guerrillas in this area have been completely unable to disturb the Japanese lines of communication.

2. Japanese losses have been serious.

3. The ordinary Chinese are dumbly acquiescent to the Japanese domination.

4. The Japanese have put to warlike use large numbers of peaceful craft.

5. The Special Service Section is managing puppet government organizations, importing Buddhist Monks for the education of Chinese children and is reported to be marketing narcotics, all with a basic political purpose.

Respectfully yours,   C. E. GAUSS

793.94/14198 : Telegram

The Consul General at Hong Kong (Southard) to the Secretary of State

HONG KONG, October 26, 1938—10 a. m.
[Received 10 : 06 a. m.]

11. Referring to the Department's telegram of October 24, 7 p. m., general opinion among the more conservative and best informed contacts of this office in Hong Kong is that the rapidity and ease of the Japanese invasion of South China and occupation of Canton was mainly contributed to by the following factors:

[58] Neither printed.

1. Cantonese conviction that the prestige of the British Government would deter the Japanese from undertaking any South China action likely to injure Hong Kong commercially or otherwise.

2. Cantonese conviction that the Hong Kong British were so strongly sympathetic with the Chinese cause and were so affectionately devoted to Canton and Canton trade, as illustrated by demonstrations of the general kind reported in our despatches numbers 243 and 273 of July 26th and September 1st,[59] that British influence and even force could be depended upon to keep the Japanese out of South China.

3. Cantonese conceit and conviction that Chiang Kai Shek considered South China so invaluable to his own strength and prestige that he would on the first threat of invasion promptly send sufficient forces to make up for Cantonese lack of defense preparations.

4. Cantonese reliance on British and other military opinion that the Japanese could not undertake invasion of South China with less than a quarter million men which force, as the Cantonese were assured by these various experts, could not possibly be spared for the purpose.

5. The much too fulsome and exaggerated praise and dramatization of Chinese patriotism and military prowess chanted almost universally by the foreign press and observers which deluded the always vain Cantonese into an undue conceit that the Japanese would take them at that valuation and thus hesitate to venture an invasion.

6. Ignorance by the Cantonese of what really would be required in the way of modern military defense against a potential invasion, their unwillingness to accept expert foreign advice and direction in the matter, and inability to bring themselves to parting with the considerable money which appropriate defense measures would have cost.

7. Cantonese disinclination seriously to prepare for defense under the influences or beliefs outlined in paragraphs 1 to 6 above particularly when such preparations would interfere with their pursuit of financial gain from the situation developed by the hostilities.

The foregoing paragraphs represent opinions concentrated from a wide variety of reputable sources and while this office has no reason to doubt their general accuracy they can not be supported by factual evidence. Among the additional factors which might be considered as exceeding opinion and approaching fact to some degree are the following:

8. Japanese bribery of both civil and military officers in Kwangtung either with money or promise of high place in a Japanese controlled government for which plans have long been made. This has been a consistent allegation mainly by Japanese and other foreigners in Hong Kong and was specifically and positively stated to me by the contact mentioned in my despatch No. 150 of April 1st [2d][60] whose statements to me as then reported were discussed in Canton's No. 131 of April 5th.[60] I personally am convinced that bribery played probably a leading part in the case of invasion and occupation and there have been various guarded references to that influence in most of the Hong Kong newspapers which have to defer to the local government's consideration for Chinese feelings.

---

[59] Neither printed.
[60] Not printed.

9. The lack of interest of the Cantonese in supporting Chiang Kai Shek, which I have long heard, by Japanese contacts, by the presumably well informed Eugene Chen family, and by British and Americans well informed but without special bias.

10. General civic inertia, grafting, and jealousy alleged to exist among Kwangtung civil and military officials.

Of all the above suggested factors, several of which could be contributory, bribery is thought by this office to have been the decisive one and there is now strong circumstantial evidence in Hong Kong that the Cantonese have decided to encourage public emphasis and proof of the bribery factor if for no other reason than that they are deeply stung by persistent charges of military ineptitude and lack of courage whereas their previous boasting has been unceasingly to the contrary. This office concurs with most informed local sources in a conviction that the South China leaders must have known for months that a Japanese invasion was inevitable, even if for no other reason than to cut the flow of munitions from Hong Kong, and have been incredibly lax in failing to make at least reasonably effective defense preparations for which they had undoubted facilities.

Repeated to Canton, Chungking, Peiping.

SOUTHARD

793.94/14201 : Telegram

The Ambassador in China (Johnson) to the Secretary of State

CHUNGKING, October 26, 1938—11 a. m.
[Received 1 : 36 p. m.]

514. Department's 4, October 24, 7 p. m., to Hong Kong. It is my belief that following factors account for rapidity of Japanese invasion of Kwangtung. Excellent weather conditions which at this time of year prevail at Bias Bay. Thus road and dry conditions of rice fields making use of mechanized equipment possible. Japanese landed in force well prepared accomplishing military surprise; Chinese who were on inside of circle were apparently uncertain as to point where blow would be delivered. Best Cantonese troops and leaders were in Yangtze Valley. Local jealousy hampered Cantonese leaders in preparing defense. Japanese had complete command of air and were able to bomb also machine gun roads over which Chinese forces were compelled to advance to meet invasion. Mechanized equipment unhampered got ahead of infantry. I have not heard any evidence to convince me of treachery on large scale sufficient to account for what has happened. I believe stupidity and ineptitude of Chinese leadership chiefly responsible.

JOHNSON

793.94/14221 : Telegram

The Consul General at Canton (Linnell) to the Secretary of State

CANTON, October 26, 1938—11 a. m.
[Received October 28—6 a. m.]

19. Department's October 24, 7 p. m. There are persistent rumors that the Japanese troops were able to get through to Canton in the short time it took them to do so by reason of the treachery of some commanders of sections of the Chinese Army who did not place their forces as ordered or did not make as strong a defense of their positions as they might have done. Chinese officers attached to headquarters admitted to me that several such officers were shot by order of General Yu Han Mou during the fighting around Tamshui and Waichow.

In my opinion a large factor in the defeat was the terrific bombardment of the Chinese troops, [by?] heavy artillery, bombardment from the air and machine gunning from armored tanks all at the same time. It appears that most of the Kwangtung troops had had little or no experience under fire and that their leadership was weak. I talked with the major in command of a Chinese battalion which was on October 20 attacked by airplanes and tanks simultaneously about 20 miles from Canton. He says the battalion was almost completely wiped out in a short time and the remnants scattered throughout the countryside, the tanks unit involved came in Canton the next day as reported in my telegram October 21, 6 p. m.[61] Only a few troops have as yet come to Canton, the commanding officer Lieutenant General Furusho is still in Tsengcheng. No news has reached Canton as to present disposition of either Chinese or Japanese troops but it is believed that the former have fallen back across Canton–Hankow Railway and gone toward northern Kwangtung.

The manner in which Canton was evacuated en masse in about 24 hours together with statements made this office by Chinese leads me to believe that this evacuation was decided upon some time before as a policy to be carried out if the Japanese came near the city and undoubtedly the police went from home [*house?*] to house telling all the people that they must get out at once as the town would be blown up and burned by the Chinese.

There is no indication whatever that the higher Chinese officials civil or military went out [*over?*]: on the contrary, all indications are that they are loyal to China and ordered scorched earth policy to be carried out on Canton to prevent the Japanese from getting any good out of their occupation of city.

Repeated to Chungking.

LINNELL

[61] Vol. IV, p. 508.

793.94/14185 : Telegram

The Consul General at Hankow (Josselyn) to the Secretary of State

HANKOW, October 26, 1938—4 p. m.
[Received October 26—7 a. m.]

19. Six Japanese destroyers preceded by sea sleds and followed by other naval craft have arrived at Hankow in the river opposite the ex-Concession. Japanese Army detachments have arrived at the Japanese Concession, Hankow. Conditions quiet.

Repeated to Chungking, Peiping and Shanghai.

JOSSELYN

893.102S/1724

Memorandum by the Chief of the Division of Far Eastern Affairs (Hamilton)

[WASHINGTON,] October 26, 1938.

Commander Struble of the Bureau of Operations, Navy Department, telephoned the contents of a message, a transcription of which is attached,[61a] received by the Navy Department from the Commander-in-Chief, Asiatic Fleet, in regard to a request made of the Commander-in-Chief that the Fourth Marines assume the responsibility of "B" sector in the International Settlement at Shanghai. Commander Struble said that the Navy Department proposed to telegraph the Commander-in-Chief approving of his action in not granting the request. Commander Struble stated that Admiral Leahy,[62] before sending the proposed instruction to the Commander-in-Chief, wished to learn the Department's views.

Mr. Ballantine, after having consulted with Mr. Hamilton, Mr. Hornbeck and the Secretary, telephoned Commander Shelley (in the absence of Commander Struble), stating that the Department concurred in the Navy Department's proposal to approve of the Commander-in-Chief's action.

M[AXWELL] M. H[AMILTON]

793.94/14213 : Telegram

The Consul General at Canton (Linnell) to the Secretary of State

CANTON, October 26, 1938—5 p. m.
[Received October 27—12: 25 p. m.]

20. Fires are still burning in various sections of Canton particularly in the area around Silk Street and Blackwood Street, back of the

---

[61a] Not printed.
[62] Admiral William D. Leahy, Chief of Naval Operations.

French hospital, Y. M. C. A. and in several places on Honam Island. The Japanese have very few soldiers in Canton as yet, probably only one regiment and are making little attempt to patrol whole city and practically no attempt to put out fires or stop looting. Last night they took over from British and French naval units the Shakee Bund district and are today patrolling that. Observers report looting in that area greatly increased since Japanese took charge. Americans in Tungshan report that Japanese soldiers with Chinese coolies to carry burdens are systematically breaking into houses in that part of the city and carrying off loot in carts and motor trucks.

It is reported that there are many cases of rape by Japanese soldiers in the villages south of Canton and many women and girls are fleeing from those villages.

A few Chinese have been shot by Japanese soldiers for refusing to carry burdens and for not coming to shore in their boats when signalled.

The Japanese have sent a notice to Shameen that no cameras will be allowed to be used in the city after tomorrow morning and that foreigners should not go into the city before 7 a. m. and after 5 p. m.

Repeated to Chungking, Peiping, Hong Kong.

LINNELL

793.94/14202 : Telegram

The Consul General at Hankow (Josselyn) to the Secretary of State

HANKOW, October 26, 1938—7 p. m.
[Received October 26—3 : 22 p. m.]

20. The Japanese Army is all around the ex-Concession area and are demanding admission at the various gates. American sailors were withdrawn back to their ship at 6 o'clock tonight except for eight without arms who are remaining at Navy Y. M. C. A. and will stand guard at gate to International Hospital in ex-Russian Concession. The general outlook in regard to the refugee zone is that there are certain places therein which the Japanese are determined to occupy.

Repeated to Chungking and Peiping.

JOSSELYN

793.94/14254

President Roosevelt to the President of the Chinese Executive Yuan (Kung)[63]

WASHINGTON, October 26, 1938.

MY DEAR DR. KUNG: Mr. K. P. Chen has kindly delivered to me your letter of August 30 in which you inform me of the nature of

---

[63] Letter transmitted through the Chinese Ambassador on October 29.

his visit to this country and thoughtfully avail yourself of the occasion to convey cordial personal greetings to me. I recall with pleasure the call which you made upon me last year and appreciate very much your friendly message.

Since his arrival, Mr. Chen has been engaged in discussions with the Treasury Department and I am sure that the matters brought forward by him are receiving most careful and sympathetic consideration.

Your expression of gratitude for the humanitarian services which the American people have rendered Chinese who have suffered as a result of the unfortunate conflict in China is appreciated as are also your generous comments concerning our efforts to contribute toward the attainment of international peace. It is my hope and firm conviction that the friendly and mutually beneficial relations which have always existed between China and the United States will through cooperative endeavor continue to develop in strength.

With kind regards [etc.]　　　　　FRANKLIN D. ROOSEVELT

793.94/14208 : Telegram

The Consul General at Hong Kong (Southard) to the Secretary of State

HONG KONG, October 27, 1938—9 a. m.
[Received October 27—4 a. m.]

18. With further reference to the Department's telegram of October 24, 7 p. m., Hong Kong English newspapers have since the start of the Japanese invasion of South China commented editorially their amazement and puzzlement over the unopposed Japanese advance and have, with the exception of the *Hong Kong Daily Press* which is understood to have Chinese financing, been inclined to find an explanation in bribery or other factors uncomplimentary to Chinese self-esteem. As indicative of a possible change of thought and argument, which could be more inspired than sincere, there is quoted the following excerpt from an editorial in the usually quite independent *China Mail* of October 26:

"Between the puzzling circumstances associated with the surrender of Canton last week and the decision yesterday to refuse battle for the Wuhan cities there are obvious parallels: so striking that we may begin to wonder [whether?] first judgments have not done a grave injustice to Kwangtung's military leaders. If it is fair to assume that the decision to abandon Hankow was based upon high policy and strategical considerations, it is not unreasonable to conjecture whether some of the reports which came through during the weekend, to the effect that General Yu Han Mou retired in direct obedience to orders from High Command, did not, after all, contain more than a germ of truth. An objective study of China's military problems must confirm this much: that nothing is really changed by the fall of Canton or Hankow, Japan having once entered upon the invasion of South China."

It is our well considered opinion that Hong Kong Government policy favors press comment as favorable as possible to the Chinese.

Repeated to Canton, Chungking, Peiping.

SOUTHARD

793.94/14205 : Telegram

The Consul General at Hankow (Josselyn) to the Secretary of State

HANKOW, October 27, 1938—10 a. m.
[Received October 27—7:15 a. m.]

21. No incidents arising out of the Japanese occupation of Wuhan and involving Americans have thus far been reported. The Japanese troops are said to have been orderly last night in the Chinese city as well as in the refugee zone. By nightfall yesterday they were in full possession of the ex-German Concession. They now have troops billeted in the ex-Russian and ex-British Concessions. This morning a large Japanese force marched through the former British concession.

There are now more than 35 Japanese naval vessels and transports, not including sea sleds and other miscellaneous small craft, in harbor. More are arriving.

Repeated to Chungking, Peiping, Shanghai.

JOSSELYN

793.94/14216 : Telegram

The Ambassador in China (Johnson) to the Secretary of State

CHUNGKING, October 27, 1938—11 a. m.
[Received 1:20 p. m.]

515. Department's 360, October 25, noon, to Tokyo. It is my opinion that the Munich Agreement came as a surprise to the Japanese who had long planned an invasion of South China for the purpose of putting an end to the stream of munitions that was flowing into China through Hong Kong and Canton. I do not believe that it precipitated that decision although Chinese reliance upon an assumed Japanese unwillingness to affront British at Hong Kong contributed doubtless to their failure to prepare for such an invasion and contributed to ease which attended Japanese military advance. Nor do I feel that Munich Agreement has necessarily contributed to increasing truculency on the part of Japanese since this has existed from the first. A review of Japanese military activities since beginning of hos-

tilities will I think justify one in believing that invasion of mainland is outward manifestation of a revolt in Japan which has almost succeeded in placing the Japanese military in control of the Government or at least that part of Government which functions in regard to China and the mainland. Resignation of Ugaki over proposed creation of China Bureau independent of Foreign Office and therefore presaging the establishment of Government for China independent of Japanese relations with other nations and whole set of treaties regulating those relations is measure of success of this revolt. Army's attitude from the beginning has been consistently opposed to existence of national government in China and continuance of third power rights, interest and influence in China. Japanese military have successfully prevented shipment of American owned goods caught by hostilities on the Yangtze between Nanking and Kiukiang (wood oil belonging to Werner G. Smith), Japanese prevented *Monocacy* proceeding [from] Kiukiang to Shanghai, arguing that this barrier was prize of war (see message 0019–0004 *Oahu* to Commander-in-Chief of August 19 [64]). Recent communication regarding Yangtze and Pearl Rivers was consistent with this earlier pronouncement which was addressed to the American Government concerning the movements of one of its national ships. Japanese Army in China and its leaders in Japan have not, from the first, had any regard for treaties between Japan and other powers or between China and third powers and by setting up in Japan an independent bureau to deal with China affairs and governments in China subordinate to Japanese Army control have consigned such questions to that other Government of Japan with which we have ordinary contact only through such recognized channels as the Ministry of Foreign Affairs. Munich agreement was I have no doubt greeted by Japanese military party with relief as an indication that at least from Great Britain and France it would meet with little or no opposition, but it did not give rise to this policy.

Shanghai please repeat to Tokyo. Repeated to Shanghai.

JOHNSON

793.94/14214 : Telegram

The Counselor of Embassy in China (Lockhart) to the Secretary of State

PEIPING, October 27, 1938—1 p. m.
[Received 3 : 20 p. m.]

640. Embassy's 620, October 13, 1 p. m.[65]

1. The Japanese claim to be completing a "mopping up" campaign in Shansi. Their claim to have again captured Yuanchu is not con-

---

[64] Vol. IV, p. 171.
[65] Not printed.

tradicted. Their claim that, following the capture October 2 of Wutai town, North Shansi, the mountain of that name was captured about 2 weeks later and the Eighth Route Army Headquarters in that vicinity was driven away with a loss to the Chinese of considerable amounts of ammunition and supplies appeared true.

2. The Japanese forces in South Shansi have not yet, according to their latest statements, been able to effect a crossing of the Yellow River into northern Honan or eastern Shensi, although they have made repeated attempts since early September. Now that Canton and Hankow have fallen, and the route from Soviet Russia via Sinkiang and Sian, Shensi is one of the few remaining channels of supplies for the National Government and the Chinese Communist forces, observers here generally expect that the Japanese will shortly make increased efforts to effect a crossing and drive against Sian.

3. Repeated to Chungking. By mail to Shanghai, Tokyo.

LOCKHART

893.515/1331 : Telegram

The Secretary of State to the Consul General at Shanghai (Gauss)

WASHINGTON, October 27, 1938—6 p. m.

594. Your 1347, October 18, 6 p. m. In response to the inquiry of the British Embassy, please inform the Embassy orally and informally that you have no comment to make other than to say that you understand that the silver in question is not specifically included in any arrangement now in effect between the American and Chinese Governments.

HULL

793.94/14215 : Telegram

The Consul General at Hankow (Josselyn) to the Secretary of State

HANKOW, October 27, 1938—7 p. m.
[Received October 27—5 : 25 p. m.]

23. At a conference this morning between British and Japanese authorities it was agreed that British Navy assisted by foreign volunteers and Chinese police would continue to police former British Concession except Bund to be policed by Japanese military representative. Japanese soldiers are forbidden to enter former British Concession. These measures to continue until arrival of adequate Japanese military police.

Japanese have evicted refugees from godowns, et cetera, in the former German Concession and have demanded that refugees be removed to the Chinese city.

Looting by Chinese reported from native city. Japanese soldiers are commandeering whatever they please from Chinese in ex-German Concession and probably in native city.

A so-called all Hupeh Self-Protection Corps was yesterday established presumably to assume puppet government functions. The head of this organization is Hu Tsung Chun who claims to be a former divisional commander under Wu Pei Fu. He stated that he arrived Hankow 1 month ago.

Repeated to Chungking, Peiping, Shanghai.

JOSSELYN

793.94/14239 : Telegram

The Ambassador in Japan (Grew) to the Secretary of State

TOKYO, October 28, 1938—9 a. m.
[Received 10 : 40 p. m.]

688. Telegrams of this general nature should always be made available to the Commander-in-Chief.[66] Department's 360, October 25, noon.

1. As having direct applicability to the question of the bearing of the Munich Agreement and its aftermath on recent developments in the Far East, please review our 655, October 10, midnight. Subsequent developments in Europe have not borne out the hope, which was current when our telegram was sent, that stabilization of Europe was within close reach, yet it was precisely that possibility which aroused apprehension in this country lest the Munich Agreement Powers eventually intervene in the Far East. In fact it was suggested by the Japanese press that the Hankow offensive was being prosecuted with increased vigor in anticipation of such possible intervention. This connection between the Munich Agreement and events in the Far East was the only one which was given any notice whatever in Japan. The suggestion that the Munich Agreement had repercussions on Japanese policy the reverse of that above mentioned would be purely speculative.

2. We believe that the Munich Agreement had no direct bearing on the attack on Canton. By reference to our 643, October 4, 4 p. m., paragraph 4, it will be observed that my British colleague had already obtained knowledge of the preparations then being made for this attack, and, considering the elaborate precautions taken to preserve Japanese military secrets, it is highly probable that these preparations had been in hand for a substantial period of time (certainly

---

[66] A common means of transmission between the Embassy in Japan and the Department of State was via the Consulate General at Shanghai and the U. S. Navy radio there. This telegram was intended to be made available to the Commander in Chief, U. S. Asiatic Fleet, at Shanghai.

not less than 2 weeks) before Craigie got wind of them—and therefore before the Munich Conference was talked of. That the attack on Canton was a sound strategic move was so obvious that it had been expected for the past 12 months. An appraisal of the reasons for making the attack at the time actually chosen will be found in our 665, October 13, 5 p. m. However, we do not at all exclude as an additional reason for making the attack at this time the lack of British resoluteness disclosed during the protracted discussions prior to the Munich Conference.

3. We are not in a position to appraise, in relation to the Munich Agreement, recent expressions of Japanese intention to preempt prior position for their shipping on Chinese rivers. Such expressions are of course completely contradictory of previous declarations that the Yangtze River would be thrown open to international commercial navigation upon the capture of Hankow. Although we have not as yet done so, we intend shortly to invite the Foreign Office to comment in the light of its previous declarations on the statement recently made in this connection by Minister Tani to Gauss.

4. The advertisement of the Shiunso is only the most recent in a series directed against Great Britain during the past year by this organization. Two years ago the organization was preoccupied with Soviet Russia, and previously with American policy during the Manchurian conflict. The fact that its former threats have not been fulfilled should serve to place the fulminations of this organization in accurate perspective. Nevertheless, the extent and depth of the anger and resentment of the Japanese public against Great Britain should not be minimized. This feeling is no new development but has been vigorously manifested during the past year or more, as reported in several of our telegrams and despatches. Its existence has been frankly admitted to my British colleague on several occasions by the Minister for Foreign Affairs (please see, among other reports, our 543, August 18, 2 p. m., paragraphs 2 and 3 [67]).

5. As the Department is aware, my British colleague is convinced that the Germans are inciting the Japanese to take an increasingly uncompromising attitude vis-à-vis the British. Information which Japan derives from Germany with regard to British difficulties and involvements in Europe might, and probably does, affect the timing and extent of Japanese actions in China, but we do not believe that potential objectives of Japanese policy in China are capable of change one way or another by whatever advice or information Germany might give.

---

[67] *Ante*, p. 265.

6. Our 670, October 15, 11 a. m.[68] may be found to throw considerable light on this general subject.

7. Finally, in our analysis of the attitude of Japan towards foreign interests and foreign commercial activities in China, we should constantly bear in mind the fact that there exist marked discrepancies between the views of the home Government and of the military authorities in the field. We can hardly reject as diplomatic persiflage the assurances given us by such substantial statesmen as Prince Konoye (see our 640, October 3, 4 p. m.,[69] paragraph 3) who himself is a thorough Nationalist, even though these assurances are being daily belied in practice. The increasingly truculent attitude of the Japanese, mentioned by the Department, is of the Japanese military in the field, not of the home Government. In dealing with Japan we are, in effect, dealing with two distinct authorities who are sometimes very far apart in their respective conceptions of foreign policy. To us who live in Japan, this is a trite statement. Ironically, the military and naval authorities are having their day. Their obvious aim is to drive all commercial interests out of China and to make of China an exclusively Japanese mart. Into such vacuum as they are able to create, Japanese commercial and industrial interests will inevitably and progressively crowd. The home Government, which alone is able to appraise the international aspects of this situation, is for the moment very nearly powerless to compel the military authorities in the field to implement its assurances.

8. The foregoing observations are presented merely as facts. It would be futile to attempt to predict the eventual outcome.

GREW

793.94/14240 : Telegram

The Ambassador in China (Johnson) to the Secretary of State

CHUNGKING, October 29, 1938—10 a. m.
[Received 12 : 10 p. m.]

519. Central News carries account [of] opening People's Political Council October 28 and digest of message from Chiang Kai Shek in which he made deductions encouraging to China from the Japanese drive into South China which he asserted evidenced increasing exhaustion and gave China military advantages. He said Chinese Government policy had always been to reconstruct West China into base for consolidation of national strength and that "the war has been going as China had previously planned—not only have military plans been completed but also political organizations have been established in the areas under Japanese occupation". He concluded by hoping

---

[68] Vol. IV, p. 67.
[69] *Ibid.*, p. 53.

256941—54——23

that members of the Council would effectively build up political and economic bases in the rear and stimulate populace in occupied areas and expressed confidence that thus "the materialization of China's plans to crush the enemy will come to pass in the near future."

Repeated to Peiping.   JOHNSON

793.94/14241 : Telegram

The Consul General at Canton (Linnell) to the Secretary of State

CANTON, October 29, 1938—noon.
[Received October 29—11 a. m.]

28.   Further reference is made to the Department's No. 4 of October 24, 7 p. m. and to my 19 of October 26.   In possible explanation of the seeming complete collapse of the Chinese defense in and around Canton when the Japanese soldiers were still at a considerable distance from the city, I would point out the essential indefensibility of assistance solely by land forces against an enemy having in addition to strong land forces and mechanized armament complete command of the air and water.

The Chinese always realized that the Japanese could by combined land, air and naval attack reduce the fortifications at Bocca Tigris and that when this was accomplished Canton could be attacked by naval vessels and guns from the Pearl River.

I believe therefore the complete abandonment of Canton, being a part of the general policy of withdrawing to interior provinces at this time and preparing to wage a long contest on guerrilla lines and pursue the policy of forcing the Japanese to extend greatly their lines of communication and wear themselves out financially and in man power, was also decided upon to save Canton from an intensive combined attack by land, water and air, which would have cost countless lives if the people remained in the city.

Complete abandonment of the city and the great destruction wrought by the Chinese on leaving was also a gesture of defiance and determination to continue the struggle elsewhere.   It was certainly not a signal of surrender.

Repeated to Peiping, Chungking, Hong Kong.

LINNELL

793.94/14232 : Telegram

The Chargé in France (Wilson) to the Secretary of State

PARIS, October 29, 1938—1 p. m.
[Received October 29—noon.]

1841.   The Chief of the Far Eastern Division of the Foreign Office expressed the opinion to me yesterday that the fall of Canton and

Hankow will fail to have decisive effect upon the outcome of the war. Chiang Kai Shek will carry out the plan which he had evolved at the beginning of hostilities for such a contingency as the present and withdraw into Szechwan. He will of course be greatly handicapped in obtaining supplies and will have to look to the overland route from Russia. He is supposed however to have a considerable stock of munitions in Szechwan.

Hoppenot states that if the Japanese were intelligent enough they might now be able to bring about peace by offering such reasonable terms that the Chinese could accept them without loss of face. However, he believes that the Japanese will not be intelligent enough to do this and that their terms will continue to be so harsh that even if Chiang Kai Shek should remove himself from the picture no Chinese leader could possibly accept them.

Hoppenot was much interested in our note to the Japanese Government of October 6.[70] I gave him the full text as received by the Department's 583 [71] inasmuch as he had seen excerpts in the press. He said that the French had encountered the same types of discrimination in their trade in North China and that the operation of exchange control in that area made it impossible for the French to carry on business there. He said that while our note was an able document he felt that the objective which we had in mind might be achieved more effectively if we would act in concert with the French and British in the Far East. He said that in his judgment the only way that the Japanese can be brought to behave more reasonably will be for the three great Western Powers to set up something in the nature of a common front, not necessarily by acting jointly but by concerting their action in such fashion as to impress the Japanese with the fact that they are taking a common stand in the protection of their interests.

He said that 2 days ago the Japanese Government through the Foreign Office in Tokyo and the Embassy at Paris had repeated its protest against the alleged continued passage of munitions over the railway in Indo-China. See my 1751, October 13, 7 p. m. He said that the note of the Japanese Embassy had been impertinent to the point of insolence. The French reply must await Bonnet's return from Marseilles but it will be in strong terms stating that the Japanese charges do not merit consideration in view of the formal French assurances that the railway has been closed to munitions traffic and due to the fact that the Japanese fail to adduce a single concrete case supporting their charges. Hoppenot said that the railway had been completely closed to the passage of munitions for over 2 months and that even material ordered by China before the outbreak of hostilities

---

[70] *Foreign Relations*, Japan, 1931–1941, vol. I, p. 785.
[71] Not found in Department files.

was not allowed passage. For instance, 10 airplanes ordered in May 1937 had arrived in Indo-China recently; the French authorities had seized the planes and cabled Paris that they were needed for the defense of the Protectorate. Paris had approved. Hoppenot stated that the Japanese through their spies knew very well what the true situation was and he believes that the renewed protests in this particular were made merely to hasten justification for military action which the Japanese will take against either Hainan or the French railway in Yunnan.

I asked if the Russians were increasing arms shipments to China. Hoppenot said that his information was that they were not increasing such shipments. He said that there had been reports from Hankow some days before the capture of the city that the Russian Mission there was not on very cordial terms with the Chinese authorities.

WILSON

793.94/14239 : Telegram

The Secretary of State to the Ambassador in Japan (Grew)

WASHINGTON, October 29, 1938—2 p. m.

371. Your 688, October 28, 9 a. m., paragraph 3, third sentence. In as much as the Department is giving current consideration to a closely related matter, please withhold action pending further instruction from the Department.

HULL

793.94/14246 : Telegram

The Consul General at Hankow (Josselyn) to the Secretary of State

HANKOW, October 29, 1938—3 p. m.
[Received October 29—12 : 35 p. m.]

30. The British Navy turned over policing of the former British Concession to the Japanese military at 11: 00 this morning in a military ceremony. A small American naval force participated. I did not know of this American participation until I saw the American seamen drawn up with the British to receive the Japanese.

A British consular officer confidentially states that the agreement for turning over the policing of the former British Concession to the Japanese Army was reached between the British Admiral here and the Japanese military without previous notice to either the Director of Special Administrative District 3 or the British Consulate General.

Difficulty is being experienced in getting refugees to move to the new refugee zone designated by the Japanese from the streets of the former concessions where they have been camping despite 3 days of rain.

Repeated to Chungking, Peiping.

JOSSELYN

793.94/14237 : Telegram

The Consul General at Canton (Linnell) to the Secretary of State

CANTON, October 30, 1938—4 p. m.
[Received October 30—1 : 45 p. m.]

34. Japanese Rear Admiral T. Sugikara arrived at Canton today on mine sweeper 18 and sent an officer to call on Captain Stapler on the U. S. S. *Mindanao*, on the British senior naval officer and the captain commanding the French gunboat *Argus*. The Japanese officer stated that no movements of vessels could be permitted at this time and the British gunboat *Cicala* was specifically refused permission to proceed to Kongmoon.

The new Japanese commander of *gendarmerie* for Canton, Colonel Hayashi, today informed the Consul General of Great Britain that the Refugee Committee would not be permitted to take from godowns at Fati any more of the rice which the bishopric of Hong Kong had purchased on October 18th from Chinese merchants. Colonel Hayashi said that the question of the ownership of this rice had been referred to Tokyo and if it was found that title was properly transferred to the bishopric at Hong Kong it would be paid for but the rice was needed for the Japanese troops.

This decision makes the problem of obtaining food for the refugees more precarious and it is understood that there is rice in the hands of the Committee to feed the present number of refugees only about 2 weeks. The refugees are rapidly increasing in number as incidents of shooting and rape occur in the villages and the women and children come to the refugee camps.

It is believed that it will be necessary to buy rice in Hong Kong or elsewhere outside China and bring it here soon. Arrangements to safeguard the rice will of course have to be made with the Japanese and more funds will be needed by the Refugee Committee to pay for it.

Repeated to Chungking, Peiping, Hong Kong.

LINNELL

CHAPTER VI: NOVEMBER 1–DECEMBER 31, 1938

Significance of appointment of new Japanese Minister for Foreign Affairs; aid to China from various countries (November 4); French suggestion of joint representations to Japan against policy of unilateral revision of treaties (November 7); President Roosevelt's assurance of American sympathy for China (November 10); Chiang Kai-shek's request for British aid (November 16, 20); signing of German-Japanese cultural convention (November 26); appraisal of situation created by Japan to date (December 1); discussion of positive steps to defend American rights and interests in China (December 5, 22); arrival in Indochina from Chungking of Wang Ching-wei, deputy leader of Kuomintang, and Japanese announcement of peace terms for China (December 23)

894.00/822

The Ambassador in Japan (Grew) to the Secretary of State

No. 3392   Tokyo, November 1, 1938.
                                               [Received November 21.]

Sir: Confirming my telegram 691, October 29, 1 p. m.,[72] I have the honor to report the appointment on October 29 of Mr. Hachiro Arita as Minister for Foreign Affairs in succession to Prince Konoye, the Prime Minister, who also concurrently held the Ministry of Overseas Affairs.

The selection at this time of Mr. Arita for the Foreign Office gives no direct information on the question whether there is to be any change, whether for better or for worse, in the future policy of Japan toward the Western Powers. As for Japan's China policy, that, as has been so truthfully said recently by Japanese leaders, is "immutable". Mr. Arita is a thoroughly honest person and will not compromise with his convictions; but one is never quite certain whether the convictions which he holds today will last the morrow. It is an open secret that, when Vice Minister for Foreign Affairs, a post which usually immediately precedes an ambassadorship, he chose to go as Minister to Austria in preference to subscribing to Japanese policy in Manchuria. Since then, he has gained the confidence of the Army, and he returns to the Foreign Office to support a policy in comparison to which the Manchuria policy was child's play. Presumably he, like most liberal Japanese, realizes that for Japan there is no road back.

Most Japanese observers were of the opinion that when the decision was taken against the opposition of General Ugaki to set up the China Organ, it would be extremely difficult if not impossible to find a senior diplomatist prepared to associate himself with that decision as a condition precedent to appointment to the Foreign Office; for to give assent would be tantamount to acquiescence in transferring the direction of Japan's relations with the Powers as well as with China from the Foreign Minister to the committee of five cabinet

---

[72] Vol. IV, p. 606.

ministers who are to be the governors of the China Organ. It might be said with a certain amount of truth that the grant of wide powers to the China Organ would merely regularize an existing practice; yet, the fact remains that a Foreign Minister who has no power of initiative in matters affecting foreign relations is not far from being an anomaly. One fair assumption to be drawn from these circumstances is that Mr. Arita, in consenting to be one of five persons who are hereafter to direct foreign relations, has views on foreign policy which do not materially differ from those of his future colleagues on the board of governors of the China Organ.

The statement made by Mr. Arita on appointment and the speculations of the press on the policy to be pursued now that Hankow has fallen are not at all informative. The statement to be issued by the Government on November 3rd [73] may clarify matters somewhat, but at the moment few persons outside the small group within the Cabinet are able to make any prediction which sounds convincing.

During a call which the counselor of the Embassy [74] made on Mr. Yoshizawa, Director of the American Bureau of the Foreign Office, he inquired whether any progress was being made in drafting a reply to my note of October 6, 1938,[75] with regard to American rights and interests in China. Mr. Yoshizawa said that lantern processions were still being held to celebrate the capture of Hankow and that, with a Minister just coming into office, he had no idea when the reply would be ready. Mr. Dooman observed that Japan had reached a fork in the road, and that she would have to choose between giving full respect to the rights in China of the United States and Great Britain, along with other Powers, and returning to a condition of seclusion not unlike that which she maintained for two hundred years under the Tokugawa Shogunate. He believed that Japan's well-being was bound up with cooperation with the United States and Great Britain, and that, although she could subsist on China, she could not expect to maintain even the present Japanese standard of living. Mr. Yoshizawa said that even the military had begun to realize that the industrial and economic development by Japan of China would be impossible without the help of American and British capital. Mr. Dooman replied that the grant of loans by Americans should hardly be given serious thought so long as the loans, if made, served only to maintain and perpetuate conditions which excluded the principle of equality of opportunity. Mr. Yoshizawa's concluding remark was significant in the light of our speculative appraisal of Mr. Arita's views: it was that he saw no solution of the issue with the United States over China

[73] *Foreign Relations*, Japan, 1931–1941, vol. I, p. 477.
[74] Eugene H. Dooman.
[75] *Foreign Relations*, Japan, 1931–1941, vol. I, p. 785.

unless the United States were to recognize the new situation in the Far East.

With an important official statement on policy promised in two days, further speculation at this time on the possibility of a change in Japanese attitude would not seem to be called for. But long experience with official statements issued by the Japanese Government gives me no grounds to expect that we shall have a clear-cut definition of Japanese attitude and objectives. If, as we expect, the announcement will consist largely of generalities, including the points enunciated by former Foreign Minister Hirota—economic cooperation between Japan and China, joint opposition to communism, and so on—a formula said to be much favored by Mr. Arita, assurance of respect for foreign rights in China, and emphasis on recognition by the Powers of the new situation in the Far East, we shall be forced by subsequent events to interpret the announcement as notice that there is to be no reversion by Japan to the conditions contemplated by the Nine-Power Treaty. The jubilation over the fall of Hankow and the confidence that dissention among the Chinese leaders will develop in the near future, coupled with the animosity toward Great Britain and to a less degree toward France, dispose me to believe that, whatever the language of the promised declaration of the Japanese Government may be, its intent will be to affirm Japanese paramountcy in the Far East.

Respectfully yours,   JOSEPH C. GREW

793.94/14280 : Telegram

The Consul General at Hankow (Josselyn) to the Secretary of State

HANKOW, November 2, 1938—2 p. m.
[Received November 3—3 : 15 a. m.]

35. Conversations before the capture of Wuhan with sources close to General Chiang Kai Shek have left the strong impression that the Generalissimo genuinely believes that he is fighting not only in defense of China but also on behalf of the democracies the vital interests of which, he feels, will be affected by the expansion and overweening ambitions of Japanese militarism. He is said to appreciate the unwillingness of the democratic powers to take military measures to check the expansion of Japanese militarism but is bitterly disappointed in these states because of their continued supply of war materials to Japan, which action he views as hostile not only to China's resistance but also as directly contrary to the national interests of the democratic powers themselves.

Before the fall of Hankow and Canton competent foreign observers here viewed China's resistance to Japan as primarily a defense of

Chinese sovereignty. They now feel that China is unmistakably fighting not only her own battle but, perforce, also that of the democracies. It is believed that the stage may soon be reached where the Japanese military may be able to convert the organizations of China now conquered into an economic base for avowed further expansion. It is questioned whether Chinese resistance, which will continue but in a weakened form, will be sufficiently effective to prevent Japanese militarism from exploiting at least those resources necessary for the aggrandizement of its military power.

Economic restraints on Japan exerted by the United States and Great Britain, these sources believe, can still check Japanese militarism before it consolidates its position in China and launches further adventures more closely affecting the democratic powers. It is suggested that once Japanese militarism has begun to draw strength from China's resources the democracies may no longer, if confronted with Japanese action jeopardizing their vital interests, be able to choose the comfortable alternative of effective persuasion through economic pressure.

Repeated to Chungking, Peiping, Shanghai.

JOSSELYN

741.94/216 : Telegram

The Ambassador in Japan (Grew) to the Secretary of State

TOKYO, November 2, 1938—6 p. m.
[Received November 2—10 : 38 a. m.]

700. 1. My British colleague [76] told me today that last summer an inter-departmental conference took place in London for the purpose of considering possible methods of retaliation against Japan as pressure to relieve Japanese encroachments on British interests in China. Three specific methods were discussed:

(*a*) A resort to the same petty tactics employed by the Japanese in placing difficulties in the way of British trade and shipping through discriminatory delays and other not illegal annoyances.

(*b*) Partial denunciation of the Anglo-Japanese treaty of commerce and navigation of 1911 [77] by rendering it inapplicable to certain outlying possessions such as Singapore;

(*c*) Total denunciation of the treaty.

2. Craigie and the British Ambassador in China [78] were respectively instructed to study this question and to report their recommendations after consulting the British Consuls in Japan and China.

---

[76] Sir Robert L. Craigie, British Ambassador in Japan.
[77] *British and Foreign State Papers*, vol. CIV, p. 159.
[78] Sir Archibald Clark Kerr.

3. A paraphrase of Craigie's telegraphic report to London which was sent some 10 days ago follows:

"Retaliation.

The opinion has been reached, after careful consideration with the senior members of my staff, that no advantage would be gained by the gradual execution of a policy of reprisals working up from petty annoyances to denunciation but that the decision should first be made whether we are prepared to accept all the consequences of denunciation and if so prepared a denunciation *in toto* should be made after fair warning to Japan.   The merit of this course is that it is justifiable on the principle that most favored nation treatment cannot continually be accorded to a country which does not fulfill its treaty obligation (i. e. Nine Power Treaty), and thus it is consonant with the recent note of the United States.[79]

I still stand by the view, however, with regard to the consequences of denunciation, that reaction would be very serious and I venture to express the view that the letter to the Departments of August 23rd somewhat underestimates the risks.   As stated in paragraph 6 of that letter, I agree that the Japanese Government would be reluctant to add to their international complications but it is my opinion that in their present mood they might even take the risk of becoming embroiled with us if a step which would in effect be indistinguishable from sanctions were to be taken by us.   Evidence of their present temper is the expedition to South China.

I doubt, however, if there is necessity of running this risk.   Since denunciation cannot come into effect for a year, no practical results can be expected before the beginning of 1940.   Although we cannot possibly say what the situation here will be then, the evidence before me makes it difficult to see whether China or Japan was nearer to financial exhaustion even before the Japanese expedition to South China.   Since, by this expedition, the Japanese have so greatly extended their commitments, it is difficult to avoid the deduction that the pace at which Japanese resources must now steadily diminish will render unnecessary any effort on our part (at the sacrifice at best of friendship after the war) to hasten the end before 1940 at all events. At the same time as we continue to maintain our condemnation of Japan's aggression and observe the terms of the League resolution,[80] I presume that our object is to maintain friendly relations with both belligerents without giving justification to either when peace comes for making claims that the other has been unduly favored by us.   I should prefer if my diagnosis is correct to put up with the temporary losses which British interests have suffered in China (many I understand have in fact not done so badly during the crisis) in order that during the peace negotiations and afterwards we may play our part. We can do this only if we do not leave a lasting grievance with the Japanese as we did with the Italians".

GREW

---

[79] Dated October 6, *Foreign Relations*, Japan, 1931–1941, vol. I, p. 785.
[80] See second report adopted October 6, 1937, by the League of Nations Assembly, *ibid.*, p. 394.

741.94/217 : Telegram

The Ambassador in Japan (Grew) to the Secretary of State

TOKYO, November 2, 1938—8 p. m.
[Received November 3—8 : 25 a. m.]

701. My British colleague has handed me a copy of a letter dated October 31, addressed by him to the Vice-Minister for Foreign Affairs,[81] of which the following is a summary :

The British Ambassador points out that the British Parliament would meet on November 1, and that he considers it of great importance to the future of Anglo-Japanese relations that something should be done at once to meet the British on at least some of the cases outstanding. He says that the Foreign Office has asked him urgently to report on the situation in view of the fact that when Parliament meets the Ministers expect to be questioned closely in regard to the fulfillment by the Japanese of the assurances so frequently given in regard to the protection of British rights and interests in China.

The Ambassador states that with the best will in the world, he is unable to return any other reply than that the Japanese Government has failed so far to meet the British desiderata in any single instance of importance. Referring to the fact that the Foreign Office has a full list of cases in which a number have been injured, and to the list of five points submitted to General Ugaki on July 26 last,[82] the British Ambassador points out that in spite of all his efforts to impress the Japanese Government with the importance of these issues, the British have in fact received no satisfaction whatever. He admits that in a number of relatively minor cases (a list of which he encloses) British property has been repaired and certain facilities given but he characterizes these as "a mere islet in an ocean of discriminatory or unfair treatment".

Sir Robert then refers to the fact that the hope has been expressed by General Ugaki and Mr. Horinouchi [83]—particularly as regards navigation on the Yangtze—that the situation would be eased by the fall of Hankow and inquires whether there is not a case here where it should be possible for the Japanese Government to give immediate satisfaction by opening up the river at least as far as Nanking. He is seriously apprehensive as to the effect upon future Anglo-Japanese relations if satisfaction is not given on this point at the earliest possible moment.

The British Ambassador deprecates the thought that he is threatening the Japanese Government with statements in Parliament in order

---

[81] Renzo Sawada.
[82] See telegram No. 494, July 27, 3 p. m., from the Ambassador in Japan, p. 239.
[83] Formerly Japanese Minister and Vice Minister for Foreign Affairs, respectively.

to secure British desiderata; on the contrary he feels sure that the British Government will make every effort to mitigate the effects of any official statements that may be made; but the facts cannot be concealed from Parliament when questions of importance are asked. He therefore repeats with the utmost emphasis that something concrete should be done by the Japanese Government to enable the British Government to say in Parliament that a satisfactory settlement has been reached on this or that important issue.

In conclusion he states that he is holding up his reply to his Foreign Office until he hears from the Vice-Minister for Foreign Affairs and he wishes to know whether the Vice-Minister believes there is any prospect of giving early satisfaction at least on the Yangtze navigation issue.

Enclosed with the letter is a list of 10 minor cases where the Japanese have evacuated British property and seven other cases which have been settled involving the seizure of launches, [assault?] cases, et cetera.

Repeated to Chungking.

GREW

793.94/14281a : Telegram

The Secretary of State to the Ambassador in Japan (*Grew*)

WASHINGTON, November 3, 1938—5 p. m.

375. 1. The press of last night and this morning carries the text of a statement made public by the Japanese Government in regard to the situation in the Far East. The opening paragraph of the statement reads as follows:

"By the august virtues of His Majesty our naval and military forces have captured Canton and the three Wuhan cities; all other vital areas in China have fallen into our hands."

The concluding paragraph reads as follows:

"Such the Government declares to be the immutable policy and the determination of Japan."

The Department desires to receive from you at the earliest possible moment a brief telegram reporting whether the Japanese Government issued such a statement and by whom or from what Government agency it was issued.[84]

2. The press today also carries reports of a speech by the Prime Minister in which the Prime Minister is said to have maintained a

---

[84] For text of statement by the Japanese Government, see *Foreign Relations, Japan, 1931–1941*, vol. I, p. 477.

close parallel with the Government statement on Chinese policy. Please telegraph the Department promptly the significant passages in the Prime Minister's speech.[85]

HULL

741.94/223

The Ambassador in Japan (Grew) to the Secretary of State

No. 3408   TOKYO, November 3, 1938.
                                          [Received November 21.]

SIR: On various occasions during the course of the present hostilities between Japan and China, I have discussed in my telegrams and despatches the relations between Japan and Great Britain as they have been affected by the hostilities. These relations have received during the past two or three months renewed attention on the part of the general public by reason of the conversations which were initiated during the month of August by the British Ambassador, Sir Robert Craigie, with the then Minister for Foreign Affairs, General Ugaki. The failure of the Japanese Government to respond favorably to the solicitations of the British Government that Japan respect British rights and interests in China has, paradoxical though it may be, resulted in exciting the press and publicists to denouncing Great Britain in as unmeasured language as though substantial concessions had been made to Great Britain. The reasons adduced for this animosity against Great Britain, which in most cases could be adduced with equal cogency against the United States, do not explain why Great Britain has been singled out for attack. There is now available a large volume of literature on this subject, but as these writings generally conform to a certain pattern, selections here and there may serve to give the Department a general idea of the reasons which are presented for the present animus against Great Britain.

There appears in the current issue of the magazine *Japan and the Japanese* an article by Dr. Oyama, who was at one time Japanese consul general at San Francisco, arguing the need for modification by Great Britain of its attitude toward Japan. He contends that it is all very well for Great Britain to insist that her rights and interests in China be respected, but that prior consideration must be the enjoyment by Japan of absolute freedom to carry on military operations in China. He states that Great Britain has:

(*a*) placed at the disposal of the Chinese Government every available facility to spread anti-Japanese propaganda;
(*b*) it has supplied arms and munitions to the Chinese Government;
(*c*) hampered Japanese military operations by refusing to remove warships and merchantmen from areas of operations.

[85] For text of speech, see *Foreign Relations*, Japan, 1931–1941, vol. I, p. 478.

Typical of the more able and thoughtful articles is one contributed to *Review Diplomatique* by its editor, Dr. Hanzawa. The writer, after citing the three points mentioned in the article by Dr. Oyama as evidence of British animosity towards Japan and of undue friendliness towards China, pronounces Britain's relations with China to be so close as virtually to constitute an alliance. Dr. Hanzawa then presents several other reasons, which probably suggest the real grounds for Japanese resentment against Great Britain. He asks whether there is not need for Great Britain to review its actions of the last twenty years against Japan. He states that he finds no great difficulty in appreciating Great Britain's desire to promote peace, to establish a system of collective security, and otherwise to promote the maintenance of the *status quo;* but he insists that it has been Great Britain which has been the ring-leader in promoting various means, such as the Washington Conference treaties and the London Naval Treaty, to bring pressure on Japan. He asks whether it is not, after all, Great Britain which has been conducting a worldwide campaign against Japanese commerce. He points out that it was free trade which made possible the evolution of Great Britain into a great commercial empire, and he asks whether it is compatible for a nation which has everything to owe to free trade to attempt to block Japanese commercial expansion in all parts of the world, but more especially in China.

In this connection my attention was recently drawn to an article which appeared in the London *Times* of September 1, 1938, from its correspondent in Japan. It is the thesis of the correspondent that the anti-British movement in Japan is one manifestation of a revolt by the younger elements in the Army and Navy and in the civil service against the older generation. He states, "In its essence, however, it has become a struggle between youthful dynamism in all departments of the national life and what is called generally the elder clique, that capable, temperate, and none too numerous oligarchy that has ruled Japan since her emergence as a modern state.["] The correspondent seems to refer in the sentence quoted to the struggle which was described in my despatch No. 2722, January 6, 1938 [86] as one between "medievalism" and Western thought. It is, however, difficult to subscribe to the correspondent's thesis that the anti-British movement is primarily a manifestation of that revolt (I say "primarily", as the greater part of his article is taken up with the development of this particular thesis), for the reason that during the past thirty or forty years the impact of the United States on Japan has been far greater than that of Great Britain and American thought and tradition exercise among the older generation as much influence as do

---

[86] *Foreign Relations*, 1937, vol. IV, p. 720.

British thought and tradition. The correspondent then ascribes as the secondary reason for the animus against Great Britain the familiar contention that Great Britain has been unduly helpful to China.

Even after reviewing the debate which wages back and forth between British and Japanese organs of public opinion, one is still left with the impression that the present state of feeling in Japan against Great Britain is one of the political curiosities of the moment. Quite apart from those factors which are being daily stressed by the Japanese publicists, such as the supply of arms and munitions by Great Britain to China, it seems to us that what has contributed more to the present state of affairs than any other are, first, the accumulation of Japanese grievances against Great Britain which began with the termination of the Anglo-Japanese Alliance and concluded with the various measures taken by or at the instance of the British Government to restrict Japanese trade, and second, the consciousness that Great Britain is determined to remain permanently a political and economic factor in the Far East.

Although my British colleague has not informed me that, in his various conversations with the Minister for Foreign Affairs, there was made clear to him the intention of the Japanese Government to avoid a separate settlement of British complaints against Japanese actions in China, I have been told by a well-informed Japanese that there is no likelihood whatever of the Japanese Government being prepared to discuss British grievances against Japan apart from Japanese grievances against Great Britain which have been stored up for a period of some years. It will have been noted from our telegram No. 700, November 2, 6 p. m. that my British colleague had reached the conclusion that from the longer viewpoint it would serve British interests if effort were made by Great Britain to avoid leaving Japan with a lasting grievance. However, it seems likely that further interpretation, by action, of the official statement of the Japanese Government published today, expressive of intent to dominate the Far East, will effectively inhibit any expectation that Anglo-Japanese relations can be guided in the near future into smooth waters.

Respectfully yours,　　　　　　　　　　　　JOSEPH C. GREW

793.94/14304 : Telegram

The Ambassador in China (Johnson) to the Secretary of State

CHUNGKING, November 4, 1938—9 a. m.
[Received November 5—4 : 29 p. m.]

526. All types of intelligent Chinese are keenly appreciative of the popular sympathy shown throughout the United States for the

Chinese people in their desperate struggle for independence and against Japanese domination. It would be useless to deny, however, that the Chinese are at a loss to explain why this sympathy does not find expression in practical form (1) by refusing to supply war essentials to Japan and (2) by extending credits to China for such commodities. Thinking Chinese would doubtless argue that self-interest alone would incline the United States to refrain from assisting the Japanese Army to invade the rights of American citizens as set forth in our note of October 6 to the Japanese Foreign Office. With reference to the matter of credits Peck [87] November 3 inquired of Tsiang, lately Chinese Ambassador in Moscow and now Director General of Political Affairs of the Executive Yuan, what assistance was being given by other countries and was told in confidence as follows: France has sold the Chinese Government 2 lots of 30 military planes each on 6 years credit. The planes are not entirely satisfactory since on arrival parts were missing and during the crisis before the Munich Agreement the Government of Indo-China temporarily detained some planes for possible use by France. On the whole this arrangement and the attitude of France are regarded as liberal and friendly. Great Britain has not extended credit but has given great assistance by permitting the passage of munitions through Hong Kong. The capture of Canton having closed this route, the British are continuing cooperation in establishing the Burma motor road which is practically completed. He said that both this route and through Indo-China are expensive, the cost per ton from the sea to Yunnanfu being about Chinese dollars 1300 and 700 respectively or roughly American dollars 200 and 100 but the Burma cost of 200 dollars may in future be decreased by improvement in details of shipping. Informant thought that the building of railways through Burma or Chinese Turkestan had no practical bearing on present needs which are urgent and immediate.

In connection with the non-aggression pact of August 1937, China obtained from the Soviet Union an unconditioned credit of 1,000,000 Chinese dollars and in the following December a credit of 200,000,000 to be repaid in Chinese commodities without time limit. China refused a Soviet request that China share its available foreign exchange. This money has all been sent [*spent?*] by the Chinese Government. Informant thought Stalin was invincibly opposed to military intervention on behalf of China although Voroshilov and Blucher [88] are both thought to advocate war against Japan. Germany has supplied China with munitions through the medium of the first barter agree-

---

[87] Willys R. Peck, Counselor of Embassy in China.
[88] Soviet Commissar for Defense and Red Army Marshal, respectively, in the Soviet Far East.

ment and a second barter agreement was concluded just before the capture of Canton which event made the shipment of German goods into China almost impossible. This second agreement is more liberal than the first in that purchases may be negotiated with individual firms instead of only with the German Government and the firms look to the German Government for payment. Informant felt that the German attitude toward this conflict is ambiguous but he discredits a rumor he reported as coming from Europe to the effect that Germany has extended a loan equivalent to 10,000,000 pounds to Japan with which to purchase 1500 planes on the condition that Japan proceed to attack the Soviet Union simultaneously with a German attack in Europe. Italian aid to China has been negligible in value. Informant made no mention of a refusal by any nation to supply to Japan commodities it needs and he seemed fully conversant with the economic conditions which would make it extremely difficult to comply with the popular Chinese desire that the United States curtail such exports. (Assistance given by the United States was not discussed, otherwise the director would undoubtedly have acknowledged gratefully the silver purchases as other informed officials have done.)

Questioned in regard to the possibility of compromise with Japan, Tsiang stated that of course the so-called Communist faction would refuse short of victory to cease fighting the Japanese invasion but he thought the general attitude of the representatives in the People's Political Council now meeting and probably of the country at large was adequately expressed by a member of the "Youth Movement" at the meeting of the second instant in saying that he would give unquestioning obedience to Chiang Kai Shek whether the latter decided for prolonged resistance or a compromise for peace. Questioned whether he thought any terms of compromise could be devised possible of acceptance by both sides, informant refrained from discussing the matter beyond observing that such terms would be very difficult to frame.

My inference from informant's statements and other circumstances is that it can hardly be believed that in practical matters any League member is seeking to implement the League resolution of October 6, 1937[89] recommending that it refrain from action likely to weaken China's power of resistance and that it consider extending aid to China (with which resolution the United States expressed itself in general accord[90]), since I understand League members have not refused to supply Japan with the mechanized equipment or materials

---

[89] See paragraph 13 of report adopted October 6, 1937, *Foreign Relations*, Japan, 1931–1941, vol. I, pp. 394, 396.
[90] See press release issued by the Department of State, October 6, 1937, *ibid.*, p. 396.

therefor that are undermining China's ability to resist. My opinion is the European nations that have assisted China including Germany and Italy, which did not join in the resolution, are convinced that the victory of the Japanese Army would result in their partial or complete exclusion from trade with China and that they privately would prefer failure of the Japanese attempt to dominate China although their aid to China is nicely proportioned to avoid provoking war with Japan. Much less can I discern any initiative among them in practical matters on behalf of the "more fundamental interest" of orderly processes referred to in the Secretary's letter to the Vice President of January 8.[91] I should say that while the United States is popularly regarded in China as being a more pronounced champion of China's independence than any European nation, nevertheless Great Britain, Russia and France are thought to be more powerful factors in the Far Eastern situation because whatever their motives their aid to China has been more widely known and more publicly opposed by Japan.

JOHNSON

793.94/14288 : Telegram

The Ambassador in Japan (Grew) to the Secretary of State

TOKYO, November 4, 1938—2 p. m.
[Received November 4—10 : 12 a. m.]

704. Department's 375, November 3, 5 p. m., and our 703, November 4, 10 a. m.[92]

1. The following are significant passages from the Prime Minister's speech.

[Here follow passages from speech printed in *Foreign Relations, Japan, 1931–1941*, volume I, page 478.]

2. For the past few weeks much attention has been given in the press and elsewhere to the need for reformulation of Japanese policy in the light of "the changed situation in the Far East" in order that (a) the foreign powers might realize that the future security of their interests in China is to be conditioned upon their recognition of the "changed situation"; (b) China be discouraged from assuming that there is to be any relaxation of Japanese determination to eliminate a government of China hostile to Japan; and (c) the need be emphasized to the Japanese people for making sacrifices which the full development of Japanese policy will entail. In our view the two statements, which might properly be regarded as a single ex-

---

[91] *Foreign Relations*, Japan, 1931–1941, vol. I, p. 429.
[92] Latter not printed.

pression of Japanese policy, address in each of these three directions a separate message. The Japanese people are told that the war has only just begun and that they will be expected to make the necessary sacrifices, an injunction which this Government pointed up by a separate warning of the Minister of Finance that taxes are to be increased. The Western Powers are warned that Japan will co-operate with only those powers which "really understand" the position of Japan and shape their policy "in accordance with the new situation in East Asia", while China is urged to abandon its leaders and associate itself with Japan in the creation of a "new order".

3. The reference in the statements to future Japanese attitude toward foreign powers must we believe be studied in the light of creditable forecasts in several papers this morning of a further statement which is reportedly to be made shortly by the Minister for Foreign Affairs, when he is to declare that "Japan can no longer acquiesce in economic and political encroachments on China by the Western Powers under the guise of the Open Door and other false principles set out in the Nine Power Treaty, and that as Japan can no longer conform to the Treaty it must be regarded as having lapsed". (Note: Necessary action by the Privy Council to permit of withdrawal from that Treaty has not as yet been taken or so far as we know requested.)   One paper adds that the Japanese Government will state in its reply to our note of October 6 that although "Japan has no objection to the maintenance in the economic field of the principle of the Open Door, it cannot admit demands regarding the principle which in reality cloak political ambitions". There is in the foregoing press stories and elsewhere sufficient warrant for the belief that the two statements issued yesterday are to be the first of a series of overt moves by the Japanese Government seeking to eliminate the Open Door as even a nominal guiding principle in the regulation of foreign rights and interests in China. Unfortunately the editorials this morning barely touch upon those portions of the statements dealing with relations with third powers, but the brief comment made tends to confirm the probable accuracy of our analysis.

4. Some surprise along with much satisfaction is reflected in editorials that it was preferred in these statements to address China in terms more conciliatory than would have been the case if there had been further emphasis on Japan's determination not to "deal with" the Chinese Government. Approval is given to the stressing of the "rebirth of the Chinese Government" and of the "creation of a new order", as contrasted with the underscoring in former statements of the "destruction of the Chinese Government" and "surrender". The conclusion is drawn by one or two papers that the invitation to the Chinese people to reconstruct the Chinese Government is clear notice

that the Japanese declaration of January 16,[93] that Japan will no longer "deal with the Nationalist Government of China", does not exclude further cooperation with the latter government if Chiang Kai Shek along with Communist and other anti-Japanese elements are eliminated therefrom.

Paragraphs 2 to 4 repeated to Peiping for Chungking.

GREW

793.94/14286 : Telegram

The Secretary of State to the Ambassador in Japan (Grew)[94]

WASHINGTON, November 4, 1938—5 p. m.

379. The Department issued to the press today a statement reading as follows:

"In response to requests by the press for comments on the statement issued by the Japanese Government [95] in regard to the situation in the Far East, the Secretary of State said that he felt it very important to view the situation in accurate and comprehensive perspective. The attitude of the United States and the position of the American Government in relations both with China and with Japan, as with other countries, are, he said, governed and guided by the generally accepted principles of international law, by the provisions of treaties to which the United States and numerous countries—among them China and Japan—are parties, and by principles of fair dealing and fair play between and among nations. This country's position with regard to the situation in the Far East has, he said, repeatedly been declared, and this position remains unchanged".

HULL

893.01 Provisional/163 : Telegram

The Second Secretary of Embassy in China (Smyth) to the Secretary of State

NANKING, November 4, 1938—11 p. m.
[Received November 4—1:20 p. m.]

179. My 178, November 2 [3], 2 p. m.[96] The conference closed yesterday morning with a 2-hour session at which Liang Hung Chih made a brief speech, Wang Keh Min read the joint "manifesto" and Wen Chung Yao made a speech.[97]

A brief summary of the manifesto follows:

[93] Foreign Relations, Japan, 1931–1941, vol. I, p. 437.
[94] The same to the Ambassador in the United Kingdom and the Chargé in France as telegrams Nos. 683 and 840, November 6, 4 p. m.
[95] Statement issued November 3, Foreign Relations, Japan, 1931–1941, vol. I, p. 477.
[96] Not printed.
[97] Members of Japanese-sponsored regimes at Peiping and at Nanking.

China has long been known as a righteous and cultured country, but during the regime of Chiang Kai Shek military power was misused and the people mistreated. Chiang united with the Communists to save himself and then commenced war, which, combined with his "scorched earth" policy, has resulted in great destruction of lives and property. Canton and Hankow have now fallen but he still continues upon one [*war?*], disregarding the sacrifice of the lives and property of his countrymen. Our country cannot be saved unless Communists are exterminated, Communists cannot be exterminated unless Chiang is overthrown, and peace cannot be attained unless Communists are exterminated and Chiang is overthrown. Peace depends upon our answer and we must arise and save ourselves.

In a joint press interview yesterday Liang Hung Chih and Wang Keh Min stated that: the general views of the conference are set forth in the joint manifesto; we have three principal tasks, namely, to work against communism, to overthrow Chiang, and to wake up our brothers and struggle for the establishment of a new China; if we are to save the country, we must overthrow Chiang and communism; the situation of the new Central Government has not been settled in this conference but will be taken up soon; relations will be established with regimes in other places from which Chiang has been or will be driven out; it is still too early to discuss definitely the participation of Mongolia and Sinkiang in our conference. Questioned as to possible peace plans, they replied "we must cultivate leading persons who can maintain peace and order." No definite statement was made in regard to the date of the next conference.

It is believed here that the new Central Government, if and when established, will be located in Nanking. Reports are current here this new Central Government will be recognized by Japan, "Manchukuo", Germany and Italy, and that the new government will request all powers concerned to give up extraterritorial rights and withdraw troops from China.

Wang Keh Min and other Peiping delegates left today for Shanghai and it is understood that they will fly to Peiping tomorrow.

Sent to Shanghai, and Peiping.

SMYTH

793.94/14405

Memorandum of Conversation, by the Adviser on Political Relations (Hornbeck)

[WASHINGTON,] November 5, 1938.

Mr. Truelle [98] called me on October 28 and said that his Embassy had a telegram from the French Foreign Office stating that the

---
[98] French Counselor of Embassy.

Chinese Ambassador in Paris [99] had stated to the Foreign Office that he and the Chinese Ambassadors at Washington and at London [1] had instructions from their Government to ask the respective foreign offices to consider making a joint or common declaration to the Japanese Government that the three Governments thus concerned would "oppose" Japanese operations in south China. Mr. Truelle wished to know whether such an approach had been made to this Department by the Chinese Embassy here.

I replied that no such approach had been made here. Mr. Truelle expressed surprise. I stated that I was not surprised. There followed some discussion of the matter, in the course of which I repeated that no such approach had been made here and therefore no consideration had been given here to any such suggestion.

This morning, November 5, the French Ambassador [2] asked for an appointment with me and stated that it was urgent. The Ambassador then came to see me and stated that the Chinese Ambassador in Paris was insistently telling the Foreign Office that the Chinese Government had instructed its Ambassadors in Paris, Washington and London to make the request mentioned above. His Foreign Office wished to know whether this Government had yet been approached by the Chinese Embassy in the sense indicated.

I replied that we had not been so approached. With the consent of the Ambassador, I called Mr. Hamilton [3] in and put the inquiry before him. Mr. Hamilton confirmed what I had said to Mr. Truelle and to the Ambassador. I then asked the Ambassador whether his Government had ascertained whether the Chinese Ambassador in London had made such an approach to the British Government. The Ambassador replied that he was uninformed on that subject. I said that it would seem reasonable to assume that his Government would have made such an inquiry and that it might be interesting both for the Ambassador and for us to know what might have transpired in that connection. The Ambassador said that he would inquire. I suggested that if and when he inquired he should assume authorship of the inquiry and not attribute it to us, as mine was an informal and unofficial suggestion and not a suggestion of the Department.

Mr. Hamilton referred to a conversation which the Chinese Minister for Foreign Affairs [4] had had sometime ago with the American Ambassador in China in which the Minister for Foreign Affairs had indicated an interest in ascertaining the reaction of the United States to the south China invasion and in which the Minister for Foreign Affairs

[99] V. K. Wellington Koo.
[1] Hu Shih and Quo Tai-chi, respectively.
[2] Rene Doynel, Count de Saint-Quentin.
[3] Maxwell M. Hamilton, Chief of the Division of Far Eastern Affairs.
[4] Wang Chung-hui.

had made a suggestion that there should be some common action by the American, the British and the French Governments in regard to the general situation in China and to observations in somewhat the same sense that had been made by officers of the French Foreign Office to our Chargé in Paris.[5] At that point, Mr. Hamilton was called away. I thereafter said to the Ambassador that, if the French Government, in having twice asked whether we had been approached by the Chinese Ambassador, was seeking to ascertain what might be our reaction to some proposal of common or joint action, I would suggest that the Ambassador carry the inquiry directly to the Under Secretary or the Secretary, as I did not wish to venture into even a tentative discussion of that point. The Ambassador replied that if he felt or found that such was the intent of his Government he would so proceed.

With appropriate exchanges of amenities the conversation there ended.

S[TANLEY] K. H[ORNBECK]

893.01 Provisional/164 : Telegram

The Counselor of Embassy in China (Lockhart) to the Secretary of State

PEIPING, November 5, 1938—4 p. m.
[Received 6 : 06 p. m.]

661. Embassy's 650, November 1, 9 a. m., and Nanking's 178, November 3, 2 p. m., and 176, November 2, 3 p. m.[6]

1. Wang Keh Min and other officials are due to return to Peiping from Nanking this morning following a visit yesterday to Shanghai. General Kita, who went with them to Nanking, is also scheduled to return.

According to several officials of the Provincial [*Provisional*] Government, the "National Conference" reported by Nanking as scheduled to be held next month in that city will have its counterpart in an assembly of "People's Delegates" here and perhaps other places. They state that out of these gatherings will probably issue invitations to the Mengchiang regime and new Canton and Hankow regimes to join the federation under the United Council. It is not, however, possible to predict the exact course such projected political developments will take, one reason being that they are experimental in nature and depend for their direction upon the outcome of rivalries among and maneuvers by concerned Japanese and Chinese. One informant states that Doihara [7] has returned here from Tokyo with approval for

---

[5] Edwin C. Wilson.
[6] None printed.
[7] Gen. Kenji Doihara.

his plan outlined in paragraph 2 of the Embassy's 650, November 1, 9 a. m., and if this proves to be true a recasting of governmental personnel and framework will result. Wang Keh Min is nevertheless expected to continue in some nominally important post because of the curious fact that although Kita and his other Japanese sponsors are reportedly tired of him because of his stubbornness, his elimination would mean a political defeat for them and victory for Doihara. As an example of Japanese difficulties with him, an officer of this Embassy has been informed by a Chinese official close to Wang that Generals Terauchi and Kita have for some time been trying to persuade Wang to sign a document "transferring" all North China railways to the Japanese in some form, such as an "indemnity" to the Japanese Government for war expenditures in this area or as a share in a development project in which nine-tenths of the ownership and control would be Japanese and a nominal [one?] tenth composed chiefly in financial returns would be Chinese. This Wang has refused to do and, although he must conform to most of their general and specific proposals in respect to the Government, he is known to quarrel with them constantly over details and over matters in which he sees some possibility of saving something for the Chinese.

3. Repeated to Chungking, Nanking, code text by mail to Shanghai, Tokyo.

LOCKHART

793.94119/453 : Telegram

The Ambassador in China (Johnson) to the Secretary of State

CHUNGKING, November 5, 1938—midnight.
[Received November 5—2: 11 p. m.]

530. Military Attaché[8] reports from Changsha that British Ambassador has arrived there reportedly with terms from Japanese alleged to be generous and which he believes to be effort by Japanese to discredit Generalissimo by having him reject them. He also reports that it is his estimate that Chinese can hold out possibly for 6 months, that Generalissimo believes Changsha-Nanchang front will hold for 2 months.

Repeated to Peiping, Shanghai.

JOHNSON

---

[8] Col. Joseph W. Stilwell.

793.94/14312 : Telegram

The Consul General at Hankow (Josselyn) to the Secretary of State

HANKOW, November 6, 1938—3 p. m.
[Received November 7—7 a. m.]

43. An informed Soviet Russian source states that the Chinese have ammunition sufficient for 6 months more of war on the present scale. Other foreign and Chinese estimates are about 8 months. Domestic production of rifle, mortar and machine gun ammunition and grenades will presumably augment the supply but only meagerly.

The same source gave the impression that no decisive assistance is to be expected from the Soviet Union. He anticipates Japanese occupation of Sian but declared with significant emphasis that any attempt to advance to Lanchow would cost the Japanese dearly.

Repeated to Chungking, Peiping, Shanghai.

JOSSELYN

793.94119/454 : Telegram

The Ambassador in China (Johnson) to the Secretary of State

CHUNGKING, November 7, 1938—noon.
[Received November 7—9 : 40 a. m.]

532. My 530, November 5, noon [midnight?]. Greenway, Secretary of the British Embassy, and Major Scott, Assistant British Military Attaché, in separate conversations on the evening of November 6 inquired of me, of Peck and of Captain Mattice [9] what information we had to peace party and peace movement among Chinese political leaders. They said that the British Ambassador has instructed them to investigate this subject. Without, of course, any previous consultation we each replied that we had not discovered any peace party or any professed advocates of compromise with Japan among Chinese political leaders. We did not deny the possibility that there might be advocates of a compromise.

Shanghai please repeat this and my message under reference to Tokyo.

Repeated to Shanghai and Peiping.

JOHNSON

[9] Capt. Earl Mattice, War Department language officer in China.

793.94/14317 : Telegram

The Chargé in France (Wilson) to the Secretary of State

Paris, November 7, 1938—7 p. m.
[Received November 7—6 : 21 p. m.]

1877. I handed Hoppenot [10] this afternoon a note containing the text of your statement to the press of November 4 (your 840, November 6, 4 p. m.[11]). He was much interested and expressed appreciation that this text had been communicated to the Foreign Office.

He referred to our conversation of November 3 regarding the Yangtze River question (my 1856, November 3, noon [12]) and stated that instructions in the sense indicated had in fact been cabled to the French Ambassador in Tokyo that same day. He expressed again the satisfaction of the Foreign Office at having been informed in advance of our contemplated action and stated that the French Ambassador in London had reported that the British Government was also greatly pleased at having been advised beforehand. The British also had instructed their Ambassador in Tokyo to take similar action.

Hoppenot said that the powers having interests in China were confronted today with a different situation from that which existed a year ago at the time of the Brussels Conference. Prior to the Brussels Conference the Japanese Government had given repeatedly assurances that it would respect the Open Door and the rights of other countries in China. The Brussels Conference therefore had considered the Far Eastern question more from the angle of what could be done to maintain the integrity of China than from the point of view of protection of their own rights in China. Today the situation is vastly different. Since Brussels, Japan has consistently acted contrary to her undertakings to respect the Open Door and now the statements made last week in Tokyo leave no doubt of the intention of the Japanese unless they are checked to create a new situation in the Far East at the expense of the rights and interests of other powers in that area. Hoppenot said that he believed that unless the United States, Great Britain, and France should take firm and concerted action to convince the Japanese that they will not accept such unilateral revision of their rights in China these three countries will find themselves in the early future completely frozen out of China.

I asked Hoppenot along what lines he was thinking [of] attempting action to convince the Japanese. He said that he was thinking about as follows: that the three powers mentioned should, at approximately the same time, let the Japanese Government know (secretly in order

---

[10] Chief of the Far Eastern Division, French Foreign Office.
[11] See telegram No. 379, November 4, 5 p. m., to the Ambassador in Japan, p. 368.
[12] Vol. iv, p. 196.

that the Japanese need not lose face) that they recognized that changes had taken place in China since July 1937 and that this fact would have to be taken into consideration in arriving at new agreements regarding the Far East. However, the recognition of changes in the situation in the Far East could not be imposed by Japan by unilateral action, and could only become effective upon agreement of the powers signatories to the Nine Power Treaty. Furthermore discussion of this question could not take place until the present conflict in China had come to an end whether this took 1 year or 2 years or longer, and of course a government representing China would have to be a party to the discussion. In the meanwhile the *status quo* regarding their rights in China must be maintained.

Hoppenot said that he believes that if something along the foregoing lines could be conveyed firmly and secretly by Great Britain, France, and the United States to Japan such action would prove effective. He believes that a move of this nature would strengthen the hands of Konoe, Arita and other civilian leaders.

As indicating that a firm stand with the Japanese proves effective, Hoppenot referred to the matter of the Japanese protest against alleged continuous passage of munitions over Indo-China (see my 1841, October 29, 1 p. m.). He said that the French reply to the Japanese Embassy had been made on November 4 and had been in strong terms refusing to take the Japanese protest into consideration. (Incidentally he stated that the Japanese had proposed the despatch of a Franco-Japanese commission to Indo-China to investigate the situation on the spot; the French Government had of course turned this down flatly.) Hoppenot then read me a Havas despatch just received from Tokyo stating that the Domei Agency had announced that the Japanese Government was now satisfied that there had been no appreciable traffic in arms across Indo-China and that the discussion with the French on this matter had taken place in a manner entirely satisfactory to Japan.

WILSON

793.94119/456 : Telegram

The Ambassador in China (Johnson) to the Secretary of State

CHUNGKING, November 8, 1938—noon.
[Received November 8—11 : 40 a. m.]

536. My 362, July 19, 3 p. m.,[13] and my 532, November 7, noon, in regard to military and political situation and present peace talk. Situation of National Government after loss of Hankow and Canton is of course most precarious. Best informed foreign military opinion

---

[13] *Ante*, p. 230.

is that Government cannot hope to continue organized resistance on any effective scale for more than 6 months and doubt is expressed concerning effectiveness of guerrilla activities. The Government cannot hope to renew supplies of munitions or gasoline in adequate amounts after present supplies are exhausted. However, I doubt whether there is a leader of the National Government who could at present come to terms with the Japanese on any basis satisfactory to the latter and command sufficient prestige to carry the people with him. Such a peace, if made, would leave the Japanese still under the necessity of continuing hostilities on a fairly large scale and over a fairly long period of time to disarm the people and restore order, so that conditions under such a peace would not differ from conditions as they are at present.

Repeated to Shanghai, Peiping.

JOHNSON

793.94/14406

President Roosevelt to Generalissimo Chiang Kai-shek [14]

WASHINGTON, November 10, 1938.

MY DEAR GENERAL CHIANG: I have received your cabled message of October 15 in which you bring to my attention the distressing circumstances and consequences of the conflict in China and make reference to certain discussions now proceeding in Washington.

For many years, I have, as you know, had a strong personal and official interest in China. My official interest dates from the time when I was Assistant Secretary of the Navy, and my personal interest, which far antedates my official interest, stems from both the early association of my forebears with the Far East and my long affection for the Chinese people. As President my interest has continued and during the past fifteen months the hardships and suffering of your countrymen have aroused my deep sympathy and their fortitude has inspired my admiration. The American people, I am sure, share my interest and my feelings of sympathy and admiration. These sentiments on our part have found expression in various types of effort toward alleviating the sufferings of the Chinese people, in support of principles which we believe should govern the efforts of every nation in its relations with all others, and in discouragement of practices not in harmony with those principles.

The friendly feeling of the Chinese people and the American people toward each other has been an important fact in international relations, and that friendly feeling prevails and is vigorous today.

---

[14] Transmitted by the Department to the Chinese Embassy on November 18.

With regard especially to the current conflict between China and Japan, the American Government has repeatedly voiced its objection to use of force in disregard of treaty rights and obligations and has contended that with peace there must be coupled law and justice. I am sure that you realize that, notwithstanding the strong sympathies of this country and our desire that peace with justice shall prevail in the Far East, action by the American Government must conform to methods which are consistent with this country's laws, with the current opinion of our people, and with our estimate of what is practicable.

With the views and considerations which I have briefly outlined above in mind, I can assure you that with regard to the discussions in Washington to which you refer, the matters brought forward are receiving most careful and sympathetic consideration, and furthermore that an early attainment of a just peace in the Far East is and will continue to be my earnest hope.

With kind personal regards [etc.]   FRANKLIN D. ROOSEVELT

793.94/14364 : Telegram

The Ambassador in China (Johnson) to the Secretary of State

CHUNGKING, November 16, 1938—10 a. m.
[Received 2 : 35 p. m.]

546. My 545, November 16, 9 a. m.[15]

"The Japanese occupied Canton with two motives in mind. The first is the effect of such occupation upon China, and the second is the effect upon Great Britain. To strike at China is of secondary importance while to strike at Great Britain is of major importance. By occupying Canton, Japan only cuts the Canton–Hankow Railway and blockades the waterways, impeding transportation and stopping supplies of munitions. Canton, too, is an important base for nautical resistance, and Japan hopes by its occupation to break down the morale of the Chinese. However, the cost of landing and maintaining her forces there will not be compensated by the above results alone. But in striking a death blow at Britain's historical prestige and traditional morale, she immeasurably enhances her own position and value. The present blow to Great Britain is not as great in effect as it will be in the future. Japan hopes that as Britain's power and prestige suffer in South China, hers will rise proportionately in the eyes of the Chinese and all Asiatic peoples.

Thus she hopes to occupy completely the historical place formerly enjoyed by Great Britain during the last hundred years as the dominant factor in Far Eastern affairs.

---

[15] This telegram stated: "I am sending you in a separate telegram an *aidemémoire* of conversation between Generalissimo and Sir Archibald Clark-Kerr on November 4." (793.94/14360)

By the successful occupation of Canton, Japan hopes that the old reliance of China upon Great Britain will now be abandoned in favor of Japan. Japan thinks that if she can break down British influence in South China she can break it down elsewhere. And the British Government and people may well ponder what the answer will be.

What I want to know is, 'what will be Great Britain's Far Eastern policy in view of this latest move on Japan's part?'

Will Great Britain view the occupation of Canton in the same light as they view the occupation of Manchuria, North China and Shanghai?

Moreover what will Great Britain do in view of these latest developments?

I would like to have a definite answer to this question.

In view of the fact that Great Britain's interests and prestige are threatened, will she quietly accept this *fait accompli* or will she demonstrate in no unmistakable terms her real intentions unequivocally, to safeguard her economic and political interests in the Far East, and above all to follow her historical policy of upholding high principles to which she has committed herself, or will she abandon these principles and sacrifice her standing?

China has been laboring lonehandedly for the past 16 months. We have looked to Great Britain and hoped for help, but up to the present we have received nothing tangible. We appreciate [the?] sending munitions through Hong Kong and upon a mutual[ly?] advantageous basis, but that avenue has now been closed.

As long as South China was not attacked we made allowances for Britain's hesitancy to extend practical aid to this Government, now that Japan has cut off British trade there is no reason why Britain should hesitate to extend help to us.

As time goes on our people and the Chinese Army will become more and more disappointed in view of the absolute lack of concrete and tangible evidence of British support. And the advantage is something which the Chinese Government will be constrained to take into account.

I would like to know whether Great Britain will adhere to her obligation as a member of League of Nations, live up to her [historic?] and traditional standards and extend economic or some other practical help to China?

I would like to have this answered in a definite 'yes' or 'no'.

For the past 16 months [we have been?] hearing a lot of eloquence about loans and in addition have been put off from time to time with excuses that loans were impossible because of Parliamentary complexities. But the whole world witnessed the granting almost overnight to Czechoslovakia of a loan similar in nature to that asked for by China.

Now the moment has come when we must have definite knowledge of Great Britain's intentions.

If Great Britain [should go back?] alike upon us and her principles, then I shall never bring up this question again. Nor shall I ever mention anything concerning Great Britain's Far Eastern policy. Nor shall I consult Great Britain as to China's future policy or attitude, or anything concerning the Far East.

I can hardly believe, however, that an Empire which produced such statesmen as Dodson [*Disraeli?*] and Gladstone could fail to see the significance of the repercussions of the occupation of Canton, and the inactivity of Great Britain upon her future in the whole of Asia.

This must be the life of [or?] the death turning point in British Far Eastern policy. Whether Britain extends aid to us or not, the British should realize that China today is unified as never before, and that we are determined to carry on prolonged resistance. Japan is unquestionably striving to have peace, on terms, however, not beneficial to Great Britain, and thus excluding her from Asiatic affairs, Japan would be willing to concede the gains she has acquired since hostilities began. If that question comes up, what is China's answer going to be?

If Japan wins the war, the old and outstanding interests of Great Britain in China will be finished.

We must know what Great Britain's answer is to be, because upon it depends the future policy of the Chinese Government. There are several roads open to us.

One thing that must be kept in view is that Japan, having occupied Canton, will probably occupy Hainan Island. What such a move will portend to Hong Kong can be left to the imagination.

In view of the importance of the questions raised in this conversation, will you kindly communicate immediately with the British Government and let me have a reply?"

Repeated to Shanghai. Shanghai repeat to Tokyo.

JOHNSON

793.94/14365 : Telegram

The Ambassador in China (Johnson) to the Secretary of State

CHUNGKING, November 16, 1938—11 a. m.

[Received 2 : 47 p. m.]

547. Reference my 546, November 16, 10 a. m. McHugh [16] arrived here on November 15 in company with the British Ambassador by car from Changsha where he was present during Clark-Kerr's conversation with Chiang Kai Shek on November 4 and 5. Clark-Kerr went to Changsha to see Chiang in response to a request made by the latter during their last meeting at Hankow late in July. He did not go, as was generally suggested in the press, to present Japanese peace proposals or to proffer Great Britain's good offices for a settlement of the present conflict.

McHugh had two very lengthy and frank conversations with Clark-Kerr at Changsha on November 6 and 8 as well as daily contact with Donald [17] during the entire period plus a family lunch with Chiang, Madame Chiang, and Donald on November 8. He is submitting a detailed written report covering these conversations which includes a verbatim copy of the *aide-mémoire* of the first conversation between

---

[16] Capt. J. M. McHugh, U. S. M. C., Assistant Naval Attaché in China.
[17] W. H. Donald, Australian adviser to Generalissimo Chiang Kai-shek.

Chiang Kai Shek and Clark-Kerr on November 4. This document which is quoted verbatim in my 546, November 16, 10 a. m. was made available to McHugh by Donald after the former had obtained permission from the British Ambassador to see it.

Clark-Kerr had expressed to McHugh a desire for a general talk the night he arrived. This took place at noon the day after the above meeting with Chiang but the arrival of other guests soon after the talk opened forestalled McHugh's intention to sound out Clark-Kerr on the details of his interview. McHugh learned from Donald on the following morning of the existence of the *aide-mémoire* and the general tone of its contents, but Donald stated he could not reveal it without Clark-Kerr's permission. McHugh then sought another interview with Clark-Kerr that afternoon when the latter spoke to appropriate authorities of the details of his conversation and gave permission for him to see the *aide-mémoire*.

McHugh gained the impression during this conversation as well as from the document itself plus his talks with Donald that Chiang Kai Shek had presented an ultimatum to London and he still believes that both Donald and Madame Chiang hold this viewpoint. During his second conversation with British Ambassador, however, which followed McHugh's lunch with Chiang, Clark-Kerr stated emphatically that Chiang had not made his statements in the form of a threat. Instead Chiang had asserted his desire to date signifies friendly relations with the democratic powers; that he had confidently expected that they, particularly Great Britain, were bound to come to the assistance of China; but that the time had now arrived when he had to have a specific statement of Britain's intentions as well as tangible evidence to present to the people of China at the forthcoming plenary session of the Kuomintang which is scheduled to take place in Chungking early in December. He suggested as an initial move on Britain's part a loan to support Chinese currency. The British Ambassador informed McHugh that he had sent a subsequent telegram himself to London after despatching the *aide-mémoire* to make clear that Chiang's statements had not conveyed any tone of belligerency or threat.

In his conversation on the 8th with Chiang Kai Shek, McHugh inquired specifically if he were to be permitted to infer that the statements made to the British Ambassador applied with equal force to the United States. Chiang after a moment's hesitation replied that he thought that question should await an opportunity for him to confer directly with the American Ambassador.

In talking with Madame Chiang and Donald later after luncheon, McHugh again inquired if the statement did not apply with equal force to the United States. Chiang replied: "At least, they should take them as the handwriting on the wall". McHugh then referred to the Generalissimo's statement that he had reason to believe that Japan would afford China very easy peace terms in return for an aboutface toward the British. McHugh inquired how this could be sold to the people of China who have been so generally aroused against Japan and asked if it could be brought about by inflammatory speeches on the part of Chinese officials against the British. He interpolated the suggestion that this appeared possible in view of the remarkable change in the attitude of the people towards foreigners today as with the latter part of the last decade.

Madame Chiang evaded the suggestion that public opinion in China could be aroused and directed from the top. She stated that she and the Generalissimo had worked very hard to bring about a favorable feeling toward foreigners. She added, however, that she believed the people would accept peace with Japan if the Generalissimo told them it was the best thing for China.

Donald informed McHugh later that the Generalissimo will attend the Kuomintang Congress at Chungking in December and that foreign policy for the coming year will be decided.

Chiang expressed his present firm determination both to Clark-Kerr and McHugh to carry on with resistance. He claims to have divisions available which he intends to dispose as follows: 60 east of the Peiping–Hankow–Canton Railway; 60 west thereof; and 60 in reserve under reorganization. He asserted that he expected to carry on active guerrilla warfare in the areas east of the railways; that although frontal resistance will be offered to the Japanese as they advance, it is not his intention to attempt to hold any place in force in the future, surrendering to them any large point they choose to attack. He thereby hopes to gain the offensive by placing the Japanese under constant threat of attack on all fronts, and claims he will choose his own ground for battle.

He again asserted that he has supplies sufficient to continue the war for another year at the present rate [of] consumption. He admitted that many of his best divisions were seriously depleted and that he did not expect to assume the offensive for some weeks yet. He is apparently prepared to surrender both Changsha and Hengyang to the Japanese if they choose to advance on those points in sufficient force. He obviously is imbued with the experience he had in chasing the Communists and intends to employ on a grand scale against the Japanese the tactics he learned from those campaigns. He appeared to have recovered from signs of the strain he exhibited during the latter days in Hankow and to be physically fit and confident. He exhibited no concern over the situation in the south; claimed that a counter-attack was already under way; and stated that Samshui had been reoccupied on the previous evening (November 7).

In response to a question about the situation in Szechwan, Madame Chiang scoffed at the idea that any threat to national unity existed there, pointing to the fact that the Generalissimo went there practically alone 4 years ago in the face of similar rumors and moved around at will. She added that he had even taken action against the opium traffic which was Liu Hsiang's chief source of revenue and asserted confidently that he could return again at will. Both she and Donald derided suggestions of a possible break up behind the front, insisting that Chiang controls the army through the younger officers which he educated and asserting that no leader, either civil or military, could possibly command sufficient force to question his authority.

Repeated to Shanghai. Shanghai please repeat to Tokyo.

JOHNSON

793.94/14362 : Telegram

The Ambassador in Japan (Grew) to the Secretary of State

TOKYO, November 16, 1938—10 p. m.
[Received November 16—12 : 15 p. m.]

734. 1. Although Ambassador Johnson has very likely reported on the recent conversations between Chiang Kai Shek and the British Ambassador to China, I nevertheless give the following brief summary as told me by Craigie who asked that it be communicated exclusively to the Department.

2. The Generalissimo seemed full of confidence with regard to the future proposed basis of the hostilities against Japan. He stated emphatically that the rapid fall of Canton had not been "bought" but was due to inefficiency and to the fact that expected British support had not been forthcoming. He said, however, that the fall both of Hankow and Canton had been foreseen and discounted and that China could continue the hostilities for another year.

3. Such continuance, however, would depend upon a currency loan from Great Britain or the United States or both.

4. If no such assistance is forthcoming, China will be obliged to seek other friends, namely, either (a) Soviet Russia or (b) Japan itself. He implied that if China eventually finds it necessary to throw in her lot with Japan, it will mean the future exclusion of all other foreign interests from China.

5. Craigie attaches importance to point (b) above in the light of the appeal broadcast by the Japanese Prime Minister to the Chinese nation referred to in paragraph 2 of our 728, November 15, 3 p. m.,[18] paragraph numbered 2.

No repetition.

GREW

---

[18] Not printed.

793.94/14367 : Telegram

The Ambassador in China (Johnson) to the Secretary of State

CHUNGKING, November 17, 1938—10 a. m.
[Received 7 : 18 p. m.]

550. During a short conversation November 16, 11 a. m., with Gen-eral Chang Chun, formerly Minister for Foreign Affairs and now Chiang Kai Shek's representative in Chungking, Peck inquired con-cerning the present state of the conflict with Japan and the following is a summary of his appraisal:

As a thorough student of Japanese institutions, informant did not think Japan financially capable of continuing present military ex-penditures indefinitely nor on the other hand is Japan financially exhausted. He thought the gold reserves of Japan probably amounted to not more than 300 million yen whereas military expenditures in the last 2 years had been between 10 and 20 billion but Japan has not exhausted such extreme measures of finance as nationalization of wealth and forced conversion of all Japanese foreign investments and further use of note reserves. He thought that restrictions on foreign trade had lowered the national income to a dangerous level. Japan's vulnerable point therefore is reached through foreign economic pres-sure. China's threefold need is for men, money and munitions. The supply of men is inexhaustible and given financial support and muni-tions China can fight indefinitely and is sure of ultimate victory. China has sufficient rifles and ammunition, hand grenades and such materials to last over an extended period but desperately needs other equipment in which it is lacking. Japan's aim in the present war is as much to eradicate foreign interests and influence in the Far East as to subjugate China. This fact as well as the repeated official expres-sions of sympathy and approval on the part of foreign powers leads China to regard foreign assistance in the struggle as logical and de-served. He thought an international conference say under the Nine-Power Treaty would afford an effective method of approach to the matter and recalled that the Chinese Government had suggested this.

China is not afraid to do the fighting but without money and munitions its advantage in man power is nullified. If foreign assist-ance were to be forthcoming, informant thought it would be neces-sary for the United States and Great Britain to take the initiative singly or jointly. He deplored apparent inability of these two coun-tries to work together in this crisis. France obviously feels great fear of Japan and is now refusing even to permit the disembarkation of non-military motor vehicles in Kwangchou while transportation of munitions over the Yunnan Railway is severely restricted. Inform-ant expressed no resentment against Germany or Italy but irritation at the failure of Great Britain to grant China a loan. He thought the plea of the British Government that Parliamentary approval of a loan would have to be obtained did not carry weight because Great Britain had granted to Czechoslovakia without any hesitation a loan similar to the one asked for by China and moreover the Government has a clear majority in Parliament. He expressed appreciation of the moral support given to China by the present administration in the United States and the hope that since the recent elections had left the administration with a strong majority in Congress this moral support might soon be accompanied by material support in the forms indicated. Informant said Japan's military man power is known exactly to the Chinese Government and is not inexhaustible but he emphasized that even with superior human resources China stood in great need of foreign aid in finances and munitions if victory against the attack on China and on European and American interests in China were to be assured. He asked that Peck report his observations and said he was to receive the British Ambassador the same morning and would make similar statements to him.

Repeated to Peiping, Shanghai. Latter repeat to Tokyo.

JOHNSON

793.94/14374 : Telegram

The Ambassador in China (Johnson) to the Secretary of State

CHUNGKING, November 18, 1938—9 a. m.
[Received 9: 10 p. m.]

553. Picture of Generalissimo in my 547 of November 16, 11 a. m. is of a man committed to a prolonged and bitter resistance to Japanese conquest with or without assistance from the outside; one who believes that in the end resistance will be successful and that he is not only fighting for the independence of his own people but that the success of his efforts will mean much in the future of those third powers who come to his aid now (and to that extent he is fighting their battles for if he loses he argues that Japan plans to monopolize all commercial opportunities to its own advantage). The Generalissimo reveals himself as a Protestant Chinese Nationalist, he desires assistance in his struggle, feels deeply that such aid is due him from the democratic nations, whose interests he identifies with China's, but will not accept aid with strings attached. Corroborative of this I recite the following. Donald told McHugh at Changsha that Russians had informed Chiang that they had 100 planes at Lanchow and were prepared to send more if he would continue resistance to the Japanese. Chiang retorted that he intended to continue resistance whether they

helped him or not. This appears to be the nearest their Government has come to presenting a *quid pro quo* to Chiang as both Donald and Madame Chiang have denied repeatedly to McHugh that Moscow has ever made specific proposals and have insisted that China has paid for all help received to date.

Please also refer to my 218, April 26, 2 p. m.,[19] when British Ambassador appears definitely to have dropped a hint that British financial help might be trending provided Generalissimo dropped Kung.[20] McHugh informs me that in conversation with British Ambassador on journey to Chungking latter stated that on one of his visits to Hankow, McHugh and I believe that (one) [*was?*] about the middle of July, the Generalissimo told Ambassador that he would be glad to receive and consider any advice which the British Ambassador might have to offer. Later Generalissimo asked the British Ambassador to visit him and asked him whether he had advice to give whereupon the Ambassador stated that if request was serious he would advise the Generalissimo to bring the Young Marshal [21] out of retirement; call all the Soong family [22] to Hankow; line them up there and present a solid front to Japan. He suggested that Kung be retained as President of the Executive Yuan (which he said he did to save Kung's face, but obviously implied that he would relieve Kung of financial responsibility), give Madame Sun Yat Sen a responsible place in the Government, suggesting a special post as Minister of Cooperation, and generally reorganize the Government along the representative lines used in selecting the delegates to the People's Political Council which had just met in Hankow. He advised Chiang specifically to award posts according to merit and to include all factions rather than to give the plums to his former comrades. British Ambassador stated Generalissimo received these suggestions coldly, commenting that Madame Sun would only be a mouthpiece for the Communists. He told McHugh he had met Madame Sun in Hong Kong; had liked her best of the whole family; and that she had expressed her desire to go to Hankow if invited.

It is my belief that this was an attempt by the Generalissimo to find out what might be considered necessary to put British Government in a mood to make loan available (he was already disappointed with outcome of Kung–Wang [23] efforts to obtain financial assistance in the

---

[19] *Ante,* p. 157.

[20] H. H. Kung, President of the Chinese Executive Yuan and Minister of Finance.

[21] Chang Hsueh-liang, who kidnapped Generalissimo Chiang Kai-shek in December 1936 at Sian and was detained thereafter.

[22] Madame H. H. Kung, Madame Sun Yat-sen, Madame Chiang Kai-shek, and their brother, T. V. Soong, former Minister of Finance.

[23] C. T. Wang, former Chinese Ambassador in the United States.

United States and had recalled Wang), and that the British Ambassador's reply was a second hint that financial assistance would be forthcoming from British sources provided Soong assisted by Rogers (of Bank of England) might have the management thereof and that a second time the Generalissimo refused assistance with strings attached.

It is my belief that the Generalissimo is convinced that the time has come when China, in dire need of compactness, must choose the source of such assistance, and that he has attempted to portray vividly to the British Ambassador the remonetizing or losses that will accrue to Great Britain as the result of its decision whether or not to assist China in time of need and thus determine the future direction of China's economic associations.

I understand that *aide-mémoire* quoted in my 545 [*546*], November 16, 9 [*10*] a. m., was sent to Hu Shih [24] with instructions not to show it until instructed.

Shanghai please repeat to Tokyo.

McHugh asks that substance of my 545, November 16, 9 a. m.,[25] and my 546, November 16, 11 [*10*] a. m., be made available to ONI.[26]

Repeated to Peiping, Shanghai; Shanghai repeat to Tokyo.

JOHNSON

793.94/14373 : Telegram

The Ambassador in Japan (Grew) to the Secretary of State

TOKYO, November 19, 1938—noon.
[Received November 19—8 : 15 a. m.]

741. Our 734, November 16, 10 p. m. In further conversation today with my British colleague I asked him whether he believed there was any truth in the rumors published in Japan that his Government was now considering a re-orientation of policy looking towards the development of Anglo-Japanese collaboration in China instead of further supporting the Chinese National Government. Craigie replied emphatically in the negative. I asked him whether he thought there was likelihood of a British loan to support the Chinese currency as proposed by Chiang Kai Shek to the British Ambassador. Craigie said he knew of no present concrete developments in that connection but that the present trend of thought in London leaned towards the building of the railway from Lashio in Burma into Yunnan and Szechuan which he thought would be financed by various members of the old consortium. He said that this was a long term policy and that while overt plans in that direction would at first cause a bitter

---

[24] Chinese Ambassador in the United States.
[25] See footnote 15, p. 377.
[26] Office of Naval Intelligence, Navy Department.

outcry from Japan the building of the railway would in due course give Great Britain, France and such powers as might participate an important leverage in their relations with Japan. He, however, told me in strict secrecy that from the purely strategic point of view a good many British military authorities are opposed to the construction of such a railway because in certain contingencies it might be captured by the Japanese and used for an invasion of Burma. Craigie believes, however, that some further concrete step in support of Chiang Kai Shek will soon have to be taken by Great Britain if they wish to avoid his being driven into the Japanese camp.

GREW

693.001/514

The Ambassador in China (Johnson) to the Secretary of State

No. 91   CHUNGKING, November 19, 1938.
                          [Received February 16, 1939.]

SIR: I have the honor to enclose, as of possible interest to the Department, a copy in translation of a leading article [27] appearing in the *Hsin Hua Jih Pao* on November 9, 1938, which endeavors to give an assessment of the Anglo-American position in China in the light of Prince Konoye's announcement of November 3. Briefly, this journal considers that Prince Konoye's announcement amounts to a negative reply to the American Government's note of October 6; that it constitutes a threat to American and British interests in the Far East; that the present situation has come about partly as a result of the compromise policy of the present British Government, which is compared unfavorably with what is described as the more positive though hampered policy of the American Government; that the gradual expansion of Japanese activity in the Pacific area will bring Japan into inevitable conflict with the United States and Great Britain; and that, therefore, it is only necessary for China to continue its resistance until such time as succor, produced of Japan's overweening ambition and pressure exerted by the people of the friendly Powers upon their government, arrives.

In this connection, the foregoing views are largely shared by the entire Chinese press of Chungking. Numerous articles have been published which stress the progressive encroachment of the Japanese upon American and European rights and interests in China; which speculate upon the nature of the reaction of the Powers concerned to these Japanese advances; and which urge upon the Powers vitally interested—principally the United States and Great Britain—the necessity of taking prompt and effective steps to safeguard their

---

[27] Not printed.

rights and interests in China, either by way of direct assistance to China or by the application of economic sanctions to Japan.

The *Hsin Hua Jih Pao*, as the Department is aware, is a daily newspaper of the Chinese Communist party, which commenced publication at Hankow in January 1938. Since the fall of Hankow, this newspaper has begun publication in Chungking.

It may be well briefly to discuss the policy of this newspaper. In internal affairs, its main consideration is the furthering of the "united front" which it holds to be essential for the final ousting of the Japanese from the Asiatic continent. In consequence, it gives the appearance of supporting the National Government, especially insofar as the prosecution of hostilities is concerned. It constantly praises the person and principles of Sun Yat Sen, professing to see in the latter the fundamentals for the regeneration of the Chinese nation along democratic lines. Through democracy, it hopes to achieve the Communist aim—a socialistic republic. At present, it warmly supports the leadership of General Chiang Kai-shek and is willing apparently to remain under his banner so long as he continues to resist Japan. While it harbors a strong suspicion against the Kuomintang, which it conceives to be following a policy of hampering the activities of the Communist party, "united front" considerations prevent it from adopting a critical attitude toward that political group. Its strongest attacks are directed toward so-called peace advocates, against whom the National Government is urged to take the most drastic measures. It continues to advocate suffrage, freedom of assembly, speech and press, and unrestricted political party activity.

In the sphere of foreign affairs, its basic policy is, of course, anti-Japanese and pro-Soviet Russian in the order named. Its thesis is that the Japanese invasion will overreach itself in western China and that prolonged resistance will in the end so exhaust the Japanese that the latter will be driven out of China and off the Asiatic continent. Prolonged resistance is expected to be maintained through the agency of the "united front" and the development of the mass movement and education among the population; negatively, it advocates steps to prevent the Japanese from utilizing the areas which the latter have occupied.

This organ maintains a policy of the utmost friendship toward the Soviet Union, hailing it as China's greatest friend and benefactor in a period of darkest trials and tribulations. News of the Soviet Union, copiously furnished by Tass News Agency, is accorded a premier place in the news columns; while no opportunity is lost to comment favorably upon the aims and policies of the Soviet Union. Its policy toward Great Britain and France has been friendly, though somewhat cool since the Munich agreement, which is held to have constituted a vital democratic concession to the Berlin–Rome–Tokyo axis. Its attitude toward the United States is studiously cordial, though it has complained about the sale of arms to Japan and the failure of the United States to take a more positive policy in the Far East. It is violently critical of Germany and Italy, holding them to be allies of Japan against China and the Soviet Union. In short, this newspaper pleads for a coalition of the democracies, including China and the Soviet Union, to curb what it terms the "Fascist group."

In the economic field, this organ calls for relief of the peasantry in the form of lower taxes, reduced rents, and reasonable rates of interest. In common with the Kuomintang, it calls for the development of the Northwest and the Southwest as economic bases for future resistance against Japan, and advocates improved communications. Though the Chinese Communist party undoubtedly wishes for the socialization of industry and the redistribution of land, the Communist newspaper has refrained from noticeable comment thereon.

It is believed that the views of the *Hsin Hua Jih Pao*, as described above, in general, represent the policy of the leaders of the Chinese Communist party today, a policy which appears to have as its basis the sinking of differences with the Kuomintang, at least temporarily, in order to establish a national unity that can avert Japanese domination of China and of the Chinese people.

Respectfully yours,   NELSON TRUSLER JOHNSON

793.94/14376 : Telegram

The Ambassador in China (Johnson) to the Secretary of State

CHUNGKING, November 20, 1938—10 a. m.
[Received November 21—1 : 30 p. m.]

557. My 553, November 18, 9 a. m. In response to his request I called upon the Chinese Minister of Foreign Affairs November 19, 4 p. m., and he told me that he wished to give me a summary of conversations that had recently taken place between the British Ambassador in Changsha about 10 days ago and General Chiang Kai Shek and between the British Ambassador and himself during the last 2 or 3 days following the arrival of Sir Archibald Clark-Kerr in Chungking. What follows is the substance of Dr. Wang's remarks.

Sir Archibald and the Generalissimo had two or three long conversations, but they might be reduced to this one point : China's situation had become so serious that it was essential for the Chinese Government to have a definite yes or no answer to the question whether Great Britain intended to continue its past attitude of inaction in reference to the Sino-Japanese conflict, or whether Great Britain intended to declare firm adherence to the Nine Power Treaty and other treaties bearing on the Far Eastern situation, to give China positive assistance in the form of a loan or otherwise, and to execute the League resolutions with reference to the conflict. General Chiang said that knowledge of Great Britain's intentions in regard to these matters was essential for the proper formulation of China's own foreign policies, especially in view of the meeting of the Executive Committee of the Kuomintang Party which would occur in Chungking in December, for at this time the Government must submit its policies for discussion. Dr. Wang said that General Chiang's remarks to Sir Archibald were not in any sense an ultimatum but rather an attempt to convey to the British Ambassador a sense of the crisis that had been reached and an earnest plea to Great Britain to act promptly on behalf of that country's own interests and in fulfillment of its announced position in relation to the matters enumerated. Dr. Wang observed that he had asked Sir Archibald whether he had communicated to his Government a report of the conversations with General Chiang and Sir Archibald replied that he had.

Dr. Wang said that he himself in view of Great Britain's great material interests in the Orient, possession of Hong Kong, Singapore and other colonial areas, its investment in China, et cetera, had conversed with Sir Archibald at length on these same subjects. Sir Archibald had also talked with Dr. Wang Ching Wei,[28] General Chang Chun and other leaders. Dr. Wang said that as in the earlier case he would not go into the details and ramifications of his conversations with the British Ambassador but would reduce them to as small a compass as possible; he had informed the British Ambassador (1) that China had reached a point where it was imperative for China to know in order to shape its present policy whether Great Britain would make a formal specific and public declaration maintaining their adherence to the Nine Power and other treaties on which the international situation in the Far East is based; (2) that it was imperative that Great Britain inform the Chinese Government at once and positively whether a loan would be granted to China; (3) that it was imperative also that the British Government indicate whether it is intended to take some measure of reprisal short of war against Japan in retaliation for the injuries inflicted by Japan on Great Britain's prestige, rights and interests in the Far East; and (4) that it was necessary that the British Government inform the Chinese Government whether it would take immediate steps to execute the various League resolutions in regard to the Sino-Japanese conflict including resort to article 16 of the League Covenant providing for sanctions against Japan.

---

[28] Deputy leader of the Kuomintang (Nationalist Party).

Dr. Wang said that these statements to the British Ambassador were neither a threat nor an ultimatum but merely set forth assurances that must be given and actions that must be taken by Great Britain if China were to frame its policy in the conflict intelligently. Of course, he said, it was the earnest hope of the Chinese Government that Great Britain would at once give the assurances and take the measures described above.

The Minister for Foreign Affairs further said that he had pointed out to the British Ambassador that the Chinese Government was surprised that while Great Britain and France had simultaneously with the United States sent strong representations to the Japanese Government protesting against the closing of the Yangtze to navigation, Great Britain had not addressed to the Japanese Government any communication similar to the note of the American Government of October 6th [29] protesting against violation of the Open Door policy; he observed to me that unless effective measures were taken at once no open door or closed would longer exist because Japan would be the only nation having any authority or opportunities in China.

Dr. Wang said that the policy of the Japanese Government in respect of China had recently undergone another drastic change; after months of dispute over the so-called "China bureau" the idea of creating such an organ had been dropped and there had been a "bureau of the new system in Asia", composed of the Ministers of War, Navy and Foreign Affairs and the Premier, a super Cabinet under direction of the army and navy to control the execution of Japan's "holy" policy toward not China alone but the whole of Asia. He added that public statements made by Japanese statesmen and private conversations held by himself with various of the highest Japanese leaders in Tokyo 3 years before proved that the "holy" policy of Japan was that of eradicating from the whole of Asia all Occidental interests and influence. He said that the then Japanese Minister of War had calculated that experts thoroughly understood China's aspiration to maintain its integrity and independence and would assist China to the fullest extent in achieving this, but on one condition, that is, that China cease to rely on the United States and Great Britain culturally, economically, or politically, [and] depend only on Japan. Dr. Wang asked that I regard this information as given to me in strict confidence.

Dr. Wang said that he had received through the Japanese Domei agency the Chinese translation of the complete text of the Japanese Government's reply [30] to the American protest of October 6th, and although he had not had time to read it he gathered that it rejected

---

[29] *Foreign Relations*, Japan, 1931–1941, vol. I, p. 785.
[30] Dated November 18, *ibid.*, p. 797.

practically all of the contentions made in the American note; he also referred to the fact that the Japanese replies [31] to the protests in regard to the continued closing of the Yangtze River to foreign navigation had rejected all the claims advanced by the powers; he wondered therefore what steps would be taken by the American Government in the face of this rebuff.

Dr. Wang said that he hoped that I would report to my Government the purport of his remarks, and that he most earnestly hoped that the United States would cooperate in this crisis.

I desire to add that Dr. Wang expressed no disappointment with the American attitude, actions, or failure to act in reference to the conflict but on the contrary said that he had plainly indicated to the British Ambassador the feeling of the Chinese Government that Great Britain had failed to afford the United States adequate support in the more advanced position we had taken on behalf of the established treaty position in the Far East. The Minister made it evident that Chiang and he are preparing to face a possible demand in the Executive Committee meeting for a reorientation of policy and to defend their course of relying for moral and material support on the Western Powers particularly the United States and Great Britain. In this connection I told the Minister that the position of the American Government toward the treaty situation and the present conflict has been made crystal clear in public statements including that of November 4 [32] and by our official actions all of which he might use in his address at the Committee meeting, but I added that no one would be able to forecast the future actions of the American Government in pursuance of its announced policy since these would be determined by circumstances.

Repeated to Shanghai and Peiping. Shanghai repeat to Tokyo.

JOHNSON

711.94/1229

Memorandum of Conversation, by the Military Attaché in Japan (Creswell) [33]

TOKYO, 22 November, 1938.

1. Colonel Nishi, head of the American Section of the General Staff, called this morning and spent something over an hour in discussing various phases of present American-Japanese relations. The gist of his remarks is as follows:

---

[31] See note of November 14, *Foreign Relations*, Japan, 1931–1941, vol. I, p. 795.
[32] *Ibid.*, p. 481.
[33] Copy transmitted to the Department by the Ambassador in Japan in his covering despatch No. 3500, December 2; received December 17.

a. The present dislocations to foreign and other trade are results of the necessities of a military situation in which, to use the Yangtze River as an example, the need for secrecy in the preparation and conduct of operations is such as to render it very unwise to permit circulation of individuals of other than Japanese nationality within the zones of the armies or along their lines of communication. In the past, operations have been frequently harmed through the activities of persons who had been permitted opportunities for observation in reporting their observations to the Chinese. The success of the military operations is so vital that they cannot afford to expose them to any hazards that can possibly be eliminated. The situation is one in which "they must go on", as any turning back would mean defeat, and every effort is being made to bring a quick end to present conditions in order that the work of rehabilitation may be started.

b. The earnest desire of the Japanese government is to bring about stable conditions in order that the pursuits of peace may be resumed. It has no desire to exclude any nation from the enjoyment of any trade or any benefits which can be derived from free competition. Under such conditions the Japanese have no fear for the economic future as there are many lines of endeavor in which they can compete successfully by reason of their advantages in proximity and in lower manufacturing costs, and that naturally, the losers in such competition will find the scope of their activities considerably curtailed. However, there is no desire to exclude activities in which the Japanese cannot compete as such action would only result in hampering the work of reestablishment. It is very likely that what has happened in Manchuria will be repeated in China; that certain forms of foreign trade will be eliminated as a result of Japanese competition but that, by reason of the betterment of conditions in general and the raising of Chinese purchasing power, the general total of foreign trade will be increased.

c. The present situation marks a turning point in American-Japanese relations, and it is hoped that the discussions may be carried on in a manner which will have a calming effect on the two peoples. It is likewise hoped that the United States will not be dragged into an adoption of the British attitude as a result of a combination of the present anti-Japanese feeling, new animosities engendered by the present problem, and a dislike for Nazi or Fascist ideas which are commonly represented as being rampant in Japan at present. The American antipathy to these doctrines is a natural one and resentment at efforts toward their propagation in the United States is understandable. Japan therefore, though neither Nazi nor Fascist, but finding points which it can admire in both, has carefully refrained from any attempt to spread any political doctrine in the United States.

d. American resentment at the present disturbance to trade is likewise entirely natural and thinking Japanese can have no objection on that score. However, it is felt that the present representations of the American Government may reflect an "economic fear", and that the Japanese Government is anxious to allay the suspicions growing out of such apprehension. In order to accomplish this end, it is important that both the Japanese and American peoples act with forbearance and an appreciation of each other's problems.

2. *Comment*

a. Colonel Nishi stated that he had come to the office in a private capacity in order to discuss these matters concerning which he is deeply concerned, and in order to present certain aspects of "military necessity" to an office accustomed to their demands.

b. Whether the visit was voluntary or directed by some higher authority cannot be determined. There can be no doubt however as to the seriousness with which Colonel Nishi presented his case, or the emphasis with which he stated that there is no thought of eliminating any foreign enterprise which can stand up under open competition. It is interesting to note that he brought up the same point regarding the increase of American trade in Manchuria as did the Foreign Minister in conversation with the Ambassador.[34]

c. As a soldier, Colonel Nishi is firmly of the opinion that the military situation must be settled before any great resumption of commercial activities can be accomplished. When it was suggested that some slight concessions in favor of foreign trade, and some relief from existing restrictions would go a long way toward bettering American opinion and removing causes for apprehension, he invariably returned to the contention that any freedom of movement by persons sympathetic toward the Chinese cause would constitute a grave hazard to the success of military activities.

d. The whole conversation may be summed up as a plea for understanding, a disclaimer of a desire to eliminate foreign interests, and an expression of the hope that the American people may find it possible to bear with the situation until the day when a resumption of normal conditions will operate toward a return of those trade conditions which all desire to see resumed.

HARRY I. T. CRESWELL
Lieut-Colonel Acting General Staff

---

[34] See memorandum of November 21, *Foreign Relations*, Japan, 1931–1941, vol. I, p. 806.

793.94119/469

Memorandum by the Ambassador in Japan (Grew)[35]

[TOKYO,] November 25, 1938.

My British colleague said to me today that a few weeks ago he had been told by "certain important sources" that if Great Britain would undertake mediation, the Japanese Government would be willing to consider peace with the Chinese Nationalist Government on three general conditions:

a. Withdrawal of Japanese troops from China.
b. Equal trade opportunity in China for all nations.
c. Discontinuance of all anti-Japanese activity and propaganda in China.

On the basis of this information Sir Robert Craigie called on Prince Konoye secretly on November 1 and said that if the information were correct, his Government would be willing to consider mediation on the aforesaid conditions on Japanese initiative. The Prime Minister replied that Japan did not at the present time desire such mediation.

At the end of this interview with the Prime Minister it was mutually agreed that if any publicity should occur, the Japanese Government would deny that Great Britain had offered mediation. The English interpreter, Mr. Tsuchiya, confirmed this understanding to the Ambassador.

A few days later, Mr. Shiratori[36] approached Sir Robert at the club and spoke of Great Britain's "offer of mediation" which Mr. Shiratori said was of course out of the question at the present time.

In a conversation day before yesterday with the Minister for Foreign Affairs, Mr. Arita mentioned the matter in the same vein. Sir Robert told him the facts and protested at the publicity recently given to this subject in *Yomiuri*.

Sir Robert thinks that Mr. Shiratori was probably the source of the publicity, having heard of the secret interview, but that Mr. Arita himself might have taken offense because, although Sir Robert's appointment with Prince Konoye was made on the evening before the announcement of Mr. Arita's appointment, the interview actually took place after Mr. Arita had assumed office.

---

[35] Copy transmitted to the Department by the Ambassador in his covering despatch No. 3493, December 2; received December 17.
[36] Toshio Shiratori, former Japanese Minister in Sweden.

862.42794/2 : Telegram

The Ambassador in Japan (Grew) to the Secretary of State

TOKYO, November 26, 1938—noon.
[Received November 26—2:45 a. m.]

751. 1. A cultural convention between Japan and Germany was signed at Tokyo on November 25 (second anniversary of the Anti-Comintern Pact) by the Minister for Foreign Affairs and the German Ambassador.[37]   It consists of a preamble in which the contracting parties express intention to strengthen "bonds of friendship and mutual confidence" by "deepening their manifold cultural relations" and of four articles which in effect provide for promotion of relations in the fields of "science and fine arts, music and literature, youth movements, sports et cetera.["]

2. The convention probably carried no secret clauses but it is obviously a significant indication of the trend toward closer political association of Japan and Germany and a part of program of preparation to move, *pari passu* with closer association with each other of Great Britain and France toward a definite Japanese-German political arrangement.

3. My British colleague tells me that he has "absolutely reliable" information that negotiations are now proceeding for a marked strengthening of the German-Italian-Japanese Axis but that Italy is showing some reluctance. Craigie regrets that he cannot give me the source but said that he is sworn to secrecy.

GREW

741.94/225 : Telegram

The Ambassador in Japan (Grew) to the Secretary of State

TOKYO, November 26, 1938—3 p. m.
[Received November 27—7 a. m.]

752. The local press has recently carried reports to the effect that the Japanese Ambassador in London had persuaded the British Government of the advantage of cooperation with Japan in the Far East.

In this connection my British colleague showed me this morning a telegram from his Government stating that no such message has in any way been inspired by any official or any department in London. Shigemitsu [38] has recently held conversations with Sir H. Wilson [39] and with Leith-Ross [40] and it is believed that he subsequently made some communication to the London representative of Domei.   The

----

[37] See *Documents on German Foreign Policy, 1918–1945*, ser. D, vol. IV, pp. 680 ff.
[38] Japanese Ambassador in the United Kingdom.
[39] Chief industrial adviser to the British Government.
[40] Chief economic adviser to the British Government.

British Government would not be surprised if reports of this nature voice a number of hopes whether justifiedly or not which get into the Japanese press transformed into statements of fact. The British Government adds that the American Government and myself may rest assured that the British Government has no intention of being inveigled into negotiations for a deal with Japan inimical to the rights or interest of China or of any other third party.

GREW

793.94/14429 : Telegram

The Ambassador in Japan (Grew) to the Secretary of State

TOKYO, November 29, 1938—5 p. m.
[Received November 29—7 : 10 a. m.]

755. 1. The following statement was issued last night by the Cabinet.

"The Cabinet this afternoon decided on its fundamental policy for regulating Sino-Japanese relations in connection with the construction of a new order in East Asia which the Five Minister Conference has been considering."

2. We have been unable to obtain any authoritative or otherwise reliable indication of the nature of this "fundamental policy", and as we understand that general indications of the character of this policy are to be given out in the next few days, we believe that an appraisal of various conjectures now current would not be helpful to the Department. We learn, however, from a reliable source that the policy is to be discussed in a conference to be held shortly in the presence of the Emperor which if true is an indication of the significance of the policy (see our 28, January 14, 5 p. m.[41]).

Repeated to Shanghai for Chungking.

GREW

893.00/14288

The Ambassador in China (Johnson) to the Secretary of State

No. 95
CHUNGKING, November 29, 1938.
[Received December 23.]

SIR: I have the honor to transmit, as of possible interest to the Department, a digest [42] of the text of the resolutions said to have been adopted at the Enlarged Sixth Plenary Session of the Central Executive Committee of the Chinese Communist Party, which was held at Yenan, Shensi, with practically all the important leaders of the Party in attendance, in late September and early October of this

[41] *Ante*, p. 22.
[42] Not printed.

year. These resolutions were published in the November 23 edition of the *Hsin Hua Jih Pao*, the official newspaper of the Chinese Communist Party which is now established at Chungking.

The importance of these resolutions is believed to lie in the fact that they appear to commit the Chinese Communist Party categorically to a vital compromise of political policy vis-a-vis the Kuomintang. In other words, the Chinese Communist Party has come to the conclusion that the vital task of today lies in the defeat of the Japanese, and they have accordingly committed themselves to an almost complete reorientation of policy in order to achieve the united front which they consider to be essential to the achievement of the final victory. It is essential to note, however, that they maintain the right to preserve their independent political organization—a fundamental tenet of that group; and that their ultimate aspiration is a San Min Chu I democracy, under which the Chinese Communist Party will be enabled to pursue an independent, free existence without let or hindrance.

Competent Chinese and foreign observers at Chungking are generally of the opinion that the resolutions, as set forth above, genuinely reflect the present day attitude of the Chinese Communist leaders, who are sincerely desirous, even at the expense of fundamental principles, of cooperating with other anti-Japanese elements in the task of expelling the Japanese from Chinese territory.

In the interest of timeliness, this despatch is being sent to the Department by airmail. A complete translation of the resolutions is in the course of preparation and will be forwarded at an early date.

Respectfully yours, NELSON TRUSLER JOHNSON

893.05/412

The Chinese Ministry for Foreign Affairs to the American Embassy in China [43]

[Translation]

[CHUNGKING,] November 29, 1938.

The Ministry of Foreign Affairs presents its compliments to the American Embassy and, with reference to the forcible attempts of Japan to seize the various Chinese courts in the concession areas at Shanghai, has the honor to recall that the Ministry has repeatedly discussed the matter with His Excellency Nelson Trusler Johnson, American Ambassador, as well as having detailed officials to proceed to the Embassy to conduct negotiations. The request to adopt a stern

---

[43] Copy transmitted to the Department by the Embassy in China apparently without covering despatch; received March 2, 1939.

attitude firmly rejecting Japanese interference has already aroused the attention of the American Embassy.

The establishment of the Chinese courts in question and the exercise of their functions are based upon international agreements signed by the various powers concerned; they possess an intimate relation to the peace of the concessions. Once they are seized by Japan, not only will Chinese citizens in the concessions be exposed to danger, but also foreign nationals without extraterritorial rights and even foreigners with extraterritorial rights, will be greatly threatened; in fact, this would amount to control of the whole of the concessions and cannot be regarded with indifference.

A confidential report has recently been received to the effect that Japan's attempts forcibly to seize the various Chinese courts in the concessions at Shanghai have been more intensified, and there is talk that it will open Hongkew as a *quid pro quo* for the taking over of the courts. If this information is true, it is thought that the various parties affected will be able to foresee the consequences. The Ministry has the honor, therefore, especially to request that the American Embassy take note of the matter and that it continue to adhere to its previous policy in relation to the Chinese courts of exhausting all efforts for their protection; that is, that it firmly reject Japan's illegal interference, in order to uphold international agreements. The Ministry is appreciative of the Embassy's friendliness in the matter.

SEAL OF THE MINISTRY OF FOREIGN
AFFAIRS OF THE REPUBLIC OF CHINA

793.94/14433 : Telegram

The Ambassador in Japan (Grew) to the Secretary of State

TOKYO, November 30, 1938—3 p. m.
[Received November 30—7 : 05 a. m.]

757. Our 756, November 30, noon.[44] Yoshizawa, who is the informant referred to in our 755 [45] and 756, has just telephoned to say that a conference in the presence of the Emperor of five Cabinet Ministers and officers of Imperial Headquarters on the new Japanese policy did take place today. (The fact that a high official of the Foreign Office did not have direct prior knowledge of this important event is indicative of the secrecy with which the plan for the holding of this conference was carried.) He added that a public announcement with regard to the new policy would be issued shortly.

Repeated to Shanghai for Chungking.

GREW

---

[44] Not printed.
[45] Dated November 29, 5 p. m., p. 397.

893.51/6730 : Telegram

The Ambassador in Japan (Grew) to the Secretary of State [46]

TOKYO, December 1, 1938—8 p. m.
[Received December 1—5:25 p. m.]

760–762. 1. As a result of the recent modification in policy announced by the Japanese Government and also as a result of the recent conversations between Chiang Kai Shek and the British Ambassador in China, my British colleague and I have had several informal talks by way of endeavoring to appraise the new situation. We are agreed on the following points:

(*a*) If any assistance is to be given by our respective Governments to Chiang Kai Shek there is little time to be lost if the assistance is to be effective.

(*b*) There is every indication that the discrimination against foreign interests in China will be continuous and progressive.

(*c*) Japan is under the governance of the military elements and the trend toward some authoritarian government is becoming progressively more pronounced. The restraining influence of the civilian and liberal elements has become so feeble that it may be entirely eliminated from our calculations.

(*d*) There is in process a strengthening of the anti-Comintern feeling. (Craigie is convinced that the further agreement which is in view between Germany, Italy and Japan can only be designed to strengthen political and possibly military ties and will be directed more against the democratic powers than against Soviet Russia. My feeling is that Germany and Japan and Italy if they can bring her along intend to keep step with any further strengthening of the ties between Great Britain and France.)

(*e*) Although there are indications that the hostilities are exerting a progressive strain on Japan's economic structure, reliance on this factor alone to bring about moderation of Japanese policies would be illusory.

2. Craigie further feels that, although the impact of a strengthened totalitarian combination would first fall on British interests in the Far East, it would only be a question of time before the "vital interests" of the United States also became affected. He is convinced further that the hardening of the Japanese attitude is due not only to recent military victories but to the conviction in military and naval circles that the democracies are not prepared to risk war under any circumstance. My position on these two points is that they are matters of opinion or of impressions and do not fall within the realm of demonstrable fact.

3. Craigie proposed that we jointly recommend to our respective Governments that there is little to be lost—and much may be gained—

---

[46] The three sections of this message, transmitted as telegrams Nos. 760–762, are printed as one document.

from resolute action taken jointly by the United States and the British Empire (preferably with French cooperation) to maintain our position, rights and interests in the Far East. The measures which he proposed for recommendation to our Governments were: (a) joint currency loan to China; (b) denunciation of respective treaties of commerce with Japan with a clear indication of the reasons for this step; (c) raising of the French embargo on the passage of munitions through Indochina.

4. I have told Craigie that after very carefully and thoroughly considering the problem for several days I am not able to conform to his suggested recommendations.

5. I said first that my Government is in possession, from many sources, of all available facts upon which to formulate and carry out its policies and actions and furthermore that it is in a far better position than I am to estimate the desires and restraints of American public opinion. These factors alone would deter me from making such a recommendation as he proposed even if I believed in the wisdom and efficacy of retaliatory measures.

6. As a matter of fact, however, I expressed to Craigie my belief that in the present temper of the Japanese Government, of the Japanese military and of a preponderant element of the Japanese public, such sanctions as he lists would defeat their own object and would simply result in making the Japanese more intransigent than ever against the interests of the participating nations. I could not estimate the practical effect of loans to the Chinese nationalists but any practical effects accruing from the denunciation of our respective commercial treaties with Japan would take a long time to register. I expressed doubts over the soundness of Craigie's belief that concerted action by the three powers along the lines he had suggested would lead to a satisfactory reorientation of Japanese policies. I admitted that he might be right but on the other hand I could not bring myself to believe that our Governments can afford to discount completely the statements which Arita has made to both of us that the primary objective of Japan in bringing about "the new situation" in the Far East [47] is to place herself in a position successfully to resist external pressure exerted through economic measures. It would seem to me extremely hazardous to assume that the program which Japan is carrying out at such enormous costs would be allowed to collapse upon there being brought about precisely that situation which the program was intended to meet.

7. I told Craigie that ever since the hostilities in China began I had endeavored to render maximum protection to American interests but

---

[47] Cf. memorandum of November 19, *Foreign Relations*, Japan, 1931–1941, vol. I, pp. 801, 804.

at the same time to avoid recommendations or action which in my opinion would steer the United States into dangerous channels which American public opinion would not countenance. In all conscience therefore I found myself unable to go along with him in the recommendations which he proposed.

8. I then talked frankly of the marked difference in the respective positions of the United States and Great Britain in the Far East. I pointed out that the United States and Great Britain have common interests and concern in the broad field of influencing of policy such as the Open Door and that in the specific field of Far Eastern politics they oppose violation of the territorial and administrative integrity of China. They furthermore have a common interest in specific issues which have been created in China in violation of the above mentioned principles. There are, however, other political and economic considerations which do not affect the two countries in equal degree, and it seemed to me that such defensive measures as Great Britain might consider necessary to protect British interests might not necessarily commend themselves to the United States.

9. Craigie replied that he fully recognized the justice of my position and that he did not wish to press me unduly. He said that it is only his deep sense of the gravity of impending events and his feeling that there is now no time to be lost that led him to put forward his suggestions.

10. The Department will undoubtedly recognize the fact that Craigie's complete frankness with me called for equal frankness on my part and that in my personal observations to him I was in no manner committing my own Government.

No repetition.

GREW

711.94/1228

The Ambassador in Japan (Grew) to the Secretary of State

No. 3496　　　　　　　　　　　　　　　Токуо, December 2, 1938.
　　　　　　　　　　　　　　　　　　　　　[Received December 17.]

SIR: I have the honor to report that, prior to his departure on November 29 to assume his duties as Ambassador at Washington to replace Mr. Saito, Mr. Kensuke Horinouchi delivered an address before the America–Japan Society of the Kwansai at Osaka on November 18, and also before the America–Japan Society in Tokyo on November 22.

There are transmitted herewith [48] a clipping from the *Japan Chronicle* of November 19 and a clipping from the *Japan Advertiser*

---

[48] Enclosures not reprinted.

of November 23 in which are published Mr. Horinouchi's addresses. As may be expected the two speeches are very similar, with only such changes as were demanded by the locality in which the Ambassador-designate spoke. It is, however, significant that on both occasions he made reference to the "new order in East Asia" for which Japan is striving, based upon cultural and economic "coordination between Japan, Manchukuo and China". This is, of course, recognizable as Mr. Arita's "Japan–Manchukuo–China bloc" to which he has recently made reference in conversations with my British colleague and myself.* Thus it may be expected that Mr. Horinouchi goes to Washington as a proponent of the "New Policy", involving modification of the open door and equality of opportunity in China and the scrapping of the Nine Power Treaty.

Respectfully yours,   JOSEPH C. GREW

762.94/264

The Ambassador in Japan (Grew) to the Secretary of State

No. 3502   TOKYO, December 2, 1938.
                                              [Received December 17.]

SIR: There has recently been a marked renewal of activities along the lines of the Berlin–Rome–Tokyo axis and evidence of a strengthening of the relations between Japan and the states with totalitarian or authoritarian forms of government—Soviet Russia always excepted. These activities are, of course, somewhat seasonal, as the month of November marks the anniversaries of the anti-comintern pacts with Germany and with Italy, but this fact alone would not account for Japan's increasingly strong swing toward those and other non-democratic states.

Celebrations here began on November 6, which marked the first anniversary of the Italo-German-Japanese anti-comintern pact, and ended on November 25, the second anniversary of the conclusion of the German-Japanese anti-comintern pact, with the signature, in Tokyo, of a cultural convention with Germany. This pact, which is similar to one signed at Rome on November 23 between Germany and Italy, consists of a preamble in which the contracting parties express the intention to strengthen "bonds of friendship and mutual confidence" by "deepening their manifold cultural relations", and of four articles which in effect provide for the promotion of relations in the fields of "science and fine arts, music and literature, youth movements, sports,

---

*Embassy's telegrams No. 744, November 18 [*19*], 8 p. m., and No. 759, December 1, 3 p. m. [Footnote in the original; telegrams printed in vol. IV, pp. 93 and 98.]

et cetera". The text of the convention, together with the Foreign Office's statement accompanying its publication, as it appeared in the *Japan Advertiser* of November 26, is enclosed.[49]

This convention probably carries no secret clauses but, as remarked in the press (*Nichi-Nichi* of November 25, 1938), "necessarily pushes the anti-comintern pact another step forward". As stated in the Embassy's telegram reporting its signature,* the convention is obviously a significant indication of the trend toward a closer political association of Japan and Germany and a part of a program to move, *pari passu* with each other of Great Britain and France, toward a definite Japanese-German political arrangement.

Since the fall of Canton and the Wuhan cities and the advent of Mr. Arita as Foreign Minister it has become evident that Japan's policy and attitude toward the United States, Great Britain, and France with respect to their rights and interests in China have undergone a marked change. Whereas, up to that time, at least the fiction of support of the Nine Power Treaty, the Open Door, and the principle of equality of treatment was maintained by Japan, this has since been dispelled through the adoption by Japan of a policy of creating "a new order in East Asia" which involves the establishment of a Japan–China–"Manchukuo" bloc and a demand for a modification of the principles of the Open Door and equality of opportunity in China. This reorientation in policy toward the powers with interests in China is part and parcel of Japan's broader policy of attempting to create in East Asia a Japan-dominated self-contained economic and political entity similar to the United States, Russia, or the British Empire. It is now the intention of Japan, as revealed by the Foreign Minister in a recent strictly confidential conversation,† to place itself in a position of security against the possible application of sanctions either by the League of Nations or "by nations inside and outside the League". Adherence to such a policy would logically tend to find Japan on one side and those powers having interests in China, that is, the United States, Great Britain, and France, on the other side. Furthermore, to the extent to which these three countries, which are incidentally the leading democracies, draw closer to one another—not only in respect of East Asia but in other fields, notably Europe—to the same degree is Japan induced to draw closer to the countries opposed to the democracies, namely Italy and Germany, whose interests in China are, incidentally, negligible. Italy and Germany, too, are outside the League of Nations, along with Japan; and those two countries, with

---

[49] Not reprinted.
*Embassy's telegram No. 751, November 26, noon. [Footnote in the original.]
†Embassy's telegram No. 744, November 16 [*19*], 3 [8] p. m. [Footnote in the original; telegram printed in vol. IV, p. 93.]

their strong navies and air forces, are becoming more and more potentially valuable to Japan as the risk of pressure from Great Britain and France in the East increases with Japan's announced policy of demanding a revision of the principles which have hitherto provided a measure of protection for foreign rights and interests in China.

It is interesting to note how greatly developments in Europe have favored Japan and how recent events there have drawn Japan into what is becoming the anti-democratic camp. While it is true that the Berlin–Rome–Tokyo axis was founded upon a common anti-communist ideology, and that it outwardly retains the anti-comintern form, events of world importance, based upon a fundamental cleavage in thought between those countries whose interests lie in the direction of maintaining the post-war *status quo* and those in whose interests it is to alter it, have aligned the anti-comintern states against the democracies. In the Far East it is the democracies whose interests are being threatened in China by Japan. In Europe it is the democracies whose interests have been and are being threatened by Germany and Italy. The Czechoslovak crisis thus provided an ideal moment for the powers who control the destinies of Japan to launch, simultaneously with the establishment of a China Board, a new policy which is developing into a virtual protectorate over all of China with the continued existence, to say nothing of the protection, of the rights and interests of the foreign powers in that area in the hands of the Japanese military. The results of the Munich Conference were interpreted by Japan as an admission by the democratic states of their inability to match the strength of the Berlin-Rome axis, and this gave further impetus to the policy of strengthening Japan's ties with that axis.

Still another factor in this policy is the growing sympathy on the part of Japan with the nations in Europe having authoritarian forms of Government. The China incident has hastened the establishment of the virtually unchallenged supremacy of the military in the government of Japan. Those liberal or civilian elements whose influence may have been felt, at least beneath the surface of things, prior to the outbreak of the hostilities with China, are today reduced to utter impotence, and something closely approaching an authoritarian form of government under the shogunate of the military may be said to have arrived.

Japan's gravitation toward the circle of authoritarian states has for some time been manifest. It will be recalled that in 1936 a cultural pact was signed between Japan and Poland; this closely followed the signature of the anti-comintern pact with Germany and was Japan's second step toward emerging from its political isolation and a bid for solidarity with a country whose policy was anti-Soviet. It is also interesting to note that Poland's form of government then, as now, closely approached the authoritarian form.

It may be added parenthetically that the news that Poland had, on November 26, suddenly decided to extend her non-aggression pact of 1932 with Soviet Russia until 1945, was badly received by the press here and this action was interpreted as Poland's withdrawal from the anti-comintern bloc. In fact, so much stir was caused in the editorial columns of the local newspapers that the Polish Ambassador, Mr. Thaddeus de Romer, called upon the Vice Minister for Foreign Affairs on the following day to reassure him that Poland's action was not to be construed as prejudicial to the friendly relations with Japan.

On November 15 a cultural pact was concluded between Japan and Hungary, another state verging on the authoritarian. This pact, incidently, is reported to take effect upon the same day as the pact with Germany, on November 25.

Japan's association, in varying degrees of intimacy, with the authoritarian states is therefore apparent; this is due somewhat to her sympathy for that particular ideology. The fact, however, that those states, each in its own way, shares some of Japan's own problems is of course the real reason behind this association. Germany and Italy have no axe to grind in the East; they are, moreover, opposed in Europe by the same powers, England and France, as, with the addition of the United States, are opposed by Japan in China. Thus Germany, Italy, and Japan, who were originally drawn together by the common denominator of anti-communism, are now being bound more closely by their common opposition to the so-called democratic states, and this process will probably continue until something occurs in the political field to reverse the circle now in operation. Such a move might, for instance, be a successful attempt on the part of Great Britain to wean Italy away from the Berlin–Rome axis. At this point, however, we enter the realm of pure speculation.

Respectfully yours,   JOSEPH C. GREW

711.94/1234½

Memorandum Prepared in the Department of State [50]

[WASHINGTON,] December 5, 1938.

Diplomatic representations to Japan have not caused Japan to respect American rights and interests in China. Japan continues to injure those rights and interests. In view of this, it is suggested in various quarters that the United States should supplement its diplo-

---

[50] The memorandum was requested by the Under Secretary of State and submitted to him by Assistant Secretary of State Sayre, together with the memorandum of December 22, p. 425.

matic representations by embarking on a course of retaliatory measures against Japan.

Any action along this line, if taken, should be based, it is believed, upon the principle of taking measures of self-defense against a country which is causing serious injury to American rights and interests, and be not based upon the principle of taking punitive action against an aggressor nation.

It may be helpful in determining the advisability and practicability of embarking upon a course of retaliation to list possible steps which the United States might take. Such a list follows, with comment in regard to each such possible step.

[Here follow sections on "Executive action," "Cessation of gold purchases from Japan," "Embargo on credit," "Place Japan upon the 'black list'," "Give notice of termination of our commercial treaty of 1911 with Japan," "Revision and subsequent application of section 338 of the Tariff Act," "Embargoes on exports and imports," "Exchange control," and "Imposition of special duties against Japanese ships".]

CONCLUSION

Mr. Sayre, Mr. Hawkins, Mr. Livesey and Mr. Hamilton [51] have collaborated in the preparation of this memorandum.

They believe that a comprehensive and thoroughgoing program of retaliation is not desirable at this time.

Their reasons for this conclusion are:

(1) Such a program of retaliation would involve serious risk of armed conflict. Neither our interests in the Far East nor the effect of current events in the Far East upon our general world interests seems to warrant incurring such a risk.

(2) The embarkation by this Government upon such a program would be followed necessarily by widespread domestic economic dislocation and also would involve the risk of overthrowing the principles of commercial policy to which this Government is committed. The latter would be particularly true in the case of the adoption of some form of exchange control.

(3) They believe the whole-hearted international cooperation, especially on the part of the British Empire, would be necessary to accomplish the objectives in mind, and they do not believe that close and thoroughgoing European cooperation can be secured.

The views set forth above represent conclusions as to the subject of commercial retaliation as a whole. It is believed, however, that our choice of a course of action need not necessarily be confined to the alternatives of a complete and effective program of retaliation or no

---

[51] Respectively Assistant Secretary of State, Chief of the Division of Trade Agreements, Assistant Adviser on International Economic Affairs, and Chief of the Division of Far Eastern Affairs.

action at all. It is suggested that this Government might advisedly consider adopting certain intermediate steps which would undoubtedly be taken seriously by the Japanese and possibly have a sobering effect upon the Japanese, although such steps could not be expected to cause Japan to desist from its program of aggression in China. The measures under reference are governmental action in discouragement of loans or credits to Japan and, if the problem discussed in the last paragraph of Section 5* can be satisfactorily disposed of, the giving of notice of termination of our commercial treaty with Japan. It is believed that these measures might not lead to retaliation by Japan. These measures would seem to be in a category entirely different from direct retaliatory measures such as the restriction or exclusion of Japanese trade, restrictions upon the exportation of certain commodities to Japan, etc. Restrictions upon trade with Japan affect the personal fortunes of firms and individuals in Japan and therefore create a solid basis for national resentment of the type which leads to counter-retaliation. The two measures mentioned, however, affect no interest immediately, are not unfriendly acts, and do not put this country in a position from which it must advance (but at the same time they would serve to clear our decks). Although there is little likelihood that American funds will be invested in Japan in the near future, the time may come when Japan will become more attractive as an investment field. Unless there is some settlement in the Far East based on the principles in which this Government believes, the Department could not view with equanimity the investment of American funds in Japan or Japanese-controlled areas. It seems preferable that a Government policy of discouraging loans or credits be announced while there is no substantial objection to it. A ban on loans and credits could be defended from either the isolationists' or internationalists' point of view. In regard to the cancellation of the commercial treaty, Japan is traveling rapidly along the road marked out by Germany, and Japan's commercial methods are becoming so alien to those of the United States that the United States can hardly avoid denouncing the commercial treaty with Japan before another year or two has elapsed, and denunciation before that time might well be considered.

It is believed that announcement of a Government policy of discouraging loans or credits to Japan and the giving of notice to Japan with regard to termination of the commercial treaty are measures warranting favorable consideration. No definite recommendation is made as to whether either or both of these measures should be adopted immediately or at some given time in the future for the reason that it

---

*Note: Arranging for some satisfactory method of continuing to admit Japanese merchants to this country. [Footnote in the original.]

is considered important that decision with regard to adoption of the measures be correlated with consideration of other matters, both domestic and external, affecting our relations with Japan.

It is suggested, further, that endeavor might well be made at this time to obtain revision of Section 338 of the Tariff Act of 1930 [52] along the lines indicated in section numbered 5. The question whether the revised section should be applied against Japan need not be decided at this time.

The study made of the retaliatory steps which the United States might take against Japan has brought to mind the question of the advisability of the United States extending aid to China. Although no detailed study has been given to that question by those collaborating in the preparation of this memorandum, it seems to them that the extending of aid to China would not be likely to involve complications as serious as those which would result should the United States adopt a thorough-going and comprehensive program of retaliation against Japan. The granting of aid to China would not cause widespread domestic economic dislocation in this country and would not involve the risk of overthrowing the principles of commercial policy to which this Government is committed. Moreover, it is believed that, although Japan would undoubtedly resent the extension of aid by the United States to the Chinese Government, Japan's resentment would not be likely to express itself in as drastic a form as would be the case should the United States adopt a comprehensive program of retaliation against Japan. It is realized, however, that embarkation by the United States upon a definite course of extending aid to the Chinese Government involves important questions of policy (such as the question of the advisability of deviating from the course hitherto pursued by the United States of not taking sides in a material way in the conflict between China and Japan, the question whether congressional authority would be needed, the question whether Congress and the country would support such a course, etc.). An examination of these questions of policy is outside the purview of this memorandum.

740.00/524½

The Under Secretary of State (Welles) to President Roosevelt [53]

WASHINGTON, December 5, 1938.

MY DEAR MR. PRESIDENT: In one of the last conversations I had with Sir Ronald Lindsay before he left on his vacation, I asked if his Gov-

---

[52] 46 Stat. 590, 704.
[53] Photostatic copy obtained from the Franklin D. Roosevelt Library, Hyde Park, N. Y.

ernment had any specific information with regard to the agreement recently reported to have been concluded between Germany, Japan, and Italy.

The British Chargé d'Affaires [54] today called to see me with a personal and confidential message from Sir Alexander Cadogan which he was instructed to decode himself and to burn after he had read it to me.

This message was to the following effect: That in the agreement recently signed between the three powers,[55] the first article provided for mutual support in the event that any one of the three powers became involved in a diplomatic dispute with any third power or powers. The second and last article provided for mutual economic, diplomatic, and political support if one of the three powers were to be threatened by any third power or powers.

My attention was specifically called to the fact that in the German-Japanese anti-Comintern agreement the U. S. S. R. was specifically mentioned, whereas in the new agreement any third power is included.

I was further informed that a secret supplementary treaty had been drafted by the Japanese Government and had been submitted to the other two powers. This proposed secret agreement specified just how much support was to be rendered in the contingencies envisaged in the two articles of the agreement above mentioned, and just how far such support should be carried. The British Government was advised that the Italian Government has so far insisted that there be a year's delay before any decision was reached on this Japanese suggestion, and that the German Government has up to the present remained non-committal. I was further informed that the Japanese were very strenuously urging that an agreement be reached on this supplementary treaty without any further delay.

Believe me [etc.]   SUMNER WELLES

741.94/232

The Ambassador in Poland (Biddle) to the Secretary of State

No. 840   WARSAW, December 7, 1938.
                                           [Received December 27.]

SIR: I have the honor to refer to my despatch No. 778 of November 4, 1938,[56] and to report the following information which has just come to light.

---

[54] V. A. L. Mallet.
[55] This report was in error. A treaty of alliance between the three powers was under discussion but was not signed. For German documents on these discussions, see *Documents on German Foreign Policy, 1918–1945*, ser. D, vol. IV, chs. 4 and 8, *passim*.
[56] Not printed.

In conversation with Minister Beck [57] last night he significantly remarked that he had learned from authoritative Japanese quarters that the Japanese Government felt the hour was approaching when it might be possible to bring about an Anglo-Japanese agreement in connection with their respective interests in China. The Japanese were very hopeful of bringing this about but were concerned lest the United States place obstacles in the way. In fact, the Japanese felt that if the United States did not oppose such an agreement, the British and Japs might come to terms within a reasonable period of time.

(The foregoing remarks rendered even more interesting a report which Polish officialdom had received a few days ago to the effect that the Japanese Government had told British Ambassador Craigie that they regretted relations between their two countries were drifting apart, and that the Japanese Government was anxious to amend this condition, due to pressure from Germany to seal the Anti-Comintern Pact with a military alliance.)

The Minister then remarked that in his opinion Britain's ability to concentrate effectively on a Western European appeasement and pacification was hampered mainly by her difficulties in the Far East. Britain could not be expected to handle both problems effectively at the same time until she had attained the desired standard of rearmament—and that was still some time off. In fact, times had changed since those days when Britain used to be able to treat with problems one by one as they arose within her Empire. London then sat back calmly while her diplomats and troops localized difficulties and effected a settlement. Nowadays, however, the high pressure politics of Germany, Italy, and Japan were pinpricking Britain at points all over the political chessboard whereat British interests crossed those of the other three countries. The Minister reiterated with emphasis his opinion that under present circumstances Britain was not in a position to handle effectively the situations in the West and the East at the same time. Therefore an Anglo-Japanese agreement in the Far East might give Britain a freer hand to concentrate her efforts in the West. The Minister then significantly mentioned that he would be greatly interested to ascertain what American official attitude might be towards a possible Anglo-Jap agreement.

The Minister's manifested interest on this score discloses, to my mind, his present efforts to appraise at long range the potential turn of events in the Far East, in the light of their bearing upon affairs in Western Europe, and upon Poland's position in particular. Accordingly, I interpret his aforementioned interest to mean that he is

---

[57] Josef Beck, Polish Minister for Foreign Affairs.

now undoubtedly planning Poland's course for the next few months. He must therefore take into consideration the possible outcome of events in the Far East. Accordingly, I perceive Beck feels that if the United States were not actively to oppose an Anglo-Japanese accord, such an accord might augur an eventual free hand for Japan vis-à-vis Soviet Russia, which in turn might hamper the Soviet's ability to cooperate effectively with Poland in protecting the Soviet's and Poland's respective Ukrainian minorities against German pressure. In such case, as well as in the event of British and French continued disinterest in Eastern Europe, Poland might be afforded no "out" from what might appear to be its only alternative, namely, collaboration with Germany in the setting up of an independent Ukrainian state at the expense of Polish, the Soviet's and Rumania's Ukrainian minorities.

On the other hand, I perceive Beck feels that if the United States were to oppose actively an Anglo-Japanese agreement, Japan's hand would not be free to act against the Soviet—at least for some time to come. Hence, in turn, Moscow might be freer to attend (a) to a much needed reconsolidation of the Soviet's internal structure, and (b) to the protection of the Soviet's Ukrainian minority against German machinations. In this case Poland might conceivably be afforded effective Soviet collaboration in protecting their respective Ukrainian minorities, and in such light a possible "out" from aforementioned forced collaboration with Germany.

Of pertinent bearing on the substance of Minister Beck's aforecited remarks, his Chief of Cabinet, Count Lubienski, who joined our conversation, stated that his recent talk with an American journalist disclosed the latter's opinion that American public opinion would be resentful of an exclusively Anglo-Jap agreement with regard to their respective interests in China. In response, Minister Beck significantly said that this opinion recalled to his mind the expressed opinion of former Japanese Minister to Poland, Hito, to effect that Japan was making a great mistake in attacking China first—she should have gone after Soviet Russia in the first instance—China later. Japan would undoubtedly encounter a longer campaign in China than expected; in such case, a consequent drain on the Japanese Army's strength and Tokyo's treasury, potential provocation of anti-Jap feeling among the democracies, and other world events of direct or indirect unfavorable bearing on Japan's position during a protracted campaign might conceivably play in Moscow's ultimate favor.

Respectfully yours,   A. J. DREXEL BIDDLE, JR.

893.01 Provisional/173 : Telegram

The Ambassador in China (Johnson) to the Secretary of State

CHUNGKING, December 8, 1938—9 p. m.
[Received December 8—7 : 03 p. m.]

586. Following is Embassy's reply to a telegraphic inquiry from Hankow dated December 7, 10 a. m., seeking instructions concerning consular relations with officials of newly formed regimes:

"[Reference?] Hankow's December 7, 10 a. m., in its telegrams of December 15, 7 p. m., 1937 [58] and January 19 [*18*], 1938,[59] to the Embassy at Peiping in regard to relations of consular officers with officials of the new regimes in China, the Department stated that American consular officers should avoid any action which might imply recognition of new political regimes. But in view of the need of the maintenance of the very complicated relations, the Department suggested that calls might be received and returned by sending or by taking in person if deemed expedient a personal calling card with the personal name of original caller inscribed thereon. In emphasizing its desire that contacts be kept on a personal and informal basis, the Department declared that it does not deem it practicable to issue instructions governing every contingency but relies upon the discretion and resourcefulness of officers to meet the requirement of the foregoing desiderata.

Sent to Hankow, repeated to Canton, and Amoy for guidance. Johnson."

JOHNSON

793.94/14557

The Consul General at Shanghai (Gauss) to the Secretary of State

No. 1871
SHANGHAI, December 9, 1938.
[Received January 3, 1939.]

SIR: I have the honor to refer to my despatch No. 1848 of December 1, 1938,[60] entitled "The Central China Development Company", and to enclose a copy of a Domei press report of November 28, 1937,[60] announcing the arrival at Shanghai on that date of Mr. Kenji Kodama, President of the Central China Development Company, accompanied by the Vice President of the company, Mr. Kaname Hirasawa, and by Messrs. Saburo Sonoda and Kyoichi Aburaya, directors of the company. Mr. Kiyoshi Kanai, another director, joined the party at Shanghai. A statement prepared for the press which Mr. Kodama gave out upon his arrival at Shanghai is also enclosed.[60]

---

[58] No. 400, *Foreign Relations*, 1937, vol. III, p. 811.
[59] No. 18, *ante*, p. 35.
[60] Not printed.

In this statement, Mr. Kodama did not repeat the phrase "we are not interested in monopolies", which he is reported to have used in his press interview on November 9, 1938,* at Tokyo, Japan, upon his appointment as President of the Central China Development Company. In fact, he made therein no reference at all to the monopolistic character of the subordinate companies of the firm.

Mr. Kodama's statement, "we do not mean to threaten in any way third Power rights and interests in China", will probably not reassure Occidental businessmen interested in the Central China market. Local American businessmen consider that Japanese restrictions on their freedom of movement and on their trading activities in the Shanghai hinterland have already deprived them of many of their rights and interests.

Mr. Kodama also stated that the Central China Development Company "desires to be the guiding factor in the economic reconstruction work of Central China by financing and managing the fundamental enterprises for production and trade." If this goal is achieved, the Central China Development Company will probably control most of the manufacturing and trade in the Yangtze Valley.

So far as this office knows, no non-Japanese individual or organization has yet indicated any desire to invest in the subsidiaries of the Central China Development Company. The possibility that these firms may function more to aid Japanese economic penetration into Central China than for profit, and lack of confidence in the future value of the Yen may act as deterrents to any such investments. Hence, it will not be surprising if Mr. Kodama's hope for the investment of foreign capital in the subsidiaries of the Central China Development Company is not fulfilled.

Mr. Kodama is quoted as saying to reporters upon his arrival at Shanghai,† "I intend to look about so as to formulate an idea of the existing situation." He and his party planned to proceed to Nanking on November 30, 1938, for a two day visit. No announcement of his return to Shanghai has come to the attention of this office and it is believed that his visit up the Yangtze River has been extended.

Mr. Kodama's statement contains little that is new, and Occidentals in Shanghai, who fear the effects of this firm and its subsidiaries upon their businesses, find nothing encouraging therein.

Respectfully yours,   C. E. Gauss

---

*Reuter's despatch in the *North China Daily News*, Shanghai, November 10, 1938. [Footnote in the original.]

†See Enclosure No. 1. [Footnote in the original; enclosure not printed.]

893.041/166 : Telegram

The Ambassador in China (Johnson) to the Secretary of State

CHUNGKING, December 9, 1938—noon.
[Received 9:35 p. m.]

588. Following is Embassy's translation of a third person note received from Chinese Ministry of Foreign Affairs under date of November 29:

"The Ministry of Foreign Affairs presents its compliments to the American Embassy and, with reference to the forcible attempts of Japan to seize the various Chinese courts in the Concession areas at Shanghai, has the honor to recall that the Ministry has repeatedly discussed the matter with His Excellency Nelson Trusler Johnson, American Ambassador, as well as having detailed officials to proceed to the Embassy to conduct negotiations. The request to adopt a stern attitude firmly rejecting Japanese interference has already aroused the attention of the American Embassy.

The establishment of the Chinese courts in question and the exercise of their functions are based upon international agreements signed by the various powers concerned; they possess an intimate relation to the peace of the Concessions. Once they are seized by Japan, not only will Chinese citizens in the Concessions be exposed to danger, but also foreign nationals without extra-territorial rights and even foreigners with extra-territorial rights, will be greatly threatened; in fact, this would amount to control of the whole of the Concessions and cannot be regarded with indifference.

The confidential report has recently been received to the effect that Japan's attempts forcibly to seize the various Chinese courts in the Concessions at Shanghai have been more intensified, and there is talk that it will occupy Hongkew as a *quid pro quo* for the taking over of the courts. If this information is true, it is thought that the various parties affected will be able to foresee the consequences. The Ministry has the honor, therefore, especially to request that the American Embassy take note of the matter and that it continue to adhere to its previous policy in relation to the Chinese courts of exhausting all efforts for their protection; that is, that it firmly reject Japan's illegal interference, in order to uphold international agreements. The Ministry is appreciative of the Embassy's friendliness in the matter."

The Embassy is acknowledging the foregoing note and stating that copies have been transmitted to Washington and Shanghai.

Repeated to Shanghai. Copy by mail to Peiping.

JOHNSON

893.041/166

Memorandum by the Adviser on Political Relations (Hornbeck)

[WASHINGTON,] December 10, 1938.

I am driven to the conclusion that much of what is being done by "the Japanese authorities" in China [61] is being done at the instance of and by order of the Army and the Navy without any particular reference to or instruction or authorization of the "home government" in Tokyo; in other words, that there are for practical purposes now two Japanese Governments, one in Japan and the other in China, the one in Japan being parent to and ally and associate of the one in China but being possessed of much less than absolute authority over and control of its offspring. This situation makes matters increasingly difficult for all concerned—except the headstrong Japanese offspring, their naval and military authorities in China. It also increases the chances of foreign powers (both governments and peoples) being fooled by assurances given by the Japanese Government in Japan.

STANLEY K. HORNBECK

793.94/14492 : Telegram

The Chargé in China (Peck) to the Secretary of State

CHUNGKING, December 12, 1938—noon.
[Received December 12—6 a. m.]

595. Embassy's 557, November 20, 10 a. m., and previous on Chiang-Clark-Kerr conversations at Changsha. A reliable Chinese official told a member of the Embassy staff on December 11 that the British Government has now replied to the Chinese Government. He stated that the British note is couched in non-committal terms and cannot for this reason be considered as satisfactory. He added however that the tenor of the note is not categorically negative and that it "leaves the way open" for further consideration.

Repeated to Shanghai and Peiping. Shanghai repeat to Tokyo.

PECK

793.94/14501 : Telegram

The Ambassador in Japan (Grew) to the Secretary of State

TOKYO, December 14, 1938—5 p. m.
[Received December 15—3: 25 a. m.]

783. Our 757, November 30, 3 p. m., last sentence.

1. Absence of recent telegrams from China and the complete silence maintained by the Japanese press on this subject make it difficult for

---

[61] See telegram No. 588, December 9, noon, from the Ambassador in China, *supra.*

us to appraise recent events affecting the Japanese plans to set up a new central Chinese Government. However, yesterday the Vice Minister for Foreign Affairs [62] informed us confidentially and off the record that the Foreign Office considers Wu Pei Fu's [63] refusal to head the proposed new government to be a blessing in disguise as the Foreign Office favors a federal form of government for China and not one which would have assimilated the existing regimes at Peiping and Nanking. Sawada said that all negotiations with Wu have ceased, that Wu is not popular in Central and South China and that there is available no Chinese who would receive as Chief of Government general support in all Japanese occupied parts of China. He further said that the Foreign Office envisages the establishment of local governments additional to those already set up and the linking together of these governments by a "Central Committee" the members of which would elect a chairman from among themselves.

2. In view of the foregoing the decision to postpone indefinitely the proposed announcement (which was to have been made by the Prime Minister on December 11) with regard to the policy decided upon by the conference held on November 30 in the presence of the Emperor may now be put down with a reasonable degree of certainty to drastic changes in the Japanese plans occasioned by Wu Pei Fu's decision.

GREW

793.94/14506 : Telegram

The Counselor of Embassy in China (Lockhart) to the Secretary of State

PEIPING, December 15, 1938—3 p. m.
[Received 7 : 43 p. m.]

722. 1. The Counselor of the Japanese Embassy volunteered last night the following statement to an officer of this Embassy :

(*a*) He hoped that the current conversations between the Japanese Foreign Minister and our Ambassador in Tokyo would soon reach a solution; he felt that a solution would be possible if the American Government did not "hold too closely to the Stimson policy".

(*b*) The Japanese military considered that policy intolerable and progress could be achieved only by "backing away from it somewhat".

(*c*) The Japanese Government had much appreciated American attitude in North China which was an area to which the Japanese attach great importance.

(*d*) When we were fairminded and patient in regard to happenings in North China the news spread very quickly and had a noticeable effect upon the Japanese military and others in Japan;

---

[62] Renzo Sawada.
[63] Military leader in retirement since 1926.

(e) Conversely a stiffer attitude would have an unfavorable effect;

(f) For example while he found it possible "to mitigate" the difficulties caused by incidents involving Japanese military and Americans he had failed to accomplish anything in respect to incidents involving British subjects because he had to inform the military that British diplomatic officers adopted an unbending attitude toward Anglo-Japanese problems.

2. The Counselor also offered a long dissertation on economic and trade problems the burden of which was that trade control was absolutely necessary for China, but was not necessarily discriminatory.

3. In a separate conversation the Japanese First Secretary stated to the American Secretary that (1) he was heartily sick of his work here; (2) he was no longer a diplomatic officer but an attaché of the Japanese military; (3) his Embassy had to consult the military in regard to every matter that arose between his Embassy and the American and British Embassies; (4) in addition various Japanese military officers concocted "ridiculous economic schemes" with which they burdened the Japanese Embassy; (5) for example, he himself was now wasting a great deal of time investigating, at the insistence of the Japanese military, the means and cost of softening North China's notoriously hard water; (6) foolishness of this sort found a corollary in the political field; (7) for example Japanese plans for a new central government for China, including the plan to make Wu Pei Fu President, were now topsy turvy and hopelessly confused.

4. Repeated to Chungking.   Code text being sent to Tokyo.

LOCKHART

793.94/14503 : Telegram

The Ambassador in Japan (Grew) to the Secretary of State

TOKYO, December 15, 1938—7 p. m.
[Received December 15—9:30 a. m.]

786. 1. During the last few days the Japanese papers have given much space to despatches from London and Washington to the effect that economic reprisals by the United States and Great Britain against Japan are being given active consideration and to feature articles on this subject apparently as a result of the Foreign Office or some other official source as they contain points not mentioned in published press despatches.   References are being made to the return of Ambassadors Johnson and Kennedy,[64] increased British export guarantees to cover war supplies to China, reported approaching American credit loan to China, et cetera, as indications of the trend of official American and British thought.

---

[64] From China and the United Kingdom, respectively.

2. The *Asahi* which has shown itself to be unusually well informed states that the Department is now studying the possibility of restricting or excluding imports from Japan on the basis of section 338 of the Tariff Act, that evidence is accumulating of Anglo-American discussions looking towards concerting reprisal measures, and that the Japanese Ambassadors at Washington and London have been instructed to ascertain the intentions of the American and British Governments. It further states that the Minister for Foreign Affairs will shortly resume his conversations with Craigie and me and that after further expounding the Japanese thesis he will urge "reconsideration of plans for Anglo-American economic sanctions against Japan".

3. Although these articles stress that Japan will not completely close the door in China their tone is not compromising.

Repeated to Shanghai for Chungking and Peiping.

GREW

793.94/14504 : Telegram

The Ambassador in Japan (Grew) to the Secretary of State

TOKYO, December 16, 1938—3 p. m.
[Received December 16—6 : 53 a. m.]

787. Our 786, December 15, 7 p. m.

1. The press reports that the Minister for Foreign Affairs is to have a further conversation with Craigie and me on or about Tuesday, December 20.

2. Does the Department desire, in the likely event of Arita initiating further discussion of the Japanese position, that I say anything more than to repeat the statements which I made to him at our last interview (see our 773, December 8, 7 p. m.[65]) ?

3. Craigie informs me that he is cabling his Government to ask whether he is to receive further instructions and to say that in the absence of instructions he will state to Arita that the British Government cannot assent to any abridgment of the principle of equality of opportunity or to any unilateral modification of the Nine Power Treaty.

GREW

---

[65] Not printed, but see memoranda of December 8, *Foreign Relations, Japan, 1931–1941*, vol. I, pp. 813 and 814.

793.94/14509 : Telegram

*The Counselor of Embassy in China (Lockhart) to the Secretary
of State*

PEIPING, December 16, 1938—3 p. m.
[Received December 17—5 a. m.]

725. 1. According to information, an officer of the Soviet Embassy
has stated to a reliable informant [of] this Embassy that

(a) According to information from Embassy in Tokyo interference
by the Japanese Navy has been responsible for delay in,

(1) formulation and execution of definite plans for establishment of the projected "central government" for China and,
(2) active operation of the new East Asia Bureau;

(b) the navy's interference is due to,

(1) its desire to obtain its share of credit for participation in
the control of China affairs in general and to exert influence in
those affairs, including the new federal regime, which the Japanese hope to establish and,
(2) its opposition to Japanese military drive against the so-
called "Red line" running south from West Suiyuan through
Kansu.

2. In connection with the last consideration, the Japanese Army
is reportedly preparing for a drive through West Suiyuan and south
from Wuyuan, Suiyuan, through Ninghsia to Lanchow, as part of its
effort to cut, (a) the channel of Chinese supplies from Soviet Russia
via Sinkiang and Sian, and (b) an alleged channel recently opened
from Urga. Recent air raids against Wuyuan and Ningyuan are
cited by some foreign observers as preparatory activities in this connection and there have been other indications that such an offensive
was being planned as an alternative to the projected drive against
Sian from South Shansi which has so far failed to materialize because
the Japanese forces have not been able after repeated attempts for
3 months to effect a crossing of the Yellow River (See Embassy's 691,
November 23, 5 p. m., paragraph 3 and 685, November 18, 4 p. m.[66]).
Repeated to Chungking, code text by mail to Tokyo.

LOCKHART

793.94/14504 : Telegram

The Acting Secretary of State to the Ambassador in Japan (Grew)

WASHINGTON, December 16, 1938—8 p. m.

422. Your 787, December 16, 3 p. m., paragraph 2. In the contingency mentioned, the Department desires that you continue to main-

[66] Neither printed.

tain the position of this Government as expressed to the Japanese Government both in writing and orally.

WELLES

893.796/258 : Telegram

The Counselor of Embassy in China (Lockhart) to the Secretary of State

PEIPING, December 19, 1938—3 p. m.
[Received 8:20 p. m.]

729. The formation of a Sino-Japanese aviation company, the China Aviation Company, with services projected for Peiping–Shanghai, Shanghai–Hankow, Shanghai–Canton, Peiping–Dairen and Peiping–Tatung, was announced here on December 17th. The capital of the new company is reportedly to be jointly invested by Peiping Provisional, the Nanking Reformed and the Mongolian Autonomous Governments, the Hui Tung and the Japan Air Transport Companies, the capital to be 6 million yen of which the three Governments will contribute only 250,000 each. As the managing director and other high officials as well as a great part of the personnel are to be Japanese and as participation in the investment is said to be small and restricted to the above official bodies, the new company may be considered as a further monopolistic venture on the part of the Japanese envisaged by and within the framework of the North China Development Company. The Hui Tung Company organized in 1936 will be merged into the new company.

LOCKHART

793.94/14522 : Telegram

The Chargé in China (Peck) to the Secretary of State

CHUNGKING, December 20, 1938—11 a. m.
[Received December 21— 6 a. m.]

610. The Embassy learns from reliable sources that the Generalissimo at a meeting, convoked on December 18, issued a forceful rebuke to the civil officials of the National Government for what he termed their frivolous attitude, inefficiency, corruption and waste in the face of a grave national crisis and pointing to life being led by the soldiers in the field, strongly admonished his listeners to be diligent, honest, eschew all amusements, and in short to pull together with the army in the war. A statement worded in a similar vein, and published in the local press, was issued by General Chen Cheng, close collaborator of Chiang Kai Shek, on December 16.

It would appear that this move presages a "moral purge" of civil officialdom and a reemphasizing of the tenets of the New Life movement.

Repeated to Peiping.

PECK

793.94/14530 : Telegram

The Consul General at Canton (Myers) to the Secretary of State

CANTON, December 20, 1938—3 p. m.
[Received December 21—4 : 27 p. m.]

87. On morning of December 20th a Canton Peace Maintenance Commission was installed under Japanese auspices at Canton in ceremony at Sun Yat Sen Memorial Hall with former Sun Yat Sen associates Peng Tung Yuan as chairman and Lu Chun Yu as vice chairman. About 5,000 Chinese of poorer classes, many presumably assembled under Japanese direction, attending [*attended?*] the meeting, where Japanese and "5 barred" flags were displayed and at which Japanese military, naval, consular and newly installed Chinese "Commission" officials urged cooperation with new regime. Congratulatory telegrams from Japanese officials in Tokyo and members of Japanese sponsored regimes in Manchuria, Peiping and Nanking were read. The German Vice Consul attended formally attired, but, except for French Vice Consul who was present unofficially, no other consular officers attended.

Following inaugural ceremony there was a parade through Canton streets of Japanese Army trucks carrying apathetic looking Chinese holding flags; there were armed Japanese guards in many of the trucks.

Recently an Imperial messenger arrived in Canton from Tokyo.

Repeated to Chungking and Peiping.

MYERS

793.94/14520 : Telegram

The Ambassador in Japan (Grew) to the Secretary of State

TOKYO, December 20, 1938—10 p. m.
[Received December 20—6 : 30 p. m.]

795. My 787, December 16, 3 p. m., paragraph 3, Department's 422, December 16, 8 p. m.

1. The Minister for Foreign Affairs has not yet asked either my British colleague or me to call upon him.[67]

---

[67] For the Ambassador's memoranda of conversation on December 26 with the Japanese Minister for Foreign Affairs, see *Foreign Relations, Japan, 1931–1941,* vol. I, pp. 631 and 818.

2. Following is a brief résumé of the instructions received by Craigie from his Government dated December 17:

(*a*) In view of the unofficial nature of the Foreign Minister's memorandum (of December 8) which was probably intended to test our reactions, no official representations should be made as coming from the British Government but an early opportunity should be taken to indicate that profound dissatisfaction has been caused in England by the Minister's expressed views. If these views were to become known to the public they would tend to increase the already mounting distrust and misgiving resulting from recent press articles outlining Japanese intentions;

(*b*) British inability to agree to arbitrary and unilateral modification of existing treaties might well be stressed, thus affording Arita opportunities to suggest revision by discussion if he desires to do so. The onus to make first proposals would thus be placed on Japan;

(*c*) Lord Elibank, who is not a member of the Government, characterized Japanese actions in China as "economic aggression" and advocated certain measures of economic retaliation. We deplore practice of Japanese news agencies and press of divorcing from their context statements by public men in England in order to create ill-feeling in Japan. Any acts of economic retaliation which are advocated or contemplated arise from failure of Japanese to implement previous assurances. Such acts of retaliation do not furnish excuse for further Japanese acts of discrimination and exclusion. The impulse to advocate retaliatory measures would automatically disappear if causes of just complaints in China were removed and a definite forward step would have been taken in improving our mutual relations. British Government has up till now exercised great restraint in replying to questions in Parliament but will be unable indefinitely to restrain public opinion in view of growing mistrust. If any gesture is called for Japan should surely take the initiative;

(*d*) Your [*The?*] arguments already used against necessity for monopolistic control in China might well be amplified. In time of war no power except China could prevent Japan's access to raw materials in that country. To assume the contrary would presuppose a defeated Japan whose communications with China were severed and in that event Japanese control and ownership would be of no avail. No argument therefore exists for departing from principle of equal opportunity. The only requirements are an independent, stable and well disposed China, free from domination by any power, and a powerful and undefeated Japan. Community interests of many powers in China should be welcomed as a stabilizing factor which would in no way obstruct Japanese aim to secure necessary raw materials. (End résumé of Craigie's instructions.)

3. Craigie today expressed to me the hope that I would cable to Washington the substance of his instructions and seek authority to present the situation to Arita in a similar light.

4. I told Craigie of the nature of my own instructions and added that in my opinion the views of my Government had been fully and adequately presented and recorded and that in the light of the present attitude of the Japanese Government nothing was to be gained by

continual debate over the same points and issues. I said I felt that the time had come when general representations or debate were futile and that while I would continue at every opportunity to maintain the position of my Government, as already fully expressed to the Japanese Government both orally and in writing, I felt that a dignified reserve was now desirable while awaiting the development of the many factors which are constantly at work in shaping the future situation.

5. Craigie was impressed by this attitude but he nevertheless believes that the present situation is inviolable and while he is emphatically in favor of economic measures of pressure he feels that a "safety valve" would be afforded by a continuance of friendly debate with the Foreign Minister with regard to the practical application of the "new order". Craigie says that he has reason to believe that the army is interested only in securing permanent access to raw materials and that the pressure on the Government to exclude foreign trade in general from China springs from other, non military, elements. (I myself find it very difficult to accept this hypothesis.)

6. I may add that Craigie in this and in previous conversations has been unable to suppress a latent eagerness to find a compromise settlement with the Japanese on the basis of (a) satisfying Japanese plans for the development of sources of raw material in China and (b) nonimpairment of British and other foreign trading rights in China. His opinion, as reported in the second sentence of paragraph 5, was fathered, I believe, more by this eagerness than by any conclusive indication of the Japanese Army's exclusive interest in raw materials. In the light of Craigie's thoughts on this point, I am apprehensive of embarking on discussions along the lines suggested in paragraph *b* of his instructions.

7. As a result of our talk today Craigie will, unless called for by Arita, postpone visiting the Minister until after the holidays. He expressed the hope, however, that I would inform him of any reply received from Washington to my present telegram in order that he might explain to his Government his own decisions.

GREW

793.94/14531 : Telegram

The Chargé in China (Peck) to the Secretary of State

CHUNGKING, December 21, 1938—9 a. m.
[Received 7:47 p. m.]

608. Further reference Department's No. 4, October 24, 7 p. m., to Hong Kong and Embassy's 514, October 26, 11 a. m. The Embassy learns from Arthur Young [68] that the following reasons are advanced

---

[68] American adviser to the Chinese Ministry of Finance.

in Chinese official circles for the ease with which the Japanese invasion of South China was accomplished:

1. The Chinese conviction that the Japanese would not strike at Canton for fear of international complications.

2. The consequent despatch of the bulk of the regular Cantonese army to the north for participation in the defense of Hankow leaving the defense of Kwangtung to local militia.

3. The surprise and speed with which the attack was executed.

4. The completeness of Japanese preparations in which extremely strong artillery and aviation support played a leading part; and the ineptitude of the South China military leadership.

He stated there was positively no evidence of Chinese treachery. He added that following commencement of attack on Canton the Generalissimo transferred an unknown number of troops from the Hankow area to South China but that this move came too late to stem the invasion, although further Japanese advances into western and northern Kwangtung were thereby prevented. However, this diversion of troops to the south was alleged to have hastened the fall of Hankow by 2 months.

PECK

711.94/1234½

Memorandum by the Adviser on Political Relations (Hornbeck) to the Assistant Secretary of State (Sayre)

[WASHINGTON,] December 22, 1938.

MR. SAYRE: Referring to your memorandum of December 15,[69] and making of record certain statements which I made in conference this morning, I may say:

I concur in the lines of reasoning on which this memorandum moves, and I have no criticism of or comment to offer upon what appears in the first twenty pages. With regard to the statement in conclusion (pages 21–25), I concur in the views there expressed except as indicated hereunder:

I share the view that "a comprehensive and thoroughgoing program of retaliation is not desirable at this time"; but I would underscore the words "at this time", and I would add that I consider it highly desirable that a plan be made at this time for a comprehensive and thoroughgoing program of measures of material pressure which might be applied, beginning with some one step and proceeding as the situation may unfold to other steps, by way of preparation for action which might soon need to be begun.

---

[69] Not printed; it invited comment on the memorandum dated December 5, p. 406.

I dissent from the view that "Such a program of retaliation would [underscoring mine] involve serious risk of armed conflict." My view is that adoption of such a program, and letting it be known that the program is in existence and may be carried out, might contribute substantially toward obviating the development of a situation in which danger of armed conflict would become an actuality. I grant that the formulation of such a program might create a risk. But I think that continuance of this Government's part of acquiescence in Japan's impairment of our rights and destruction of our interests in China is more sure to contribute to the creation of a risk than would be the adoption by this Government of a program of resistance to Japan by means of material pressures. In my opinion, unlawful and aggressive acts cannot anywhere be opposed—even by words alone—without some degree of risk arising. It is my conviction, however, that resolute opposition is less dangerous than timorous opposition or acquiescence; and I believe that a bold stand by the American Government would on the one hand have very prompt support from the American public and on the other hand have a definite though not conclusively determining effect toward deterring the Japanese from going to extremes.

I dissent from the view that "wholehearted international cooperation, especially on the part of the British Empire, would be necessary, to accomplish the objectives in mind . . ." [70] To begin with, the immediate objective is to prevent the Japanese from taking extreme action against our rights and interests (along with those of other powers) in China. The more remote, as contrasted with the immediate, objective is to prevent a collapse of Chinese resistance to Japan and the concomitant of an early military victory by the Japanese which would place them for the time being in unopposed military occupation of the whole of China. Sharing the view that "close and thoroughgoing European cooperation" cannot be secured, I nevertheless do not believe that such cooperation is necessary—provided the United States would take and would make clear that it had taken and would continue in a determined position of refusal either to assent to or to acquiesce in disregard of its rights and destruction of its interests in China. This country has the capacity and it could be brought to have the will to bring to bear upon Japan material pressures of such weight that the Japanese, contemplating the prospect of those pressures being applied, would very substantially modify the program to which they have recently and openly declared themselves committed.

I find the suggestion, but absence of a recommendation, that endeavor might be made now to obtain revision of Section 338 of the

---

[70] Omission indicated in the original.

Tariff Act of 1930 on lines indicated; also, that possible denunciation of the commercial treaty of 1911 might be considered. I would go further. I would urge that the first of these suggestions be acted upon forthwith. I would urge that a decision be made that denunciation of the treaty of 1911 be authorized, now, notification to be given if, when and as developments in the situation may be such as to lead to the conclusion that the moment is opportune and the act desirable.

S[TANLEY] K. H[ORNBECK]

893.00/14286 : Telegram

The Chargé in China (Peck) to the Secretary of State

CHUNGKING, December 23, 1938—9 a. m.
[Received 10 : 45 a. m.]

613. The Embassy is reliably informed that Wang Ching Wei left Chungking for Yunnanfu December 19 and that he has since gone to Hanoi where he is remaining indefinitely. It is reported that his sudden and secret departure is attributable to a growing rift between him and H. H. Kung which is said to have originated at the Chungking session of the People's Political Council during which Kung was roundly criticized. Kung is reported to believe that Wang Ching Wei is directly or indirectly responsible for the attacks launched upon him.

It is believed unlikely in local circles that Wang Ching Wei will return to Chungking so long as Kung who is reported to be unpopular in most official quarters remains in office. However, it is doubtful whether the Generalissimo can be prevailed upon to relieve Kung of his official duties particularly in view of family relationships and in the face of recent financial arrangements. There is no suggestion locally that Wang Ching Wei's departure can be construed as indicative of a design to align himself with Japan or with puppet organizations.

Repeated to Peiping.

PECK

793.94119/470 : Telegram

The Ambassador in Japan (Grew) to the Secretary of State

TOKYO, December 23, 1938—2 p. m.
[Received December 23—8 : 05 a. m.]

802. 1. We are informed by Associated Press and United Press that they have already telegraphed to the United States the complete text of the statement issued last night by the Prime Minister.[71]

---

[71] For text, see *Foreign Relations, Japan, 1931–1941*, vol. I, p. 482.

2. With one exception, the papers vie with each other in commending the "moderate and magnanimous" character of the Japanese peace terms, which are summarized as follows:

(*a*) China's recognition of Manchukuo;

(*b*) Conclusion of Sino-Japanese agreement to combat communism which would grant Japan the right to station troops in specified parts of China and would designate Inner Mongolia as a "specified anti-communist area";

(*c*) Economic cooperation between Japan and China, including the "freedom of residence and trade on the part of Japanese subjects in the interior of China" and "China should extend to Japan facilities" for the development of natural resources "especially in the regions of North China and Inner Mongolia".

It is generally agreed that these peace terms, along with disclaimer of intention to demand indemnity from China and to seize any part of China, should effectively convince the United States and Great Britain that "the lawful activities in China of third countries which recognize the new order in East Asia will not in any way be restricted" (*Yomiuri*). The *Kokumin Shimbun*, however, deplores failure to set forth in the statement details of ways and means by which the Japanese peace conditions are to be carried out, and it is concerned lest the full expectations of Japan be misunderstood. It stresses that the basic principle of the "new order" policy is to eradicate completely those "conditions which place China under European and American dominance", and it hopes that this point will be emphasized in subsequent official statements.

3. The possibility of the Japanese Government having been influenced in the direction of moderation, by adverse reaction abroad to Japan's economic defense program, is indirectly suggested in a feature article in the *Nichi Nichi*, which states *inter alia:*

"It is believed that last night's statement will be effective toward removing the necessary fears of third countries with regard to their economic interests in China. The Government will accordingly profit by every opportunity and will use every means to assure these powers, and of course China, that Japan will endeavor to bring about a settlement of the conflict on the basis of the terms set forth in the statement."

4. Our own comment on this statement, as on other recent Japanese utterances, is that, being couched in too general terms and hedged about with qualifying clauses, it commits Japan to nothing specific. We believe that it has been thus framed to permit Japan all possible latitude to move as circumstances warrant. The peace terms, as such, are not new and, in the absence of a concrete plan for implementation, cannot be appraised. It will be, of course, the guarantees which will be demanded from China for the latter's observance of these terms, that will actually define them.

5. The question, to whom is the statement addressed, naturally arises. We do not believe that it was addressed primarily to the Chinese Government, although it might be supposed that it was formulated partly with an eye to encouraging those elements in the Chinese Government which are reported to be weary of the conflict. Again, it was probably intended to provide a means by which the regimes in China might observe the proprieties in accepting the Japanese terms. However, it would seem to us that the audience which the Japanese Government had chiefly in mind was the United States and Great Britain. The moderate language of the statement and the tone of the press comment both suggest that the statement was intended as an invitation to these countries to explore ultimate Japanese intentions.

Repeated to Shanghai for Chungking and Peiping.

GREW

793.94/14586

The Ambassador in Japan (Grew) to the Secretary of State

No. 3533   TOKYO, December 23, 1938.
[Received January 9, 1939.]

SIR: Toward the end of November 1938 there was much talk in Japan, in the press and elsewhere, of the formulation of a fundamental policy toward China. Various leaders and various governmental bodies were reported to have the problem under consideration, though only the most generalized statements with regard to what was going on were obtainable. On the evening of November 28 the Cabinet gave out a statement (Embassy's telegram 755, November 29, 5 p. m.) to the effect that "The Cabinet this afternoon decided on a fundamental policy for regulating Sino-Japanese relations in connection with the construction of a new order in eastern Asia which the five-minister conference has been considering." On November 30, amid measures of secrecy which deceived even responsible highly placed officials (Embassy's telegrams 756, November 30, noon,[72] and 757, November 30, 3 p. m.), a conference in the presence of the Emperor was held. These are rare occurrences and take place only for decisions of the first importance (despatch 2746, January 22, 1938[73]).

Still no public explanation was made, although there were several announcements portending an important statement in the near future. During the "interest build-up", which continued for several days, it was noteworthy that on December 1 the *Japan Times* ran a special story about Wu Pei-fu in which the statement was made that "Some

---

[72] Not printed.
[73] See footnote 41, p. 24.

observers predict that he may consent to become 'President of the Federal Republic of China' in the areas now under Japanese occupation." Other papers carried similar articles. A few days later it was given out to the press that the Premier would make a declaration of major importance in a speech at Osaka on December 11 which would be broadcast widely. When that date arrived a press release said that the Premier would not be able to make the trip because of ill health; and on December 12 the press was officially informed that the declaration had been indefinitely postponed.

Meantime information from various sources was leading the Embassy to believe that the conference in the presence of the Emperor as well as the other discussions within the government conducted in such secrecy had had to do at least in part with efforts to establish in China a new regime, nominally led by Chinese, for the governing of the occupied areas. This belief was in considerable part borne out and confirmed by statements made to the Counselor of the Embassy by the Vice Minister for Foreign Affairs on December 13 (Embassy's telegram 783, December 14, 5 p. m.). The Vice Minister stated confidentially and off the record that the Foreign Office believes that the refusal of Wu Pei-fu to become head of the new government which had been proposed is in reality a blessing for Japan. He gave it as the opinion of the Foreign Office that a federated form of government is the most promising form of government for China, not a regime made over from the union of the Nanking and Peking groups. The Vice Minister further gave an intimation of the system of government envisaged for China by the Foreign Office when he referred to the possibility of establishment of a central committee the members of which would represent a large number of local governments additional to those already set up, a chairman being elected from among the members of the committee.

On the evening of December 22 the Premier gave out an important statement [74] embodying the conditions which Japan asserts that she demands of China (despatch 3535, December 23, 1938,[75] enclosure 3). The press was given to understand at the time of the release that the conditions had been approved by the November 30 conference in the presence of the Emperor.

It seems probable that when the November 30 conference made its decisions of basic policy toward China it also approved the recognition of a government of China for the occupied areas, probably to be headed by Wu Pei-fu. Obviously the recognition of an established regime at the same time as the announcement of basic policy as conditions governing the relations of Japan with the newly established

---

[74] *Foreign Relations*, Japan, 1931–1941, vol. I, p. 482.
[75] Vol. IV, p. 110.

regime would have offered to the Japanese public and to the foreign world a dramatic development, and there seems little doubt that, had Wu Pei-fu been cooperative, such would have been the result. Wu Pei-fu's refusal then apparently caused postponement of announcement even of the basic conditions approved by the November 30 conference, in the hope that some new solution for setting up a government of China might be found. By December 22 it was nevertheless found advisable to announce the basic conditions without taking simultaneous action in recognition of a regime.

Piecing together the fragments of information which have come to the Embassy's attention in explanation of this sequence of happenings, the Embassy inclines to the view that General Doihara was sponsor of a plan for installing Wu Pei-fu as head of a single government for the occupied areas of China; that General Kita was sponsor of a plan for installing Wang Keh-min as head of such government; that General Doihara was able to win the support of the Japanese Government to his plan; that the plan miscarried on account of Wu Pei-fu's refusal to cooperate; that the establishing of a single regime for the governing of the occupied areas has had to be deferred and is now not being actively pressed; and that the present prospect is for a loosely federated form of government, without a dominating individual Chinese leader. A fair assumption is that, as Japanese pressure for the immediate setting up of a government has apparently relaxed, the December 22 announcement of basic conditions, separately from any act of recognizing of a regime, is further indication that the setting up of a single government is not imminently expected.

Respectfully yours, JOSEPH C. GREW

894.00/836

The Ambassador in Japan (Grew) to the Secretary of State

No. 3549   TOKYO, December 23, 1938.
                                        [Received January 9, 1939.]

SIR: With reference to my despatch No. 3300, October 4, 1938,[76] I have the honor to report that the Koa-in (Asia Promotion Board), which is the name finally decided upon for the central organ established to administer all affairs connected with China, has been officially organized. There are enclosed [77] for the Department's information the Embassy's translations of the Imperial Ordinances for the official organization of the Asia Promotion Board and for the official organi-

---

[76] Not printed.
[77] None printed.

zation of the affiliated offices as well as a list of the officials appointed.

The Board, organized under the presidency of the premier, is to administer during the China incident, with the specified exception of diplomatic matters, the following affairs:

1. Political, economic and cultural affairs which, in connection with the China incident must be managed in China.
2. Matters having to do with the establishment of policies in connection with the above affairs.
3. Affairs relating to the supervision of the North China Development Company and the Central China Promotion Company and to the control of Japanese businessmen in China.
4. Affairs related to the maintenance of unity among Government offices in their relations with China.

The vice presidents are specified in the ordinance to be the Ministers for Foreign Affairs, War, Navy, and Finance. A director general, to be accorded the treatment of an official of *shinnin* rank, is to be the general administrative officer. General Yanagawa has been appointed to this important position.

The general organization of this board largely conforms to that of former projected organizations which have been fully reported to the Department by various despatches, particularly my No. 3300, October 4, and there is little additional comment which can be made at this time. It may be, however, of some significance to point out the extensive preparations for the establishment of "affiliated offices" in China, a liaison committee for the purpose of facilitating unity in the policies of the various Government offices regarding China and the provision for the participation in the work of the Asia Promotion Board by Army and Navy officers on the active list, such officers to retain their active service standing. The strong position held by the military in relation to the Asia Board is evidenced by the appointment of General Yanagawa, General Suzuki, and other military officers to important positions. It is yet too early to predict to what extent the supervision by the Cabinet will be effective, or whether the scope of this Board may be broadened until it equals or surpasses a ministry in importance.

The progress in the organization of this central organ has been very slow, however, during the latter part of November, it was announced that the Cabinet had finally approved the proposed organization of an official organ for the control of relations with China and that the name to be adopted would be the Koa-in (Asia Promotion Board). On December 2, it was reported that the Privy Council had approved the draft plan, but at the same time had attached a statement of "its hopes" to the effect that the greatest consideration be given to the functioning of the Board, the selection of its personnel, and the relations between the Board and "local agencies", and further that every care be taken to avoid friction with the diplomatic authorities. The Committee's approval was followed shortly thereafter by the formal approval of the Privy Council and the Imperial Ordinances were promulgated on December 16. The Board reportedly began functioning immediately. While the Imperial Ordinance states that the Board is to function "during the China Incident", a Government spokesman reportedly stated in reply to a question posed by the Privy Council Committee that the end of the China incident will be fixed by Imperial decision and that the Asia Promotion Board may exist even if the emergency is brought to an end. It is also obvious from various press reports of Government statements that the emergency will not be considered to have ended with the termination of active hostilities but that the necessity for such organizations as the Asia Promotion Board will continue until Japan's policies and programs for a new order in East Asia have been realized. This has been interpreted by Government spokesmen to mean until the program for the reconstruction and development of China and the economic, political, and cultural cooperation of Japan, "Manchukuo" and China has been effected.

Respectfully yours, JOSEPH C. GREW

793.94119/471 : Telegram

The Chargé in China (Peck) to the Secretary of State

CHUNGKING, December 24, 1938—noon.
[Received 11:10 p. m.]

618. Central News Agency release of December 23, Chungking, quotes a spokesman of the Chinese Foreign Office as having commented as follows in regard to the statement issued by the Japanese Prime Minister: [78]

"The latest statement by Prince Konoye is in no wise different from previous declarations made by the Japanese Government. It thus shows that the basic policy of Japan, namely, the policy of destroying the independence and integrity of China and of closing the Open Door in this country, has remained unchanged.

Prince Konoye professes, on the one hand, the respect of his Government for the sovereignty of China, but, on the other, he announces the determination of Japan to continue her military operations in China, to consolidate the puppet regimes set up by the Japanese Army, and to force China into signing an anti-communist pact. His declared objects falsify the avowed intention of his Government to respect the sovereignty of China.

While declaring that Japan has no territorial designs on China, Prince Konoye demands in the same breath the right to station troops in China and the transformation of inner Mongolia into a so-called

[78] *Foreign Relations*, Japan, 1931–1941, vol. I, p. 482.

'special anti-communist district.' Such demands constitute but a disguised attempt at the political dismemberment of China.

With regard to the so-called rights of domicile and trade in the interior of China, the Japanese desire may appear to be harmless on the surface. But if one were to consider the presence of Japanese troops in China and their domination of the puppet government, it should not be difficult to visualize Japan's true intentions in this country. That is to say, Japan is intent on using her military forces and the bogus regimes to push with all her might a comprehensive scheme of economic penetration covering the whole of China and exclusively for Japan's own interest. This line of action is identical with that followed in her exploitation of Manchuria.

The declaration that Japan does not wish to monopolize the economic rights in China now to restrict the economic interests of third powers, is entirely insincere, being merely intended to ease the international atmosphere which has become increasingly unfavorable to her. One needs only to look at the present condition of the so-called 'Manchukuo' and the recent Japanese economic establishments in China as well as the extent of destruction of third power interests to realize that Japan's declaration is not to be trusted."

The Chinese press today comments widely and in a similar vein on Prince Konoye's statement and generally makes the point that China will continue to offer resistance until Japan relinquishes her present policy toward China.

Repeated to Peiping for Tokyo.

PECK

793.94/14533 : Telegram

The Chargé in China (Peck) to the Secretary of State

CHUNGKING, December 24, 1938—3 p. m.
[Received December 26—2 : 30 p. m.]

619. The Embassy is reliably informed that prior to coming to Chungking on or about December 10 the Generalissimo went to South China where he convoked a conference which was attended by over 200 ranking officers and at which detailed plans were formulated for the defense of northern Kwangtung and of Kwangsi. Chang Fa Kwei was designated as Commander-in-Chief of the South China forces with Yu Han Mou and Li Han Hun, newly appointed Kwangtung Provincial Government Chairman, as vice commanders. The South China forces are reported to comprise 28 regular divisions including 6 central, 12 Cantonese and 10 Kwangsi, in addition to a formidable auxiliary force in the Self Defense Corps. It is anticipated that no serious effort will be made to defend the coastal areas adjacent to Pakhoi and Kwangchowwan or even Nanning and this whole area is now being laid waste and the inhabitants required to evacuate in order to impede Japanese military operations. However, it is ex-

pected that strong resistance will be offered if the Japanese endeavor to penetrate deeply into Kwangsi.

Repeated to Peiping for Tokyo.

Chiang Kai Shek left Chungking December 20 to investigate military conditions at Sian and other points in the northwest. It is reported that he will soon return to Chungking. In this connection it is learned that the Chinese will make no strong effort to hold their present Yellow River defenses or Sian, although Hanchung in South Shensi will be defended by powerful forces the nucleus of which is said to be composed of 11 intact and well trained divisions under the command of General Hu Tsung Nan.

It is generally believed in Chungking that the failure of the Japanese military to follow up the capture of Hankow with a concerted drive on Changsha and Hengyang, the center of Chinese resistance in Central China, constituted a repetition of the costly error in strategy committed during the fall of Nanking. The Embassy has received information from official and private sources which discloses that the Chinese military forces were badly demoralized during the fall of Wuhan and Canton and that the Japanese would have met with negligible resistance if they had continued to advance beyond Yochow. However, the present "breathing spell" has enabled the Generalissimo to reorganize his forces and it is generally believed that Japanese penetration into western Hunan and Hupeh will meet with firm resistance.

To the failure of the Japanese to press the military advantages accruing from the fall of Wuhan and Canton [may be?] added another factor of vital import to China's resistance: namely, the granting of American credits to China and reports of similar British action have been construed by the Chinese as indicating the commencement of action by those powers to prevent Japan from achieving its aims in the Far East, and it now seems clear that this conviction has immensely stimulated and stiffened the Chinese will for prolonged resistance.[79]

PECK

893.00/14287 : Telegram

The Chargé in China (Peck) to the Secretary of State

CHUNGKING, December 25, 1938—noon.
[Received December 25—11 : 35 a. m.]

620. Embassy's 613, December 23, 9 a. m. The First Secretary of the British Embassy informed me December 24, 9 p. m., that Donald had informed him that Chiang Kai Shek wished to state to the British

---

[79] See pp. 519 ff.

and American Governments that nothing Wang Ching Wei might do or say represented the Chinese Government in any way. Being unable to reach me quickly Donald asked the British Secretary to transmit this message to me for the Department.

The Embassy is reliably informed that General Chiang returned to Chungking on the afternoon of December 24 from his trip of inspection in the northwest.

Repeated to Peiping for Tokyo.

PECK

793.94119/472 : Telegram

The Chargé in China (Peck) to the Secretary of State

CHUNGKING, December 27, 1938—10 a. m.
[Received 9 : 17 p. m.]

622. My 618, December 24, noon. The Chinese press and Central News Agency today published an incomplete version of a speech attributed to General Chiang Kai Shek which was delivered at the weekly memorial meeting of the Central Tangpu in Chungking on December 26.

General Chiang is reported to have referred to the recent statement of the Japanese Prime Minister as a disclosure of Japanese intrigue aimed at the dismemberment of China and to have stated that this and other recent Japanese official utterances have served to give the Chinese people a deeper understanding of Japanese ambitions and have thereby strengthened the determination of the Chinese people to continue resistance without surrender or compromise.

He is also said to have stated that Minister Wang Ching Wei went to Hanoi for medical treatment, that Japanese and German rumors that he is on a mission on behalf of the National Government to discuss peace terms with the Japanese are entirely false and that Mister Wang's trip has not the slightest connection with National Government or party affairs. General Chiang is quoted as having alluded to Mister Wang's meritorious service to the state and to have expressed the hope that if Mister Wang had his own views on national policy he should feel free to return and to discuss them with members of the Government and the party.

Repeated to Peiping for mailing to Tokyo.

PECK

693.001/445 : Telegram

The Ambassador in Japan (Grew) to the Secretary of State

TOKYO, December 28, 1938—noon.
[Received 1:20 p. m.]

811. Our 805, December 24 [*27*], 9 a. m.[80]

1. My British colleague has made available to me his telegram to London reporting his conversation on December 26 with the Minister for Foreign Affairs, of which the following is an outline:

(*a*) Craigie left with the Minister for Foreign Affairs an informal paper based on and expanding his instructions, which are set forth in summarized form in paragraph 2 of our 795, December 20, 10 p. m.

(*b*) Afterward, commenting on this paper, [Arita] stated that the British Government's declared intention to examine sympathetically China's request for financial assistance, and British desire to achieve an equitable settlement of the Sino-Japanese conflict were mutually contradictory. In view of the precarious position of the Chiang Kai Shek government and its inability to offer substantial security, any loan to China in the present circumstances assumed a political significance. Craigie insisted that the British credit extension to China was a purely commercial transaction, and that to refuse such commercial arrangements with China would be incompatible with the maintenance of neutrality.

(*c*) The discussion with regard to the Japanese statements of policy involving the principle of equal opportunities in China were substantially similar to the discussion between Arita and myself.

2. Craigie's report of a discussion which was held on the point brought out in paragraph 6 of my 795, is as follows:

"His Excellency seemed particularly interested in my slightly elaborated version of paragraph 4 of your telegram No. 800 and admitted that Japan's primary concern was to develop in China the raw materials of which she had special need and the trades connected therewith. I suggested that it should surely be possible to evolve some means of doing this without treading on anybody's toes and with the willing assent of the Chinese Government. I still could not understand why His Excellency thought it necessary to spoil his case by threatening trade discrimination even though at the moment we were only being shown the thin end of the wedge. Mr. Arita would not admit that his instrument was a wedge and expressed hope that if I had any suggestion to make by which Japan could attain her legitimate needs without any departure from the principle of equality of opportunity, he hoped I would not hesitate to make it.["]

Repeated to Chungking.

GREW

---

[80] Not printed; see memorandum of December 26, *Foreign Relations*, Japan, 1931–1941, vol. I, p. 818.

793.94119/474 : Telegram

The Consul General at Shanghai (Gauss) to the Secretary of State

SHANGHAI, December 28, 1938—noon.
[Received 2:10 p. m.]

1500. Domei News Agency quotes a statement reportedly issued by the Japanese expeditionary forces in Central China which the agency characterizes as a commentary on Premier Konoye's recent statement of policy.

The Japanese military command is quoted as being prepared "to receive and shake hands with anyone whether or not affiliated with the Kuomintang or its armies who is desirous of taking part in the huge task of reconstructing a new China". The statement also expresses the gratification of the Japanese military authorities for the work of the "Reformed Government" and asserts the Japanese forces are now engaged in dealing a "finishing blow" to Chinese troop reorganization. Of particular interest is that portion of the statement which reads "the Government statement elucidating the fundamental policies which will guide the readjustment of Japanese relations with a new China is a most appropriate measure in view of the current situation. This, however, cannot be regarded as indicating any new developments occurring or any prospects of their taking place within the occupied areas of Central China."

These views if correctly quoted would appear to indicate that in so far as the Japanese military command in Central China is concerned no new development may be expected and that Japanese policy in the Central China area actually will continue to move in the grooves already established by the Japanese military authorities regardless of policy pronouncements given out in Tokyo.

Repeated Peiping, Chungking and Tokyo.

GAUSS

793.94/14546 : Telegram

The Ambassador in Japan (Grew) to the Secretary of State

TOKYO, December 29, 1938—1 p. m.
[Received December 29—9:45 a. m.]

812. 1. The Minister for Foreign Affairs will issue on New Year's Day a message, of which the following is an outline with quotation of significant portions. It is requested that no public reference to this message be made until released on January 1.

(a) The first three paragraphs refer to the occupation by Japan of important areas in China, to the conversion of the Chinese Government into a provincial regime, to the development in China of a movement hostile to Chiang Kai Shek and to the establishment by Japan of a new order "by sweeping away old conceptions of the Orient as a colony for occidental capitalistic countries and by modifying international policies based on such ideas".

(b) Turning next to international cooperation against communism the message states "at this point the Japanese nation must express its heartfelt thanks to Germany and Italy who understand the position of Japan in eagerly pushing on toward the great objective of anti-communism. They accurately recognize the actual state of affairs in East Asia and show a sincere attitude in extending helping hands to the pacific construction works in this part of the world".

(c) Reference is made to American and British attitude in the following terms: "Especially is it a matter of deep regret that some third powers are adopting policies of open assistance to the National Government, thus putting off the termination of hostilities . . .[81] furthermore, in view of the fact that some powers, in their eagerness to safeguard their rights and interests in China, have presented unreasonable requests regardless of the actual state of affairs in the zone of hostilities or are trying to readjust the new situation, created by the hostilities, on the basis of anachronistic ideas, we deeply feel the necessity of making strenuous efforts in the future to correct the misunderstandings of these powers and to officials of the [sic] international relations".

2. The only features of this message which are in any way new are, first, the reference to "occidental capitalistic countries" in an uncomplimentary context and one which would suggest that Japan maintains economic and political systems different from those maintained by such countries, and second, the suggestion that Germany and Italy, "by recognizing the actual state of affairs in East Asia" may expect to enjoy more fully than others the right of the Open Door in China.

Repeated to Chungking.

GREW

893.01 Provisional/181 : Telegram

The Counselor of Embassy in China (Lockhart) to the Secretary of State

PEIPING, December 30, 1938—4 p. m.
[Received December 31—7 a. m.]

746. Embassy's 704, December 3, noon,[82] and last sentence 722, December 15, 3 p. m.; Tokyo's 783, December 14, 5 p. m. which has just been received by mail.

---

[81] Omission indicated in the original.
[82] Not printed.

1. The recent lack of concrete developments in connection with the projected "federal" government for the occupied areas is here generally attributed to (a) failure of interested Japanese political agents to come to agreement concerning both the personnel and the form of such government; (b) strong opposition to Wu Pei Fu by Chinese leaders of the present Peiping regime sponsored by General Kita; (c) lack, other than Wu, of more or less suitable Chinese personnel to constitute a federal regime and General Doihara's resultant persistence in attempting to arrange for the assumption of the executive office by Wu Pei Fu on the ground that he is the only present possibility and; (d) failure to reach complete agreement on the part of Wu, of his Chinese adherents and of his Japanese sponsors as to his emergence from political retirement and the Japanese *quid pro quo* therefor.

2. All available sources including adherents of Wu and members of the Peiping regime profess that these various difficulties have resulted in a decision by the authorities in Tokyo to postpone concrete political action in respect to a new central government for China for 1 or 2 months.

3. Some of Wu's adherents, however, are still working for his emergence and state that Wu Pei Fu is still considering the matter. This may be wishful thinking on their part and most observers feel that if the plan to make Wu Pei Fu head of a new federal regime has not been abandoned it has been indefinitely postponed because of : (1) lack of accord between the various Japanese and Chinese chiefly concerned as mentioned above or, (2) Wu's insistence upon terms to which the Japanese will not agree or, (3) both these conditions. Meanwhile a group of Wu's adherents is preparing for Wu's signature a manifesto appealing for peace, denouncing Chiang Kai Shek and possibly criticizing Wang Keh Min, head of the Peiping regime. It is too early to say whether Wu Pei Fu will actually issue such a manifesto.

4. The sum total of these factors is that the situation continues to be one of confusion concerning which no predictions can safely be made. A widespread impression exists here that the federal government plan is losing favor with the Japanese Government and that it will probably be a long time before events shape themselves towards anything much beyond the development of regional regimes connected if at all only very loosely by some such organ as the present United Council.

5. Repeated to Chungking, Nanking, Shanghai, Tokyo.

LOCKHART

793.94119/477 : Telegram

The Commander in Chief, United States Asiatic Fleet (Yarnell), to the Chief of Naval Operations (Leahy)[83]

[SHANGHAI, December 31, 1938—10 : 55 a. m.]
[Received January 1, 1939—7 a. m.]

0031. Mr. Wang Ching Wei, Chairman Central Political Council and Deputy General Executive of Kuomintang, who has long favored early termination of hostilities has, according to a report carried by Domei, the official Japanese news agency, addressed a statement to General Chiang Kai Shek and the supervising committees of the Kuomintang Party urging immediate action to exchange views with the Japanese Government for the restoration of peace. He suggests that the Chinese Government accept latest Japanese proposals as a basis for discussion and that China propose terms, including first a responsible solution of the issue of the four northern provinces; second, anti-Comintern collaboration; third, economic cooperation. He states that China must insist that the Japanese Army withdraw completely from China except that during the period of anti-Comintern collaboration Japanese troops may be stationed in Inner Mongolia. Japanese proposals have already been rejected, according to statements of General Chiang and other Chinese spokesman made public on 27 December, so it is probable that Mr. Wang's opinions are not shared by other important leaders. This is substantiated by Mr. Wang's sudden departure from Chungking.

DEVELOPMENTS WITH RESPECT TO "MANCHOUKUO";[84] BORDER HOSTILITIES BETWEEN JAPANESE AND SOVIET TROOPS

793.943 Manchuria/50

The Secretary of State to the Belgian Ambassador (Van der Straten-Ponthoz)

The Secretary of State presents his compliments to His Excellency the Belgian Ambassador and has the honor to acknowledge the receipt of the Ambassador's communication of January 24, 1938,[85] making inquiry in regard to the attitude and point of view of the American Government toward the question of the abolition of extraterritorial rights in Manchuria.

---

[83] Copy of telegram transmitted to the Department by the Navy Department.
[84] For previous correspondence, see *Foreign Relations*, 1937, vol. III, pp. 915 ff.
[85] Not printed.

Following the signature of the Japan–"Manchukuo" agreement of November 5, 1937, providing for the abolition of Japanese extraterritoriality rights in Manchuria and the manifesto of the "Manchukuo" régime issued on the same date indicating the intention of that régime to abolish as from December 1, 1937, the extraterritorial rights of all foreigners in Manchuria,[86] the Department of State informed American consular officers in Manchuria that, should they receive notice from the "Manchukuo" authorities in regard to the termination of extraterritorial privileges or, in the absence of such notice, should a case arise involving the assertion by the local authorities of jurisdiction over American nationals or their property, they should promptly notify the Department.

Having received information that an American concern operating in Manchuria had been requested by the "Manchukuo" authorities to register in accordance with a newly promulgated "Law Concerning Foreign Juridicial Persons", the Department instructed the American consular officer at Mukden to register with the authorities at Hsinking emphatic objection to any attempt by the "Manchukuo" régime to exercise jurisdiction over American nationals and to point out that this Government considers any law which contemplates assertion of such jurisdiction as inapplicable to American nationals and firms in view of the extraterritorial rights of nationals of the United States in Manchuria which are granted by treaties between the United States and China. The American Ambassador at Tokyo was instructed to make similar representations to the Japanese Foreign Office.

Subsequently, the Department sent further instructions to American consuls in Manchuria to the effect that while the American Government does not assent to laws of the "Manchukuo" régime and has not modified in any way its position in regard to the broad general principles involved, the consuls should, as a matter of expediency, when specific cases should arise affecting American business interests and upon request by the representatives of the American interests concerned, intercede with the appropriate authorities toward obtaining a favorable interpretation of the laws or such modification thereof as might be within the discretionary authority of administrative officials.

WASHINGTON, January 25, 1938.

---

[86] See telegram No. 733, November 6, 1937, 11 p. m., *Foreign Relations*, 1937, vol. III, p. 935.

761.94/1014 : Telegram

The Counselor of Embassy in China (Lockhart) to the Secretary of State

PEIPING, February 6, 1938—1 p. m.
[Received February 6—7 a. m.]

91. Following from Harbin.

"2, February 5, 11 a. m. The Soviet Acting Consul General informed me last night that the decision of his Government to restrict parcel post service to and from Japan and Manchuria was an act of reprisal for the detention of a Soviet mail plane which had inadvertently landed near Mutanchi aerodrome on December 19, and that unless the plane, its crew of two, and its cargo of 11,000 letters are released within 2 weeks, stronger reprisals may be expected. He did not specify their probable nature. He emphatically denied the Japanese contention that the plane was armed.

He also said that on January 30 and 31 four clashes occurred near Hunchun and Aigun when Russian troops were compelled to fire on, drive back, Japanese soldiers trespassing on Russian territory, and that although no casualties were reported, he filed a strong protest with the Foreign Office delegate in Harbin.

Neither the incidents nor the protest in the circumstances reported by the press."

LOCKHART

893.01 Manchuria/1508

The Consul at Harbin (Merrell) to the Ambassador in China (Johnson) [87]

No. 36   HARBIN, February 17, 1938.

SIR: I have the honor to enclose translations of two official press releases [88] which appeared in the February 12 issue of the *Harbin Times* * containing detailed information regarding a communist roundup in Manchuria in April 1937 and the investigations which followed. The arrests were reported at the time by the Consulate General† but little information was then available as to the reasons for them, although it was generally supposed that they were aimed at communist organizations. The press ban has been removed, and details have been given to the public.

Before discussing the articles, it should first be stated that this office is of the opinion that they are substantially true, despite the notorious inaccuracy of the Harbin press and the ambiguity of official

[87] Copy transmitted to the Department by the Consul at Harbin in covering despatch No. 39, February 17; received April 18.
[88] Neither printed.
* Russian language Japanese-owned daily. [Footnote in the original.]
† Despatch No. 325 of April 23, 1937; No. 502 to the Department. [Footnote in the original; for despatch No. 325, see *Foreign Relations*, 1937, vol. III, p. 918: covering despatch No. 502 not printed.]

pronouncements in "Manchukuo". There has never been any doubt that the well-equipped bandits received material assistance from Russia, and although the present release may not contain the whole truth, its general accuracy can hardly be questioned. Another point deemed worthy of note is that in no place is there any indication that the various communist organs discovered in Manchuria were in any way connected with Chinese Communists now operating in northwest China; it is alleged throughout that the communists of Manchuria received their orders directly from the Comintern, and scrupulous care is taken to avoid mention of the Soviet Government.

It is stated that 482 persons, mostly of the Chinese race, were arrested in all; of these, 85 received death sentences, 64 were sentenced to hard labor for various periods, 31 have not yet been sentenced, 26 will not receive sentences, 135 are still under investigation, and the remainder have been set free.

The release to the press states that communist activity in Manchuria was started well before the Mukden Incident of September 18, 1931, with headquarters in Mukden, and that after the occupation of that city by the Japanese the agents were forced to transfer their main activities to Harbin and North Manchuria. It is alleged that the bandit depredations which were so serious in the years following 1932 were instigated by the Comintern and carried out by such local organizations as the "Manchurian Regional Committee of the Chinese Communist Party" and similar groups. It would therefore appear that the "anti-bandit campaigns" which have been reported by this office and by the Consulate General at Mukden for the past four or five years were in reality campaigns against armed communist groups which received substantial assistance from Russia. These drives have to a great extent been successful, as depredations in North Manchuria so far this winter have been much less than anticipated, and Mukden reported last year that large-scale banditry was decidedly on the wane in South Manchuria. This would appear to bear out the contention of the authorities that they seized the principal communist leaders.

It is not surprising that the articles fail to mention the mutinies in the "Manchukuo" Army during July and August 1937, and their probable instigation by agents of the Comintern.‡ According to information believed to be reliable, the mutinies, in the Harbin area at least, were only discovered through the arrest in the Chinese city of communist agitators during the latter half of July 1937. These arrests were undoubtedly connected with the anti-red activities now made public.

---

‡Despatch No. 359 of September 22, 1937; No. 554 to the Department. [Footnote in the original; neither printed.]

Although the assertion is made that communist activity has been brought to a standstill in Manchuria by the recently announced arrests, it remains to be seen whether such is really the case. Russians in the employ of the Japanese forces have said that large scale smuggling goes on across the border, especially in the Pogranichnaya (Suifenho) region, and it seems hardly likely that the Comintern will cease attempting to harass Japan and "Manchukuo". Although direct evidence is lacking, there is reason to suppose that many of the incidents and armed clashes which have taken place on the Russian border resulted from attempts of the Japanese to put a stop to this activity.

Respectfully yours,   GEORGE R. MERRELL

893.01 Manchuria/1499 : Telegram

The Ambassador in China (Johnson) to the Secretary of State

HANKOW, February 22, 1938—noon.
[Received February 22—7 a. m.]

118. Following statement is published in Hankow press 22d.

"Hankow, February 21. A spokesman of the German Embassy issued the following statement today:

The declaration of German Chancellor Adolf Hitler made on February 20 before the Reichstag reveals clearly that the recognition of Manchukuo by Germany in no way can be interpreted as an act directed against China. The reasons for the recognition are as follows:

(1) Germany wants to disassociate herself from the policy of the League of Nations;

(2) Germany intends to base her policy on facts and realities. She believes that this is the best for all peoples;

(3) Germany is determined now as before to remain neutral in the present conflict in East Asia and to maintain her traditional friendship towards China;

(4) Germany has no political or territorial designs in East Asia but solely economic;

(5) The German-Japanese relations are based only on the mutual understanding of fighting against Bolshevism."

Sent to Shanghai. Shanghai please transmit by mail to Tokyo.

JOHNSON

893.01 Manchuria/1498 : Telegram

The Ambassador in Japan (Grew) to the Secretary of State

Tokyo, February 22, 1938—6 p. m.
[Received February 22—7 : 10 a. m.]

122. The German Chargé told me that he called this morning on the Minister of Foreign Affairs [89] and stated, under instructions from his Government, that Germany will recognize Manchukuo.

Repeated to Shanghai for Hankow and Peiping.

GREW

893.01 Manchuria/1500 : Telegram

The Consul at Dairen (Turner) to the Secretary of State

Dairen, February 23, 1938—5 p. m.
[Received February 23—8 : 55 a. m.]

I am informed in confidence by my German colleague that Hitler's decision to recognize Manchukuo comes as a surprise to him and to Knoll, Reich trade representative in Hsinking, and is contrary to their recommendations. He hazards the opinion that the German Foreign Office is equally taken by surprise.

By mail to Tokyo, Peiping and Mukden.

TURNER

793.943 Manchuria/52

Memorandum by the Chief of the Division of Far Eastern Affairs (Hamilton)

[Washington,] February 23, 1938.

The new Counselor of the Belgian Embassy, Baron Hervé de Gruben, called and left with me the attached paper [90] as an informal memorandum indicative of the views of the Belgian Government toward the declaration of the "Manchukuo" government in regard to the abolition of extraterritoriality in Manchuria. Baron de Gruben referred to the fact that some time ago we had furnished the Belgian Ambassador information in regard to the attitude of this Government toward the question of extraterritorial jurisdiction in "Manchukuo".[91] Baron de Gruben said that the Belgian Government had made known its views in the matter to the "Manchukuo" authorities. In reply to inquiry, he said that the Belgian Government had made no approach in the matter at Tokyo.

M[AXWELL] M. H[AMILTON]

---

[89] Koki Hirota.
[90] *Infra.*
[91] See note to the Belgian Ambassador, January 25, p. 441.

793.943 Manchuria/52

The Belgian Embassy to the Department of State

[Translation [92]]

MEMORANDUM

The Belgian Government has taken note of the declaration which the Government of Manchukuo made on November 5, 1937, on the occasion of the signature of the treaty relating to the termination of extraterritoriality between Manchukuo and Japan as well as of the interview which Mr. Chuichi Ohashi gave to the press on the subject of the status of foreign nationals in Manchukuo.

The Belgian Government cannot admit that the treaty of November 5, 1937, can have as a consequence the abolition in Manchukuo of the privileges of extraterritoriality which Belgian nationals enjoy by virtue of the treaties always in force.

793.943 Manchuria/51 : Telegram

The Secretary of State to the Ambassador in Japan (Grew)

WASHINGTON, February 24, 1938—6 p. m.

68. Your 93, February 9, 10 p. m., via Shanghai.[93] Department feels that, as representations in regard to some of the laws mentioned in your telegram under reference have been made, and as our general position with regard to laws of this kind which violate the "Open Door" principle has repeatedly been brought to the attention of the authorities at Hsinking and at Tokyo, and as we have registered at both places emphatic objection to any attempt on the part of the authorities of Manchuria to exercise jurisdiction over American nationals and made full reservation with regard to the treaty rights of the United States and its citizens, no useful purpose would be served by further action by this Government at this time.

HULL

793.943 Manchuria/53 : Telegram

The Consul General at Shanghai (Gauss) to the Secretary of State

SHANGHAI, March 3, 1938—10 p. m.
[Received March 3—1 : 58 p. m.]

354. Following from Tokyo.

"March 3, 6 p. m. Reference Department's 319, November 28, 3 p. m.,[94] extraterritoriality in Manchuria.

---

[92] File translation revised by the editors.
[93] Not printed; it reported British representations to the Japanese Government on the subject of treaty rights in Manchuria.
[94] *Foreign Relations*, 1937, vol. III, p. 941.

The Foreign Minister has replied to my note of December 2 [1?], 1937 [96] (see despatch No. 2689 of December 9, 1937 [97]) under date of March 1.[98] The Foreign Minister's note in translation refers to the subject matter of my note and concludes with the following paragraph.

'The policy of the Government of Manchukuo in this instance, which concerns the treatment of nationals of third countries and juridical persons of third countries, is a matter in which the Japanese Government is not concerned and the Japanese Government, accordingly, regrets that it is not in a position to make any explanation'.

Please repeat to Peiping, Hankow and to the Department as our No. 146, March 3, 6 p. m. Grew".

GAUSS

893.01 Manchuria/1504 : Telegram

The Ambassador in Germany (Wilson) to the Secretary of State

BERLIN, March 8, 1938—5 p. m.
[Received March 8—2 : 20 p. m.]

97. The Director of the Political Section of the Foreign Office in the course of a conversation today stated that the Chancellor's statement concerning Germany's recognition of Manchukuo in his February 20 speech, Embassy's 67, February 21, 4 p. m.,[97] paragraph 7, was solely a declaration of intention, that no formal action had yet been taken but that he envisaged such action in the relatively near future and believed it would take the form of a note from the German Ambassador at Tokyo to the Minister of Manchukuo at that capital proposing an exchange of diplomatic representatives.

WILSON

893.506 Manchuria/41 : Telegram

The Secretary of State to the First Secretary of Embassy in China (Salisbury), at Peiping

WASHINGTON, April 8, 1938—6 p. m.

102. Your despatch 1499, December 22, 1937.[97] The West Coast Life Insurance Company in a letter to the Department dated March 25 [97] has represented to the Department that recent legislation in Manchuria if enforced may render it necessary for the Company to discontinue the transaction of new business and that exchange restrictions are being placed in effect which in a number of instances will prevent policy holders residing in Manchuria from maintaining

---

[96] *Foreign Relations, Japan, 1931–1941*, vol. I, p. 154.
[97] Not printed.
[98] For text, see *Foreign Relations, Japan, 1931–1941*, vol. I, p. 154.

their insurance contracts in force owing to their inability to remit premiums in the currency of the policy. It is requested in the letter that, as the time limit for compliance with the new laws is May 31, immediate action be taken by the Department.

The Department desires that the Embassy instruct Harbin to review the situation with the Company's local agent, and take or ask Mukden to take such action as may be appropriate along the lines indicated in the Department's 405 to the Embassy of December 23, 7 p. m.[99] The Consul should report briefly by telegraph the extent and nature of present and prospective restrictions upon the Company's business and the action taken by the Consul, if any.

HULL

893.506 Manchuria/42 : Telegram

The First Secretary of Embassy in China (Salisbury) to the Secretary of State

PEIPING, April 14, 1938—3 p. m.
[Received 3:20 p. m.]

234. Following from American Consulate General at Harbin:

"April 11, 11 a. m. Reference is made to the Department's No. 102 dated April 8, 6 p. m. to the Embassy at Peiping regarding the West Coast Life Insurance Company.

The company's agent reports that exchange restrictions are no problem at present; he felt able to remit all of his accumulation of premiums collected in local government currency, and now accepts only drafts in foreign currency presented by policy holders, who readily give [*get?*] permits to pay premiums or loans. He expects this condition to continue.

He is not writing new policies, which must be in local currency unless special permission is granted. The company will not authorize policies in local currency, and so far has not given him the necessary authority to apply at Hsinking for permission to write policies in foreign currency and remit the premiums. Such permission would be valid only until June 1, when the new legislation comes into force, but he feels that it would be granted readily and would establish a precedent for similar permission following full compliance with the laws after the date mentioned.

On January 13, February 7 and 11 the Consulate General forwarded to the company's Shanghai branch, at its request various translations of the pertinent law, the insurance business law, and a discussion of the situation. These, together with the agent's recommendations and legal advice which it is understood have been forwarded, should be enough to enable the company to decide the question of compliance. No question of consular representations has arisen; the American Government has already protested the application of these laws to American nationals; and as other American firms are taking steps

---

[99] *Foreign Relations,* 1937, vol. III, p. 951.

toward registration with this office acting in a notarial capacity only, the Consulate General does not think it expedient to intervene on behalf of one company until such time as it suffers from direct official action. An authorized representative of the company (the agent here has no power) should apply for registration; or if registration not desired, he should settle with the authorities the now uncertain status of an office maintained for collection purposes only."

Copy by mail to Mukden.

SALISBURY

761.94/1037 : Telegram

The First Secretary of Embassy in China (Salisbury) to the Secretary of State

PEIPING, April 20, 1938—11 a. m.
[Received April 20—2 a. m.]

245. Following from American Consulate General at Harbin.

"April 15, 5 p. m. Reliable Japanese and official Soviet sources independently stated that several days ago about 10 Japanese armed planes from the Korean garrison violated the Soviet frontier near Hunchun. One was grounded, perhaps shot down, and is being held by the Soviet authorities. The unarmed mail plane captured in December in Manchuria has never been released.

North bound Japanese troop movements indicate a possible crisis, although they may be spring transfers. The press has not mentioned this incident and is relatively quiet regarding Russia in general.

Virtually all news items regarding military activities in China have been suppressed, and no foreign newspapers from Tientsin and Shanghai have been received since April 5."

SALISBURY

762.93 Manchuria/16 : Telegram (part air)

The Ambassador in Germany (Wilson) to the Secretary of State

BERLIN, May 12, 1938—6 p. m.
[Received May 13—7 : 30 a. m.]

241. The semi-official German news agency released this afternoon the following announcement:

"Carrying out the declaration of Fuehrer and Reich Chancellor in his Reichstag speech of February 20 of this year that Germany would recognize Manchukuo, a treaty was signed on the 12th of this month in the Foreign Office by Secretary of State Baron von Weizsaecker and the Trade Commissioner of Manchukuo.

The treaty stipulates the immediate assumption of diplomatic and consular relations between the two States and provides further for the early beginning of negotiations regarding a consular, trade and shipping treaty".

WILSON

793.94/13009 : Telegram

The First Secretary of Embassy in China (Salisbury) to the Secretary of State

PEIPING, May 13, 1938—3 p. m.
[Received May 13—7 a. m.]

291. The following telegram has been received from the American Consul at Harbin:

"15. May 12, 3 p. m. Yesterday 1000 carts and horses and many more coolies were impressed in Harbin for use probably on the eastern border. Chinese with a knowledge of Japanese or Russian were taken from their places of employment, which is legal under the national defense mobilization law enforced yesterday.

It is reported that the Okamura Division (Second Division) which has been stationed in Harbin for about a year has left for the East.

Japanese residents feel that a war with Russia is more likely now than several months ago, and they say that Japanese forces in Manchuria exceed those in China. The war feeling in Harbin is stronger than it has been for over 2 years, with Japanese civilians admitting that if it comes it will be brought about by their own leaders. Repeated to Tokyo."

SALISBURY

762.93 Manchuria/17 : Telegram

The First Secretary of Embassy in China (Salisbury) to the Secretary of State

PEIPING, May 14, 1938—9 a. m.
[Received May 14—7 a. m.]

292. The following telegram has been received from Mukden:

"39, May 13, noon. Hsinking announces that German-Manchukuo Treaty of Amity was signed yesterday at Berlin[1] by Kato, representative of Manchukuo in Germany, and the German Vice Minister of Foreign Affairs and that Treaty contains four articles as follows:

Article 1. Each country being of independent and equal status, it will cause Consuls to be exchanged with and stationed in the other and will afford them the same treatment as Consuls of the several countries.

Article 2. The nationals of each country shall be assured freedom of residence, movement, and business in the other country and each government shall afford to nationals of the other country protection of life and property.

Article 3. In order to promote their friendly relations the two Governments agree that immediately after the signing of the present treaty they shall begin negotiations for commerce.

Article 4. The text of the present treaty shall be in the Manchurian and German languages.

---

[1] Text printed in *Reichsgesetzblatt* (Berlin), 1938, pt. II, p. 286. The telegraphed version is an inexact summary of the German text.

Hsinking bulletins state that the treaty will go into effect following ratification by the Heads of each State which is expected to take place towards the end of this month. They add that nothing definite has been arranged as to place or scope of negotiations provided by article 3."

SALISBURY

893.77 Manchuria/135

The Secretary of State to the Ambassador in Japan (Grew)

No. 1509   WASHINGTON, May 28, 1938.

SIR: The Department refers to a communication, under date June 25, 1937, addressed to you by Ambassador Johnson in which it was suggested that you take up with the appropriate Japanese authorities the question of the failure of the South Manchuria Railway and its subsidiary organizations to discharge certain obligations to American nationals and firms. As reported in Mukden's despatch to the Embassy at Peiping, No. 220 of March 23, 1938, (a copy of which was sent to you) [3] the latest representations in respect of one of these obligations, the payment of certain Chinese Eastern Railway pensions, have been definitely rejected. It will be noted that Vice Consul Davies,[4] in accordance with the suggestion advanced by Consul General Adams,[5] recommends that it be intimated to the appropriate Japanese authorities that, in view of the failure of the State Railways and the South Manchuria Railway to honor certain obligations, World Trade Directory Reports on these concerns might necessarily be revised to show a poorer credit rating.

Before giving consideration to this or any other specific suggestion for action which might appropriately be taken by this Government as a consequence of the failure of the South Manchuria Railway Company to discharge what appear to be legitimate obligations to American firms and individuals, the Department would welcome an expression of the Embassy's opinion in regard to the possibility that the officers of the company might give further consideration to the claims in question if they were made aware of the likelihood that their present attitude, in the event that it became generally known in American financial circles, might prejudice the business standing of the company in this country to an extent out of proportion to the small sums involved in these claims. If, in the Embassy's opinion, a discreet intimation along these lines to the appropriate Japanese authorities either by the Embassy, or by the Consul at Dairen, or by both, would be likely to serve a useful purpose, you are authorized in your discretion to make such an approach and to instruct the Consul at Dairen

---

[3] Not printed.
[4] Then at Mukden.
[5] Then at Harbin.

to make a similar approach to the head office of the South Manchuria Railway there.

Very truly yours,   For the Secretary of State:

R. WALTON MOORE

765.94/92 : Telegram

The Ambassador in Japan (Grew) to the Secretary of State

TOKYO, June 23, 1938—6 p. m.

[Received June 23—11:45 a. m.]

404. 1. We obtained from a confidential and trustworthy source copies of drafts of various agreements now under negotiation between Japan and Manchukuo on the one hand and Italy on the other.[6] These projected agreements are:

(*a*) Treaty of Commerce and Navigation between Italy and Manchukuo supplemented by

(*b*) Barter arrangements between Italy, Japan–Manchuria.

(*c*) Arrangement for exchange clearance.

(*d*) Protocol of signature.

These drafts were prepared by Japan–Manchuria and were presumably presented to the Italian commercial mission as a basis for discussion. We do not know what changes have been agreed upon. According to the most recent press reports, the chairman of the mission returned to Hsinking on June 21 to propose certain textual changes in the agreed upon drafts, and he is to return to Tokyo for further discussions, after which the agreements are to be signed.

2. Draft (*a*) above substantially follows the standard form for treaties of commerce and navigation. Among the points which might be specially noted are:

(*a*) There is no reference to extraterritorial privileges of Italian nationals in Manchuria. Access to courts is guaranteed.

(*b*) Unconditional most-favored-nation treatment in respect of imports is provided, but exemption from that provision of special privileges accorded by either party to an adjoining state, special privileges arising out of any customs union, and special privileges accorded to colonies and possessions is stipulated.

(*c*) "An equitable share" is guaranteed in the laying down of import and export quotas.

3. Draft (*b*) provides that all commercial exchanges between Japan and Italy and Manchuria and Italy are to be regulated by the agreement, which is to run for a period of 1 year, subject to extension for a further period of 1 year. The draft contemplates a balancing of trade between Japan–Manchukuo and Italy, and requires to that end

---

[6] Signed at Tokyo July 5.

454 FOREIGN RELATIONS, 1938, VOLUME III

compilation of exports by categories from each party to the other. A statistical summary attached to draft (*b*) indicates that Japan–Manchuria were prepared to accept Italian goods to the total value of yen 34,000,000 including yen 19,000,000 for arms and munitions and yen 3,000,000 for motor vehicles, and that Japan–Manchukuo proposed exports to Italy, largely of primary and semimanufactured commodities, to the value of lira 200,000,000, as against lira 150,000,000, acceptable to Italy.

4. The other two drafts are not of exceptional interest.

5. Our informant states that the discussions included the possible purchase by Japan from Italy of airplanes to the value of 30,000,000 yen, but that this transaction has fallen through.

Please furnish paraphrase to Navy Department.

GREW

893.20 Manchuria/28 : Telegram

The First Secretary of Embassy in China (Salisbury) to the Secretary of State

PEIPING, June 29, 1938—4 p. m.
[Received June 29—10 : 35 a. m.]

395. Following from Mukden:

"45, June 28, 4 p. m. My telegram June 28, 11 a. m.[8] Japanese Army Headquarters Jehol City this noon announced that Chinese communist army units which had been hovering about Manchurian southwest border since middle of the month have invaded Hsinglunghsien (the newly created prefecture comprising the corner projecting into Hopeh Province due south of Jehol City) but are surrounded by Japanese and Manchurian troops."

Repeated to Hankow and Tokyo.

SALISBURY

893.20 Manchuria/31 : Telegram

The First Secretary of Embassy in China (Salisbury) to the Secretary of State

PEIPING, July 5, 1938—3 p. m.
[Received 7 : 56 p. m.]

417. Embassy's 411, July 2, 4 p. m.[8] Following from Mukden.

"47, July 2, 11 a. m.
Your June 29, 4 p. m. I am reliably informed that Ma Chan Shan's command has made contact with revolted troops and there is fighting

---

[8] Not printed.

going on in southwest Jehol with Chinese in control of some localities. Police detachments from Mukden are reported to have been sent south evidently to help maintain order behind disturbed zone."

Repeated to Embassy, Hankow, Tokyo.

SALISBURY

761.93 Manchuria/112 : Telegram

The First Secretary of Embassy in China (Salisbury) to the Secretary of State

PEIPING, July 16, 1938—11 a. m.
[Received July 16—7 a. m.]

447. Following from Mukden:

"July 15, 6 p. m. 49. According to urgent Kokutsu reports, Hsinking is greatly aroused over occupation on 12th and fortification since by Soviet soldiers of a hill 4 kilometres within Manchurian territory 40 kilometres slightly east of south of Hunchun commanding Tumen Railroad. Reports say that 30 Russian soldiers are now completing defenses of occupied point supported by detachments on east and northern slopes within Soviet territory who also are erecting defenses. Reports add that Hsinking has protested to Soviet Consul General at Harbin and requested withdrawal invading forces.

I am reliably informed Manchurian tribes [*Government?*] regards Soviet action as direct challenge and is ready to use force if invaders do not withdraw."

SALISBURY

761.93 Manchuria/114 : Telegram

The Chargé in the Soviet Union (Kirk) to the Secretary of State

Moscow, July 16, 1938—7 p. m.
[Received July 16—5 : 10 p. m.]

184. Embassy's telegram 181.[9] Japanese Embassy here states that the incident was caused by some 40 soldiers undertaking military operations on July 11 within Manchurian territory at a point southeast of Vladivostock near Changkufeng.

According to further information from the Embassy, the protest to the Soviet Foreign Office stated that in view of its special relations with Manchuria and of certain provisions of the Portsmouth Treaty [10] Japan could not remain indifferent to the action of the Soviet soldiers and requested that the soldiers in question be withdrawn. The Japanese Embassy was informed last night by the Foreign Office that the soldiers are within Soviet territory and this statement has been com-

---

[9] Not printed.
[10] Signed September 5, 1905, *Foreign Relations*, 1905, p. 824.

municated to Tokyo by the Embassy. The Japanese Embassy emphasizes the reasoned and cautious nature of the action of the Japanese Government in this matter.

KIRK

761.93 Manchuria/117 : Telegram

The First Secretary of Embassy in China (Salisbury) to the Secretary of State

PEIPING, July 19, 1938—7 p. m.
[Received July 19—10:10 a. m.]

454. Following from Harbin:

"25, July 19, 11 a. m. The Acting Soviet Consul General minimizes the importance of the recent incident on the eastern border, and asserts that it is 'another Japanese bluff'. He said that he refused to accept the protest and demand for evacuation of Soviet troops lodged with him by the Harbin delegate of the Foreign Office because it was done by telephone at 10 p. m., July 14, and because Russian troops had not crossed the border anyway. This probably explains why the Manchukuo government has received no reply to the protest, as stated in the press. He departed today on home leave as scheduled.

The hill, said to have been occupied by Russian soldiers, has not been occupied before, according to a report to Soviet and to Manchukuo officials, and hence probably is not as important strategically as reported in the Japanese press. This office feels that perhaps the incident is being played up by the Japanese because no satisfactory news is coming out of China.

Repeated to Mukden, Tokyo."

Repeated to Embassy Hankow, Consulate General Shanghai.

SALISBURY

761.93 Manchuria/118 : Telegram

The Chargé in the Soviet Union (Kirk) to the Secretary of State

MOSCOW, July 21, 1938—4 p. m.
[Received July 21—10:11 a. m.]

194. My telegram No. 187, July 18, 2 p. m.[11] The Embassy is reliably informed that the Japanese Ambassador, who has just returned from a trip abroad yesterday, renewed his Government's protest against the action of the Soviet troops and strongly insisted on their withdrawal and a return to the *status quo ante*. He is furthermore said to have indicated that if this were done his Government would be willing to set up a joint commission to delineate the frontiers in the area where the incident took place.

KIRK

---

[11] Not printed.

761.93 Manchuria/126 : Telegram

The Ambassador in Japan (Grew) to the Secretary of State

Tokyo, July 25, 1938—5 p. m.
[Received July 26—11 : 40 a. m.]

487. Soviet-Manchurian border incident at Changkufeng. The Military Attaché [12] has submitted the following memorandum on the situation:

"1. According to information which has reached this office, the Japanese Government is at present giving considerable thought to the question of whether military operations subsequent to the fall of Hankow should be pushed to the extent of attempting the actual physical destruction of the Chiang Kai Shek regime, or whether the situation could be better handled by a relative suspension of offensive operations after the fall of Hankow and a resumption of political activity directed toward a reorganization of Central China along political lines on the assumption that, with the fall of Hankow, the Chiang government will in this event have been crushed.

2. It has also been reported that there is a relation between the above question and the recent border incidents, the most important of which is the occupation of the hill at Changkufeng by Russian troops. In regard to this incident, it is reported that there are two factions in the Government, one advocating positive action with a view to actually forcing the Russian troops out of the occupied position, and the other advocating caution and the adoption of a watchful policy to be accompanied however by certain precautionary moves on the part of Japanese troops in the vicinity.

3. In other words, viewing the two questions as related, one school of thought advocates the suspension of military operations beyond Hankow and a strong handling of the border situation while attempting the political downfall of Chiang Kai Shek, while the other leans toward avoiding border operations in order to operate more vigorously toward a complete destruction of the Chiang government, and with it the likelihood of future Russian operations in support of that government.

4. While it is difficult to determine what may be the Japanese course of action in the present situation, as that course will obviously be determined by Japanese estimates as to Russian motives in the present border activities, it is none the less apparent that these activities have constituted a sort of diversion which demands careful consideration in its relation to operations in China".

The Embassy has learned from a thoroughly reliable source that since Shigemitsu [13] presented to Litvinoff [14] the Japanese demands for the settlement of the incident and those demands were rejected, the Japanese Government has done nothing further than to pursue a policy of what our informant termed "watchful waiting". According to our informant, a popular version of the affair is that the Russians

---

[12] Maj. Harry I. T. Creswell.
[13] Japanese Ambassador in the Soviet Union.
[14] Maxim Litvinov, Soviet Commissar for Foreign Affairs.

in occupying the position at Changkufeng were sounding out the Japanese with a view to ascertaining whether they were prepared for hostilities on a grand scale, which he added was similar to the assertion made at the time last year when the Japanese occupied the islands in the Amur River that Japan was sounding out Russia with a view to ascertaining whether it was prepared for hostilities on a grand scale.

Shanghai please repeat to Hankow as our 487, July 25, 5 p. m.

Department please send copy to War Department.

GREW

761.93 Manchuria/124 : Telegram

The Chargé in the Soviet Union (Kirk) to the Secretary of State

Moscow, July 26, 1938—9 a. m.
[Received July 26—6: 45 a. m.]

202. My telegram No. 199, July 24, 4 p. m.,[15] and previous. In the course of a conversation last night Litvinov discussed briefly the present Soviet-Japanese controversy. He said that the Soviet soldiers had every right to occupy the position to the west of Lake Khasan, that maps of long standing in the possession of Soviet Government proved definitely the Soviet contention and that, therefore, there was no reason why the soldiers should be withdrawn as the Japanese had requested. However, he said that he did not believe that this incident would result in hostilities, that the Soviet Union had no intention of "attacking" the Japanese and that he was informed that the Japanese military authorities were opposed to precipitating a conflict with the Soviets. Litvinov added that he had told the Japanese Ambassador that he would examine any proofs of the Japanese contention that the Ambassador might care to submit (see my 195, July 22, noon[15]) and that he supposed that the Japanese Government was now working on further representations to the Soviet Government which would encourage some adjustment of the controversy.

KIRK

761.93 Manchuria/127 : Telegram

The Ambassador in Japan (Grew) to the Secretary of State

TOKYO, July 26, 1938—1 p. m.
[Received July 26—7: 13 a. m.]

488. General statement. Our 487, July 25, 5 p. m., via Shanghai, Changkufeng incident. My German colleague[16] who from his former

---

[15] Not printed.
[16] Maj. Gen. Eugen Ott, German Ambassador in Japan.

position as Military Attaché enjoys the closest relations with the Japanese military told me this morning that high Japanese officers have informed him that they want no trouble with Soviet Russia at present because they are too much occupied in China and that no broadening of the incident will be permitted to develop.

GREW

761.93 Manchuria/131 : Telegram

The Chargé in the Soviet Union (Kirk) to the Secretary of State

Moscow, July 30, 1938—1 p. m.
[Received July 30—6:20 a. m.]

210. My 204, July 28, 11 a. m.[17] A Tass report in today's *Pravda* states that on July 29, 4 p. m. two Japanese-Manchurian detachments crossed the Soviet frontiers and attempted to occupy the heights 2 kilometres to the north of Lake Khasan but were driven out by Soviet border guards after a skirmish which resulted in some killed and wounded on both sides. The report continues that the Soviet Chargé d'Affaires in Tokyo has been instructed to make a firm protest to the Japanese Government, to demand punishment for those guilty and also to warn the Japanese Government that the Soviet Government holds it fully responsible for the consequence of the action of its functionaries in Manchuria.

KIRK

761.93 Manchuria/132 : Telegram

The Ambassador in Japan (Grew) to the Secretary of State

TOKYO, July 31, 1938—5 p. m.
[Received July 31—6:30 a. m.]

506. Domei released this afternoon a communiqué from the Kwangtung Army Headquarters at Hsinking reporting a serious clash which occurred yesterday afternoon at 4:30, lasting until 5 this morning, between the Soviet troops and Japanese-Manchukuo troops at Changkufeng. The Japanese-Manchukuo troops are reported to have taken the Soviet positions on the hill at Changkufeng and driven off the Soviet troops to the eastward. The communiqué reports approximately 200 Russian casualties, 30 having been found dead on the field, as well as a number of Japanese casualties.

Repeated to Peiping for Hankow.

GREW

---

[17] Not printed.

761.93 Manchuria/133 : Telegram

The First Secretary of Embassy in China (Salisbury) to the Secretary of State

PEIPING, July 31, 1938—5 p. m.
[Received July 31—7 a. m.]

Following from Mukden:

"July 31, 2 p. m. My July 15, 6 p. m. Following information provided my informant by the Kwangtung Army. Japanese forces yesterday repelled Russian forces which penetrated Manchurian territory north of disputed position, and in addition after batteries newly established at this point opened fire on them. Russian heavy tanks also were in action. This morning same batteries shelled Korean village across Tumen and exchange artillery fire is in progress, seven Japanese casualties up to last night."

Repeated to Ambassador and Tokyo.

SALISBURY

761.93 Manchuria/134 : Telegram

The Chargé in the Soviet Union (Kirk) to the Secretary of State

Moscow, August 1, 1938—10 a. m.
[Received August 1—6: 30 a. m.]

212. My 210, July 30, 1 p. m. Tass reports in today's Soviet press that on July 31 Japanese military forces violated the Soviet border on the heights west of Lake Khasan and that Japanese troops opening unexpected artillery fire during the night suddenly attacked troops of the border guard of the Soviet Union stationed on the frontier. The Japanese occupied Soviet territory to a depth of 4 kilometres. On the heights west of Lake Khasan a clash took place which lasted for several hours. The report adds that the Japanese military forces received a severe repulse and the Japanese troops suffered heavy losses in men and materials. The losses of the Soviet troops are being investigated.

KIRK

761.93 Manchuria/135 : Telegram

The Chargé in the Soviet Union (Kirk) to the Secretary of State

Moscow, August 1, 1938—2 p. m.
[Received August 1—11: 20 a. m.]

215. Referring to my 210, July 30, 1 p. m.; and 212, August 1, 10 a. m., an official of the Japanese Embassy today stated that the following information has been received from Tokyo in regard to the

incidents reported in the Soviet press and referred to in my telegrams under reference. According to this information, 10 Soviet soldiers on July 29 at 9 : 30 a. m. crossed the Manchurian frontier about 2 miles north of Lake Khazan and were repulsed by Japanese troops. The Japanese troops then withdrew behind the frontier but at 4 p. m., the Soviet forces again attacked with tanks and artillery and were again repulsed by the Japanese forces, who this time remained in the disputed area. On July 31st, the Soviet troops in the same area returned to the attack, supported by artillery fire and tanks, and, after a skirmish which lasted several hours, were thrown back by the Japanese troops. The Soviet losses were 60 killed and the Japanese 30 killed, and the Japanese captured 10 or 11 Soviet tanks. In connection with this engagement the Japanese forces on the same day occupied the town of Changkufeng, the original center of disturbances.

The official of the Japanese Embassy added that messages from Tokyo which he assumed were in relation to the foregoing developments had just reached the Embassy.

KIRK

761.93 Manchuria/137 : Telegram

The Chargé in the Soviet Union (Kirk) to the Secretary of State

Moscow, August 2, 1938—8 a. m.
[Received August 2—7 : 39 a. m.]

217. Referring to my telegram No. 216, August 1, 8 p. m.,[18] following statement issued during the night. According to information received by Tass from authoritative sources, the account of the clash between the Soviet and Japanese detachments in the region of Lake Khasan has been as follows: on July 29 after the Japanese detachment was ejected on the hill Bezimiannya occupied by them the Japanese concentrated their troops consisting of one division against Zaozernoi (Changkufeng) hill which is situated in Soviet territory.

On July 31 at 3 a. m., Japanese troops under cover of artillery fire suddenly attacked Soviet frontier posts and compelled them to retreat from Zaozernoi hill. Simultaneously the Japanese artillery began to bombard the adjacent heights and the road behind them in order to prevent Soviet reinforcements from approaching. Aided by artillery Japanese infantry succeeded in penetrating 4 kilometres into Soviet territory. In a few hours Soviet regular troops which had come up ejected the Japanese from Soviet territory. On both sides there are wounded and killed. Japanese lost 400 killed and wounded. The Japanese abandoned on Soviet territory 5 cannon, 14 machine gun, 157 rifles with ammunition. On the Soviet side there

---

[18] Not printed.

256941—54——30

were 55 wounded, 13 killed.   In addition one Soviet tank and cannon also were disabled.   It is assumed that a Soviet pilot who parachuted from a scouting plane fell into the hands of the Japanese.   Both before the Japanese invasion and during the battle, Soviet troops never violated the Manchurian border which deprived them of the chance of encircling the invaders or taking them on the flank.

The Soviet Chargé d'Affaires in Tokyo was instructed to present an energetic protest to the Japanese Government and to call its attention to the possible threatening consequence of the actions of the Japanese militarists unwilling to respect the inviolability of Soviet territory the boundaries of which have been established by Russo-Chinese agreements and clearly delineated in the maps bearing the signatures of representatives of China annexed thereto.

KIRK

761.93 Manchuria/140 : Telegram

The Consul at Harbin (Merrell) to the Secretary of State

HARBIN, August 2, 1938—10 a. m.
[Received August 2—7 a. m.]

31. The Kwantung Army officially released at 2:30 last night a statement to the effect that during the afternoon Soviet planes bombed the railway and bridges along the Tumen River both in Manchuria and Korea and that five of them were shot down.

An American visitor in Hsinking last week declared the officials there were relieved when the tension appeared to be relaxing.   He was certain that the Russians were the aggressors.   It therefore follows that the present incident, if reported correctly by the Kwantung Army, is undoubtedly causing great concern in Hsinking and Tokyo, as all evidence indicates that the Japanese do not desire a Soviet war at the present time.

It has been reliably learned that civilian movements in the affected districts in Manchuria and Korea have been strictly controlled for the past 10 days.

Repeated to Mukden, Tokyo.

MERRELL

761.93 Manchuria/141 : Telegram

The Ambassador in Japan (Grew) to the Secretary of State

TOKYO, August 2, 1938—6 p. m.
[Received August 2—10:55 a. m.]

508. Our 506, July 31, 5 p. m.

1. The clash which occurred on the Soviet border reportedly resulting in the shooting down of five Soviet airplanes by Japanese forces

has, we understand, been fully reported to the American press by local correspondents. In response to inquiry by us, the Foreign Office and the War Office both stated that all information received in official Japanese quarters has been made available to the press.

2. The latest incident along with developments at Changkufeng is not being sensationally played up in the Japanese press. This attitude of restraint on the part of the press probably reflects the strong hope expressed to us by officials that the situation can be prevented from becoming aggravated.

GREW

761.93 Manchuria/168

Memorandum by the Assistant Chief of the Division of Far Eastern Affairs (Ballantine) of a Conversation With the Counselor of the Japanese Embassy (Suma)

[WASHINGTON,] August 2, 1938.

Mr. Suma called at his own request to acquaint me confidentially with information he had received from his Government in regard to the situation on the Siberian-Manchurian border. Most of the information was a repetition of Japanese official communiqués which have already been reported in the press and by our Embassy at Tokyo. Mr. Suma showed me a map of the border region where the recent incidents have occurred and said that when the Japanese Ambassador at Moscow protested against the Russian occupation of Changkufeng the Russians produced a copy of a map which they said accompanied the Hunchun Treaty of 1868 [19] and which showed that the disputed place was in Russian territory. Mr. Suma said further that in 1906 when a Russo-Japanese agreement was concluded [20] Ambassador Motono had been furnished by the Russian Government with copies of maps defining the borders and that according to these maps the disputed place was in Manchuria. The map which Litvinoff showed to Ambassador Shigemitsu was not among the maps which had been furnished the Japanese Government in 1906.

I said that our information in regard to this situation was derived from official communiqués of the two sides issued in the press and that I had understood from these communiqués that the Japanese did not intend to take military measures to recover the disputed territory. Mr. Suma said that that was the case up to the time that certain Manchurian gendarmes were arrested by the Soviet authorities on the 30th which was the direct cause of the subsequent fighting. Mr. Suma said

[19] Variously reported as concluded in 1869, 1884, or 1886; extract printed in the Moscow *News*, August 8, taken from *Pravda*.

[20] For Russo-Japanese agreement of July 30, 1907, see *British and Foreign State Papers*, vol. CI, p. 462.

that according to latest reports Soviet airplanes had made incursions into Korean territory. They had gone as far as Rashin and had dropped bombs at the port of Yuki. Mr. Suma said that the Japanese Government was making every effort to reach a peaceful settlement and had reasonable hopes that such a settlement would be reached. He said that of course it was impossible to make any predictions but he was hopeful of a satisfactory outcome.

J[OSEPH] W. B[ALLANTINE]

761.93 Manchuria/143 : Telegram

The Chargé in the Soviet Union (Kirk) to the Secretary of State

[Extract]

Moscow, August 2, 1938—10 p. m.
[Received August 2—5 : 02 p. m.]

219. My 217, August 2, 8 a. m.

. . . .

I understand that the messages received by the Japanese Ambassador yesterday (see my 215, August 1, 2 p. m.) instructed him to protest in person to Litvinov against the violation of Manchurian territory by Soviet troops and to resume discussion on the general controversy; that the Japanese Ambassador considered it inadvisable for him to approach Litvinov personally at the present time and sent instead a secretary of the Embassy to deliver the protest to an official of the Foreign Office. The Soviet official, however, is said to have declined to discuss the matter with the Japanese representative stating that the matter was too serious to be discussed between subordinates.

KIRK

761.93 Manchuria/144 : Telegram

The Chargé in the Soviet Union (Kirk) to the Secretary of State

Moscow, August 3, 1938—noon.
[Received August 3—8 : 50 a. m.]

220. My 217, August 2, 8 a. m. Following Tass communiqué published in Soviet press this morning:

"At dawn on August 2 the Japanese Army again launched an attack on the height of Zaozernaya [Changkufeng] situated on Soviet territory and the struggle for the possession lasted throughout the entire day. Whenever the Japanese forces penetrated into Soviet territory they were subjected to artillery fire and aerial bombardment from the Soviet side which caused them enormous losses.

The accounts spread by the Japanese telegraph agencies and newspapers of flights of Soviet bombing planes over Manchurian and

Korean territories are strongly denied by the competent Soviet circles. They point out that from the very beginning of the conflict the Soviet Government has declared that it intends to defend only territory belonging unquestionably to the Soviet Union and that the air forces as well as the infantry in strict observance of this directive have held themselves the entire time exclusively within the borders of the Soviet Union. They suggest that the above mentioned accounts have been purposely spread by the Japanese militarists in order to justify their repeated attacks on Soviet territory and the enormous losses which they are suffering. The opinion is also advanced that the Japanese authorities in their provocative actions are being encouraged by certain Japanese diplomats. In these circumstances it is considered inevitable that the further continuation of military actions is fraught with the most serious consequences." [21]

KIRK

761.93 Manchuria/152 : Telegram

The Chargé in the Soviet Union (Kirk) to the Secretary of State

Moscow, August 3, 1938—midnight.
[Received August 3—8 : 35 p. m.]

223. I understand that the Japanese Ambassador is maintaining the position referred to in my 219, August 2, 10 p. m., and has not sought an interview with Litvinov in regard to latest developments in the controversy on the basis that the position on both sides was clearly stated in his interview of July 20. It is further understood that the Japanese Ambassador while reaffirming Manchukuo claim to the territory in dispute is stating here that the Japanese Government has no desire to acquire further territory in the region nor to bring about an enlargement of the conflict. In would appear from the foregoing that in so far as diplomatic negotiations in Moscow are concerned both the Soviet and Japanese Governments have not advanced beyond the positions assumed at the beginning of the controversy.

KIRK

761.93 Manchuria/153 : Telegram

The Ambassador in Japan (Grew) to the Secretary of State

TOKYO, August 4, 1938—6 p. m.
[Received August 4—10 : 06 a. m.]

516. Embassy's 508, August 2, 6 p. m., Soviet border clash.

1. The featuring by the press of reports on the Soviet border incident is running a poor second to reports on the advance towards Hankow. Systematic and effective use is being made of Domei reports

---

[21] In telegram No. 225, August 4, noon, the Chargé in the Soviet Union reported that this last sentence should read: "In these circumstances the further continuation, fraught with extremely serious consequences, of military actions is considered inevitable." (761.93 Manchuria/149)

from each important capital to the effect that dominant opinion at such capital does not expect the incident to develop into war. Particular interest attaches to reports that Moscow is not excited and that the Soviet press appears to be belittling the incident. At the same time Japanese Army releases purporting to be simply factual accounts are currently published and they make it clear that the scale of fighting has been dangerously extensive. One release published today states that the Soviet forces in the vicinity of Changkufeng include 3 battalions of infantry and 1 mechanized brigade with more than 200 tanks. Soviet air raids involving large numbers of planes, over points in Manchuria and Korea, continue to be affirmed.

2. The populace shows no desire for war against the Soviet Union and appears to be calm. However, apprehension is evidenced among officials and other informed Japanese, who feel that, as it is now the Soviet's turn to move, the decision for war or peace rests with Moscow.

We learn from the Foreign Office that Litvinov is evading the Japanese Ambassador, which would seem to support press despatches from European capitals that the Soviet Government has not as yet made its decision. It was also stated at the Foreign Office that Japan will, whatever the consequences, tolerate no violation of the frontier. Nevertheless, there appears to be moderate optimism that war will not eventuate.

3. As there is available in Tokyo no information from sources other than Japanese, we are in no position to decide whether we wish to modify our views on Soviet-Japanese relations expressed in our despatch 2822 of March 18 [22] and in other reports. It would appear, however, that the Soviet forces have, by moving into an area the ownership of which has been for some time in controversy, initiated this dangerous situation. Whether the motive was to divert Japanese forces from operations against China, as has been suggested, or some other, the Soviets have apparently precipitated a situation which may become impossible either for the Soviet Union or Japan to control.

Repeated to Peiping for Johnson.

GREW

761.93 Manchuria/155 : Telegram

The Chargé in the Soviet Union (Kirk) to the Secretary of State

Moscow, August 4, 1938—10 p. m.
[Received August 4—5 : 30 p. m.]

228. Reference my telegram 223, August 3, midnight. A member of the Japanese Embassy informed me today that the Japanese Ambassador acting under instructions from his Government called on

---

[22] Not printed.

Litvinov this afternoon and made the following proposals in the name of the Japanese Government which were also presented to the Soviet Chargé d'Affaires in Tokyo.

1. The immediate cessation of hostilities in the area to be followed by discussions through diplomatic channels in regard to the means of establishing a truce.

2. Following the cessation of hostilities and the establishment of a truce, the Japanese Government was prepared to discuss the question of the frontier in that region on the basis of the merits of the case, and each side would then present documentary and other evidence to substantiate its claim to the region in dispute. Litvinov, according to the official of the Japanese Embassy, without definitely rejecting the entire Japanese proposal, stated that the Soviet Government could agree to no cessation of hostilities until the Japanese troops had withdrawn behind the frontier line shown on the map annexed to the Hunchun Treaty, which had been published yesterday in the Soviet press, but that following withdrawal behind what the Soviet Government had maintained and continued to maintain was the correct frontier line, the Soviet Government would then be glad to bring about the immediate cessation of hostilities and discuss with the Japanese Government the exact demarcation of the frontier.

My informant added that the discussion lasted over 2½ hours and consisted largely of reiterations of the respective positions indicated above without making any progress towards their reconciliation. He believed, however, that while no progress had been made in today's conversation it did not mean that the door was shut for future conversations between the two Governments. The Japanese Ambassador, I understand, is reporting to his Government and does not intend to seek a further interview with Litvinov pending the receipt of further instructions from Tokyo.

KIRK

761.93 Manchuria/157 : Telegram

The Chargé in the Soviet Union (Kirk) to the Secretary of State

Moscow, August 5, 1938—10 a. m.
[Received 12 : 20 p. m.]

229. My 288, August 4, 10 p. m. Following is translation of Tass report published in today's press:

"Yesterday, August 4, the Japanese Ambassador in Moscow, Mr. Shigemitsu, called on the People's Commissar for Foreign Affairs, Comrade Litvinov, and with reference to the clash in the region of Lake Khasan, declared that the Japanese Government had the intention of resolving the 'incident' by peaceful means as a local incident. Under instructions from his Government, the Ambassador therefore is proposing to terminate military actions by both sides and to transfer the question to negotiations through diplomatic channels.

Comrade Litvinov replied that if in reality the Japanese Government had peaceful intentions then the activities of the Japanese military authorities are not at all in conformity thereto. The armed incursion into Soviet territory and the night attack on the Soviet frontier post accompanied by the use of artillery could only ironically be called peaceful actions. The incident had arisen only as a result of these activities and had they not occurred there would have been no incident. If the Japanese will terminate the attacks on Soviet territory and the bombardment thereof and will recall those remnants of its armed forces which may still be on Soviet territory, there would then be no reason for the Soviet forces to continue its counter military activities and then the Soviet Government will be prepared to proceed to the diplomatic consideration of those proposals which the Japanese Government may wish to make to it. However, the inviolability of the Soviet frontier established by the Hunchun Agreement and the map annexed thereto must be preliminarily guaranteed.

The Ambassador said that he had intention to renounce the dispute concerning the frontier and concerning the responsibility of one side or the other, because of the [apparent omission] there was no common views on both sides on that score. He recognizes the validity of international treaties but Manchukuo, after its separation from China, has its own data. Japan has now seen for the first time the map annexed to the Hunchun Agreement. It would be unreasonable, therefore, to decide the incident on the basis of such a map. However, the Japanese Government is prepared to proceed to concrete negotiations on the spot concerning the treaty and the map. Negotiations had already taken place previously concerning the abstract delineation of the frontier between Japan and the Soviet Union and an agreement had been reached concerning the composition of mixed commissions. If the question is based only on maps, then there would have been no reason to speak of mixed commissions. In the meantime, it is necessary to speak in a practical sense concerning the termination of military activities and of the reestablishment of the situation existing prior to July 11.

To this, the People's Commissar declared as follows:

'Frontiers between states are defined exclusively by international agreements and maps and not by the subjective opinions or wishes of governments and military circles or by unofficial data. The official documents produced by the Soviet side have been countered on the Japanese side by nothing more than a declaration concerning its desire for a different frontier. The frontier between the Soviet Union, Manchuria and Korea can only be that which has been established by agreements and treaties concluded with the Chinese Government and by maps annexed thereto. The occupation of Manchuria by Japan does not give the latter the right to demand an alteration of the frontier. In any event, the Soviet Government has not agreed and will not agree to a reexamination of the frontier. It is not our fault if Tokyo has not in its possession the treaties and maps which were in the possession of the Commission and should be in that of Manchuria. But if, in fact, they are not available, then the Ambassador could, of course, have asked us to give him copies of these treaties and maps for examination. But the Japanese Armed Forces had preferred instead the path of direct action and had penetrated beyond the line indicated on the map. The Soviet Government does not withhold its consent to the creation of mixed commissions under the definite conditions stated by it. The question then did not refer to the establishment of a new frontier but to the demarcation (the establishment of frontier signs) or the redemarcation of the grades on the basis of the existing agreement and map. If the Japanese forces will declare to us clearly its [*their*] recognition of the Hunchun Agreement, then we will be prepared to include in the work of the Mixed Commission the grades indicated therein but only for redemarcation. There can be no question of the substitution of the Hunchun Agreement by another. In regard to the termination of military activities, if there will be reestablished the situation existing prior approximately to the 29 of July, that is prior to the attempts by Japanese to force the heights of Bezymyannaya and subsequently Zaozernaya, and if the Manchurian side will cease attacks on Soviet territory lying behind the line indicated in the Hunchun Treaty and the bombardment of that territory and the remnants of the Japanese forces which may still remain on that territory will be withdrawn, then the military activities on the Soviet side will also cease for they would become without object since we need no Manchurian territory. The Japanese could have convinced themselves after the night seizure of the height of Zaozernaya that no preparations of any kind for offensive actions had been made there and that even no fortifications of any kind had been constructed. This, best of all, bears witness to the peaceful intentions of the Soviet side. The Soviet peoples, however, will not be reconciled to the presence of foreign troops on even a small piece of territory which they consider indisputably theirs, and will not hesitate before any sacrifices in order to free it from them. Therefore, as long as the attacks on Soviet territory and the bombardment thereof continue or as long as there is to be found even one Japanese soldier thereon, the Soviet Government must reserve to itself liberty of action. The Ambassador surely has understood and will accurately convey to his Government what is required in order to terminate the military activities. Later on, the Japanese Government may receive a copy or photostatic copy of the Hunchun Agreement and map and [*in order?*] to convey appropriate instructions to the authorities on the spot.[']

The Japanese Ambassador promised to inform his Government of the conversation."

Certain foreign circles in Moscow profess to see in the above conversation between Litvinov and the Japanese Ambassador evidence of the possibility of some slight lessening, for the moment, of the tension between the two countries. The sole basis for this belief would appear to be the mere fact that after many days of an apparent interruption of diplomatic contact between the Soviet and Japanese Governments, while military operations continued, conversations were held yesterday both in Moscow and Tokyo. While it is recognized that these conversations do not appear to have marked any advance toward a solution and that both sides are maintaining their original stands, there is some inclination here, however, to see evidence of a weakening in the Japanese position in that that Government made the initial move in yesterday's conversations and apparently refrained on that occasion from further specific protests against alleged Soviet violations of Manchurian territory or from any categorical claim that the territory in dispute was without question Manchurian. In so far as the Embassy is aware there would appear to be no evidence of any modification of the Soviet position that the portion of territory in dispute is incontestably Soviet and therefore its possession is not a subject for negotiation or possible compromise.

KIRK

761.93 Manchuria/158 : Telegram

The Chargé in the Soviet Union (Kirk) to the Secretary of State

Moscow, August 5, 1938—6 p. m.
[Received August 5—2:06 p. m.]

231. Referring to my telegram No. 228, August 5 [4], 10 a. m. [p. m.], during my interview with Litvinov today he informed me that the Soviet Government "knew" that Japan did not desire a war with the Soviet Union and that the Soviet Government had no intention of receding from its position which it felt was right. He added that such controversies would continue as long as the Fascist nations existed unless combined action could be taken against them and that the only manner of dealing with those nations was to meet force or threat of force with the same weapons.

Soviet military circles confirm the above opinion that the Japanese will not go to war over this incident and reiterate the determination of the Soviet Government to take all necessary measures to force the withdrawal of the Japanese troops from Soviet territory. The same circles stated this morning that the struggle was still going on; that it was believed that on the Japanese side one Japanese division was involved and intimated that the Soviet forces consisted of border troops together with some detachments of one Red Army division but that the total number did not equal one whole division.

KIRK

761.93 Manchuria/159 : Telegram

The Chargé in the United Kingdom (Johnson) to the Secretary of State

LONDON, August 5, 1938—9 p. m.
[Received August 5—3:30 p. m.]

730. In the course of a conversation at the Foreign Office today the Embassy was informed that they had no reliable information regarding the Russo-Japanese hostilities on the Manchukuo border. Both parties to the dispute were "such accomplished liars" and there was no satisfactory way to judge the relative merits of their stories. The Foreign Office felt that neither of the two Governments as distinct from their respective commanders in the area under dispute desired war and the British Government hoped and was inclined to believe that this dispute would be settled in one way or another like the previous border disturbances.

On the other hand the Chinese were not unnaturally equally anxious that the disturbances would lead to a further war and were doing whatever they could toward that end by spreading alarming reports and otherwise aggravating the situation.

The Foreign Office said that it seems there were no maps attached to the 1860 Russo-Chinese Treaty,[23] the Russians contended that in the treaty of 1886 reaffirming the earlier one the maps attached showed Changkufeng in Russian territory. The Japanese, however, state that in 1908 Russia handed them copies of these maps which did not show the disputed hill in Russian territory. The Japanese ask therefore why in 1938 Russia should submit maps purporting to be those of the 1886 treaty which do not conform to the maps given to the Japanese 30 years ago.

The Foreign Office said that they did not know to whom to attribute this clash. One could accept any one of a number of interpretations but there were too many unknown factors to weigh the interpretations with any accuracy. Possibly Russia was gambling that Japan would not dare risk a real fight and this disturbance would prevent Japan from sending troops from Manchuria to the Chinese battle areas. By the same token the Foreign Office said that Japan might be gambling that Russia would not risk a real war.

The *Times* in a leading editorial on the subject says: "All previous similar clashes have petered out in a drizzle of diplomatic protests, rumors of troop movements and half-hearted proposals for a boundary commission", and that the odds are against the Changkufeng affair departing very far from this precedent. It thinks it is understandable that the desire for a settlement should be more apparent in Japan than in Russia. Other puzzling features of the affair are that considering the strategic importance of the hill it escaped having its ownership established long ago. The *Times* says Russia may have wished to make a diversion in the north to relieve the pressure on the Chinese but this explanation is weakened by two considerations: (1) The Japanese have for some weeks past been reinforcing on the frontier, and (2) that the self-contained expedition now advancing on Hankow would hardly be much affected by a flurry in the north. A likely culprit or hero is a military commander on the spot who took the initiative in search of glory. Two years ago it would have been safe to assume that he was a Japanese but today it was an even chance. But the *Times* believes a study of the events leading to the clash suggests that the Japanese took the initiative and that the ardor of the Russians in taking up the challenge may well have been enhanced by the conviction that to die in battle is better than to be shot against a wall. The article concludes that everything considered the Japanese militarists may emerge from this scrape in a slightly chastened frame of mind.

JOHNSON

---

[23] Signed at Peking, November 2/14, 1860, *British and Foreign State Papers,* vol. LIII, p. 970.

761.93 Manchuria/162 : Telegram

The Chargé in the Soviet Union (Kirk) to the Secretary of State

Moscow, August 7, 1938—5 p. m.
[Received August 7—2 : 42 p. m.]

236. My telegram No. 234, August 7, noon.[24] A member of the Japanese Embassy confirms the report that the Japanese Ambassador has been instructed by his Government to seek an interview with Litvinov and that the meeting would probably take place today. He was unable to divulge the purport of the instructions or state whether they related to a protest on the part of the Japanese in regard to the bombardment of Korean villages or to the general subject of the conflict.

The same official said that a few days ago the local Soviet authorities in Khabarovsk had demanded the closing of the Japanese Consulate General in that city and had requested the Consul General to leave immediately and that the Consul General had left under protest on August 6 for Vladivostok. He added that the closing of the Khabarovsk Consulate had been under consideration in connection with the request of the Soviet Government for the closing of several Japanese Consulates in the Far East, as has been previously reported, but that the present action of the local authorities had been taken without previous warning and in entirely arbitrary fashion.

KIRK

761.93 Manchuria/163 : Telegram

The Chargé in the Soviet Union (Kirk) to the Secretary of State

Moscow, August 7, 1938—11 p. m.
[Received August 7—5 : 05 p. m.]

237. My 236, August 7, 5 p. m. In a communiqué issued tonight entitled "Staff Report of the First (Primoria) Army" it is stated that 1 day following the so-called peaceful offer of the Japanese Ambassador on August 4th the Japanese troops opened an intensive fire on Soviet territory from the heights behind Lake Khasan. Artillery fire from Manchurian territory covered the offensive operations of the Japanese infantry against the Soviet troops who responded with artillery fire. The communiqué continues that after 3 or 4 hours the Japanese artillery was silenced and the Soviet detachment aided by aviation cleared the remaining Japanese troops from Soviet territory and Soviet troops occupied frontier points.

KIRK

---

[24] Not printed.

761.93 Manchuria/164 : Telegram

The Chargé in the Soviet Union (Kirk) to the Secretary of State

Moscow, August 7, 1938—midnight.
[Received August 7—8 : 40 p. m.]

238. My 236, August 7, 5 p. m. Litvinov and the Japanese Ambassador held a conference this evening lasting for more than 3 hours. According to a version of this conference given out orally by the Domei representative to a foreign press correspondent which is the only account of the conversation so far available, the conversation was largely devoted to a re-statement and elaboration of the previous contentions of the two Governments and the basis on which each maintained some solution might be reached and apparently ended without any agreement.

It is stated that a Tass communiqué giving the Soviet version of the conversation will be published tomorrow.

KIRK

761.93 Manchuria/169 : Telegram

The Chargé in the Soviet Union (Kirk) to the Secretary of State

Moscow, August 8, 1938—11 a. m.
[Received 2 p. m.]

239. My 238, August 7, midnight. Following is translation of Tass communiqué published this morning:

[Here follows a lengthy report of conversation between the Japanese Ambassador and the Soviet Commissar for Foreign Affairs on August 7, in which the positions stated by each were substantially a reiteration of those reported in previous telegrams.]

The [Japanese] Ambassador promised to consider the contents of the conversation which had taken place and to revert thereto. Thereupon Comrade Litvinov made the following declaration to the Ambassador:

At the same time that the Japanese Government had advanced proposals concerning the cessation of military operations on one portion of the frontier, on another portion and this time in the regions of Grodekovo a Japanese company with three machine guns suddenly attacked the Soviet border detachment guarding height 588.3 situated on Soviet territory and occupied it. The Soviet reinforcements which came up were fired upon by machine guns on the part of the Japanese company, which having fled to Manchuria territory left on the height 10 Japanese grenades and 50 used grenade cases. During the fight several Red Army men were killed and wounded. There were obviously killed and wounded also on the Japanese side. After numerous protests in connection with similar incidents it would be useless to limit oneself to a new protest. In view of the foregoing it appears essential to declare that the Soviet Government does not intend in the future to permit the unpunished, periodic killing and wounding of its border guards nor the even temporary occupation of Soviet territory by Japan forces and that it fully intends in the future in similar instances to use the most severe measures, including the use of artillery and aviation. Let the Japanese Government oblige the Kwantung and Korean Armies to respect the existing frontier. It is time to put an end to the endless "incidents" and clashes on the frontier.

Insofar as the Embassy is aware, the Soviet press has published no account of the incident in the vicinity of Grodekovo referred to by Litvinov in the above communiqué.

Today's *Pravda* prints under the title "Japan's Militarism is Drawing Japan into a War with the Soviet Union" the first important editorial which has appeared in the Soviet press devoted exclusively to actual conflict in the Far East. This editorial after reviewing the course of events since the 29th or improving the Soviet version thereof and the diplomatic conversations which have taken place between Shigemitsu and Litvinov since that date reiterates the Soviet position as outlined in the above communiqué. After announcing that Soviet territory has been cleared of the remnants of the Japanese forces, the editorial inquires rhetorically what guarantees there are that the Japanese militarism will not renew its attack and states "therefore if the Japanese Government is in fact animated, as the Japanese Ambassador declared on August 4th, by peaceful intentions, then it must give clear and precise guarantees that the attacks on Soviet territory will not be repeated." After repeating the Soviet conditions for a solution of this conflict the editorial emphasizes that the Soviet Government however has not consented and will not consent to a reexamination of the frontier. In conclusion the editorial states *inter alia* that "there can be no doubt but that the popular masses of Japan and also those elements of the ruling camp who soberly evaluate the international and internal situation of their country are not interested in war with the Soviet Union. One must believe that the Japanese militarists know this well. But evidently precisely for that reason the adversaries who are striving at all costs to involve Japan in a war with the Soviet Union are proceeding further and further in provocative activities."

KIRK

761.93 Manchuria/174 : Telegram

The Chargé in the Soviet Union (Kirk) to the Secretary of State

Moscow, August 9, 1938—3 p. m.
[Received August 9—1 : 30 p. m.]

243. My telegram No. 239, August 8, 11 a. m. I understand that the Japanese Ambassador is manifesting greater pessimism follow--

ing his last conversation with Litvinov and professes to be unable to understand Litvinov's attitude toward the Japanese proposal for cessation of hostilities in view of the fact that Litvinov stated that there were no Japanese troops at that time on Soviet territory and consequently the Soviet insistence on the removal of Japanese troops from territory claimed as Soviet as a condition precedent to any agreement had, on the basis of this admission, been met. I understand further that the Ambassador states that the communiqué of the interview while substantially correct failed to mention that the Japanese Ambassador had refused to accept Litvinov's version that Japanese troops had attacked on August 5 and that Japanese forces had provoked the incident at Grodekovo and had said that in both instances Soviet troops had taken the initiative. It is furthermore reported that the Japanese Ambassador admitted yesterday that the Russian troops were believed to be in occupancy of some part but not all of the Height Changkufeng.

The declaration, as published in the communiqué of August 8 to the effect that Litvinov after stating that no Japanese troops were on Soviet territory did not meet the Japanese proposal for an immediate cessation of hostilities, has given rise to speculation in foreign circles as to the possible motives actuating this stand. The following opinions have been suggested possible explanation: (1) That Litvinov's statement and the military communiqué were not in accordance with the facts and that Japanese troops were still in occupancy of what the Soviet Government considers to be Soviet territory; (2) that as fighting was presumably still continuing Litvinov envisaged the possibility that before the cessation of hostilities could be actually effected the military situation might alter in favor of the Japanese and that contrary to his previous stand he would then be in the position of having agreed to a cessation of hostilities while Japanese troops were actually in occupation of Soviet territory, or (3) that the Soviet Government or Litvinov in the hope of exacting further concessions from the Japanese in regard to the general question of border incidents along the entire frontier is not desirous at the present time of terminating the incident. In support of the last explanation, it may be pointed out that the last paragraph of the Soviet communiqué on the conversation introduced an element heretofore not present in the Soviet demands, namely, that some general assurance will be sought from the Japanese against the recurrence of similar frontier incidents in the future.

Up to the present, at least from the published communiqués of the Soviet Government and from other information available to the Embassy, there appears to be no evidence that the Soviet Government intends to recede from the position which it has maintained since the beginning of the controversy and there is an intimation in the request for a general assurance as indicated above that the Soviet Government may even be broadening its original position. In this way the Soviet Government, on the supposition that the Japanese do not intend to engage in a general war with the Soviet Union at the present time, may be endeavoring to secure as complete a diplomatic victory as possible in the present instance and may be manifesting an uncompromising attitude in this controversy with a view to enhancing Soviet prestige in general throughout the world at this particular moment. As regards Litvinov's personal role in the present controversy, the consideration should not be excluded that the firm attitude which he has displayed may be motivated by a desire for the maximum of success with a view to enhancing his own standing with the Kremlin and his personal reputation abroad.

KIRK

761.93 Manchuria/191

Memorandum of Conversation, by the Secretary of State

[WASHINGTON,] August 9, 1938.

The Japanese Ambassador [26] called on his own request. He said he and his wife were down from Hot Springs, Virginia, for a few days and that while here he desired to call, both to pay his respects and to point out the Japanese position with respect to the controversy between Japan and Soviet Russia over the frontier near the Tumen River. The Ambassador said that there had been a Treaty of 1860 and later a Treaty of 1886, that the Treaty of 1886 left the Changku-feng mountain or hill on the Japanese side; that the Soviets claim it to be on their side of the line; and that the Soviet claim is based on a change in the bed of the river. He said that early in July the Soviets moved some troops to Changkufeng hill and occupied it; that there has been desultory fighting since that time; that on yesterday the press reported the Soviets in possession of this hill, while today the Ambassador understands the Japanese are in possession of it. He said that this hill affords an artillery range not only across the Tumen River but to and beyond the railroad running from Rashin on the coast to Hsinking, which is the chief inlet and outlet of Japan into Manchuria and on into North China. The Ambassador two or three times emphasized the view that his country is very desirous of making this a local incident and nothing more; that to this end his Government has proposed to the Soviet Government that the two governments agree that, as a first step, fighting shall be stopped; that they then agree on the withdrawal of troops from a given area to be decided upon; that finally a commission be agreed upon which would set about to solve the trouble. The Ambassador several times re-

___

[26] Hirosi Saito.

peated his statement that Litvinov is very incorrigible in effect; that he insists that before any steps towards a cessation of clashes and fighting shall take place the Japanese must withdraw from Changkufeng hill and back beyond what the Soviets claim is the present border line between the two countries. The Ambassador said that he cannot fathom the mind of Litvinov in thus being so disturbing. He then said that Litvinov might, of course, think that the closer alliance between Great Britain and France would be calculated to sever the alliance between France and Soviet Russia and therefore they would make this demonstration in order to stimulate and unify and encourage the Soviet people. He then said that Litvinov, of course, might be prompted upon the theory that he would divert Japan from its movements toward Hankow and other points in southern and central China; that this idea could only be based upon the theory that Japan is more or less worn down in her military strength and power.

I inquired as to how many troops the Russians have in this Pacific area and he replied that they already had 250,000, have since increased the number to 300,000, and are bringing in more troops from the interior of the Soviet Union. I inquired how many aeroplanes the Soviets have in this area, and he replied 1000. He then answered another question by saying that the Soviets have a number of submarines near Vladivostok. The Ambassador said that several Soviet aeroplanes have flown over Korea up to Rashin and Yuki and have dropped some bombs, including some on an interior point between; but that Japan has declined to send up a single aeroplane thus far. The Ambassador appeared very much worried about the offensive attitude of the Soviets. He did not say whether the Japanese would go on in an effort to hold the Changkufeng hill or whether they would give way in the interest of peace. He only repeated more than twice Japan's extreme desire to restrict this clash to a local incident.

C[ORDELL] H[ULL]

761.93 Manchuria/178 : Telegram

The Chargé in the Soviet Union (Kirk) to the Secretary of State

Moscow, August 11, 1938—9 a. m.
[Received August 11—6 : 30 a. m.]

247. My 245, August 10, 3 p. m.[27] Following is text of military communiqué issued last night.

"Communiqué of First (Primoria) Army. On August 9 Japanese troops again undertook number of attacks on Height Zaozernaya (Changkufeng) occupied by our troops, the Japanese troops were repulsed with great losses to them. The disposition of our troops

---

[27] Not printed.

run along the frontier line with the exception of the height of Bezymyana where Japanese forces form a wedge into our territory for approximately 200 meters and where our troops in their turn form a wedge into Manchurian territory for about 300 meters. In the entire area exchange of artillery fire is continuing."

KIRK

761.93 Manchuria/179 : Telegram

The Chargé in the Soviet Union (Kirk) to the Secretary of State

Moscow, August 11, 1938—10 a. m.
[Received August 11—6 : 50 a. m.]

248. Referring to my telegram No. 247, August 11, 9 a. m., following is text of Tass communiqué issued early this morning:

"Yesterday, August 10, the Japanese Ambassador Mr. Shigemitsu again visited the People's Commissar for Foreign Affairs, Comrade Litvinov, after an exchange of opinions, the People's Commissar made in the name of the Soviet Government the following proposals.

1. The Japanese and Soviet forces shall cease all military activities on August 11 at 12 noon local time. Instructions to that effect to be issued immediately by the Governments of the Soviet Union and Japan.

2. Japanese as well as Soviet troops shall remain on those lines which they occupied at midnight local time on August 10.

3. For the redemarcation of the portion of the frontier in dispute there shall be created a mixed commission of two representatives from the Soviet Union and two representatives from the Japanese-Manchurian side with an umpire selected by agreement of both parties from among the citizens of a third state.

4. The Commission for the Redemarcation shall work on the basis of agreements and maps bearing the signatures of plenipotentiary representatives of Russia and China".

Ambassador Shigemitsu accepted in full the first two proposals having refused arbitration. Litvinov pointed out that the most effective guarantee of the achievement of an agreement for redemarcation would be the presence on the Commission of an unbiased disinterested umpire but in view of the objection of the Ambassador he did not insist upon arbitration. This agreement is considered to have been reached on the third point also.

An agreement was not reached on the question of the basis of the work of the Commission for Redemarcation. Ambassador Shigemitsu proposed to use as a basis also other material which up to the present time had not been presented to the Soviet Union and concerning which it therefore had no knowledge. Mr. Shigemitsu promised however to inquire of his Government on this question and to amicably answer at the earliest possible moment.

KIRK

761.93 Manchuria/183 : Telegram

The Chargé in the Soviet Union (Kirk) to the Secretary of State

Moscow, August 12, 1938—10 a. m.
[Received August 12—6 : 54 a. m.]

252. My 250, August 10 [*11*], 2 p. m.[29] Tass communiqué issued last night states that as agreed between the Soviet Union and Japan on August 10 hostilities in the zone of Lake Khasan ceased on August 11 at 13:30 local time. The first meeting of military representatives of both sides for the purpose of fixation of the position of troops took place south of Height Zaozernaya (Changkufeng) on the evening of August 11. The next meeting is scheduled for 12 noon August 12.

KIRK

761.93 Manchuria/185 : Telegram

The Chargé in the Soviet Union (Kirk) to the Secretary of State

Moscow, August 14, 1938—2 p. m.
[Received August 14—11 a. m.]

254. My telegram No. 245, August 10, 3 p. m.[29] There has been no further editorial comment on the Japanese conflict and reference thereto in the Soviet press has been confined to the publication of favorable foreign comment. This favorable reaction is also reflected in Soviet circles.

Although judging from the communiqué issued on August 11 the conclusion reached in the conversation between Litvinov and the Japanese Ambassador wherein the cessation of hostilities was agreed upon represented to some extent a compromise on both sides, it is generally regarded that Litvinov's proposal constituted at least a diplomatic recession from the position which he had maintained up to that moment.

Litvinov had firmly insisted upon the withdrawal [of] the Japanese troops from the territory under contention and upon the recognition by the Japanese of the line drawn on the map annexed to the Hunchun Treaty. On the basis of the Soviet military communiqué (see my 237, August 7, 11 p. m., and 247, August 11, 10 [*9*] a. m.) it would appear that the tactical position of the Soviets was less favorable on August 10 than on August 7 inasmuch as Japanese troops were admitted to be on Soviet territory on the former date. Litvinov however agreed on August 10th to a cessation of hostilities without apparently insisting upon complete satisfaction as to the conditions hitherto maintained by him. The query therefore arises as to the reasons which prompted this modification of the former position.

[29] Not printed.

In foreign circles here the opinion is prevalent that military developments constituted an important factor in the final negotiations. According to this view, Litvinov had been instructed by the Kremlin, on the assumption that the Japanese did not want war, to adopt a firm stand in his conversations with the Japanese Ambassador and, even in the face of the serious possibilities inherent in such tactics, not to deviate from that stand, during the course of the military operations, unless so instructed. On August 10th, however, notwithstanding the implications of the communiqués, the military situation was apparently found to be in fact favorable to the Soviets with the added possibility that reinforced opposition from the Japanese side might jeopardize that advantage and therefore a cessation of hostilities was regarded as acceptable or desirable from the Soviet point of view. Litvinov therefore was ordered by the Kremlin to bring about a quick termination of the deadlock in the dispute although it involved a certain compromise of the diplomatic position heretofore maintained by the Soviet Government and accordingly the accord outlined in the communiqué of August 11 was reached. In support of this view attention is called to the rapidity in which the decision was apparently put into operation as evidenced by the lack of information in military circles as to the actual termination of hostilities on August 11 (see my 249, August 11, 11 a. m.[30]).

In regard to the controversy as a whole, aside from the simple explanation that the incident arose from and was developed on the basis of the local issues involved, with special reference to the strategic importance of the disputed position, the possibility is also suggested that the Political Bureau was interested in exploiting the effect throughout the world and in Central Europe in particular of a demonstration of force on the part of the Soviet Union. On the other hand, it is suggested that as the incident developed the Japanese were not averse to making a reconnaissance of the present fighting ability and morale of the Red Army at the present time and that furthermore the Kwantung Army for its part was ready to engage in a reconnaissance of this nature on the Far Eastern front. These factors may be more clearly developed in the course of the process of negotiating the concrete questions as to frontier and treaty matters which are still involved in a final settlement of the present controversy.

A more comprehensive evaluation however of the various considerations which may have prompted the Soviet Government throughout this controversy would depend upon a clearer definition of the policy of the Japanese Government than the negotiations here have so far revealed and in particular upon more accurate information than is at present available in Moscow in regard to the positions held by

---

[30] Not printed.

the respective military forces in the later stages of the conflict as well as concerning the actual combat efficiency of the Red Army as demonstrated in the course of the hostilities.

KIRK

761.93 Manchuria/193 : Telegram

The Chargé in the Soviet Union (Kirk) to the Secretary of State

Moscow, August 15, 1938—noon.
[Received August 15—10 : 10 a. m.]

255. My 254, August 14, 2 p. m. The following is translation of a Tass communiqué entitled "Concerning the Events in the Region of Lake Khasan" published today.

At the first meeting of the military representatives of the Soviet Union and Japan on August 11 of this year the military authorities of the Soviet Union declared that despite the cessation of military activities on August 11 at 1 : 30 p. m. local time a unit of Japanese forces had violated the agreement concerning the truce and taking advantage of the truce had advanced forward 100 meters and occupied a portion of the northern slope of the Height Zaozernaya (Changkufeng). Despite the protest of the military representatives of the Soviet Union and their demand for the immediate withdrawal of the Japanese forces to their previous position Japanese military representatives categorically refused to carry out this legal demand. In view of the fact that on the sector indicated the forces of both sides are perhaps within 4 or 5 meters of each other and that armed conflict might spontaneously be renewed at any moment, the military representatives of both sides on the spot decided mutually at this place to withdraw the forces of each side to a distance of 80 meters. On receiving information to this effect the Soviet command in the Far East in conformity with the agreement concluded concerning a truce issued orders for the immediate return of our units to their previous positions which they occupied at midnight on August 10 with instructions to demand from the Japanese authorities the withdrawal of the Japanese forces. This instruction was carried out by our command.

At the same time Litvinov brought this violation of the truce by the Japanese forces to the attention of the Japanese Ambassador and demanded that they withdraw in this sector not less than 100 meters and warned that unless this was carried out then the Government of the Soviet Union would consider the truce had been violated through the fault of Japan.

At the moment the Japanese forces have been withdrawn from the above mentioned point.

On August 12 and 13 meetings again took place between the military representatives of the Soviet Union and Japan who fixed the disposition of the forces of both sides. However, the proposal of the military representatives of the Soviet Union on August 13 to sign a protocol and map fixing the disposition of the forces of both sides was refused by the Japanese military representative who declared that they were awaiting instructions from their high authorities and that another more authoritative commission will probably arrive for that purpose. Thereupon the military representatives of both sides separated. No new meetings took place on August 14. The region of the conflict is quiet at the present time. On August 13 at the request of the Japanese military representatives and with the agreement of the military representatives of the Soviet Union a mutual exchange of dead took place. According to the calculations of the command on the Soviet side, there were 236 dead and 611 wounded. According to the estimation of our command the losses of the Japanese forces amounted to 600 dead and 2500 wounded.

KIRK

761.93 Manchuria/200 : Telegram

The First Secretary of Embassy in China (Salisbury) to the Secretary of State

PEIPING, August 17, 1938—1 p. m.
[Received August 17—6 a. m.]

501. 1. American correspondent of the Associated Press who has just returned from Changkufeng area states that: (*a*) Following minor skirmishes the first serious fighting occurred July 29, when Soviet planes bombed the railway along the Tumen River; (*b*) Soviet troops which had momentarily occupied Changkufeng Hill were subsequently driven off the hill by Japanese under instructions; (*c*) Soviet troops who had taken the hill and succeeded at least once and possibly twice in reoccupying a part or all of the hill temporarily; (*d*) Japanese troops were in occupation of the crest of the hill when hostilities ceased which made them victors in a military sense; (*e*) the Japanese also gained a diplomatic victory in that, although the original Russian contention was that the boundary went through the crest of Changkufeng, by the truce arrangements the boundary accepted by the respective forces was east of Changkufeng Hill and between the hill and the lake which is east of the hill. He said he thought that Soviet casualties were, as stated by the Japanese, far greater than Japanese casualties because the Soviet troops made several attacks over difficult terrain including swamps at either end of the lake, but Japanese statements concerning bombing of Korean villages were questionable as there was little actual damage to civilian life and property. Three disabled Soviet tanks were visible on the hill but no facilities were provided to enable a view of Soviet planes stated to have been brought down, which he believed to have been three in number. He said that the accuracy of Soviet artillery and the speed of Soviet planes were remarkable and that both could easily have done more damage to the Japanese side if the Soviet had evidently not wished to aggravate the situation too greatly.

2. He said (*a*) the fighting on the Japanese side was done by the Korean Army; (*b*) the Kwantung Army was now massing large numbers of troops near the border and expected further trouble; (*c*) military and civilian Japanese in Manchuria generally did not connect the border incidents with the hostilities in China but considered them as a separate problem arising from the General Lyushikov [31] affair; that is, the alleged Lyushikov's statements derogatory of the Soviet military establishment made it seem necessary to the Far Eastern Soviet commanders (1) to demonstrate to Stalin that they were loyal to him and prepared to defend Soviet territory, and (2) to demonstrate to the Japanese that the report of their weakness was false and that they were prepared for any contingencies.

3. He said that in his opinion further serious friction between Soviet and Japanese troops were inevitable.

4. Repeated to Chungking, Tokyo, Shanghai.

SALISBURY

761.93 Manchuria/195½ : Telegram

The Chargé in the Soviet Union (Kirk) to the Secretary of State

Moscow, August 18, 1938—11 a. m.
[Received August 18—6 : 46 a. m.]

260. My 255, August 15, noon. Tass report published in Soviet press today stated that the Counselor of the Japanese Embassy in Moscow has informed the People's Commissariat for Foreign Affairs that the agreement for a truce in the region of Lake Khasan has been put into effect and that the forces of both sides at the present time are at some distance from each other. The communiqué adds that, in view of the foregoing, the Japanese Embassy had proposed that should further questions arise which require meetings between the representatives of the Japanese and Soviet military commands, such meetings should be arranged through diplomatic conversations between Moscow and Tokyo and that the Counselor of the Japanese Embassy was informed that this proposal was acceptable.

KIRK

761.93 Manchuria/205 : Telegram

The Chargé in the Soviet Union (Kirk) to the Secretary of State

Moscow, August 24, 1938—2 p. m.
[Received August 24—8 : 40 a. m.]

267. My 260, August 18, 11 a. m. I understand that in the course of the negotiations between Litvinov and the Japanese Ambassador

---

[31] Chief of Far Eastern Krai of Soviet Commissariat for Internal Affairs; he deserted to Manchuria.

during the past few days an agreement was reached as to delegates of the Boundary Commission to discuss the frontier in the region of Lake Khasan. The question however of the nature of the documents and other evidence admissible as a basis of the work of the Commission is apparently still pending as Litvinov insists that the accords concluded between Russia and China with the maps annexed thereto should be the sole basis for negotiation whereas the Japanese Ambassador maintains that other material should be considered as well.

There has been no reference to developments in regard to this general subject in the Soviet press since the publication of the communiqué reported in my telegram under reference.

KIRK

761.93 Manchuria/223

The Chargé in the Soviet Union (Kirk) to the Secretary of State

No. 1650   Moscow, September 14, 1938.
                                            [Received October 4.]

SIR: With further reference to my confidential despatch No. 1577 of August 18, 1938,[32] and to previous correspondence regarding the recent Soviet-Japanese hostilities in the vicinity of Changkufeng on the Soviet-Manchurian border, I have the honor to inform the Department that no further information has been published in the Soviet press regarding the appointment of the members of the commission agreed upon for the demarcation of the area in dispute, nor regarding the still moot point as to the data which the commission is to take into consideration in the performance of its task. The Embassy has been reliably informed, however, that conversations on this subject, which have been progressing between the Japanese Ambassador, Mr. Shigemitsu, and Mr. Litvinov, have been interrupted by the departure of Mr. Litvinov on September 5 for Geneva. It has been learned from the Japanese Embassy here that substantial agreement has been reached concerning the personnel of the commission and that announcement with regard thereto will shortly be made. It would appear, however, that the matters affecting the composition of the commission and its work have been relegated for the time being at least to a place of relative unimportance and that little publicity regarding the functioning of the commission need be expected.

On the basis of information which has been made available here the attitude of Germany has been made more clear in relation to the hostilities which recently ceased and in particular with regard to the scope of any obligations which might have been expected of it by

---

[32] Not printed.

Japan as a result of the "Anti-Comintern Pact".[33] It appears that the German Foreign Minister, Herr von Ribbentrop, during the earlier stages of the hostilities avoided seeing the Japanese Ambassador owing to the German Government's unwillingness to define too closely its attitude toward the controversy. The Japanese Ambassador, however, sought an interview so insistently that he was at last received by Herr von Ribbentrop at his country place and given merely non-committal expressions of the sympathetic attitude of Germany toward Japan. According to the Embassy's information the Ambassador subsequently conveyed to representatives of the press that the Foreign Minister had given him assurances of more than moral support for Japan on the part of Germany. When word of this reached Herr von Ribbentrop he is stated to have sent for the Ambassador and informed him that the press reports were at variance with the facts of their conversation and that Germany would not only not render material assistance but counseled Japan's moderation in relation to the incident.

The Changkufeng incident has received no attention from the Soviet press since the date of my despatch above mentioned other than an occasional article containing comment laudatory of the Soviet troops and giving details of some of the fighting.

Respectfully yours,   A. C. KIRK

761.93 Manchuria/231 : Telegram

The Chargé in the Soviet Union (Kirk) to the Secretary of State

Moscow, November 10, 1938—2 p. m.
[Received November 10—9 : 30 a. m.]

387. Voroshilov, People's Commissar for Defence, in a speech delivered on Red Square November 7 published in *Izvestiya* today in referring to the Lake Khasan incident characterized the Japanese as "our stupid neighbors" and reminded them and "all other restless and impertinent enemies" that the next time they attempted to violate Soviet territory the Red Army would not be obligated to confine military action to the area attacked by the enemy but that it "is more convenient and easier for us to crush the enemy on his own territory." This warning was also contained in the *Pravda* and *Izvestiya* editorials today. Voroshilov continued that the fighting forces of the Soviet Union were fully aware of the present situation and that consequently they were continually perfecting their defence.

Pravda of November 7 published so-called orders issued by Voroshilov and by Frinovski, newly appointed People's Commissar for

---

[33] Signed at Berlin, November 25, 1936, *Foreign Relations*, Japan, 1931–1941, vol. II, p. 153.

Navy, stating *inter alia* that a Fascist crusade is organizing against the Soviet Union and emphasizing the determination and ability of the Soviet Union to defend its frontiers.

KIRK

760C.93 Manchuria/6 : Telegram

The Counselor of Embassy in China (Lockhart) to the Secretary of State

PEIPING, December 7, 1938—5 p. m.
[Received December 8—4 : 07 p. m.]

56. Hsinking today released Japanese text of notes exchanged between Polish and Manchurian Ambassadors at Tokyo alluded to in my 54, October 19, 5 p. m.[35] Notes provide that pending conclusion of formal treaties covering such matters the two Governments agree on condition of reciprocity:

(1) to accord most-favored-nation treatment to each other's Consuls;
(2) to accord to each other's nationals most-favored-nation treatment in principle in respect to travel, residence, occupation, personal and property rights and social organization;
(3) that the most-favored-nation treatment principle referred to in the preceding article shall not be applicable insofar as it affects joint defence with an allied nation or "special indivisible relations with contiguous countries based on military, political, racial and like conditions;"
(4) to extend favorable treatment to each other's trade and economic activity pending signing of a commercial treaty.

In releasing the text the Premier and high Hsinking officials, in addition to the usual solemn congratulation, gloated over the first legal admission by a third nation of their country's indivisible relationship with Japan and presumably North China.

Repeated to Chungking.

LOCKHART

760C.93 Manchuria/7

The Ambassador in Poland (Biddle) to the Secretary of State

No. 846   WARSAW, December 14, 1938.
[Received December 30.]

SIR: I have the honor to forward herewith a copy of the Warsaw *Monitor Polski*, the official journal of the Polish Republic, dated December 7, 1938, which contains on pages 2–4 the text in the English language of the notes exchanged at Tokyo on October 19, 1938, be-

[35] Not printed.

tween the Polish and the Manchukuoan Ambassadors at that capital providing for consular relations and regulating right of establishment and trade between Poland and "Manchukuo".

Competent officials of the Polish Ministry of Foreign Affairs stated to the Embassy that this exchange of communications "is not regarded as constituting formal recognition of 'Manchukuo' by Poland, but rather as meeting in a practical way the problems inevitably arising out of the residence in 'Manchukuo' of numerous Polish nationals and the trade between Poland and 'Manchukuo'." I understand that the British Embassy at Warsaw inquired of the Polish Foreign Office whether this exchange amounted to recognition and was informed that it did not in words somewhat similar to those used in the later comment to a member of my staff and quoted above. Officials of the Foreign Office likewise observed that this exchange had been improperly interpreted in some circles in implying to Poland the intent to recognize "Manchukuo" thereby.

It is, however, quite generally accepted at Warsaw, as pointed out in my despatch No. 741 of October 19, 1938,[36] that Poland by this exchange has paved the way for *de jure* recognition of "Manchukuo" and that such recognition will take place in the not too distant future unless unforeseen events of political character interfere to make such action highly undesirable from the Polish point of view.

Respectfully yours, A. J. DREXEL BIDDLE, JR.

893.77 Manchuria/139

The Ambassador in Japan (Grew) to the Secretary of State

No. 3534   TOKYO, December 22, 1938.
[Received January 9, 1939.]

SIR: With reference to the Department's instruction 1509 of May 28, 1938 on the subject of the failure of the South Manchuria Railway and its subsidiary organizations to discharge certain obligations to American nationals and firms, I have the honor to enclose herewith translation of a note from the Japanese Foreign Office under date of December 15, 1938 [37] in response to the Embassy's inquiry of June 16, 1938.

When the Embassy received the Department's instruction, information with regard to failure of payment of pensions had already come

---

[36] Not printed.
[37] Not printed. The note stated that the pensions in question were discontinued under a regulation that pensions would be terminated if the recipient resided over a year in any place outside the Soviet Union or China and that the decision of the courts mentioned in the Embassy's note was given in 1927 prior to the application of this regulation and therefore was considered to have no connection in this case.

to the Embassy from the Embassy at Peiping, on the basis of which this Embassy had addressed a third person note to the Japanese Foreign Office on June 16, 1938. The discretionary authorization contained in the Department's instruction was therefore not immediately availed of, the Embassy deciding instead to await reply of the Japanese Foreign Office. In the months which have intervened, the Foreign Office has repeatedly assured the Embassy that a reply would be received within a week's time, and in consequence further action was postponed.

The Foreign Office's reply raises a question of fact with regard to the court decision cited, and the Embassy will make inquiry into the matter before taking further action.

Respectfully yours, JOSEPH C. GREW

CHINA'S APPEAL FOR SANCTIONS AGAINST JAPAN UNDER THE COVENANT OF THE LEAGUE OF NATIONS [38]

793.94 Advisory Committee/130 : Telegram

The Chargé in the United Kingdom (Johnson) to the Secretary of State

LONDON, January 1, 1938—5 p. m.
[Received January 1—1:45 p. m.]

3. During my conversation this morning with the Foreign Secretary,[39] he mentioned that he had seen the Chinese Ambassador last night and that with reference to the forthcoming meeting of the League Council the Ambassador had asked for his views regarding the Committee of Twenty-three. Mr. Eden told the Chinese Ambassador that he felt there was no real work under present circumstances for the Committee to do and that it would be a mistake for it to be convened without the interested governments having been sounded out beforehand. Mr. Eden suggested in particular to the Chinese Ambassador that he get in touch with his own colleagues at Washington and Paris with a view to ascertaining the views of the United States and French Governments.

Mr. Eden will leave Monday for a holiday in the south of France and possibly may not return to England until after the meeting of the League Council on January 17 which he will attend. It is understood that in his absence the Prime Minister [40] will be in direct charge of the Foreign Office.

JOHNSON

---

[38] For previous correspondence, see Foreign Relations, 1937, vol. IV, pp. 1 ff.
[39] Anthony Eden.
[40] Neville Chamberlain.

793.94 Advisory Committee/131 : Telegram

The Chargé in the United Kingdom (Johnson) to the Secretary of State

LONDON, January 4, 1938—2 p. m.

[Received January 4—12 : 55 p. m.]

6. My 3, January 1, 5 p. m. A conversation at the Foreign Office last evening threw some additional light on the rather general statement made to me by the Foreign Secretary on January 1st regarding his conversation with the Chinese Ambassador. It seems that the Chinese Ambassador had spoken to Mr. Eden of the forthcoming meeting of the League Council and had asked for his view regarding the advisability of calling for a meeting of the Advisory Committee of Twenty-three which the delegations, it was said, obviously desired should take place.   The Chinese Ambassador had made it sufficiently clear that the object of a meeting of the Advisory Committee in his view was that it should serve as a preclude [prelude?] to a proposal for imposing sanctions on Japan and specifically sanctions on oil.   He evidently hoped for favorable reaction from Mr. Eden. As stated at the Foreign Office, Mr. Eden's reply to the Ambassador was definitely intended to discourage him from any such idea, for he pointed out to him the impracticability of raising such a question at this time and the serious complications which might result therefrom in Anglo-American, Anglo-French and Anglo-Dutch relations.   He also advised the Chinese Ambassador that in his opinion there was no real work which the Advisory Committee could do to good purpose at this time and that before the Ambassador considered such a step as requesting the Committee to convene he should be very sure what the reaction of the principal interested powers would be.   It was to this end that Mr. Eden suggested to him that he should, through his colleagues in Washington and Paris, endeavor to ascertain the views of the United States and French Governments.

I was told also that the Soviet Ambassador recently informed Mr. Eden that his Government has been able to provide a certain amount of war material for China but not very much and that he, the Soviet Ambassador, supposed that Great Britain, France and the United States were doing likewise within certain limits. The Ambassador expressed his opinion that unless aid in war material could reach China from foreign sources, her struggle against Japan was a hopeless one.   Mr. Eden, it seems, concurred in this opinion. The Foreign Office pointed out to me, however, that in fact there are no supplies of war material except rifles and a certain number of Lewis guns, which are available for export from this country; that it was impossible for British sources to furnish Chinese requirements in aircraft or submarines which had been requested by the Chinese Ambassador. The present scale and progress of British rearmament make the prompt supply of any such material impossible.

The foregoing was given me simply as confidential information which might possibly be of interest to the Department.

JOHNSON

793.94 Advisory Committee/134 : Telegram

The Consul at Geneva (Bucknell) to the Secretary of State

GENEVA, January 27, 1938—2 p. m.
[Received 2 : 10 p. m.]

13. Having heard a report that the Chinese were considering making a request for the reconvening of the Advisory Committee I took occasion to inquire of Hoo [41] regarding this possibility. He told me in confidence that the representatives of certain governments were in favor of reconvening the Advisory Committee while others were suggesting the possibility of a further meeting of the Brussels Conference.[42] Hoo did not volunteer the names of these governments and I did not feel it opportune to press him on the subject. He added, however, while he could not say definitely what action would be decided upon, in his personal opinion he did not think the Committee of Twenty-three would be convened since it was difficult to see what could be obtained from this action nor did he see at the moment the probability of a reconvening of the Brussels Conference. He also said that Litvinoff,[43] Eden, Delbos [44] and Koo [45] would meet this afternoon to discuss the situation.

He concluded by saying that China was anxious to obtain some form of assistance and that Koo would probably make a declaration before the Council, the tenor of which has not yet been decided and may depend on the result of the meeting this afternoon. Hoo promises to keep me informed of any decisions taken.

BUCKNELL

---

[41] Victor Chitsai Hoo, Chinese Minister in Switzerland.
[42] For correspondence, see *Foreign Relations*, 1937, vol. IV, pp. 1 ff.
[43] Maxim Litvinov, Soviet Commissar for Foreign Affairs.
[44] Yvon Delbos, French Minister for Foreign Affairs.
[45] V. K. Wellington Koo, Chinese Ambassador to France.

793.94 Advisory Committee/136 : Telegram

The Consul at Geneva (Bucknell) to the Secretary of State

GENEVA, January 28, 1938—9 p. m.
[Received January 28—8 p. m.]

18. Lord Cranborne [46] having expressed the desire to see me, I called on him this afternoon. He was with Mr. Stevenson of the British delegation.

Lord Cranborne said that he was terribly sorry to hear that the Minister [47] was ill and therefore was not in Geneva and said that he would be glad if I would give him a message on his behalf. He said that the British, French, Russians, and Chinese had had a meeting this morning and that the Chinese were pressing for some further action on the part of League.

He said that it was pretty definite that a Council resolution would be presented reaffirming the resolution adopted by the Committee of Twenty-three and by the Assembly and in addition calling upon states to collaborate in the action recommended by that Committee of necessity of "refraining from taking any action which might have the effect of weakening China's power of resistance." [48] He pointed out that such collaboration would mean the end of efforts of conciliation. He said that the Chinese had been anxious to apply article 17 [49] with its "full regalia" which would, of course, pave the way toward sanctions. This, Lord Cranborne felt, was difficult and perhaps dangerous since Japan would in all probability refuse an invitation to appear and state her case and would probably not be favorably received. The Chinese finally pressed for "one small step in advance," that is, consultation regarding such collaboration.

The question of possible consultation remained to be considered. He emphasized the fact that no decision had been reached in this respect although he felt that in the event a resolution calling for collaboration of states to refrain from hindering China was adopted the Chinese would immediately press for the further step to consult as to what means this collaboration should take.

Such consultation could take one of four forms: (1) By a reconvening of the Committee of Twenty-three which Cranborne thought was unwise since he did not feel that very much could be accomplished by this means; (2) a reconvening of the Brussels Conference which he thought was perhaps a better move; (3) a private and informal meet-

---

[46] British Parliamentary Under Secretary of State for Foreign Affairs.
[47] Leland Harrison.
[48] See point 13 of report, adopted October 6, 1937, by the League of Nations Assembly, *Foreign Relations, Japan, 1931–1941*, vol. I, p. 394.
[49] Of the League Covenant, *Foreign Relations*, The Paris Peace Conference, 1919, vol. XIII, pp. 69, 91.

ing of interested governments which would presumably include the United States; and (4) some committee set up by the Council.

He said that Eden was anxious at all costs to avoid embarrassing the United States and that he felt it wise to inform Harrison of the situation in order that Washington might be "tipped off." He said that the British position had always been at Brussels and elsewhere that they were prepared to take such action as they felt would be effective but were not prepared to take action which they felt would not be effective.

He said that while one object of the Chinese was to obtain a political gesture another was perhaps that the Chinese wanted to line up the various interested powers to see to what extent they could receive aid from each, that is, that they would say that they needed so many guns, so many tanks, so many airplanes, et cetera, and would then ask each power what it could supply although he thought that inquiries of this kind had already been addressed to those governments.

Throughout the conversation Cranborne was evidently anxious to obtain any indication of what the American attitude would be with regard to the new Chinese move. I refrained from saying anything more than that I would be glad to transmit the information to Mr. Harrison.

Cranborne concluded by saying that he was most anxious to keep the United States Government fully informed and to avoid in any way embarrassing it and that he would continue to keep it informed of any developments.

I telephoned the above information to the Minister in Bern who asked me to telegraph it to the Department and to explain that he has been ill with sinus but hopes to be able to get about within the next few days.

Department's instructions are requested.

Later in the afternoon Stevenson informed me that Cranborne wished to speak to me again and I was received by Eden and Cranborne.

Eden said that following Cranborne's conversation with me there had been another meeting later this evening and that after an extended discussion particularly with regard to the last paragraph the following draft resolution was agreed upon subject to approval of the British and French Governments:

"The Council.

Having taken into consideration the situation in the Far East, Notes with regret that hostilities in China continue and have been intensified since the last meeting of the Council.

Deplores this deterioration in the situation the more in view of the efforts previously made by the Chinese National Government to promote the unity and prosperity in China.

Recalls that the Assembly has expressed its moral support for China and has recommended that members of the League should refrain from taking any action which might have the effect of weakening China's power of resistance and thus of increasing her difficulties in the present conflict and should also consider how far they can individually extend aid to China;

Invites those states represented on the Council to whom the situation in the Far East is of special interest to consider, in consultation with other similarly interested powers the possibility of any further steps which may contribute to a just settlement of the conflict in the Far East."

Eden remarked that if this draft was approved by the governments it would be passed at the meeting of the Council tomorrow morning. Following this action one of the two following procedures would be adopted: (1) the three powers, Great Britain, France and Russia would consult and then make some joint approach to other interested powers, principally intervening [*interviewing?*] United States and Holland, or (2) that these two governments would be approached through the usual diplomatic channels. He said that for himself he very much favored approaching the governments through diplomatic channels since the first alternative had too much the flavor of presenting an agreed upon program by joint or concerted action. He inquired what I thought my Government would prefer. I replied that I was unfortunately not in a position to express an opinion whereupon he said that he thought he would take it upon himself to say in the private Council meeting preceding the public session tomorrow that in his opinion the second alternative would be much more agreeable to the United States Government.

In discussing the draft resolution he said that he thought that on the whole it was not a bad draft and laughingly remarked that no punitive measures of any kind were mentioned and that the action contemplated might even take the form of consultation with Japan for example or any other of a dozen different procedures. He said that Delbos had remarked that the resolution meant in fact that they were afraid to shake the bad boy out of the tree but that if they could get another and powerful partner they would shake him out very quickly. I received the impression that the draft resolution was more agreeable to the English than to the French who apparently preferred certain changes. Eden said that he thought that the present plan would rather wipe out the other possibilities of consultation described to me by Cranborne and set forth in the first part of this telegram.

BUCKNELL

793.94 Advisory Committee/137 : Telegram

The Consul at Geneva (Bucknell) to the Secretary of State

GENEVA, January 29, 1938—noon.
[Received January 29—8 : 55 a. m.]

20. My 18, January 28, 9 p. m. The Polish permanent delegate telephoned this morning and asked me to come around as soon as possible. He said that he wanted to speak very privately and unofficially and asked if I could say whether the attitude of the United States Government with regard to the Sino-Japanese dispute had grown any stronger since the Brussels Conference and if they were now prepared to take a stronger line. He said that the British delegation were telling him that this was the case but that his own information did not support this.

I replied that I regretted that I was not in a position to express any opinion with regard to any change in the attitude of the American Government which has been consistent all along.

Komarnicki then went on to say that he objected very much to the way the British, French, and Russians were attempting to put over the draft resolution in the Council, which he considered not only objectionable but highly dangerous. If it was decided to apply article 16, well and good, but to ask him to agree to and give his blessing to Soviet aid to China which might reach dangerous proportions was something that he did not feel he could do. Such a resolution would be subject to many interpretations and he felt that some of these interpretations might be exceedingly dangerous. His attitude would probably be greatly changed if he had any assurance that the United States Government were in favor of or interested in such a resolution and its implications but failing this he opposed it bitterly.

He went on to say that the British-French-Russian move was pure bluff; that Eden, Beylard [*Litvinov?*], Delbos were anxious to achieve a personal triumph in the Council so that they could go home to their governments and point with pride to what they had achieved here but that for his own part he did not feel that conference of [*or?*] his Government should or could contribute to such a bluff. It was impossible for Poland to be a pawn in a political game which did not concern her and which contained such dangerous possibilities.

Poland he said objected to having three powers sit down in secret, decide upon a draft and then present it to the other members of the Council for them simply to accept whether they liked it or not. On what article of the Covenant was this draft resolution based? What was hoped to be accomplished by it? Poland had the greatest moral sympathy for China but a war between China and Japan did not directly affect Poland. He had no intention of voting for a resolution which might bless a Russian adventure with Japan.

I repeated that I was not in a position to express any opinion on the subject of either the draft resolution or of any change in the American French [*sic*].

Council meeting has been postponed until 5 this afternoon.

BUCKNELL

793.94 Advisory Committee/139a : Telegram

The Secretary of State to the Consul at Geneva (Bucknell)

WASHINGTON, January 29, 1938—1 p. m.

6. The Chinese Ambassador [50] has just called and asked what our attitude would be toward a further Nine Power Treaty Conference. I told the Ambassador that the answer to this question was self-evident. I added, however, that of course if there should be called a duly constituted meeting of the parties to the Nine Power Treaty [51] the American Government would attend and if, by way of illustration there should be called in a duly constituted way a meeting of the Advisory Committee, the American Government would follow its previous practice. I then emphasized to the Ambassador that the really important consideration in connection with matters of this sort was whether any useful purpose would be served by the calling of a conference or a meeting, and whether the interests of peace in general as well as the interests of China would be furthered. I said that the Ambassador knew the importance of those preliminary questions as well as I. I pointed out that assembling of conferences or committees with achievement of nothing definite or constructive serves only to harm the cause of peace. I referred to a press report from Geneva that various foreign governments contemplate approaching the American Government in regard to a proposal to extend credits to China for the purchase of arms and munitions. I said to the Ambassador that he knew the situation in this country in regard to a question of that sort and that I of course assumed that the representatives of any governments which might have presented to them for consideration any such plan would have knowledge and understanding of the situation here in this regard.

It is possible that the Chinese Ambassador here may cable a report of his conversation with me to the Chinese representative at Geneva and that as a result you may be approached by the representative of some government interested in the matter. In such event you should be guided by the foregoing and discreetly discourage any impression that this Government feels that any useful purpose would be served by a reconvening of the Brussels Conference at this time.

---

[50] C. T. Wang.
[51] Signed at Washington, February 6, 1922, *Foreign Relations*, 1922, vol. I, p. 276.

Please repeat to Harrison for his information; also repeat to the Embassies at London and Paris for their information.

HULL

793.94 Advisory Committee/139 : Telegram

The Consul at Geneva (Bucknell) to the Secretary of State

GENEVA, January 29, 1938—4 p. m.
[Received January 29—1 : 10 p. m.]

22. My telegram No. 18, January 28, 9 p. m. Stevenson of the British delegation has just informed me that following extended discussion this morning the last paragraph of the draft resolution has now been changed to read as follows:

"Is confident that those states represented on the Council for whom the situation is of special interest will lose no opportunity of examining, in consultation with other similarly interested powers the possibility of any further steps which may contribute to a just settlement of the conflict in the Far East".

Stevenson said that this change had been largely due to the insistence of the French although the British had also accepted it. Koo was apparently rather unhappy at the change which he considers weakens an already weak statement. The amended resolution will now be referred to the Chinese Government for approval. It is expected that opposition will continue in the Council to the resolution even as amended. The principal opposition it is thought comes from the Pole.

Stevenson explained that the object of the above change was to make the resolution "less imperative" as far as the United States was concerned.

In view of the above the Sino-Japanese conflict will not be considered at this afternoon's session of the Council and will be postponed at least until Monday and perhaps even later if no agreement can be arrived at by that time.

BUCKNELL

793.94 Advisory Committee/138 : Telegram

The Consul at Geneva (Bucknell) to the Secretary of State

GENEVA, January 29, 1938—7 p. m.
[Received January 29—4 : 20 p. m.]

23. My January 29, 4 p. m. Hoo, the Chinese permanent delegate, said this evening that he presumed that I had read both the first draft of the proposed Council resolution and the amendment.

I said that I had. He asked if I could express any opinion as to the reaction of my Government. I explained that I was not in a position to express any opinion whatsoever.

Hoo then went on to say that the French had been insistent upon weakening the draft resolution and as far as he could see were not willing to do anything at the moment due to the fact that they feared an Italian belligerent act sometime in March. He said that as an excuse they kept repeating that they could not do anything because the United States was unfavorable toward any action and would be unwilling to cooperate in any way but that he was convinced that the real reason was that they were anxious about the European situation.

He said that Litvinoff had been very favorably disposed toward the Chinese case and that even the British had appeared disposed to do at least something but the French had been making all sorts of excuses and, in addition to saying that they were unable to move because of the United States' attitude, had warned about the intransigent attitude that the Poles would adopt if any strong resolution were agreed upon.

He promised to keep me informed of any developments.

Eden is expected to leave Geneva tonight.

With reference to my telegram 20, January 29, noon, I am informed by a usually reliable source that Beck [52] has left Geneva and that when the resolution is presented to the Council the Poles will abstain but will take the opportunity to protest against a procedure whereby the great powers decide an important matter in secret and then present the other members of the Council with a *fait accompli*.

BUCKNELL

793.94 Advisory Committee/140 : Telegram

The Consul at Geneva (Bucknell) to the Secretary of State

GENEVA, January 30, 1938—7 p. m.
[Received 7 : 30 p. m.]

26. Department's telegram No. 6, January 29, 2 [1] p. m., my telegram No. 23, January 29, 4 [7] p. m. Stevenson of the British delegation informed me today that the status of the Chinese Council resolution remained unchanged from yesterday. He went on to say that as he had pointed out in our last conversation (see my 22, January 29, 4 p. m.) the Chinese were rather unhappy over the amendment of the last paragraph of the resolution but had referred it to the Chinese Government from which no reply had yet been received.

---

[52] Polish Minister for Foreign Affairs.

He hoped and expected that the Chinese would agree to it and would not be so "silly" as to attempt to press an appeal under article 17 which procedure in his opinion would be ill-advised. He continued that in the event a favorable Chinese reply was received in time another Council meeting would probably be held tomorrow afternoon. If the resolution was adopted by the Council he expected that the next step would be for Moscow, London, and Paris to consider what steps they were in a position to take which would most likely be followed by an approach to Washington through diplomatic channels to ascertain whether or not the American Government would join in such steps as had been regarded as possible by the other three governments.

Having previously discussed the Department's 6, January 29, 2 [1] p. m., with the Minister in Bern, I took advantage of an opportunity during the course of my conversation with others to refer to the Secretary's conversation with the Chinese Ambassador saying that the Secretary in referring to our attitude toward a further Nine Power Conference had said that he felt that the really important thing was whether any useful purpose would be served by further conferences or meetings and whether the interests of peace in general as well as the interests of China would be thus furthered. I added that the Secretary had pointed out that assembling of conferences or committees with achievement of nothing definite or constructive serves only to harm the cause of peace. Stevenson remarked that this appeared to be a remarkably sound view of the matter.

Eden left Geneva last night and Delbos this morning.

Repeated to London, Paris. Code copies to Berlin, Rome.

BUCKNELL

793.94 Advisory Committee/142 : Telegram

The Consul at Geneva (Bucknell) to the Secretary of State

GENEVA, January 31, 1938—1 p. m.
[Received January 31—11 : 14 a. m.]

27. Quo Tai Chi and Wellington Koo[53] informed me this morning that the amended Council resolution was unacceptable to their Government. They said that the first resolution was bad enough but that the second one was impossible; there would be another meeting this afternoon of the representatives of China, Great Britain, France and Soviet Russia. The Chinese were somewhat despondent about what could be accomplished and said that they were in a most difficult position and that perhaps it would be better to have no reso-

---

[53] Chinese Ambassadors in the United Kingdom and France, respectively.

lution at all if this was the best that could be obtained. The French, they said, had consistently tried to hold back the British from agreeing to any strong action saying in effect that if the British were involved in the Far East what would happen to poor France all by herself in the Mediterranean? They said it was evident that France was greatly concerned with regard to possible trouble with Italy.

The Chinese had been greatly concerned regarding press report from the United States to the effect that France, Great Britain, Soviet Russia and China were trying to cook up some program of furnishing money and munitions to China which these states would attempt to force upon the United States. These reports they described as completely without any foundation.

They said that the American attitude was very well known and that there was not and would not be any attempt to force the victim's hand. They said that the British had consistently insisted that nothing be done to embarrass or displease the American Government. The Chinese also described as fantastic reports that the Council had consulted the United States Government with regard to the resolution and said that the facts of the case were that all of the four powers now holding discussions on the subject in Geneva had agreed that the United States Government should be kept fully advised of any developments here purely for their information and in the hope that we might be in a position to take some parallel or independent action along the lines of anything that was finally decided by the other three powers.

They asked me if I had received any reaction from my Government with regard to the Council resolution or other developments in Geneva. I then asked if they had had any report of the conversation that the Chinese Ambassador in Washington had with the Secretary of State on Saturday. They replied in the negative and I then explained that the Chinese Ambassador had asked the Secretary what our attitude would be toward a further Nine Power Treaty Conference and that the Secretary had replied that if there should be called a duly constituted meeting of the powers to the Nine Power Treaty the American Government would attend and if by way of illustration there should be called a meeting of the Advisory Committee the American Government would follow its previous practice. I explained that the Secretary had emphasized that the really important consideration in connection with matters of this sort was whether any useful purpose would be served by the calling of conferences or a meeting and whether the interests of peace in general as well as the interests of China would be furthered. I concluded that the Secretary had pointed out that assembling of conferences or committees with the achievement of nothing definite or constructive serves only to harm the cause of peace. They thanked me for telling them this and said that it seemed quite evident that under present circumstances the Secretary felt that it would be useless to have another meeting of the Nine Power Conference or a further meeting of the Committee of Twenty-three.

A Council meeting is scheduled for 6 p. m., today.

Repeated to London and Paris, mailed Berlin and Rome.

BUCKNELL

793.94 Advisory Committee/143 : Telegram

The Consul at Geneva (Bucknell) to the Secretary of State

GENEVA, January 31, 1938—6 p. m.
[Received January 31—2 : 15 p. m.]

30. The Chinese delegation issued the following statement to the press this evening:

"In view of the various reports in the press regarding the Sino-Japanese conflict, the League, and the United States of America, the spokesman of the Chinese delegation issued the following statement to clarify China's position as well as the general situation.

In asking the League to take effective action vis-à-vis Japanese aggression in China, the Chinese Government has been pursuing a legitimate and logical course in accordance with the Covenant of the League of Nations.

The efforts of the Chinese delegation at Geneva have been so directed and it is ridiculous to attribute to it the intention of maneuvering for the intervention of the United States of America. It is equally grotesque to say, as was reported in the press, that the Chinese delegation, or for that matter, any delegation attempted to involve France and the United States in the war in connection with the Sino-Japanese conflict.

During the deliberations of the members of the Council it was suggested—and the suggestion was an agreeable one to the Chinese delegation—that Washington should be informed as before of the discussions at Geneva as undoubtedly the United States have a very deep interest in the Far East. Such a step was considered all the more necessary as the results of the Geneva discussions would, it was hoped, furnish the American Government with useful elements for exercising its own judgment.

It is unnecessary to emphasize that the American policy of independent judgment and parallel action is well known here. Therefore recent reports which have appeared in the press implying or alleging that certain delegation or a group of delegations has been maneuvering to force the American Government to concerted action with the League are entirely unfounded."

BUCKNELL

793.94 Advisory Committee/144 : Telegram

The Consul at Geneva (Bucknell) to the Secretary of State

GENEVA, January 31, 1938—10 p. m.
[Received January 31—7 : 50 p. m.]

31. My 27, January 31, 1 p. m. I saw Cranborne immediately after the Council meeting this afternoon and he referred to a reported statement that the Secretary had given to the press regarding the American attitude toward furnishing arms and munitions to China alone. I told him that I had no knowledge of such statement. He said that he hoped that the Chinese would now adopt the amended resolution and that he would let me know as soon as any decision was arrived at.

Stevenson has just telephoned and informed me that at the meeting this afternoon the four interested powers had after wrangling for 2 hours agreed to a resolution. The first two paragraphs are the same as reported in my No. 18, January 28, 9 p. m. The third paragraph has been changed to read as follows:

"Deplores the deterioration of the situation the more in view of the efforts and achievements of the National Government of China in her political and economic reconstruction".

The fourth paragraph remains the same. A new fifth paragraph reads:

"Calls the most serious attention of the members of the League to the terms of the above-mentioned resolution".

The last paragraph remains practically the same except that the word "feasibility" has been inserted in the place of "possibility" in the last sentence.

Stevenson described the change in the third paragraph as a little bouquet for the Chinese but said that the changes agreed upon made no difference whatever in substance. The resolution is being circulated confidentially tonight and will be considered by the Council at its meeting tomorrow afternoon.

Repeated to London, Paris. Cipher text to Rome, Berlin by mail.

BUCKNELL

793.94 Advisory Committee/145 : Telegram

The Consul at Geneva (Bucknell) to the Secretary of State

GENEVA, February 1, 1938—3 p. m.
[Received February 1—1 p. m.]

34. My 31, January 31, 10 p. m. The Council met in private session this morning to discuss the Council resolution in the matter of the

Chinese appeal.   Peru and Ecuador objected to the resolution at some length, Ecuador in regard to the last paragraph, saying that he must refer to his Government before he could accept it and Peru protested against a few powers agreeing upon such an important declaration and then submitting it for the acceptance of the other members of the Council.   It is now thought that Peru will probably join Poland in abstaining when the matter is put to a vote in public session while Ecuador's position will depend upon the attitude of his Government. A public meeting of the Council has been set tentatively for 6 o'clock this evening but in the event that Ecuador's position has not been cleared up by that time it is possible that the meeting may be postponed until noon tomorrow.

With reference to the reported statement that the Secretary was supposed to have given to the press regarding the American attitude towards arms and ammunition to China mentioned in the first paragraph of my telegram referred to above, it appears that the French stated that they had received a telegram to the effect that the Secretary had made a very strong statement to the press that the United States Government would not in concert or alone furnish arms and ammunition to only one side in the Sino-Japanese conflict.   This the Secretary was supposed to have done on Saturday.[54]   Since Lord Cranborne had asked me to give him any press statement on this subject that I might receive, I gave him a copy of the Secretary's reply at his press conference on Saturday to a question contained in Radio Bulletin 24, January 29 with regard to press reports from Geneva to the effect that Great Britain, France and the Soviet Union had consented to help arm China and were going to consult the United States on such a decision.[55]   Cranborne commented that the French seemed rather to have overdrawn the matter but that he hoped that the resolution as agreed upon last night would go through without difficulty since he felt that this would be agreeable to the United States Government.   He asked if I did not agree with him and I replied that I was not able to express any opinion with regard to the matter.

Repeated to London, Paris, cipher text by mail to Rome, Berlin.

BUCKNELL

---

[54] January 29.
[55] From Department of State press conference report: "The Secretary replied that no communications had been received from any of these Governments on this subject any more than we have any new foreign policy on this subject."

793.94 Advisory Committee/147 : Telegram

The Consul at Geneva (Bucknell) to the Secretary of State

GENEVA, February 2, 1938—4 p. m.
[Received February 2—11:40 a. m.]

38. My 36, February 1, 7 p. m.[56] Council adopted without change resolution reported in my 31, January 31, 10 p. m., and declared the present session closed.

Peru and Poland abstained largely because, they said, of the procedure whereby a declaration of this nature was prepared in secret by a small number of the members of the Council and then presented for their acceptance without sufficient time to consider it or its implications.

Ecuador accepted the resolution upon instructions from his Government. He said that he had referred the matter to his Government because the implications in the last paragraph had not been clear as to what responsibilities might devolve upon Ecuador if she accepted it.

Koo brought the Chinese position up to date from the time of his last summation to the Council and enumerated a list of Japanese atrocities directed not only against the Chinese people but also the citizens and interests of foreign powers in China. He also pointed to the fact that unchecked Japanese aggression in China could only serve detrimentally to affect the cause of peace in Europe. In accepting the resolution he said that he did so confidently believing that greater effect than heretofore will be given to the terms of the Assembly resolution referred to and that the proposed examination will be pursued with energy and promptness. He reserved his right to ask the League to adopt positive measures under the Covenant and further stated that his acceptance was also based upon the understanding that the Council remained seized of the appeal of the Chinese Government invoking articles 10, 11 and 17 of the Covenant.

Cranborne explained that the procedure followed had been adopted merely to save time and that no one had any thought of disregarding the views of any member of the Council.

BUCKNELL

---

[56] Not printed.

793.94 Advisory Committee/150 : Telegram

The Consul at Geneva (Bucknell) to the Secretary of State

GENEVA, February 11, 1938—11 a. m.
[Received February 11—8:30 a. m.]

44. The Secretary General [57] has communicated to members of the League and of the Advisory Committee a communication from the Chinese delegation protesting against renewed indiscriminate bombing by Japanese planes of open villages around Canton. The communication states "These continued air bombings appear to us not only cruelty to humanity but also flagrant defiance of League resolution as well as present strong world opinion against slaughter civilians through aerial attacks".

BUCKNELL

793.94/12975 : Telegram

The Consul at Geneva (Bucknell) to the Secretary of State

GENEVA, May 7, 1938—11 a. m.
[Received May 7—9:10 a. m.]

79. Secretary General has received a note from Chinese permanent delegate bringing up the nature of Japanese outrages in Sino-Japanese conflict. Hoo asks that this be circulated to members of the League and to members of the Far Eastern Advisory Committee.

BUCKNELL

793.94116/40 : Telegram

The Consul at Geneva (Bucknell) to the Secretary of State

GENEVA, May 13, 1938—6 p. m.
[Received May 13—4 p. m.]

93. I am reliably informed that in a secret session of the Council this morning Koo pressed for mutual assistance to China and also asked that an international commission be sent to the northern front to investigate Chinese charges concerning the use of poison gas. The British are understood to have demurred at the appointment of a commission of inquiry but a committee of the Council has been appointed to draft a resolution referring to the previous resolution on assistance to China and urging both sides to refrain from the use of poison gas. It may also contain some reference to recent Chinese successes. In this connection the Japanese delegation has issued a press statement denying the Chinese charges respecting poison gas and accusing the

---

[57] Joseph Avenol, French.

Chinese of making preparations for its use. It is rumored that the British have agreed to discuss privately in London a Chinese request for commercial credits.

BUCKNELL

793.94/13023 : Telegram

The Consul at Geneva (Bucknell) to the Secretary of State

GENEVA, May 14, 1938—10 p. m.
[Received May 14—8:35 p. m.]

95. The Council this evening in public session passed unanimously (Poland abstaining) the following resolution:

["]The Council,
Having heard the statement by the representative of China on the situation in the Far East and on the needs of the national defense of China;
I. Earnestly urges members of the League to do their utmost to give effect to the recommendations contained in previous resolutions of the Assembly and Council in this matter, and to take into serious and sympathetic consideration requests they may receive from the Chinese in conformity with the said resolution;
Expresses its sympathy with China and her heroic struggle for the maintenance of her independence and territorial integrity, threatened by the Japanese invasion, and in the suffering which is thereby inflicted on her people.
II. Recalls that the use of toxic gases is a method of war condemned by international law, which cannot fail, should resort be had to it, to meet with the reprobation of the civilized world; and requests the governments of states who may be in a position to do so to communicate to the League any information that they may obtain on the subject."

Koo said he accepted the resolution on the understanding that the Council remain seized of the Chinese appeal under articles 10, 11 and 17 of the Covenant. He made an appeal for "financial and material aid and facilities for purchase, transport and transit of arms and military supplies, facilities which should in no case be less than those which she enjoyed before the commencement of the present hostilities with Japan".

Bonnet [58] in supporting the resolution said that "acting in accordance with the Assembly resolution and with the resolutions of the Council, France has so far as was possible endeavored to give her aid to China and any recommendation which the Council may in this connection make to states members will be taken into very serious and sympathetic consideration by France". He then referred to the inten-

---

[58] Henri Bonnet, French Minister for Foreign Affairs.

tion of the French Government to make a considerable contribution to the anti-epidemic work in China and called attention to the protection already accorded Chinese refugees in the French Concession[s?].

Halifax [59] likewise supported the resolution and referring to previous resolutions stated "His Majesty's Government have done their best within the limits which the situation in the United Kingdom imposes upon them to implement to the full their obligations to China under these resolutions. I can assure Mr. Koo that His Majesty's Government will continue as they have done in the past to give, in the words of our resolution today, serious and sympathetic consideration to any requests they may receive from the Chinese Government in conformity with these resolutions". Council session was then closed.

At the close of the meeting Quo and Koo in private conversations expressed themselves as pleased with the result of the Council's action, feeling that an advance had been made in their favor as compared with previous sessions, particularly as regards the statements of Bonnet and Halifax.

Koo informed Minister that Halifax had just told him that arrangements for credits mentioned in my No. 93, May 13, 6 p. m., would be concluded "in a manner satisfactory to the Chinese".

BUCKNELL

893.48/1608 : Telegram

The Consul at Geneva (Bucknell) to the Secretary of State

GENEVA, August 2, 1938—4 p. m.
[Received August 2—11:45 a. m.]

164. My telegram 143, June 28, 6 p. m.[60]

1. Smets [61] informs me that it has been decided not to convene an early meeting of Committee for Technical Collaboration with China to consider Chinese request. A meeting will be held probably in September to consider matter.

2. Chinese have now further requested that League undertake work of planning necessary conservancy measures to control floods resulting from destruction of dykes of Yellow River which are seriously affecting provinces of Anhwei, Honan and Kiangsu. The Chinese communication states that occupation of part of these areas by Japanese forces greatly hampers efforts of Chinese Government for conservation and relief measures. The latest Chinese request has been referred to the Committee for Communications and Transit now in

[59] Viscount Halifax, British Secretary of State for Foreign Affairs.
[60] Not printed.
[61] Charles E. Smets, member of the League Secretariat, Economic and Financial Section.

session for a preliminary opinion as to the technical conditions in which such a task if accepted could be undertaken under responsibility of the League.

3. Smets pointed out that both the Chinese and Japanese accuse the other of having destroyed the dykes and said that in his private opinion it would be difficult for the League to undertake this work because of (1) political considerations; (2) the lack of sufficient technical information to enable League engineers to draw up a sound plan and (3) a lack of funds.

BUCKNELL

793.94116/85 : Telegram

The Consul at Geneva (Bucknell) to the Secretary of State

GENEVA, August 9, 1938—7 p. m.
[Received August 9—1 : 50 p. m.]

167. My telegram 93, May 13, 6 p. m. Secretary General has now received a communication from Chinese permanent delegate alleging the use of poison gas by Japanese on Matang front during period July 2 through 5. This communication is accompanied by a medical report supporting Chinese allegations. The note requests that Secretary General transmit communication to members of Council, Assembly and Advisory Committee "for their information and consideration."

BUCKNELL

793.94116/96 : Telegram (part air)

The Consul at Geneva (Bucknell) to the Secretary of State

GENEVA, September 7, 1938—9 p. m.
[Received September 9—8 : 10 a. m.]

181. My 167, August 9, 7 p. m. Chinese permanent delegate has addressed a further communication to Secretary General containing additional information concerning alleged use of poison gas by Japanese troops in China. Communication states that after the first use of gas at Matang gas has continued to be used on many occasions up to and including present drive on Hankow. Note asks that communication be circulated to members of Council, Assembly and Advisory Committee.

BUCKNELL

793.94/13835 : Telegram

The Consul at Geneva (Bucknell) to the Secretary of State

GENEVA, September 8, 1938—5 p. m.
[Received September 8—1: 30 p. m.]

182. Hoo informs me that Chinese delegation has been instructed to press for immediate application of article 17 of the Covenant probably at meeting of new Council to be elected during Assembly. (The Council remains seized of Chinese appeal under articles 10, 11 and 17.) He said that China up to present had been persuaded not to press for application of this article on grounds that they would receive help from individual countries. This help had not been forthcoming and the Chinese were now determined to insist upon immediate application of article 17.

He added that it had not yet been decided whether China would again raise the question of Japanese aggression before the Assembly.

BUCKNELL

793.94/13874 : Telegram

The Consul at Geneva (Bucknell) to the Secretary of State

GENEVA, September 13, 1938—4 p. m.
[Received September 13—1: 10 p. m.]

192. My telegram 182, September 8, 5 p. m. In a conversation with Quo Tai-chi concerning the Chinese request for immediate application of article 17 which has now been embodied in a formal note to the League, he explained that China had so far refrained from insisting upon the application of article 17 as a result of pleas of various members of the League to save them from embarrassment and of promises of individual aid for China. Now, however, since with the exception of Russia these promises of aid had not been carried out, public opinion in China was insisting upon some direct action on the part of the League and the delegation had accordingly been instructed to press for the immediate application of article 17.

In view of the fact that under present circumstances it would be highly embarrassing for the League to agree with the Chinese request for an application of article 17, which would automatically lead to article 16, and equally embarrassing to the Chinese to have such a request refused, it may well be that the present Chinese move is designed for bargaining purposes and that they hope that by their insistence upon the application of article 17 that Great Britain and France particularly may be forced into more concrete measures of assistance to the Chinese Government.

BUCKNELL

793.94/13894 : Telegram

The Consul at Geneva (Bucknell) to the Secretary of State

GENEVA, September 16, 1938—10 p. m.
[Received September 16—9 p. m.]

205. In concluding his speech before the Assembly this afternoon on the various aspects of the war in China, Koo, in addition to requesting financial and material aid to China, urged (1) the immediate application of article 17; (2) an embargo against Japan of arms, munitions, airplanes, oil, essential raw materials, and financial credits and (4) [*3*] measures to deter Japan from the use of poison gas and the bombing of the civilian population. As regards the third point he asked for the despatch of a commission of neutral observers to watch the situation on different fronts and report to the League for consideration.

Code text to Paris, London, Berlin.

BUCKNELL

793.94/13903 : Telegram

The Consul at Geneva (Bucknell) to the Secretary of State

GENEVA, September 17, 1938—9 p. m.
[Received September 17—4: 10 p. m.]

208. My 192, September 13, 4 p. m. At a private meeting of the Council today China requested early consideration of the Chinese appeal under article 17. A reliable Secretariat official said he considered the Chinese move as motivated partly for bargaining purposes and partly to satisfy a growing anti-League sentiment in Government circles in China. He considered it would be difficult for the Council to refuse to give an invitation to Japan. Japan would almost certainly not accept but he felt certain that no serious demand would be made for the application of article 16. He did not know however what formula would be used to avoid its automatically coming into effect. It will be noted that in accordance with paragraph 3 of article 17, article 16 would be applicable only after a formal recognition that Japan had resorted to war. An allusion to this was made by Hoo in a recent conversation with me who suggested that if formal recognition of a state of war should be made it might have some bearing upon the application of the American neutrality law.[62]

Speculation that the Russians may have instigated the Chinese move are discounted in usually reliable circles.

BUCKNELL

---

[62] As amended May 1, 1937; 50 Stat. 121.

793.94/13913 : Telegram

The Consul at Geneva (Bucknell) to the Secretary of State

GENEVA, September 19, 1938—7 p. m.
[Received September 19—2:45 p. m.]

211. The Council today agreed to telegraph an invitation to the Japanese Government in accordance with paragraph 1 of article 17. It was agreed that no action in accordance with paragraph 2 of that article was necessary at this time in view of the fact that an inquiry into the circumstances of the dispute had already been made by the League.

BUCKNELL

793.94/13914 : Telegram

The Consul at Geneva (Bucknell) to the Secretary of State

GENEVA, September 19, 1938—8 p. m.
[Received September 19—3:40 p. m.]

212. My telegram 211, September 19, 7 p. m. I learn that at the private meeting of the Council this afternoon no opposition was made to the Chinese request for the application of article 17. Poland was not represented on the Council on the ground it is understood that Poland's term has expired. It is believed here that the real explanation of Poland's taking this position is a desire to avoid being represented on the Council in the event of a Czech appeal or protest to the League.

BUCKNELL

793.94/13917 : Telegram

The Ambassador in Japan (Grew) to the Secretary of State

TOKYO, September 20, 1938—10 p. m.
[Received September 20—11:07 a. m.]

610. 1. No authoritative Japanese comment on the action of the Council of the League in inviting Japan to accept the obligations of members in settling its dispute with China is available. There is unanimous expectation that the Cabinet, which will probably meet tomorrow, will decide to reject the invitation.

2. Reports of the action by the League have not been prominently displayed. First impressions here are that economic sanctions will not, in the anticipated event of Japan's refusal, be carried out and that the action under reference is primarily a gesture calculated to mollify China.

Repeated to Hong Kong for Chungking.

GREW

793.94/13933 : Telegram

The Consul at Geneva (Bucknell) to the Secretary of State

GENEVA, September 22, 1938—11 a. m.
[Received September 22—9 : 10 a. m.]

223. My telegram No. 211, September 19, 7 p. m. The Secretary-General this morning received a telegram from the Japanese Foreign Minister [63] stating that in the view of the Japanese Government the measures envisaged by the Council would not serve to bring about a just settlement and that therefore the Japanese Government would be unable to accept the invitation addressed to it by the Council.

BUCKNELL

793.94/13934 : Telegram

The Ambassador in China (Johnson) to the Secretary of State

CHUNGKING, September 22, 1938—noon.
[Received September 22—8 : 40 a. m.]

459. Minister of Foreign Affairs [64] invited me to see him this morning to tell me that in view of probability that Japan would refuse invitation which League is extending under article No. 17 of the Covenant, China would request the League to apply article 16 which calls for sanctions. He said he was anxious to know attitude of United States. Said China was looking to the United States to take a leading and important part befitting its known stand in any ultimate settlement of Far Eastern situation and expressed belief that application by the League of sanctions against Japan under article 16 would offer an opportunity to the United States to back up action of the League by such parallel action as might be possible for us. I attempted to explain legal difficulties involved but said that I would communicate his message to you.

JOHNSON

793.94/14003

Memorandum by the Chief of the Division of Far Eastern Affairs (Hamilton) of a Conversation With the Counselor of the Chinese Embassy (Ing)

[WASHINGTON,] September 22, 1938.

Mr. Ing called by appointment. He said that the Ambassador had asked him to call to inquire whether the American Government would be willing to support the League action in invoking article 17 of

[63] Gen. Kazushige Ugaki.
[64] Wang Chung-hui.

the Covenant and whether the American Government would take parallel action with members of the League to impose sanctions to restrain aggressors and maintain the peace of the world.

In reply, I said to Mr. Ing that the situation was not quite that which one would take it to be from his questions; that according to our information the League had, pursuant to Article 17 of the Covenant, extended an invitation to Japan to accept the obligations of membership in the League for the purposes of the Sino-Japanese dispute and that newspaper reports stated that Japan had decided to decline this invitation. I said further that, as Mr. Ing knew, questions relating to Article 17 of the League Covenant were matters for consideration and determination by the League and that this Government was not a member of the League. I said that the general attitude and policy of this Government had been made clear repeatedly; that they were known to the Ambassador and to the Chinese Government; and that I would therefore not undertake to elaborate in regard to them. I mentioned several times that the only action taken by the League so far was to address an invitation to Japan pursuant to Article 17 of the Covenant. (My purpose in calling attention to this fact was to indicate that until the League had decided on the question of further action there existed only a hypothetical basis for the questions which Mr. Ing had asked.) I said that I could make no comment other than as indicated above. I said that I would, however, make note of the questions propounded by the Chinese Government and would bring those questions, together with the comments which I had made, to the attention of higher officers of the Department.

Toward the end of his call Mr. Ing told me that he was asking these questions under instruction from the Chinese Government. I then repeated the statements which I had previously made, as set forth above.

M[AXWELL] M. H[AMILTON]

793.94/13984

Memorandum of Conversation, by the Chief of the Division of European Affairs (Moffat)

[WASHINGTON,] September 23, 1938.

The Chinese Ambassador called to say goodbye. He pointed out that China was appealing for League assistance against Japan under Article 17 of the Covenant, and added that he had received instructions to try and persuade the American Government either through approaching the British and French Council Delegates at Geneva, or the British and French Foreign Offices to support the Chinese position at the League. I told the Ambassador that while I would, of course, report his request to my superiors nonetheless I saw little chance of its being favorably acted on as we were not members of the League and had always made it a point carefully to refrain from advocating any procedure on a member of the League under the Constitution of that body. He asked if Mr. Harrison were not sitting with the Council as observer. I told him no, that he was in Geneva, that he was a member of the Committee of twenty-eight, that his Deputy was a member of the Committee on Technical Aid to China but that he did not sit with the Council in any way except on one occasion when he would meet with them to cast his vote on the composition of the Permanent Opium Board.

The Ambassador said he was also going to mention his plea to other officials in the Department but had brought it up with me also as the League of Nations fell within the purview of the Division of European Affairs.

P[IERREPONT] M[OFFAT]

793.94/13971

Memorandum of Conversation, by the Adviser on Political Relations (Hornbeck)

[WASHINGTON,] September 23, 1938.

The Chinese Ambassador called and said that he had come to say goodbye. Mr. Hornbeck expressed regret that the Ambassador was leaving.

The Ambassador brought up—as he had brought up with Mr. Moffat and Mr. Hamilton—the subject of China's appeal to the League under Article 17. He expressed the hope that the American Government would volunteer to the League a suggestion that the League act vigorously, with an indication that the United States would give such action support (by concurrent or parallel action). Mr. Hornbeck referred to the tremendous preoccupation of the leading powers members of the League with the European situation and to the embarrassments of those among them that are most friendly to China.

The Ambassador then suggested that the United States might ask for a reconvening of the Brussels Conference under the Nine Power Treaty. Mr. Hornbeck asked whether the Ambassador had considered the probabilities with regard to the responses that would be made by the various powers, especially the more important of them, to an inquiry or invitation toward that end; also, whether any advantage would accrue either to the cause of peace in general or to the cause of China in particular through the making by the American Government of such a gesture, with the probable immediate consequences thereof. The Ambassador indicated that consideration of those questions would lead to a not very optimistic conclusion.

The Ambassador then made some pleasant observations on the subject of his sojourn in Washington as Ambassador. Mr. Hornbeck inquired whether the Ambassador would go, in China, to Chungking. The Ambassador replied in the affirmative.

With exchanges of appropriate amenities the conversation was brought to a close.

S[TANLEY] K. H[ORNBECK]

793.94/13964 : Telegram

The Consul at Geneva (Bucknell) to the Secretary of State

GENEVA, September 27, 1938—5 p. m.
[Received September 27—1 : 40 p. m.]

242. The Council in secret session this afternoon set up a drafting committee composed of Russia, Great Britain, France and Greece. I am informed in strict confidence that this Committee with the assistance of China will draft a resolution to be submitted to the Council which will be along the following general lines. (1) It will recall the fact that the Japanese refusal referred to in my 223, September 22, 11 a. m. presents a new legal situation; (2) it will refer to the resolution adopted by the Assembly Committee last year [65] in which Japan was declared the aggressor; (3) will state that article 16 is now applicable and, (4) will leave it to each member of the League to decide in view of its own circumstances in what manner and to what extent it is prepared to apply this article.

BUCKNELL

793.94/13970 : Telegram

The Consul at Geneva (Bucknell) to the Secretary of State

GENEVA, September 28, 1938—3 p. m.
[Received September 28—11 a. m.]

245. I am reliably informed that in a secret meeting of the Council this morning a resolution along the lines reported in my telegram 242, September 27, 5 p. m., was opposed by Belgium and Sweden on the ground that it was inconsistent with their declared policies respecting article 16. The resolution has again been referred to a

---

[65] See final paragraph of report adopted October 6, 1937, *Foreign Relations, Japan, 1931–1941*, vol. I, pp. 384, 394.

drafting committee which will endeavor to meet this objection. The Chinese delegate informs me that the question is one of wording but not of substance.

BUCKNELL

793.94116/105 : Telegram

The Consul at Geneva (Bucknell) to the Secretary of State

GENEVA, September 28, 1938—5 p. m.
[Received September 28—1:55 p. m.]

247. The Chinese permanent delegate informs me that China will introduce the following resolution at the next meeting of the Council:

"The Council, having regard to the second part of its resolution adopted on May 14th 1938, which recalls that the use of toxic gases is a method of war condemned by international law, which cannot fail, should resort be had to it, to meet with the reprobation of the civilized world, and requests the governments of states, who may be in a position to do so, to communicate to the League any information that they may obtain on the subject;

Taking note of the information contained in the various communications of the Chinese representative on the subject; and of his statement on the urgent need for the constitution of a commission of neutral observers in China to investigate the cases of the use of poisonous gas in China, watch the situation in respect thereto, and make reports for examination;

Invites the governments of the states represented on the Council and on the Advisory Committee having official representatives in China to instruct them to constitute themselves into a committee to conduct the necessary inquiry in consultation with the competent authorities of the Chinese Government, watch the situation in regard to resort to this illegal practice, and submit reports from time to time for examination and consideration."

BUCKNELL

793.94/13934 : Telegram

The Secretary of State to the Ambassador in China (Johnson)

WASHINGTON, September 28, 1938—6 p. m.

259. Your 459, September 22, noon. The Counselor of the Chinese Embassy called at the Department on September 22 at the request of Ambassador Wang. He inquired whether the Government of the United States was willing to support the action of the League of Nations in invoking Article 17 of the Covenant and whether this Government would be prepared to act along parallel lines with League members to impose sanctions with the object of restraining aggressor nations and maintaining world peace. The Counselor was informed

that our general attitude and policy with regard to matters concerning action by the League had been made clear to the Ambassador and to the Chinese Government and therefore require no elaboration now. His attention was invited to the fact that questions relating to Article 17 of the Covenant call for consideration by the League, of which the American Government is not a member, and (with a view to indicating that until the League may have decided on its course of action there exists only a hypothetical basis for the questions which the Counselor had asked) to the further fact that the only action thus far taken by the League had been to address an invitation to Japan pursuant to Article 17.

On September 23 Ambassador Wang informed an officer of the Department that the Chinese Government hoped that the League members would take action, in accordance with the Covenant, helpful to China and believed that a confidential approach from the American Government to the British and French Governments in regard to the matter would prove helpful.

HULL

793.94/13975 : Telegram

The Ambassador in China (Johnson) to the Secretary of State

CHUNGKING, September 29, 1938—9 a. m.
[Received September 29—8 a. m.]

570. My 469, September 28, 1 p. m.[66] In my interview with the Minister for Foreign Affairs yesterday he informed me that he had received word that League had voted to apply sanctions against Japan and he again expressed the hope that United States would support the League in any way within its power.

JOHNSON

793.94116/106 : Telegram

The Consul at Geneva (Bucknell) to the Secretary of State

GENEVA, September 29, 1938—8 p. m.
[Received September 29—5 : 33 p. m.]

254. My 247, September 28, 5 p. m. The Council in secret session this afternoon adopted the resolution to be introduced into the Council in public session tomorrow which is as quoted in my telegram referred to above with the exception of the last paragraph thereof. The last paragraph as finally adopted reads:

---

[66] Not printed.

"Invites the governments of the states represented on the Council and on the Advisory Committee having official representatives in China to investigate through the diplomatic channel so far as this may prove practicable and by the most appropriate method such cases as may be brought to their notice and to submit all relevant reports for examination and consideration."

BUCKNELL

793.94/13980 : Telegram

The Consul at Geneva (Bucknell) to the Secretary of State

GENEVA, September 29, 1938—9 p. m.
[Received September 29—8 : 50 p. m.]

255. My telegram No. 245, September 28, 3 p. m. The Council in secret session this afternoon decided to submit a report instead of a resolution to the Council tomorrow in regard to the Chinese appeal under article 17. The report is in general in accordance with my telegram referred to above but is considerably "watered down". Please instruct whether Department desires full text [67] consisting of about 500 words by telegraph when adopted tomorrow.

BUCKNELL

793.94/13986 : Telegram

The Consul at Geneva (Bucknell) to the Secretary of State

GENEVA, September 30, 1938—11 p. m.
[Received September 30—8 : 22 p. m.]

259. My 255, September 29, 9 p. m. The Council this afternoon adopted a report [68] declaring that in view of Japan's refusal of the invitation extended under article 17 and of the fact that the Assembly had already found Japanese military operations in China to be "illicit", article 16 is applicable. The report states that League members are entitled not only to act as before on the basis of the Assembly's previous findings but are also now entitled to adopt individually the measures provided for in article 16. It declares, however, that the coordination of the measures that have been or may be taken can not yet be considered. Sweden, Belgium, and Latvia voted for the report but with reservations referring to their previous statements regarding application of article 16.

Koo said that while the report did not completely satisfy his Government the declaration that article 16 was applicable marked a step forward. He reserved the right to ask at a later date that the Council take steps to coordinate action of states in carrying out

---

[67] The Department assumed publication of text in the press.
[68] See League of Nations, *Official Journal*, November 1938, p. 878.

provisions of the article and accepted the report subject to the understanding that the Council remained seized of the Chinese appeal.

BUCKNELL

793.94116/107 : Telegram

The Consul at Geneva (Bucknell) to the Secretary of State

GENEVA, September 30, 1938—midnight.
[Received September 30—7 : 10 p. m.]

260. My No. 254, September 29, 8 p. m. The Council today adopted the resolution providing for investigation of Chinese charges of use of poison gas by Japanese without change in text already reported. British stated that this was best method of inquiry at least in first instance and China in accepting resolution reserved the right to ask Council to take further action if present procedure proved to be ineffective. Council session closed tonight.

BUCKNELL

793.94/14607

Memorandum of Conversation, by the Chief of the Division of Far Eastern Affairs (Hamilton)

[WASHINGTON,] December 30, 1938.

Participants: Dr. Chang-Lok Chen, Counselor of the Chinese Embassy,
Mr. Tswen-ling Tsui, First Secretary of the Chinese Embassy,
Mr. Hamilton

Dr. Chen called at his request. He was accompanied by Mr. Tsui. Dr. Chen said that the Chinese Embassy had received instructions from the Chinese Ministry of Foreign Affairs directing the Embassy to approach the Department in regard to the forthcoming meeting of the Council of the League of Nations on January 16, to state that the Sino-Japanese conflict would come up for consideration again at this meeting of the League Council, to point out that the Chinese Government realized that the United States was not a member of the League but that in the opinion of the Chinese Government the governments members of the League Council naturally looked to the United States for an indication of attitude in regard to a matter of this character, and to express the hope of the Chinese Government that this Government would by such means and in such way as might be practicable and appropriate take steps, either directly or indirectly, toward causing the governments represented on the

League Council to take more definite action than had hitherto been taken in the way of assisting China and of checkmating Japan.

I referred to the fact that Mr. Tsui had been in to see me a number of months ago on this same subject.[69] I said that as the Chinese Government realized the United States was not a member of the League. I said also that the attitude of this Government and the principles of policy in which this Government believes had been made clear to the American people and to the world in the published statements and addresses of the Secretary of State and of the President. I said that I would of course make record of Dr. Chen's approach under instruction from his Government and refer the matter to higher officers of the Department.

Dr. Chen, in closing the interview, said that his Government wished to lay this matter before us and that he realized that decision as to whether any action by this Government along the line indicated was practicable and appropriate, and, if so, in what way this Government would bring its influence to bear, was a matter for decision by this Government.

M[AXWELL] M. H[AMILTON]

CONSIDERATION OF POSSIBILITIES OF FINANCIAL AID TO CHINA; EXTENSION OF CREDIT BY EXPORT-IMPORT BANK

793.94/11984

Memorandum by the Secretary of State of a Conversation With the Chinese Ambassador (C. T. Wang)

[WASHINGTON,] January 3, 1938.

The Chinese Ambassador came in upon his own request. I first inquired about the general situation in China. He seemed not to have any particular information, more than what I already had. He then said that Chiang Kai-shek [70] is relinquishing his position as head of the civil department of the Government in order to give his entire attention to military operations, and is placing Dr. H. H. Kung [71] in charge of the civil affairs of the Chinese Government. The Ambassador next offered his personal view that Chiang Kai-shek should have taken this step six months ago.

I inquired as to when, in the opinion of the Ambassador, the Chinese Government would feel obliged to move from Hankow to Chungking. He replied that he did not think they would move from Hankow at all soon; that they would not move until and unless the

---

[69] See memorandum of September 22, p. 511.
[70] As President of the Chinese Executive Yuan (Premier).
[71] Chinese Minister of Finance.

capture of Hankow was more or less imminent. I then asked as to what the Japanese situation with respect to Hankow seemed to be. He said that the Japanese had not advanced farther in that direction than to a point not far above Wuhu and was showing no disposition at present to move ahead. I inquired whether he had any late information about conditions in Nanking, and he said that he did not.

I then inquired whether his Government is getting any supplies through French Indo-China, and he said he understood that a certain amount is being gotten across by making detours. I was not much impressed with the earnestness of this statement. I inquired what would be done with the locomotive being shipped from this country this week, and he replied that it would be shipped to Hong Kong; that it could not go across the narrow-gauge road in French Indo-China.

I inquired if the Ambassador knew what the Russian state of mind is with respect to the Chinese-Japanese situation. He said he had nothing new upon that subject. Another inquiry was whether in his judgment the internal troubles in Russia are creating a feeling on the part of all other nations that Russia would be correspondingly engrossed without any definite program relating to international foreign policy, especially in the Far East. To this he readily agreed.

The Ambassador then brought up the question he had in mind in coming to the Department today, and he proceeded to say that at the Brussels Conference some weeks ago [72] Dr. Wellington Koo [73] took up with the representatives of Britain, France, and the United States, the necessity for a loan from these three governments for China, of five hundred million dollars with which to purchase munitions, arms, and implements of war, and that the impression was left with Dr. Koo that the matter would be given further attention by this Government and presumably a more definite answer made than Mr. Norman Davis [74] had given in Brussels. Before making reply to the Ambassador's question, I inquired as to the amount and location of the gold and silver reserves of China. He was vague as to the amount. He said they had certain amounts in certain cities in China, also in London, in Hong Kong, and in the United States. I inquired then as to how long the Chinese Government could go forward on its own resources, incidentally citing the fact that it had proceeded already for six months. The Ambassador replied that it could probably go on another six months on its own resources, and he then proceeded to emphasize the view that it was important and

---

[72] See *Foreign Relations*, 1937, vol. IV, pp. 155 ff.
[73] Chinese Ambassador in France.
[74] American delegate.

necessary that the Government should look ahead and plan accordingly; hence the desirability and urgency to ascertain about the possibilities of the requested loan of five hundred million dollars. In that connection, I remarked that of course the Ambassador was thoroughly familiar with the fact that our entire market for arms, ammunition, and implements of war, is open in this country; that transportation is easily possible; that we are carrying forward our silver purchases from China; that the Export-Import Bank is discounting certain commercial paper for locomotives, etc. The Ambassador agreed with expressions of appreciation on behalf of his Government.

I then recurred to his inquiry, and said I was sure that he recalled the conversation which took place at Brussels, to the effect that Mr. Norman Davis had stated that only Congress could authorize a loan in any amount by the Government of the United States, while the British then or thereafter indicated that they were completely preoccupied at the time in producing armament supplies for themselves. I then said that there had been no developments with respect to this matter since the Brussels conversations; that I could not undertake to speak for Congress in regard to possible legislation authorizing a loan; that, in the circumstances, I would not be frank, as I always desired to be, if I offered any comment as to the situation beyond what was said at Brussels, except that this is a matter which comes under the authority and jurisdiction of Congress. The Ambassador indicated he understood this view, and then suggested that perhaps the President and the executive branch might have influence with Congress in carrying out a program such as he was proposing. I replied that in some and possibly many instances this would be true, but that the Congress itself is giving increasing attention to our foreign affairs and especially to conditions in the Pacific area, and that it would have definite opinions in regard to the question of a loan and hence would not be susceptible of influence by the opinions of the executive or other branches of the Government; that in any event I could not and would not, in justice to all concerned, undertake to comment as to the future in this connection but only stand on what has been said to the effect that the Congress alone has jurisdiction and must be looked to for the necessary legislation. The Ambassador sought to induce me to say that the matter was still under advisement and that there were possibilities of a different decision in the future. To this I again promptly brought him back to my statements which I have just recorded and I made the matter most definite by a further statement that I was not called upon to speak except as to the present; that I had spoken definitely as to the present; and that the future would have to take care of itself. The Ambassador did not seem at all surprised.

With reference to the report of the Japanese Government's peace terms to the Chinese Government, I remarked that, having been confined at my apartment with a severe cold for some days, I had not seen and conferred with the President in the meantime; that I was informed the Chinese Ambassador had had a conference with the President and, in order that there might be no crossing of wires, I might inquire whether the Chinese Ambassador had discussed the Japanese peace proposals in the presence of the President; if so, whether the President had offered any comment whatever relative to the merits of the reported peace proposals. The Ambassador replied without hesitation or equivocation that the peace proposals were brought up in his talk with the President, but that the President said not one word touching the merits or demerits of the peace proposals. I did not say to the Chinese Ambassador that my inquiry was due to the fact that a despatch from Johnson in China, repeating a report that had reached him, was to the effect that the President had in fact commented on the merits of the peace proposals and had indicated definitely to the Chinese Ambassador that the Chinese Government should view them as favorable proposals.[75]

C[ORDELL] H[ULL]

893.51/6564 : Telegram

The Secretary of State to the Ambassador in the United Kingdom (Kennedy)

WASHINGTON, January 6, 1938—9 p. m.

8. The British Ambassador [76] has informed the Department today that his Government had advised him that the Chinese Ambassador in London,[77] in talking with the Secretary for Foreign Affairs [78] last Monday, had said the Chinese Government was negotiating with the United States Government for a loan of 125 million dollars for 10 years at 3 percent and to be issued at 90; and that yesterday he told the British Foreign Office that an agreement had been signed in Washington for a loan of 150 million dollars, but that he could not definitely say whether the United States Government were concerned or not.

There is no foundation for this report as far as the American Government is concerned, and the Department has no knowledge of any loan arrangement with private parties. The Department is so informing Sir Ronald Lindsay.

---

[75] See telegram No. 128, December 31, 1937, 2 p. m., from the Ambassador in China, *Foreign Relations*, 1937, vol. III, p. 847.
[76] Sir Ronald C. Lindsay.
[77] Quo Tai-chi.
[78] Anthony Eden.

In his most recent talk with the Chinese Ambassador in Washington on this subject, the Secretary of State, while pointing out the constant purchases of Chinese silver by the American Tresaury, had made clear that any government loan would require the passage of legislation.

If Butterworth [79] should be questioned about the report by the British Treasury, he may state that no such loan transaction is under discussion with this Government.

HULL

893.51/6584

Memorandum by the Under Secretary of State (Welles) of a Conversation With the Counselor of the Chinese Embassy (Ing)

[WASHINGTON,] January 8, 1938.

Owing to the absence in New York of the Chinese Ambassador, I asked the Counselor of the Embassy to come to see me this morning. I told Dr. Ing that on January 5 the British Ambassador in Washington had advised me that he had just received a cable from Mr. Eden informing him of a conversation which Mr. Eden had had on January 3 with the Chinese Ambassador in London. The latter had stated that the Chinese Government was negotiating with the United States Government for a loan of 125 million dollars for ten years at 3 per cent to be issued at 90. I told Dr. Ing that on the following day I had been further informed by the British Ambassador that he had been advised by Mr. Eden of a further conversation which the latter had had on January 5 with the Chinese Ambassador in London in which the latter had said that an agreement had been signed in Washington for a loan of 150 million dollars but that the Ambassador could not say definitely whether the United States Government were concerned or not.

I told Dr. Ing that after consultation with the Secretary of the Treasury [80] I had informed the British Ambassador that no conversations, no negotiations, and no agreement for a loan had taken place between the United States and the Chinese Governments. I said to Dr. Ing that undoubtedly some strange misapprehension and misunderstanding had occurred and that since we wanted, of course, to avoid any type of misunderstanding with the Chinese Government, it seemed to me that it would be helpful if the Chinese Embassy here would communicate with the Chinese Ambassador in London and let him know that there was no foundation for the information which

---

[79] William W. Butterworth, Second Secretary of Embassy in the United Kingdom.
[80] Henry Morgenthau, Jr.

he had conveyed to the British Foreign Secretary in so far as the United States Government was concerned.

Dr. Ing told me that he would immediately communicate our conversation to the Chinese Ambassador and ask that the latter take the action with regard to his colleague in London which I had suggested.

S[UMNER] W[ELLES]

893.51/6593 : Telegram

The Ambassador in China (Johnson) to the Secretary of State

HANKOW, February 27, 1938—3 p. m.
[Received February 27—9 : 55 a. m.]

130. My 95, February 8, 2 p. m.[81] I learned from source near Soong [82] that C. T. Wang is being recalled for apparently misinforming Government about prospects for loan in the United States which Kung [83] hoped to apply to purchase of planes.

JOHNSON

893.51/6594 : Telegram

The Consul General at Hong Kong (Southard) to the Secretary of State

HONG KONG, February 28, 1938—4 p. m.
[Received March 1—12 : 30 p. m.]

Referring to my strictly confidential telegram of December 2, 9 a. m.,[84] Hong Kong and Shanghai Banking Corporation state that shipments of Chinese Government silver to London were finished by mid-February, they estimate the total shipments as follows: 318½ million silver dollars; 6 million dollars in silver bars; and 133½ million dollars worth of subsidiary coins. It is not known how much silver these subsidiary coins will yield when melted. No further arrivals of Chinese Government silver at Hong Kong are anticipated.

By mail to Hankow, Tokyo, London.

SOUTHARD

---

[81] Not printed.
[82] T. V. Soong, chairman of the Board of Directors, Bank of China, and formerly Chinese Minister of Finance.
[83] H. H. Kung, President of the Chinese Executive Yuan (Premier) and Minister of Finance.
[84] *Foreign Relations, 1937*, vol. IV, p. 626.

893.51/6598 : Telegram

The Ambassador in the United Kingdom (Kennedy) to the Secretary of State

LONDON, March 23, 1938—1 p. m.
[Received March 23—9 : 15 a. m.]

236. Department's 8, January 6, 9 p. m. The Chinese Ambassador tells me that he has again approached the British authorities with a view to obtaining a loan of 20,000,000 pounds. In particular he has gone into the matter with Leith-Ross [85] and offered as security mines in the southwest provinces which have the advantage of being [inaccessible?] to the Japanese. The Chinese Ambassador emphasized that if such a loan was not obtained China could not carry on with its currency much longer.

Leith-Ross states that he held out no hope to the Chinese of a loan but that he suggested that something might be done in the matter of arranging commercial credits for the mineral produce. At the moment Hong Kong is the point of export and Leith-Ross said that the Japanese might well interfere with such shipments but that it might prove practical to get certain ores out through Burma.

Mr. Quo Tai-chi also stated that the Japanese are now counterfeiting Chinese currency in order to bring it into disrepute and thus disorganize Chinese finances.

KENNEDY

893.51/6599 : Telegram

The Ambassador in China (Johnson) to the Secretary of State

HANKOW, March 23, 1938—4 p. m.
[Received March 23—2 : 32 p. m.]

170. Grant Forbes called on me today. He brought a letter from his [uncle] Cameron Forbes.[86] I do not know whom he represents but believe that he is working with and for a financial group of which Jean Monnet [87] and T. V. Soong have been dominating and moving spirits. Forbes stated that he had been discussing with Kung possibilities of a material credit arrangement which I believe was based on China's holdings of silver, but that Kung had made conditions so difficult that he thought his principals would not approve. Forbes stated he was awaiting reply to a telegram. He suggested to me that American Government might be well advised to grant Chinese forces aid in the form of munitions. I told Forbes that I saw no chance of

---

[85] Sir Frederick Leith-Ross, chief economic adviser to the British Government.
[86] Former Ambassador in Japan.
[87] French banker.

256941—54——34

this; that furthermore I had on all occasions attempted to make quite clear to the Chinese that they could not expect any such aid from American sources.

JOHNSON

893.51/6607

Memorandum of Conversation, by the Adviser on Political Relations (Hornbeck)

[WASHINGTON,] March 24, 1938.

The Chinese Ambassador called this afternoon in consequence of an intimation made by Mr. Hamilton [88] in a conversation with Mr. Leonard Hsu [89] this [*yesterday*] morning in connection with the question of a possible loan by the Bankers Trust Company to China (see Mr. Hamilton's memorandum [90]).

The Ambassador said that, as Mr. Hornbeck knew, he, the Ambassador, was endeavoring to make the most effective use possible of China's financial resources, especially China's stock of silver, toward establishing credits and making possible purchasing by the Chinese Government in the United States. He said that he was trying to make each dollar's worth of China's silver stock do the work of two dollars. He said that the United States Treasury had been very helpful in its purchasing of silver. He said that he now had under way a negotiation with the Bankers Trust Company for a loan of from $10,000,000 to $25,000,000; this loan to be secured 50 percent by deposit of silver either with the Bankers Trust Company or elsewhere and 50 percent by resources of the Bank of China; the loan was to be for three (?) years and was to bear interest at from 3 to 4 percent; the negotiations had reached a point at which, before going further, he wanted to obtain the "blessing of the Department of State." He said that approach had been made to Mr. Hamilton on the subject and that now he, the Ambassador, would very much like to have the Department's view.

Mr. Hornbeck said that such a question involved consideration of a number of factors. He said that the American Government has been pursuing in regard to China and Japan, in the light of the fact that those two countries are engaged in hostilities, and in the light of the further fact that there is on the statute books of the United States a "Neutrality Act," [91] a course designed to conform first of all to the desire of the American people that this country shall not become in-

[88] Maxwell M. Hamilton, Chief of the Division of Far Eastern Affairs.
[89] Chinese Industrial Commissioner in the United States.
[90] Not printed.
[91] As amended May 1, 1937; 50 Stat. 121.

volved in armed conflict and that, where there is armed conflict, this country shall not encourage or contribute to the prolonging of the conflict. This Government is trying, Mr. Hornbeck said, to maintain and preserve on behalf of this country a position of neutrality. The people of this country are opposed in principle to the furnishing of funds, furnishing of munitions, etc. For good reasons, the President has seen fit not to make proclamation putting into effect provisions of the Neutrality Act; but the Administration is being guided by the spirit of that Act. Markets in this country are open to foreign governments which, engaged in hostilities, seek to raise funds and to make purchases of munitions, etc., but encouragement is not being given by the Government to such transactions. We had reached, before the Japanese-Chinese hostilities began, a point where the Department of State had ceased to pass upon the question of loans abroad. We had become very conservative on the subject of "giving our blessing" to projects contemplating loans abroad.

Mr. Hornbeck then went on to say that, speaking in all friendliness, he wondered whether the Ambassador had given full consideration to various possible effects, as regarded China's interest, which might flow from the obtaining by China at this time of loans in this country. He said that, among other things, Japanese agents have been very active toward obtaining loans and credits for Japan; there has been on the part of American financial interests perhaps more of a disposition to be interested in possible Japanese financing than in possible Chinese financing; there have been informal approaches to agencies of the American Government toward ascertaining the attitude of the Government; and, in general, the Government has discouraged rather than encouraged embarkation by American interests upon such projects. If the Chinese Government succeeded in floating a loan or loans in this country, would not persons interested in possible Japanese financing become more active and be likely to be more successful in that field than has hitherto been the case?

The Ambassador said that he thought that Japan had already succeeded in getting a good deal of financial assistance, especially credits in this country. He said that he had taken into consideration the possibilities which Mr. Hornbeck had mentioned.

Mr. Hornbeck said that the most conspicuous of the transactions of Japan had been in sale of gold. He wondered why China did not simply sell more silver. He was not overlooking the Ambassador's statement that he wanted a dollar's worth of silver to do the work of two dollars; but advantages gained along that line would be advantageous only for a short time: what the Ambassador had in contemplation was a short-term loan, and it is amazing how soon payment on short-term loans becomes due. The Ambassador said that he had in contemplation other loans which, when and as negotiated, would make possible payments when due.

There followed some further discussion of points of which mention is made above; and Mr. Hornbeck finally said that, as the Ambassador would realize from what had been said, the Department was not in position either to give a blessing to or to make an objection to entry by the Bankers Trust Company upon a loan project. The Ambassador asked whether this meant that the Department "did not object." Mr. Hornbeck said that that was not exactly the meaning: he repeated that the Department was not in position definitely to "make an objection to," i. e., to veto.

Mr. Hornbeck then brought up another subject (the matter of Bernhard and Company: record of which is made in a separate memorandum [92]).

S[TANLEY] K. H[ORNBECK]

893.51/6614

Memorandum of Conversation, by the Adviser on Political Relations (*Hornbeck*)

[WASHINGTON,] March 29, 1938.

Participants: Mr. Charles E. C. Freyvogel ⎱ Vice Presidents of
Mr. O. Parker McComas ⎰ the Bankers Trust
Mr. Feis [93] Company, New
Mr. Hornbeck York, N. Y.

Messrs. Freyvogel and McComas called by appointment (made at the instance of and by the Chinese Ambassador).

Mr. McComas referred to a project of which the Department already had some information, a project for a loan by the Bankers Trust Company to the Chinese Government. He said that he and Mr. Freyvogel had come to the Department with regard to political aspects of this project. In the course of the conversation he outlined the project as one whereby the bank would loan China $10,000,000; China would deposit silver to the value of $5,000,000 and the Bank of China would deposit securities covering the balance plus perhaps a 20 percent margin; and, the Bank of China would undertake to deposit additional security if and as needed to cover a proper ratio. Mr. McComas said that he assumed that the Chinese wanted this loan "for propaganda purposes." He later explained this as meaning that the Chinese Government wished to be able to say to their own people, in

---

[92] Dated March 24, not printed.
[93] Herbert Feis, Adviser on International Economic Affairs.

connection with financing in China, and also to the world at large, that they were getting assistance from the United States (or from American sources).

Mr. Hornbeck said that in his opinion it is impossible to draw a clear line between economic qualities and political qualities in a matter of loans to foreign governments: he therefore wished to ask some questions which would bear on what might be regarded as the economic or commercial side of this project. He asked questions with regard to the proposed security, especially the part to be offered by the Bank of China, and with regard to activities of the Bankers Trust Company and other banks in New York in connection with or in relation to financing of Chinese and of Japanese business, both public and private, and financing of exports from this country to China and Japan. Mr. McComas and Mr. Freyvogel replied with apparent frankness to these questions. It was brought out that the project under consideration, if undertaken, would constitute the first making of an outright loan by American banks to either of the countries involved since the outbreak of the present Chinese-Japanese hostilities.

Mr. Hornbeck inquired whether Mr. Feis would ask questions or make comments. Mr. Feis expressed the view that there could be no advantage or profit to China from a loan of the character described.

The point that China was seeking this loan "for propaganda purposes" was again brought up, and the observation was made that the Chinese Ambassador envisaged this loan as an entering wedge or a stepping stone to the making of other and bigger loans.

Mr. Hornbeck said that the Chinese Ambassador had spoken to him about this project and had described it as involving from $10,-000,000 to $25,000,000. Mr. McComas said that $25,000,000 had been mentioned when the Chinese Ambassador first broached the subject and that $10,000,000 had been later talked about as a starting point.

Mr. Hornbeck then asked just what inquiry, if any, Messrs. Freyvogel and McComas would feel disposed to put to the Department. Mr. McComas said that it was because this project, if proceeded with, would have a political aspect and would involve a question of national policy, the project being different from ordinary commercial financing, that they had come to the Department. He indicated that they wanted to know what would be the Department's attitude.

Mr. Hornbeck said that the Chinese Ambassador had made much the same inquiry, soliciting a "blessing" from the Department for the project, and that he had given the Ambassador an account of this Government's attitude and policy and had told the Ambassador that he would say much the same thing to the representatives of the bank when they called. He then gave an exposition of policy and procedure in the light of the existence of the Neutrality Act and of public opinion in regard to subjects to which that act relates. He said that the old practice of the Department's giving consideration to projects for foreign loans and expressing itself in terms of "no objection" or to the contrary has been discontinued. He said that, with the points which he had mentioned in mind, the parties interested in such a possible project would realize that the Department was not prepared to take a position with regard to the matter and, with those same points in mind, each of the parties must decide for itself.

Mr. McComas said that it was clear that the project had substantial political implications, would involve national policy to a considerable extent, and that Mr. Feis and Mr. Hornbeck could understand what would be his and Mr. Freyvogel's position (which he implied would be unfavorable toward proceeding with the project); he added that he would explain the whole matter to his associates at the bank. Mr. Hornbeck said that he wanted to make sure that it would not be reported that the Department had taken a position either pro or contra the project: we could not say that we were favorable to it and we would not say that we were opposed to it. Mr. McComas and Mr. Freyvogel said that this was understood.

S[TANLEY] K. H[ORNBECK]

893.51/6615

The Ambassador in the United Kingdom (Kennedy) to the Secretary of State

No. 157   LONDON, April 7, 1938.
                                                [Received April 16.]

SIR: I have the honor to report that, in the course of a conversation about other matters, Sir Frederick Leith-Ross reiterated the statement reported in the Embassy's 236, March 23, 1 p. m. He went on to say that there were now 170,000 coolies working on the Burma-Yunan road which was scheduled to take three and would, in fact, only take five months to complete. This added channel of communication should prove quite helpful to China, which at the moment was receiving most of its munitions from Europe via French Indo-China by road or by rail. Leith-Ross said that Chiang Kai-shek had six months' supply of munitions and he was now also getting supplies from Russia, including some quite useful tanks. Nevertheless the Chinese, through Dr. Sun-Fo,[94] were pressing hard for money with which to purchase further supplies.

Leith-Ross inquired about our purchases of Chinese silver and asked whether our action as regards Mexico would affect the position. He

---

[94] President of the Chinese Legislative Yuan.

said that he personally wished the British Government could undertake similar purchases but when it was suggested that the Government of India could do so (paragraph 2, Embassy's 267, March 30, 7 p. m.[95]), he said that India already had more silver than it wanted. Leith-Ross explained that the offers which the Chinese had made here as regards silver were on the basis of pledged silver as security, and he therefore wondered whether American arrangements with the Chinese precluded them from selling silver on the market or elsewhere. He did not indicate that the British Government was prepared to buy silver, but he implied that it certainly could not consider entering into transactions on the basis of pledged silver for that would mean a loan, which was out of the question since it would require Parliamentary sanction.

Leith-Ross seemed both pleased and encouraged at the resistance the Chinese had offered. He also said that in his opinion they had done a commendable job as regards their currency: it had been held a very long time under trying conditions, and was only now slipping. He expressed the hope that the foreign banks would take some risks and help the Chinese by not attempting to cover themselves against every contingency. For instance, small transactions now affected the exchange rate and, therefore, it would be well if the foreign banks would carry small foreign exchange transactions between allotments.

Respectfully yours,

For the Ambassador:

HERSCHEL V. JOHNSON
Counselor of Embassy

693.006/38 : Telegram

The Ambassador in China (Johnson) to the Secretary of State

HANKOW, April 11, 1938—2 p. m.
[Received April 11—8 : 50 a. m.]

199. Young [96] inquires whether Department is in position to express any views for his guidance as to attitude of American Government in case China should decide to curtail unessential imports in order to safeguard currency and economic situation and strengthen war effort. He considers it would be much preferable to utilize prohibitions in so far as properly applicable and to limit use of restrictive or prohibitive tariffs because (first) prohibitions less likely to become permanent trade barriers and (second) danger that tariffs would cause marking up internal prices and tend to initiate general price rise which so far has not gone far but might develop due to general condi-

---

[95] Not printed.
[96] Arthur N. Young, American adviser to the Chinese Ministry of Finance.

tions and increased note issue since last summer. He hopes American Government would not feel obliged to object on treaty or other grounds to imposition of certain temporary prohibitions if deemed necessary since acquiescence would be concrete manifestation of sympathy with China.

I may add that I feel that something of this kind is inevitable; that the suggested action seems least harmful of possible actions that might be taken. I hope that United States can take a sympathetic attitude under serious situation now facing Chinese Government.

Young says that he does not know that above steps will be taken. He has told no one of this inquiry.

JOHNSON

693.006/38 : Telegram

The Secretary of State to the Ambassador in China (Johnson)

WASHINGTON, April 15, 1938—noon.

125. Your 199, April 11, 2 p. m., in regard to possible curtailment by China of unessential imports.

You may orally and confidentially inform Young that the Department is confident that, in connection with any measures which China may take for the protection of her national economy, the Chinese Government would give due consideration to American interests and would avoid any discrimination against those interests.

HULL

893.51/6631 : Telegram

The Ambassador in Japan (Grew) to the Secretary of State

TOKYO, June 18, 1938—7 p. m.
[Received June 18—8 : 53 a. m.]

389. Under the title "Rumored Large American Loan to China" the editorial in this morning's *Asahi* is given to a discussion of the American attitude toward the current conflict. Information from Hong Kong and Shanghai, it states, reports American loans of 25 million on the security of silver deposited with the United States and of 500 million dollars on the security of banking rights, mining, and other collateral. The editorial finds it not unlikely that Chinese negotiations for loans in the United States have made some progress even if these details are inaccurate. It asserts that a business basis for such loans is lacking and that they are possible only as political loans made by the American Government. Discussing the probabilities in accuracy of the report, it deduces that probably the report arises from a new silver purchase agreement. The editorial thereupon

goes into the American policy of purchasing Chinese silver, states that the American policy is keeping Chinese currency up in spite of lack of foreign trade, and asserts that the Chiang Kai Shek régime is thereby being sustained. Recent intensification of American opinion against Japan is admitted.

If I am approached with regard to this loan rumor, I shall be guided by the Department's 338, December 10, 1937.[97]

Repeated to Shanghai for Hankow.

GREW

893.51/6631 : Telegram

The Acting Secretary of State to the Ambassador in Japan (Grew)

WASHINGTON, June 20, 1938—8 p. m.

201. Your 389, June 18, 7 p. m.

1. The Treasury Department knows nothing whatsoever about the 500 million dollar transaction mentioned. With regard to the reported American loan to China on the security of silver, the Treasury Department states that there is no new feature in the arrangements with China; no credit is being extended on silver; and the Treasury is making periodic purchases in relatively small amounts in accord with its general policy of buying gold and silver the world over whenever offered, upon delivery in New York.

2. At the press conference today the Acting Secretary, in reply to an inquiry in regard to the report that a 500 million dollar loan is impending to China, advised the correspondents to consult the Treasury Department but added off the record that it was his understanding, after talking with the Treasury Department, that there was not a word of truth in the report.

3. You are authorized in your discretion to inform inquirers that the reports mentioned in your telegram under reference are without basis in fact so far as the information available to this Government is concerned.

WELLES

893.51/6636 : Telegram

The Chargé in the United Kingdom (Johnson) to the Secretary of State

LONDON, June 23, 1938—6 p. m.
[Received June 23—2:04 p. m.]

551. Embassy's 528 of June 17, 6 p. m.[98] In the course of a conversation, the British Treasury referred to the desirability of making

---

[97] *Foreign Relations*, 1937, vol. III, p. 785.
[98] Not printed.

funds available to China and confidentially described the position here as follows:

The Foreign Office was strongly in favor of a loan but the Cabinet had not been able to make up its collective mind. The Chancellor of the Exchequer [99] was not in favor of taking any action which would offend the Japanese and yet would not have important benefits for China. Simon, therefore, recommended the making either of a substantial loan or none at all. But any large sum would have to have a British Government guarantee and there lay the stumbling block.

The British Treasury felt that not less than £10,000,000 and preferably £20,000,000 would constitute a sum sufficient to facilitate food and other purchases and strengthen the Chinese exchange position.

The British Treasury did not conceal its chagrin at the delay in facing up to this situation and took the line that until the British Cabinet made up its mind it could not appropriately approach the United States regarding joint action.

Asked about the reaction in Japan to any such project, the British Treasury stated that it would no doubt be hard to explain but since the Japanese had always maintained that they favored the bringing of stability to China's exchange, it might be defended on that score though the defence would certainly be weak and transparent.

The British Treasury mentioned that Russia had accorded China some £8,000,000 of barter credits.

JOHNSON

893.51/6642 : Telegram

The Ambassador in France (Bullitt) to the Secretary of State

PARIS, July 7, 1938—noon.
[Received 2:25 p. m.]

1077. I discussed with Bonnet [1] last night the action of the French Government in landing troops on the Paracel Islands and the action restricting Japanese exports to France (reported in my 1040, July 1, 3 p. m.[2]). Bonnet said that these two actions did not indicate any change in French policy vis-à-vis Japan and that they were not in any way related. The action with regard to Japanese exports was due solely to the refusal of the Japanese to permit French exporters to get their money out of Japan.

Bonnet went on to discuss the situation in China and said that he believed that Chinese resistance could and would continue indefinitely

---

[99] Sir John Simon.
[1] Henri Bonnet, French Minister for Foreign Affairs.
[2] Not printed.

provided China could obtain a loan for the purpose of maintaining Chinese currency in foreign exchange markets. Incidentally the same statement has been made to me by a number of competent observers who have recently come to Paris direct from China.

Bonnet added that he was now satisfied the British were doing everything they could to support Chiang Kai Shek. He said that he was certain that both Great Britain and France would be prepared to advance money to the Chinese Government at the present time if the United States should be able to take similar action. I gathered that he did not envisage a joint loan but that he felt both England and France would grant loans to the Chinese Government if it should be possible for our Export Import Bank or some other agency public or private to grant a loan. The action of the three Governments would be separate but simultaneous.

I am not sufficiently in touch with our present policies vis-à-vis the Far East to know whether this idea is in the realm of practical politics. Recently I have been impressed, however, by the statements of men returning from China to the effect that Chinese resistance may collapse because of this monetary difficulty and that a sum of 100 million dollars would be sufficient to enable the Chinese Government to continue resistance.

I should be obliged if you could give me some slight indication of our policy in this regard.

BULLITT

893.51/6643 : Telegram

The Ambassador in the United Kingdom (Kennedy) to the Secretary of State

LONDON, July 11, 1938—8 p. m.
[Received July 11—4 : 16 p. m.]

623. Embassy's 551, June 23, 6 p. m. I had a conversation with Halifax [3] today at his request. The British are considering a loan up to $100,000,000 to the Chinese for the support of currency. He asked me whether I thought the United States would join in this and I said of course I had no way of knowing what the Government would do. He asked me my personal opinion and I told him I thought it was extremely unlikely.

I asked him how he was going to reconcile the position of supporting currency for the Chinese and backing a nonintervention committee in Spain [4] and also advising the Japanese that this loan was only to

---

[3] Viscount Halifax, British Secretary of State for Foreign Affairs.
[4] For correspondence regarding the Spanish Civil War, see vol. I, pp. 149 ff.

help currency and not meant as a hostile gesture to the Japanese. He told me that he did not think the Spanish policy was at all contrary to the policy already set out, on which they were on record as supporting, that everything should be done that could be done to help the Chinese. He said that the Japanese had already approached the British with the idea of joint guardianship of the Chinese financial status, but the British were unwilling to participate.

Frankly, however, he is very worried about the Japanese situation and the prospect of a situation arising in Hong Kong which would be another sore spot and might mean trouble—even worse than the present Spanish bombings.

I asked him what he had actually called me over there for and he said to get my personal reactions rather than the Government's reactions. He said that he is in the toughest spot he has been in to advise the Cabinet on this particular question because he is convinced that unless the British do something on currency the Chinese will go bad financially and that the party will be over as far as the Japanese are concerned. If on the other hand the Chinese get some help for their currency they would go along for a year and at that time a better settlement all around could be made.

I am sending this on to you for your information because I am convinced that Halifax did me the honor of trying to get my personal reactions on the problem rather than as Ambassador, but if there is anything further you want me to do on it, please advise.

Halifax is of the opinion that things have eased up over here considerably but, as I went out the door, he said "I feel that I am such a bad prophet that anything can happen any time and show up the British. I know nothing about what is going on".

KENNEDY

893.51/6643 : Telegram

The Secretary of State to the Ambassador in the United Kingdom (Kennedy)

WASHINGTON, July 13, 1938—6 p. m.

350. Your 623, July 11, 8 p. m., especially penultimate paragraph. I believe that it would be useful for you, when next you see Halifax, to take occasion to say to him that your Government has indicated to you that it finds interesting the information that the British are considering a loan to the Chinese for support of currency and welcomes this indication of the line along which the British Government's thought is proceeding. You should state that your Government feels that assistance of various legitimate types to China at this time should

serve the best interests of the world and that much is being done in this country, some of it with publicity and some without, that is deliberately calculated to be of assistance to China directly or indirectly or both, and that broadening and intensification of such activities are in prospect. Say further, that we believe that a currency loan would be helpful to the Chinese; but we also feel that the making of such a loan jointly or collectively would tend to accentuate adverse Japanese susceptibilities and retard progress toward resolving the fundamental issue inherent in the Chinese-Japanese conflict; that we feel that the problem of assistance can best be dealt with by each country in accordance with its capacity and in its own way, without the disturbing implications of and the delaying complications inherent in joint action; that, moreover, numerous difficulties would attend the floating privately in this country of such a loan at this time and the Government is not in a position to make or to participate in the making of a loan by official action. We are giving and will give assistance along different lines. Some of these will not be conspicuous and will in large measure escape publicity. Well known, however, is the assistance which this Government has afforded to the purchasing in an otherwise unsupported market, of Chinese silver, a type of assistance which in all probability will continue. Substantial assistance has been and probably will be given through the agency of the Export Import Bank. Also, considerable amounts of money have been and are being given by private organizations for relief, medical work, and associated activities for relieving the suffering of Chinese civilian population. We are confident that within the limitations of our policy of non-interference and non-intervention the assistance which has been and which may be rendered by this country will in the long aggregate prove to be of very substantial value to the Chinese. We thoroughly believe that assistance by each country in its own way, without fact or appearance of joint action and with a minimum of publicity, will be most potentially efficacious towards the desired end of peace with stability. Please emphasize especially the point that assistance of that type and along those lines is being given and more of such is in prospect by and in this country.

You might in your discretion add, with special reference to Halifax's apprehension regarding Hong Kong and regarding possible collapse of Chinese resistance, that in our estimates we consider not likely a Japanese attack upon Hong Kong while vigorous Chinese resistance continues and we see little reason now to expect or apprehend a collapse in the near future of Chinese resistance.

HULL

893.51/6643 : Telegram

The Secretary of State to the Ambassador in the United Kingdom
(Kennedy)

WASHINGTON, July 14, 1938—10 p. m.

356. Department's 350, July 13, 6 p. m. Unless already done take no action, pending further instruction. Inform Department whether action taken.[5]

HULL

893.51/6721

Memorandum by the Adviser on Political Relations (Hornbeck) of a Conversation With the President of the Export-Import Bank (Pierson)

[WASHINGTON,] July 15, 1938.

Mr. Pierson and Mr. Hornbeck met in Judge Moore's[6] office in response to a call by Judge Moore for a conference which was also to have been attended by Judge Moore and Mr. Hackworth,[7] who were called elsewhere at the moment.

Two matters were discussed.

1. Mr. Hornbeck brought up the question of possible assistance by the Bank toward sale of trucks to China. Reference was made to conversations held in May in consequence of which Mr. Hamilton had recorded in reference to a proposal involving sale by the Chrysler Corporation of approximately one thousand trucks (see Mr. Hamilton's memorandum of May 21[8]) that "After consideration, FE, EA and PA/H[9] recommend that the Department's attitude be that, should the Bank consider the proposition to be a sound one from a business point of view, we do not wish to interpose objection."

Mr. Pierson said that he had talked as late as yesterday with a representative of the Chrysler Corporation and had given no intimation that the Bank might be in a position to give assistance.

Mr. Hornbeck said that there has been developing an increasing feeling that, from the point of view of the general interests of the United States, it would be undesirable that China be defeated by Japan, and, hence, a tendency to feel that effort should be made toward giving China assistance when, where and as legitimate methods

---

[5] Ambassador Kennedy reported in telegram No. 639, July 15, noon, that no action had been taken (893.51/6644).
[6] R. Walton Moore, Counselor of the Department of State.
[7] Green H. Hackworth, Legal Adviser of the Department of State.
[8] Not found in Department files.
[9] Symbols used in the Department. PA/H stands for Adviser on Political Relations, Hornbeck; EA, Adviser on International Economic Affairs; and FE, Division of Far Eastern Affairs.

may be available. Mr. Pierson said that he had long since had that view. Mr. Hornbeck said that in some quarters the question of "neutrality" is raised, but that, in his opinion, our whole course thus far in relation to the Chinese-Japanese hostilities has been based on the theory that, "war" not having been declared and the "Neutrality Act" not having been put into operation, there exists no question of neutrals and belligerents and we are entitled to carry on with "business as usual" under limitations of political expediency and appropriateness rather than limitations which would apply in international law if we admitted or affirmed that the Chinese-Japanese hostilities constitute "war". Mr. Pierson made the comment that on the whole the course thus far has been guided and shaped by the fact that no country has declared, affirmed or admitted that these hostilities constitute "war". He thought that we should plan our course with a view to our future security.

Mr. Pierson and Mr. Hornbeck were both of the opinion that it would be lawful and legitimate and would serve a useful purpose for the Bank to facilitate sale of trucks, etc.; also, of the opinion that sale and purchase in not too large lots would be the most practicable way of going about the matter.

2. Mr. Pierson said that the Chinese Ambassador had come to him recently with an approach on the subject of wheat and cotton credit: The Ambassador had said that China, due to hostilities, floods, etc., was looking forward to a hard winter and would need food and clothing. Mr. Hornbeck interjected an expression of doubt whether the Chinese Government would want wheat and cotton for purpose of consumption: Whether they did not have in mind selling what they might procure of those commodities toward raising cash with which to purchase arms and munitions. Mr. Pierson said that this possibility had also occurred to him. He continued, however, to the effect that he had replied to the Ambassador that we could hardly consider the question of the wheat and cotton but we might give consideration to a question of flour and cloth.

There followed some discussion, in the course of which Mr. Pierson raised the question whether the old wheat and cotton credit ($50,-000,000, of which $17,000,000 were used) might not be revised: By that procedure it might be possible to avoid certain types of adverse criticism and to simplify the consideration which would need to be given to the question of security. Mr. Hornbeck said that it had been his understanding that the old credit transaction had been completely closed. Mr. Pierson said that such had been the understanding,—but he seemed to think that it might be possible to re-open.—There followed some discussion of the point that, if we wish to help China in pursuance of a political objective of our own, the balance between the political and the economic aspects of whatever financial transaction with China may be under consideration must necessarily shift somewhat, with primary emphasis on the political rather than on the economic aspects (objectives and methods) of the matter.

S[TANLEY] K. H[ORNBECK]

893.51/6645 : Telegram

The Ambassador in the United Kingdom (Kennedy) to the Secretary of State

LONDON, July 15, 1938—2 p. m.
[Received July 15—noon.]

640. Hansard text of parliamentary announcement made by the Chancellor of the Exchequer yesterday afternoon in answer to an arranged question is as follows:

"Various proposals have been made by the Chinese Government for obtaining a loan in this country. As stated in the reply given to the honorable member on 14th April last, if in present circumstances the Chinese Government found it possible to obtain a loan from British financial institution, any request for government approval would be sympathetically considered. His Majesty's Government have no power themselves to grant or guarantee a loan without special legislation which in present circumstances they have not seen their way to introduce."

In answer to extemporaneous questions Sir John Simon indicated that in reaching this decision British interests had been fully considered and also the terms of the League of Nations resolutions "have been kept very fully in mind."

Asked whether he did not feel that "in view of all that has happened in the Far East the claim of China to assistance in the form of a loan is at least as great as that of Turkey", the Chancellor of the Exchequer replied:

"The circumstances of each case of course have to be weighed and the circumstances of the present case are very grave and serious but there is the consideration which must not be overlooked that in the case of Turkey we were dealing with a loan to a country which is not engaged in hostilities."

I understand that the decision embodied in the above statement was made by the Cabinet on Wednesday. An official of the British Treasury implied that the Cabinet had been impressed by the desirability of avoiding antagonizing Japan gravely unless Great Britain was in a position to defend its Far Eastern interests without jeopardizing those in Europe and in the Mediterranean.

KENNEDY

893.51/6653 : Telegram

The Ambassador in France (Bullitt) to the Secretary of State

PARIS, July 26, 1938—5 p. m.
[Received July 26—1 : 50 p. m.]

1166. The Chinese Ambassador Wellington Koo called on Secretary Morgenthau [10] this morning. In the course of the conversation which ensued at which I was present the Chinese Ambassador stated that although the morale of the Chinese Army and the civilian population was admirable the financial resources of China were becoming exhausted. It therefore was a matter of vital importance to the Chinese Government to obtain financial aid.

The negotiations for a loan in England had collapsed. The French had indicated their willingness to give a loan or credit provided Great Britain and the United States should give a loan or credit.

The Secretary of the Treasury stated to the Chinese Ambassador that while he could make no promises of any sort he felt that it might be advisable for the Chinese Government to send Mr. K. P. Chen,[11] with whom he had negotiated in the past with pleasure, to the United States for the purpose of inquiring into the possibilities of obtaining a credit for the purchase of flour and grain goods.

The Secretary of the Treasury suggested also that if Mr. K. P. Chen should come to the United States he should inquire into the methods of purchasing now employed by the Chinese Government.

The Chinese Ambassador was most grateful for these suggestions and said that he would communicate with his Government immediately.

BULLITT

―――――――――

893.51/6661

The Ambassador in the United Kingdom (Kennedy) to the Secretary of State

No. 860

LONDON, July 28, 1938.
[Received August 5.]

SIR: I have the honor to refer to telegram No. 640, July 15, 2 p. m. and previous correspondence regarding the request by China for a loan from Great Britain, and to transcribe below the pertinent portion of the speech made by the Prime Minister [12] in the House of Commons on July 26, 1938, (Hansard Col. 2971 [*2961*]).

"The right hon. Gentleman asked me, Can we show what we are doing to carry out our obligations under the League resolutions? and

―――――――――

[10] The Secretary of the Treasury was on a visit to Europe.
[11] Chairman of the Foreign Trade Commission, Chinese Ministry of Finance.
[12] Neville Chamberlain.

he made special reference to the request of China for a loan. We considered long and anxiously whether we should be justified in introducing the special legislation which would have been necessary if this Government had granted or guaranteed such a loan, and we came finally to the definite conclusion that we should not be so justified in the case of a loan, which would have been based upon security of hypothetical value, and as to which it was by no means certain that, if it were granted, it would achieve the objects which were intended. The fact that we have not been able to grant or guarantee a loan to China does not exclude all forms of assistance, financial or otherwise, and there are various proposals which have come to us from China for assistance in another way, which are not open to the objections at any rate which we found to a loan, and which are now under examination by the Government Departments concerned."

An inquiry of the British Treasury elicited the fact that the Prime Minister's speech had been written particularly with an eye to the Opposition's criticism of his policy, and that the "various proposals" which are "now under consideration by the Government Departments concerned" have only to do with the Export Credits Guarantee Department, (Embassy's 652, July 19, 6 p. m.[13]).

Incidentally, in the course of a conversation between Sir Frederick Leith-Ross, Economic Adviser to the British Government, and Dr. Herbert Feis, Adviser on International Economic Affairs, the former indicated that he had pushed for a British Government guaranteed loan and he seemed definitely of the opinion that action of this type was for the moment settled. This particular conversation did not touch upon the possibility of more indirect measures of assistance. But Sir Frederick Leith-Ross indicated that his initiative was prompted at least as much by the wish to safeguard the Chinese currency against a marked decline, as by the thought of providing funds for military purposes for the Chinese Government and he expressed the considered opinion that if the Chinese currency broke decidedly this would lead to such a withholding of trade bills as to weaken critically the Chinese Government.

Respectfully yours,

For the Ambassador:
HERSCHEL V. JOHNSON
Counselor of Embassy

893.48/1613

Memorandum of Conversation, by the Secretary of State

[WASHINGTON,] August 3, 1938.

The Chinese Ambassador came in on his own request. He referred to the loan arrangement between this Government and that of China

---

[13] Not printed.

in 1933, for cotton and wheat in particular, in the amount of 50 million dollars. He said that some 18 million dollars of this amount had been consumed by these purchases and the matter left in abeyance as to the balance of the 50 million dollars of purchases. The Ambassador said he desired very earnestly to request that this remaining 32 million dollars of credit be further utilized by purchases from this country of cotton cloth and flour for the urgent relief of nearly 100 million of the Chinese population. He made a plea about the distress in his country and the increasing need for this cloth and foodstuff, adding that this full amount of credit was not utilized on account of good crops in 1935 and 1936. He was very earnest in his representations. I replied that I would look into the matter during the next few days and talk with him further; that this would be the best step to pursue before any formal note from his government should be presented to us on the subject. With this he was in accord.

I then inquired of the Ambassador as to when he thought the Japanese would reach Hankow. He replied that it would be some time yet. I inquired as to how long the Chinese would be able to provide themselves with essential military supplies, and he replied that they could go on indefinitely in view of the financial cooperation of this and other countries. He then emphasized that the large Chinese population which came within range of the Japanese invasion would be, however, in urgent need of the cotton cloth and flour for which he was asking.

He asked what we knew about the Japanese-Soviet frontier situation.[14] I answered that we knew nothing more than what we saw in the papers.

C[ordell] H[ull]

893.51/6659 : Telegram

The Ambassador in China (Johnson) to the Secretary of State

Hankow, August 5, 1938—10 a. m.
[Received August 5—7 a. m.]

399. My 387, July 30, 10 [*11*] a. m.[15] Following from Hong Kong.

"August 4, 3 p. m. Following from McHugh.[16]

Buck[17] sent secret letter dated July 14th to Kung from Washington via Treasury office here stating he had seen both Secretaries Hull and Morgenthau and assuring Kung that China has excellent friends

---

[14] For correspondence concerning border hostilities between Japanese and Soviet troops, see pp. 441 ff.
[15] Not printed.
[16] Capt. James Marshall McHugh, U. S. M. C., Assistant Naval Attaché in China.
[17] Prof. John Lossing Buck, of Nanking University, special representative in China of the Treasury Department.

in the Administration. He quoted both Morgenthau and the latter's assistant adviser Lockhead as stating that the only chance of China obtaining a loan would be to send K. P. Chen to Washington to negotiate an agricultural commodity loan. He stated that Morgenthau has complete confidence in Chen and said the Secretary feels that because of Chen's straightforwardness and intimate knowledge of financial problems he could negotiate with him as with no one else.

Buck urged that Chen be sent in September to meet the Secretary when he returns from Europe and that Chen be supplied definite information on the need for and use of a commodity loan. He stated that he thought the loan could be as great as China could possibly use in terms of commodities. He added that there also was a good possibility of obtaining credits on Chinese products if same were stored in the United States. Buck will return here August 10 to continue to act as special agent for Treasury."

JOHNSON

893.51/6673½

The Ambassador in France (*Bullitt*) *to President Roosevelt* [18]

PARIS, August 8, 1938.

DEAR MR. PRESIDENT: From a multitude of reliable sources, I have been informed during the past two months that the Chinese will be at the end of their financial resources by the first of next January, unless they can obtain credits abroad. Chiang Kai-shek's will to fight and the courage of the Chinese people remain unbroken; but there will be just no money to buy anything. I have had this information in a series of messages from Chiang Kai-shek, T. V. Soong, and Doctor Kung transmitted to me by the Chinese Ambassador here, and I have had the same information from a horde of detached observers.

As you will recall, some months ago Bonnet said to me that he hoped it might be possible for the United States to extend some sort of a credit or loan to China and that he was certain that if we should be willing to act, both France and Great Britain would act simultaneously though not jointly. Two days ago, Bonnet reiterated this to me. He added that he was certain that either England, France, or the United States could give credits to China without provoking any serious Japanese reaction. The Japanese were too involved in China and were too fearful of Russian attack to dare to act against either England, France, or the United States.

This reasoning seems to me sound. I believe we should, however, avoid putting ourselves out on any long limb. I do not think we should sell the Chinese arms or munitions on credit, but I believe we should give the Chinese Government a credit of one hundred million

---

[18] Photostatic copy obtained from the Franklin D. Roosevelt Library, Hyde Park, N. Y.

dollars for the purchase of flour and gray goods in the United States.

We shall have to take a loss on our wheat and cotton anyhow. If we sell the Chinese Government flour instead of wheat and gray goods instead of cotton, we shall get the benefit of the first processing and even if we should lose the hundred million, it would be money well spent.

I have talked over this idea with Henry Morgenthau and find that he is entirely in accord with me. As you know, he suggested to the Chinese Ambassador in Paris that the Chinese Government should send K. P. Chen to Washington and I have just received information that Chen will reach Washington about the same time that Henry returns.

If you should approve of this proposal, I suggest that you should let me know in advance so that I could try to push Bonnet into making good his statements to me with regard to the readiness of the French Government to take simultaneous and similar action.

I have thought about this a lot and I feel certain that we ought to do it. I hope you will too.

Love and good luck.

Yours affectionately,   BILL

893.51/6661 : Telegram

The Secretary of State to the Ambassador in the United Kingdom
(Kennedy)

WASHINGTON, August 10, 1938—5 p. m.

437. In the light of your 710, August 3, 10 a. m.,[19] and your mail despatch No. 860, July 28, just received, the Department assumes that, notwithstanding the British Government's decision reported in your 640, July 15, 2 p. m., there may be under consideration proposals which would involve assistance by the Exports Credit Guarantee Department, as indicated in UP press dispatch from London of July 31. The Embassy will of course keep the Department currently and fully informed of any developments in this connection.

HULL

893.48/1618a : Telegram

The Secretary of State to the Consul General at Hong Kong
(Southard)

WASHINGTON, August 10, 1938—7 p. m.

Please forward to the Ambassador at Chungking by first available safe hand code text of message as follows:

---

[19] Not printed.

"For your strictly confidential information. With reference to the statement contained in your 370 of July 25, 4 p. m.,[20] the Chinese Ambassador has not seen fit to inform the Department of any developments concerning these matters.

On August 3, however, he called at his request on the Secretary and, referring to the cotton and wheat credit of 1933 in the amount of $50,000,000, said he desired earnestly to request that the balance of this credit which had not been utilized amounting to $32,000,000 be now made available for purchases of cotton cloth and wheat flour for the relief of 100,000,000 of the Chinese population. The Secretary replied that he would look into the matter during the next few days and have a further talk with the Ambassador.

While the Department is prepared to explore in this connection such lines of possible action as appear to be practicable and appropriate, there are of course various difficulties in the way of carrying out the Ambassador's proposal for renewing the credit arrangement of 1933.

As you know, this Government is already affording material assistance to the Chinese Government through silver purchases in an otherwise unsupported market. Also, the extension of limited credits in appropriate cases has been and is being considered by the Import and Export Bank. Our Ambassador at Paris has been informed by the Chinese Ambassador there that, pursuant to a suggestion by the Secretary of the Treasury, Mr. K. P. Chen will shortly proceed to Washington for the purpose of looking into possibilities of obtaining a credit for the purchase of agricultural commodities."

HULL

893.48/1619

Memorandum of Conversation, by the Secretary of State

[WASHINGTON,] August 11, 1938.

The Ambassador of China called at his own instance and inquired what progress I was making in regard to his request some days ago for the further extension of $30,000,000 of credit to his Government for the purchase of flour and cotton cloth. I replied that I had been giving the matter full attention; that the credit situation had assumed a different form from what it once was prior to the exhaustion of 18 million dollars of the original 50 million dollars of credit; and that it presented difficult questions in more than one respect. I said that I had called on my associates to give the matter early and sympathetic attention; and that, of course, I would be glad to acquaint the President with the Ambassador's visits here and his request. I concluded with the statement that it would be some days before we could reach a conclusion—that we might do so next week. The Ambassador was very urgent in his tone and demeanor.

C[ORDELL] H[ULL]

---

[20] Not printed; it reported alleged loan discussions.

893.48/1631½

Memorandum of Conversation, by the Chief of the Division of Far Eastern Affairs (Hamilton)

[WASHINGTON,] August 21, 1938.

I called on the Chinese Ambassador at his residence. I referred to the approaches made by the Ambassador to the Secretary several days ago at which time the Ambassador had raised the question of a credit of approximately $30,000,000 being extended to the Chinese Government for the purchase of flour and cotton cloth. I referred also to the fact that the Secretary had informed the Ambassador that this question was a very complicated one and involved consideration of many factors, financial, economic and political. I said that at some stage in the process of considering the matter it would probably be appropriate that technical experts of this Government study various phases of the question. I said that in the Far Eastern Division we had been giving thought to the question which the Ambassador had raised and that it seemed to us that our thinking might be clarified if we could obtain from the Ambassador information in regard to certain points.

I then asked the Ambassador whether there was contemplated an agreement along the lines of the R. F. C. credit of 1933.[21] The Ambassador replied in the affirmative.

I thereupon asked the Ambassador whether it was contemplated that the goods would be used in China and not elsewhere. The Ambassador again replied in the affirmative.

The Ambassador interposed that he would like to give me a little background in regard to this whole matter. He said that last June when Dr. H. H. Kung was in Washington, Dr. Kung and the Ambassador had talked to Mr. Jones of the R. F. C. and to Mr. Pierson of the Export-Import Bank in regard to the question of China obtaining credits for materials to be used in constructive enterprises in China. The Ambassador continued that before consideration had been given to this proposal, the fighting broke out on July 7 at the Marco Polo bridge; that thereafter the whole matter remained in abeyance, chiefly because of uncertainty as to the question whether this Government would invoke the Neutrality Act; that early in December, when it appeared that it was not likely that the Neutrality Act would be invoked, the Chinese Ambassador furnished the Export-Import Bank with a list of goods desired by the Chinese Government for constructive purposes in China, the total purchase price to aggre-

---

[21] A press release was issued on June 4, 1933, by the Reconstruction Finance Corp. regarding its extension of a $50,000,000 credit to China for the purchase of U. S. cotton and wheat (893.48/708).

gate approximately $50,000,000. The Ambassador said that no affirmative action had been taken by the Export-Import Bank. The Ambassador said that in view of this fact it had occurred to him that it might be more practicable for this Government to extend a credit for relief purposes. He said that although his Government did not, he personally understood the questions presented to this Government by reason of the Neutrality Act. He said that he had therefore presented this question to the Secretary.

The Ambassador said that in his conversation with the Secretary he had mentioned flour and cotton cloth as merely illustrative. He said that his Government would be interested in obtaining on credit raw cotton (which is widely used by the Chinese people for padding of clothes during the winter), wheat, medicines, and perhaps other things. He said that his Government would be interested in purchasing trucks which could be used to transport the relief supplies to the main centers of distribution (and possibly to interior points).

In reply to my inquiry as to the purpose to which the Chinese Government would put such goods, he said that such goods would be utilized for the relief of the Chinese people who had been rendered destitute as a result of the hostilities. I inquired whether it was not a fact that most of these destitute people were in areas controlled by the Japanese military. He replied in the negative. He said that Japan controlled only the cities and certain railway lines, and that the people in the country were not under Japanese control. (Comment: It remains the belief of officers of FE that the majority of the people who need relief are in areas not controlled by the Chinese Government.) The Ambassador indicated that the Chinese Government might wish to utilize some of these goods for relief purposes at Shanghai and at Tientsin and in other areas under Japanese control but that the major portion of the commodities would be utilized in territory under the control of the Chinese Government.

I asked the Chinese Ambassador how his Government would take care of the problem of distribution, and where and by what means would delivery be effected in China. The Ambassador said that even should the Japanese take Hankow, supplies could be sent in through French Indo-China and through Burma. I pointed out that this would probably be expensive and not very rapid. I asked how the supplies would be distributed into the interior. He said that it was his idea that the village magistrates and American missionaries might be utilized. I remarked that there would still remain a very difficult problem of distribution.

I asked the Ambassador what quantities of goods the Chinese Government could use. He said that he could not answer that question.

He said that if and when the Secretary was in position to inform him that this Government was favorably disposed in principle, he would wire his Government for details and information as to the amounts and types of goods which the Chinese Government needed for relief purposes.

I said to the Ambassador that it was my understanding that the Chinese Government needed at the present time above all else foreign exchange and money with which it could purchase commodities abroad. I said that I did not see how the Ambassador's proposal would assist China in these respects. The Ambassador agreed that his proposal would not furnish the Chinese Government with foreign exchange. He said, however, that his proposal would relieve the Chinese Government from the necessity of spending sums of money for the relief of destitute Chinese. I remarked to the Ambassador that in a time of national emergency, such as that now confronting China, was it not true that, while the Chinese Government assisted in a modest way in the problem of relief, the destitute people were cared for primarily by their own families and by charitable organizations. The Ambassador maintained that the Chinese Government was expending considerable sums of money on relief.

I said to the Ambassador that if cotton goods were furnished, they presumably would take the form of gray goods which normally require further processing. I asked how and where this processing could be done, inasmuch as most of the Chinese mills were in Shanghai and Tientsin. The Ambassador made no definite reply to this question, other than to say that the Chinese Government might like to obtain cotton as well as cotton goods.

The Ambassador repeated that his proposal represented merely a general idea and that if and when the Secretary was in position to inform the Ambassador that this Government was favorably disposed in principle, the Ambassador would wire his Government for details. The Ambassador said that the matter was urgent inasmuch as winter would soon be confronting the Chinese destitute population and as two or three months would probably be required to work out the details and to effect deliveries in China.

As of interest in this general connection, the Acting American Commercial Attaché to China [22] reports under date July 14 [23] that there had come to his attention press reports in regard to wheat or flour loans or credits. The Acting Commercial Attaché states that Mr. John Earle Baker, an American who is directing the work of the China International Famine Relief for the Chinese Government,

---

[22] A. Bland Calder.
[23] Not found in Department files.

"states that at most for relief purposes, and not for any commercial purpose, for distribution in Shanghai to refugees his committee could now use only about 6,000 tons spread over one year". The Acting Commercial Attaché comments further as follows:

"A Chinese Government wheat and flour loan with Shanghai as the destination would seem now to be out of the question as this is in Japanese occupied territory, in fact the report above which states that most of the Chinese mills are now in Japanese occupied territory is true. If American loan wheat or flour were to be shipped to Chinese controlled territory at the present time, transportation problems of a serious nature would enter in, deliveries would have to be made to South China (which is not a flour consuming but a rice consuming area) and thence by inland transportation to distant bread consuming points in the interior. It is believed too many complications would be involved under present conditions of transportation and high costs thereof to warrant the consideration of such a plan at this time."

As of further interest, there are quoted below excerpts from a despatch of June 24, from the American Consul General at Hankow,[24] as follows:

"There is enclosed a leaflet issued by the International Red Cross Committee for Central China on June 1, 1938, being a survey of the war refugee situation by the Committee's advisor on war refugee relief. This report constitutes a sober, dispassionate survey and is based on replies to questionnaires sent out by the Red Cross Committee as well as on personal investigation by the author and other members of the Committee. It shows that, although the number of persons who have moved as a result of the war undoubtedly runs into millions, yet the actual number of refugees in Central China receiving or in need of help in refugee camps is much less than might be expected. The reason for this is that many times the number of refugees being cared for in camps are receiving assistance from their fellow country-men in ways which are not immediately obvious. That is to say, large numbers of refugees are being cared for by their family or by their clan, others by their provincial guild or by one or other of the many Chinese charitable organizations such as the Red Swastica Society. The report gives the number of refugees in camps in Wuhan (Hankow, Wuchang and Hanyang) as 40,000 and states that this is the largest concentration of refugees in Central China."

"Evidence that there is a great movement amounting almost to a migration, chiefly westward, of Chinese people is given by missionaries who come to this office from their stations in Honan and Hupeh. Many of these refugees have some funds; more are totally without funds and are dependent on charity along the road."

M[AXWELL] M. H[AMILTON]

---

[24] Not printed.

893.48/1631½

Memorandum by the Chief of the Division of Far Eastern Affairs (Hamilton) to the Secretary of State

[WASHINGTON,] August 23, 1938.

MR. SECRETARY: Pursuant to your suggestion, I saw the Chinese Ambassador and endeavored to obtain further information in regard to the Ambassador's proposal that this Government extend credits to China for relief purposes.

As you will note from the attached account of my conversation with the Ambassador,[25] the Ambassador has only a very general idea but stated that if and when you were in position to inform him that this Government was favorably disposed in principle, he would wire his Government for details.

The chief difficulty would appear to revolve about the practicability of effecting distribution.

It seems to me that the most practicable way of proceeding with consideration of the matter would be to await the return to Washington of Secretary Morgenthau, who returns on August 29, and then to discuss various possibilities with him. The question whether Mr. K. P. Chen is or is not coming to the United States may be important in this connection.

M[AXWELL] M. H[AMILTON]

893.51/6670 : Telegram

The Ambassador in the United Kingdom (Kennedy) to the Secretary of State

LONDON, August 30, 1938—7 p. m.
[Received August 30—5 : 45 p. m.]

840. Department's 437, August 10, 5 p. m.

1. The references made in my 710, August 3, 10 a. m.[26] are still representative of the broad outlines of the situation.

2. The present situation was discussed with the Foreign Office which suggested that Butterworth consult the Export Credit Guarantees Department which in turn outlined the position as follows:

(a) P. W. Kuo[27] has been pressing for credits which would in effect amount to an advance of about pounds 10,000,000. The scheme envisages the setting up of an organization in China having monopolistic control of the export of certain mineral and agricultural produce

---

[25] *Supra.*
[26] Not printed.
[27] Chinese Vice Minister of Finance and representative in London of the Ministry.

and effecting an arrangement similar to the Anglo-Turkish *comptoire* but as implied in the Embassy's previous communications the deal is by no means on the point of consummation. It has not been fully worked out; the Export Credit Guarantees Department is not convinced that they will be able to obtain sufficient security and they are not without doubts about the benefit to the Chinese of taking trade out of the hands of individual professionals and canalizing it under the guidance of amateurs. Furthermore the Anglo-Chinese merchant and banking houses are not without influence here and they might well make difficulties.

The exact status at the moment is that Kuo is pressing the Export Credit Guarantees Department for a letter to be sent to the Chinese Ambassador in London defining the British terms and the British anticipate "a painful interview" with him tomorrow for they believe that the writing of such a letter would carry with it something of the same objections that led them to reject the proposal for a British Government guaranteed loan and they fully expect that any such letter would be "waved in the face of the Japanese." Furthermore the British are aware that the Chinese Embassy in Paris has been attempting to work out a proposal along somewhat similar lines without the knowledge of the Chinese Embassy in London. On the other hand the Chinese Embassy in London to mislead their Paris colleagues has indicated that everything has been settled here.

Furthermore the Export Credit Guarantees Department itself is having difficulties. It was set up as a nonpolitical commercial body with an advisory committee of businessmen, and now in the face of increasing pressure from the Foreign Office, and to some extent the Treasury, to undertake operations for reasons which are difficult to defend on their commercial merits, it is somewhat hamstrung. Its advisory committee of businessmen naturally do not wish to accept responsibility for losses incurred for political causes; and in any case it cannot by statute give credits for armaments.

The Export Credit Guarantees Department states therefore that in the given circumstances no decisive action can be taken about the above in the next few weeks anyway. A Cabinet decision may well prove the propelling factor.

(*b*) Tentative discussions have been taking place regarding the Marsman proposition (Embassy's 652, July 19, 6 p. m.[28]). The Marsman group claim that their Chinese associates are in a position to obtain funds for the construction of the railway from the Burmese border to Chengtu. They look to the Export Credit Guarantees Department for about pounds 2,500,000 worth of rolling stock and equip-

---

[28] Not printed.

ment and offer as security a first charge on the revenue for the whole line. The Export Credit Guarantees Department has the same opinions of the Marsman group as reported in the Embassy's telegram No. 652 and they have been unable to ascertain the Marsman group's exact status, whether it is acting as co-principal or merely in a consultative capacity. This Department likewise is inclined to the view that this line is a long range peace time project and that whereas it might open up an important trading area and save some 2,000 miles of sea journey, it is difficult to envisage its construction and completion in the present circumstances. The Burmese are represented as not being actively favorable to the proposition, although some observers predict that such a line would turn Rangoon into an important entrepot center.

(c) The Export Credit Guarantees Department consider an improvement in the Burmese-Yunnanfu motor road and motor equipment as offering the most practical immediate procedure. Hall-Patch [29] considers that the Chinese order for trucks will eventually go to United States manufacturers because of price. Thorneycroft has, however, put up a proposition to the Chinese and the Export Guarantees Department for 100 trucks, 25 percent in cash, the remainder in monthly installments over a 2-year period.

(d) A. G. Marshall who arranged the Leno Goldfield–Marshall settlement has now been turning his interest from Russia to China. He has put up various tentative propositions which were described as being designed to get a prior commitment from the Export Credit Guarantees Department with a view to including [inducing?] the Chinese to come in. None of them is yet considered as likely to mature and bear fruit.

KENNEDY

893.51/6702

Memorandum of Conversation, by the Chief of the Division of Far Eastern Affairs (Hamilton)

[WASHINGTON,] September 6, 1938.

The British Ambassador called at his request. He said that he had called on the Secretary on Saturday last in reference to other matters and that the Secretary had indicated that we were giving thought to the question of the possibility of extending credits to China for the purchase of commodities of a type which could not be used for military purposes. The Ambassador said that he had not discussed with the Secretary this question but that in turning the matter over in his mind he wondered whether he should have pursued the matter further with

---

[29] Edmund L. Hall-Patch, financial adviser to the British Embassy in China.

the Secretary. He asked whether I could give him any further information in the matter. He said that the Chinese Ambassador at London had informed the British Foreign Office that at the forthcoming meeting of the League Assembly [30] the Chinese would press for definitive action on the subject of the extension of assistance to China. He added that the Chinese Ambassador at London had indicated that some assistance would be forthcoming from the American Government.

I said that as the Ambassador was aware the Chinese Ambassadors at London, Paris and Washington had from time to time approached the governments to which they are accredited with various proposals for the extension of loans or credits to the Chinese Government. I said that the most recent such approach to this Government by the Chinese Ambassador here had taken the form of a suggestion that this Government extend credits to China for the purchase of commodities to be utilized for the relief of the many millions of destitute, homeless Chinese. I said that we have been giving the matter thought. I referred to the fact that some weeks ago the British Government had decided adversely in reference to a proposal that the British Government extend a loan to China. I said that it was my understanding that the Export Credit Guarantee Department of the British Government had been and was continuing to give certain consideration to various proposals involving the extension of credit to China for the purchase of certain types of commodities. I said that here we had a somewhat similar situation and that these proposals if and when they were put forward received attention. The Ambassador inquired whether it would be possible under existing legislation for the American Government to extend a credit to China for the purchase of commodities to be used for relief purposes. I said that I thought such action would be possible if the Government should decide that it was advisable to take the action. The Ambassador then remarked that the American Government had previously, in 1933, extended a credit to the Chinese Government. I assented. The Ambassador asked whether I thought a decision would be reached by us in the near future before the meeting of the League Assembly. I expressed doubt whether early action was to be expected and I said that the whole proposition was still just a general idea which was receiving thought but that the matter had not progressed to a point where we had come to grip with practical details. I said that if a decision should be reached to go ahead with the matter, we would probably wish to get in touch with the British Government. I also said that I would report the Ambassador's call to the Secretary, having especially in mind my statement that if and as our consideration

[30] See pp. 508 ff.

proceeded to a point where affirmative action on our part appeared likely, we would probably wish to get in touch with the British Government.

M[AXWELL] M. H[AMILTON]

893.51/6681

Memorandum of Conversation, by the Adviser on International Economic Affairs (Feis)

[WASHINGTON,] September 6, 1938.

Participants: Mr. Ralph M. Carson of Davis, Polk, Wardwell Gardiner and Reed, 15 Broad Street, New York.
Mr. Feis.
Mr. Hamilton—for part of conversation.

Mr. Carson called upon me this afternoon. He explained that coordinated approaches were made to the Guaranty Trust Company by the Chinese Ambassador, the Chinese Consul General in New York, and Mr. Hsu in regard to a bank loan of $10,000,000 for three years, secured by a cash deposit of the same amount to be made to the Guaranty Trust Company by the Chinese Government. Mr. Carson stated that since there could be no apparent benefit of a financial character to the Chinese in this transaction, the Guaranty Company was naturally puzzled and would appreciate having any sidelights which the Department may be able to throw on the matter.

I stated that as far as official statement went, the Department had "no comment to make". Mr. Carson asked whether any difficulty would arise under the Johnson Act.[31] I replied that the Department of Justice and not the State Department was the branch of the Government responsible for the interpretation and application of this Act. However, as far as I was acquainted with the Attorney General's rulings on the subject, China did not fall within the scope of the application of the Act.

He said that in the discussion among themselves as to the reasons why the Chinese Government might wish to enter into this transaction, various possibilities presented themselves; among others were the following: (*a*) the Chinese Government thought that through this transaction they might be laying the basis for later and other loan transactions; (*b*) the Chinese thought the mere announcement of a loan arrangement would have an encouraging moral effect in China and possibly influence decisions in other monetary centers. I commented that these might be possibilities, and suggested also the transaction might arise from the apparent somewhat competitive

---

[31] Approved April 13, 1934; 48 Stat. 574.

eagerness of the various Chinese diplomatic representatives abroad to secure help for China.

In reply to Mr. Carson's question as to whether previous transactions of this character had come to the attention of the Department, I stated that several had, though differing somewhat in detail; that they had however all dissolved at some point.

The discussion also touched upon the question of whether the Chinese Ambassador would have the authority to make the actual deposit of funds, and Mr. Carson said he believed that special credentials would be required.

Mr. Carson indicated that he did not think the Guaranty Trust Company would close the transaction because of its difficulty of understanding what purpose may lay behind it.

In the course of this conversation, Mr. Hamilton joined us and I summarized the substance of the preceding to him, and he agreed.

H[ERBERT] F[EIS]

893.51/6678 : Telegram

The Consul General at Hong Kong (Southard) to the Secretary of State

HONG KONG, September 6, 1938—4 p. m.
[Received September 7—7 a. m.]

Following from McHugh.

"Rogers [32] informs me that Kung intends to have Wellington Koo present a demand at the coming session of the League of Nations on September 9 that China be granted a loan similar to those which have been made to various European countries in the past and to threaten withdrawal if the demand is refused. Informant states that he tried to point out to Kung, first, that there is no present hope of such a loan being granted since London has already rejected the idea and is the dominating influence in the League today, second, that such a plea would only give away China's present financial crisis to Japan and encourage the Japanese to redouble their efforts in the war just at the time when they are not at all sure of themselves and, third, that the League has served China well in many ways to date and China will have real need of its assistance in the reconstruction work to follow the present conflict. Nevertheless, Kung remains bitter on the question of the failure of western nations to help China and determined to proceed with the idea.

Rogers himself then [*has?*] recently cabled the British representative at Geneva and suggested that the League forestall China's action by offering to suspend her annual subscription amounting to 1,400,000 Swiss francs, getting other member states to make up the deficit in the League of Nations budget if necessary. He found an adverse

---

[32] Cyril Rogers of the Bank of England.

reply to this awaiting him here on arrival but states that he hopes to approach the question from another angle and obtain favorable consideration. [McHugh.]"

Sent to Chungking.

SOUTHARD

893.48/1638

Memorandum by the Secretary of State of a Conversation With the Chinese Ambassador (C. T. Wang)

[WASHINGTON,] September 7, 1938.

During the Ambassador's call he inquired as to what progress had been made looking towards selling China some supplies, such as, flour, cotton cloth, etc. I replied that the matter has been receiving consideration from day to day; that it is not without its difficulties; and that a number of departments of the Government are considering all angles of the proposition. The Ambassador expressed his earnest hope that it might be brought to a favorable conclusion before he goes away, and pressed me to give him some intimation about the probable outcome. I said it was not possible for me to do so at this stage.

C[ORDELL] H[ULL]

893.51/6682 : Telegram

The Consul General at Hong Kong (Southard) to the Secretary of State

HONG KONG, September 9, 1938—9 a. m.
[Received September 10—7 a. m.]

Following from McHugh. Financial mission composed of K. P. Chen, T. M. Hsi and two secretaries now scheduled leave by clipper September 9. Morgenthau indicated disapproval of Y. C. Ku and it became necessary to find a substitute. Selection of Hsi who is the general manager of the Central Bank was opposed by Rogers and Soong because of his lack of aggressiveness plus recent loss of grip due to war strain. The untimely death of Sing Loh Hsu who was en route to Chungking for final instructions and who was scheduled to replace Chen left no alternative.

General confusion and lack of active appreciation of China's actual financial crisis have characterized the situation since the invitation first came more than a month ago. Chen's delay in starting appears to have been due mainly to inability to get clear instructions and full powers from Kung, rather than because of ill-health although he is not well. Rogers has mentioned frequently of late that Kung had no plan or policy for meeting the crisis and demurred even on supplying

Chen with frank statement of present Chinese position plus concrete suggestions for presentation to Morgenthau. He claims that ideas for a possible cash advance by the United States against future deliveries of wood oil, wolfram or other commodities were first suggested to Chen by Nicholson.[33] He undertook study of them and has since evolved rough plan on wood oil but admits he still lacks complete information. Rogers independently had worked out several such ideas months ago for presentation to London and since arrival here has tried to coach Chen. He states that London rejected all schemes when he was there in June because they anticipated the present crisis in Europe and felt that the slightest move on their part might disturb the delicate balance of relations with Hitler.

News of Chen's trip has in the meantime leaked out in Chinese circles and he has been harassed by visitors who believe that the United States is about to pour money into China and want to share in spoils (there is reason to suspect that the associates of Kung are conniving in this respect [ )]. Campbell was approached on September 7 by one C. H. Lee, wealthy mine owner, who admitted close friendship with Kung and former business association with C. T. Wang. He inquired if it would be possible to send a message direct to Morgenthau to offer him a chance to purchase antimony or other minerals direct with no question of loan. He promised to return in a few days with specific proposition. Rogers had mentioned to me that prior to leaving Chungking Kung had proposed instructing K. C. Li to make informal inquiries in Washington as to what Morgenthau might have in mind which former strenuously opposed.

Rogers gave me the following figures on Chinese position direct from composite balance sheet of the Central Bank: total sales of foreign exchange in the market since last August equaled pounds sterling 53 million; monthly sales have dropped from a peak of over pounds sterling 5 million in February to 1.7 in July. He estimated it would be 1.4 million for August and thought they could reduce it even further. Reserves have diminished however to about pounds sterling 5 million. Monthly service of foreign loans requires 400,000. Both he and Young assert that the Chinese dollar appears undervalued at its present level and that the relative stability since early in June has been accomplished at comparative small cost. They also state that thus far internal prices have not risen greatly and that the note issue has increased only about 25 percent. [McHugh.]

Repeated to Embassy at Chungking.

Southard

---

[33] M. R. Nicholson, Treasury Department Attaché in China.

893.51/6683 : Telegram

The Ambassador in the United Kingdom (Kennedy) to the Secretary of State

LONDON, September 14, 1938—5 p. m.
[Received September 14—12 : 16 p. m.]

924. In the course of a conversation at the British Treasury today reference was made to the information supplied by the Export Credit Guarantees Department reported in No. 840, August 30, 7 p. m. The British Treasury stated that the situation had not been materially advanced and seemed pessimistic about the possibility of effecting any substantial arrangement for the reason that "the Chinese did not really want British goods but munitions and even if they had any security to offer, the Export Credit Guarantees Department was not by statute able to deal in armaments."

KENNEDY

893.48/1651

Memorandum of Conversation, by the Secretary of State

[WASHINGTON,] September 15, 1938.

The Chinese Ambassador called on his own request. He said that before taking his leave as Ambassador he was much interested to know what I could tell him further and finally about the question of the relief transactions between our two Governments which are now under discussion. I replied that this Department and other interested departments are giving all phases of the matter steady attention. I then said that the matter could not be further dealt with until the Chinese financiers, who, it was my understanding, are on their way to this country to confer with the Treasury, reach here and such conference is held. The Ambassador seemed fully to understand. He then bade me goodbye.

C[ORDELL] H[ULL]

893.51/6703

Memorandum by the Chief of the Division of Far Eastern Affairs (Hamilton) of a Conversation With the Counselor of the Japanese Embassy (Suma)

[WASHINGTON,] September 20, 1938.

Mr. Suma called by appointment. He said that information which the Japanese Embassy had received from Shanghai was to the effect that the Chinese had recently concluded a loan or some financial arrangement for $20,000,000.00 with the Chase Bank in New York City and that a group of Chinese bankers was coming to the United States as a financial mission to arrange for credits. Mr. Suma said that it would seem strange to him for such a loan to be made by a New York bank at this juncture and he indicated that he did not take the report seriously. I said that I had seen no recent report of any such loan. I asked whether he referred to the reports in the American papers to the effect that a mysterious group of Chinese had come to this country on a financial mission. He said that he had noticed the reports in the American papers but that quite apart from those reports the Embassy had received from Shanghai the information which he had outlined above. I said that as he was aware there were certain matters with regard to which it was appropriate for this Department to speak; there were other matters with regard to which it was appropriate that the Commerce Department or the Navy Department speak; and that in regard to the reports about this group of Chinese bankers, we commented in response to inquiry that this was a matter for the Treasury Department. I said that I had noticed in the newspapers today statements to the effect that the Secretary of the Treasury had said that he would receive a group of Chinese bankers today. I said that until the Treasury Department wished to give out further information, we had no comment to make. Mr. Suma referred to one newspaper report to the effect that T. V. Soong was a member of the Chinese party. I said that if the press report to the effect that Mr. Morgenthau would receive the Chinese group today was correct, probably the newspapers would carry the names of the members of the Chinese group.

M[AXWELL] M. H[AMILTON]

893.51/6693 : Telegram

The Ambassador in the United Kingdom (Kennedy) to the Secretary of State

LONDON, September 22, 1938—7 p. m.
[Received September 22—4 p. m.]

995. In view of the report in the Radio Bulletin of a conference between a Chinese financial delegation and the Secretary of the Treasury, I wish to refer to my 924, September 14, 5 p. m., and previous communications regarding the status of Anglo-Chinese discussions for British financial aid to China. At the same time I venture to give you my feeling which is based on nothing tangible that the group of Cabinet Ministers and permanent officials, who threw their weight against the giving of a British guaranteed Government loan in July, is now even more strongly opposed to British intervention. No doubt the critical European situation has strengthened their belief in the rightness of their previous decision but even before the Czech situa-

tion came to a head Sir Charles Addis,[34] for example, who is nothing if not favorably predisposed to the Chinese, in a confidential talk with a British banker emphasized the view that in the long run Great Britain would have to work with and to some extent through the Japanese in fostering its interests in China and he went on to comment on the fact as significant that the Japanese had not broken up the Maritime Customs organization [35] and that this would eventually furnish an important means through which "we can rebuild".

With the above in view an opportunity was taken to talk with Leith-Ross. He implied that no substantial financial aid for the Chinese was contemplated but he added the proviso that in the event of a European war such assistance would certainly be given. Inasmuch as Leith-Ross had personally advocated the British Government guaranteed loan it may be of interest in connection with the above that he stated that the recent Japanese actions in Tientsin had disillusioned some of those who were hopeful that Japan would ultimately cooperate with other interested powers in China. Leith-Ross went on to say that he understood that whereas the Chinese still had a substantial amount of foreign exchange most of it was earmarked against commitments already entered into. Although there was still a steady trickle of silver coming in from private hoardings his estimate was that the Chinese Government would have very little silver available for sale in the new year. Chinese exports through the south were still holding up comparatively well and the Chinese had been quite competent in obtaining the resulting foreign exchange. But he expressed surprise that the Chinese had continued to service their foreign obligations and did not expect them to do so much longer.

Leith-Ross was impressed by the resistance the Chinese had put up over Hankow and was not at all sure whether it would be taken within the Japanese time limit. He estimated Japanese casualties in China thus far at about a quarter of a million, 60% of which were due to disease. Since the recent change of tactics Japanese losses had been increasingly heavy, nevertheless there were this week new indications that they might extend their operations to the south. He estimated this would require a further 200,000 troops and such a move might be "in China's ultimate interest" and he reiterated his belief that in the long run the Japanese would not be victorious.

He said that he understood that some of the Chinese Government's financial advisers feared that the internal financial situation might reach a point which would cause the Chinese to lose faith in their currency and banking system which would in turn cause a loss of faith in the authority of the present Chinese forces. This might make

---

[34] Representative of the British group of the China Consortium.
[35] For correspondence concerning the Maritime Customs organization, see pp. 626 ff.

them willing to work under puppet Government control.   However, the British Embassy in China did not agree with this view; they felt that Chinese nationalism was sufficiently aroused so that the average Chinese would stick by his currency almost regardless of its backing and continue to oppose Japan.   Leith-Ross felt that on this question the situation turned and he indicated that he had pointed out to the Japanese here the unwisdom of their taking steps to undermine the Chinese currency; that if they brought chaos to China they in turn would suffer as well.   In this connection the head of the Yokohama Specie Bank in London had called to see Leith-Ross and made strong protestations to the effect that Japanese commercial and financial interests and in particular his bank were strongly opposed to any action which would seriously undermine the Chinese dollar and he went on to inveigh in the usual manner against the Japanese militarists.

Incidentally it is Tani [36] in Shanghai who from time to time makes approaches to the British respecting Anglo-Japanese aid for the margin and control of Chinese currency.

KENNEDY

893.51/6696

Memorandum by the Adviser on International Economic Affairs (Feis) to the Secretary of State

[WASHINGTON,] September 22, 1938.

MR. SECRETARY: The Secretary of the Treasury informed me today that conversations were being held with Mr. Chen and his mission in an effort to define any possible action of use to China and within the scope of practicability for this Government.   Up to the present, I think the discussions have dealt with silver and the possibility of speeding up purchases.   The Secretary asked whether I thought Mr. Hull would care to receive Mr. Chen on a purely courtesy visit. I expressed the judgment—subject to correction—that Secretary Hull would rather not at the present moment, in view of the fact that there would be nothing specific to tell him and the extreme pressure of events.   I suggested that later on when the discussions had defined any possibilities of action would be a better time.

The Secretary of the Treasury said that Chen was being completely candid with him and that the Chinese situation was getting desperate. and he thought this was the very last chance we would have of making a contribution to the Chinese ability to sustain themselves.   He referred to the consequences of having the Western Pacific so completely under Japanese control.

---

[36] Japanese Minister at Large in China.

He said that as soon as the discussions had defined themselves he would ask Mr. Hamilton and myself to come over to receive a report.

H[ERBERT] F[EIS]

893.51/6709

Memorandum of Conversation, by the Counselor of the Department of State (Moore)

[WASHINGTON,] September 24, 1938.

The Chinese Ambassador accompanied by his Counselor called upon me this morning to discuss the prospects for receiving any form of assistance from the American Government. Dr. Feis was present at my request.

The Ambassador referred to the strong indications given to him by both the President and the Secretary of the Treasury of their disposition to furnish some form of assistance. He said that he understood that the question of whether this would, or would not, be done is dependent upon whether the State Department would give consent; and that he was seeking a clear understanding of the situation prior to his prospective departure.

After reference was made to the importance to China of our silver buying program, a short outline of the situation as it stood at the present moment was given to the Ambassador. He was informed that one reason certain possible forms of action previously had proved abortive was the lack of knowledge on the part of this Government of facts essential to determine the feasibility or desirability of various suggestions; and that now systematic discussion was going on between the Chinese Commission and the Treasury Department in an effort to ascertain all the facts pertinent. It was anticipated when and as the Treasury had reviewed the whole factual situation, and had given thought to all the possibilities, that the question would again come before the State Department.

The Ambassador expressed the view that one type of assistance—relief assistance [37]—could be treated in the vanguard of the discussions taking place or apart from them. He reiterated that he had received the impression both from the President and the Secretary of the Treasury that all the important information necessary for relief effort was at hand, and that the matter was simply one for decision. He had in mind particularly a reinstatement of the earlier wheat and cotton loan whereunder shipments of foodstuffs, fabrics (or he added raw cotton), medical supplies, and trucks to distribute these products could be effected. He indicated the view that these products could

---

[37] See also vol. IV, pp. 571 ff.

be shipped primarily to Hong Kong for distribution in the various areas under Chinese Government control. However, he added, in response to a direct question, that the Chinese Government would also consider it useful to have these products distributed as far as North China, through Tientsin and Shanghai—provided the military authorities would permit.

He re-emphasized the sense of urgency in view of the near approach of winter, saying that the prospect that tens of millions of his countrymen would suffer from intense cold and hunger during this winter, unless assistance could be given. He, therefore, said that he hoped any study of the subject would not be unduly prolonged.

R. W[ALTON] M[OORE]

893.51/6706

Memorandum by the Adviser on International Economic Affairs (Feis)

[WASHINGTON,] September 28, 1938.

Mr. Carson, of Davis, Polk and Wardwell, telephoned me yesterday afternoon to inform me that the credit transaction between the Guaranty Trust Company and the Chinese Government, which was discussed with me some weeks ago, would be completed today. The contract would be signed by the Chinese Ambassador. It provided for a loan by the Guaranty Trust Company of $10,000,000 for I believe two years, at a low rate of interest, against the security of $10,-000,000 of United States Government bonds to be put up by the Chinese Government.

I conveyed to him, as in our previous conversations, our perplexity as to the motives of the Chinese Government for entering into such a transaction. Mr. Carson said that as far as they could understand the matter, it was being carried out for psychological reasons, and that since it was seemingly legitimate business, the Guaranty had decided to execute it. After consulting with Mr. Hamilton, I informed Mr. Carson the Department had "no comment to make" on the transaction.

In view of the fact that the Treasury is now in discussion with the Chinese financial mission, I conveyed word of the prospective transaction to the Treasury. Mr. Lochhead of the Treasury telephoned me this morning and stated that he had passed the information on to the Secretary of the Treasury, and had been requested to say that the Treasury likewise had "no comment to make" about the transaction.

However, he said that the Treasury had curiosity in regard to its terms and character, and thought it possible, for example, that the

Chinese Government didn't actually have the bonds, but might first be credited with the $10,000,000, with them would buy the bonds, and deposit the bonds as security. In the wish to get further information, Mr. Lochhead asked me if I would not tell the interested parties this morning that the Treasury was desirous of further details, and to ask them to telephone such details to the Treasury. I said I would do so.

I telephoned Mr. Havens Grant of the same law firm this morning (Mr. Carson being away from New York), and Mr. Grant said he would immediately telephone Mr. Lochhead.

H[ERBERT] F[EIS]

893.51/6711 : Telegram

The Consul General at Shanghai (Gauss) to the Secretary of State

SHANGHAI, October 4, 1938—6 p. m.
[Received October 4—10:48 a. m.]

1294. There is a persistent rumor in local foreign banking circles today to the effect that a wheat and flour or wheat and cotton loan amounting to approximately $50,000,000 United States currency has been concluded or is about to be concluded between the Central Government of China and the Government of the United States. The local exchange market is very nervous and this office has received several inquiries from banks and business houses regarding the reliability of this rumor.

Inasmuch as such a loan would likely have a marked effect upon the official Japanese attitude towards American interests in China, any information that the Department may feel can properly be communicated to me confidentially or otherwise would be helpful.

Copy of text by mail to Peiping and Chungking.

GAUSS

893.51/6720

Memorandum by the Secretary of State of a Conversation With the British Ambassador (Lindsay)

[WASHINGTON,] October 20, 1938.

The Ambassador, during his call, said that the Ambassador of China at London had called at the Foreign Office and represented that this Government was doing different important things in aid of China and that the British Government was not making any particular showing in this direction; that his earnest appeal was that something be done by Great Britain. The Ambassador then handed me what he called a copy of his oral conversation relative to this Chinese matter [38] and suggested that I transmit it to the Far Eastern Division for their examination and that he would then call on them and discuss the matter more in detail. I replied that I would be glad to do this. I also said that it was not necessary for me to refer to the large purchases of silver from China by this Government or to the campaign led by President Roosevelt for a million dollars of relief,[39] in practical effect, for China, or to our attitude of opposition to the sale of military airplanes, et cetera, to Japan by the private producer.[40] I finally added that my associates in the Far Eastern Division would be glad to go into any details with him.

There was some comment on the international situation, especially as it relates to economic recovery, but little new, however, in addition to what has frequently been said by and between us on these subjects in the past.

C[ordell] H[ull]

893.51/6716

The Chairman of the Board of the Reconstruction Finance Corporation (Jones) to the Secretary of the Treasury (Morgenthau) [41]

Washington, October 24, 1938.

Dear Mr. Secretary: Reference is made to our conversation regarding a suggested loan of $20,000,000 by the Export-Import Bank to a Chinese owned American trading company, the loan to be guaranteed by the Government of China or the Bank of China and the proceeds used to buy agricultural products and manufactured goods in this country for export to China.

In 1934 we agreed to lend China $50,000,000 to be used in the purchase of cotton and wheat. Only $17,105,385.80 of this credit was used. In 1931 the Grain Stabilization Corporation, a Government agency, sold China 15,000,000 bushels of wheat for a consideration of $9,212,826.56. The unpaid portions of these credits were taken over by the Export-Import Bank in April 1936.

In April 1937, a loan of $1,600,000 was authorized for the purchase of locomotives in this country. Disbursement of $733,200 on this loan was made in April 1938. It matures monthly over a period of five years.

It will be seen that our total Government credits to China since September 1931 aggregate $27,051,412.36. $14,419,892.36 has already been repaid and the balance is being paid as it matures. $3,801,055.62, including interest, has been paid since September 30, 1937, the last payment having been made September 30, 1938.

[38] *Post*, p. 625.
[39] See vol. iv, pp. 571 ff.
[40] See pp. 613 ff.
[41] Copy transmitted to the Department by the Chairman of the Board of the Reconstruction Finance Corporation.

While it is not possible to foresee the outcome of the present situation in China, it is probably safe to assume that China will pay her debts, and if none of the purchases in this country would be in conflict with the Neutrality Act, I see no reason why the credit should not be made. Particularly since it is contemplated the borrowers will sell to American importers Chinese products necessary for us to import, for delivery within the period of the maturity of the note, approximating the amount of the credit.

The Export-Import Bank would need to be put in funds through the purchase by the RFC of its preferred stock in the amount of the credit. The President approving, the Bank is prepared to make the loan under suitable provisions to assure the disbursement of the funds in this country for the purchase of American products.

Sincerely yours,   JESSE H. JONES

893.515/1337

Memorandum of Conversation, by the Chief of the Division of Far Eastern Affairs (Hamilton)

[WASHINGTON,] November 9, 1938.

Mr. Lochhead of the Treasury Department telephoned and said that Chinese bankers now in this country discussing financial matters with the Treasury Department had recently stated informally to him that the Chinese Government had certain silver at Shanghai which was available for sale to the U. S. Treasury; that the U. S. Navy transport *Chaumont* was now in Chinese waters; that the *Chaumont* would probably need ballast on its return trip to the United States; that the Treasury might care to purchase this silver from the Chinese Government and have it transported to the United States on the *Chaumont;* and that if the Treasury Department was interested in this, it might also be interested in making similar arrangements for the purchase of silver now at Tientsin. Mr. Lochhead said that he had told the Chinese bankers that this would not, in his opinion, be a purchase by the Treasury Department of silver, but would be the purchase of a diplomatic incident which would go outside the range of pure Treasury business. Mr. Lochhead said that he had indicated to the Chinese bankers that the Treasury Department wanted to keep matters on a strictly financial basis.

Mr. Lochhead said that this whole matter had been handled by the Chinese bankers and by him in an informal and unofficial way. He said that he thought we would be interested in the approach made by the Chinese bankers and that, as he had mentioned to me once before in regard to the silver at Shanghai, the Treasury Department was in position, if we should so desire, to become interested in this silver.[42]

---

[a] See also memorandum of October 21, p. 327.

I told Mr. Lochhead that I thought that his rejoinder to the Chinese bankers would dispose of the matter and I thanked him for his thoughtfulness in informing us in regard thereto.

M[AXWELL] M. H[AMILTON]

893.51/6736⅛

Memorandum by the Adviser on International Economic Affairs (Feis) to the Secretary of State

[WASHINGTON,] November 12, 1938.

MR. SECRETARY: The Secretary of the Treasury last evening requested me to bring before you the following—stating that he had tried to get in touch with you after the Cabinet meeting and later in the afternoon and had failed both times and that he was requesting me to bring the matter before you for the sake of expedition since it would come under discussion at his luncheon meeting with the President on Monday next, November 14.

He stated that the discussions which he had been conducting with Mr. Chen (and incidentally with Jesse Jones, Chairman of the R. F. C., and various American oil companies) in regard to a plan whereunder advances would be made to the Chinese Government, indirectly through corporations set up in the United States and China, against future shipments of tung oil from China, had been virtually completed the day before Canton fell into Japanese hands. He had suspended discussion to watch developments.

The project had then again been discussed with the President. The President had stated that if satisfactory assurances were received from Chiang Kai-Shek that resistance from [to] Japan would continue, he would carry through the project. The President had authorized him to communicate this word to Chiang Kai-Shek through Chen. He had done so. The assurances were now received in the form of the attached letter.[43] The Secretary of the Treasury was of the opinion that the President's promise had been directly passed to the head of the Chinese Government.

Upon the receipt of this message from Chiang Kai-Shek Mr. Morgenthau had informed the President and asked him to ascertain whether the Secretary of State would "acquiesce". I attach the documents given me by the Secretary of the Treasury describing the projected transaction.[43a]

H[ERBERT] F[EIS]

---

[43] Not attached to file copy of memorandum, but see letter of October 15, from Generalissimo Chiang Kai-shek to President Roosevelt, p. 321.
[43a] Not attached to file copy.

893.51/67362½

Memorandum by the Chief of the Division of Far Eastern Affairs
(Hamilton)

[WASHINGTON,] November 13, 1938.

It is assumed that all officers of this Government who have considered the tung oil project in question desire that China be not defeated by Japan and that Japan not succeed in subjugating China. That certainly is the attitude of the writer of this memorandum. However, in examining the project in as nearly an objective manner as possible, factors as follows appear to be important.

1. *The project is in my opinion not practical and is unsound from a business point of view.*

The Chinese Government still controls about 75–80% of the wood-oil producing territory in China. However, the chief exporting center, Hankow, is under Japanese control, as are the chief communication outlets for this commodity, the Yangtze and Pearl Rivers. Hunan and Szechuan Provinces are the main producing areas. Hunan is in process of being conquered by the Japanese and will probably fall to them within two or three months. By the time the Chinese Government could put into operation any plan for assembling and exporting wood oil, its supplies would not be sufficient to meet the terms of the arrangement and it would be faced with very difficult transportation problems. The transportation facilities which would be available would not, in my opinion, be adequate and transportation could be effected only in an uneconomic way.

2. *The project would project the United States into the conflict without, however, having any decisive effect upon the outcome.*

The project would mean the abandonment by the United States of the course of non-involvement and impartiality which has heretofore been followed. It would thus mean action contrary to the thought underlying and the spirit of the Neutrality Act. But it would not vitally affect the outcome of the hostilities. If the United States wishes to do that, it must throw its whole weight behind China.

A tremendous event has occurred in China and it would be a mistake, in my opinion, to underestimate it. Japan has occupied the entire coast and all the most important centers. Whether Japan will be able in the long run to pacify the country and make effective its control, only time will tell, but the positional military struggle is nearing an end.

3. *It is questioned whether Congress and the country would approve such a project.*

It is believed that the isolationist and non-involvement sentiment in the Congress and in the country is still strong. Congress might with warrant take the position that it did not appropriate funds to be used for the purpose of enabling the United States to assist one party in a foreign conflict. Congress might see fit to restrict the Government agency (the Export-Import Bank) actively handling the project in such a way as to impair the future usefulness of the agency (in, for example, South America). Should the attitude of Congress and the country be unfavorable, the fact that the Administration had approved the project might serve to give added support to those who favor the adoption of the Ludlow amendment [44] and might have seriously adverse effects on the question of our neutrality legislation.

4. *The project might conflict with the provisions of the Nine Power Treaty.*[45]

If the Chinese Government is to furnish the United States with large quantities of wood oil, the Chinese Government must virtually monopolize sales in and exportation from the territory it controls. As pertinent to the question of China setting up such a monopoly and the United States being party thereto, there is quoted article III of the Nine Power Treaty, as follows:

"With a view to applying more effectually the principles of the Open Door or equality of opportunity in China for the trade and industry of all nations, the Contracting Powers, other than China, agree that they will not seek, nor support their respective nationals in seeking—

"(*a*) any arrangement which might purport to establish in favour of their interests any general superiority of rights with respect to commercial or economic development in any designated region of China;

"(*b*) any such monopoly or preference as would deprive the nationals of any other Power of the right of undertaking any legitimate trade or industry in China, or of participating with the Chinese Government, or with any local authority, in any category of public enterprise, or which by reason of its scope, duration, or geographical extent is calculated to frustrate the practical application of the principle of equal opportunity.

"It is understood that the foregoing stipulations of this Article are not to be so construed as to prohibit the acquisition of such properties or rights as may be necessary to the conduct of a particular commercial, industrial, or financial undertaking or to the encouragement of invention and research.

"China undertakes to be guided by the principles stated in the foregoing stipulations of this Article in dealing with applications for economic rights and privileges from Governments and nationals of all foreign countries, whether parties to the present Treaty or not."*

[44] For text of the so-called "Ludlow Resolution", see Department of State, *Peace and War: United States Foreign Policy, 1931–1941*, p. 400, footnote 38.

[45] Signed at Washington, February 6, 1922, *Foreign Relations*, 1922, vol. I, p. 276.

*Note: Article XV of the Chinese-American Treaty of 1844 might also be considered pertinent. [Footnote in the original; for text, see Hunter Miller (ed.), *Treaties and Other International Acts of the United States of America*, vol. 4, p. 564.]

5. The project would serve to worsen relations between the United States and Japan.

Japan would naturally view the project unfavorably. She would probably make representations to this Government against what she would call an unfriendly act. Japan would also probably intensify her action in China against American lives and interests. New frictions and incidents between Japanese and Americans would be likely to develop, in China and to some extent in Japan. What the reaction of the American people to the worsened situation would be I do not know: the American people might call for stronger action by their Government; equally, they might press for isolationism. The adoption of this one project would not, in my view, lead to armed conflict between the United States and Japan. It would, however, lessen whatever chance there is of salvaging some of our rights and interests in China through processes of reason, argumentation, patience and skillfully applied pressure.

Japan might declare war against the Chinese Government, set up a blockade against third-power shipments, and by declaring war bring about invocation of our Neutrality Act. Would invocation of that Act stop the project in question? It would render illegal further carrying on of private transactions of that character. Should a governmental transaction be carried through, even though it might be exempt technically from the provisions of the Neutrality Act?

It is my view that to adopt a course of assistance to China now, after Japan has almost completed its positional warfare, would be of no decisive aid to China and would be a profitless irritant to Japan, unless the United States is prepared to give really substantial and long-continued assistance to China. And if that decision be made, it should be made with realization that that course may lead to armed conflict with Japan.

It seems to me that the wise course for the United States to pursue in regard to Japan's actions in China is not to aid China, but bring pressure to bear upon Japan. Such a course would not be taking sides. We would retaliate against Japan because of Japan's injuring American rights and interests. In my opinion, such retaliatory measures should be applied patiently and judiciously over a considerable period of time. They might have very little, if any, immediate effect upon the outcome of the conflict between Japan and China. They would, however, assist in there gradually emerging in China a situation whereunder the United States might continue to enjoy some measure of general equality of treatment.

I am not one of those who believes that war between the United States and Japan is inevitable. Nor even that war need be probable. I believe that the United States must keep itself amply strong in arms to ensure that Japan realize our strength. And with that strength in the background, I believe that the United States by tactful, patient handling of problems in relations between the two countries can avert, without loss of dignity, an armed conflict.

M[AXWELL] M. H[AMILTON]

893.51/6736⅜

Memorandum by the Adviser on Political Relations (Hornbeck)

[WASHINGTON,] November 14, 1938.

In considering the tung oil project, the American Government should, in my opinion, first of all give intensive consideration to certain political aspects of the problem presented and related problems. The political implications and possibilities of the project are far more important, both as regards our foreign relations and as regards our internal situation, than are the economic aspects of the matter. In this memorandum I shall speak, briefly, only of certain of the political aspects.

It is an important interest of the United States that Japan not gain control of China. It therefore would be to our interest that Chinese resistance to Japan's effort to gain that control continue. The Japanese nation today is animated by concepts and is pursuing objectives which are in conflict with the concepts and the legitimate objectives of the people of the United States. The Japanese are embarked upon a program of predatory imperialism. Unless the Japanese march is halted by the Chinese or by some other nation, the time will come when Japan and the United States will be face to face and definitely opposed to each other in the international political arena. It is desirable that the development of such a situation be prevented. It therefore is desirable that the United States act toward the preventing of such a development.

The American Government should formulate and adopt a program of action (a diplomatic "war plan") toward averting an armed conflict between the United States and Japan. In the conducting of our relations with Japan and with China we should not take haphazard and unrelated steps. Such action as we may take in the realm of use of words should be related to action which we may plan to take in the realm of material pressures (positive or negative, or both). It should be our objective to have Japan's predatory march halted. Our course of action should, therefore, be a course in opposition to that march. That march will be halted only by the power of resistance of material obstacles and material pressures. Any nation which definitely opposes that march should be prepared in last analysis to use, if it prove necessary, armed force. The Chinese have already found resort to armed force necessary. China's resistance may possibly be overcome by Japanese armed force. Resistance which may be made by other countries may in the long run have to take the form of armed force. This country, therefore, in formulating its course of action should make it its business to be prepared if necessary to use armed force.

The American Government has during recent years been opposing Japan by use of words (appeal to principles, to rules of law, to provisions of treaties, etc.). Our Department of State may be able to get the better of the Japanese Foreign Office—though even that is not certain—in the field of argumentation, but victories on our part in that field will not halt the forward march of Japan's military machine. The fact is that unless the United States expects and intends to use weapons stronger than those of argument, continuance on our part along that line is almost certain to lead to the development of a situation in which this country will have either to accept a diplomatic defeat or find itself forced to resort to arms. The more we talk and the longer we refrain from resort to some substantial measures of positive (material) pressure toward preventing the Japanese from taking or destroying our rights, titles and interests in the Far East, the more likely will it be that resort by us to such measures at some future time—if and when—will be replied to by the Japanese with resort to armed force against us, which would, in turn, compel us to respond with armed force.

The most practicable course for us to follow would be that of giving assistance to the Chinese and withholding those things which are of assistance to the Japanese, toward prolonging and strengthening China's resistance and curtailing Japan's ability to continue military operations against China. If and when, however, we commit ourselves to that line of action, we should do so wholeheartedly and with determination. We should not take some one step without expecting, intending and being able to take further steps, many further steps, in the same direction. Such steps should include a combination of diplomatic, economic and potential military pressures. If this Government wishes to embark upon such a course, it should be prepared to consider seriously the taking of such steps as denunciation of the U. S.–Japan Commercial Treaty of 1911,[46] repeal of the Neutrality Act, retaliatory tariff measures against Japan, placing of embargoes upon trade and shipping between Japan and the United States, disposal of our naval resources in such manner as to indicate to the Japanese Government and nation that we "mean business."

---

[46] Signed February 21, 1911, *Foreign Relations*, 1911, p. 315.

The tung oil project is a project the objective of which is to give assistance to China. The amount of assistance which would be given by the consummation of this transaction alone would not be sufficient substantially to influence the situation in which resides our problem. If this Government, speaking and acting for the American people, is prepared to move forward with a comprehensive program along such lines as are indicated above, consummation of the tung oil project would be in line with and consistent with such an attitude and intention. But unless such is the case, consummation of the tung oil project would achieve so little and be accompanied by hazards and possibilities of complications so great that consummation of that project would not, it is believed, be advisable.

Decision whether to consummate or not to consummate this project should be made not on the basis of the inherent merits or demerits of the project and not on the basis of the desire of this country that China be not defeated by Japan but on the basis of and in the light of a decision by the American Government to exert itself actively and intensively toward throwing the weight of this country's capacity into a general effort to halt Japan's predatory advance. It is the belief of the undersigned that the American Government should consciously and definitely commit itself (the Government) to such an effort and that it should formulate a comprehensive general plan of procedure toward that end.

STANLEY K. HORNBECK

893.51/6736½

Memorandum by the Secretary of State [49]

[WASHINGTON,] November 14, 1938.

The Treasury Department's barter and credit proposal with regard to China is almost purely political. It would not be considered—certainly by Japan—as a mere commercial transaction, but as a transaction one of the major purposes of which would be to aid China in her military activities against Japan.

Naturally, all American Government officials are equally desirous of getting rid of surplus production and they are also equally anxious to see Japan defeated in her purpose by the exercise of force to dominate the Far East and repudiate and render inoperative the Nine Power Treaty. In these circumstances all of our Government officials, therefore, would be equally disposed to see this Government indulge in any word or act consistent with its situation and short of the serious risk of becoming involved as a party in the military

---

[49] Submitted to President Roosevelt and the Secretary of the Treasury.

conflict between China and Japan that would be calculated to discourage the Japanese military objective and to encourage Chinese military resistance.

Japan, viewing as she undoubtedly would the proposed transaction as one of definite aid to China in the fighting against Japan, would complain bitterly and charge the United States with having made itself a party to the conflict on the side of China. The military clique in control would map Japan's actions in return and they would in all probability include increasing injuries to American citizens and American interests in China, and perhaps one or more methods of retaliation. This transaction and the incident relating to it when combined with other acts, which might follow, of injury and possible retaliation by Japan would result in a serious possibility of this country being drawn ultimately into the war, as stated.

If it is desired to go forward with these possible developments in view, then it would be all-important that the American people and the Congress be disposed and ready to support this new policy, and this would include the sending of the Navy farther beyond Hawaii than at any time in similar circumstances within recent years.

Great Britain and France are and for a time will be preoccupied with Western European exigencies. China is understood to have adequate military supplies for the next six to ten or twelve months. There would be time for further developments and their full consideration in the meantime.

I cannot in the light of all the foregoing, as well as numerous other pertinent facts and circumstances which I have not the time now to enumerate, either advise or concur in the course proposed.

893.51/6736½ : Telegram

The Acting Secretary of State to the Secretary of State [50]

WASHINGTON, December 2, 1938—1 p. m.

13. The President has informed me and he has also informed the Secretary of the Treasury that he desires to go ahead with the tung oil project. I have conferred with the Secretary of the Treasury and have suggested that implementation be held in abeyance until the President returns to Washington next week. The Secretary of the Treasury has agreed to this suggestion. Upon the return of the President to Washington I propose to call to his attention again the views which you expressed in your memorandum of November 14 and to raise for his consideration the question of general policy and pro-

---

[50] The Secretary of State, who was Chairman of the American delegation to the Eighth International Conference of American States, was aboard the S. S. *Santa Clara* en route to Lima to attend the Conference.

cedure in reference to the Far Eastern situation and the question whether he desires to continue for the time being the policy and procedure which this Government has heretofore followed and to proceed with the tung oil project as an isolated act.

The problem presented is, as you know, especially complicated by virtue of the fact that positive commitments have been exchanged between very high officials on both sides. In view of this fact along with other considerations, our opinion and Treasury opinion at this moment lean toward treating the project under consideration, if consummated, as an independent and self-contained commercial transaction.

I should greatly appreciate any suggestions or comments in addition to those contained in your memorandum of November 14 which you would like to have me present to the President.

WELLES

893.51/6733 : Telegram

The Ambassador in the United Kingdom (Kennedy) to the Secretary of State

LONDON, December 3, 1938—2 p. m.
[Received December 3—11:15 a. m.]

1389. 1. In a conversation this noon Cadogan [53] said the British Cabinet had under consideration a proposal looking toward the support of the Chinese currency.

2. The Chinese Ambassador here had approached the British Government regarding a loan, suggesting specifically that if British banks could provide a minimum of 3 million pounds to establish an equalization fund to support the Chinese currency, Chinese banks would supply an equal amount. The Hong Kong [and] Shanghai Bank would make the British loan under a Government guarantee.

3. Cadogan went on to say that the Ambassador had indicated that a larger loan, either 5 or 10 million pounds, would, of course, be better. Cadogan, however, intimated that the British Government, if it acted at all, would not be disposed to go beyond the 3 million figure.

4. Cadogan said he was uninformed as to whether the Chinese had approached us on this subject but if the British Government knew whether we were contemplating parallel action, this would naturally have an effect on their decision.

5. He expressed the opinion that the British had an interest in the maintenance of the Chinese currency and that the British Govern-

---

[53] Sir Alexander M. G. Cadogan, British Permanent Under Secretary of State for Foreign Affairs.

ment had a right to look to the Japanese. He added that he thought the Japanese however recognized its value in their own interest. But he did not know whether they would object.

6. He indicated that the Government here would greatly appreciate receiving our reaction.

KENNEDY

893.51/6736⅜ : Telegram

The Secretary of State to the Acting Secretary of State

ON BOARD S. S. "SANTA CLARA," December 4, 1938—3 p. m.
[Received 7 : 16 p. m.]

8. Your 13, December 2. I cannot of course pass upon the finality of any commitments which may have been taken towards the Chinese Government.

My judgment remains that it is unlikely that the arrangement would be accepted by American opinion as an isolated commercial transaction and Japanese Government circles will certainly not so regard. It probably will impede any neutrality legislation if it is done. We should be clearly prepared to deal with the grave possible consequences if the Japanese Government should decide to retaliate and I believe it important that this aspect of the matter as set forth in the memorandum presented to the President again be further considered.

HULL

893.51/6738

Memorandum of Conversation, by the Chief of the Division of Far Eastern Affairs (Hamilton)

[WASHINGTON,] December 5, 1938.

Participants: Mr. Hall-Patch, Financial Adviser to the British Embassy in China;
Mr. Bewley, Financial Counselor, British Embassy, Washington;
Mr. Hornbeck; Mr. Adams; [54]
Mr. Hamilton; Mr. Jones. [55]

Mr. Hall-Patch, Financial Adviser to the British Embassy in China, called upon Mr. Hornbeck by appointment made through the British Embassy. Mr. Bewley accompanied Mr. Hall-Patch. Mr. Hornbeck asked Mr. Hamilton to be present.

---

[54] Walter A. Adams of the Division of Far Eastern Affairs.
[55] Joseph M. Jones, Jr., of the Division of Far Eastern Affairs.

Mr. Hall-Patch inquired whether Mr. Hornbeck would prefer to ask him questions or to have him proceed with general comments in regard to the situation in China and in Japan. Mr. Hornbeck suggested that Mr. Hall-Patch give us the benefit of his general comments and said that as Mr. Hall-Patch proceeded with these comments we might wish to ask certain questions.

Mr. Hall-Patch talked first about the currency situation in north China. He said that in north China the Japanese military was determined to have its way and to regard north China as more or less a possession of Japan. He said that, contrary to the advice of Japanese financiers and of Japanese commercial and trading circles, the Japanese military had insisted on inaugurating in north China a new currency which was tied to the yen. Mr. Hall-Patch said that if the Japanese military were successful in making this new currency completely effective, foreign trade in north China would be stopped, because in his opinion the new exchange could be made effective only as a result of the setting up of a very rigid system of exchange control accompanied by general control of import and export trade. He said that he thought this new currency system in north China would work to the economic disadvantage of Japan but that the Japanese military was insistent that the new currency supplant the old currency. He mentioned the fact that the existence of the concessions at Tientsin and the continued circulation in the concessions of the old standard currency were definite obstacles in the way of the success of the new currency. He observed that so long as the foreign traders could continue to use this old currency, they might hold on in north China. He mentioned definite measures which the British and the French at Tientsin were taking (or were considering taking) to keep some of the old currency in circulation.

With regard to central China, Mr. Hall-Patch said that the situation there was different from that obtaining in north China in that in central China the Japanese Army had not as yet insisted upon introducing the new currency. He said that there were substantial elements among the Japanese which opposed the introduction into central China of the new currency. He mentioned Mr. Kodama, the head of the new Japanese Central China Development Company, as one of those who strongly opposed the introduction of the new currency into central China. He expressed the view that those elements among the Japanese who did not wish to see the new currency introduced into central China had a reasonable prospect of having their view prevail unless the Chinese Government currency should collapse. He intimated that he did not see how the Chinese Government could prevent such a collapse for very much longer, because the Chinese Government's only means of maintaining its currency were remittances from abroad and the sale of Chinese Government silver, the supply of which was now not large. He said that in his opinion the collapse of the Chinese Government currency would be a serious blow to Japan as well as to the Chinese Government; also that such collapse would be a particularly heavy blow to foreign trade.

In reply to inquiry, Mr. Hall-Patch said that it was his estimate that the will to resist still continued among the Chinese who he thought would henceforth engage in very little positional fighting. He said that some disintegration had already set in among the Chinese within the occupied areas and that he expected this disintegration to continue as the months passed. He said that in his opinion the Japanese needed to get some respectable Chinese to head the new régimes which they were setting up in China; that if they could get such a respectable Chinese, some of the Chinese merchant and banking classes as well as peasants would probably incline to discontinue their active opposition to the Japanese. He said that such Chinese as the Japanese had up to the present been able to persuade to come forward as officials of new régimes were not respected by any element among the Chinese.

In reply to a further inquiry, Mr. Hall-Patch said that in his opinion the chances as matters stand are that the Japanese will attain their objective in China. He said that he thought achievement of this would, however, require a matter of ten to twenty years, after which he felt that the Chinese would gradually throw off the Japanese yoke. He said that during this period of from ten to twenty years it was his view that Japan would become an increasing menace to the rest of the world.

With regard to the question whether in his opinion it was possible for foreign governments to take effective action to restrain Japan, he expressed the view that thoroughgoing economic embargoes on both imports from and exports to Japan would be effective but that he did not think such action was possible. He said further that if such action should be taken he thought it likely that Japan would take positive action of a military character against one or more of the countries which adopted such redressive action against Japan. He said that even the more conservative element in Japan was now as a result of the fall of Canton and Hankow "flushed" with the sense of victory.

As illustrative of the type of action by other countries which the Japanese particularly resented, Mr. Hall-Patch said that sometime ago a group of Japanese had formed a British incorporated company; that the company had secured the right from one of the provinces in Australia to mine certain rich deposits of iron ore; that subsequently the Australian Commonwealth Government had had a geological survey made of Australia and had found that the deposits of iron ore in Australia were not nearly so large as had been thought previously; that the Commonwealth Government had thereupon informed the Japanese-controlled company which had obtained the provincial government's sanction to carry on mining operations that it (the Commonwealth Government) could not approve the contract; that the Japanese Government had made strong representations to the Commonwealth Government pointing out that the Japanese had entered into the contract in good faith, that a large amount of Japanese capital had been put into the enterprise, that it was inconceivable to the Japanese Government that the Commonwealth Government had not been aware of the permission granted by the provincial government, and that the Commonwealth Government had previously asserted its belief in the principle that raw materials should be made available to countries not possessing such raw materials. Mr. Hall-Patch said that he anticipated that the Japanese Government would carry this matter to London. (His account of this matter gave the impression that he thought well of the Australian action.)

Inasmuch as Mr. Hornbeck had another appointment, Mr. Hall-Patch and Mr. Bewley went to Mr. Hamilton's office where Mr. Adams and Mr. Jones joined them. After Mr. Hornbeck had seen his additional caller, Mr. Hornbeck also came to Mr. Hamilton's office.

In reply to questions, Mr. Hall-Patch gave further interesting information in regard to the details of the currency situations in north and central China.

Mr. Hornbeck referred to reports which had come to our attention that there was a difference in opinion between British investment circles in China and British trading circles in China as to the policy which the British Government should follow. Mr. Hall-Patch said that he was not aware of any difference and he said that British investment circles as well as British trading circles had some months ago reached the point in their thinking where they believed that Japanese success in the hostilities with China would mean the ousting of British investment and trading interests in China. Mr. Hornbeck referred to information which had reached us to the effect that the British Foreign Office had some time ago been in favor of making a currency loan to China but that interests in the city had opposed such action and had been successful in having their viewpoint prevail. Mr. Hall-Patch said that he believed that the fundamental difficulty in regard to a currency loan was that such a transaction would not be sound from an economic point of view and he expressed the view that, if British financial circles in the city had opposed such a step, they had done so on purely economic grounds. He said that the British Export

Credit Guarantee Department was still struggling with the question of extending credits to China and that the chief difficulty in all such matters was the question of security. He said that the question of security was also the chief obstacle in connection with plans for building the Burma–Yunnan Railway. He said that in Great Britain no new credits were being extended to Japan; that existing credits were being continued but when they came up for renewal were being shortened as to the period of time; and that the whole trend was to place business with Japan on comparatively a cash basis.

Mr. Hall-Patch asked whether we could see any objection to his raising with the Treasury Department the question of the current exchange between the British and American Governments of more detailed statistics in regard to capital movements and exchange operations between the United States and the Far East than appear in the Treasury Department's *Statistics of Capital Movements between the United States and Foreign Countries and of Purchases and Sales of Foreign Exchange in the United States.* Data in regard to China and Japan are not given separately in that publication, as are the data for several European countries, but are classified in the geographical area of "Far East (including China, Japan, Netherlands East Indies, Straits Settlements, and the Philippine Islands)". Mr. Hornbeck stated that he could see no objection to a discussion of the question with the Treasury Department.

As he was leaving, Mr. Hall-Patch said that he expected to go to London and after about six months to return to this country. He said that he hoped to have a further talk with Mr. Hornbeck upon his return. Mr. Hornbeck assured Mr. Hall-Patch that he would be very glad to see him.

Mr. Hornbeck and Mr. Hamilton thanked Mr. Hall-Patch for his courtesy in calling and for having given officers of the Department the benefit of his comments and of his knowledge of current developments in China.

M[AXWELL] M. H[AMILTON]

893.51/6760

The British Embassy to the Department of State [58]

AIDE MÉMOIRE

Sir A. Cadogan informed the United States Chargé d'Affaires in London on December 3rd that to their regret His Majesty's Government were still not quite ready to furnish considered views in regard

---

[58] Handed to the Adviser on Political Relations, on December 8, by the British Chargé.

to possible punitive measures of retaliation or pressure on Japan. It had, however, occurred to them, he said, that third party interests in China might derive a certain measure of protection and benefit if, quite apart from economic and financial reprisals, steps were taken to support the Chinese currency. The Chinese Government had in fact recently requested that British banks should make a contribution of at least £3,000,000 sterling to a currency stabilisation fund, an equal amount being put up by Chinese banks. A small committee of Chinese and British bankers would control policy and the operation of it through the two British banks i. e. the Hong Kong and Shanghai Bank and the Chartered Bank of India, Australia and China. The Chinese Government intimated unofficially at the same time that if foreign support could be increased to five or ten million pounds, the margin of safety would make the Chinese dollar impregnable over a long period.

The United States Chargé d'Affaires was informed that His Majesty's Government were in fact considering a proposal to introduce legislation to guarantee a contribution of £3,000,000 by the Hong Kong and Shanghai Banking Corporation to the projected fund. Appropriate arrangements would of course be made to try to ensure that the fund if set up would be utilised solely for the purposes for which it was said to be necessary.

So far His Majesty's Government have reached no conclusion in the matter but their decision on the question of a contribution to a currency stabilisation loan would be greatly influenced by the knowledge that the United States Government were willing to take parallel and simultaneous action.

WASHINGTON, December 7, 1938.

893.51/6736⅜

Memorandum by the Acting Secretary of State [61]

[WASHINGTON,] December 9, 1938.

I send you herewith the papers I have just received from Mr. Oliphant.[62] The question came up in Cabinet meeting this afternoon and I gather that the President would like this put through without further delay. Consequently, we should be in a position to express our views with regard to this proposed contract and with regard to the other papers not later than next Monday.

S[UMNER] W[ELLES]

---

[61] Addressed to the Adviser on Political Relations and the Chief of the Division of Far Eastern Affairs.
[62] Herman Oliphant, General Counsel to the Treasury Department; papers not identified but they referred to the proposed tung oil agreement.

893.51/6736½

Memorandum of Conversation, by the Chief of the Division of Far Eastern Affairs (Hamilton)

[WASHINGTON,] December 12, 1938.

As directed by Mr. Welles, I called on Mr. Oliphant this morning and returned to him the papers in regard to the tung oil transaction which Mr. Oliphant sent to Mr. Welles on December 9. At the same time I gave Mr. Oliphant the original of the attached memorandum and told him that we felt definitely that an amendment along the lines set forth in the memorandum should be made. I told him also that we would like to see the contract amended so as to provide that title should pass to the American corporation upon delivery of the commodity in the United States and I said that we would feel very much happier if this change could be made.

Mr. Oliphant said that they would have to study these questions. I asked that the Treasury Department be so good as to inform Mr. Welles what the Treasury Department, upon completion of its study, purposed doing in regard to the two points which I had mentioned. Mr. Oliphant said that this would be done.

Subsequently Mr. Oliphant telephoned and asked whether our points would be met if there should be substituted in the contract for the proviso at the end of Article 3 the proviso appearing at the bottom of page 4 of the memorandum [63] which I had left with Mr. Oliphant, and if the provision with regard to the passing of title should be amended to read "and title shall pass to the buyer upon arrival alongside wharves in ports of the United States to be designated by the buyer in its absolute discretion." I said that these amendments would satisfactorily take care of the two points we had raised. Mr. Oliphant then asked whether the contract, with these two amendments, was satisfactory from our point of view. I replied that of course we had not undertaken to pass upon the business aspects of the contract or upon the contract as a whole but had examined it merely from the point of view of the treaties and from the point of view of where it seemed advisable that title pass to the American corporation. I repeated that from these two points of view the amendments which Mr. Oliphant had said would be made were satisfactory to us.

Mr. Oliphant then asked whether he should telephone Mr. Welles or whether I would inform Mr. Welles. I said that I would do so.

M[AXWELL] M. H[AMILTON]

---

[63] Last paragraph of memorandum.

[Annex—Memorandum]

PROPOSED AGREEMENT BETWEEN AN AMERICAN CORPORATION AND A CHINESE CORPORATION FOR THE SALE BY THE LATTER TO THE FORMER OF A STIPULATED AMOUNT OF TUNG OIL TO BE FINANCED IN PART BY A LOAN BY THE EXPORT-IMPORT BANK TO THE AMERICAN CORPORATION

If the proposed agreement is a contract between two private corporations, none of its terms, as disclosed in the draft agreement, would seem to involve definite conflict with any treaty of the United States although it is not improbable that it might be opposed as contrary to the general purpose of Article III of the Nine Power Treaty to which reference is made hereinafter.

However, if it could be established that the Chinese corporation represents or acts for or at the instance of the Government of China it would be difficult to avoid the conclusion that the financing of the transaction by an agency of the United States would in practical effect involve an agreement between the Government of China and the Government of the United States, the principal objective of which would seem to conflict with the provisions of two treaties to which the United States is a party.

This statement is based on the provision of Article 3 of the draft contract which provides:

"that the amount of oil required to be delivered under this contract in any one year shall not exceed three-fifths of the total oil produced in China during that year."

When it is considered that the area in which the supply of oil must be obtained represents only a part of the tung oil producing area of China and that a considerable quantity of that production is needed for local consumption it will be apparent that the supply deliverable under the contract might exhaust all of the available supply in the area in which the contract may be given effect. This would close or seriously restrict the market to all other prospective purchasers and would seem to be inconsistent with Article XV of the treaty of 1844 between the United States and China and Articles I, II and III of the Nine Power Treaty of 1922.

Article XV of the treaty of 1844 provides that:

"The former limitation of the trade of Foreign nations to certain persons appointed at Canton by the Government, and commonly called hong merchants, having been abolished, citizens of the United States engaged in the purchase or sale of goods of import or export are admitted to trade with any and all subjects of China without distinction; they shall not be subject to any new limitations nor impeded in their business by monopolies or other injurious restrictions."

The rights which are granted to the United States by Article XV of the treaty of 1844 are equally available to British, French, Japanese and a number of other governments under most-favored-nation provisions of their respective treaties with China and would appear to afford a basis of protest both to China and to the United States if all or the greater part of the available supply of tung oil should be preempted by the United States or its nationals.

Such a result would also appear to conflict with the provisions of (1) Article I of the Nine Power Treaty which obligates the United States:

"To refrain from taking advantage of conditions in China in order to seek special rights or privileges which would abridge the rights of subjects or citizens of friendly states . . ." [66]

(2) Article II of the Nine Power Treaty under which "the contracting powers (including China) agree not to enter into any treaty, agreement, arrangement, or understanding, either with one another, or, individually or collectively, with any Power or Powers which would infringe or impair the principles stated in Article I"; and (3) Article III of the Nine Power Treaty in which "the Contracting Powers, other than China, agree that they will not seek, nor support their respective nationals in seeking—

"(a) any arrangement which might purport to establish in favour of their interests any general superiority of rights with respect to commercial or economic development in any designated region of China;

"(b) any such monopoly or preference as would deprive the nationals of any other Power of the right of undertaking any legitimate trade or industry in China, or of participating with the Chinese Government, or with any local authority, in any category of public enterprise, or which by reason of its scope, duration or geographical extent is calculated to frustrate the practical application of the principle of equal opportunity."

In view of the fact that the proviso in Article 3 of the draft contract renders uncertain the quantity of oil to be supplied and affords no certain and authoritative basis for determining the quantity which the seller could be held legally obligated to deliver, it is suggested that the purpose of the article as now drafted could be accomplished no less effectively and any ground for objection on treaty basis be eliminated by amending the article to read somewhat as follows:

"3. Quantity. 220,000 tons (of 2,000 pounds each), or so much thereof as may be lawfully available to the seller for export, to be supplied, as nearly as practicable, in accordance with the following schedule:

---

[66] Omission indicated in the original.

First year	25,000 tons
Second year	35,000 tons
Third year	45,000 tons
Fourth year	55,000 tons
Fifth year	60,000 tons

Total   220,000 tons"

Another amendment of the article which would seem to accomplish the same purpose would be to revise the proviso to read somewhat as follows:

"Provided however, that the amount of oil required to be delivered under this contract in any one year shall not exceed the quantity lawfully available to the seller for export during that year."

893.51/6739a : Telegram

The Acting Secretary of State to the Ambassador in Japan (Grew) [67]

WASHINGTON, December 15, 1938—7 p. m.

419. 1. This afternoon the Reconstruction Finance Corporation issued a statement to the press as follows:

"Jesse Jones today announced that the Export-Import Bank has authorized credits to the Universal Trading Corporation of New York up to $25,000,000, the proceeds to be used in financing the exportation of American agricultural and manufactured products to China, and the importation of wood oil from China. The loans will be guaranteed by the Bank of China and mature over a period of 5 years. The funds will be disbursed as needed.

Mr. Jones further announced that of the $50,000,000 loan authorization to China in 1934, only $17,105,385.80 was used. In April 1937 a loan of $1,600,000 was authorized for the purchase of locomotives in this country. This loan matures monthly over a period of 5 years. In 1931 the Grain Stabilization Corporation sold China 15,000,000 bushels of wheat for a consideration of $9,212,826.56.

All of these credits are now handled by the Export-Import Bank. The total actual disbursements for loans to China since 1931 have been $27,051,412.36. $14,419,892.36 has been paid and the balance is being paid as it matures. $3,801,055.62, including interest, has been paid since September 30, 1937, the last payment having been made September 30, 1938."

2. If anyone makes inquiries or representations to you in regard to this transaction, you should read to them the statement which the Reconstruction Finance Corporation has issued to the press as quoted above and state that the transaction is accurately described in that statement and is a genuine and legitimate commercial transaction.

[67] The same telegram was sent, December 15, 7 p. m., as No. 650 to the Consul General at Shanghai for the Embassy in China at Chungking and Peiping.

Should any Japanese characterize this transaction to you in any way as an unfriendly act, you should state that you take decided exception to any such characterization of it. You should add that you regard with amazement any such characterization by a Japanese of an essentially commercial transaction consummated for the purpose of legitimately serving American industrial enterprises and American consumers.

WELLES

893.51/6740 : Telegram

The Ambassador in Japan (Grew) to the Secretary of State

TOKYO, December 17, 1938—2 p. m.
[Received December 17—6:45 a. m.]

789. Department's 419, December 15, 7 p. m.

1. Reports concerning the grant of credit loan to the Universal Trading Corporation were prominently featured in the papers yesterday afternoon. This morning the papers carry despatches from London and elsewhere stressing that the credit loan, along with the British guarantee covering shipments to China, evidence coordinated action by the United States and Great Britain toward protecting their interests in China.

2. The *Hochi* this morning carries a feature story substantially similar to those mentioned in our 786, December 15, 7 p. m.[68] It concludes with the statement that the Minister for Foreign Affairs[69] will, during his interviews next week with the British and American Ambassadors, emphasize that "the firm determination of the Japanese Government to set up a new order in the Orient will not be shaken" by "British and American assistance to Chiang Kai Shek and efforts to exert economic pressure on Japan".

3. An editorial this morning in the *Asahi*, which is the only one which has thus far appeared, describes the circumstances as set forth in the announcement of the Reconstruction Finance Corporation and concludes that the credits to the Universal Trading Corporation, which it characterizes as a "phantom corporation," is substantially similar to the British export guarantee to China. "In American financial circles the view is held that this loan was made to China, with Japan held in view and for the purpose of increasing China's power of resistance, that it is a political loan, and that it is intended to be a gesture in the direction of Japan in connection with questions arising over the principle of the Open Door and equality of opportunity. It is reported that Anglo-American discussions are taking

---

[68] *Ante*, p. 418.
[69] Hachiro Arita.

place with a view to concerting measures in the nature of economic reprisals against Japan. In addition to these measures the United States, it is understood, is considering various measures which the President is authorized by law to take in the event of any foreign nation discriminating against American goods." The various forms of retaliatory action which are reported to be under consideration between United States and Great Britain are then reviewed, and the editorial concludes: "International assistance to Chiang Kai Shek in his efforts to continue resistance is now beginning to take shape. Apart from Soviet Russia it goes without saying that the prime mover is Great Britain. Whether the United States will pull Britain's chestnuts out of the fire is an open question, but one fact is clear, and that is that the grant of British and American credit loans to China will help the expiring Chiang Kai Shek spiritually, more than materially, and that these loans derive only from a malicious desire to stimulate Chiang to continue resistance."

Repeated to Shanghai for Peiping and Chungking.

GREW

893.5151/550

Press Release Issued by the Treasury Department on December 19, 1938

Secretary Morgenthau announced today that the arrangement announced July 9, 1937, under which the Central Bank of China has been enabled, under conditions which safeguard the interests of both countries, to obtain dollar exchange for stabilization purposes has been extended for a further period beyond December 31, 1938.

893.51/6745 : Telegram

The Chargé in China (Peck) to the Secretary of State

CHUNGKING, December 19, 1938—noon.
[Received December 20—12:15 a. m.]

607. Department's 6 [650], December 15, 7 p. m.[70] News of the granting of credits to be used in financing the exportation of American products to China which reached Chungking almost simultaneously with reports from London of the imminent granting of British credits to China was greeted in Chinese official and private circles with marked elation. The Minister of Finance is reported in the press as having expressed gratification "at this further evidence of America's friendly interest in China's progress and development, which China will not forget". "This credit," Dr. Kung is quoted as saying,

[70] See footnote 67, p. 586.

"will further the development of China's economic potentialities and will enlarge American trade in China".

The local press has given much prominence to the matter of which the motive [view?] of the *Ta Kung Pao* on December 17 is representative. This journal emphasizes that the credit is purely commercial, that it constitutes a fresh testimonial of Sino-American friendship, that China despite financial difficulties will continue to fulfill its financial obligations, and that though purely a commercial transaction it will have the political effect of dealing a blow to Japanese aggression. This paper expresses the hope that the granting of these credits will cause Great Britain to follow suit. The *China Times* comments that the significance of the granting of credits lies not in their amount but in their implications which in its view amount to the first step on the part of Great Britain and the United States in making a "concrete reply" to Japan's wish to set up a new order in East Asia and that they constitute a warning that "Chinese cooperation with the European powers and the United States cannot be destroyed." The fact that the credits came after the fall of Wuhan is noted and the conclusion drawn that Anglo-American recognition of the National Government has not been affected by military or political developments. The extension of Anglo-American credits to China is held not only to manifest the traditional friendship existing between China and these Anglo-Saxon powers but to reflect the commencement by Great Britain and the United States of steps to implement the League resolutions to assist China.

Repeated to Peiping for mailing to Tokyo.

PECK

893.51/6742 : Telegram

The Ambassador in Japan (Grew) to the Secretary of State

TOKYO, December 19, 1938—6 p. m.
[Received December 19—8 a. m.]

793. Department's 419, December 15, 7 p. m. The following statement, as furnished to us by Hugh Byas,[n] was made this afternoon by the Foreign Minister in reply to questions at a press conference with the foreign correspondents:

"Mr. Arita: An early cessation of hostilities in China is earnestly desired not only from the standpoint of peace in East Asia but for the sake of the nationals of third powers in China as well as of the 300,000,000 Chinese. Reported foreign loans to the Chiang Kaishek régime though they may be purely trade propositions will necessarily lead to the prolongation of hostilities and the consequent embarrassment and inconvenience of foreign nationals. The report

[n] Tokyo representative of the *New York Times* and the London *Times*.

256941—54——38

of an American loan is therefore an opportunity to say what we cannot but say: it is a regrettable act on the part of the United States which has hitherto acted with discretion and understanding in Chinese affairs; and if, as the United States papers say, it is a political gesture of the United States towards Japan, I think there will be nothing more dangerous.

The Japanese people may regard that the present loan is really intended as economic pressure by a powerful economic unit, and its results will prove quite contrary to what is expected by America. At least the Japanese people will undoubtedly find new grounds for strengthening the proposed new order in East Asia.

Personally, I am surely not inclined to regard the loan as a political gesture towards the activities of Japan.

Asked if those remarks would apply to a loan by Great Britain and how he would regard the prospect of common economic pressure by the United States and Great Britain, the Minister replied: 'I say exactly the same thing; this applies to a British loan. But personally I am inclined not to regard that kind of loan as a political gesture'."

GREW

───────────

893.51/6744 : Telegram

The Consul General at Shanghai (Gauss) to the Secretary of State

SHANGHAI, December 20, 1938—noon.
[Received December 20—7 : 15 a. m.]

1486. Reference my No. 1485, December 19, 4 p. m.,[72] regarding local reaction to extension of credit.

Abend of *New York Times* informs us he was told this morning by Horiguchi of Domei News Agency that it had been decided that Shanghai would be the principal theater of Japanese retaliatory action against American and British interests and that more severe restrictions would be imposed upon American and British trade in this area. Abend also states that information of a similar nature was given to him in confidence this morning by Kita, First Secretary of Embassy and Japanese Embassy spokesman here.

Repeated to Peiping and Chungking. Code text by air mail to Tokyo.

GAUSS

───────────

893.51/6761

Memorandum by the Acting Secretary of State[73]

[WASHINGTON,] December 20, 1938.

I have spoken with Mr. Wayne Taylor[74] regarding the discussions which the Treasury Department has had with Mr. Bewley concerning

───────────

[72] Not printed.
[73] Addressed to the Adviser on Political Relations and to the Chief of the Division of Far Eastern Affairs.
[74] Fiscal Assistant Secretary, Treasury Department.

the British currency loan to China. Mr. Taylor tells me that he has indicated to Mr. Bewley that the opinion of the Treasury Department is that in view of the recent commercial credit of the Export-Import Bank involving the tung oil transaction, this government is not disposed for the time being to consider any further steps of the kind suggested by the British Government.

I consequently suggest that there is no need to reply in writing to the British *aide-mémoire* [75] left with me and that you may inform Mr. Mallet orally that the views of the Department of State coincide with the views expressed by the Treasury Department to Mr. Bewley.

893.51/6762

Memorandum of Conversation, by the Adviser on Political Relations (Hornbeck)

[WASHINGTON,] December 20, 1938.

Under instruction by the Under Secretary, Mr. Welles, I made oral reply to Mr. Mallet today. I said that I understood that the Treasury Department had been talking with Mr. Bewley of the British Embassy in regard to the matter to which this *aide-mémoire* refers and that I was under instruction to say that the views of this Department coincided with the views which the Treasury Department had expressed. I asked whether, in these premises, this oral reply on our part would be satisfactory to the British Embassy. Mr. Mallet said that it would and that he would report to his Government, as the Department's reply, what I had said.

S[TANLEY] K. H[ORNBECK]

EFFORTS OF CHINA TO SECURE WAR MATERIAL FROM OTHER COUNTRIES [76]

893.24/371

Memorandum Prepared in the Division of Far Eastern Affairs

[WASHINGTON,] March 12, 1938.

Very little definite information is available in regard to arms and munitions entering China during recent months. However, an evaluation of such data as are available makes possible the following general statements.

Considerable quantities of war materials have been and are entering China by three routes. In order of probable importance these are Hong Kong, Lanchow via Sinkiang, and French Indochina.

---

[75] Dated December 7, p. 581.
[76] For previous correspondence on the export of military material to China, see *Foreign Relations*, 1937, vol. IV, pp. 520 ff.

Germany, Russia, Italy, and France appear to be supplying the largest quantities and smaller amounts are of Belgian, Danish, Czechoslovakian, American, and Swedish origin.

A more detailed summary of the information on file follows.

Routes of Entry

Possible routes still available to China for the import of war materials are: (1) Alma Ata or Serglopol (on the Turksib Railway) by highway or air to Urumchi to Lanchow; (2) Semipalitinsk or Irkutsk by highway or air to Uliassutai to Lanchow; (3) Verkhne–Udinsk by rail to Urga and thence by highway or air to Lanchow. From Lanchow a highway leads to central China via Sian. (4) Hong Kong by rail, highway, or steamer to Canton and from there to central China by rail. (5) Haiphong (French Indochina) by rail to Yunnanfu and thence by highway to central China or from Haiphong by rail to Langson and from there by highway to Lungchow (Kwangsi), Nanning, Kweilin, and central China. (6) Another possible route which apparently has been used very little, if at all, is from Rangoon by rail to Myitkyina or Lashio, or by river steamer to Bhamo and thence by mule caravan to Tailfu, 440 kilometers west of Yunnanfu, from which city there are motor roads to central China. This route is, of course, impractical for anything but small arms and ammunition and is slow (60 days or more from Rangoon to central China). (7) A few supplies are reported to have entered by way of Macao (thence by highway to Canton) and (8) Kwangchowwan from where they are shipped by highway to a redistribution point on the West River.

Countries of Origin

Licenses issued for the export of arms and munitions from the United States to China for the periods indicated were as follows:

December 1937	$290, 618. 27
January 1938	380, 083. 50
February 1938	1, 918, 613. 83
March 1–14, 1938	76, 002. 95
	$2, 665, 318. 55

Applications now pending which may be acted upon favorably in the near future total only $104,430.00. The value of American arms (this term is used in a broad sense and includes military equipment and munitions of war) entering China may actually be higher than these figures would indicate, as Hong Kong has reported that there are believed to be arms agents there selling American arms originally exported to South America but refused by the consignees there. Where these arms are stored at present is unknown. There are also at Hong Kong rumors that American arms are arriving there via Australia and Manila.

Official British figures (communicated to the Ambassador at Tokyo about February 1) show that of the war materials passing through Hong Kong 62% are of German origin, 21% Italian, 12% French, 3% British, and the remaining 2% American and Belgian. Although there is little information in regard to the origin of arms entering via Indochina, it appears probable that they are almost entirely of French, Belgian, and possibly Czechoslovakian manufacture. Assuming that all supplies entering via Lanchow are Russian, the countries supplying arms to China may be ranked roughly as follows: Germany or Russia, Italy or France, Belgium, Great Britain, Czechoslovakia, United States, Sweden, Denmark. A large order for automatic weapons including 7.92 mm. machine guns, anti-aircraft and anti-tank guns, and 20 mm. automatic cannon has been placed with the Danish Industrial Syndicate. The size of this order is indicated by the fact that seven Chinese officers have been sent to the factory in connection therewith. These supplies are to be shipped by sea from Hamburg, but it is not known whether deliveries have yet begun. The absence of Denmark from the British list of countries of origin mentioned above would seem to indicate that no part of the order had arrived at the time that list was compiled, a date which is not definitely known but which is probably near the first of the present year. There have been several definite figures mentioned in reports but it is not believed that listing them would greatly help in understanding the situation as they do not pretend to be accurate, refer to different periods, and bear no indication as to the type of supplies which they include.

[Here follow sections on Hong Kong, Lanchow, and Indochina.]

711.00111 Regis. Lic./1222

Memorandum of Conversation, by the Chief of the Office of Arms and Munitions Control (Green)

[WASHINGTON,] March 25, 1938.

After consulting Mr. Hornbeck [78] and Mr. Hamilton,[79] I asked the Chinese Ambassador [80] by telephone this morning to call at my office. He said that he would come immediately.

After some preliminary conversation of no significance, I told the Ambassador that I was disturbed by the fact that during the current month licenses had been granted authorizing the exportation to Japan of arms to the value of $893,983.06, whereas the corresponding figure

[78] Stanley K. Hornbeck, Adviser on Political Relations.
[79] Maxwell M. Hamilton, Chief of the Division of Far Eastern Affairs.
[80] C. T. Wang.

in respect to China was only $176,044.31. I explained why the Department had adopted the policy of publishing monthly statistical summaries of licenses issued by this office, and I pointed out that the figures which I had just given him, with such modifications as might result from licenses issued between now and the end of the month, would be published during the first week in April.[81] I reminded him that one of the arguments which had been recently emphasized by persons who desired the immediate application of the Neutrality Act [82] to China and Japan was that it was no longer physically possible for China to import arms purchased in the United States and that therefore the invocation of the act would penalize Japan without affecting exports to China. I said that, although I realized, of course, that China was still finding it possible to import arms, nevertheless a publication of these figures might tend to give the opposite impression and might result in further agitation in this country for the immediate invocation of the Neutrality Act. I suggested that, if the Chinese Government had already placed any further orders for arms in this country which might be ready for export in the near future, it might be advisable for the companies with which the orders had been placed to apply for export licenses within the next few days in order to increase the valuation of arms authorized for export to China before the publication of the March statistics.

The Ambassador said that he entirely agreed with me as to the result which the publication of these figures might have. He said that he would see to it that applications for further export licenses were made within the next few days if his Government had placed any further orders for arms in this country. He disclaimed any knowledge of the orders which might have been placed and under which applications for licenses might be made.

.   .   .   .

J[OSEPH] C. G[REEN]

893.24/370 : Telegram

The Chargé in France (Wilson) to the Secretary of State

PARIS, April 2, 1938—noon.
[Received April 2—10:30 a. m.]

522. With reference to press report that the French Government had recently suspended munitions supply to China over the Hanoi-Yunnanfu Railroad, an official of the Far East section of the Foreign Office has told us that there has been no change in policy, which is to

---

[81] Released April 4; see Department of State, *Press Releases*, April 9, 1938, p. 455.
[82] Joint resolution approved May 1, 1937, amending earlier legislation; 50 Stat. 121.

approve applications for shipments ordered prior to last August and started before October. It appears however that it has been possible for some subsequent shipments to evade this control and there have been other shipments originating in French Indo-China which are not strictly subject to it. Shipments from France must be approved by the Defense Ministries also and of late these have been authorizing very few arms exports, with the result that the French munitions supply to China has been considerably diminished principally because of France's own military needs but has not been interrupted.

Our informant added that the French were still fearful that the Japanese might endeavor to cut off this supply altogether by bombing the railroad from planes based on carriers off Hainan. They thought the attack would be confined to that part of the line beyond the French frontier but as the entire railroad belonged to them they wished to avoid giving provocation.

WILSON

893.24/427

Memorandum Prepared in the Division of Far Eastern Affairs

[WASHINGTON,] April 20, 1938.

Military supplies from abroad enter China principally by three routes: (*a*) Lanchow; (*b*) French Indochina; and (*c*) Hong Kong.

Lanchow. (*Kansu*).

A radio report just received from an American military observer who made a special trip to Lanchow gives information as follows:

Shipments of military supplies from Russia passing through Lanchow are estimated to average less than 25 tons daily. The material consists of aircraft supplies, including gasoline, bombs of various sizes up to approximately 1,500 pounds, machine guns and ammunition for artillery and small arms. During December, 1937, 15 anti-aircraft guns and a few searchlights were received. Six light tanks arrived this year but there have been no further shipments of artillery. A total of 300 airplanes of all types, which is believed to be the entire shipment expected, has already arrived at Lanchow. Trucks in use on this route have a capacity of three tons. They are guarded by armed Russians en route and by Chinese guards at halting points. From 120 to 150 truckloads of material are now arriving weekly. Strict secrecy on these shipments is being maintained and information is most difficult to secure.

It is estimated by officers of the War Department that the ammunition and aviation gasoline entering China by Lanchow is primarily for the use of the Russian equipment, such as airplanes, anti-aircraft guns and tanks shipped by the same route. The present flow of munitions is believed to be sufficient to maintain those weapons in action. If the tonnage capacity, as indicated above, of this route is utilized for general munitions, it is believed that the volume would be sufficient to supply the needs of only about three and a half divisions (45,000 to 55,000 men) engaged in military operations.

The American military observer who visited Lanchow has been directed by the War Department to forward more detailed information via air mail. This air mail report should reach Washington in approximately 2 weeks.[83]

French Indochina.

Military supplies entering China via French Indochina are shipped by two routes: (*a*) by rail to the Kwangsi border (Lungchow) and from there by motor direct to central China or to a transshipment point on the Canton–Hankow Railway; and (*b*) by rail to Yunnanfu.

A radio report just received from an American military observer who made a special trip to Lungchow (on the Kwangsi side of the Kwangsi–Indochina border) gives information as follows:

Since February 7 an embargo has been established on shipments by rail of munitions from other than French sources. After March 1 the embargo also included French material. While the French Colonial Ministry is reported to have authorized munitions shipments, the local Governor General is reluctant to permit their passage for fear of Japanese reprisals. The embargo does not apply to articles which can be classed as commercial. Under this liberal interpretation, airplane engines, engine parts, gasoline, oil and many other articles may be shipped. A highway from Dongang, on the railway in French Indochina, to Kweilin, capital of Kwangsi, via Nanning, able to take five-ton loads, is now complete. A hard surfaced road connects Dongang with Haiphong. A water route is also open via Wuchow.

The American military observer who visited Lungchow has been directed by the War Department to forward more detailed information via air mail. This air mail report should reach Washington in approximately 2 weeks.[84]

With regard to the statement that since February 7 an embargo has been established on shipments by rail through French Indochina, the American Embassy at Paris telegraphed on April 2 that according to the French Foreign Office there had been no change in French policy which is to approve applications for shipments ordered prior to last August and started before October. The Embassy reported further that there had been some evasion of the French control and that other shipments which originated in French Indochina were not strictly subject to the control. The Embassy stated that because of

---

[83] Dated April 16, not printed.
[84] Dated April 15, not printed.

France's own military needs the French munitions supply to China had been considerably diminished.

With regard to Yunnanfu, the American Consul at that place reported under date January 29 that there had arrived at Yunnanfu a shipment of war materials consisting of 32 light tanks, 6 or 8 airplanes, and 1800 tons of explosives, mostly bombs. The Consul reported further that he understood that another shipment of 1500 tons was then at Haiphong awaiting transportation to Yunnanfu.

Hong Kong.

It has recently been learned that the Government of Hong Kong is forwarding fortnightly to London data in regard to war material passing through Hong Kong. The American Embassy at London has been asked by telegraph to request that the British Government supply it with these data fortnightly or monthly. No reply has as yet been received from the Embassy at London.

Under date February 25 the American Consul General at Hong Kong reported that, based on first-hand observation, the traffic in war materials via Hong Kong appeared to be substantial and continuous. The Consul General forwarded a report by the Hong Kong correspondent of a Japanese newspaper giving a list of supplies reported to have reached China through Hong Kong between February 1 and February 15. The Consul General expressed the opinion that these figures were not greatly exaggerated. The figures are as follows:

From America: 15 cases of machine guns for aeroplanes, 500 tons of gunpowder and other explosives.

From Britain: 27 aeroplanes, 700 tons of gunpowder and other explosives, 250 tons of quasi-explosives, 26 tanks, 500 cases of sulphuric acid, 2 motor lorries, 15 anti-aircraft guns, 1,500 tons of bridge material, 100 tons of railway material, 200 tons of other war supplies.

From Denmark: 6 cases of machine guns for aeroplanes, 2,000 tons of quasi-explosives.

From Germany: 20 motor lorries, 200 tons of railway material, 100 tons of other war supplies.

From Holland: 1,500 tons of quasi-explosives, 150 motor lorries, 100 tons of bridge material, 1,000 tons of railway material, 400 tons of bombs.

From Italy: 5,000 tons of ammunition, 100 cases of sulphuric acid, 300 tons of other war supplies.

From Norway: 25 cases of machine guns, 1,000 cases of sulphuric acid, 115 motor lorries, 500 tons of bridge material, 50 tons of barbed wire.

As further indicative of the volume of traffic through Hong Kong of military supplies and related materials, there is enclosed a list of certain exports to China from Hong Kong for the period November

1937 to January 1938, inclusive, as supplied by Hong Kong port authorities.[85]

Burma.

A further route which may become of importance in connection with the supply of arms and munitions to China is from Rangoon to Lashio, railhead in Burma, and thence by motor truck to Yunnan. A motor highway, approximately 550 kilometers in length, is now being built from the Burma border to Tali, a city in western Yunnan from which highways lead to central China and Szechwan via Yunnanfu and Kweichow. Recent reports from the Consulate at Rangoon indicate that some 200,000 coolies are working on this road and that strict orders have been issued for its completion by May. It is believed, however, that even if a road of some sort is completed by that time it will not be practicable for use by motor vehicles during the rainy season from June to November. It is also believed that the potential importance of this route has been exaggerated in the press, as the geographical difficulties in the way of construction and maintenance are enormous.

The non-completion of a motor road connecting Burma and Yunnanfu does not, of course preclude the possibility that small arms and ammunition may be brought in by pack animals over the route to be followed by the road or over the main caravan routes from Bhamo and Myitkyina. It would probably take in the neighborhood of 60 days to transport goods from Rangoon to central China over either of these routes.

Chinese Arsenals.

Chinese Government arsenals can manufacture limited quantities of small arms of all types, machine guns, trench mortars, light artillery, and ammunition for these weapons. Hand grenades and airplane bombs up to 300 pounds are also manufactured. China must of course import certain raw materials to complete the manufacture of these munitions.

Conclusion.

The information so far received is not sufficiently comprehensive to afford a basis for making an estimate as to the volume of military supplies entering China from abroad. Upon receipt of the air mail reports from the American military observers who visited Lanchow and Lungchow and of an air mail report expected from the Consul at Rangoon, and if the British Government furnishes the information which has been requested of it in regard to the transit through Hong Kong of military supplies, there may be available data on the basis of which an estimate can be made.

---

[85] Under date of February 12, not printed.

711.00111 Lic. $\frac{\text{Douglas Aircraft Co. Inc.}}{93}$ /118

Memorandum by the Chief of the Office of Arms and Munitions Control (Green) [86]

[WASHINGTON,] May 31, 1938.

Mr. Richard M. Mock, American representative of N. V. Nederlandsche Vliegtuigenfabriek Fokker, called me by telephone from New York this morning. He referred to the pending application by the Douglas Aircraft Company for a license to export three planes to Outer Mongolia. He said that Mr. Douglas had sent a telegram to the Douglas representative in Hong Kong and had instructed him to proceed to Hankow to confer with the Chinese authorities with a view to having them send appropriate instructions to the Chinese Ambassador in Washington, in order that the latter might inform the Department that his Government wished an export license to be issued. He said that Mr. Douglas had now received a telegraphic reply from his representative at Hong Kong saying that his visit to Hankow had been fruitless as the Central Government was unwilling to send instructions to its Ambassador to Washington until the Urga Government had requested it to make arrangements to admit the planes. This, it was understood, the Urga Government was unwilling to do as it considers itself independent of the control of the Central Government in respect to such matters.

Mr. Mock said that he was leaving tomorrow for Europe, and that he hoped that when the situation had been made clear to his principals they might find it possible to persuade the Urga Government to take action. He said that he feared, however, the Urga Government would refuse to take the necessary action and Outer Mongolia would hereafter purchase planes exclusively in countries which were not so meticulous in the issuance of export licenses.

This is an absurd situation. I shall take up the question once more with the Chinese Ambassador if FE [86a] thinks that such action might possibly serve any useful purpose. For my part, our past experience leads me to the conclusion that further conversation with the Ambassador would probably be of no avail. I suggest, therefore, that we should consider the advisability of making an exception in regard to these planes. The President's Proclamation of January 31, 1922 [87] delegates unlimited authority to the Secretary of State to prescribe exceptions. If an exception were made permitting the granting of an

---

[86] Addressed to Division of Far Eastern Affairs.
[86a] Division of Far Eastern Affairs.
[87] *Foreign Relations, 1922,* vol. I, p. 726.

export license without awaiting an expression of approval from the Chinese Embassy, the license could be legally issued forthwith.

I should appreciate it if I might discuss this situation with you at your convenience.

J[oseph] C. G[reen]

711.00111 Lic. $\dfrac{\text{Douglas Aircraft Co. Inc.}}{93}$ /121

Memorandum of Conservation, by the Chief of the Office of Arms and Munitions Control (Green)

[Washington,] June 8, 1938.

Major Victor E. Bertrandias, Export Sales Manager of the Douglas Aircraft Company, Incorporated, called at my office this morning. He said that the statement which Mr. Mock made to me on May 31, in regard to the efforts of the Douglas representative in Hong Kong to persuade the Chinese Government to instruct its Ambassador in Washington to inform the Department that it desired that a license be issued authorizing the exportation of three planes to Outer Mongolia, were based on a telegram received from Hong Kong. He said that, since my conversation with Mr. Mock, Douglas had received a letter from its agent in Hong Kong which told in considerable detail of his conversations in Hankow and of his failure to persuade the Chinese Government to take action. To the utter astonishment of the Douglas agent, and according to the agent to the utter astonishment of our Ambassador,[88] the Chinese had said that they would not request that a license be issued authorizing the exportation of the planes to Outer Mongolia and had added a suggestion that this Government obtain assurances from the Soviet Government that the latter had no objection to the importation of these planes into Outer Mongolia and, if such assurances were received, that it proceed to issue the necessary license.

J[oseph] C. G[reen]

893.24/446

The Acting Secretary of War (Johnson) to the Secretary of State

Washington, June 15, 1938.

Dear Mr. Secretary: Reference is made to your letters of March 2 and 7, 1938,[89] asking that data as to the volume of military supplies entering China via Lanchow, Kansu and Lungchow, Kwangsi be

---

[88] Nelson T. Johnson.
[89] Neither printed.

secured for the information of the President. In a letter dated April 20, 1938 [90] I informed you of the contents of radio reports received from American military observers sent to those points. Since then additional information has been received which enables me to give you a more complete estimate of the munitions traffic into China. Therefore the following information is submitted.

It is estimated that over 75 per cent of the military supplies imported into China since the start of the hostilities have been routed through Hong Kong. The routes of entry for the remainder in order of their importance are French Indo China, Russian Turkestan, Kwangchowan (French leased territory on the Kwangtung coast 220 miles southwest of Hong Kong), Macao, and Burma. A negligible amount of military supplies may enter China from Siberia via Urga. Similarly small quantities may pass through the Japanese blockade into ports on the China Coast.

Extensive road and railway construction and improvement are now in progress with a view toward bettering communications with countries bordering China and so facilitate shipments of military supplies. In Yunnan, the caravan route from Talifu to Burma is being improved into a road suitable for wheeled traffic, and an extensive road net is being constructed connecting Yunnanfu, the terminus of the French railway from Hanoi, with roads leading north, east and west. In Kwangsi railroads and roads are under construction connecting the railway terminus at Langson, French Indo China, with the Canton–Hankow railway via Nanning and Kweilin. The long route from Russian Turkestan has in large part been made suitable for heavy hauls in all weathers.

The material imported consisted primarily of the following:

(a) Aircraft and aircraft supplies.
(b) Explosives and other components for the manufacture of bombs, artillery ammunition, trench mortar ammunition, small arms ammunition and hand grenades.
(c) Small arms ammunition.
(d) Artillery ammunition.
(e) Machine guns and small arms.
(f) Antiaircraft guns and ammunition.
(g) Antitank guns and ammunition.
(h) Artillery and trench mortars.
(i) Tanks and armored cars.
(j) Aircraft bombs.

Little artillery (other than as indicated above) has been imported since the start of hostilities.

Germany, until its recent decision to cease shipping munitions to China, furnished the largest percentage as well as the largest variety

[90] Not printed.

of military supplies. Other countries furnishing munitions in order of their probable importance are Russia, Italy, England, France, United States, Belgium, Sweden, Austria, Switzerland, and Denmark. The heavy German participation in the munition trade to China is probably due to a barter agreement between the two countries concluded in 1935 and to the presence of the German advisers. Practically all the materials purchased from Germany can be procured elsewhere provided China can secure the necessary credit or provide foreign exchange.

Chinese claim they now have sufficient supplies on hand for one more year of warfare.

It is believed that the military supplies now being imported into China together with the reserve on hand are sufficient to maintain the Chinese forces in defensive operations on the present extensive scale. It is estimated that a minimum reserve of four months' supply of essential military supplies are now in China either in arsenals and supply dumps or en route thereto.[91]

From the standpoint of supply, continued large scale Chinese operations are contingent upon the maintenance of China's purchasing power abroad, upon keeping the present route via Hong Kong open until efficient substitute routes can be established, and upon continued Chinese occupation of the areas containing important Government arsenals, particularly those in the Hankow area.

Sincerely yours,

LOUIS JOHNSON

711.00111 Lic. $\frac{\text{Douglas Aircraft Co. Inc.}}{93}$ /123

Memorandum by the Chief of the Office of Arms and Munitions Control (Green)

[WASHINGTON,] June 21, 1938.

The attached telegram of June 21 [92] from Mr. Richard M. Mock, American representative of N. V. Nederlandsche Vliegtuigenfabriek Fokker, seems to indicate definitely that there is no chance that the Urga Government can be induced to ask the Chinese Government to instruct its Ambassador to request the Department to issue a license authorizing the exportation of the three planes which the Douglas Aircraft Company wishes to export to Outer Mongolia. I suggest, therefore, that, in view of the considerations set forth in my memorandum of May 31, we consider the possibility of taking immediate action to facilitate the exportation of those planes. I suggest that appropriate procedure might be for me to inform the Chinese Am-

---

[91] The Under Secretary of State, Welles, in transmitting this letter to President Roosevelt on June 24, stressed this paragraph.

[92] Not printed.

bassador orally of the situation which has developed and to tell him that, unless we receive within two or three days a definite request from his Government that the necessary export licenses be not issued, we propose to issue them.

J[OSEPH] C. G[REEN]

711.00111 Lic. $\frac{\text{Douglas Aircraft Co. Inc.}}{93}$ /124

Memorandum of Conversation, by the Chief of the Office of Arms and Munitions Control (Green)

[WASHINGTON,] June 24, 1938.

I called the Chinese Embassy by telephone yesterday afternoon intending to request the Chinese Ambassador to come to see me in order to discuss with him the matter of the three DC–3 commercial passenger transport airplanes which the Douglas Aircraft Company, Incorporated, desires to export to Outer Mongolia. Mr. Ing, Counselor of the Embassy, told me that the Ambassador was out of town and would be away several days. I therefore asked him to call.

Mr. Ing called this morning.

I explained the situation to him, emphasizing particularly that, if the necessary export license were not issued, the only practical effect would probably be that an American manufacturer would lose the business and that planes would be purchased in some other country and sent to Outer Mongolia without the permission, and perhaps even without the knowledge, of his Government. I said that, in view of the situation which had arisen, the Department proposed to issue the necessary export license unless we were informed within the next few days that his Government objected to its issuance.

Mr. Ing said that he did not believe that his Government had any objection and that, if the Ambassador approved, he proposed to inform me by telephone on Monday that the Embassy had nothing to say further than that it had received no instructions in the premises.

It was obvious from what Mr. Ing said that he personally approved the procedure which I had suggested and that he hoped that the necessary export license would be issued.

J[OSEPH] C. G[REEN]

711.00111 Lic. $\frac{\text{Douglas Aircraft Co. Inc.}}{93}$ /127

The Secretary of State to the Chinese Ambassador (C. T. Wang)

The Secretary of State presents his compliments to His Excellency the Chinese Ambassador and, with reference to a conversation between the Counselor of the Chinese Embassy and the Chief of the Office of Arms and Munitions Control on June 24, 1938, regarding the desire of the Douglas Aircraft Company, Inc., to export three Douglas DC–3 commercial passenger transport airplanes to Outer Mongolia, has the honor to inform him that license No. 2412 was issued to the Douglas Aircraft Company, Inc., on June 27, 1938, authorizing the exportation of two of these aircraft to Amsterdam, the Netherlands, for reexport to Urga, Outer Mongolia, China, and that the country of destination of another aircraft, for the export of which to the Netherlands a license was issued to the Douglas Aircraft Company, Inc., on January 28, 1938, has been changed to show that the aircraft will be reexported to Urga, Outer Mongolia, China.[93]

WASHINGTON, June 29, 1938.

711.00111 Lic. $\frac{\text{Douglas Aircraft Co. Inc.}}{93}$/131

Memorandum of Conversation, by the Chief of the Office of Arms and Munitions Control (Green)

[WASHINGTON,] July 2, 1938.

Mr. Zaung Teh Ing, Counselor of the Chinese Embassy, called me by telephone this morning. He read me a translation of a telegram from the Chinese Foreign Office in regard to the exportation of three DC–3 planes to Outer Mongolia. The telegram stated that the Foreign Office had informed our Ambassador a month ago that it could not give permission for the importation of planes into Outer Mongolia unless the Outer Mongolian Government would request that such permission be granted, and that the situation remained unchanged.

Mr. Ing said that he had received the note addressed to the Ambassador on June 29 informing him that the export license had been issued and that he supposed that that settled the matter.

I referred to our conversation on June 24 and said that in view of what I had told him at that time we had decided to issue the license unless his Government expressed strong objection to such action.

Mr. Ing said that as he read the telegram from the Foreign Office it was not intended to express objection. He pointed out that it merely stated that the Central Government could not grant permission.

I gathered from Mr. Ing's tone that the Embassy was not in any degree displeased at the issuance of the license.

J[OSEPH] C. G[REEN]

[93] On September 23 the Secretary of State informed the Chinese Ambassador that a license for the export of six such aircraft to Urga had been issued to the Douglas Aircraft Company, Inc., on September 22.

893.24/439

The Consul at Rangoon (Brady) to the Secretary of State

No. 95   RANGOON, July 26, 1938.

[Received August 9.]

SIR: I have the honor to report that it is authoritatively stated that the question of duty on war materials that may be shipped through Burma in transit to China is receiving the consideration of the Government. Under regulations now in effect such materials would be subject to full tariff rates on importation into Burma, and there would be no drawback on re-exportation to China (despatch No. 52 of March 3, 1938 [94]). A drawback of seven-eighths of the duty is allowed on goods in general. It is considered probable that a concession will be made to China, but a decision in the matter has not yet been reached.

The Collector of Customs is authority for the statement that no advance shipments of arms or ammunition or other war materials for China have entered Burma.

Customs statistics covering the first half of July 1938 show only usual imports of arms and ammunition for dealers, valued at Rupees 4,372 ($1,617). The United States shared to the extent of $904, that amount representing the value of 40,400 rifle and revolver cartridges, 12,000 shotgun shells, and 18 rifles and two shotguns. The other imports were chiefly shotgun shells and were from Great Britain.

Respectfully yours,   AUSTIN C. BRADY

893.24/460

The Vice Consul at Saigon (Palmer) to the Secretary of State

No. 69   SAIGON, August 19, 1938.

[Received September 6.]

SIR: I have the honor to report that war materials are continuing to be received at Haiphong and to be despatched from there across the border into China. Details as to the quantities of the various commodities comprising the traffic are not known.

Presumably no munitions are being accepted by the railroad line which runs to Yunnanfu (because of an agreement with the Japanese). Airplanes, gasoline, etc. are not on the list of banned articles. Munitions are generally routed by rail from Haiphong through Hanoi to Langson, on the border, where they are transshipped by motor truck into China. There is said to be an extremely heavy traffic over this route.

---

[94] Not printed.

The French cargo ship *Min* of the Messageries Maritimes arrived at Haiphong from France early in the second week of August with a very large cargo of munitions. (The vessel's tonnage is: displacement, 18,006; gross, 7,997). To minimize the risk of an explosion in the port of Haiphong, the vessel's cargo was discharged with great despatch and the railroad service was practically given over to transporting it—to the exclusion of all other goods—into China.

Respectfully yours,   JOHN PEABODY PALMER

893.24/466

Memorandum by the Second Secretary of Embassy in France
(Higgins)[95]

PARIS, September 2, 1938.

Since the beginning of the Sino-Japanese War there has been a Chinese Munitions Purchase Commission in Berlin. I have seen this morning a memorandum sent by it to the Chinese Embassy here giving the terms of a German offer for the sale of a quantity of munitions for immediate delivery to the Chinese Government. This stuff is urgently needed. The memorandum is dated September 1, 1938. The material offered for sale consists of:

1. 120 75–millimeter field pieces at approximately 4,000 pounds sterling apiece.
2. Shells for the above.
3. 60 105–millimeter field pieces (presumably howitzers) at approximately 5,000 pounds sterling apiece.
4. Shells for the same.
5. 100,000 Mauser rifles and ammunition at 14 pounds sterling apiece.

The material is all new and of the most recent models. Calculating from the above figures, it will be noted that the total order would amount to over eleven million dollars. Terms are 25 percent cash and the rest credit, F. O. B. Rotterdam. The Munitions Purchase Commission is at present engaged in trying to make arrangements to get together the necessary cash, approximately three million dollars.

L[AWRENCE] H[IGGINS]

---

[95] Copy transmitted to the Department by the Ambassador in France in covering despatch No. 2894, September 2; received September 16.

893.24/480 : Telegram

The Ambassador in Japan (Grew) to the Secretary of State

TOKYO, November 2, 1938—9 p. m.

[Received November 2—1 : 03 p. m.]

702. Japanese protest concerning shipment of arms via French Indo-China. My French colleague [96] confirms the report that he was recently called to the Foreign Office by Prince Konoe who as Foreign Minister protested in general terms against the alleged shipment of arms and munitions for the Chiang Kai Shek Government through French Indo-China. The Foreign Minister stated that a similar *démarche* was being made simultaneously through the Japanese Ambassador at Paris. Prince Konoe stated that if such shipments were not stopped "certain steps would have to be taken" but he did not specify what those steps would be.

The French Ambassador replied in a general denial of the allegation that any arms or munitions had been shipped into China through French Indo-China since the frontier had been closed by the Indo-Chinese Government to all munitions traffic and demanded specific evidence.

By the way of elaborating on this question my French colleague informs me that in every case where specific complaints have been made of such contraband shipments the French Government has investigated with the greatest of care and in no single instance has the allegation of the Japanese been found to be true. He said that allegations involving individual instances of shipments undoubtedly arose from false information given for a fee by irresponsible individuals to Japanese consular officials in French Indo-China. He further stated that in his opinion the general allegation of shipment of arms through French Indo-China originated with and was kept alive by certain interested circles in Japan probably with the support of the navy in whose interest it was to furnish any excuse to further the southward advance policy by the seizure of Hainan Island and a blockade of the Gulf of Tongking.

Arsene-Henry has reported fully to his Foreign Office but he has as yet received no reply.

Repeated to Shanghai for Chungking.

GREW

---

[96] Charles Arsene-Henry, French Ambassador in Japan.

893.24/483 : Telegram

The Consul General at Hong Kong (Southard) to the Secretary
of State

HONG KONG, November 8, 1938—9 a. m.
[Received 2:15 p. m.]

61. The French Consul at Hong Kong has notified shipping companies verbally that the transit of "war materials" through Kwangchowwan and Haiphong is suspended. This prohibition includes motor trucks, presumably only those for military use, but the instructions received by my French colleague are not clear on that point and he has written requesting clarification thereof. He has informed the local representative of General Motors that motorcars would be allowed to pass through these two ports but presumably only when they are not destined to the Chinese Government. A shipment of 12 American motor trucks from Hong Kong to Kwangchowwan consigned to the Highway Bureau of Szechwan Province was not allowed to land by the French authorities and has returned to this port.

The opinion has been expressed in some quarters that the French will be very strict regarding the movement of war materials including trucks through Kwangchowwan but to a lesser degree at Haiphong since at the latter port there is a 4% ad valorem transit tax which is not collected at Kwangchowwan.

The port of Pakhoi could be used but at present only two lighters are available there and the Japanese would not long tolerate the shipment of any kind of war materials through the port of Pakhoi.

Repeated to Peiping, sent by mail to Saigon, Chungking, Yunnanfu.

SOUTHARD

893.24/486 : Telegram

The Consul at Rangoon (Brady) to the Secretary of State

RANGOON, November 12, 1938—8 p. m.
[Received November 12—2 p. m.]

T. L. Soong, a brother-in-law [of] Chiang Kai Shek, is here to establish purchasing, shipping and banking headquarters, transferring his Government's activities previously centered Hong Kong. War supplies brought by British vessel are from Russia, other ships reported to be on the way.

BRADY

893.24/491 : Telegram

The Ambassador in China (Johnson) to the Secretary of State

CHUNGKING, November 15, 1938—10 a. m.
[Received November 15—7 a. m.]

544. Arthur Young [97] informs me that the French having stopped the transshipment through French Indo-China of arms and munitions destined for China, the Chinese Government has made representations to the French Government pointing out that such a measure in effect constitutes in [an?] application of a form of sanctions against China.
Repeated to Peiping.

JOHNSON

893.24/493 : Telegram

The Chargé in France (Wilson) to the Secretary of State

PARIS, November 16, 1938—7 p. m.
[Received November 16—7 p. m.]

1937. The Chinese Ambassador [98] told me yesterday that his Government would be greatly concerned over the closing of the French Railway in Indo-China to the passage of war supplies. With the cutting of the Canton–Hankow Railway the French Railway becomes of vital necessity to the Chinese Government. He said that he had spoken with Bonnet [99] at various times recently requesting that some way be found to permit in secret the passage of supplies, that Bonnet had promised to take it up with Daladier [1] but that on the tenth of this month Bonnet had informed him that it would be impossible for the French to permit any war material, even that ordered before the outbreak of hostilities, to pass over the railway.

Wellington Koo said that the French Government was frightened that the Japanese would make reprisals if the French relaxed control over the railway. He had asserted to Bonnet that the Japanese were in no position to risk an attack on French possessions in the Far East. Bonnet, however, insisted that France could not act alone and that only if France were guaranteed the support of the United States and Great Britain could she risk offending the Japanese.

The Chinese Ambassador said that he had suggested to Bonnet that this matter might be discussed during the Chamberlain–Halifax [2] visit next week. Bonnet promised to take it under consideration.

---

[97] American adviser to the Chinese Ministry of Finance.
[98] V. K. Wellington Koo.
[99] Henri Bonnet, French Minister for Foreign Affairs.
[1] Edouard Daladier, President of the French Council of Ministers (Premier).
[2] Neville Chamberlain, British Prime Minister, and Viscount Halifax, British Secretary of State for Foreign Affairs.

Wellington Koo said that he had the definite impression that Bonnet was so concerned with the European situation and with domestic affairs in France that he paid but slight attention to Far Eastern questions and left them to others in the Foreign Office.

WILSON

651G.11251/9 : Telegram

The Acting Secretary of State to the Chargé in France (*Wilson*)

WASHINGTON, December 1, 1938—5 p. m.

896. Your 1972, November 22, 5 p. m.[3] The following telegram has been received from the Consul at Yunnanfu:[4]

"It is reported here that motor trucks are now included in the list of war materials the transshipment of which through French Indo-China is allegedly prohibited. Purchasers here of American trucks are being seriously inconvenienced by this situation. It is rumored that difficulty can be avoided by paying the full Indo-China import duty on trucks instead of only the usual 4 per cent transit tax. If this is the case it would indicate discrimination against American trucks as it is understood that French trucks are not subject to import duty in Indo-China. A representative of the Owult Motor Car Company has recently arrived in Yunnanfu for the alleged purpose of establishing a branch agency here. This would not appear to be warranted unless that Company contemplated large scale sale of trucks as the sale of passenger cars at present is inconsiderable. French Consulate here professes to know nothing about this matter but I have already received one complaint in this regard."

The Ford Motor Company and the Rubber Export Association of Akron, Ohio have asked the Department to intervene with the French Government to obtain permission for the shipment in transit through French Indo-China of automobiles, trucks and automotive products.

This Government deprecates the placing of restrictions on trade involved in the reported action of the French authorities. We perceive no warrant for discrimination by the French authorities, in the matter of transit, between American cars or trucks and French cars or trucks, as indicated in Yunnanfu's telegram quoted above. Moreover, as France has ratified the Convention and Statute on Freedom of Transit, signed at Barcelona on April 20, 1921,[5] the French Government, even though the United States has not ratified that convention and statute, is in principle obligated to facilitate transit shipments.

Unless you perceive reasons to the contrary, therefore, it is desired that you discuss this matter informally with the appropriate French authorities and report by telegram to the Department.

WELLES

---

[3] Not found in Department files.
[4] Paul W. Meyer.
[5] League of Nations Treaty Series, vol. VII, p. 11.

651G.11251/11 : Telegram

The Ambassador in China (Johnson) to the Secretary of State

CHUNGKING, December 5, 1938—9 a. m.
[Received December 5—6 a. m.]

577. With reference to recent telegrams on the question of transshipment of war supplies through French Indo-China, the Counselor of the French Embassy in Chungking volunteered the following information in a conversation with a member of my staff on November 30:

(*a*) a law in effect before beginning of hostilities provided that military supplies could not be shipped through Indo-China unless sanctioned by the Governor General;

(*b*) following start of hostilities the Japanese informed the French authority that they were aware of foregoing law and also of transshipments of arms and munitions through Haiphong to China. The Japanese considered this activity to be of an unfriendly character, particularly as it involved official sanction on the part of a high French official, and requested that it be stopped;

(*c*) subsequently the French Government broached the subject at the Brussels Conference of 1937 with a view to seeking American and British assurances of assistance in case of a Japanese move against French interests in the Far East, but the United States and Great Britain refused these commitments; and

(*d*) the French Government therefore decreed that military supplies for which orders had been placed before the end of October 1937 would be permitted to pass through Indo-China, but that those ordered after that date would be denied shipment.

The informant stated that in his opinion any relaxation in the restrictions now imposed would have to be carried out gradually. He added that after the fall of Canton the Chinese authorities had endeavored to ship approximately 1,000 motor trucks into China via Haiphong and Kwangchouwan and inasmuch as facilities at those ports were limited congestion had occurred. To ameliorate this condition the French authorities had taken steps to limit such shipments, an action which had been misconstrued by the Chinese as an extension of the restrictions applying to transshipments through French territory. He alluded to this as an erroneous conception and said that the French Government had no intention of restricting the passage of commercial products through French territories to China.

Repeated to Peiping for Tokyo.

JOHNSON

651G.11251/10 : Telegram

The Chargé in France (Wilson) to the Secretary of State

PARIS, December 5, 1938—4 p. m.
[Received December 5—2 : 23 p. m.]

2049. Department's 896, December 1, 5 p. m. I have discussed this question with Hoppenot, Chief of the Far Eastern Division at the Foreign Office. He states that motor trucks are not included in list of war materials the transshipment of which through Indo-China is prohibited. He also states that the "rumor" that difficulties can be avoided by paying the full Indo-Chinese import duty is entirely untrue because in fact no difficulties exist.

He says that the only types of trucks which are refused transit are those manifestly designed or capable of being used for military purposes such as caterpillar types, those fitted with gun mounts, et cetera. He says that after the capture of Canton permission was refused for a short time for the transit of all trucks through Indo-China because such a large number of them were diverted there that time was required to sift out the "non-military" trucks from the "military" trucks. Instructions since then have been given to the Governor General of Indo-China to authorize the transit of all "non-military" trucks and motorcars.

Hoppenot asserts that there is therefore no discrimination as between American cars and trucks and French cars and trucks and adds that if we will furnish him with information regarding any specific case in which difficulties are encountered he will be glad to send the necessary instructions to the Governor General.

WILSON

893.24/511 : Telegram

The Consul at Rangoon (Brady) to the Secretary of State

RANGOON, December 13, 1938—9 p. m.
[Received December 13—2 : 30 p. m.]

First war munitions over Chinese road part of shipment German and Czechoslovak machine guns ammunition valued at about $112,000. Norwegian steamer has delivered 1300 tons of Italian explosives arms and ammunition. British steamship due to arrive January with cargo of French war materials.

BRADY

651G.11251/13 : Telegram

The Consul General at Hong Kong (Southard) to the Secretary of State

HONG KONG, December 22, 1938.
[Received December 22—12: 20 p. m.]

Following telegram has been received from the American Consul at Saigon.

"December 22, 11 a. m.   Restrictions on transit automobiles and trucks by road from French Indo-China into China removed by order of the Governor General made known orally last night.   Only transit and registration taxes required."

Repeated to Chungking, Peiping.

SOUTHARD

BOMBING BY THE JAPANESE OF CIVILIAN POPULATION IN CHINA; APPEAL BY THE DEPARTMENT OF STATE TO AMERICAN FIRMS NOT TO EXPORT AVIATION MATERIAL TO JAPAN[6]

793.94116/44

The Chinese Ambassador (C. T. Wang) to the Secretary of State

WASHINGTON, June 1, 1938.

SIR: Acting under instructions of the Chinese Government, I have the honor to convey to you the following communication:

Since the beginning of the Japanese military aggression in China not a day has passed without the Japanese aircraft severely bombing Chinese open towns and inflicting heavy loss to the civilian life.   For the past several days the Japanese airplanes have continuously raided Canton, one of the most populous cities in China and deliberately bombed and machine-gunned residential sections of the city far from any military objectives killing and wounding several thousand noncombatants including a great number of women and children.   The action was indeed savagely cruel and the scenes were indescribably appalling.

It may be recalled that on September 28, 1937, the Assembly of the League of Nations by a resolution[7] declared that no excuse could be found for the aerial bombardment of open towns in China by the Japanese aircraft which had aroused horror and indignation throughout the world and solemnly condemned such action.   The bombing of

---

[6] For further correspondence in 1938 regarding the bombing of civilians in China, see *Foreign Relations*, Japan, 1931–1941, vol. I, pp. 564 ff.
[7] For League resolution of September 27, 1937, see *ibid.*, p. 506.

Canton at present has proved even more daring, barbarous and disastrous than any of the previous visitations by the Japanese aircraft. And it is certain that if the Japanese are allowed to go their own way, such air raids will yet be repeated over Canton and other cities with even more terrible loss of human life.

China once more appeals to the conscience of the world. It is the earnest wish of the Chinese Government that on humanitarian if on no other grounds the American Government and other Governments take such urgent and effective measures as will make Japan cease the wholesale slaughter of human beings by aerial bombardment.

Accept [etc.]   CHENGTING T. WANG

793.94116/46 : Telegram

The Ambassador in Japan (Grew) to the Secretary of State

TOKYO, June 4, 1938—noon.
[Received June 4—4:55 a. m.]

356. My British colleague [8] informs me that he has been instructed by his Government to concert with our French colleague and myself with a view to making parallel representations to the Japanese Government in protest against the recent allegedly indiscriminate bombing of Canton. The Minister for Foreign Affairs [9] is absent from Tokyo at the Ise Shrine but Craigie feels that the matter is too urgent to await possible action by myself and he therefore proposes to make his own representations to the Vice Minister for Foreign Affairs [10] this afternoon. I told him that I had as yet received no instructions but would inform him immediately if such instructions should be received. He believes that the British Ambassador in Washington [11] has already brought this matter to the attention of the Department. Craigie proposes to leave with the Vice Minister the following *aide-mémoire:*

"*Aide-mémoire.*—The recent air raids made upon Canton by Japanese airplanes and the large number of civilian casualties caused thereby have attracted considerable notice in the United Kingdom.

According to official reports based on careful inquiry which have reached His Majesty's Government in the United Kingdom, the raids of the 28th, 29th and 30th of May resulted in death to some 450 persons and injury to over 1,000; out of 60 or more sites bombed during these 3 days not 10 were of military importance and it would appear that less than one-third of the bombs were directed at airdromes, industrial plants and fairly open country.

---

[8] Sir Robert L. Craigie, British Ambassador in Japan.
[9] Gen. Kazushige Ugaki.
[10] Kensuke Horinouchi.
[11] Sir Ronald C. Lindsay.

In a statement issued to the press on the 1st June the Ministry of Foreign Affairs, after claiming that the Japanese air squadrons had not attacked the civilian population for whose safety they were ever solicitous, suggested that any loss of civilian life had resulted from the aimless firing of Chinese anti-aircraft guns: that this was not so is shown by the fact that foreign doctors in Canton state that less than one percent of the wounds suffered as a result of the raids were from anti-aircraft shell fragments.

The fact that the great majority of the objectives struck by bombs were without justifiable military importance combined with the heavy death roll of civilians has aroused great feeling in the United Kingdom which cannot help but affect good relations between Great Britain and Japan. It is therefore the earnest hope of his Majesty's Government that the Japanese Government will discontinue such indiscriminate bombing of Chinese towns.

At the same time His Majesty's Government desire to enter a protest against the flight of Japanese airplanes over the British Concession at Shameen".

Repeated to Shanghai for Hankow. GREW

793.94116/47 : Telegram

The Ambassador in Japan (Grew) to the Secretary of State

TOKYO, June 6, 1938—4 p. m.
[Received June 6—7 : 30 a. m.]

357. Our 356, June 4, noon, bombing of Canton. My British colleague has supplied me with the substance, as follows, of his telegram to London describing his conversation on June 4 with the Vice Minister for Foreign Affairs:

"I spoke to Vice Minister today as instructed, pointing out that in view of urgency of matter I had thought it best not to await return of Minister for Foreign Affairs to Tokyo. I made use of the information contained in the various telegrams from His Majesty's Consul General at Canton.

His Excellency inquired whether our representations were based on grounds of humanity? I replied in the affirmative, adding that they were also made in the interests of Anglo-Japanese relations, having regard to the most unfavorable impression made on British public opinion by the appalling loss of life amongst the civilian population.

Vice Minister stated that reports received from Japanese Navy indicated the utmost care had been taken to confine attacks to military objectives and that no Japanese planes had flown over Shameen. Nevertheless, in view of my statement that official reports we had received were based on personal investigation and not merely on accounts from Chinese sources, Vice Minister promised that careful inquiry would be made into the facts on which His Majesty's Government's representations had been based." [12]

Repeated to Shanghai for Hankow. GREW

---

[12] Further British representations were made on June 6 and 8.

793.94116/46 : Telegram

The Secretary of State to the Ambassador in Japan (*Grew*)

WASHINGTON, June 6, 1938—7 p. m.

185. Your 356, June 4, noon.

1. The British Ambassador here has approached the Department in regard to this matter. In reply the Department is taking note of the facts that the British approach to us was decided upon prior to the public statements made on June 3 by the Secretary and by the Acting Secretary [13] in which there were reiterated this nation's emphatic reprobation of ruthless bombing of unfortified localities and that the British have already taken action at Tokyo. The Department is also informing the British Ambassador that while we are in thorough accord with the views motivating the British *démarche* and with the humanitarian objectives of the British Government, we do not feel that any useful purpose would be served by repeating statements which this Government has just made and which have undoubtedly been made known to the Japanese Government.

2. The Department desires that you keep in mind the deep humanitarian interest of this Government and of the American people in the subject of bombings of civilian populations, and the Department authorizes you in your discretion, if and when an appropriate occasion should arise, to bring this interest to the attention of the Japanese Government.[14]

HULL

793.94116/50 : Telegram

The Ambassador in Japan (*Grew*) *to the Secretary of State*

TOKYO, June 8, 1938—11 a. m.
[Received June 7—10:41 p. m.]

364. Our 359, June 6, 6 p. m.[15] My French colleague now informs me that he has presented an *aide-mémoire* to the Japanese Government protesting vigorously against the bombing of the French hospital at Canton.

Copy by mail.

GREW

---

[13] For statement by the Acting Secretary of State, see *Foreign Relations,* Japan, 1931–1941, vol. I, p. 595.

[14] For Ambassador Grew's reply, see telegram No. 368, June 9, 7 p. m., *ibid.,* p. 596.

[15] Not printed.

793.94116/44

The Secretary of State to the Chinese Ambassador (C. T. Wang)

WASHINGTON, June 8, 1938.

MY DEAR MR. AMBASSADOR: I have noted with sympathetic concern the contents of your note of June 1, 1938, in regard to the aerial bombardment by Japanese aircraft of unfortified localities in China.

Public opinion in the United States regards as barbarous methods which are currently being used in the conduct of hostilities in the Far East and in Europe in the form of ruthless bombing of unfortified localities with the resultant slaughter of civilian populations. Several times during the past year, the Government of the United States has expressed the views of this country to that effect, and on June 3, 1938, this Government, taking cognizance of recent aerial bombings in China and in Spain, reiterated this nation's emphatic reprobation of such methods and acts.[16]

I assure you that this Government is deeply desirous that methods and acts of an inhumane character be avoided, and that it will continue to exert its influence in all practicable ways toward that end.

I am [etc.] CORDELL HULL

700.00116/354a : Telegram

The Secretary of State to the Ambassador in Japan (Grew)

WASHINGTON, June 11, 1938—2 p. m.

192. At the press conference on June 11 the Secretary, in reply to a question whether the Secretary could add anything to a story in the press that he was considering some plan in connection with bombings pointed toward discouraging the sale of American bombing planes abroad, stated that in reference to the bombing of civilian populations and the danger to Americans and American interests abroad we have put out repeated public statements condemning the bombing of civilian populations, that the present attitude is to maintain that position, to say to everybody that we do condemn the bombing of civilian populations or its material encouragement, and that we say that abroad and at home to the American people and especially to the manufacturers of bombing planes. In reply to a question whether the administration or the Government will frown upon all future sales of American airplanes that could be used for bombing purposes, the Secretary indicated that our attitude will discourage sales to regions where airplanes are being used to bomb civilian populations.

HULL

---

[16] See statement by the Acting Secretary of State, June 3, 1938, *Foreign Relations*, Japan, 1931–1941, vol. I, p. 595.

700.00116/354b : Telegram

The Secretary of State to the Ambassador in Japan (Grew)

WASHINGTON, June 12, 1938—2 p. m.

193.   Department's 192, June 11, 2 p. m.   During the past several weeks purchasing by Japan in this country of military planes has steadily increased.   On June 9 licenses were issued for the exportation of 14 planes.   Moreover, Japanese interests recently approached an American company with a view to the immediate purchase of an exceptionally large number of bombers and there has been every indication that further very large purchases by Japan of military aircraft, including bombers, have been in contemplation.   This situation is inconsistent with the abhorrence with which this Government and the American people view the current bombings of civilian populations and the attendant danger to Americans and American interests abroad, as consistently and repeatedly expressed by high officers of this Government.

HULL

700.00116/377

Memorandum by the Chief of the Office of Arms and Munitions Control (Green)

[WASHINGTON,] June 13, 1938.

In compliance with instructions received, I began this morning to get in touch with manufacturers and exporters of airplanes and aeronautical equipment to inform them orally of this Government's desire that they do not sell or export such articles to countries engaged in bombing civilian populations from the air.

There are 27 persons and companies registered as manufacturers of airplanes, airplane parts, etc.; 34 persons and companies registered as exporters of airplanes, airplane parts, etc.; and 86 persons and companies registered as both manufacturers and exporters of airplanes, airplane parts, etc.   Of these 148 persons and companies, the most important in this connection would appear to be the following:

[Here follow list and report on individual contacts.]

J[OSEPH] C. G[REEN]

793.94116/65 : Telegram

The Chargé in the Soviet Union (Kirk) to the Secretary of State

Moscow, June 21, 1938—noon.
[Received June 21—7:40 a. m.]

158. The principal Moscow papers today carry a Tass communiqué from Tokyo stating that a Soviet Chargé d'Affaires on June 17 made representations to the Japanese Vice Minister for Foreign Affairs regarding the "bombardment of unprotected peaceful populations and unprotected peaceful cities of China by the Japanese Army and especially by Japanese aviation". According to the communiqué, the bombardment of Canton resulting in "many thousands of victims including a huge number of women and children victims" was especially referred to in the representations and it was pointed out that "the operation of Japanese aviation in Canton is a completely unjustified act of brutal violence and that it has called forth a feeling of the deepest indignation in the public opinion of all civilized countries in the world including the Soviet Union". The Chargé d'Affaires expressed his Government's strong hope that such attacks against unprotected populations and peaceful towns in China will be stopped.

KIRK

700.00116/376

Memorandum of Conversation, by the Chief of the Office of Arms and Munitions Control (Green)

[WASHINGTON,] June 24, 1938.

Mr. Tswen-ling Tsui, Second Secretary of the Chinese Embassy, called at my office this morning. He said that the Ambassador, who was out of town, had requested him to call in order to ask my advice. He said that the Ambassador had just learned that the Japanese Government had closed a contract with an American manufacturer for 50 bombing planes. He wished to know whether I thought it would be wise for the Embassy to address a note to the Department, asking that everything possible be done to prevent the exportation of those planes.

I said that the Ambassador must be fully familiar with recent statements made by the Secretary and Mr. Welles [17] in regard to the bombing of civilian populations and the sale of bombing planes to countries engaging in that practice. I said that he had undoubtedly correctly inferred from those statements that we were doing everything possible to discourage sales and shipments which would be of material assistance in the bombing of civilian populations. I said further that, in

---

[17] For Mr. Welles' statement of June 3, see *Foreign Relations, Japan, 1931–1941,* vol. I, p. 595.

view of the many delicate questions involved and in view of the fact that we were already making every effort which we considered appropriate in the circumstances to carry out our announced policy, I did not believe that a note from the Chinese Ambassador on the subject of Japanese purchases would serve any useful purpose.

Mr. Tsui said that he would report our conversation to his Ambassador, and he expressed the opinion that, in view of what I had said, the Ambassador would decide not to take up the matter formally.

J[OSEPH] C. G[REEN]

793.94116/66: Telegram

The Chargé in the Soviet Union (Kirk) to the Secretary of State

Moscow, June 27, 1938—4 p. m.
[Received June 27—11:46 a. m.]

164. My telegram 158, June 21, noon. A foreign newspaper report received here confirmed by the local Domei correspondent states that the Soviet protest was rejected by the Japanese Foreign Office which called the attention of the Soviet Chargé d'Affaires to the continued assistance given to China by Soviet aviation. The Japanese Embassy here is noncommittal as to truth of this report.

KIRK

793.94116/70: Telegram

The Ambassador in Japan (Grew) to the Secretary of State

TOKYO, June 28, 1938—9 p. m.
[Received June 28—noon.]

424. 1. My British colleague informs me that the Minister for Foreign Affairs has expressed appreciation of the facts and figures and direct observations of the British Consul General in Canton concerning the indiscriminate bombing of that city which Craigie has periodically brought to the Minister's attention. The Ambassador thinks that the true facts were obscured here and that the precise information which he has furnished to the Foreign Minister has resulted in more carefully controlled bombing operations.

2. In this connection Debuchi [18] told me 2 days ago that the Foreign Minister had informed some 200 members of the House of Peers of the form and manner in which our representations concerning the bombing of Canton had been made (see our 368, June 9, 7 p. m.[19]) and that our procedure had created a very favorable impression. Ob-

[18] Katsuji Debuchi, former Japanese Ambassador in the United States.
[19] *Foreign Relations*, Japan, 1931–1941, vol. I, p. 596.

viously the only proper criterion of the value of such procedure lies in the results. We gather from widespread comments that our approach was listened to with considerable respect and that a liaison officer has been sent out to exert some form of greater control of future bombing operations.

Repeated to Shanghai for Hankow.

GREW

793.94116/75 : Telegram

The Ambassador in Italy (Phillips) to the Secretary of State

ROME, July 1, 1938—6 p. m.
[Received July 1—1 : 20 p. m.]

164. The *Osservatore Romana* announced today that the Apostolic delegate at Tokyo had been directed to make representations to the Japanese Government urging that the Japanese Army use every effort to avoid useless bombardments of open cities. It adds that the Japanese Foreign Minister has given assurances that all means permitted by military developments will be used to guarantee the safety of noncombatant civilians adding that any proposals which may be of value in this connection will be willingly considered.

PHILLIPS

700.00116/407

Memorandum of Conversation, by the Assistant Chief of the Office of Arms and Munitions Control (Yost)

[WASHINGTON,] July 26, 1938.

Mr. Leighton Rogers, President of the Aeronautical Chamber of Commerce, called this afternoon to discuss further the steps taken by his organization to prevent the export of aircraft and aircraft parts to countries engaged in the bombing of civilian populations.

Mr. Rogers said that he believed that about ninety-five percent of the companies in the industry were prepared to cooperate with the Department in carrying out the policy voiced by the Secretary on June 11.[20] He said that a few manufacturers, however, would probably desire to continue to export to Japan small quantities of aircraft engines, propellers, and other parts to be used as replacements on commercial airlines in Japan which these companies had been supplying over a long period of years. Mr. Rogers expressed the hope that the Department would see fit for the present not to protest against small shipments of replacement parts which were obviously to be used on commercial airlines only.

---

[20] See telegram No. 192, June 11, 2 p. m., to the Ambassador in Japan, p. 617.

I replied that the Department could not, of course, prevent exports of aircraft and aircraft parts to Japan and that it limited itself to reiterating to persons who made application for export licenses the terms of the Secretary's statement of June 11 and the Department's letter of July 1.[21]   I added that we were currently issuing licenses for very small quantities of replacement parts and would not be unduly alarmed if an occasional application for such a license were presented to us, but that, if such shipments should increase in ensuing months, it would, of course, give rise to the presumption that the industry was not observing the Secretary's policy.

C[HARLES] W. Y[OST]

894.24/327

Memorandum of Conversation, by the Secretary of State

[WASHINGTON,] August 27, 1938.

The Chinese Ambassador called on his own request.   He said he desired to thank this Government for its protest to Japan against the destruction of a passenger plane and a number of lives.[22]   He handed me the attached copy of a message [23] received by the Chinese Embassy as to the facts.

The Ambassador then brought up the question of the Sino-Japanese situation and, after expressing his appreciation of what this Government has been doing, especially in relation to the purchase of silver, he said he believed this country was now in a state of mind and that the time was ripe for further action along the lines of restraining shipments of important materials, as well as munitions, to Japan, and he hoped this Government would feel justified in taking up the matter. I said that, of course, I could make no commitments whatever in regard to this; that I would keep in mind what he said and bring it to the attention of my associates, especially in the Far Eastern Division.   I reminded him that, of course, shipments of most of our aeronautical supplies to Japan have ceased except those under contract.   He seemed thoroughly to understand this.   I inquired what would be the state of mind of other important governments abroad, such as those in Europe, in regard to his suggestion.   He said he had no information of a recent nature but that he would be glad to see our Government take the matter up with the British and other governments.   I suggested that

---

[21] For text of letter, see *Foreign Relations, Japan, 1931–1941*, vol. II, p. 201.   The Secretary had submitted draft of letter on June 16 to President Roosevelt for approval; the following notation was made by the President: "CH OK FDR". (700.00116/375)

[22] See press release of August 26, *ibid.*, vol. I, p. 619.

[23] Not printed.

those governments are very much preoccupied during present weeks with the Czechoslovak and Spanish situations, and that in any event I would suggest that his Government might more appropriately perhaps take the matter up through its ambassadors and other representatives at European capitals. He said that might be well enough.

He then inquired when the President would return, and I replied that he would be back on Tuesday morning next. He said he would be glad if the State Department would make an engagement for him to see the President; that he desired to bring up this same important point with him. I replied that I would be glad to confer with the Protocol officials, or he could do so as he preferred. He said that he would be glad to see them himself.

In reply to my question, the Ambassador stated that it would be some time yet before Hankow would be occupied by the Japanese.

C[ORDELL] H[ULL]

793.94116/97 : Telegram

The Ambassador in Japan (Grew) to the Secretary of State

TOKYO, September 9, 1938—5 p. m.
[Received September 9—7 a. m.]

593. Our 590, September 8, 11 p. m.,[24] paragraph 5, proposals for the avoidance of bombing civilian populations. My British colleague has given me the following:

"In the British view the fundamental principles might provisionally be defined as follows: in order that bombing may be legitimate there must at least be: (*a*) an objective recognized as legitimate, and (*b*) an intention to attack that objective and not some other objective, and (*c*) a reasonable prospect that any bombs dropped will in fact hit the objective.

Correspondingly, the following at least should be definitely inadmissible: (*a*) the intentional bombing of civilian populations, (*b*) the plea that the presence of a legitimate objective in the neighborhood of a civilian center justifies general bombing of the area, even when there may be a hope of hitting that objective *inter alia*, and (*c*) a general and indiscriminate release of bombs even with the hope that they may hit a suspected legitimate objective, when it is not possible at the time to distinguish and identify that objective with certainty, or alternately when there is no reasonable expectation that the damage done will be restricted to the military objective.

In connection with (*c*) in preceding paragraph, an antiaircraft gun in the British viewpoint constitutes so small a target that it is normally only at point blank range and from a very low altitude that anyone could identify it with certainty and bomb it with a reasonable prospect of hitting it."

GREW

---

[24] *Ante*, p. 280.

894.24/348

*The Counselor of the Department of State (Moore) to Representative
George H. Tinkham, of Massachusetts*

WASHINGTON, September 20, 1938.

MY DEAR MR. TINKHAM: I have your letter of September 9, 1938 [25]
in which you quote two questions asked by a resident of your congressional district in regard to the export of war materials to Japan.

The first question is "Could the United States Government in any
way without the consent of Congress forbid the export to Japan of all
war material?". My understanding is that your constituent is alluding to arms, ammunition, and implements of war as referred to in
Section 1 of the Neutrality Act.[26] The answer to the question, in that
case, is that the Government is not authorized to forbid the export
to any country of such articles, except when the President issues a
proclamation in accordance with the provisions of that section. If
your constituent is referring to commodities other than arms, ammunition, or implements of war, the answer is that this Government has
no statutory authority to restrict the export of such commodities to
any foreign country.

The second question is " . . . [27] why could not the State Department
request the cessation of all such exports (as it has done in regard to
bombing planes) and then publish widely in the Press the names of all
those who disregard the request?". In answering this question it may
be stated that the Department's action in urging the manufacturers
and exporters in this country of airplanes and aeronautical equipment
not to sell or export their products to countries whose armed forces
are engaged in the bombing of the civilian population from the air
was based upon this country's general and unreserved condemnation,
to which the Secretary has given expression repeatedly in public
utterances, of that type of activity. Only in such exceptional cases
does the Department take action of that advisory character.

Sincerely yours,

R. WALTON MOORE

894.24/452

The British Embassy to the Department of State

AIDE-MÉMOIRE

On October 17th the Chinese Ambassador in London, acting on
instructions, requested that His Majesty's Government should implement their commitments under relevant League of Nations Resolu-

---

[25] Not printed.
[26] 50 Stat. 121.
[27] Omission indicated in the original.

tions by immediate and positive action against Japan. They might declare an embargo on the export of arms and raw materials, or they might apply pressure to that same end on manufacturers particularly in regard to aeroplanes, steel and oil. The Ambassador said that some time ago the United States Government had made known its attitude that aeroplanes should not be sold to Japan; and the Department of Commerce had discouraged traders from giving credit. The effect of these measures had been appreciable, and it was understood that further administrative steps of a similar nature were in contemplation. The Ambassador hoped that it might be possible for His Majesty's Government to take parallel action to the same purpose in consultation with the United States Government.

It would be greatly appreciated if His Majesty's Government could be furnished with details regarding the actions or intentions of the United States Government in the directions mentioned by the Chinese Ambassador in London.

WASHINGTON, October 20, 1938.

894.24/452

The Department of State to the British Embassy

AIDE-MÉMOIRE

Reference is made to the British Embassy's *aide-mémoire* of October 20, 1938, in regard to an approach made to the British Government by the Chinese Ambassador at London.

With regard to the reference in the *aide-mémoire* to this Government's attitude toward the sale of airplanes and to the action of the Department of Commerce in discouraging credits, the facts are as follows:

On June 11 the Secretary of State made a statement definitely condemning the bombing of civilian populations from the air. The Department of State has brought that statement to the attention of manufacturers and exporters of airplanes or aeronautical equipment and has informed those manufacturers and exporters that this Government is strongly opposed to the sale of airplanes or aeronautical equipment which would materially aid or encourage the bombing of civilian populations from the air in any countries in any part of the world and that the Department would with great regret issue any licenses authorizing exportation, direct or indirect, of any aircraft, aircraft armament, aircraft engines, aircraft parts, aircraft accessories, aerial bombs or torpedoes to countries the armed forces of which are making use of airplanes for attack upon civilian populations.

In June last the Department of Commerce issued a circular to its district offices in which the belief was expressed that, in view of the increasing severity with which exchange restrictions in Japan were being enforced, it appeared advisable that exporters in the United States should have a confirmed irrevocable letter of credit in their hands before accepting orders for shipments to Japan.

With regard to the general attitude of this Government toward the present conflict in the Far East, this Government has, since the commencement of that conflict, consistently supported in appropriate and practicable ways principles of policy and objectives which it believes should be controlling in relations between states, and it is continuing to give study to appropriate ways and means calculated to obtain respect for and observance of those principles and objectives.

It is assumed that the British Government will inform this Government as to steps likely to be of interest to this Government which the British Government has taken or may have under contemplation in the directions mentioned in the British Embassy's *aide-mémoire* of October 20.

WASHINGTON, November 9, 1938.

REPRESENTATIONS TO THE JAPANESE GOVERNMENT WITH RESPECT TO THE INTEGRITY OF THE CHINESE MARITIME CUSTOMS AND SALT REVENUE ADMINISTRATIONS [28]

693.002/437 : Telegram

The Secretary of State to the Ambassador in Japan (Grew)

WASHINGTON, January 4, 1938—6 p. m.

2. Your 699, December 31, 7 p. m.[29] After giving careful consideration to the explanation and comment contained in your telegram under reference and while appreciating the motives which prompt the British to put forward their proposal, we do not feel that we can actively lend our support to that proposal. We are disinclined to participate in joint discussions in Tokyo which, although limited only to "general principles governing an arrangement" might in effect commit us to support of a specific plan which we would be expected to join in persuading the Chinese to accept. We feel that it is preferable that both you and Gauss [30] continue to exert every effort, through approaches and informal discussions in Tokyo and Shanghai respectively, to convince the Japanese that in the interest of all con-

[28] Continued from *Foreign Relations*, 1937, vol. III, pp. 848–915; see also *Foreign Relations*, Japan, 1931–1941, vol. I, pp. 735 ff.
[29] *Foreign Relations*, 1937, vol. III, p. 913.
[30] Clarence E. Gauss, Consul General at Shanghai.

cerned the integrity of the customs, both with regard to administration and revenues, should be respected.

Having in mind the possibility that control of the Chinese customs organization in areas occupied by Japanese forces may be handed over to some professedly independent régime for whose actions the Japanese authorities might disclaim responsibility, the Department is of the opinion that it is highly important that you endeavor to obtain the assurances mentioned in its 339, December 12, 3 p. m.[31] We feel that you would be warranted in requesting that the Japanese authorities give those assurances before they take further steps to pursue to a conclusion the negotiations now in progress at Shanghai with Chinese Customs officials.

Repeated to Shanghai and Hankow.

HULL

693.002/438 : Telegram

The Consul General at Shanghai (Gauss) to the Secretary of State

SHANGHAI, January 9, 1938—11 a. m.
[Received 7:40 p. m.]

45. Last evening Sir Frederick Maze, the Inspector General of Customs, sent me with a covering letter a strictly confidential statement which he has prepared and forwarded also to the French Ambassador and the British Chargé here. While the statement is somewhat involved in parts, the essential features I summarize below:

The Inspector General indicates that should the situation continue along present lines he would remain at his post until compelled by *force majeure* to leave when if possible he would remove the Inspectorate elsewhere. He believes, however, that he will soon be confronted with the situation of a provisional government claiming jurisdiction in China and will be face to face with refusing to transfer his allegiance to that regime in which case he would doubtless be succeeded by a Japanese. However, should the powers desire for the purpose of preserving the integrity of the service that he remain temporarily, he would do so and extend limited recognition to the provisional régime pending a final settlement of Sino-Japanese affairs. In this case the powers should attempt to persuade the Chinese Government to offer no objection to that course and the powers would presumably make representations however to the *de facto* régime in regard to their treaty rights and controversial matters such as preferential duty treatment. If the powers were not prepared to take the outlined action the Inspector General might be forced to resign. If the powers wish the inspectorate and the various and great prerogatives so closely con-

---

[31] *Foreign Relations*, 1937, vol. III, p. 900.

nected with the customs to be preserved, they should be prepared to assume the attitude of 1911 when the Inspector General was treated not only as a servant of the Chinese Government but as a trustee of foreign interests.

The Inspector General foresees the early establishment of the provisional régime in Shanghai and considers that the powers should intimate to him the course of action he should follow. He expressed the hope that I would "continue to exercise your valuable influence in favor of the integrity of the service and the so-called inspectorate system". I shall not reply unless otherwise instructed.[32] I feel that the present Inspector General is inclined too much to seek the instructions and support of the three interested powers with reference both to the Chinese Government and the Japanese. It is probable however, that he will have to face the situation outlined under which a provisional Chinese government set up by the Japanese will demand his adherence.

Repeated to Hankow and Peiping.

GAUSS

693.002/439 : Telegram

The Consul General at Shanghai (Gauss) to the Secretary of State

SHANGHAI, January 9, 1938—5 p. m.
[Received January 9—4 : 10 p. m.]

46. In conversation this noon with the Japanese Consul General concerning the customs situation at Shanghai, he told me that he expects instructions from Tokyo within a few days and will then be in a position to resume conversations. He referred to a brief conversation we had held a week ago when he had mentioned to me (rather casually) that it was the Japanese idea here that all revenues should be deposited in the Yokohama Specie Bank and the payment of all loan and indemnity quotas suspended until the cessation of hostilities as their payment regularly might sustain Chinese credit abroad. He recalled that I had promptly and emphatically dismissed any such idea as entirely unacceptable and he later so reported to Tokyo recommending that the quotas be paid regularly as due. He said he hoped his instructions would permit this. I commented that I was interested to know this but that we are interested not only in loan and indemnity payments but in the integrity of the customs and we desire assurances on a number of important points which have been made known to his Foreign Office by the Ambassador at Tokyo and which I again outlined briefly on the basis of the Department's 393

---

[32] Notation by Walter A. Adams, of the Division of Far Eastern Affairs: "Decided after discussion not to instruct Gauss to reply to Inspector."

[*339?*] of December 12, 3 p. m.[33] to paragraph 2. My colleague seemed to be of the opinion that the Shanghai Customs situation might find its solution in the extension to include Shanghai of the jurisdiction of the provisional government at Peiping. His remarks this noon on this and other matters suggest to me that he expects the present unsettled situation at Shanghai to continue for some time and that it is not the present intention to include Shanghai under the puppet regime set up for North China.

Repeated to Hankow and Tokyo.

GAUSS

693.002/440 : Telegram

The Ambassador in Japan (Grew) to the Secretary of State

TOKYO, January 10, 1938—11 a. m.
[Received January 10—6 : 30 a. m.]

14. Department's 390, December 31, 5 p. m.,[34] disregard of customs requirements for Japanese goods and vessels.

I took this matter up informally with the Minister for Foreign Affairs [35] in the course of conversation on other matters this morning. The Minister said that this question was now under discussion and it is hoped that some solution will shortly be found. The problem he said is to separate incoming war supplies for the Japanese forces from other goods. I pointed out the damaging effect upon the Customs Administration of the present procedure. I took occasion once again to repeat to the Minister that a disruption of the Chinese customs service and inability of the customs to meet foreign loan and indemnity quotas would bring most unfortunate consequences to all concerned. Hirota said that the matter is now under discussion and he implied, altogether without specific assurances, that the final result would be entirely satisfactory to American interests.

Repeated to Shanghai.

GREW

693.002/441 : Telegram

The Consul General at Shanghai (Gauss) to the Secretary of State

SHANGHAI, January 10, 1938—noon.
[Received 4 : 11 p. m.]

48. Reference my telegram No. 45, January 9, 11 a. m. At a meeting this morning the British Chargé d'Affaires said that his instructions had been to advise the Inspector General to keep his Embassy

---

[33] *Foreign Relations*, 1937, vol. III, p. 900.
[34] *Ibid.*, p. 913.
[35] Koki Hirota.

fully informed and follow its advice and the Embassy would give him such support as possible. French Ambassador has no instructions but is seeking them along similar lines. Both diplomatic representatives are informing their Governments of the purport of the statement communicated to you by my No. 45.

Repeated to Hankow and Peiping.

GAUSS

693.002/445 : Telegram

The Ambassador in China (Johnson) to the Secretary of State

HANKOW, January 11, 1938—11 a. m.
[Received 1 : 37 p. m.]

22. Shanghai's 45, January 9, 11 a. m., and 48, January 10, noon. I have in various ways refrained from offering any advice to the Chinese Government as to what it should do about the Customs Administration, confining myself on such occasions as have offered to the statement that it is our hope that the integrity of the Customs Administration may be preserved. On one occasion Minister for Foreign Affairs [36] volunteered to me the information that, in reply to representations made by the British Ambassador that Sir Frederick Maze be given authority to reach some settlement with the Japanese which might subsequently be submitted to the Chinese Government for its approval, he had stated that Chinese Government was unwilling to relinquish its right to examine and approve any plan prior to its acceptance. It is my belief that Chinese Government will be unwilling to give its official approval to any plan which deprives it of control over Customs Administration and of customs fund.

Repeated to Peiping and Shanghai. Peiping please repeat to Tokyo.

JOHNSON

693.002/450 : Telegram

The Consul General at Shanghai (Gauss) to the Secretary of State

SHANGHAI, January 14, 1938—7 p. m.
[Received January 14—4 : 45 p. m.]

78. Minister of Finance [37] has telegraphed Inspector General of Customs expressing appreciation of efforts of the commissioners concerned in maintaining the *status quo* of the Tientsin and Chinwangtao customs but stating that, (1), no orders should be accepted from and no agreement of any kind should be negotiated and concluded with

---

[36] Wang Chung-hui.
[37] H. H. Kung.

the bogus government; (2), no changes should be made in the present customs system rules and regulations; (3), present tariffs should not be revised without authority, these three conditions being the minimum that should be held in maintaining the Customs Administration and under no circumstances be compromised. Commissioners of Customs to be instructed accordingly.

2. Inspector General has replied that the commissioners are being instructed, that no written agreement whatever has been made with the bogus government, that in order to maintain sovereign rights and credit at home and abroad by preserving the integrity of the service as the Government's agents throughout China, et cetera, it may become advisable at some ports to yield to *force majeure* in non-essentials, and that to stimulate trade and help revive economic conditions seriously upset by hostilities, the Inspector General may later submit some tariff proposals for approval of the Government.

Repeated to Hankow and Peiping.

GAUSS

693.002/451 : Telegram

The Ambassador in Japan (Grew) to the Secretary of State

TOKYO, January 17, 1938—3 p. m.
[Received January 17—7 a. m.]

36. Department's 6, January 11, 7 p. m.,[38] importation of kerosene to China from Japan duty free and placed on the market.

Full representations were made by me to the Minister for Foreign Affairs this morning in which I emphasized the discriminatory character of the importation as well as the damaging effect upon the Customs Administration. I pointed out that this was another flagrant act of discrimination inconsistent with the repeated assurances of the Japanese Government and stated that my Government expects the Japanese Government to take appropriate and prompt steps to assure the carrying out of those assurances. The Minister said that he would promptly take the matter up with the proper authorities.

I previously discussed the matter with my British colleague who stated that the question had been taken up at Tientsin with the local authorities on January 11th and that he would find an opportunity to refer to the question orally here.

Repeated to Peiping for Tientsin and Shanghai.

GREW

---

[38] *Foreign Relations*, Japan, 1931–1941, vol. I, p. 737.

693.002/453 : Telegram

The Consul General at Shanghai (Gauss) to the Secretary of State

SHANGHAI, January 20, 1938—6 p. m.
[Received 11 p. m.]

113. I learn that a representative of the Japanese Consul General today informed the Commissioner of Customs that the customs arrangements for Shanghai are to be as follows:

Deposit of revenues in Yokohama Specie Bank in the name of the Commissioner, authorization for payment of cost of collection including consideration of a quota for cost of Inspectorate General, and authorization to meet Shanghai quota of foreign loan and indemnity payments such quota to be established in consultation with the customs. Balance of revenue to remain in the account in anticipation of later organization of a regional government in this area. Commissioner replied that he must consult the Inspector General. Developments will be reported.

Sent to the Department, repeated to Tokyo, Hankow and Peiping.

GAUSS

693.002/452 : Telegram

The Consul General at Shanghai (Gauss) to the Secretary of State

SHANGHAI, January 20, 1938—7 p. m.
[Received 9 : 15 p. m.]

114. Reference my 45, January 9, 11 a. m., and 48, January 10, noon. British Chargé d'Affaires has replied to Inspector General to the effect that it is not possible to give advice beforehand on hypothetical situations, that British Government are doing their utmost by representations at Tokyo to prevent creation of a separate tariff in North China or any other action which would disrupt Customs Administration, that in their view if these efforts are unsuccessful the Inspector General must decide what measures are essential to secure integrity of the Administration in its international form and the service of foreign loans and indemnity, that they also regard deposit of revenues in a neutral bank as most important, that difficulty of the position of Inspector General is, however, recognized and he is assured that provided he keeps Embassy informed and is guided by its advice the British Government will support him to the best of their ability in any difficulties which may supervene and they will continue to impress upon Kung the necessity of taking a realistic view of the situation and will endeavor to secure ultimate acceptance by Chinese of any arrangement finally reached. French Ambassador will reply along somewhat similar lines.

I learn from a confidential source that the Japanese have insisted that all foreign customs staff at Tsingtao shall be Japanese and that the Inspectorate General has acquiesced; also that the Japanese insist that the Commissioner at Chefoo shall be a Japanese and that this requirement also will probably be met.

Repeated to Hankow and Peiping.

GAUSS

693.002/454 : Telegram

The Consul General of Shanghai (Gauss) to the Secretary of State

SHANGHAI, January 23, 1938—1 p. m.
[Received January 23—8:20 a. m.]

126. Reference my 113, January 20, 6 p. m., regarding customs. Inspector General of Customs has now communicated to the British and French diplomatic representatives and to me a letter from the Commissioner of Customs outlining the Japanese proposals, as reported in my 113. Inspector General thinks these proposals if officially confirmed by the Japanese and accepted by the Chinese Government, and if scrupulously observed, would protect foreign obligations and provide for financial upkeep of the service but he questions whether they will prove acceptable to the Chinese Government as the Shanghai revenue which is normally about 50% of the total for all China would be placed in a bank functioning under Japanese law and the arrangement for Shanghai might in due course be extended to most if not all principal ports of China and thus give Japan control over funds which in the past have served Chinese domestic loans and administrative expenses. He suggests that the holding of such balances by Japan might facilitate their diversion toward payment of the large unsecured and inadequately secured Chinese debts to Japan. He also recalls that the question of custodian banks for customs revenues has long been the subject of international discussions, the last occasion being at the Tariff Conference in 1926 when Japanese made proposals which would have given them predominant positions through their interest in unsecured debts. However, he considers the proposals offer a basis of discussion and they will in due course be submitted to the Chinese Government. Meanwhile he desires that our respective governments be informed.

Repeated to Tokyo, Hankow and Peiping.

GAUSS

693.002/516

The Chinese Embassy to the Department of State

The spokesman of the Ministry of Finance of the Chinese Government issued on January 24, 1938, the following statement in regard to the reported revision of tariff in North China:

"The announcement made by the Peiping puppet regime that modified tariff will be enforced in North China beginning from tomorrow is the most serious matter which, it is hoped, will receive the immediate attention of the world powers whose interests, besides China's, are directly menaced. For many years, the Customs Administration has been responsible for the payment of China's foreign obligations secured on the customs revenue. The Japanese invasion of Manchuria in 1931 has already caused serious impairment of the administrative integrity of the Chinese customs service. Notwithstanding the promise Japan made to pay from the revenue collected in Manchuria certain quotas for the payment of foreign obligations, she has not carried it out. Japan is now trying to disrupt the Chinese customs service entirely by instigating the Peiping puppet regime to modify the tariff. This move would not only destroy the integrity of the Chinese national fiscal administration, but also seriously jeopardize the interests of the foreign governments and bond-holders of all nationalities. The tariff changes made by the Peiping puppets are reported to involve considerable reductions, but obviously they are made in favor of the Japanese commodities particularly. Once the action of making such tariff changes in China by illegal organizations is not challenged, there will be little doubt that the Japanese have in their hands the powerful weapon to keep the commodities from other countries out of that part of China which is under the Japanese influence. The Ministry of Finance has wired instructions to the Customs Inspectorate General not to recognize the illegal change of tariff in North China."

WASHINGTON, January 24, 1938.

693.002/467 : Telegram

The Consul General at Shanghai (Gauss) to the Secretary of State

SHANGHAI, January 26, 1938—1 p. m.
[Received 8 : 32 p. m.]

140. Reference my No. 132, January 24, 8 p. m.[39] Inspector General of Customs last evening sent me copy of a telegram he said he had sent to the Minister of Finance reading in substance as follows:

"The Inspector General begs to suggest that with a view to encouraging trade and helping to restore the economic life of the country the Government should authorize him to reintroduce the 1931 tariff with some slight modifications. This should neutralize action of

---

[39] Not printed.

bogus government in north and by insuring equality of treatment for merchants of all nations would be welcomed by foreign officials and merchants alike, who have always maintained that present tariff rates are too high. Foreign powers mainly interested in equality of treatment and as reduction of rates is obviously to the advantage of their nationals they are unlikely to oppose such reduction. If Government declines to adopt Inspector General's suggestion trade will be diverted from Shanghai and other ports to Tientsin and Tsing-tao from whence goods will penetrate by rail and by road through all occupied areas to the detriment of the Government's prestige and expectations."

2. At a meeting this morning with the French and British diplomatic representatives the latter told us that the foregoing message has actually not been sent as he desires first to consult London and if his Government is prepared to support the suggestion he wishes to give such support at the time the suggestion is presented. Neither he nor French Ambassador believes that the Minister of Finance will be fully prepared to approve suggestion. They both expressed the opinion that further representations should be made at Toyko in opposition to tariff changes by the Peiping régime or Japanese military.

Repeated to Tokyo, Hankow and Peiping.

GAUSS

693.002/468 : Telegram

The Consul General at Shanghai (Gauss) to the Secretary of State

SHANGHAI, January 26, 1938—7 p. m.
[Received 8 : 20 p. m.]

146. Reference my 126, January 23, 1 p. m., regarding Shanghai customs. At a meeting with French Ambassador and British Chargé d'Affaires this morning the latter stated British view on Japanese proposals substantially as follows:

(1) That every effort should be made to resist deposit in Yokohama Specie Bank but he has authority to give way in the last resort at any time on condition that revenues so deposited in that bank be controlled by a board of officials in which case officials should be in joint names of the Inspector General and board of officials and not in name of Commissioner of Customs. In response to my inquiry it was stated that the proposed board of officials would be nominated by interested governments.

(2) Withdrawals for expenses should include appropriate share for expenses of Inspector General.

(3) Quotas should be determined not by Japanese in consultation with customs but by representatives of interested powers including Japan in consultation with customs or by the proposed board of officials if that system is adopted. Quotas should be subject to fre-

quent and regular revision, his suggestion being review every month on basis of revenue collected for previous 2 or 3 months.

(4) Domestic loans should continue to be serviced from any customs surplus but if Japanese will not agree he is authorized not to insist but should do all he can to insure that any surplus is held in suspense account definitely earmarked for domestic loans.

2. The British earnestly desire however that we should all insist that foreign loan and indemnity quotas shall be deposited directly into the neutral bank or banks and only the excess revenue go into Yokohama Specie Bank if necessary. British Chargé d'Affaires agrees.

3. Japanese authorities have not yet informed or discussed proposals with any of the interested foreign representatives.

Repeated to Tokyo, Hankow, and Peiping.

GAUSS

693.002/469 : Telegram

The Consul General at Shanghai (Gauss) to the Secretary of State

SHANGHAI, January 27, 1938—3 p. m.
[Received January 27—12 : 20 p. m.]

152. Reference my No. 140, January 26, 1 p. m. British Chargé d'Affaires informs me today that the telegram from the Inspector General to the Minister of Finance has now gone forward. He has not stated whether he is indorsing the proposal.

Repeated to Hankow, Peiping and Tokyo.

GAUSS

693.002/471 : Telegram

The Consul General at Shanghai (Gauss) to the Secretary of State

SHANGHAI, January 28, 1938—9 p. m.
[Received January 28—7 : 58 p. m.]

166. Reference my 132, January 24, 8 p. m.,[40] 140, January 26, 1 p. m. and 155 [*152*], January 27, 7 [*3*] p. m., regarding customs. British Chargé d'Affaires has received instructions that his Foreign Office is not prepared to advise Commissioner of Customs at Tientsin as to attitude he should adopt to the new tariff and Commissioner must decide for himself whether or not the circumstances amount to *force majeure;* that he should urge the Minister of Finance to accept proposals of Inspector General of Customs regarding 1931 tariff ; and that he should protest in strong terms to Japanese authorities in North China against proposed alteration of the tariff basing his protest on

---

[40] Not printed.

treaty right to a uniform national tariff at all ports and consequent illegality of this action by a local authority whether recognized or not. He adds that a protest is being made at Tokyo.

Repeated Shanghai, Tokyo, Hankow and Peiping.

GAUSS

693.002/468 : Telegram

The Secretary of State to the Consul General at Shanghai (Gauss)

WASHINGTON, January 29, 1938—4 p. m.

86. Your 146, January 26, 7 p. m. With regard to the British views, the Department perceives no objection in general to your lending such support to those views as you deem appropriate and advisable, with the understanding of course that we are not prepared to commit ourselves to an arrangement which calls for the nomination by the American Government of an official or officials on the proposed board; but it would not appear to be advisable to press the British views to the point of jeopardizing discussions or negotiations looking toward the adoption of an arrangement on the basis of the Japanese proposals.

The Department has confidence that you, bearing in mind its various instructions on the subject, will be able to exert your influence to the end that a settlement may be reached which in so far as possible respects our position with regard to preservation of the integrity of the customs and the safeguarding of the customs revenues, with special reference to the servicing of foreign loan and indemnity quotas.

HULL

693.002/472 : Telegram

The Consul General at Shanghai (Gauss) to the Secretary of State

SHANGHAI, January 29, 1938—4 p. m.
[Received January 29—3 : 43 p. m.]

170. I discussed Shanghai customs question this morning with Japanese Consul General who confirmed the conversation with the customs on lines reported in my No. 113, January 20, 6 p. m. and stated he "hopes" after Shanghai question is settled arrangements will be made release loan and indemnity quotas at Tientsin but adds he has no jurisdiction in that matter. He has no intention of submitting Shanghai arrangements to interested foreign representatives here before making them effective. He believes loan and indemnity quotas for Shanghai should be fixed for a fairly long period—6 months or a year—and not be subject to frequent revision. He asserts he cannot agree to deposit of revenues in any other than Yokohama Specie Bank

and considers assurance of payment of foreign loan and indemnity quotas should satisfy foreign interests. I emphasized the American interest in the integrity of the customs and again outlined the assurances desired by the American Government.

2. I am inclined to believe that if pressed the Japanese may ultimately agree to periodic transfer of foreign loan and indemnity quotas to foreign banks after they have first been deposited in the Japanese bank.

Repeated to Tokyo, Hankow, and Peiping.

GAUSS

693.002/458 : Telegram

The Secretary of State to the Ambassador in Japan (Grew)

WASHINGTON, January 30, 1938—1 p. m.

31. Reference Shanghai's 132, January 24, 8 p. m., and Peiping's 48, January 22, 3 p. m.[41] (forwarded to you by mail), which lists some of the reductions in tariff rates and quotes an announcement by the "Provisional Government of China."

1. The Department is of the opinion that the matter under reference is one in regard to which the principally interested powers will wish to take action. The Department desires therefore that you consult with your principally interested colleagues, especially your British colleague, and when you have ascertained that one or more of them are prepared to make representations in regard to the matter, that you hand the Japanese Government a note reading substantially as follows:

"The American Government has from time to time since the outbreak of the present conflict in China made known to the Japanese Government its very real interests in the preservation of the integrity of the Chinese customs and in the safeguarding of the customs revenues. The American Government has repeatedly urged that no action be taken or countenanced by the Japanese authorities which might undermine the authority of the customs administration, disrupt the customs service, or impair the ability of the Customs to continue the service of foreign loan and indemnity quotas and to meet administrative expenses. This Government has expressed a desire to receive from the Japanese Government certain assurances, including an assurance with regard to the continuance of existing custom tariffs and procedure.

The American Government has recently received information from its representatives in China to the effect that a provisional regime in Peiping has caused a revision to be made of Chinese customs rates on certain articles entering into the foreign export and import trade of North China. This Government, regarding the Government of China as the only authority which can legally cause a revision to be made in the Chinese customs tariff, is constrained to invite the attention of the

---

[41] Neither printed.

Japanese Government to this arbitrary and illegal assumption of authority by the provisional regime in Peiping, and to point out that the action of the provisional regime may have a seriously adverse effect upon the integrity of the Chinese Customs, with regard both to administration and to revenues, and that the revision of rates does violence to the principle of a uniform Chinese tariff at all ports.

The Japanese Government shares with the American Government and with other Governments a long established and well recognized interest in the integrity of the Chinese Customs administration, and the American Government has expressed its confident belief that the Japanese Government reciprocates the earnest desire of the American Government that the integrity of the Chinese Customs be respected. The action of the provisional regime at Peiping in revising rates of duty seriously threatens the integrity of the Customs. For the creation and the acts of the provisional regime the Japanese Government has an inescapable responsibility; and when those acts are of a character, as in the case of the revision of the rates of duty, which affect the interests of foreign governments, it is to the Japanese Government that those governments must address their representations.

The American Government is impelled, therefore, to state to the Japanese Government that it perceives no legality or legitimacy in the assumption of authority by the provisional regime, and that it profoundly regrets that the Japanese Government has not exercised that restraining influence which it is in position to exercise upon the authorities of the provisional regime. In the light of the existing situation, the American Government will be compelled to consider the Japanese Government responsible for any adverse effects which a revision of the rates may have upon American rights and interests, including therein trade with China and the servicing from customs revenues of foreign loans and indemnity quotas."

2. Since preparing the foregoing instruction the Department has received from the British Embassy an *aide-mémoire* [42] which conveys the information that the British Ambassador at Tokyo has been instructed to make a protest in strong terms to the Japanese Government against the introduction of the new tariff. When you ascertain that your British colleague is prepared to act in accordance with his instructions, you are authorized to present a note along the lines suggested to the Japanese Government.

Repeated to Shanghai for repetition to Hankow and Peiping.

HULL

693.002/473 : Telegram

The Ambassador in Japan (Grew) to the Secretary of State

TOKYO, January 31, 1938—4 p. m.
[Received January 31—6 : 20 a. m.]

59.   Department's 31, January 30, 1 p. m., integrity of Chinese customs. My British colleague received his instructions today and is pre-

---

[42] Dated January 29, not printed.

pared to act. I have therefore today presented to the Japanese Government a note conforming precisely to the Department's text.[43]

Repeated to Shanghai for repetition to Hankow and Peiping.

GREW

693.002/477 : Telegram

The Consul General at Shanghai (Gauss) to the Secretary of State

SHANGHAI, February 1, 1938—9 p. m.
[Received February 1—6 : 50 p. m.]

179. Inspector General of Customs has today reported to the Minister of Finance that the Tientsin and Chinwangtao customs have been obliged to yield to *force majeure* and submit to enforcement of the reduced tariff rates. He has urged Government to defer any action or decision. Evidently anticipating some drastic move by the Minister of Finance, he asks that the foreign representatives use their influence to dissuade Chinese Government from any precipitate action.

2. Inspector General has also sent me précis of a long message from Commissioner of Customs at Tientsin [44] who says that the Peiping régime and the Japanese military are now moving to obtain the release of foreign loan quotas in order to separate such quotas from the remaining revenue which will be treated as surplus to be dealt with by the Peiping régime as it pleases. Commissioner believes Peiping régime would reject any move to reintroduce the 1931 tariff. He recommends that in order to prevent disruption of the customs service and consequent inevitable loss to foreign bondholders the customs be placed under international control. Inspector General points to the 1912 arrangement under which control was placed temporarily in the hands of the Inspector General and states that adoption of that plan or of the suggestion of the Tientsin Commissioner for International Control is a matter for the foreign powers to decide in collaboration with the Chinese Government and he asks that the matter be made known to our governments and their views obtained.

3. I report the matter as requested but consider it would be futile to attempt to induce China and Japan to agree to any scheme of international control of the customs or to reintroduce the arrangement of 1912. The Japanese military are determined to obtain customs revenues for use in areas under their control and apparently regard the release of foreign loan quotas as a liberal concession to foreign inter-

---

[43] See *Foreign Relations, Japan, 1931–1941*, vol. I, p. 738; the Department on January 31 also replied to the British Embassy's inquiry on this subject. For reply of the Japanese Foreign Office, on March 22, see *ibid.*, p. 742; it replied likewise to British and French representations.
[44] W. R. Myers.

ests. The customs situation is moving rapidly to a crisis. I believe the full weight of foreign effort should be devoted to obtaining from the Japanese Government at Tokyo broad assurances similar to those being sought by the United States. The interest here seems to be in opposing the use of Japanese instead of British banks of deposit for the customs revenues collected at Japanese occupied ports. It is also evident that foreign customs officials are principally concerned as to their own future.

Repeated to Hankow and Peiping. Not repeated to Tokyo.

GAUSS

693.002/481 : Telegram

The Ambassador in China (Johnson) to the Secretary of State

HANKOW, February 2, 1938—noon.
[Received 4:41 p. m.]

72. Shanghai's 166, January 28, 9 p. m. MacKillop of British Embassy informs me Moreno [*that he?*] saw Kung on February 1 and recommended to him acceptance of Maze's recommendation that 1931 tariff as amended be put into effect in the interest of uniformity of tariff. Kung told MacKillop that he would give matter further consideration after receiving views of British Government upon following four points: (*a*) Chinese Government would have no assurance that Japanese would permit 1931 tariff to be applied in North China. Japanese on contrary might extend to Shanghai and other occupied areas schedule now applied in North China. (*b*) Chinese Government by this action might be drawn into undignified competition with puppet governments in reduction of rates. (*c*) Lower rates would diminish securities for loan obligations and increase burden of Central Government which is already making up deficiency of revenue of customs. It is understood that present customs revenue just about equals service of foreign loans and cost of administration. (*d*) Lower rates would stimulate imports and increase strain on national currency by creating demand for foreign exchange.

MacKillop states that his conversation with Kung took place before publication here of interview given by General Matsui [45] in Shanghai on February 1 to Woodhead [46] in which Matsui is reported to have said that it was originally his purpose to take over the Shanghai customs immediately but that he had resorted to more moderate lines because of the *Panay* and *Ladybird* incidents. [47] Matsui

---

[45] Japanese Commander in Chief in Central China.
[46] British journalist and editor of *Oriental Affairs*, Shanghai.
[47] See *Foreign Relations, 1937*, vol. IV, pp. 485 ff., and *Foreign Relations, Japan, 1931–1941*, vol. I, pp. 517 ff.

is reported to have stated that because negotiations were dragging he might have to revert to his original attitude, as every day's delay was a day lost in restoring war-stricken areas and financial resources furnished by Chinese customs were necessary in order to finance new Chinese regime. It is MacKillop's belief that appearance of Matsui interview will destroy any chance of favorable consideration by Kung of Maze recommendations.

I had a conversation yesterday with Arthur Young [48] who informs me that he has consistently recommended against deposit of customs funds in Japanese bank, and that he has recommended against adoption 1931 tariff as recommended by Maze. Young states that question is whether Japanese will take over customs or not, and that suggested measures will not in the end affect Japanese decision but may prejudice Chinese position vis-à-vis Japanese taking over of customs.

Repeated to Peiping and Shanghai. Shanghai please repeat to Tokyo.

JOHNSON

693.002/478 : Telegram

The Ambassador in Japan (Grew) to the Secretary of State

TOKYO, February 2, 1938—8 p. m.
[Received February 2—10 : 05 a. m.]

69. Our 37, January 17, 4 p. m.[49] My British colleague yesterday presented a memorandum to the Vice Minister for Foreign Affairs [50] reciting the action of a Chinese organization, acting under the orders of the Japanese military authorities at Shanghai, in taking over the Chinese Government internal revenue administration in the International Settlement and the previous voluntary agreements with the Chinese Government concerning the payment of the consolidated tax. The memorandum requests that the Japanese authorities will take no action and will countenance no action by any provisional régime in the areas from which the legitimate Chinese authority has withdrawn which would fail adequately to take into account the obligations of the Chinese Government under the aforementioned agreements.

Repeated to Shanghai.

GREW

[48] American adviser to the Chinese Ministry of Finance.
[49] Not printed.
[50] Kensuke Horinouchi.

693.002/479 : Telegram

The Ambassador in Japan (Grew) to the Secretary of State

Tokyo, February 2, 1938—9 p. m.
[Received February 2—10 : 35 a. m.]

70. Our 59, January 31, 4 p. m., integrity of Chinese customs. My French colleague yesterday evening addressed to the Japanese Government a note along lines similar to ours but containing an additional paragraph stating in translation :

"In view of the influence exercised at Peiping (*sic*) by the Imperial Government, my Government considers in addition that it will be obliged to hold the Imperial Government responsible for damages to French rights and interests which may result from an arbitrary revision of the customs tariffs in China".

The Vice Minister for Foreign Affairs informed my British colleague yesterday that the tariff revision had been effected to meet the difficult economic situation obtaining in China and that there were precedents for such action during former periods of famine. Craigie [51] obtained Horinouchi's oral admission that the Provisional Régime in North China could not have taken such a step without the approval of the Japanese Army; Craigie then pointed out that the responsibility rested squarely on the Japanese Government which should have consulted the other interested powers before permitting such action.

Repeated to Shanghai for Hankow and Peiping.

GREW

793.94/12292 : Telegram

The Consul at Chefoo (Allen) to the Secretary of State

Chefoo, February 3, 1938—10 a. m.
[Received February 3—6 a. m.]

Naval landing parties from a force of nine Japanese naval vessels are completing occupation of Chefoo. Japanese have hoisted Japanese flag over all Chinese public buildings. Commissioner of Customs intends to protest against raising of Japanese flag over Chinese customs on grounds of international interest in customs and customs revenue. I do not believe that Japanese action constitutes an infringement of American rights in customs integrity and customs revenue which would warrant a protest from me at this time. Posters distributed by Japanese forces show five barred flag and bear Chinese characters "Republic reborn Peking".

ALLEN

---

[51] Sir Robert L. Craigie, British Ambassador in Japan.

693.002/483 : Telegram

The Counselor of Embassy in China (Lockhart) to the Secretary of State

PEIPING, February 3, 1938—7 p. m.
[Received February 3—3 : 56 p. m.]

85. Shanghai's 179, February 1, 9 p. m. The British Embassy states that a protest will be made to the Japanese Consul General at Tientsin and that an officer of the Embassy on January 31 called on the Japanese Counselor in Peiping and made representations on the subject. The original Foreign Office instructions were to protest to the Provisional Government in Peiping but the British Counselor at Hankow directed that a call be made on the Japanese Embassy instead. The local office of the British Embassy is not hopeful that the Japanese will yield in their position on the customs.

Repeated to Ambassador and Shanghai.

LOCKHART

693.002/482 : Telegram

The Secretary of State to the Consul General at Shanghai (Gauss)

WASHINGTON, February 3, 1938—7 p. m.

109. Your 189, February 3, 11 a. m.,[52] quoting Tokyo's 66, February 2, 5 p. m., on the subject of disregard by Japanese vessels of Chinese Customs requirements.

If the discrimination described in the British *aide-mémoire* continues, please telegraph the Department a brief statement that can be made the basis of a further approach by the American authorities to the Japanese authorities in regard to the matter.

Please repeat your reply to Tokyo.

Repeated to Tokyo.

HULL

693.002/484 : Telegram

The Consul General at Shanghai (Gauss) to the Secretary of State

SHANGHAI, February 3, 1938—9 p. m.
[Received February 3—7 : 50 p. m.]

197. Japanese Consul General recently urged the Inspector General of Customs to instruct the Shanghai Commissioner to deposit the Shanghai revenues in the Yokohama Specie Bank. Inspector General

---

[52] Not printed; this telegram quoted a British *aide-mémoire* to the Japanese Government protesting the landing of commercial cargoes by Japanese ships at Shanghai without payment of customs.

replied that the customs revenues are largely mortgaged for service of foreign obligations, that Japan is not the only power interested, that a group of powers oppose deposit of their shares in the Japanese Bank, that the Chinese Government also objects, and that it is impossible for him to conclude an arrangement with one power to which other powers object and the Japanese should therefore endeavor to obtain withdrawal of that objection.

2. Japanese Consul General inquired of me this morning whether the American Government object to deposit of revenue in the Japanese Bank. I answered that the natural reply to his question is to inquire what assurances the Japanese Government is prepared to give in response to the request of the American Government as made at Tokyo and repeated by me to him here. He admitted that he did not know the attitude of his Government on the American request, commented that some of the assurances would be difficult to give, but asserted that the Japanese are prepared to release foreign loan and indemnity quotas. In the long discussion which followed I suggested that it would seem a reasonable compromise to release the foreign loan and indemnity quotas in other than the Japanese Bank since he asserts that such quotas will be released, but I emphasized that from my point of view the question of the assurances we desire is much more important than the question of the nationality of the bank of deposit. I also directed attention to reports that the Japanese are not contributing to the customs revenues, their ships and merchants not paying tariffs and customs duties. He replied that he was anxious to get the matter of the Shanghai customs settled so that this situation could be corrected.

Repeated to Tokyo, Hankow, and Peiping.

GAUSS

693.002/485a : Telegram

The Secretary of State to the Ambassador in Japan (Grew)

WASHINGTON, February 3, 1938—9 p. m.

37. Shanghai's 179, February 1, 9 p. m. (which Shanghai has been requested to repeat to you), and Shanghai's 113, 146, and 170 in regard to Customs.[53]

In the light of your knowledge of the Department's position in regard to the Chinese Customs, the Department desires that you discreetly bring to the attention of your British and French colleagues, without reference to source, the views expressed in paragraph 3 of Shanghai's 179; that you frankly discuss with them, on a basis of

---

[53] Telegram No. 113, January 20, 6 p. m., p. 632; No. 146, January 26, 7 p. m., p. 635; No. 170, January 29, 4 p. m., p. 637.

expediency and the realities of the situation, the possibility and advisability of concentrating on defensive efforts in regard to the major issues relating to and involving preservation insofar as possible of the administrative machinery of the customs and provision for the servicing of foreign loans and indemnity quotas, as contrasted with effort to preserve the existing situation at all points and in all features; and that you endeavor to obtain favorable consideration of the proposal that approaches be made to the Japanese Government by each of you individually along the following lines:

The Department suggests that you acquaint the Japanese Foreign Office with the fact that you have information with regard to the character of the Japanese proposal made at Shanghai to the Commissioner of Customs for a settlement of the Customs problem; that in connection therewith but without indicating approval or disapproval of the proposal you refer in general to the assurances which we have expressed a desire to receive from the Japanese Government (Department's 339, December 12, 3 p. m.[54]); and that you express an earnest and emphatic desire to receive from the Japanese Government positive assurances that no action will be taken or countenanced which will disrupt the Chinese customs service or jeopardize the servicing of foreign loan and indemnity quotas from Customs revenues, but that on the contrary in any arrangement reached the administrative machinery and procedure of the Customs will be carefully preserved and the payment on an equitable and unconditional basis of foreign loan and indemnity quotas will be provided for.

Please inform the Department and Shanghai of the result of your discussions and approach, if made, to the Japanese Government.

Repeated to Shanghai.

HULL

693.002/488 : Telegram

The Ambassador in China (Johnson) to the Secretary of State

HANKOW, February 4, 1938—2 p. m.
[Received 2:45 p. m.]

83. My 72, February 2, noon, and Shanghai's 140, January 26, 1 p. m. Following is paraphrase of telegraphic instruction sent by the Minister of Finance to the Inspector General of Customs February 2:

"After studying your telegram received January 29 I authorize you to make the following counterproposal if it becomes necessary for you to take action before the Government has received and studied any opinions expressed by the Governments of France, Great Britain and the United States: The entire customs revenue of all occupied areas may be deposited as a temporary measure in two or more foreign banks

---

[54] *Foreign Relations*, 1937, vol. III, p. 900.

to act as co-trustees and these banks, one of which may be the Yoko-hama Specie Bank, shall utilize the revenue in the first place to meet the cost of customs services; then in respect of all obligations paid from the customs revenue and secured thereon as of July 1, 1937, con-tributions shall be provided toward contractual payments proportion-ate to average collections prior to July 1, last; in the third place, if there is any surplus remaining, the conclusion of hostilities shall be awaited before surplus is paid out. The willingness of China to make all reasonable concessions to protect the service of obligations and the integrity of the customs is shown by this proposal.

The Government still wishes to await and consider any views which may be expressed by the foreign governments, but in the meantime for your guidance and information it makes the following comment: Depositing customs' funds in the Yokohama Specie Bank would be tantamount to delivering them to the Japanese, as shown by what has occurred at Tientsin and elsewhere. Moreover, the Japanese have indicated that over and above such sums as they themselves choose to make available for foreign obligations they would seize such funds, and there further is indication in the statement recently made by General Matsui that the Japanese would make adjustment of negotia-tions and would thereafter reduce even payments whose amount is specified under individual agreements and are thus not open to dis-pute. If the demands of the Japanese were accepted they would force the payments to themselves or to a bogus régime of most of the revenue collected by the customs which would be an invidious position. The result would be impairment of the credit of the Government and of the rights of bondholders both of which the Government in spite of great difficulties is trying to maintain."

Repeated to Peiping and Shanghai. Shanghai repeat to Tokyo.

JOHNSON

693.002/485 : Telegram

The Ambassador in China (Johnson) to the Secretary of State

HANKOW, February 4, 1938—3 p. m.
[Received February 4—10:55 a. m.]

84. Kung left by air for Hong Kong today. He has summoned Maze to meet him in Hong Kong. Arthur Young proceeds Hong Kong tomorrow. It is expected that customs matter will be discussed. Young is advising Kung against compromise on the ground that com-promise begs the issue which is "will Japanese take customhouses and administration by force?" He believes Kung should instruct Com-missioners of Customs to refuse to collect new tariffs established by Japanese fostered régimes, or to deposit collections with Yokohama Specie Bank at behest of Japanese, lest Chinese discover that they have transferred customs to Japanese or to régimes fostered by them.

Repeated to Peiping and Shanghai. Shanghai please repeat to Tokyo.

JOHNSON

693.002/487 : Telegram

The Consul General at Shanghai (Gauss) to the Secretary of State

SHANGHAI, February 4, 1938—6 p. m.
[Received February 4—3 : 45 p. m.]

207. Reference my No. 140, January 26, 1 p. m. Inspector General now writes me that the question being urgent and the Ministry of Finance having pressed him for further information wishes to know with as little delay as possible, (1), the view of the American Government vis-à-vis suggested reintroduction of 1931 tariff with some modifications and (2), whether there are any articles not including those dealt with by the Peiping *de facto* government on which the American authorities and nationals wish to see rates different from those given in the 1931 tariff.

Repeated to Hankow and Peiping.

GAUSS

693.002/486 : Telegram

The Consul General at Shanghai (Gauss) to the Secretary of State

SHANGHAI, February 4, 1938—8 p. m.
[Received February 4—3 : 50 p. m.]

208. Referring to Department's 109, February 3, 7 p. m., the situation is as stated in the communication quoted in Tokyo's 66, February 2, 5 p. m.[56] I understand a similar situation existed at Tientsin until the customs yielded to the demands concerning deposit of revenues. Also see last two sentences of my 197, February 3, 9 p. m.

Repeated to Tokyo.

GAUSS

693.002/486 : Telegram

The Secretary of State to the Ambassador in Japan (Grew)

WASHINGTON, February 5, 1938—3 p. m.

42. Shanghai's 208, February 4, 8 p. m. The Department desires that you make an approach to the Japanese Government, in such manner as you consider appropriate, in regard to this matter, using the information contained in the British *aide-mémoire* quoted in your 66, February 2, 5 p. m., as confirmed by Gauss [56] as a basis for your approach. You may make mention of the situation described in the two concluding sentences of paragraph 2 of Shanghai's 197, February 3, 9 p. m., and point out that it is utterly indefensible that the Japanese

---

[56] Not printed.

should make observance of customs procedure at Shanghai contingent upon acquiescence in their wishes in regard to settlement of the Shanghai customs issue.[57]

Repeated to Shanghai.

HULL

693.002/467 : Telegram

The Secretary of State to the Consul General at Shanghai (Gauss)

WASHINGTON, February 5, 1938—4 p. m.

116. Your 207, February 4, 6 p. m., and Hankow's 83, February 4, 2 p. m. The Department does not wish to proffer views in regard to the suggested reintroduction of the 1931 tariff or in regard to different rates for specific items in that tariff and you may so inform the Inspector General. You may also inform him of our very real interest in the customs issue and of our hope that there may be reached a solution which, insofar as practicable, will preserve the present customs administrative machinery and procedure and make adequate provision for the servicing of foreign loan and indemnity quotas.

Please repeat the above telegram to Hankow, Peiping and Tokyo for their information. Please also repeat your 207, February 4, 6 p. m., to Tokyo.

HULL

693.002/491 : Telegram

The Ambassador in Japan (Grew) to the Secretary of State

TOKYO, February 7, 1938—7 p. m.
[Received February 7—10 : 18 a. m.]

83. Department's 37, February 3, 9 p. m.

1. My British colleague informs me that he is willing to make to the Japanese Government an approach along the lines of pressing for the assurances with regard to the customs at Shanghai which the American Government has already requested. He feels, however, that we should when making those representations express disapproval of the arrangement which the Japanese have proposed. He points out that the Japanese have already given oral assurances that foreign rights and interests in the customs would be respected but that in fact the arrangement which they are pressing the Commissioner of Customs to accept violates that assurance. Craigie is informed from Shanghai that there has been a substantial decrease in revenues and that the Japanese desire, notwithstanding the fact that the foreign

---

[57] For the American Embassy's *aide-mémoire* dated February 7, see *Foreign Relations*, Japan, 1931–1941, vol. I, p. 739.

loans and indemnity quotas should be the first charge on the revenues, to decrease these quotas *pari passu* with the decrease in revenue. He believes that we could quite properly say to the Japanese that the arrangements relating to the service of the foreign debts and indemnities can only be modified by the Japanese Government (as by the Chinese Government) with the assent of the powers which have acquired rights in this matter in virtue of past agreements.

2. It seems to us that Craigie's point is well taken. If the Department shares that view, will it be disposed to authorize modification of the suggested line of approach so as to include disapproval of the proposed Japanese arrangement?

3. My French colleague is cabling for instructions.

Repeated to Shanghai for Hankow.

GREW

693.002/497 : Telegram

The Consul General at Shanghai (Gauss) to the Secretary of State

SHANGHAI, February 8, 1938—6 p. m.
[Received February 8—5 : 41 p. m.]

223. Japanese Consul General today sent a letter to the Commissioner of Customs asking him to arrange to deposit customs revenues in the Yokohama Specie Bank and stating that "the Japanese authorities will not allow any amount of money to be transferred without" their authorization from revenue accounts now in other banks except funds for defraying the Shanghai customs expenses. The letter, which is in poor English, then goes on to say that the Japanese authorities have no intention of having withheld from foreign loan and indemnity services such payments from the revenue accounts which they, the Japanese authorities, agree are reasonably allotted from the Shanghai customs. The letter as interpreted or explained by the Consul General's representative does not preclude withdrawal of funds for foreign loan and indemnity services from revenues now in the British bank but makes such withdrawal subject to authorization by the Japanese authorities who will consider whether it represents a reasonable allotment from the Shanghai revenue.

Repeated to Tokyo, Hankow and Peiping.

GAUSS

693.002/491 : Telegram

The Secretary of State to the Ambassador in Japan (Grew)

WASHINGTON, February 9, 1938—8 p. m.

51. Your 83, February 7, 7 p. m. You state that the British Ambassador is informed from Shanghai that there has been a substantial

decrease in revenues and that the Japanese desire, notwithstanding the fact that the foreign loans and indemnity quotas should be the first charge on the revenues, to decrease these quotas *pari passu* with the decrease in revenue. The Department has not hitherto received any information in regard to this proposed decrease of quotas and before replying to your telegram under reference would appreciate the receipt of any additional information which you and Shanghai may be able to provide.

The Department has received today from the British Embassy here an *Aide-Mémoire* [58] giving among other things the following information:

(1) General Matsui has stated in a press interview that ample financial resources drawn upon the Customs revenues are to be placed at the disposal of the new Chinese regime and that foreign loan services will have to suffer;

(2) The Japanese Minister for Foreign Affairs has told a Committee of the Lower House that the Japanese Government will supervise the Shanghai Customs and take over a fixed part of the revenue;

(3) The British Ambassador at Tokyo has been given to understand that the revenue is to be made to bear the expenses of "other administrations" as well as the Customs administration before the loans are served.

Any comment, confirmation or additional information which you and the American Consul General at Shanghai may be able to give in regard to the foregoing three points will be appreciated by the Department. Early reply requested.

Repeated to Shanghai.

HULL

693.002/499 : Telegram

The Consul General at Shanghai (Gauss) to the Secretary of State

SHANGHAI, February 10, 1938—7 p. m.
[Received February 10—4 : 10 p. m.]

235. At a meeting this afternoon which I attended by invitation, French Ambassador and British Chargé d'Affaires agreed to suggest that the Inspector General of Customs communicate officially to the representatives of the three powers the letter outlined in my telegram No. 223, February 8, 6 p. m. whereupon British and French representatives propose to reply that no action should be taken without consultation with interested powers and that so far as concerns funds for foreign loan and indemnity payments no action should be taken without their permission to give effect to the Japanese demand that funds shall not be transferred without Japanese approval from the

---

[58] Dated February 9, not printed.

present banking account of the Shanghai customs.   I stated I would report to the Department for instructions.   British Chargé d'Affaires told us that his Government is insistent that no customs revenues shall be placed in the Yokohama Specie Bank and that his Government is seeking agreement to this position at Washington and Paris.   French Ambassador expressed the opinion that if the desired assurances are given at Tokyo it might be possible to make an arrangement under which revenues could be deposited in the Japanese bank.   With all due respect for the British view, I feel that I should say to the Department that the situation appears to be heading rapidly toward the point where the Japanese will take steps to compel deposit of the revenues in the Japanese bank and we shall find them there without any assurances or guarantees.

Repeated to Tokyo, Hankow and Peiping.

GAUSS

693.002/502 : Telegram

The Ambassador in Japan (Grew) to the Secretary of State

TOKYO, February 11, 1938—4 p. m.
[Received February 11—11 : 25 a. m.]

99. Department's 51, February 9, 8 p. m.—Chinese customs Shanghai.

1. We have no further information regarding decrease in Chinese customs revenues and the proposed decrease of quotas for indemnity and loan services.

2. With respect to the three points contained in the *aide-mémoire* of the British Embassy referred to in the Department's telegram under acknowledgment, the British Ambassador states with regard to point 1 that he furnished this information based upon a published interview given Woodhead by General Matsui on January 28 at Shanghai.

3. With regard to point 2 the Ambassador stated that he based this information on a report of a statement made by the Minister for Foreign Affairs before a committee of the Diet which appeared in the press of February 3 reading in translation as follows:

"Reverting to the Shanghai situation the Foreign Minister said in answer to other questions 'negotiations on customs are now in a deadlock.   The position of this country is that a close watch should be kept on customs revenue rather than actually taking over the whole revenue.   What revenue is taken will be deposited with the Specie Bank.   In answer to the question whether the Government has any plan of using Shanghai customs revenue for reconstruction of the city I can say only that there is at present a great decline in revenue, due to the military campaign.   This causes me to believe that the customs revenue cannot be used at least to any satisfactory degrees in reconstructing Shanghai.' "

4. We noted the foregoing press report but did not think nor do we now think that it warranted the conclusion arrived at by the British Ambassador.

5. Regarding point 3 the British Ambassador in a conversation with Mr. Horinouchi on February 7 pointed out that Japan having temporarily taken over at certain Chinese ports the rights of the National Government in respect of the Chinese customs should in equity also assume the obligations of that Government and that so far as China's obligations to foreign powers are concerned Japan has promised to respect all foreign rights and interests in China. On the foregoing basis Japan should recognize that the service of the foreign debt and indemnities constitute a first charge on the customs revenue apart from normal deductions for running expenses and that therefore Japan should recognize that the arrangements relating to the service of the foreign debt can only be modified by the Japanese Government with the assent of the powers which have acquired rights by virtue of past agreements. Craigie informs us that although Horinouchi was prepared to agree that Japan had assumed obligations in respect of customs quota of the Chinese Government he would not agree that Japan should previously discuss with other governments any proposed change in quota. Craigie states that he gathered from Horinouchi's evasive reply that the Japanese authorities in Shanghai intended to use the customs revenues to service other administrations as well as the Customs Administration before the loans were serviced.

6. Craigie told me today that he considers the customs situation critical and hopes that I will be in a position to act in concert with himself and the French Ambassador as soon as possible. My French colleague is prepared to act as soon as my own instructions are received.

Repeated to Shanghai for Hankow.

GREW

693.002/505 : Telegram

The Consul General at Shanghai (Gauss) to the Secretary of State

SHANGHAI, February 11, 1938—8 p. m.
[Received February 11—6 : 45 p. m.]

244. Reference your 129, February 9, 8 p. m.[59] Hall-Patch, Financial Adviser, British Embassy, told me yesterday afternoon he has definite information from officer of Japanese Consulate General with whom he discussed matter several days ago that the Japanese have

---

[59] This telegram repeated the Department's No. 51, February 9, 8 p. m., to the Ambassador in Japan, p. 650.

intention of decreasing Shanghai quotas for foreign loan and indemnity services *pari passu* with decrease in revenue. I had received no such intimation from the Japanese or from the customs.

The essence of the press interview given by Matsui is correctly stated in your message. I am telegraphing separately full text.[60]

I have no information on other points mentioned.

Repeated to Tokyo.

GAUSS

693.002/506 : Telegram

The Consul General at Shanghai (Gauss) to the Secretary of State

SHANGHAI, February 12, 1938—10 a. m.
[Received February 12—7:20 a. m.]

247. Referring further to your 129, February 9, 8 p. m.,[61] customs revenues for all China have decreased from a monthly average of about 34 million Chinese dollars during the first 7 months of last year to slightly more than 14½ million monthly average during last 5 months of the year. Estimated revenue for January this year 15½ million. Whereas Shanghai formerly contributed about 45% of the total revenue, it now contributes about 25%. Cost of customs administration is roughly 40 million dollars a year. Total payments due from customs revenue in 1938 in respect of obligations with regard to service as of July 1st, 1937, estimated to be the equivalent of 88 million Chinese dollars for foreign loans and indemnities and 130 million for internal debt.

Not repeated to Embassy.

GAUSS

693.002/507 : Telegram

The Consul General at Shanghai (Gauss) to the Secretary of State

SHANGHAI, February 12, 1938—8 p. m.
[Received February 12—5:16 p. m.]

252. Recent assertions by the Japanese authorities here that the failure of the Tientsin customs to remit funds for foreign loan and indemnity service was due to a decision made by the Customs Commissioner at Tientsin led to inquiry as a result of which the British Chargé d'Affaires has obtained and sent to me and to the French Ambassador in strict confidence copy of a letter dated October 22 addressed by the Commissioner of Customs at Tientsin to the Japanese Consul General there in which he states:

---

[60] Telegram No. 245, February 11, 9 p. m., not printed.
[61] See footnote 59, p. 653.

"Throughout the duration of the present hostilities between the Japanese Empire and China and until the questions arising out of these hostilities are settled these specified collections will continue to be deposited with the Yokohama Specie Bank and it is understood that withdrawals therefrom shall consist of moneys for regular and accepted current local expenses. In regard to such of these moneys as are marked for loan obligation purposes, their disposal is left to my discretion, but it is not my intention to make any withdrawals in this connection pending the settlement arising out of the present hostilities and therefore any question regarding them does not arise."

Repeated to Tokyo and Hankow.

GAUSS

693.002/499 : Telegram

The Secretary of State to the Consul General at Shanghai (Gauss)

WASHINGTON, February 13, 1938—noon.

134. Your 235, February 10, 7 p. m. Should the Inspector General of Customs communicate to you the letter outlined in your telegram No. 223, February 8, 6 p. m., the Department desires that, if such communication calls for any response beyond an acknowledgment, you reply that the American Government does not wish to advise the Chinese Maritime Customs administration in regard to the attitude which it should adopt in the matter.

For your information and guidance, the Department gives below the substance of an *aide-mémoire* which it is handing to the British Embassy here [62] in response to the latter's question whether the United States Government would support a proposal to the Japanese and Chinese Governments that customs funds in areas controlled by the Japanese be deposited in the Hong Kong and Shanghai Banking Corporation and that control of those funds be vested in a body of officials nominated by the interested powers.

The Department replied that it would not be in position to take the proposed action but, realizing that the British Government might wish to continue with the proposal, desired to avoid any procedure that would tend to prejudice the British position. The Department stated that it was accordingly instructing the American Ambassador to Japan and you to consult with your British colleagues and, if the latter so desired, to hold in abeyance for the present further approaches to the Japanese authorities; that Mr. Grew and you were being further instructed that in case your British colleagues did not wish a postponement of further American approaches to the Japanese

---

[62] The Department's *aide-mémoire* of February 13 was in reply to the British Embassy's inquiry of February 9; neither printed.

authorities you were authorized, either alone or accompanied by similar but separate action on the part of your British and French diplomatic and consular colleagues, to acquaint the Japanese Government with the fact that you have information in regard to the character of the Japanese proposal made to the Commissioner of Customs at Shanghai for a settlement of the Customs problem; to refer to the assurances which the American Government has already requested of the Japanese Government; and to re-express an earnest and emphatic desire to receive from the Japanese Government positive assurances that no action will be taken or countenanced that will disrupt the Chinese Customs service or jeopardize the servicing of foreign obligations secured on the Customs revenues and that the servicing of such obligations will be considered and treated as first charges on the Customs revenue after the deduction of the costs of maintaining the Chinese Maritime Customs.

The French Embassy here has informally approached the Department in regard to this subject, and you and Tokyo may acquaint your French colleagues with the Department's position as set forth in this and previous telegrams.

HULL

693.002/510 : Telegram

The Ambassador in China (Johnson) to the Secretary of State

HANKOW, February 14, 1938—11 a. m.
[Received February 14—10 : 35 a. m.]

102. I am reliably informed that an instruction has been issued to the Inspector General of Customs by the Minister of Finance that he is to instruct Commissioners of Customs in occupied territory to decline to apply new tariff recently proclaimed for application in such areas, on the ground that Chinese customs service is entrusted with responsible duty of enforcing a uniform tariff at all parts of China in accordance with China's treaty obligations, and of remitting revenues to the Inspector General for the purpose of meeting obligations for which revenues are pledged. Commissioners of Customs are also instructed to notify the public that payment of new tariff is not recognized by the Chinese Government.

Repeated to Shanghai and Peiping. Shanghai please repeat to Tokyo.

JOHNSON

693.002/509 : Telegram

The Ambassador in Japan (Grew) to the Secretary of State

TOKYO, February 14, 1938—7 p. m.
[Received February 14—10 : 17 a. m.]

106. Department's 58 of February 13, noon.[63]

1. In our draft *aide-mémoire* to the Japanese Foreign Office we are including the sentence "Mr. Grew is aware of the character of certain proposals recently made by the Japanese authorities at Shanghai to the Commissioner of Customs for a settlement of the customs problem." (See telegram above cited.) We are also including the phrase "on an equitable and unconditional basis". (See Department's 37 of February 3, 9 p. m.)

2. When we showed the draft to the British Ambassador this afternoon he stated that the inclusion of the above sentence and phrase would prejudice the British position as he thought that it would convey to the Japanese authorities the idea that after desired assurances were obtained the Japanese would feel free to work out a plan which would not provide for full payment of the loan and indemnity services and would thereby leave the way open for the Japanese to scale down loan and indemnity payments in accord with decreased revenues.

3. The British Ambassador stated that without our backing of the British view the "whole thing would be lost".

4. The British Ambassador also asked if he could be informed in confidence why we did not wish to support the British plan rather than to seek further assurances along the lines we propose to follow.

5. In view of the British objection we are holding representations in abeyance for the present. Please inform us if and when the Department now desires that action be taken.

Repeated to Shanghai.

GREW

693.002/509 : Telegram

The Secretary of State to the Ambassador in Japan (Grew)

WASHINGTON, February 15, 1938—6 p. m.

59. Your 106, February 14, 7 p. m. You may omit from your *aide-mémoire* the sentence and phrase quoted in paragraph 1 of your telegram.

You should say to the British Ambassador, as from the Department, that in regard to his inquiry why this Government does "not wish to

---

[63] This telegram repeated the Department's No. 134, February 13, noon, to the Consul General at Shanghai, p. 655.

support the British plan rather than to seek further assurances along the lines we propose to follow," that this Government considers that the British plan, even if this Government were wholeheartedly to "support" it, would be rejected by the Japanese; that the British plan involves insistence upon one or more measures to which this Government believes that the Japanese Government will not under the existing circumstances assent; and that the procedure which this Government suggests and which it is prepared to follow is one calculated, in this Government's opinion, to stand a fair chance of gaining the assent of the Japanese. Say that this Government, on the basis of your views and the views of the American Consul General at Shanghai and the views of the Department, all of which are in substantial agreement, believes it advisable to concentrate on the points most to be desired, especially the maintenance of the integrity of the Customs Administration. Say that, in case the "whole thing" or any part of it is "lost", the factors responsible for that eventuation will be numerous; and that among those factors, absence of this Government's "backing of the British view" will in our opinion have had less of contributory effect than will refusal of the British to respond to any other than the British view.

The Department desires that you hold in abeyance the approach to the Japanese Government authorized in the Department's 37, February 3, 9 p. m., and 58, February 13, noon,[64] until, in your judgment, action may be taken without prejudicing the position of the British Government in regard to the Customs situation.

Repeated to Shanghai.

HULL

693.002/512 : Telegram

The Consul General at Shanghai (Gauss) to the Secretary of State

SHANGHAI, February 16, 1938—3 p. m.
[Received February 16—1:37 p. m.]

263. Reference my 235, February 10, 7 p. m. regarding Shanghai customs. Inspector General has today informed the Commissioner of Customs that he understands conversations are proceeding in Tokyo between interested diplomatic representatives and Japanese Government regarding the question of bank of deposit of customs revenue, that Inspector General is not in a position to take action himself or to authorize the Commissioner to do so, that it is not possible for him to conclude an agreement with one power which is not acceptable to other powers whose interest in indemnities and loans on the customs exceed those of Japan, and he suggests therefore that the matter be deferred pending conclusion of negotiations at Tokyo. Commissioner

---

[64] See footnote 63, p. 657.

is expected to reply to Japanese Consul General in the sense of the foregoing which was drafted in consultation with the British Embassy.

Repeated to Tokyo, Hankow and Peiping.

GAUSS

693.002/514 : Telegram

The Ambassador in Japan (Grew) to the Secretary of State

TOKYO, February 17, 1938—6 p. m.
[Received February 17—8 : 55 a. m.]

112. Department's 59, of February 15, 6 p. m., Chinese customs.

1. The considerations outlined by the Department were imparted to the British Ambassador today.

2. Craigie was informed recently by the Vice Minister for Foreign Affairs that revised instructions have been sent to Okamoto [65] which Horinouchi believes will be more acceptable to foreign interests. These instructions envisage *inter alia* the deposit in the Yokohama Specie Bank only of the customs revenues taken in districts now under Japanese occupation, all other customs revenues to be deposited in the Hong Kong [and] Shanghai Bank. If Lawford [66] declines to accept the new proposal, Okamoto is, according to Craigie, directed to discuss the matter with the foreign representatives in Shanghai. Horinouchi implied that these instructions might be even further amended if they fail to meet the views of the foreign interests.

3. Our *aide-mémoire* was presented to the Foreign Office this afternoon.[67]

Repeated to Shanghai for Hankow and Peiping.

GREW

693.002/517 : Telegram

The Ambassador in China (Johnson) to the Secretary of State

HANKOW, February 21, 1938—3 p. m.
[Received February 21—10 : 47 a. m.]

117. My 102, February 14, 11 a. m. I understand British Embassy, complying with instructions from London, will tell Kung this evening that British Government strongly disapproves the proposed instructions to Maze because they confront Commissioners with alternatives of signing [*resigning?*] or breaking the formal integrity of the customs.

JOHNSON

---

[65] Japanese Consul General at Shanghai.
[66] British Commissioner of Customs at Shanghai.
[67] *Foreign Relations*, Japan, 1931–1941, vol. I, p. 740.

693.002/507 : Telegram

The Secretary of State to the Consul General at Shanghai (Gauss)

WASHINGTON, February 23, 1938—5 p. m.

159. Your 252, February 12, 8 p. m.   The Commissioner's letter of October 22 would seem to afford a superficial basis for an assertion that the failure of the Tientsin Customs House to remit its quota for the servicing of foreign obligations secured on the Customs revenue was the result of the Commissioner's own decision.

Please confer with your British colleague and, having in mind the manner in which the text of the letter became known, telegraph the Department whether information is available which would make the record reflect the true situation in regard to remittances.   All reports received indicate to the Department that the letter represents part of an arrangement forced upon the Commissioner by the Japanese.

Please repeat this telegram and your reply to Hankow and Tokyo.

HULL

693.002/525 : Telegram

The Consul General at Shanghai (Gauss) to the Secretary of State

SHANGHAI, February 24, 1938—11 a. m.
[Received 3 : 05 p. m.]

309. I discussed the customs situation yesterday afternoon with the Japanese Consul General who says he has received no instructions in regard to the assurances we desire and that any such assurances must, of course, be given at Tokyo.   He suggested that customs revenues in Japanese occupied ports be deposited in the Japanese bank while those in Chinese ports be placed in the British bank, and that the interested foreign representatives should now determine the quotas due from each port for service of foreign obligations, saying that it can also be arranged to release quotas from other Japanese occupied ports.   He desires that quotas be fixed for a year and that they be based upon revenues for the past 5 or 6 months.   I pointed out that if the assurances we desire are given and implemented in good faith it will be a simple routine process for the Inspectorate General to determine monthly or every 2 months what amounts are due from each port for servicing loan obligations.   I again complained of the extremely unsatisfactory situation here under which the customs are restricted in functioning and Japanese ships and Japanese merchants are not paying tonnage dues and customs duties.   I also stated that reports indicate continued smuggling in North China.   He asserted that smuggling in the north has been stopped and he is anxious to settle the customs question here and suppress irregular practices.

2. It seems to me obvious that what the Japanese now desire is to obtain for their own purposes of customs revenues over and above the lowest possible fixed quotas for customs expenses and foreign obligations, leaving all other questions to be dealt with in future by the puppet governments of their creation.

Repeated to Tokyo, Hankow and Peiping.

GAUSS

693.002/526 : Telegram

The Ambassador in China (Johnson) to the Secretary of State

HANKOW, February 25, 1938—4 p. m.
[Received February 25—9 : 30 a. m.]

124. My 117, February 21, 3 p. m. I am authoritatively informed that Kung, replying to British Ambassador's advice, has stated in substance as follows:

"The Chinese Government considers that Japanese interference with performance of China's treaty and loan agreement obligations—introduction of new tariff, seizure of customs revenue and application of pressure to make Customs Administration subservient to Japanese wishes—should appear as acts of violence and not as compliance by Chinese customs officials as tools of the Japanese. Chinese Government asks British Government what action it would be prepared to take that might be effective in avoiding a serious eventuality which Chinese Government believes will result from a policy of acquiescence in Japanese wishes on the part of customs services.

In view of British suggestions of disobedience by Commissioners, Chinese Government asks British Government to emphasize to any person or persons of British nationality disobedience of orders issued by lawful Chinese authority with a view to maintenance of China's treaty and loan obligations would involve disloyalty of high traditions of service and would be particularly reprehensible at this particular juncture. Chinese Government asks British Government to bring all practicable pressure to bear, with a view to prevention of disloyalty which would have unfortunate consequences for British and other foreign as well as Chinese interests."

JOHNSON

693.002/528 : Telegram

The Ambassador in Japan (Grew) to the Secretary of State

TOKYO, February 25, 1938—8 p. m.
[Received February 25—3 p. m.]

133. Our 123, February 23, noon,[68] via Shanghai. Chinese customs. My British colleague has given me in confidence the substance of new telegraphic instructions from his Foreign Office dated February 24 paraphrased below which he will take up tomorrow with the Vice Minister for Foreign Affairs.

---

[68] Not printed.

Without indicating that he has given me this document for any reason other than to keep me informed of developments he evidently hopes that these modified proposals may commend themselves to and possibly receive the support of our own Government. He tells me that the French Ambassador is prepared to make representations in support of these proposals but Craigie has asked him to abstain from doing so lest the impression be created that the American Government alone is out of sympathy with the British position which would inevitably weaken his own representations.

Paraphrase of British telegram.

With regard to the deposit of funds in return for sufficient safeguards it appears that the time has come for us to make a concession. We believe that if possible this concession should be restricted to depositing in the Yokohama Specie Bank the Japanese share in the loan services as well as the surplus after the foreign loan obligations have been met in full.

We would be prepared to consider an alternative only if this desideratum is impossible to secure. Such an alternative would provide that the complete revenues in the occupied areas be deposited in the Yokohama Specie Bank but that an undertaking be given that there shall be regularly transferred to the interested foreign banks the quotas accruing with respect to foreign obligations. This second alternative could however only be contemplated if formal assurances in writing were given you by the Japanese Government to the following purport: (End paraphrase).

"(1) That the full services of foreign obligations will be maintained without interruption on due dates provided that revenue collections are sufficient but otherwise unconditionally.

(2) That foreign obligations will be treated as a first charge on revenue after the cost of maintaining the customs administration.

(3) That foreign loan quotas will be settled by agreement with all the powers concerned at weekly or monthly intervals as may be agreed and amounts so settled shall be transferred forthwith by the Yokohama Specie Bank to the banks nominated by the powers concerned or responsible for the service of the loan, i. e. in our case there would be paid to the Hong Kong and Shanghai bank the quota[s] in respect of the British Boxer indemnity and in respect of the loans serviced by the bank.

(4) That any preventive launches, et cetera, still detained will be returned to the customs.

(5) That customs authority shall be exercised in regard to all Japanese non-military imports.

(6) In addition to the above it is highly desirable to have a uniform tariff for all China. An assurance that the Japanese authorities will arrange for this with the Inspector General of Customs on the 1931 basis or otherwise would help to relieve our anxiety regarding the integrity of the Customs Administration."

(Paraphrase) Provided that you receive written assurances from the Japanese Government covering the first five points, and if possible, the sixth point, the financial adviser in Shanghai would then be authorized by us to waive further objection on the part of the British Government [to] a local discussion of the details. Of course no responsibility for the attitude of the Chinese Government or of the other interested parties would thereby be implied.

There must be a perfectly clear understanding that any arrangement on either of the foregoing bases would be only for the duration of the present hostilities and therefore of a temporary character. (End paraphrase.)

GREW

693.002/531 : Telegram

The Consul General at Shanghai (Gauss) to the Secretary of State

SHANGHAI, February 27, 1938—noon.
[Received February 27—7 a. m.]

324. Reference my 313, February 25, 1 p. m.[69] I have now seen copy of personal letter from Commissioner at Tientsin to Inspector General from which it appears that while at the very first an arrangement could have been made for regular remittances for foreign obligations, the long delay resulted in stiffening of attitude of military who insisted on a statement that no remittances would be made until end of hostilities, to which the Commissioner says he agreed in order to save the situation.

Repeated to Tokyo, Hankow.

GAUSS

693.002/534 : Telegram

The Ambassador in China (Johnson) to the Secretary of State

HANKOW, February 28, 1938—noon.
[Received 5 : 25 p. m.]

134. Shanghai's 252, February 12, 8 p. m., Department's 159, February 23, 5 p. m. and Shanghai's 313, February 25, 1 p. m.[70] Following information imparted to me by Arthur Young may throw some light on situation:

Arthur Young states that in October there was discussion in Shanghai regarding instructions which should be sent to Commissioner of Customs at Tientsin in connection with discussions emanating from Tientsin as the result of instructions sent to the Commissioner quoted in my 804, October 13, 3 p. m.[71] Young states that on October 15 British Consul, Tientsin, reported that strong objection was taken by Japanese authorities to the fact that arrangements for

---

[69] Not printed; this telegram was an inconclusive reply to Department's telegram No. 159, February 23, 5 p. m. p. 660.
[70] Telegram No. 313 not printed.
[71] *Foreign Relations*, 1937, vol. III, p. 873.

custodian bank covered all China and Consul doubted whether even the original proposal of putting the money into Yokohama Specie Bank would be acceptable. Maze appears to have suggested in view of the above that only safe way to ensure agreement would be to authorize the Commissioner to make the best local settlement of the case. Kung would not agree to this. Eventually, as the result of discussions in Shanghai between Kung, Hall-Patch, Hall [72] and Young, Maze instructed Commissioner at Tientsin on October 19 that Minister of Finance was unable to authorize any concession beyond that set out in the six points which Department will find covered in my 804, October 13, 3 p. m. This instruction was followed by another on October 19 sent by Maze to the Commissioner of Customs at Tientsin which apparently had the approval of Kung. It stated that if Commissioner of Customs [at] Tientsin failed to secure agreement along lines of six points and in view of the difficult position in which he was, Commissioner of Customs was privately authorized as a final alternative to use his discretion in depositing the Tientsin and Chinwangtao customs revenue locally "in a reliable bank of good standing, but remittances for cost of collection, foreign and internal loans, and the indemnity and regular local obligations such as conservancy and quantity are to be made therefrom as due and if considered necessary by you. Any balance remaining is to be left to accumulate in the bank." Arthur Young informs me that the "due and if" in the above quotation were omitted in the process of transmitting this instruction to Commissioner of Customs at Tientsin, and that Commissioner therefore interpreted message as giving him complete discretion. He deposited funds in the Yokohama Specie Bank without obtaining any assurances from the Japanese, hence situation which has now developed. Letter dated October 22 addressed by the Commissioner of Customs at Tientsin to the Japanese Consul General, quoted in Shanghai's 252, February 12, 8 p. m., was doubtless the result of Commissioner of Customs' exercise of discretion which he thought he had because of the instruction which he received from the Chinese representative and which was dated October 19.

JOHNSON

693.002/536 : Telegram

The Consul General at Shanghai (Gauss) to the Secretary of State

SHANGHAI, March 1, 1938—8 p. m.
[Received March 2—7 a. m.]

340. On January 28th the National City Bank reported the customs authorities here had refused to issue a permit to reship a cargo of

---

[72] Monroe B. Hall, Consul at Shanghai.

automobile tires from Shanghai to Hong Kong and that it was their understanding such refusal was based upon instructions issued by the Japanese military authorities to the customs to prevent shipment from Shanghai of any so-called war materials which might reach the Chinese market. Another American firm a few days later reported a similar case involving a shipment of tires to Hoihow.

These cases were immediately taken up with the Commissioner of Customs who on February 1st replied in part as follows: "The Japanese authorities who are now in military control of this area have informed me that they cannot allow reshipment of tires to Hong Kong or to South China ports".

On February 2 I addressed a letter to the Japanese Consul General regarding the matter and requested an explanation of this reported interference by the Japanese authorities with legitimate American trade. On February 18th a further request was made for an immediate reply. I am now in receipt of the Japanese Consul General's reply dated February 28th the pertinent portions of which read as follows:

"I have the honor to inform you in reply that upon the complete encirclement of Shanghai by the Japanese forces the Japanese military authorities instructed the Shanghai Maritime Customs to prohibit the reshipment from Shanghai of military supplies which are liable to fall into the hands of the Chinese troops or being utilized by the Chinese for military purposes. Since the reshipment of the goods belonging to the said American firms has been prohibited by the Shanghai Maritime Customs in accordance with the instructions of the Japanese military authorities, I regret to inform you that I am not in a position to enable the said goods to be reshipped from Shanghai to South China or Hong Kong. I have to add however that the Japanese authorities have no intention whatever to impede legitimate and bona fide business transactions by nationals of third powers and therefore are now trying to devise such means as to preclude as far as possible any unnecessary pressure on legitimate business transactions resulting from the application of the said prohibition."

A few cases involving goods other than tires have been reported but upon representations being made to the Commissioner of Customs permits to reship have generally been granted which would seem to indicate that while the prohibition in respect of tires is absolute there is considerable elasticity in regard to other goods. In this connection I learn from the acting British Commercial Counselor that British firms have experienced somewhat similar difficulties but that no shipments of tires have been involved, that all cases of other types of goods have been successfully arranged with the customs and that in consequence it has not been necessary thus far to make any representations to the Japanese authorities.

Repeated by mail to Tokyo.

GAUSS

693.002/532 : Telegram

The Secretary of State to the Ambassador in Japan (Grew)

WASHINGTON, March 3, 1938—5 p. m.

76. Your 133, February 25, 8 p. m., containing in its penultimate paragraph six points outlined by the British Government as the basis for representations by the British Ambassador.

The Department notes from your 137, February 27, 4 p. m., and 138, February 28, noon,[73] that the British Ambassador has made the representations above referred to, that the Japanese have replied, and that discussions are in progress.

The following comment upon the six points is offered for your guidance in discussions with your British and French colleagues and, as the situation develops, in possible further approaches by you in your discretion to the Japanese authorities:

With regard to numbered points 1 and 2, the Department would approve endeavors to obtain from the Japanese Government assurances of the character described.

With regard to points 4 and 5, the Department notes that the Japanese are giving these points consideration but are asking that they not be insisted upon as a part of the proposed arrangement. In regard to point 4, the Department would approve efforts to obtain from the Japanese assurances of the character described, as indicated in the Department's 339, December 12, 3 p. m., to you.[74] In regard to point 5, the Department would also approve efforts to obtain assurances from the Japanese in regard to the observance of customs requirements for Japanese goods imported into China, as indicated in the Department's 109, February 3, 7 p. m., to Shanghai, which was repeated to you, and in the Department's 42, February 5, 3 p. m. to you.

With regard to point 3, the Department's attitude is, as indicated to the American Consul at Shanghai in Department's 86, January 29, 4 p. m., that the American Government is not prepared to participate officially or to nominate an official to participate in an arrangement for the allocation of foreign loan quotas. If the assurances covered in points 1 and 2 are obtained and faithfully observed, it would appear that the general objectives of point 3 would be attained.

With regard to point 6, the Department's position was covered in its telegram to you, No. 31, January 30, 1 p. m., and in the Department's telegram to Shanghai No. 116, February 5, 4 p. m. (which Shanghai was asked to repeat to you), indicating that the American Government regards the Government of China as the only authority which can legally cause a revision to be made in the Chinese customs tariff and

---

[73] Neither printed.
[74] *Foreign Relations*, 1937, vol. III, p. 900.

that the Department does not wish to proffer views in regard to the suggested reintroduction of the 1931 tariff.

Repeated to Shanghai.

HULL

893.51 Salt Funds/169 : Telegram

The Consul General at Shanghai (Gauss) to the Secretary of State

SHANGHAI, March 9, 1938—4 p. m.
[Received March 10—7 a. m.]

371. Dr. Lockhart, the American Associate Director General of the Chinese Government Salt Administration, has today handed to me (for the Ambassador) and at the same time is handing to the British, French and German diplomatic representatives and to the representatives of the American, British, French and German banking groups interested, a memorandum outlining the very serious effect upon the Salt Administration and upon the system of regular monthly remittances of revenues for the unprotected foreign loans in particular resulting from hostilities and Japanese military occupation of certain districts.

2. The memorandum states that the Chinese and foreign Salt Administration officers at Kalgan, Taiyuanfu, Hangchow, Tsinanfu, Yangchow and Panpu[75] have been compelled to evacuate their posts as a result of actual hostilities or of chaotic conditions associated therewith; that the Chinese officers at Tientsin and Wuhu have also been obliged to evacuate; that the Associate District Director at Tientsin, a Japanese subject, participated apparently under compulsion in the seizure of the records and in the subsequent unlawful transfer of funds of the Changlu District Directorate to the control of an office allegedly functioning under the Peiping Provisional Government; that this same officer is reported to have assumed the designation of Associate Director General in North China and as such has appointed a fellow Japanese until recently at Amoy and a former Chinese salt officer as directors of the Shantung District; that at Tsingtao one or possibly two Japanese officers of the service are understood to have been appointed to the eastern areas of Shantung Province; and that with the forcible evacuation of senior foreign and Chinese personnel from the affected districts the administrative procedure governing production, storage, and release of salt against duty payment has either been brought to a standstill or taken over by the *de facto* authorities of the locality for their own benefit.

3. The salt revenue affected districts for the fiscal year ended June last totaled over 116,477,000 Chinese dollars or 54% of the aggregate for the whole country. The foreign loan quotas due from these Jap-

---

[75] North Kiangsu on Lunghai Railway.

anese occupied districts total over 563,000 Chinese dollars each month and are in arrears to a total of about 290,000 Chinese dollars to March 1 this year.

4. Although the Japanese Consular authorities at Tientsin assured the deputy of the Directors General last August that foreign loan interests would be respected there had been no other indication that the authorities set up at Tientsin intend to resume remittance of quotas.

5. Furthermore a foreign loan surtax imposed since 1931 to safeguard the loan service from impairment through currency depreciation has not been forthcoming from Japanese occupied districts. During the fiscal year ended June 30 last this surtax from the districts now Japanese occupied amounted to over 4,600,000 Chinese dollars.

6. The following foreign loans serviced from the salt revenue are jeopardized by the existing situation: Anglo-French loan of 1908, Hukuang loan of 1911, Crisp loan of 1912, Vickers Marconi loans of 1918 and '19, Chicago Bank loan of 1919, and Pacific Development Corporation loan of 1919.

7. The memorandum emphasizes importance of salt revenue and maintenance of integrity of the Salt Administration in relation to China's international credit, continued service of foreign loans, and continued stability of China's domestic currency and finance. The interference with normal functioning clientele involves reduction in staff whose experience and energy have hitherto been vital factors in maintenance and increase of salt revenue and consequent support of loans secured thereon.

8. Memorandum is submitted as basis for consideration of what specific action should be taken toward preservation of integrity of the Administration and of the significant international interests represented thereby.

9. I add the following for your further information: the Chinese Director General of the Salt Administration with part of staff withdrew some time ago to Hong Kong and has been ordered to proceed to Hankow and Chungking. Lockhart remains at Shanghai temporarily in connection with foreign loan interests principally. The attitude of the Ministry of Finance appears to be one of desiring the withdrawal of the Administration from occupied areas to prevent development of organization and revenue by the Japanese. This would more or less tie Lockhart's hands in any negotiations with the Japanese should they become necessary. He has not been approached by Japanese. There are reports that the special service bureau of the Japanese Army or its puppet governments will set up a salt bureau for Kiangsu, Chekiang and Anhui.

Repeated to Hankow, Peiping and Tokyo.

GAUSS

693.002/552 : Telegram

The Ambassador in China (Johnson) to the Secretary of State

HANKOW, March 10, 1938—10 a. m.
[Received March 10—7 a. m.]

151. My 124, February 25, 4 p. m. Doctor Young showed me yesterday a copy of a letter addressed to Doctor Kung by Mr. MacKillop of British Embassy which contained in substance the following:

British note stated that policy which Kung suggested must lead to the forcible seizure and disruption of the customs by the Japanese; that this will result in the suspension of service of foreign obligations and destroy China's credit. British note states that the only means of avoiding Japanese control of customs in occupied areas (which Japanese are in a position to do) is to arrive at some arrangement which will preserve non-Japanese administration, provide due service of foreign obligations, and enable collections to be enforced. British note added that the object of the discussions at Tokyo and Shanghai is to secure as far as possible these essentials, and stated that it was the desire of the British Government that the utmost effort should be made to persuade Doctor Kung to acquiesce in any arrangements that it might be possible to reach in those negotiations.

Doctor Young remarked to me that British Government was asking Kung to accept some arrangement which might be arrived at through negotiations concerning which Doctor Kung was being kept in complete ignorance.

JOHNSON

___

893.51 Salt Funds/170 : Telegram

The Ambassador in China (Johnson) to the Secretary of State

HANKOW, March 12, 1938—10 a. m.
[Received March 12—7 a. m.]

154. Shanghai's 371, March 9, 4 p. m. It is my opinion that in dealing with the situation which faces the Salt Administration we should remain as aloof in the matter of offering advice to the Chinese as we have been in regard to the Customs Administration. Chinese Government is unable to do anything for administration of this tax in areas occupied by the Japanese. Foreign governments are in no position to substitute themselves individually or in combination for Chinese control. Japanese are prepared and in fact desire to substitute Japanese control for Chinese control of these taxes. Under the circumstances it seems to me that we must in the end hold Japanese responsible for any claim which our nationals have upon the revenues in question.

Repeated to Peiping, Shanghai. Shanghai please repeat to Tokyo.

JOHNSON

893.51 Salt Funds/169 : Telegram

The Secretary of State to the Consul General at Shanghai (Gauss)

WASHINGTON, March 16, 1938—5 p. m.

209. Your 371, March 9, 4 p. m. Please transmit the following telegram to Tokyo:

"Shanghai's 371, March 9, 4 p. m. The Department suggests that in your discretion and following conference with your interested colleagues, you make an oral approach, supported by an *aide-mémoire*, to the Japanese Foreign Office in regard to this matter. It is suggested that you bring to the attention of the Japanese Government in detail but without divulging source the occurrences and situation described in paragraphs 2 and 3 of Shanghai's telegram under reference and that you state (1) that American loans amounting to more than U. S. $15,000,000 are secured on the revenues of the Chinese salt administration (specifically, there are three loans: the American share of the Hukuang Loan, the so-called Chicago Bank Loan, and the Pacific Development Corporation Loan); (2) that arrangements were made early in 1937 for the servicing of those loans from salt revenues, with every prospect that payment would be made in full; and (3) that in as much as the prospects of servicing those loans are being adversely affected in consequence of the action in China of Japanese armed forces, we desire to bring to the attention of the Japanese Government the substantial American interest in the Chinese salt administration and to make full reservation in regard to American rights and interests." [76]

Repeat to Hankow for the information of the Ambassador, referring to his 154, March 12, 10 a. m., and repeat also to Peiping.

HULL

693.002/575 : Telegram

The Consul General at Shanghai (Gauss) to the Secretary of State

SHANGHAI, March 24 1938—10 a. m.
[Received March 24—7 : 30 a. m.]

446. Inspector General of Customs has communicated to British and French Ambassadors and to me copy of a telegram from Commissioner of Customs at Tientsin reporting that he is informed that further tariff revision will come into force probably on May 1st and that local press indicates that the revision will include measures designed to promote trade and industry, reduction in export duties, lifting of prohibition on export of some products and some changes to encourage export trade for improvement of international receipts and payments for stabilization of new currency, stimulation of closer

---

[76] For text of *aide-mémoire*, dated March 19, to the Japanese Foreign Office, see *Foreign Relations, Japan, 1931–1941,* vol. I, p. 741; the British and French Embassies took similar action.

economic contact between China, Japan and Manchukuo, and a "simultaneous readjustment of customs structure to simplify customs procedure".

Repeated to Tokyo, Hankow, and Peiping.

GAUSS

693.002/576 : Telegram

The Consul General at Shanghai (Gauss) to the Secretary of State

SHANGHAI, March 25, 1938—noon.
[Received March 25—11 : 35 a. m.]

451. Following from Tokyo:

198. "March 24, 8 p. m. The British Ambassador called this morning and informed me that his negotiations with the Japanese Government with respect to the settlement of the Chinese customs question were coming to a close. He furnished me with a copy of the text of a proposed agreement which he has telegraphed to his Government. He believes the proposed agreement, which the Japanese would like to put into force from April 1st next, represents the maximum concession obtainable from the Japanese and that it will be generally satisfactory to the British Government although there are two or three points which may require modification. The Ambassador stated that he believed the agreement would be satisfactory to the Chinese in view of the fact that the Japanese were agreeing to the full servicing of the foreign loans and thereby helping to maintain China's credit and furthermore that the arrears on the foreign loan and indemnity service at present deposited in the Hong Kong and Shanghai Bank would be released to meet the relevant overdraft of the Central Bank of China for the loan and indemnity payments for which they act as security.

The French Ambassador has cabled the text to his Government and asked for instructions.

Craigie expressed the hope that the settlement of the customs question by the proposed agreement would prevent the Chinese from further playing of the American, British, and French Governments against Japan. Craigie then stated that he hoped that if we could not accept or approve the proposed agreement our Government would at least express no objection to it.

The proposed agreement presumably is to be initialed by Craigie and the Minister for Foreign Affairs and despatched to Shanghai to be signed by the Inspector General of Customs and the Japanese Consul General at Shanghai.

Hall-Patch, financial adviser to the British Embassy in China, is arriving in Tokyo tonight for consultation.

The text of the proposed agreement is as follows:

'1. All revenues collected by the Chinese Maritime Customs at each port within the areas under Japanese occupation to be deposited with the Yokohama Specie Bank or, where the bank has no branch, with any other bank or banks agreed upon.

2. From revenues thus deposited, foreign loan quotas to be remitted at intervals agreed upon to the Inspector General's account at the Yokohama Specie Bank in Shanghai in order to meet in full on due dates the service of such foreign loans and indemnities secured on the customs revenues as were regularly met up to July, 1937.

3. The service of foreign loans and indemnities secured on the customs revenues to be treated as a first charge on the revenues after deducting the maintenance expenses of the Customs Administration.

4. (a) Foreign loan quota for each port to be in proportion to its share of the total revenue for all ports during the 6 months period commencing September 1, 1937.

(b) Quotas to remain good for 6 months, except in the event of a radical change affecting the proportion of revenue of each port, whereupon a readjustment of the quotas is to be undertaken.

(c) Quotas for the following 6 months to be determined at the close of the first 6 months period on the basis of the actual revenue during that period.

(d) All calculations in respect of quotas to be based on Chinese customs statistics and to be determined on the above basis by the Chinese Customs Administration with the agreement of Japan and the interested third powers.

(e) Any insufficiency of revenue to meet the quota of any port within the area under Japanese occupation in North China and in Central China to be made up out of the revenue of other ports in the respective areas.

5. (a) A reserve fund in respect of North China revenues to be created from the revenues now being held at Shanghai and Tientsin of a sum, equal to the foreign loan quotas for Tientsin and Chinwangtao determined according to 3 [4?] (a) for the period commencing on the date of the suspension of remittances to the Inspector General in October last and ending on the 28th February. This fund to be deposited in the Yokohama Specie Bank at Tientsin. The Inspector General to be authorized, after consultation with the proper Japanese authorities, to make the necessary requisitions from this fund in order to make good any insufficiency of revenue to meet quota payments at any port in North China under Japanese occupation.

(b) A reserve fund in respect of the Central China revenues to be created from the accumulated balance of current revenue collections at Shanghai now deposited at the Hong Kong and Shanghai Bank. This fund, of which the amount would be equal to the fund to be created under paragraph (a) above, will be deposited in the Yokohama Specie Bank at Tientsin. The Inspector General to be authorized, after consultation with the proper Japanese authorities, to make the necessary requisitions from this fund in order to make good any insufficiency of revenue to meet quota payments at any port in Central China under Japanese occupation.

(c) The arrears on the foreign loan and indemnity service at present deposited in the Hong Kong and Shanghai Bank at Shanghai to be released to meet the refund overdraft for which they act as security.

(*d*) The arrears on the Japanese portion of the Boxer indemnity held in a suspense account at the Hong Kong and Shanghai Bank since September 1937 to be transferred to the Yokohama Specie Bank for the account of the Japanese Government.

(*e*) Future payments of the Japanese portion of the Boxer indemnity as well as the Japanese share of the reorganization loan of 1913 to be made from the Inspector General's accounts at the Hong Kong and Shanghai Bank and the Yokohama Specie Bank as in the servicing of all foreign loans and indemnities secured on the customs revenue.

(*f*) After the above-mentioned payments and adjustments have been made the balance of the customs accounts with the Hong Kong and Shanghai Bank in each port under Japanese occupation is to be transferred to the branch of the Yokohama Specie Bank in each port and utilized for future foreign loan quota payments'.

The following is a paraphrase of Craigie's telegram to his Government commenting on the proposed agreement:

'The arrangement proposed represents the best I can hope to get here and, while we need not take too seriously Vice Minister's warning in regard to impatience of local authorities, I am definitely of opinion that further bargaining now over details will only play into hands of opponents of any arrangement with foreign interests.

Under proposed arrangement we secure return to central bank of Shanghai arrears on foreign loan quotas (£6,700,000) and creation of reserve fund in addition to reserve fund for northern area. It is useless to press further for any control over surplus balances whether of arrears or of future collections, but arrangement contains no mention of how surplus is to be disposed of after deposit in Yokohama [Specie] Bank and we remain free to continue unofficial pressure on behalf of domestic loan service. I have proposed deposit of surplus in name of Inspector General (see Shanghai telegram to Foreign Office No. 482) but I do not think Japanese Government will agree. Vice Minister hopes that new currency in North China will be placed on a convertible basis before arrangement is concluded, but agrees that, failing that, a clause must be added to ensure that northern revenues are made available to the Inspector General either in Chinese legal tender or in foreign currencies necessary to these obligations.

I hope to receive simultaneously desired assurances as regards Japanese non-military imports and customs launches, except that latter must at present be confined to ports in occupied area. I am hopeful however we may gradually be able to secure release of some launches for operation off coasts of unoccupied area. Decision on 1931 tariff still hangs fire and I do not anticipate answer before end of month: but omens are favorable and I do not recommend insistence on obtaining parallel assurance on this point.

It is just possible that, after discussions with financial adviser, we may still be able to get monthly basis of calculation of quotas in return for abandonment of all claim to creation of reserve funds, but I am not sanguine of this nor am I convinced that it is wise policy.

Subject to any amendments which financial adviser may propose on points as to detail, I hope I may have your authority to agree to proposed arrangement before the end of this month. It will, I presume, ultimately take the form of an agreement between Inspector General of Customs and Japanese Consul General at Shanghai, but I should be grateful for your views on this point.'

Please repeat to Hankow and Department as our No. 198, March 24, 8 p. m. Grew."

GAUSS

693.002/583 : Telegram

The Consul General at Shanghai (Gauss) to the Secretary of State

SHANGHAI, March 28, 1938—5 p. m.
[Received March 28—9 : 19 a. m.]

469. My No. 340, March 1, 8 p. m., regarding instructions issued by the Japanese military to the customs authorities here to refuse permission to reexport automobile tires and other articles classed as war materials from Shanghai to South China ports.

I have now been informed by one of the American firms affected by this prohibition that during the past 10 days shipments of tires in small lots not exceeding 50 pieces have been passed by the customs and shipped to South China ports. Shipment of larger lots apparently still impossible. From a reliable customs source I learn that although there has been no change in the general prohibitory order issued by the Japanese military referred to above, Japanese customs authorities are easing the restrictions somewhat.

Repeated to Tokyo.

GAUSS

893.51 Salt Funds/173 : Telegram

The Ambassador in China (Johnson) to the Secretary of State

HANKOW, March 29, 1938—10 a. m.
[Received 11 : 40 a. m.]

175. Shanghai's 371, March 9, 4 p. m. [and] my 154, March 12, 10 a. m. Under date of March 22 British Embassy addressed letter to Kung referring to memorandum of the Associate Director General of the Salt Administration stating that the question of representations to the Japanese Government was under consideration. British Embassy stated that the basis of such representations would be that "apart from the interests of His Majesty's Government in existing loans secured on salt revenues and in the British staff, the preservation of the Administration is most important for future rehabilitation." British Embassy concluded by stating that under the circumstances British Embassy was anxious to urge upon Kung the importance of

preventing the disruption of the Administration and the necessity of maintaining the authority of the foreign staff. To this letter Kung replied in substance under date of March 24:

"The Chinese Government is anxious that every practicable step be taken to preserve the Salt Administration and to prevent its disruption, and will be grateful for the assistance of your Government to that end. As to the position of the foreign officers, I would point out that the present abnormal conditions, and particularly difficulties of communication, have made it impracticable in all cases fully to maintain the principles by whatever joint responsibility of foreign and Chinese officers in matter of administration; but in principle I consider that as to essential functions the joint responsibility of the Directors General and of the subordinate foreign and Chinese officials should be maintained substantially as it existed during the years prior to the outbreak of hostilities. I am issuing instructions to the Salt Administration to the effect that there should be no derogations from this principle except to such extent as is unavoidable during the emergency, and that any such derogations are only temporary in character."

Repeated to Peiping and Shanghai.

JOHNSON

693.002/584 : Telegram

The Ambassador in China (Johnson) to the Secretary of State

HANKOW, March 29, 1938—3 p. m.
[Received March 29—11 : 54 a. m.]

178. Shanghai's 451, March 25, noon. I have not observed anything in the situation here which would lead me to expect that the proposed agreement regarding Chinese customs worked out between British Ambassador and Japanese Minister for Foreign Affairs will be accepted by Chinese Government. As was to have been expected, agreement makes no provision for maintenance of domestic loans, nor any provision made regarding surplus of funds after foreign quotas and administrative expenses of customs have been taken care of. My reaction to this proposal is that we should refrain from urging Chinese Government to accept this arrangement. I see no reason on the other hand why we should attempt to oppose it.

I do not perceive any basis for hope that the settlement of the customs question by this proposed agreement would prevent Chinese from further playing off the American, British and French Governments against Japan. It has not been apparent to me that the Chinese Government has endeavored to use this question for the purpose indicated. On the contrary, it has at times seemed to me that the Japanese may be disposed to use the situation for the purpose of persuading the British, French and American Governments to use their influence with the Chinese Government to accept situations beneficial to the

Japanese and secondarily to the foreign powers but harmful to the Chinese.

Repeated to Peiping and Shanghai.

JOHNSON

693.002/585 : Telegram

The Consul General at Shanghai (Gauss) to the Secretary of State

SHANGHAI, March 30, 1938—9 p. m.
[Received March 30—3 : 15 p. m.]

480. The following telegram has been received from Tokyo:

"March 30, noon. Our 198, March 24, 8 p. m.,[77] Chinese customs. My British colleague has now learned from the Inspector General of Customs in China that the latter will not accept the responsibility of signing an agreement with the Japanese Consul General in Shanghai. Craigie therefore now visualizes the following procedure: The Japanese Government would convey to Craigie the assurances finally evolving from his negotiations and at the same time would send transcript of instructions to the Japanese Consular Officers in China who in turn would communicate these instructions involving the deposit of customs receipts in the Yokohama Specie Bank to the various Customs Commissioners. The Commissioners acting under *force majeure* would report their action to the Inspector General. Such procedure is apparently considered necessary to avoid loss of face by the Chinese officials.

Please repeat to Hankow and to Department as our No. 215, March 30, noon. Grew."

GAUSS

693.002/594 : Telegram

The Consul General at Shanghai (Gauss) to the Secretary of State

SHANGHAI, April 7, 1938—11 a. m.
[Received 4 : 52 p. m.]

508. Following from Tokyo:

233. "April 6, 7 p. m. Reference our 198, March 24, 8 p. m., Chinese customs. My British colleague has furnished me with the text of the revised summaries of the proposed customs arrangement which is the same as the text transmitted in our telegram under reference with the following exceptions. Paragraph 1. After the word 'deposited' insert 'in the name of the Commissioner of Customs'.

Paragraph 3. Insert after the word 'administration' '(including the share of the expenses Inspectorate General) as certified by the Inspector General of Customs'.

Paragraph 4, sub-paragraph (*b*) substitute the word 'amount' for the word 'proportion'.

[77] See telegram No. 451, March 25, noon, from the Consul General at Shanghai, p. 671.

Paragraph 4, sub-paragraph (*d*) to read : 'All calculations in respect of quotas to be based on Chinese customs, gross import, export, and interport duty collections and to be determined on the above basis by the Customs Administration, with the agreement of Japan and the interested third powers'.

Paragraph 5, sub-paragraph (*a*) first sentence to read 'A reserve fund in respect of the North China revenues to be created from the revenues now being held at Tientsin, the amount of the fund being equal to the foreign loan quotas for Tientsin and Chinwangtao determined according to sub-paragraph 4 (*a*)' and thence the text as given.

Paragraph 5, sub-paragraph (*b*). Insert the word 'Tientsin' instead of the word 'Shanghai' at the end of the second sentence.

Paragraph 5, sub-paragraph (*e*). Delete the words 'from the Inspector General's accounts at the Hong Kong and Shanghai Bank and the Yokohama Specie Bank' and insert the words 'in the same manner'.

Paragraph 5, sub-paragraph (*f*). Delete the words 'the branch of the Yokohama Specie Bank in each port and utilized for future loan quota payments' and insert the words 'the account of the Commissioner of Customs at the branch of the Yokohama Specie Bank in each port and utilized for future foreign loan quota payments'.

Craigie informs me that certain points are still outstanding, the most important of which is the choice to be made between the two alternative systems of which contributions of the various ports to the service of the foreign obligations shall be based. Namely, (1) quotas fixed for 6 months in advance on the basis of the receipts of the previous 6 months, together with reserve funds on which the Inspector General can call in order to make good any deficiencies and (2) a system of quotas revised monthly on the basis of collections for the preceding month but without any reserve funds. The draft text as revised is based on the assumption that the former alternative will be chosen.

The British Ambassador also furnished me with a draft copy of the Foreign Minister's note which refers to the conversations which took place between the British Ambassador and the Vice Minister regarding the Chinese customs revenues and states that the Japanese Government after obtaining the concurrence of the proper Chinese authorities in the occupied areas are now desirous of dealing with the matter on the lines set forth by the proposal and are prepared to take measures described therein on the understanding that they are of a temporary nature and for duration of the present hostilities. The note concludes with the expression of hope that the arrangements will prove acceptable to the British Government.

Craigie's draft reply acknowledges the receipt of the Foreign Minister's note and states that the arrangements proposed in the documents enclosed therewith are acceptable to the British Government.

Craigie also furnished me with a draft letter addressed to him by the Vice Minister referring to the question of China's domestic debt, the payment of duty on non-military imports at Shanghai, and the return of the customs craft seized by the Japanese forces. With respect to China's domestic debt the draft letter states that while the question of China's domestic debt lies outside the scope of any discussion relating to China's foreign obligations it is believed that the Provisional Government will in its own interest give due consideration to this question. With regard to the payment of duty on non-military imports at Shanghai the draft letter states that it is unavoidable that the Chinese customs during active hostilities should have suffered some temporary dislocation in the ports immediately affected and that it is the intention of the Japanese Government that normal conditions should be restored and that payment of duty by [on?] all Japanese imports should be ensured at the earliest possible date; and that if not possible it is hoped that interested third powers will appreciate the importance of such emergency measures as reduction or exemption of tariff on a limited number of articles urgently needed and indispensable for the restoration of devastated war areas and for the relief of the general population. With respect to the return of the customs craft the draft letter points out that the customs service has already been permitted to use some of the vessels and that the Chinese authorities in the areas under Japanese orbits will gradually become interested in ensuring the collection of customs revenues and the Japanese will be ready to cooperate to this end and in such circumstances the Chinese customs service will be permitted to use all [its?] vessels excepting those especially required for military purposes and that even the latter will be progressively released as circumstances permit.

Please repeat to Hankow and to Department [as] No. 233, April 6, 7 p. m. Grew."

GAUSS

693.002/603 : Telegram

The Consul General at Shanghai (Gauss) to the Secretary of State

SHANGHAI, April 24, 1938—9 a. m.
[Received 10:40 a. m.]

572. [Following from Tokyo:]

267. "April 23, 8 p. m. Subject to the approval of the British Government the British Ambassador has now reached agreement with the Vice Minister for Foreign Affairs on the following texts relating to the service of foreign obligations secured on the Chinese Maritime Customs. The arrangement consists of a note with enclosure from the Minister for Foreign Affairs and the British Ambassador's reply. In addition there is a confidential exchange of letters with the Vice Minister relating to the provision of exchange to facilitate the transfer of the North China quotas.

My British colleague has suggested that the texts be cabled to the Department. He considers the matter urgent because if the arrangement is not concluded soon it may not be possible to apply it to the March customs collections which he feels would greatly complicate matters.

I shall take no action unless or until instructed.

Documents. 1. Draft note from the Minister for Foreign Affairs to the British Ambassador as revised at interview with the Vice Minister on April 23.

'Your Excellency, As a result of the conversations which have recently taken place between Your Excellency and Mr. Horinouchi respecting the service of the foreign obligations secured on the Chinese Maritime Customs and other relevant matters, I have the honor to inform Your Excellency that the Japanese Government, after obtaining the concurrence of the proper Chinese authorities in the occupied areas, are now desirous of dealing with the matter on the lines set forth in the accompanying document and are prepared to effect the measures described therein. It is understood that the measures are of a temporary nature for the duration of the present hostilities and will be subject to reconsideration in the event of a radical change in the economic conditions under which the above measures are proposed.

I trust these arrangements will prove acceptable to His Majesty's Government in the United Kingdom.

I have the honor to be, et cetera.'

2. Text of draft customs arrangement:

'All duties, surtaxes, dues and other revenues collected by the Chinese Maritime Customs at each port within the areas under Japanese occupation shall be deposited in the name of the Commissioner of Customs with the Yokohama Specie Bank or, where the bank has no branch, with any other bank or banks to be agreed upon.

(2) From the import, export and inter-port duties thus deposited, foreign loan quotas shall be remitted, at intervals which should not exceed 10 days, Inspector General's account at the Yokohama Specie Bank in Shanghai in order to meet in full on due dates the service of the foreign loans and indemnities which were secured on the customs revenue in July 1937.

(3) The service of foreign loans and indemnities secured on the customs revenues shall be treated at all ports in China as a first charge on the revenues after deducting the maintenance expenses of the Customs Administration (including the share of the expenses of the Inspectorate General) as certified by the Inspector General of Customs, and such customs payments and grants (hitherto deducted from gross revenues before payment of foreign obligations) as are similarly certified.

(4) (a) Foreign loan quotas for each port shall be determined monthly in proportion to the share of that port in the total gross collections for all ports during the preceding month.

(b) Calculations in respect of foreign loan quotas shall be based on the gross import, export, and inter-port duty collections of the Chinese Maritime Customs and these quotas shall be determined as set out in (a) above by the Inspectorate General of Customs, with the agreement of Japan and the other powers concerned.

(c) Any insufficiency of customs revenue to meet quota of a port within the area under Japanese occupation in North China and in Central China shall be made up out of customs revenue of other ports in the respective areas.

(5) (a) The arrears on the Japanese portion of the Boxer indemnity held in a suspense account at the Hong Kong and Shanghai Bank since September 1937, shall be paid to the Japanese Government.

(b) Future payments of the Japanese portion of the Boxer indemnity as well as the Japanese share of the Reorganization Loan of 1913 shall be made in the same manner as in the servicing of all foreign loans and indemnities secured on the customs revenue.

(c) The balance of the customs accounts with the Hong Kong and Shanghai Bank in each port under Japanese occupation shall be transferred to the account of the Commissioner of Customs at the branch of the Yokohama Specie Bank in each port and utilized for future foreign loan quota payments.

(6) This arrangement shall come into effect on (agreed date) and shall apply to the customs collections beginning with March 1938.'

3. Draft reply by the British Ambassador to the Minister for Foreign Affairs.

'Your Excellency, I have the honor to acknowledge the receipt of the note which Your Excellency was good enough to address to me on the [date] respecting the service of the foreign obligations secured on the Chinese Maritime Customs revenues and other relevant matters.

His Majesty's Government in the United Kingdom recognize that the present position creates great difficulties for which it is urgently necessary in the interest of all countries concerned to find a solution and I have accordingly been authorized to state that the arrangements set forth in Your Excellency's note and its enclosure are regarded by His Majesty's Government, for their part, as acceptable.

I am further instructed to take this opportunity to emphasize once more to Your Excellency the interest which my Government take in the maintenance in every respect of the authority and integrity of the Maritime Customs service.

I avail, et cetera.'

4. Draft letter from Sir Robert Craigie to the Vice Minister for Foreign Affairs.

'Confidential. My dear Vice Minister, With reference to the formal notes which are being exchanged today in regard to the Chinese Maritime Customs, I should be glad if, in order to avoid future misunderstanding, Your Excellency would be so good as to give me an assurance that the quotas for foreign obligations payable by the northern ports in Japanese occupation will be remitted in a currency which will enable the Inspector General to effect the necessary transfer into the currencies in which the foreign obligations are serviced. This question arises particularly in connection with the recent decline [decision?] to create a new currency in Northern China. I may add that I feel sure that the British authorities in China will lend such assistance as they properly can in overcoming transfer difficulties in connection with the payment of the foreign loan obligations due from the northern ports. Believe me, my dear Vice Minister, yours very sincerely.'

5. Draft reply from the Vice Minister for Foreign Affairs to Sir Robert Craigie.

'Confidential. My dear Ambassador, With reference to your letter of today I am glad to be able to give you the assurance that the quotas for foreign obligations payable by the northern ports in Japanese occupation will be paid in Chinese national currency, on the understanding that the Inspector General of Customs will arrange for the supply of the necessary amount of foreign exchange for the conversion of these sums into currencies in which the foreign obligations are serviced. I also take note with pleasure of your assurance that the British authorities will take such steps as they properly can to overcome transfer difficulties in connection with the payment of the foreign obligations due from the northern ports. Believe me, my dear Ambassador, yours very sincerely.'

Please repeat to Department as our 267, April 23, 8 p. m. Grew."

GAUSS

693.002/616 : Telegram

The Ambassador in China (Johnson) to the Secretary of State

HANKOW, April 26, 1938—10 a. m.
[Received 6 : 53 p. m.]

215. Tokyo's 233 of April 6, 7 p. m.,[78] regarding Chinese customs. Young yesterday handed my copy of a letter which he addressed on April 25 to British Ambassador which referred to letter summarized in my 151, March 10, 10 a. m., and made suggestion that consideration be given to the danger that the Japanese authorities might cause Japanese fostered régimes in China to accept any arrangement regarding customs which might be agreed upon between one or more of the friendly powers and Japan—before ascertaining whether conclusion of such arrangement would be acceptable to China—and then represent that the friendly powers had in effect recognized such régimes by reaching an understanding with them regarding customs. Young urged the desirability that Chinese Government be kept advised as far as deemed practicable and be consulted before anything should be consummated between Great Britain and Japan regarding customs. Young informs me that Chinese Government has no information of negotiations in Tokyo other than oral summary communicated to Kung by British Ambassador on recent visit.

JOHNSON

---

[78] See telegram No. 508, April 7, 11 a. m., from the Consul General at Shanghai. p. 676.

693.002/613 : Telegram

The Ambassador in China (Johnson) to the Secretary of State

HANKOW, April 26, 1938—noon.
[Received April 26—11:45 a. m.]

217. My 215, April 26, 10 a. m. Arthur Young gave me on April 25th copy of a confidential memorandum which he had presented on that day to British Ambassador at the latter's request regarding customs secured internal loans issued prior to outbreak of hostilities. Memorandum states that such loans outstanding amount to about 1,800 millions and that amount required for their service in 1938 is about 130 millions; that the corresponding figures for external customs secured obligations are approximately 650 millions and 90 millions. He states that since hostilities the service of foreign obligations has absorbed nearly all the net customs revenue exclusive of sums seized by Japanese controlled agencies at Tientsin and other ports, and that central bank has advanced to the customs amounts required to make up shortage.

Memorandum points out that as a matter of legal right obligations for which customs revenue is pledged are equally valid with rank according to seniority, and that an arrangement prejudicing position of some obligations by selecting others for favored treatment and permitting diversion of revenue for purposes other than those for which revenue is pledged would cause far-reaching injury to China's credit. Memorandum emphasizes importance of domestic loans to China's financial structure, pointing out that they are an essential part of the backing of the currency and comprise practically all of the required 60% of the fiduciary reserve against note issue. Memorandum was intended to impress British with necessity of including domestic loans in matters being considered in negotiations which British Ambassador has been conducting in Tokyo.

I am personally persuaded that on or about May 1st Japanese Government may attempt to arrange with Japanese controlled régimes at Nanking and Peiping to put into effect agreement recently arrived at between British and Japanese at Tokyo, and that British will find that customs in those areas have for all practical purposes been handed over to only Chinese authorities which Japanese recognize. Whether or not this result has been contemplated by British in negotiations at Tokyo I do not know. British Ambassador doubtless sincerely believes that he has been discussing an arrangement which Japanese will accept as between them and Nationalist Chinese authorities at Hankow, but I feel certain that Japanese will not recognize Chinese

Government as party to this arrangement, but will communicate it to régimes set up by them.

Not repeated to Tokyo or Shanghai.

JOHNSON

693.002/614 : Telegram

The Consul General at Shanghai (Lockhart) to the Secretary of State

SHANGHAI, April 26, 1938—3 p. m.
[Received April 26—1 p. m.]

584. Following from Tokyo.

"273. April 26, 10 a. m. Our 267, April 23, 8 p. m.,[79] Chinese customs. In further elucidation of the documents submitted, the British Ambassador has informed us orally as follows:

With respect to [*In explanation of*] the last sentence of the first paragraph of the note from the Foreign Minister to the British Ambassador, Craigie said that the Vice Minister desired to include the sentence "in the event there should occur an abrupt fall in the currency".[80]

With respect to the final sentence in Craigie's informal letter to the Vice Minister regarding such assistance as the British authorities in China can properly render in overcoming transfer difficulties in connection with the payment of the foreign loan obligations, Sir Robert said that during his negotiations with the Vice Minister the latter had pressed for assurances that the British authorities in China would use their influence to persuade the Bank of Communications and the Bank of China to permit their Tientsin branches to sell to the Yokohama Specie Bank in Tientsin bills against their credit balances in order to provide the necessary yuan exchange for the quotas of the governments in North China. Sir Robert said that he could not agree to endeavor to persuade the banks to act along the lines desired and that he finally agreed to compromise on the understanding that the British authorities would place the matter before those banks and leave it entirely to them whether they could meet the desires of the Japanese.

Sir Robert then went on to say that he also had an understanding with the Vice Minister, outside the agreement, to the effect that the interest charges on the Tientsin–Pukow Railway loans and the Hukuang Railway loan (both British) while not covered by the proposed agreement nevertheless had a secondary lien on the customs revenues. In the event the interest should not be forthcoming due to restrictions against traffic on account of Japanese military operations, the interest service was to be paid out of customs revenues after the service had been paid on the loans constituting the first charge on the customs revenues. He said that it was quite likely that the interest service on the

[79] See telegram No. 572, April 24, 9 a. m., from the Consul General at Shanghai, p. 678.
[80] The Ambassador in Japan subsequently reported that this phrase was not included in the Japanese note.

Tientsin–Pukow Railway would have to be paid out of the customs revenues but it was not likely that the Hukuang Railway loan service would come up before 1941. He said that in order to get the Vice Minister to agree to this the Japanese required equal treatment of the 6% Treasury notes issued for compensation for public property and salt interests in Tsingtao in 1923 and the Chinese Government 8% bonds for refunding interest and foreign debt.

Sir Robert Craigie said that when putting up to his Government the proposed agreement as it now stands he stressed the fact that the conclusion of the agreement would be very helpful to all concerned as there were two schools of thought in Japan: the one dominated by the military whose tactics were to present a *fait accompli,* and the other the civilian element who believed that through negotiation and agreement much could be done in dealing with the foreign powers to assure their good will and their cooperation when and if needed and the agreement would tend to demonstrate that the policy of the latter was by far the better one. (With regard to this last paragraph please see our 239, April 11, 6 p. m.[81]).

Please repeat to Department as our 273, April 26, 10 a. m. Grew."

LOCKHART

693.002/603 : Telegram

The Acting Secretary of State to the Consul General at Shanghai
(Lockhart)

WASHINGTON, April 26, 1938—7 p. m.

283. Your 572, April 24, 9 a. m. Following for Tokyo:

"Your 267, April 23, 8 p. m.

(1) The Department does not wish to make comment upon the general terms of the agreement reached between the Japanese authorities and the British Ambassador in regard to the Chinese Maritime Customs.[82]

(2) With reference to paragraph 4 (*b*) of the agreement, the Department would not wish to authorize an American official to participate in the determination of quotas or to express approval of them as one of the requirements for making them effective. The Department is, however, definitely interested in the matter of the servicing of the foreign obligations secured on the Chinese Maritime Customs revenues and would expect the Inspector General of Customs to keep the American authorities currently informed of the quotas decided upon.

(3) The Department desires that you communicate the substance of the foregoing informally to your British colleague."

Please repeat to Ambassador, Hankow.

WELLES

---

[81] *Ante,* p. 138.
[82] The French Government gave approval of the draft agreement.

693.002/617 : Telegram

The First Secretary of Embassy in China (Salisbury) to the Secretary of State

PEIPING, April 27, 1938—noon.
[Received April 27—7 a. m.]

260. 1. An officer of the Embassy has been informed by the Italian Commissioner of Customs at Chinwangtao that the so-called situation in that area has been "liquidated" through the payment made by customs to persons unnamed (presumably Japanese military) of Chinese dollars 50,000 and that Chinwangtao and Shanhaikwan revenues together now approximate Chinese dollars 400,000 monthly as against one fourth that sum when smuggling was rife. According to the Commissioner, none of this revenue goes to the Peiping régime but is deposited in and held by the Yokohama Specie Bank.

2. The Commissioner states also that the Japanese now permit his officers to carry arms and customs cruisers and wall stations to have machine guns.

3. Repeated to Hankow and Shanghai.

SALISBURY

___

693.002/619 : Telegram

The Ambassador in Japan (Grew) to the Secretary of State

TOKYO, April 29, 1938—8 p. m.
[Received April 29—9 : 45 a. m.]

285. Department's 283, April 26, 7 p. m. via Shanghai. Chinese customs.

1. My British colleague now informs me that his Government has approved the provisional agreement set forth in our 267, April 23, 8 p. m., except for a few modifications which he discussed today with the Vice Minister for Foreign Affairs. He will send me shortly text as provisionally amended but does not consider that amendments are likely to affect American interests in any way. I shall immediately inform the Department of such alterations. He hopes that the final texts of the agreement, notes and letters will be settled tomorrow or the next day.

2. Craigie informs me that the Foreign Office has been proposing to address notes to the French Ambassador and myself inquiring if our respective governments have any objections to the agreement finally reached with the British Ambassador. Craigie expressed to Horinouchi the view that an exchange of informal letters between Horinouchi and ourselves might be preferable and hopes that this procedure will be agreeable to our Government.

3. I made no commitment but said that I would inform the Department of this proposal in anticipation of the receipt of the final texts. Unless the American Government, which has a direct interest in the integrity and disbursements of the Chinese Maritime Customs, states to the Japanese Government that it does not propose to offer any objection to the proposed arrangement, Craigie fears that the Japanese Government may be reluctant to conclude the agreement. He says there is now a real danger that, failing an early agreement, the customs at Shanghai will be taken over forcibly by the renovation government (which means the Japanese military authorities).

4. Craigie informs me that the French Ambassador has been authorized to express approval of proposed arrangement.

GREW

_____

693.002/603 : Telegram

The Acting Secretary of State to the Consul General at Shanghai
(Lockhart)

WASHINGTON, April 29, 1938—8 p. m.

289. Following for Tokyo:

"Your 267, April 23, 8 p. m. The Department interprets the fifth document listed to mean that the Inspector General of Customs will be given currency of the Chinese National Government and that with such currency the Inspector General will be expected to obtain from the Chinese Government foreign exchange for the payment of the quotas of the ports under Japanese occupation in the servicing of foreign obligations secured on customs revenue.

This would throw upon the Chinese Government the burden of providing foreign exchange for the quotas of areas in which the socalled Federal Reserve Bank is endeavoring to replace the circulation of Chinese national currency with its own notes and from which exports do not contribute to the foreign exchange fund of the Chinese Government.

The Department would welcome your comment upon the above, together with any information you may have as to whether there is any indication that the Inspector General could in fact obtain from the Chinese Government the foreign exchange required to pay the quotas of the ports under Japanese occupation."

Please repeat to Hankow for information.

WELLES

693.002/622 : Telegram

The Ambassador in China (Johnson) to the Secretary of State

HANKOW, April 30, 1938—11 a. m.
[Received April 30—7 a. m.]

224. Reference Tokyo's 273, April 26, 10 a. m.[83] Arthur Young gave me last evening copy of a letter addressed to British Embassy by Minister of Finance in reference to customs agreement negotiated by British Embassy at Tokyo. Letter referred to Reuter report that agreement was to be initialed in Tokyo on April 30 and copies would be sent to France, United States and other interested powers. Letter then asks that British Embassy inquire by telegraph as to basis for report, saying that in conversation with British Ambassador here latter had not indicated that such an agreement was imminent. Letter concludes by stating that as matter is chiefly of concern to China, Minister of Finance assumes that Chinese Government will be informed of proposed terms well in advance before understanding is concluded in order to ascertain whether terms would be acceptable. Letter states that pending receipt of information and full consideration of all aspects of situation the position of the Chinese Government will be fully reserved. British Embassy replied on April 29 that no agreement had been made, but that a draft had been drawn up which was now being considered in London.

Repeated to Shanghai and Peiping. Shanghai please repeat to Tokyo.

JOHNSON

693.002/619 : Telegram

The Acting Secretary of State to the Ambassador in Japan (Grew)

WASHINGTON, April 30, 1938—2 p. m.

152. Your 285, April 29, 8 p. m. The Department is studying this matter and expects to send you instructions on Monday. Inform Craigie that the Department reacts unfavorably to the suggestion that an inquiry be addressed by the Japanese Government to the Embassy.

WELLES

---

[83] See telegram No. 584, April 26, 3 p. m., from the Consul General at Shanghai, p. 683.

693.002/621 : Telegram

The Ambassador in Japan (Grew) to the Secretary of State

Tokyo, May 1, 1938—9 a. m.
[Received May 1—2 a. m.]

286.   Our 285, April 29, 8 p. m., Chinese Maritime Customs.   The following letter and enclosure from my British colleague were received late last night:

"30th April 1938.   Immediate.   My Dear Grew, The Ministry for Foreign Affairs are anxious, for reasons connected with the Privy Council, not to publish the actual texts of the notes or their enclosure relating to the customs and we have accordingly prepared the accompanying draft of a communiqué, which, it is suggested, might be issued in the morning papers (here and in London) of the day following the conclusion of the arrangement.   This text I have now submitted to my Government.   The inclusion of the last sentence of paragraph 1 is of course dependent on your receiving the necessary authority to inform the Japanese Government that your Government do not propose to raise any objection to these arrangements.   We have discovered today that we should have included amongst the 'duties' in paragraph 2 of the proposed arrangement a reference to the flood relief surtax in which the United States are interested.   In order to avoid a last minute alteration of the text, it is proposed to inform you, after the agreement has been concluded, that both sides regard the service of this surtax as being covered by the arrangement.

Believe me, et cetera, R. L. Craigie."

"Draft of statement to be issued by British and Japanese Governments on Chinese customs question (to be released on blank date and to be supplemented as required by each Government) :

Unofficial conversations have been taking place since February last between the British Ambassador, Sir Robert Craigie, and the Vice Minister for Foreign Affairs, Mr. Kensuke Horinouchi, regarding the service of foreign obligations secured on the Chinese Maritime Customs revenue and other relevant matters.   As a result of this exchange of views the Japanese Government have notified His Majesty's Government in the United Kingdom of the temporary measures which they propose to take, during the period of hostilities, to regulate these matters and they have received in reply the assurance that the British Government will for their part offer no objection to the application of these measures for the period mentioned.   It is further understood that the Governments of the United States and France do not propose to raise any objection to the temporary application of these arrangements.

According to these arrangements, which will be subject to reconsideration in the event of a radical change occurring in economic conditions, all revenue collected by the customs at each port within the areas under Japanese occupation are to be deposited with the Yokohama Specie Bank.   From the revenues thus deposited foreign loan quotas will be remitted to the Inspector General of Customs in order to meet in full the service of the foreign loans and indemnities secured on the customs revenue. The service of such foreign loans and indemnities will be treated as a first charge on the revenue, after deducting the maintenance expenses of the Customs Administration and certain customs payments and grants. Foreign loan quotas for each port will be determined monthly in proportion to the share of that port in the total gross collections for all ports during the preceding month.

Arrangements will also be made for the payment to the Japanese Government of the arrears on the Japanese portion of the Boxer indemnity held at the Hong Kong and Shanghai Bank since last September, for the meeting of future payments in respect of the Japanese portion of the Boxer indemnity and the Japanese share of the Reorganization loan of 1913, for the repayment of the overdraft incurred by the Inspector General since January in relation to the Shanghai share of the foreign loan service which has been accumulating in the Hong Kong and Shanghai Bank at Shanghai, and for the transfer to the Yokohama Specie Bank of the balance of the customs accounts with the Hong Kong and Shanghai Bank in each port under Japanese occupation and its utilization for the future service of foreign obligations."

GREW

693.002/623 : Telegram

The Ambassador in Japan (Grew) to the Secretary of State

TOKYO, May 1, 1938—11 a. m.
[Received May 1—7 : 10 a. m.]

287. Department's 289, April 29, 8 p. m., via Shanghai, Chinese Maritime Customs. The Department's interpretation of the fifth document transmitted with our 267, April 23, 8 p. m. is correct. According to Craigie, the Japanese Government by the arrangement under reference will contribute to the servicing of Chinese loans and indemnity payments 2 million yuan per month; the Japanese Government could not be expected to provide the foreign exchange necessary to cover the remittances and the Chinese Government must therefore furnish the foreign exchange for the Japanese contribution of 2 million yuan if the Chinese loan service and indemnity payments are to be maintained. Furthermore, according to Craigie, if the Chinese Government should refuse to provide the foreign exchange the arrangement must collapse. Craigie further states that once the arrangement becomes effective he believes that the Japanese might be prevailed upon to collect in foreign currencies 1 million yuan of the 2 million customs revenues necessary for loan and indemnity payments, which would lighten the burden on the Chinese National Government to the extent of 1 million yuan. Craigie expresses the opinion, however, that the Chinese Government will not be greatly burdened in providing the foreign exchange necessary to convert the 2 million yuan turned over monthly.

Craigie reiterated to me that he believes the arrangement will fall through unless we express no objection. He suggested as a possible formula that he orally assure the Japanese Government that we have no objection to the arrangement upon oral assurances from us to that effect.

Our only comment concerning the proposed furnishing of adequate foreign exchange by the Chinese Government is that this would appear to be a purely "pious hope" on the part of the British Ambassador but we have no knowledge that the Chinese Government has been consulted in the premises.

Repeated to Shanghai for Hankow.

GREW

693.002/624 : Telegram

The Ambassador in China (Johnson) to the Secretary of State

HANKOW, May 2, 1938—4 p. m.
[Received May 2—8 : 50 a. m.]

227. Arthur Young informs me that today British Embassy communicated text of customs agreement to Chinese Minister of Finance with summary of accompanying documents urging Chinese Government to accept or at least not oppose agreement as otherwise Japanese threaten to take over Chinese customs in occupied areas as of May 3rd whereupon Chinese will find themselves with Customs Administration in Japanese hands and used for Japanese purposes.

Chinese Government have communicated by telegraph to London, Paris and Washington objections to the implementing of agreement and reservations of rights should agreement be put into effect by British and Japanese without consulting Chinese. These instructions in two telegraphic instructions will doubtless be communicated to you by Chinese Ambassador in Washington.

Repeated to Shanghai and Peiping. Shanghai please relay to Tokyo.

JOHNSON

693.002/621 : Telegram

The Secretary of State to the Ambassador in Japan (Grew)

WASHINGTON, May 2, 1938—8 p. m.

153. Your 286, May 1, 9 a. m., and 287, May 1, 11 a. m.; Hankow's 224, April 30, 11 a. m., and the Department's 152, April 30, 2 p. m., in regard to the Chinese Maritime Customs. From the beginning our position with regard to the question of the Chinese customs has revolved around two objectives: (*a*) that the integrity of the customs

be preserved, and (b) that the customs revenue be safeguarded with special reference to the servicing of foreign loan and indemnity quotas. If and as losses are occasioned to American interests in China by the military and other activities of the Chinese or Japanese Government, this Government must look for indemnification to the Government responsible for such losses. In this customs issue we have consistently held that we did not wish to espouse any particular plan toward attaining the objectives in which we are interested. If a particular plan is put forward, is carried into effect, and operates in such a way as to bring about reasonable attainment of our objectives, we would not expect to make objection. If, however, any particular plan should not in practical operation have that result, we would wish to be free to offer objection. Moreover, should a particular plan when brought to our attention appear to be seriously objectionable we would probably so indicate to the authors or sponsors of that plan.

With the foregoing general outline of our position in mind, the Department offers certain specific observations as follows:

1. The Department naturally assumes that in any arrangement effected in regard to the Chinese Maritime Customs there would be no discrimination against the American obligations secured on customs revenues, including the flood relief surtax.

2. The Department does not understand the basis of the British Ambassador's statement that "the Japanese Government could not be expected to provide the foreign exchange necessary to cover" the quotas of the Chinese ports under Japanese military occupation for the servicing of the foreign obligations secured upon the Chinese Maritime Customs revenue. The régime set up in north China following the Japanese military occupation of that area is receiving the benefit of the foreign exchange accruing from trade and other commercial transactions in that area. As illustrative of the latter there may be mentioned an agreement between Major General Kita and the "Federal Reserve Bank" on one side and the Yee Tsoong Tobacco Company on the other for the purchase by the latter with foreign currencies of "Federal Reserve Bank notes" for the purpose of buying tobacco in Shantung. Under these circumstances it would appear to be entirely reasonable for the authorities controlling the area under Japanese military occupation to provide the foreign exchange necessary to cover the quotas of the customs ports in such area.

3. There arises the question whether, if the arrangement arrived at between the British Ambassador and the Japanese were agreed to by the American Government and if that arrangement collapsed because of China's refusal to agree thereto (and this would seem to be a not improbable contingency), would not the American Government be thereby placed at a disadvantage in its attitude of holding the Japa-

nese Government responsible for losses occasioned by the acts of the latter's forces or other agents in China?

4. In as much as the arrangement must, according to Craigie, collapse if the Chinese Government should refuse to provide the foreign exchange called for therein, the Department desires to withhold any further comment until the Chinese Government has made known its attitude toward the whole arrangement.

5. Please discuss the matter with Craigie in the light of the foregoing.

Please repeat to American Embassy, Hankow, through Shanghai.

HULL

693.002/625 : Telegram

The Ambassador in Japan (Grew) to the Secretary of State

TOKYO, May 2, 1938—midnight.
[Received May 2—8 p. m.]

289. Our No. 287, May 1, 11 a. m., Chinese customs. The British Ambassador has informed me that he completed the customs arrangement this evening with the Foreign Office and that the Foreign Office will give out to the press tonight or tomorrow morning a statement to the effect that an understanding has been reached on all points with the British Ambassador. Craigie also said the Foreign Office will give a communiqué tomorrow afternoon at 2 o'clock giving some details of the arrangement. He expressed the hope that we would be in a position to express "no objection" before the communiqué is issued.

Craigie has sent me the following letter and enclosure:

"2nd May, 1938.

My dear Grew, As we informed your Embassy by telephone this evening, the Vice Minister and I exchanged the notes and confidential letters about the customs at the Ministry of Foreign Affairs this evening at 6 : 00 p. m. For various reasons it was necessary to move very quickly in order to prevent a breakdown. For the moment we are merely informing the press of the bare fact that an understanding has been reached on all points and that this has been duly recorded. We are avoiding the word 'agreement' and the Japanese are anxious that we should avoid any reference to an 'exchange of notes', owing to possible difficulties with the Privy Council. Their thesis is that the notes merely record our understanding and are not in the form usually employed when an exchange of notes is intended to consummate a formal agreement.

You will remember that I mentioned that there were one or two points such as the character of the loans to be covered by this arrangement and methods of transferring the northern quotas to Shanghai which we had discussed in some detail during our deliberation. These points have now been recorded in an agreed record of our final conversation today and I enclose copy of this document for your strictly confidential information.

Believe me, Yours very sincerely, R. L. Craigie."

["]Record of meeting on the Chinese Maritime Customs question between Mr. Horinouchi and Sir Robert Craigie held at the Ministry of Foreign Affairs on May 2, 1938.

Point 1. Customary Grants.

To prevent any possibility of misunderstanding Mr. Horinouchi and Sir Robert Craigie agreed that the wording of paragraph 3 of the proposed arrangement was intended to cover not only the customary payments normally made by the Commissioners of Customs before remitting the balances to the Inspector General of Customs but also those payments normally made by the Inspector General himself before meeting the service of the foreign obligations.

Point 2. Method of obtaining exchange for transfer of North China quotas.

Mr. Horinouchi pointed out that the Tientsin branches of the Bank of China and the Bank of Communications have considerable credit balances at the Shanghai offices of these banks. The best way to enable the Tientsin branch of the Yokohama Specie Bank to remit the foreign loan quotas from ports in North China to its Shanghai branch would be to let the Tientsin branches of these Chinese banks sell remittance bills against these credit balances. He asked that the British authorities should use their influence to secure the cooperation of the Chinese banks to that end. Sir Robert Craigie stated that although this would involve great difficulty, the British authorities in China would be prepared to place this proposal before the Chinese banks concerned.

In reply to Sir Robert Craigie's inquiry as to what further measures would be taken for the creation of the necessary exchange, Mr. Horinouchi stated that should this prove necessary, it was intended to use in full the deposits which were to be transferred to the Yokohama Specie Bank from the Hong Kong and Shanghai Bank at Shanghai, Tientsin and Chinwangtao for the payment of foreign loan quotas due from ports in North China.

Sir Robert Craigie stated that, according to a telegram received from His Majesty's Government's Ambassador in China, the amount of the balance in the Hong Kong and Shanghai Bank at Shanghai of the Shanghai customs revenue account, the revenue surtax account and the flood relief surtax account amounted to $24,829,703.46 up to and including April 29, last. The similar balance in Tientsin and Chinwangtao was $1,762,841.85.

Point 3. Foreign obligations covered by the proposed arrangement.

Sir Robert Craigie stated that it was his understanding that paragraph 2 was intended to cover not only those loans which were directly secured on the customs revenue but also the foreign obligations having the customs revenue as a contingent security, i. e., the Tientsin–Pukow and Hukuang Railway loans. The contingent liability of the customs in respect of the latter loan did not arise until 1941, so that, so far as he was concerned, the only loans enjoying a contingent charge which would fall within the scope of the present arrangement were the Tientsin–Pukow Railway loans. Sir Robert Craigie added that the principal and interest of these loans were secured on the railway revenues, but the customs were to make good deficiencies in interest payments. The contingent liability of the customs for the remainder of the present year was 125,000 pounds; for each year 1929 to 1941 inclusive 307,000 pounds; the liability thereafter slowly decreasing.

Mr. Horinouchi replied that he was prepared to recognize the contingent interest of these loans in the customs revenue on the understanding that certain Japanese loans, which had a contingent charge on the customs revenue, should also be regarded as covered by the arrangement. As examples he quoted the two principal loans involved namely: (a) 6 percent treasury note in gold yen for the compensation of public properties and salt interests in Tsingtao (1923). (b) Chinese Government 8 percent bonds for refunding internal and foreign short term debts (1922) so-called Japanese portion of the $96,000,000 loan.

He added that the Japanese Government had no present intention of putting forward a claim that any of these loans should be serviced out of the customs revenue.

Sir Robert Craigie stated that no objection would be raised by his Government for their part in the event of the Japanese Government putting forward claims in connection with these Japanese loans. He also concurred in the view expressed by Mr. Horinouchi that the status of the various loans was not affected one way or the other by the fact that they would be regarded as falling within the scope of the proposed arrangement."

Repeated to Shanghai for Hankow.

GREW

693.002/626 : Telegram

The Ambassador in Japan (Grew) to the Secretary of State

TOKYO, May 3, 1938—11 a. m.
[Received May 3—1: 29 a. m.]

290. Our 286, Chinese Maritime Customs.[84] Craigie has just informed me that owing to a misunderstanding, his Government released last night for publication in this morning's London papers, the press communiqué containing the final sentence in paragraph 1 that: "It is further understood that the Governments of the United States and France do not propose to raise any objection to the temporary application of these arrangements." Craigie expresses sincere regret for this unfortunate occurrence and requests me so to inform you. He thought that his Government would not release the communiqué until tomorrow and that there would be plenty of time for him to have the sentence concerning the American attitude eliminated if it is true, after I had received and communicated to him the Department's final instructions. I also expressed regret and pointed out the unfortunate repercussions which might occur in case the statement under reference in the communiqué should prove to be inaccurate. I told him that I was expecting the Department's final instructions at any moment but

[84] Dated May 1, 9 a. m., p. 688.

that I had already informed him 2 days ago that the Department's reaction to his proposal for an inquiry from the Japanese Government regarding our attitude was unfavorable and that the Department had already gone on record as saying that it had no comment to make on the general terms of the arrangement.

Craigie states that the sentence quoted above will be eliminated from the communiqué to be issued in Japan today.

Repeated to Shanghai for Hankow.

GREW

693.002/629 : Telegram

The Ambassador in China (Johnson) to the Secretary of State

HANKOW, May 3, 1938—11 a. m.
[Received May 3—9 : 35 a. m.]

231. My 227, May 2, 4 p. m. Counselor [of] British Embassy has just permitted me to read communication which British Ambassador made to Generalissimo urging Chinese Government to accept or at least not oppose customs agreement. MacKillop asked me for an expression of my opinion of the agreement. I told him that I was not in a position to express any opinion officially but that personally, assuming as I had assumed, that the Japanese from the beginning had intended to take over the customs, this agreement would be interpreted as evidence of British acquiescence therein and of willingness on the part of the British Government to legalize Japanese capture of customs.

MacKillop stated that he had been instructed to ask me also whether I was in a position to take action with the Chinese Government similar to that taken by the British Ambassador. I stated that my answer to that was that I could not take such action; that thus far we had refrained from offering any advice to the Chinese as to what they should do in the matter; and that if asked by the Department for my views I would recommend against taking such action here. British Counselor stated that he had anticipated this reply, as he had all along understood my point of view.

He stated that in his interview with Kung latter had complained against British action in reaching an agreement with the Japanese without consulting the Chinese. I understand from British counselor that agreement is to be signed today.

Repeated Shanghai and Peiping. Shanghai please relay to Tokyo.

JOHNSON

693.002/627 : Telegram

The Ambassador in China (Johnson) to the Secretary of State

HANKOW, May 3, 1938—7 p. m.
[Received May 3—9 : 22 a. m.]

233. Tokyo's 289, May 2, midnight. I have just seen Kung, at his request, who is much disturbed over agreement and particularly over statement issued in London and carried in Reuter despatch received here today to the effect that the American Government will not object to the agreement. Kung hopes that this does not put us publicly in position of at least tacit approval of an arrangement made by third parties without China's consent which deprives China of control of customs and which discriminates as between bonds secured on customs.

JOHNSON

693.002/629 : Telegram

The Secretary of State to the Ambassador in China (Johnson)

WASHINGTON, May 3, 1938—6 p. m.

138. Your 231, May 3, 11 a. m. The Department approves the reply made by you to the Counselor of the British Embassy.
Please repeat to Tokyo through Shanghai.

HULL

693.002/626 : Telegram

The Secretary of State to the Ambassador in Japan (Grew)

WASHINGTON, May 3, 1938—6 p. m.

154. Your 290, May 3, 11 a. m. The *New York Times* this morning carries an account by Hugh Byas dated Tokyo, May 2, of the British-Japanese arrangement in the course of which there appears the following: "The negotiations were conducted between Japanese and British authorities only, but other interested powers, including the United States and France, have been kept informed of the progress made and have raised no objection."

Such account and the release made in London will, of course, be noted in foreign offices the world over, regardless what may be the character of the communiqué issued officially in Japan.

Referring to Craigie's expression of regret, you may state to Craigie that the Department deprecates the coloration given the arrangement in the Byas account and the London release.

HULL

693.002/632 : Telegram

The Ambassador in China (Johnson) to the Secretary of State

HANKOW, May 4, 1938—1 p. m.
[Received May 4—8 : 55 a. m.]

236. Supplementing my 233, May 3, 7 p. m., I added that during conversation Kung invited attention to the following: that while he appreciated the good intentions of the British Government in trying to protect British and Chinese interests in the customs, still the agreement would result in assisting Japan at China's expense and would place China in a very difficult situation. He remarked that this was the first time since the Washington Conference that two foreign countries had entered into an agreement concerning China without China's participation. He felt that this created a dangerous precedent. He pointed out that one of the interpretations of the agreement might be that it sanctioned Japan's violation of the interests of foreign powers by military power at their seizure of revenue, in disregard of rights of holders including foreign nationals, of internal bonds, and by altering the status of the customs.

Dr. Kung asked me specifically whether it was true that the American Government would not object to the agreement as stated in the Reuter despatch. I told Dr. Kung that I had no information in regard to the attitude of the American Government concerning this matter, and that I was not informed as to whether the American Government had stated that it would not oppose the agreement. Dr. Kung asked me to convey these views to you and I said that I would. Dr. Kung stated that the arrangement had put him in a very embarrassing position. He does not wish to alienate British sympathy. He has refused to issue any instructions to Maze in regard to matter, apparently in this matter yielding to the request of the British that he not oppose it. Young informed me this morning that local Commissioner of Customs called on Kung and stated that he had received a telegram from Maze indicating his difficulties in the light of present agreement. Kung told Commissioner of Customs that he was not issuing specific instructions; that standing instructions should be sufficient to enable Maze to know what he should do, as he was an officer of the Chinese Government. This of course leaves Maze in a very difficult situation because he will now be pressed by Japanese and British to pay over moneys deposited in his name in Hong Kong and Shanghai Bank under an agreement to which his Government is not a party.

JOHNSON

693.002/627 : Telegram

The Secretary of State to the Ambassador in China (Johnson)

WASHINGTON, May 4, 1938—5 p. m.

139. Your 233, May 3, 7 p. m. You may inform Kung orally of the substance of the first paragraph of the Department's telegram No. 153, May 2, 8 p. m., to Tokyo, which Tokyo was instructed to repeat to you. With reference to the last sentence of that paragraph, you may say to Kung in confidence that by the time the Department had received from the British clarification as to the meaning of that part of the arrangement which relates to payments from north China in national currency, the arrangement had already been agreed upon by the British Ambassador and the Japanese Foreign Office, but that the Department nevertheless definitely queried the reasonableness of that part of the arrangement. You may say to Kung also in confidence that we were asked to indicate that we had no objection to the arrangement and that we replied that we desired to withhold any further comment until the Chinese Government had made known its attitude toward the whole arrangement.

Department has repeated to Tokyo this telegram and your telegram under reference.

HULL

693.002/636a : Telegram

The Secretary of State to the Ambassador in Japan (Grew)

WASHINGTON, May 4, 1938—6 p. m.

157. 1. The Department has under consideration the question of an approach to the Japanese Foreign Office along the following lines:

(a) On November 28, 1937, the Japanese Foreign Minister gave you specific assurance that no American interests in the Chinese Maritime Customs would be harmed (your telegram 576, November 28, 4 p. m.[85]).

(b) Prior to the present Japanese military action in China, the obligations expressed in foreign currencies and involving American interests, secured on the Chinese Maritime Customs revenue, including surtaxes, were being regularly serviced.

(c) Japanese military occupation of north China has resulted in the economic separation of that area from the rest of China, and exports from that area and commercial transactions therein do not contribute to the foreign exchange resources of the rest of China.

(d) The Department is informed that the Japanese authorities are contemplating measures which will in effect exempt the Japanese-occupied area from its obligation of supplying its share of the foreign exchange necessary for the servicing of the foreign obligations secured upon the customs revenues for the whole of China.

---

[85] *Foreign Relations*, 1937, vol. III, p. 889.

(e) Such measures, if successfully effected, will so reduce the areas remaining available for the supply of the foreign exchange necessary for the servicing of the foreign obligations, secured upon the Chinese Maritime Customs revenue, as to jeopardize and render almost certain default in the servicing of the obligations in which American interests are involved, and thus completely nullify the assurance given by the Japanese Minister for Foreign Affairs to you on November 28, 1937.

(f) In summarization, an integral part of the obligations involving the Chinese Maritime Customs revenue is the payment of foreign creditors, including American, in foreign currencies; and failure of the areas in north China to assume responsibility for furnishing a fair share of the foreign currencies would in effect constitute non-fulfillment by such areas of a vital element in the obligations.

(g) With the foregoing in mind, the American Government requests assurance from the Japanese Government that the Japanese Government will not agree to or countenance any arrangement which will negative the assurance given by the Japanese Foreign Minister to you.

2. Having in mind the action of the British Ambassador in keeping us informed of the progress of the negotiations which he has been conducting with the Japanese authorities, and our desire to avoid, as far as is consistent with the protection of our interests, any embarrassment to him or to the French Ambassador, the Department offers for your consideration the suggestion that you acquaint the British and French Ambassadors with the proposed approach above outlined, and endeavor to arrive at an understanding with them in regard to such an approach. Would it, perhaps, be practicable for them, under the existing circumstances, to make parallel approaches to the Japanese?

3. Your comment upon the foregoing is requested.

HULL

693.002/633 : Telegram

The Ambassador in Japan (Grew) to the Secretary of State

TOKYO, May 5, 1938—7 p. m.
[Received May 5—9 : 23 a. m.]

294. Department's 157, May 4, 6 p. m.

1. In my discussion with Craigie of the substance of the Department's 153, May 2, 8 p. m., he brought out the fact that the Japanese had consented, in the event the Chinese Government should refuse to provide the foreign exchange necessary to remit for loan and indemnity services the 2 million yuan contributed from the customs in areas under Japanese control, to furnish foreign exchange from the customs revenues collected in foreign currencies at Shanghai which amounted to upwards of 3 to 4 million yuan monthly. He further stated that the British authorities in China for their part would

endeavor to prevail upon their nationals to continue to pay customs duties in foreign currencies which many of them apparently are now doing. We have had no previous indication from Craigie of this understanding with the Japanese.

2. In the light of the foregoing I should like to explore the matter further with the British Ambassador before expressing opinion on the approach proposed by the Department. If the Department desires that I do so I would appreciate a rush telegraphic reply,[86] as Craigie is to leave Tokyo on Saturday morning the 7th for a visit of some days to the south of Japan.

GREW

693.002/634 : Telegram

The Ambassador in Japan (Grew) to the Secretary of State

TOKYO, May 5, 1938—8 p. m.
[Received May 5—9 : 35 a. m.]

295. Department's 154, May 3, 6 p. m., Chinese customs.

1. Craigie informs me that he gave to Byas no gratuitous information concerning the attitude of the United States but that in reply to a direct question from Byas he said that we had been kept informed of the progress made in the negotiations and had not raised objections (in other words that we did not wish to comment).

2. Byas informed me today on his own initiative that such was the impression he had received from the British Ambassador but that in the hurried drafting of his telegram late at night when he could not consult me he had perhaps failed to make clear the fine distinction between a tacit and a positive attitude on our part. He said that the Foreign Office in Tokyo had given him the same information as had the Ambassador.

3. Byas proposes also on his own initiative to take occasion in his next telegram regarding the Chinese customs to say "although the United States and France have not expressed objections, and this has been confirmed by the Foreign Office, it should be understood that silence on the part of the American Government in no sense implies that it approves or supports the agreement".

4. Wishing sedulously to avoid crossing wires with the Department in matters of publicity I refrained from offering comment but if the Department feels that the publication of the foregoing statement would or would not be helpful and wishes to advise me by urgent telegram I believe that Byas will be guided by any suggestion that I may make.

Repeated to Shanghai for Hankow.

GREW

[86] The Department agreed in telegram No. 159, May 5, 6 p. m.

693.002/634 : Telegram

The Secretary of State to the Ambassador in Japan (Grew)

WASHINGTON, May 5, 1938—5 p. m.

158. Your 295, May 5, 8 p. m. In case Byas should be agreeable to substituting for the words "Although the United States and France have not expressed objections, and this has been confirmed by the Foreign Office" the words "Although the United States has not taken any position in regard to the general terms of the agreement", the Department would perceive no need to make objection to Byas publishing the statement on his own initiative.

HULL

693.002/635 : Telegram

The Ambassador in Japan (Grew) to the Secretary of State

TOKYO, May 5, 1938—9 p. m.
[Received May 5—10 a. m.]

296. Department's 153, May 2, 8 p. m., Chinese customs.

1. Instructions in paragraph 5 carried out.

2. Craigie explained to me fully the circumstances which necessitated the sudden conclusion of the arrangement on May 2nd. The Japanese Ministry of Finance acting on the advice of the military had violently objected to the offer of the Vice Minister to release the arrears on the foreign loan and indemnity service at present deposited in the Hong Kong [and] Shanghai Bank amounting to 4,000,000 yuan to meet the overdraft for which they act as security and the Finance Ministry had finally agreed to this provision only if the agreement were concluded not later than May 2nd. Horinouchi said: "We cannot longer hold the military in line".

3. Craigie told me that he had definite information from the British Ambassador in China that the Chinese Government must and would object technically to the arrangement for political reasons but that actually they would not oppose it in practice. Craigie said that he had spoken with the Chinese Chargé d'Affaires in Tokyo a month or so ago and had informed him of the general purport of the arrangement and that there seemed to be no doubt that the Chinese Government was aware that an arrangement was under consideration. (We were hitherto unaware of this conversation with the Chinese Chargé d'Affaires.)

Repeated to Shanghai for Hankow.

GREW

693.002/639: Telegram

The Ambassador in China (Johnson) to the Secretary of State

HANKOW, May 6, 1938—noon.
[Received 5:26 p. m.]

340. Department's 139, May 4, 5 p. m. Department's instructions carried out this morning. Dr. Kung informed me that Counselor of British Embassy called on him yesterday and communicated to him a message from British Ambassador to the effect that the Ambassador had no arguments which he cared to advance in rebuttal of statements which Kung had made to him, which I assumed were along the lines of those communicated in my 236, May 4, 1 p. m., but that agreement was temporary and all that could be obtained at the moment, and British Ambassador expressed the hope that Dr. Kung would not actively oppose the agreement. Since November Kung stated that he had asked British Counselor to inform British Ambassador that he appreciated all that the friendly powers had done by their active assistance which they had rendered in the interest of China's credit and the protection of the Customs Administration, but he wanted to point out that the agreement seemed to have a more important aspect than might seem at first apparent. He referred specifically to the undertakings entered into by the powers in the Nine Power Treaty, reminded the Ambassador that Great Britain had by this treaty undertaken to do nothing to abridge China's sovereignty or administrative integrity. He wondered whether this agreement meant that the British Government no longer considered the Nine Power Treaty as binding. He stated that the British Counselor demurred to this pointing out that the British Government had taken the initiative in convening the Conference at Brussels under the Nine Power Treaty; that the British Government certainly considered the Nine Power Treaty as binding. Kung then pointed out that the British Government having entered into this undertaking with the Japanese Government, it must watch the Japanese very carefully. He referred to numerous reports that the Japanese or their puppets intended to take over the customs, put up the five barred flag and appoint a superintendent of customs at Shanghai and he said that the British might discover that the Japanese might violate the Nine Power Treaty through their puppets. He said that he had told the British Counselor that he would try not to do anything to oppose the carrying out of the understanding, but that his undertaking to this effect was now contingent upon the Japanese not violating the Nine Power Treaty through the agency of their puppets.

Repeated to Peiping and Shanghai. Shanghai please repeat to Tokyo.

JOHNSON

693.002/637 : Telegram

The Consul General at Shanghai (Lockhart) to the Secretary of State

SHANGHAI, May 6, 1938—4 p. m.
[Received May 6—1 : 14 p. m.]

624. I am reliably informed that Li Chien Nan recently reported to have been appointed Chinese Superintendent of Customs at Shanghai by the so-called "Reformed Government" called on the Commissioner of Customs this morning and informed him of his appointment to the post mentioned. The Commissioner is understood to have been polite but noncommittal. At Li's request the Commissioner showed him the office of the Chinese Superintendent but Li did not indicate whether he expects to occupy the office forthwith. I understand the Commissioner denies the story published by Domei to the effect that Li informed him that the "Reformed Government" had taken over control of the Shanghai customs and that he and Sir Frederick Maze had been commissioned by that so-called government as Commissioner and Inspector General respectively. Five barred flag is not being flown over the customs.

Repeated to Hankow, Peiping and Tokyo.

LOCKHART

693.002/624 : Telegram

The Secretary of State to the Ambassador in China (Johnson)

WASHINGTON, May 6, 1938—4 p. m.

144. Your 227, May 2, 4 p. m., Chinese Maritime Customs. On May 3 the Chinese Embassy at Washington left with the Department a memorandum [87] summarizing the arrangement arrived at between the British Ambassador to Japan and the Japanese Foreign Office, and on May 5 a memorandum [87] containing the text of a *note verbale* communicated to the British Foreign Office by the Chinese Embassy at London and containing an account of personal observations made by the Chinese Ambassador at London to Leith-Ross.[88] The Department assumes that the substance of these communications is known to you. Copies of the two memoranda are being forwarded by pouch.

HULL

[87] Not printed.
[88] Sir Frederick Leith-Ross, chief economic adviser to the British Government.

693.002/638 : Telegram

The Consul General at Shanghai (Lockhart) to the Secretary of State

SHANGHAI, May 6, 1938—7 p. m.
[Received May 6—1 : 25 p. m.]

625. Reference my 624, May 6, 4 p. m. Mr. A. Tajiri, First Secretary of the Japanese Embassy, called on the Inspector General of Customs yesterday and requested him to transfer forthwith to the Yokohama Specie Bank the Shanghai customs revenue balance in the Hong Kong and Shanghai Bank. The Inspector General informed him that he could not comply with the request unless the Chinese Government first expressed no objection to such procedure. The Inspector General intimated that the recent provisional arrangement of depositing current revenue collections in the Yokohama Specie Bank is liable to cancellation in the event of the Chinese Government's dissension.

The Japanese authorities, through Tajiri, requested the Shanghai Commissioner of Customs to call on the head of the Executive Yuan of the so-called "Reformed Government" in Nanking. The Inspector General replied that he could not authorize the Commissioner to establish contact with the new régime.

In response to request for the appointment of a senior Japanese customs employee in the Financial Secretary's office, the Inspector General said that the proportion of Japanese employees in the customs establishment at Shanghai cannot be further increased at the present. Tajiri stressed the importance of settling as soon as possible the question of the transfer of funds above mentioned.

Repeated to Hankow, Peiping and Tokyo.

LOCKHART

693.002/642 : Telegram

The Ambassador in China (Johnson) to the Secretary of State

HANKOW, May 7, 1938—11 a. m.
[Received May 8—7 : 30 a. m.]

242. Following communication dated May 6 has just been received from the Foreign Office.

"The Wai Chiao Pu presents its compliments to the American Embassy and has the honor to inform the Embassy that the Chinese Government has just despatched the following communication to the British Government.

'The Chinese Government has learned that the British and the Japanese Governments have just concluded certain temporary arrangements concerning the Chinese customs. Whatever motives may have prompted the British Government to enter into these arrangements, it is regrettable that the Chinese customs, which form an important part of the administration of the Chinese

Republic, should have been taken into consideration, without China's consent, as the subject matter of an agreement between two foreign states. In this connection the Chinese Government desires to remind the British Government of their formal undertaking not to enter into any treaty or arrangement with any power or powers which would infringe or impair the sovereignty and the administrative integrity of China.

The Chinese Government must declare at this juncture that China is not in any way bound by the arrangements concerning the Chinese customs just concluded between the British and Japanese Governments and fully reserves her rights and freedom of action in matters relating to the customs'."

Repeated to Peiping and Shanghai. Shanghai please repeat to Tokyo.

JOHNSON

693.002/640 : Telegram

The Ambassador in Japan (Grew) to the Secretary of State

TOKYO, May 7, 1938—1 p. m.
[Received May 7—8 : 35 a. m.]

300. Department's 159, May 5, 6 p. m.,[89] Chinese Maritime Customs. In further discussion yesterday with my British colleague he brought out the following points.

1. His main purpose in his negotiations with the Japanese Government has been to produce an arrangement which would stand some chance of working satisfactorily in practice.

2. To depend on the Japanese to furnish the foreign exchange necessary to pay the foreign obligations of the customs would be illusory simply because the Japanese do not at least at present possess or command in North China the foreign exchange necessary for servicing the northern quotas. The Vice Minister in their discussions said that with the best will in the world they could not at present do so in practice and Craigie is convinced that this statement is correct.

3. The Chinese have up to the present produced sufficient foreign exchange to meet these obligations and in the opinion of the British experts they can continue to do so. If however it should become known in China that we were pressing the Japanese to produce this foreign exchange, this, in Craigie's opinion, would be tantamount to an invitation to the Chinese to refuse to furnish the foreign exchange necessary for the quotas of the areas in North China.

4. With reference to our 294, May 5, 7 p. m., paragraph 1, Craigie has now modified his previous statement to me (McGurk [90] was present and we agree as to what we understood Craigie to say) that the Japanese had consented in the event the Chinese Government should refuse to provide the foreign exchange necessary to remit for loan

---

[89] See footnote 86, p. 700.
[90] Joseph F. McGurk, First Secretary of Embassy in Japan.

and indemnity services the 2 million yuan contributed from the customs in areas under Japanese control to furnish foreign exchange from the customs revenues collected in foreign currencies at Shanghai. Craigie now says that he had discussed this matter with Horinouchi and that while he had nothing in writing to confirm the latter's agreement to such an arrangement it was his understanding that the question was to be left for further discussion here or in Shanghai to ascertain whether such procedure could be worked out.

5. Craigie states that it would not necessarily embarrass him if I were to make the approach to the Japanese Foreign Office outlined by the Department so long as it was done orally and without publicity but for Craigie himself to take parallel action would be merely to repeat what in effect he has been saying to the Japanese Government during the past several weeks. He considers that his negotiations over the past few months concluding with the arrangement of May 2 fully cover his side of the question and he is doubtful if the French, having approved the arrangement, would feel that they could ask for further assurances. I have not consulted my French colleague but I am inclined to agree with Craigie's estimate of the French attitude.

6. Craigie acknowledges that his arrangement may not work but he believes that it was the very best agreement that could be concluded. He hopes that we will wait to see if it does work.

Our comment follows.

7. It seems to us that the first step in considering the Department's proposed approach to the Japanese Government would be to decide whether there is available in the Japanese occupied areas other than Shanghai foreign exchange for the remittance to Shanghai in foreign currencies of quotas for servicing foreign loans and indemnities. Craigie affirms that such foreign exchange is not available and that view is substantially confirmed by reports emphasizing the difficulties which the North China régime is having on this score. The Japanese presumably cannot be persuaded to place at the disposal of the North China régime their own limited reserves of foreign exchange. For the time being, therefore, it appears improbable that the North China quotas could be remitted in foreign currencies even if the Japanese were agreeable to the proposition in principle. However, with prospects of revival of exports in North China there should be accumulated a reserve of foreign exchange which could be available in the course of time for quota remittances.

8. The British are committed to try out the arrangement which they have just made with the Japanese and Craigie made it clear to me that he could not recommend that the British Government go along with us on the proposed approach to the Japanese if made now. The French, according to Craigie, have by approving the arrangement associated themselves with the British.

9. It is therefore our view that we should withhold the proposed action while carefully watching the operation of the recent arrangement. If then the conditions envisaged by the Department should threaten to arise, our representations when made would rest on a firmer basis than they would, we believe, if made now.

10. If, however, the Department feels that some tactical advantage is to be gained by making the suggested approach now, I can see no important objection.

GREW

693.002/633 : Telegram

The Secretary of State to the Consul General at Shanghai (Lockhart)

WASHINGTON, May 7, 1938—1 p. m.

297. Reference Tokyo's 294, May 5, 7 p. m., which Tokyo has been requested to repeat to you. Department understands that the "2 million yuan contributed from the customs in areas under Japanese control" referred to in paragraph 1 of the telegram under reference is contemplated as the share of the Tsingtao, Chefoo, Tientsin and Chingwangtao customs districts which are in the area of the new "Federal Reserve Currency" and does not include Shanghai or other Yangtze river customs districts which are outside such area. With the foregoing in mind the Department desires to know whether the equivalent of 3 to 4 million yuan monthly is actually being collected at Shanghai by the customs in foreign currencies and, if so, what disposition is now being made of such collections by the bank or banks in which they are being deposited. The Department would also welcome your comment whether payment from such collections of the foreign exchange quotas of the north China ports in the area of the new "Federal Reserve Currency" would affect adversely the Chinese Government's foreign exchange resources. Also, if practicable, please ascertain whether the foreign currencies collected at Shanghai would be adequate to supply Shanghai's quota of foreign exchange in addition to the quotas of the north China ports.

In endeavoring to obtain the information desired by the Department, as indicated above, please do not disclose the information reported in Tokyo's telegram under reference.

Please repeat this telegram and your reply to Tokyo and Hankow.

HULL

693.002/650

Memorandum of Conversation, by the Secretary of State

[WASHINGTON,] May 7, 1938.

The Chinese Ambassador called upon his own request. He seemed very optimistic about the fighting in China and the future possibilities of success. He desired to discuss our interest in an attitude towards the British-Japanese arrangement relative to the Chinese customs organization. I said that we had been giving all phases of the matter every attention; that the fact we were not signatories to the arrangements but only interested in securing certain of the customs receipts did not place us in the same attitude as a signatory, but that we had been giving the matter every practical attention in the light of our situation; that we had earnestly insisted from the beginning on the preservation of the integrity of the Chinese customs organization. I said that if he desired to go into any details he might talk with Mr. Hamilton and Dr. Hornbeck, which he said he would be glad to do.

C[ORDELL] H[ULL]

693.002/643 : Telegram

The Consul General at Shanghai (Lockhart) to the Secretary of State

SHANGHAI, May 7, 1938—5 p. m.
[Received May 8—7 : 30 a. m.]

632. My number 624, May 6, 4 p. m. With reference to the report that the "Reformed Government" has taken over the Shanghai customs, the Japanese Consul General today informed the Secretary of the Consular Body that the Inspector General and the Commissioner of Customs had actually recognized the new situation. While I have not been able to ascertain whether the Inspector General and Commissioner has in fact recognized the new situation, such recognition would seem to be inevitable.

The Chinese staff of the customs threatened to walk out this morning. The Commissioner is understood to be endeavoring to persuade them not to do so and the staff is meeting to come to a decision on this point. It is understood that all foreign members of the staff propose to remain.

Repeated Hankow, Peiping and Tokyo.

LOCKHART

693.002/646 : Telegram

The Consul General at Shanghai (Lockhart) to the Secretary of State

SHANGHAI, May 9, 1938—7 p. m.
[Received May 9—2 p. m.]

633. My No. 632, May 7, 5 p. m. Threatened walk out of Chinese staff of customs was averted following statement reportedly made by the Commissioner of Customs to the staff indicating that he is still following the instructions of the National Government. Commis-

sioner is also said to have urged the staff to remain at their posts. Chinese staff all on duty today.

Repeated to Hankow, Peiping and Tokyo.

LOCKHART

693.002/651 : Telegram

The Consul General at Shanghai (Lockhart) to the Secretary of State

SHANGHAI, May 12, 1938—6 p. m.
[Received May 13—7 a. m.]

649. Department's 297, May 7, 1 p. m.

1. Inquiry made in various quarters, including the customs and the British Consulate General, fails to disclose information indicating that any foreign currency is being collected at Shanghai in payment of customs duties; hence no foreign currency belonging to the customs is being deposited in any bank except that which is being converted at the Government rate.

2. For the months of February and March Shanghai customs revenue totalled in round figures 11,800,000 local dollars and 15,500,-000 local dollars were expended in that period at the official rate of exchange for the purchase of foreign exchange to meet foreign obligations secured by the customs. With 2,000,000 monthly available from Tsingtao, Chefoo, Tientsin and Chinwangtao it is believed that the net customs revenue available for foreign obligations will be sufficient (if the Central Bank supplies the customs with exchange at the official rate as it is now doing) as under the terms of the Anglo-Japanese arrangement the present quota for the port under so-called Japanese occupation is about 54% of the total of which Shanghai's share is about 33% of the total. It is also known that revenues collected at Tientsin are increasing and are now averaging over 3,000,000 local dollars a month.

3. While the amount of foreign exchange which the Central Bank grants the customs to meet foreign obligations would not under normal circumstances be an item affecting adversely China's foreign exchange resources, it must necessarily be an important factor at present when little or no foreign exchange is accruing to the Chinese Government in the areas under Japanese occupation. The average amount of foreign exchange allowed by the Central Government each week ranges from 20% to 30% of average amount applied for which latter amount averages about 1,000,000 pounds. The Hankow authorities are becoming increasingly strict in regulating exchange and they are now beginning to designate items which may be covered as well as reducing the amounts. Japanese banks are getting very small coverage and some of the larger American and British corporations

are not able to make remittances in the full amounts applied for under the new restrictions.

4. It would seem that the question of foreign exchange for customs collections in the occupied areas rests entirely upon the action of the authorities at Hankow who administer the exchange regulations. To withhold the permits might impair Chinese Government credit and to grant necessary allotments would strengthen the Japanese hold on the customs in the occupied areas. If the Chinese make it possible to convert the customs collections in the occupied areas into foreign exchange, I believe it will be only because they do not wish to impair their credit abroad or on account of political expediency.

Repeated to Embassies Hankow, Tokyo.

LOCKHART

693.002/653 : Telegram

The Consul General at Shanghai (Lockhart) to the Secretary of State

SHANGHAI, May 14, 1938—11 a. m.
[Received 12 : 25 p. m.]

659. My 649, May 12, 6 p. m. The amount of foreign exchange acquired this year by the Central Bank of China through the sale of customs gold units for payment of customs duties, according to records furnished me by the Central Bank, has been as follows: 13,000 United States dollars and 2,781 pounds all acquired prior to March 18. Of the total about 8,000 United States dollars were obtained at Shanghai and the balance by the Tientsin branch.

The customs are collecting duties at fixed rates based on the official value of the Chinese currency.

Owing to the spread between the official rate and the open market rate existing since the currency decree of March 13, it has been considerably cheaper for importers having foreign exchange to sell it on the open market and pay duties with the resultant local currency. No foreign exchange accrues to the Chinese Government either directly or indirectly as a result of such transactions although they do serve to hold up the open market value of Chinese currency.

The spread between the official rate and the open market rate is now over 20% in Shanghai.

Repeated to Embassy Hankow only.

LOCKHART

693.002/651 : Telegram

The Secretary of State to the Ambassador in Japan (Grew)

WASHINGTON, May 14, 1938—2 p. m.

170. Your 300, May 7, 1 p. m., and Shanghai's 649, May 12, 6 p. m., Chinese Maritime Customs. After careful consideration of the information and comment contained in the telegrams under reference, the Department desires that you make an approach to the Japanese Foreign Office along the lines of the Department's telegram 157, May 4, 6 p. m.

You may inform your British and French colleagues of your action.

Repeat to Shanghai for Hankow.

HULL

693.002/655 : Telegram

The Ambassador in Japan (Grew) to the Secretary of State

TOKYO, May 17, 1938—3 p. m.
[Received May 17—6 : 31 a. m.]

316. Our 314, May 17, 11 a. m.[91] We have now fully registered our position. I am reluctantly of the opinion that further representations along these lines by us at present would accomplish no constructive results.

GREW

693.002/658 : Telegram

The Consul General at Shanghai (Lockhart) to the Secretary of State

SHANGHAI, May 18, 1938—2 p. m.
[Received May 19—7 : 30 a. m.]

680. Inspector General of Customs has received instructions from the Minister of Finance to transmit the balance of 25 million dollars local currency standing to the credit of the Shanghai Commissioner's revenues accounts with the Hong Kong and Shanghai Bank to the Central Bank of China. The Inspector General has informed the British Ambassador that "as the Shanghai Commissioner's balance in the Hong Kong and Shanghai Bank was satisfactory and been kept intact for the Chinese Government under the protection of the interested powers (notably Great Britain) it is incumbent upon me to take no action without ascertaining your attitude in this connection".

---

[91] Not printed; for memorandum of May 17 recording oral representations to the Japanese Minister for Foreign Affairs, see *Foreign Relations, Japan, 1931–1941*, vol. I, p. 743.

The Inspector General is proposing to telegraph the Minister of Finance at Hankow that in view of the political situation here, more especially with reference to the Shanghai customs issue which he states is not yet settled, he suggests that question of transfer of the above funds to Central Bank be deferred for the time being "otherwise impasse may result". He proposes to suggest that, since the balance in question has been accumulated, [and?] "has been held in safety under the protection of interested powers", their views on the subject should be ascertained before coming to a definite decision on the matter of transferring the funds.   I understand from officials of Central Bank here that the bank has granted sizeable overdrafts to the customs principally if not entirely to meet interest payments on internal loans for which the customs revenues are security.   The 25,000,000 would probably go in part to meet such overdraft.   The Minister of Finance has informed the Inspector General that the Central Bank will continue to permit the customs to draw from the Bank which will charge customs account as overdraft.

Repeated to Hankow, Peiping and Tokyo.

LOCKHART

693.002/656 : Telegram

The Secretary of State to the Ambassador in Japan (Grew)

WASHINGTON, May 20, 1938—1 p. m.

176. Your 316, May 17, 3 p. m., and 314, May 17, 11 a. m.,[92] Chinese Maritime Customs.

1. The Department concurs in the opinion expressed in your telegram No. 316, but feels it desirable that, unless you feel strongly that it is inadvisable, a *pro memoria* in regard to the matter be given the Japanese Foreign Office for the purpose of having on record an accurate statement of our position.   In such a document, it should be made clear that the American Government reserves entirely its declared position in regard to the matter.

2. If in your judgment any useful purpose would be served thereby, you might also, in such manner as you may deem appropriate, inform the Japanese Minister for Foreign Affairs that, should there be default in the service of the obligations concerned, the American Government may feel impelled, in order to clarify its position and action, to give full publicity in the United States to your approach to the Japanese Foreign Office on May 17 and to the fact that the Japanese Minister for Foreign Affairs indicated that the views of his Government differ from those expressed by you.

HULL

---

[92] Latter not printed, but see memorandum of May 17, *Foreign Relations*, Japan, 1931–1941, vol. I, p. 743.

693.002/660 : Telegram

The Ambassador in China (Johnson) to the Secretary of State

HANKOW, May 23, 1938—noon.
[Received May 23—7 : 55 a. m.]

263. Shanghai's 680, May 18, 2 p. m. Young informs me that Minister of Finance learned only within last few days of deposit of Shanghai customs receipts with Hong Kong–Shanghai Bank which apparently represents an accumulation since last November. He states that this sum could rightly have been used for payment of loan obligations, but that as matter now stands Shanghai has made no contributions to loan obligations since November, Shanghai's obligations having been met by an overdraft on the Central Bank. I understand customs agreement negotiated by British is not functioning, as Japan refuses to perform their part of agreement until Chinese turn over this balance. Young states that this sum now in Hong Kong–Shanghai Bank is causing some embarrassment in currency situation, as it has been used by bank in the form of loans, one of which was made to the Yokohama Specie Bank, thus increasing the amount of currency in circulation at Shanghai and softening the currency situation to that extent.

Repeated to Peiping and Shanghai. Shanghai please repeat to Tokyo.

JOHNSON

693.002/658 : Telegram

The Secretary of State to the Consul General at Shanghai (Lockhart)

WASHINGTON, May 23, 1938—4 p. m.

335. Your 680, May 18, 2 p. m., Chinese Maritime Customs. If you are asked to advise any Chinese Maritime Customs official in regard to action affecting the deposit in question, you should state that you do not wish to express an opinion in the matter.

Repeat to Hankow, Peiping, and Tokyo.

HULL

693.002/661 : Telegram

The Ambassador in Japan (Grew) to the Secretary of State

TOKYO, May 24, 1938—10 a. m.
[Received May 24—7 : 13 a. m.]

327. Department's 176, May 20, 1 p. m., Chinese Maritime Customs.
1. We assume that the Department does not wish us to reiterate points (a) and (b) set forth in the first paragraph of the Depart-

ment's 153, May 2, 8 p. m.   It seems to us that we have placed ourselves amply on record in regard to those points in our note of November 28, 1937,[93] copy enclosed with despatch No. 2674 of November 29,
1937 [94] and subsequent notes and conversations.

2. With regard to presenting a *pro memoria* covering the question
of foreign exchange along the lines set forth in the Department's 157,
May 4, 6 p. m., can it not be held that our position has been adequately
recorded by my oral statement to the Minister for Foreign Affairs on
May 17 and the memorandum of the conversation prepared by me immediately thereafter [95] which is on the Embassy files and a copy of
which will go to the Department by mail?   When I went to see the
Minister on May 17 I took with me a *pro memoria* setting forth the
points in the Department's 157 but I did not leave it with Hirota because as the conversation progressed I sensed that it would only serve
to increase irritation and to invite a written rebuff without accomplishing any constructive purpose.

3. At one point in our talk Hirota said: "Have you recognized the
Provisional Government of North China[?]" to which I replied in the
negative and said that in the question under discussion my Government holds the Japanese authorities responsible.   Hirota's implication, although not very clearly stated, seems to have been that we are
asking something, namely the furnishing of foreign exchange to
holders of the national currency, which is the prerogative of an independent government and that we are not entitled to demand that the
Provisional Government fulfill this function unless we are prepared to
recognize it as an independent state.   His argument while thoroughly
specious indicates that in diplomatic controversies relating to North
China Hirota will probably pursue the same tactics as he has followed
in questions relating to Manchukuo.

4. As I conceive the situation, the Japanese Foreign Office considers
that it has adequately espoused the cause of the foreign interests in the
Chinese Maritime Customs in the face of considerable difficulty with
the army which undoubtedly desired to confiscate the customs and
customs revenues in the occupied areas *in toto*.   As explained in our
285, April 29, 8 p. m., paragraph 3, and 296, May 5, 5 [*9*] p. m.,
paragraph 2, there was a moment when the issue was "touch and go"
and when the whole situation might have been lost had not the British
promptly closed their agreement.

5. Having informed my French colleague of my talk with the Minister for Foreign Affairs on May 17, I inquired whether he proposed

---

[93] *Foreign Relations*, Japan, 1931–1941, vol. I, p. 730.
[94] Despatch not printed.
[95] *Foreign Relations*, Japan, 1931–1941, vol. I, p. 743.

to take similar action with regard to the question of foreign exchange. He has written me (translation) :

"So far as I am personally concerned I do not for the present propose to raise with the Japanese the matter of which you speak. In fact up to the present I have followed very closely and have supported the negotiations carried on by our British colleague and I think that the results which he has obtained are all that we can expect."

6. I hesitate to take any step which might afford the Japanese Government an excuse, however specious, to reopen the whole question and possibly to jeopardize what has already been accomplished. The army, especially since the fall of Hsuchow, is "feeling its oats" and its future action vis-à-vis the customs as toward other matters is unpredictable, in any case, should I present the proposed document, I would anticipate a possible reply in the nature of a rebuff which might well lead unavoidably to further acrimonious correspondence with possibly deleterious results.

7. Department's paragraph numbered 2. I spoke to the Minister in our conversations of May 17 about the risk of adverse publicity in the United States. Occasion might be taken to reiterate that risk but I do not think any useful purpose would be served by using such a statement as an implied threat.

8. If, notwithstanding the considerations above set forth, the Department still desires that I present the *pro memoria*, please instruct me accordingly. I suggest that the Department may wish to consider in connection with this matter the contents of our 328, May 24, 11 a. m.[96]

Not repeated to Hankow.

GREW

693.002/662 : Telegram

The Ambassador in Japan (Grew) to the Secretary of State

TOKYO, May 24, 1938—11 a. m.
[Received May 24—7 : 34 a. m.]

328. 1. Sansom and Hall-Patch have now returned to Tokyo and Craigie sent me yesterday a letter summarizing their observations on foreign exchange conditions in North China and his views on probable results of insistence that the Japanese Government provide foreign exchange as follows:

"As regards North China the position is that the Japanese banks are at present not competing for any export bills for destinations other than Japan. This leaves the foreign banks perfectly free to acquire

[96] *Infra.*

these bills and, *pro tanto*, to finance foreign imports. As the foreign banks purchase these bills with Chinese national currency they are, in fact, providing the only support for that currency in North China, as the Hankow Government is making no allotments of exchange to Tientsin.

The Japanese authorities cannot be said to be acquiring any foreign exchange which, in the ordinary course, could be made available for the service of customs secured foreign loans. If, in existing circumstances, they are pressed to provide this foreign exchange, there seems only two courses open to them:

(*a*) To compete with the foreign banks for export bills, or, (*b*) to impose exchange control and to attempt to make the Federal Reserve Bank an effective central bank for North China. Either course would produce results inimical to foreign trade interests.

Turning to Central China there is, as you know, no Japanese sponsored currency in existence in that area, and customs duties are collected solely in Chinese national currency. It seems clearly the responsibility of the Hankow Government to exchange these collections into foreign currency for amount necessary to meet that portion of the foreign loan service chargeable to that area.

Here again if we insist, in present circumstances, on the Japanese authorities providing the foreign exchange to meet the customs secured foreign loans, they can only do so by imposing some form of exchange control, unless they provide the foreign exchange from their own reserves in Japan, which seems inconceivable. Exchange control in Central China would imply a severe restriction of imports in view of the adverse balance of trade in that area. Moreover, the Japanese would be sorely tempted to set up a new bank in Central China on lines similar to the Federal Reserve Bank in North China as a means of obtaining complete financial control in the area. If any such new bank is created in Central China, I fear it will be the final blow to the Chinese national currency and complete currency collapse would sooner or later ensue. Either exchange control or a new bank of issue in Central China would again hamper all foreign trading interests.

I quite recognize that it is most reprehensible of the Japanese to have launched a new currency in North China which can be employed in discharge of customs duties while at the same time making this currency convertible. Nevertheless, I feel that the dangers of insisting at this juncture on payment through Japanese agencies of the foreign currency necessary to meet the customs secured foreign loans may lead to measures being imposed which, on other and more general grounds, we are pointing out to the Japanese Government are undesirable and prejudicial to foreign interests."

2. Craigie feels strongly that if the Chinese Government learns that we are pressing the Japanese to furnish foreign exchange the Chinese authorities will become more intransigent.

3. We shall not repeat this telegram to Shanghai or Hankow unless the Department so directs.

GREW

693.002/663 : Télegram

The Consul General at Shanghai (Lockhart) to the Secretary of State

SHANGHAI, May 24, 1938—2 p. m.
[Received May 24—10 : 40 a. m.]

714. Hankow Embassy's 273 [*263*], May 23, noon. Inspector General of Customs informed me that he recently despatched a telegram to the Minister of Finance in which he stated that it is becoming increasingly difficult in existing circumstances to continue to withhold payment of Japanese portion of Boxer indemnity outstanding since September last and deposited in Hong Kong and Shanghai bank and that it may become necessary to ease the tension and obviate actual deadlock to consider question of releasing these deposits at an early date. The Inspector General has informed the British Ambassador at Shanghai in writing that: "I have repeatedly alluded to the impropriety of not liquidating the terms of the protocol, and resumption of the payment of Japan's share of the indemnity month by month as it falls due and if this view is supported I suggest that the representatives of the interested powers in Hankow should be advised accordingly." I shall keep the Department informed of further developments in this matter.

Repeated to Hankow, Peiping and Tokyo.

LOCKHART

693.002/662 : Telegram

The Secretary of State to the Ambassador in Japan (Grew)

WASHINGTON, May 25, 1938—5 p. m.

178. Your 327, May 24, 10 a. m., and 328, May 24, 11 a. m. in regard to the Chinese Maritime Customs. In the light of your presentation of the matter in telegrams under reference, Department is satisfied to let the matter rest for the present, pending further developments.

HULL

693.002/667 : Telegram

The Consul General at Shanghai (Lockhart) to the Secretary of State

SHANGHAI, May 26, 1938—midnight.
[Received May 27—7 : 48 a. m.]

723. 1. The Inspector General of Customs on May 24 wrote me to state that the Japanese Embassy has approached him and the Japanese military authorities are prepared to permit the resumption of normal customs procedure on the wharves in the Hongkew, Yangtzepoo and Pootung areas under certain conditions. A memorandum

submitted to the Inspector General on May 21 by the Japanese Consul General provides for the cooperation of the Japanese military and naval authorities in ensuring the payments of duty on non-military Japanese imports and in preventing smuggling under the following general conditions:

(1) Only imports customs officers to be despatched to Japanese owned wharves and Chinese wharves occupied by Japanese troops.

(2) At least one Japanese customs officer to be placed on other wharves to supervise foreign customs officers to prevent smuggling of arms and munitions.

(3) Measures to be taken at once to implement the recent Anglo-Japanese arrangement. To implement the above the Japanese Consul General suggests the prompt permanent employment of at least 85 examiners and 40 tidewaiters of Japanese nationality; also to facilitate the smooth working of the recent Anglo-Japanese arrangement, the employment of a Japanese assistant secretary or revenue accountant.

2. In his letter of transmittal to me the Inspector General states that he believes it is generally admitted that in the interests of international trade it is essential to restore normal trade conditions here and to endeavor to place the control of trade and shipping on an equal basis and he therefore suggests that the Japanese proposals merit favorable consideration.

3. Enclosure 6 to the Consulate General's despatch 1236 of February 24 on the customs situation, despatch 1272 of March 10 entitled Japanese members of the Chinese Maritime Customs and enclosure 1 to despatch 137 [*1307*] of March 30 on the Shanghai customs situation [98] supply considerable background on this matter.

Repeated to Hankow, Peiping and Tokyo.

LOCKHART

693.002/669 : Telegram

The Consul General at Shanghai (Lockhart) to the Secretary of State

SHANGHAI, May 27, 1938—6 p. m.
[Received May 27—2: 15 p. m.]

726. My 723, May 26, midnight.

1. Inspector General of Customs informs me that new rules concerning the depositing and remittance of customs revenues have been promulgated by the Minister of Finance and that these rules which are applicable to those provinces in which the customs are functioning purely under Chinese control provide that as from June 1, 1938, the ports concerned are to remit to the Inspector General's revenue account in the Hong Kong and Shanghai Bank, Shanghai, only their exact quota of the cost of meeting the installments of the foreign loan

---

[98] None printed.

and indemnity obligations secured on the customs revenue (based on the percentage duties for the preceding month), the service expenditure of the Inspectorate General of Customs and the grants regularly paid from the net revenue collected, and that the balance of the revenue collection of these ports after making these payments is to be remitted direct to Hankow for the service of internal loans.

2. The Inspector General has commented on the above in writing as follows:

"The significance of these instructions is that from 1st June 1938 revenue collected in the Chinese controlled areas will be available to meet only a part of China's foreign commitments secured on the customs revenue and that, unless I receive in time from foreign loan and indemnity quotas from ports in the Japanese controlled areas, I shall find myself unable to provide the full service of the foreign loans and the indemnity.

I propose to make during this month provision in advance for the June installment of the 4½% Anglo-German loan of 1898, due on the 4th June 1938, from revenue remittances already to hand from ports in Chinese areas, on the understanding that a proper adjustment of this operation will be made subsequently. Unless, however, in the meantime, full quotas come forward from Japanese controlled ports it will be impossible for me to meet on the 17th June 1938 the July installment of the Reorganization loan of 1913, or on the last of the month the obligations of the Boxer indemnity and the consolidation note of the United States Commodity loan of 1925 [*1931*] and 1933. In this connection I desire to point out that, whereas the estimated cost of meeting the foreign loan and indemnity obligations during July 1938, at present exchange rates, is $8,953,000, the Shanghai customs have a balance of $3,703,286.86 deposited in the Yokohama Specie Bank and of $25,287,184.68 in the Hong Kong and Shanghai Bank, the latter representing collections made prior to the 3d instant; and that at other ports in Japanese controlled areas the customs had on deposit on the 30th ultimo $16,868,367.20 in the Yokohama Specie Bank and $2,381,106.51 in the Hong Kong and Shanghai Bank. It will be understood, therefore, that if these balances could be drawn upon for remittance to my accounts there would be no immediate fear of default on the foreign loan service. I accordingly suggest for your consideration the advisability of making this situation clear to the Japanese authorities."

3. The above information was also communicated to the British and French Ambassadors at Shanghai.

4. I learn from the British Embassy that the British may propose a modification of the Anglo-Japanese agreement on the customs. I have been informed that the British Embassy made the following proposals to the Foreign Office in London under date of May [no date]:

"(1) Transfer immediately from these balances to the Central Bank the agreed quotas for Shanghai for January and February (see 5 *c* of the arrangement) and the quotas from March 1st to date for all the occupied ports as determined by the Inspector General following the agreed procedure.

(2) Inspector General to withdraw at short intervals from the balances remaining the quota due under the arrangement from the occupied ports.

(3) Until these balances have been exhausted in this manner, nothing to be drawn from Yokohama Specie Bank on account of foreign loan quotas.

(4) Costs of collection and 'customary payments' to be drawn meanwhile from the Yokohama Specie Bank.

(5) On exhaustion of the balances, further loan quota to be drawn from Yokohama Specie Bank following the agreed procedure."

5. I made no comment to the Inspector General on the matter mentioned in paragraphs 1, 2 or 4 above.

Repeated to Hankow, Peiping and Tokyo.

LOCKHART

693.002/668 : Telegram

The Consul General at Shanghai (Lockhart) to the Secretary of State

SHANGHAI, May 27, 1938—11 p. m.
[Received May 27—2 : 25 p. m.]

728.   Peiping's 322, May 26, noon.[99]

1. Inspector General of Customs has informed me that he has received information from the Commissioner of Customs to the effect that the Japanese authorities are prepared to authorize customs control north of Soochow Creek and to introduce the new tariff simultaneously on June 1. Inspector General states that if he is approached on the subject of the application of the revised tariff his position will be that he has no authority to depart from the existing tariff rates. He has inquired what the attitude of the American Government will be in the event of the "Reform Government" attempting to compel the Commissioner of Customs to collect the new rates. The Inspector General fears if he declines to comply with the demand that the new rates be collected the Shanghai Customshouse may be seized and the integrity of the customs service destroyed. He refers to the fact that he suggested some time ago to the Chinese Government the desirability of introducing the 1931 tariff on its own initiative but that no action has yet been taken.

Repeated to Hankow, Peiping and Tokyo.

LOCKHART

---

[99] Not printed.

693.002/670 : Telegram

The Consul General at Shanghai (Lockhart) to the Secretary of State

SHANGHAI, May 31, 1938—noon.
[Received May 31—7 : 35 a. m.]

736. Peiping's 321, May 25, 6 p. m.[1]

1. Commissioner of Customs informs me that, in connection with the new tariff duties, he will be prepared to accept the 1931 rates in payment of customs duties if tendered to him tomorrow. He has asked me whether I would insist that American importers should pay the old duties and I replied that obviously I had no authority to compel business men to pay the old rates if they can import under the 1931 rates, but that I would report the matter to the Department at once.

2. It seems to me that if other merchants pay the 1931 rates it would be a discrimination against American merchants if they paid the 1934 rates and that American merchants would expect most favored nation treatment. Unless I am instructed to the contrary, the matter of whether the merchants shall pay the 1934 or 1931 rates will be left entirely to their discretion. I cannot imagine any American merchant paying the 1934 rates if the local customs will accept the 1931 rates. The British attitude is substantially the same and I believe that importers of other nationalities will take the same stand.

3. I asked the Commissioner whether he had received any instructions from Hankow as to what rates he should collect and he answered in the negative. I anticipate that the Inspector General (as distinguished from the Commissioner) will ask me to inform him officially whether the Consulate General will insist upon the payment of the 1934 rates and I recommend that I be authorized to inform him that the matter will be left to the discretion of the importer himself (which in effect will be that the importer will pay the 1931 rates).

Repeated to Hankow, Peiping and Tokyo.

LOCKHART

693.002/670 : Telegram

The Secretary of State to the Consul General at Shanghai (Lockhart)

WASHINGTON, June 1, 1938—6 p. m.

357. Your 736, May 31, noon.

1. Your attention is invited to the Department's 31, January 30, 1 p. m., to Tokyo in which it is stated that this Government regards the Government of China as the only authority which can legally

---

[1] Not printed.

cause a revision to be made in the Chinese customs tariff. The Department concurs in general in your observations regarding payment of duties by American merchants but it feels that you should take no initiative in advising American merchants. If you are approached, you should inform merchants that the matter is not one in regard to which you feel called upon to give advice.

2. With regard to the question raised in paragraph 3 of your telegram it appears to the Department that the character of your reply would depend in a large measure on the character and subject matter of any letter of inquiry that you might receive from the Inspector General. If and when you receive such a letter, the Department would wish to be informed of the substance thereof before instructing you with regard to any reply that you might be called upon to make.

HULL

893.51 Salt Funds/187 : Telegram

The Consul General at Shanghai (Lockhart) to the Secretary of State

SHANGHAI, June 3, 1938—4 p. m.
[Received June 3—1: 30 p. m.]

767. 1. Dr. Lockhart, Associate Director General of the Salt Administration, informed me last night confidentially that the British Ambassador sent to the British Foreign Office a few days ago a telegram of which the following, to the best of Dr. Lockhart's recollection, is the substance:

Dr. Kung on March 24 wrote MacKillop (Counselor of the British Embassy at Hankow) that the Chinese Government would be grateful for the assistance of the British Government towards preventing by every practicable step the disruption of the Salt Administration. Embassy suggested that, if the British Foreign Office approved, it would endeavor to obtain an arrangement with the Japanese (at the same time keeping the Chinese Government fully informed in order to obviate such criticism as was directed against the Anglo-Japanese customs agreement) by which (1) the Directorate General should be maintained in Shanghai and the joint authority of the foreign officers should be fully recognized; (2) Japanese to consent to make available funds for the necessary expenses and for service of foreign loans secured on salt revenues; (3) authority of the Directorate General over district offices to be recognized and maintained; (4) if Dr. Kung should not agree to permit discussion on the above basis, efforts should be limited to obtaining assurances of continued provision for loan service through quotas as reported by the Associate Director General.

2. For the Department's confidential information, there is apparently a difference of opinion in the Salt Administration as to the feasibility of taking any steps such as suggested above or in any way

delegating any authority to the Japanese military by agreement or otherwise. A large part of the Salt Administration has already been removed to Hankow and there is a possibility that the remainder of the personnel may be required to remove there. Dr. Lockhart assures me that he will keep me fully informed of developments.

Repeated to Hankow, Peiping and Tokyo.

LOCKHART

893.51 Salt Funds/188 : Telegram

The Consul General at Shanghai (Lockhart) to the Secretary of State

SHANGHAI, June 4, 1938—1 p. m.
[Received June 4—7 : 45 a. m.]

776. My 767, June 3, 4 p. m. Associates of Dr. Lockhart informed me last night that the Minister of Foreign Affairs replied "I generally agree with the proposal." Lord Halifax [2] added, however, that he was reluctant to proceed in the matter without something in writing from Doctor Kung and he further suggested that in view of the heavy United States interests involved the British Ambassador should proceed in close cooperation with the Salt Administration and "American interests."

2. Doctor Lockhart expressed doubt, which doubt I share, that Kung will give to the British authorities any written consent to proceed along the lines set forth in my 767, June 3, 4 p. m.

Repeated to Hankow, Peiping and Tokyo.

LOCKHART

693.002/688 : Telegram

The Ambassador in China (Johnson) to the Secretary of State

HANKOW, June 8, 1938—4 p. m.
[Received 7 : 35 p. m.]

279. I am in receipt of a third person note from the Minister of Foreign Affairs dated June 6 from which I quote the following pertinent paragraphs:

"The Chinese Maritime Customs at Shanghai has recently been compelled by the Japanese to enforce an unlawful tariff as from June 1st. Japanese merchants are now paying duty according to this tariff and the other foreign merchants are beginning to do likewise. This act of the Japanese not only impairs the integrity of the customs but also decreases sharply the customs revenue due the Chinese Government. The customs revenue normally collected at Shanghai constitutes over 30% of the total of such revenue for the whole of

---

[2] British Secretary of State for Foreign Affairs.

China. If duty is collected at Shanghai and at all other places under the control of the Japanese Army according to the unlawful tariff, there will be almost a 60% decrease in customs revenue and the ability of the Chinese Government to meet its domestic and foreign loan obligations will be seriously threatened.

The Chinese Government now recommends that the receipts of the customhouses throughout the country be entrusted to an international committee appointed by the various countries interested in the foreign loans, which, together with the Inspector General of Customs, will take charge of the receipts and service the loans on behalf of the Chinese Government.

The recommendation described above is likewise entirely for the preservation of the integrity of the Chinese Maritime Customs and for the safeguarding of lawful rights of Chinese and foreign nationals. The Ministry of Foreign Affairs requests the American Ambassador to transmit this recommendation to the American Government for favorable consideration. If the levy of the unlawful tariff cannot be prevented, the Chinese Government will be obliged to reconsider ways and means for the repayment of foreign loans.

Seal of Ministry of Foreign Affairs."

Sent to Peiping, Shanghai.

JOHNSON

693.002/690 : Telegram

The Consul General at Shanghai (Lockhart) to the Secretary of State

SHANGHAI, June 8, 1938—10 p. m.
[Received June 9—2 : 05 p. m.]

798. 1. The British Ambassador has informed me that the Inspector General of Customs has notified him that in recognition of the special circumstances now existing in Shanghai with reference to the collection of customs duties and the likelihood that the present situation will continue for some time he contemplates recruiting about 22 additional examiners and 40 additional tidewaiters, all of Japanese nationality, in order to render effective control at Japanese wharves. Negotiations have been in progress between the customs and Japanese authorities for some time looking to the resumption of customs control north of the Creek and the above arrangement appears to have been a concession on the part of the customs based on a written assurance of the Japanese authorities that they are prepared to cooperate with the customs to check smuggling and generally to require all Japanese firms and individuals to pay duty on dutiable cargo.

2. The British Ambassador has informed the Inspector General that he is in agreement with the view that normal conditions should be restored on the wharves in Hongkew, Yangtzepoo and Pootung, that smuggling should cease and that all commercial cargoes and vessels of no matter what nationality should be subject to same customs

treatment. He had stated that while he is not in a position to express any views on the numbers of staff required it is expedient to recruit staff, of Japanese or other nationals, if the customs authorities believe that the attainment of the objectives requested in paragraph 1 would thereby be facilitated.

3. It is the Inspector General's intention to appoint 32 of the above-mentioned Japanese on a contract, not a permanent, basis.

Repeated to Hankow, Peiping and code text by mail to Tokyo.

LOCKHART

693.002/693a : Telegram

The Secretary of State to the Consul General at Shanghai (Lockhart)

WASHINGTON, June 10, 1938—6 p. m.

368. Please transmit the following telegram to Tokyo and repeat it to Hankow and Peiping for their information.

"Reference telegrams from Shanghai and Peiping to the Department in regard to the revision on June 1 of the Chinese customs tariff in areas under Japanese military control.

In as much as the recent revision gives rise to considerations essentially similar to those which caused the Department to issue the instruction contained in its telegram No. 31, January 30, 1 p. m., outlining its position in the matter for communication by you to the Japanese Government, we desire that, choosing whatever manner of approach you consider appropriate, you recall to the Japanese Government our statement of position set forth in the telegram under reference and state that we consider that statement applicable to the recent tariff revision.

You may in your discretion inform your British colleague of the action you propose taking and ascertain whether or not he plans to take similar action.["]

HULL

693.002/688 : Telegram

The Secretary of State to the Ambassador in China (Johnson)

WASHINGTON, June 14, 1938—3 p. m.

178. Your 279, June 8, 4 p. m. The Department desires that you ascertain whether your interested colleagues, particularly your British colleagues, received similar notes and that you obtain their views with regard to the matter. When reporting thereon, please give the Department the benefit of your comment.

It is recalled that suggestions of a similar character put forward by the British some months ago did not meet with favorable reaction on the part of the Japanese.

HULL

693.002/695 : Telegram

The Consul General at Shanghai (Lockhart) to the Secretary of State

SHANGHAI, June 14, 1938—5 p. m.
[Received June 15—8 a. m.]

838. Embassy's 279, June 8, 4 p. m., from Hankow. The British Ambassador, on reporting to the Foreign Office at London on the Chinese proposal, stated that he considers that the proposal comes too late and that it is not likely to be accepted by the Japanese Government. The Ambassador reported that the British Embassy made a somewhat similar suggestion last October but that it was not accepted by the Chinese Government and that the Chinese proposal, in his judgment, is the forerunner of a public statement by the Chinese Government that it will not in the future make good from its own funds quotas which should come from Japanese occupied ports. He holds that, in case of such a default, the Chinese Government would try to hold the foreign powers responsible on the grounds that they refused the proposal for international control. The Ambassador recommended that the Chinese Government be advised to permit the Anglo-Japanese Customs Agreement of May last to be implemented; that if such implementation takes place the Chinese Government would cancel its instructions to withhold the Japanese Boxer indemnity payments and the transfer to the Yokohama Specie Bank of part of the balances now lying in the Hong Kong and Shanghai Banks in the occupied areas; that on the other hand the Chinese Government would receive at once about $16,000,000 Chinese currency of accumulated funds and would in addition receive in future from the occupied ports their fair share of the cost of servicing foreign obligations secured on the customs.

Repeated to Hankow and Peiping.

LOCKHART

893.51 Salt Funds/189 : Telegram

The Consul General at Shanghai (Lockhart) to the Secretary of State

SHANGHAI, June 14, 1938—6 p. m.
[Received 8 : 10 p. m.]

839. Following from Tokyo:

"June 14, 2 p. m. Department's 209, March 16, 5 p. m. and Embassy's 185, March 19, 11 a. m.[3] via Shanghai. Chinese Salt Administration. My British colleague informs me that his Government has under consideration the desirability of trying to secure from the Japanese Government an assurance that it recognizes the liability of the areas occupied by Japanese forces for their proper share of the foreign loan

---

[3] Latter not printed.

quotas for the servicing of the loans secured by the revenues of the Chinese Salt Administration, and has asked me whether we propose to take any further steps in the matter.

If the Department perceives no objection, and my British colleague is authorized to proceed along similar lines, I propose to leave with the Foreign Office an *aide-mémoire* referring to our *aide-mémoire* of March 19,⁴ and stating that the American Government would welcome assurances from the Japanese Government that it recognizes the liability of the areas under Japanese control for their proper shares of the loan quotas for the servicing of the American loans secured by the revenues of the Chinese Salt Administration.

Repeat to Hankow and Peiping and to the Department as our No. 378, June 14, 2 p. m."

LOCKHART

693.002/694 : Telegram

The Consul General at Shanghai (Lockhart) to the Secretary of State

SHANGHAI, June 15, 1938—3 p. m.
[Received June 15—10:20 a. m.]

842. Following from Tokyo:

"381, June 15, 1 p. m. Department's 368, June 10, 6 p. m., via Shanghai, revision of Chinese customs tariff. Action taken by *note verbale* to Foreign Office.

My British colleague believes that no useful purpose would be served by further representations on his part and does not propose to supplement his representations reported in our despatch 2761 of February 4, 1938.⁵ Please repeat to Hankow and Peiping and to the Department as our 381, June 15, 1 p. m. Grew."

LOCKHART

693.002/696 : Telegram

The Consul General at Shanghai (Lockhart) to the Secretary of State

SHANGHAI, June 15, 1938—6 p. m.
[Received 7:35 p. m.]

845. Reference Department's telegraphic instruction 357, June 1, 6 p. m., and my 831, June 13, 9 p. m.⁶

1. Request to this office by American firms for assistance in ironing out the illegal import tariff increases affecting them are becoming numerous. Trade Commissioner Smith is now drafting a radiogram reporting that the new import schedule contains increases over 1934 schedule on 110 classifications and subclassifications, of which 24 are significant in American trade. These items will be listed, with a statement of the percentage duty increases. Authorization to discuss informally with the Commissioner of Customs methods of preventing

---

⁴ *Foreign Relations*, Japan, 1931–1941, vol. I, p. 741.
⁵ Not printed, but see telegram No. 69, February 2, 8 p. m., p. 642.
⁶ Latter not printed.

the assessment of increased rates on American goods would be helpful. Discretion to make informal representations to the Japanese authorities to this end might also prove helpful.

2. This office is informed that the Commercial Counselor of the British Embassy made informal oral representations to the Japanese Embassy on June 13 against the increased rate of import duty on butter being assessed in Shanghai under the "illegal" tariff schedule now enforced in Shanghai and that the Japanese Embassy official replied that the increase was probably the result of an oversight and quoted the increased rate of duty on sake as an example of another oversight. This information tends to support the belief that the increases affecting American trade, in some instances, for some time also have been the result of oversight.

Repeated to Hankow and Peiping.

LOCKHART

893.51 Salt Funds/189 : Telegram

The Secretary of State to the Consul General at Shanghai (Lockhart)

WASHINGTON, June 15, 1938—7 p. m.

382. Following for Tokyo: as Department's 196, June 15, 7 p. m.

"Your 378, June 14, 2 p. m.,[7] Chinese Salt Administration. The Department authorizes you, when you have ascertained that your British colleague is prepared to take similar action, to leave with the Foreign Office an *aide-mémoire* referring to your *aide-mémoire* of March 19, and stating that the American Government would welcome assurances from the Japanese Government that it is prepared to accord full respect to American interests in the Chinese salt revenues."[8]

Repeat to Hankow and Peiping.

HULL

693.002/699 : Telegram

The Consul General at Shanghai (Lockhart) to the Secretary of State

SHANGHAI, June 16, 1938—2 p. m.
[Received June 16—11 a. m.]

849. Inspector General of Customs has informed me that the Japanese Embassy has communicated to him a statement to the effect that the Japanese Vice Minister for Foreign Affairs will raise no objection to the transfer from the Shanghai Commissioner's revenue account with the Hong Kong and Shanghai Bank of a sum sufficient to liquidate the Japanese quotas of the Reorganization loans due on June 17.

---

[7] See telegram No. 839, June 14, 6 p. m., from the Consul General at Shanghai, p. 726.
[8] For American and Japanese exchange of memoranda on June 21 and August 31, see *Foreign Relations*, Japan, 1931–1941, vol. I, p. 745.

Sir Frederick Maze has informed me today that, since funds are now available for all quotas, the Reorganization loan payments will be met in full on June 17.

Sent to Hankow, Peiping and Tokyo.

LOCKHART

693.002/698 : Telegram

The Consul General at Shanghai (Lockhart) to the Secretary of State

SHANGHAI, June 16, 1938—6 p. m.
[Received June 16—11 a. m.]

850. 1. The Inspector General of Customs has informed me that strong pressure is being brought to bear for the appointment of a Japanese Commissioner [of] Customs at Amoy, together with the appointment of Japanese to practically all the important posts in the Amoy customs house. The Inspector General states that this action on the part of the Japanese represents a further attempt to impair the integrity of the customs.

2. The Inspector General has also cited as a further impairment the recent seizure of a customs cruiser by the Japanese at Tsingtao for semi-naval purposes and the recent temporary seizure of a customs cruiser at Chefoo for the same purposes. He strongly deprecates these acts on the part of the Japanese and states that their continuation is certain to result in the complete impairment of the customs service as a Chinese institution.

Repeated to Hankow, Peiping and Tokyo.

LOCKHART

693.002/701 : Telegram

The Ambassador in China (Johnson) to the Secretary of State

HANKOW, June 17, 1938—2 p. m.
[Received 7 : 33 p. m.]

301. Your 178, June 14, 3 p. m. My German and Soviet colleagues did not receive notes. Presumably they were addressed only to colleagues interested in loans secured on customs. Shanghai's 838, June 14, 5 p. m. conveys British Ambassador's comment. Impression among colleagues here is that note is intended to prepare us for Government's claim of inability to continue payments on foreign loans guaranteed on customs. This is also my opinion. It comes too late now. I do believe that we should follow suggestion of British Ambassador set forth in Shanghai's 838, June 14, 5 p. m.

Repeated to Peiping and Shanghai.

JOHNSON

693.002/688 : Telegram

The Secretary of State to the Ambassador in China (Johnson)

WASHINGTON, June 18, 1938—3 p. m.

184. Your 301, June 17, 2 p. m. and previous.

1. The Department suggests that your reply to the Chinese Government's note of June 6 embody the following points:

(*a*) The American Government continues to have active interest in the preservation of the integrity of the Chinese Maritime Customs both with regard to administrative functioning and with regard to the servicing of foreign loans and quotas.

(*b*) It is understood that British suggestion made within recent months in regard to the matter of international administration or supervision of the Chinese Maritime Customs did not have a favorable reception, and the American Government does not feel that the present offers prospects of any more favorable consideration of such a proposal.

2. When presenting your note you may add orally that the American Government would not be disposed to place any obstacle in the way of the organization of some form of international administration or supervision of the Chinese customs, provided due regard be given to American interests.[9]

HULL

693.002/696 : Telegram

The Secretary of State to the Consul General at Shanghai (Lockhart)

WASHINGTON, June 18, 1938—4 p. m.

390. Your 845, June 15, 6 p. m. The Department authorizes you to discuss the matter informally with the Commissioner of Customs and in your discretion to make informal oral representations to the local Japanese authorities in regard to the tariff increases which seem likely to affect American trade adversely.

HULL

893.51 Salt Funds/191 : Telegram

The Ambassador in China (Johnson) to the Secretary of State

HANKOW, June 22, 1938—9 a. m.
[Received June 21—7:43 p. m.]

304. Shanghai's 767, June 3, 4 p. m.; Tokyo's 378, June 14, 2 p. m.[10] and Department's 196, June 15, 7 p. m., to Tokyo.[11] The British Coun-

---

[9] Ambassador Johnson reported in telegram No. 308, June 22, 4 p. m., that the reply and oral statement were made on June 21 (693.002/703).

[10] See telegram No. 839, June 14, 6 p. m., from the Consul General at Shanghai, p. 726.

[11] See telegram No. 382, June 15, 7 p. m., to the Consul General at Shanghai, p. 728.

selor also referring to Lockhart's memorandum reported in Shanghai's 371, March 9, 4 p. m., informed me this morning that although British Embassy had received an intimation that Chinese Government would not consent to arrangement similar to that reached by British Ambassador at Tokyo and Japanese authorities in regard to customs (referred to in Shanghai's 767, June 3, 4 p. m.), he was now instructed to endeavor to obtain from the Chinese an official yes or no to this view. He referred to the fact that in March Chinese had given British Embassy assurances that it was intended to protect tenure of office of foreign employees of Salt Administration. He said that as a matter of fact such instruction had not been issued by the Chinese Government and that he had been instructed to get the Chinese to reaffirm these assurances. He stated, furthermore, that as regards paragraph 9 of Shanghai's 371, March 9, 4 p. m., British Government is of the opinion that head office of Salt Administration should be maintained at Shanghai, and I inferred that British Embassy has written to express this opinion officially to the Chinese Government.

MacKillop inquired as to my attitude in regard to these matters. I told him that we had not offered any advice to the Chinese Government in regard to the disposition of the foreign personnel of the Salt Administration; that as regards the question of obtaining from the Chinese Government its official approval or disapproval of an arrangement regarding the Salt Administration along the lines of that reached between Chairman of the Customs [*British Ambassador?*] and Foreign Office covering the customs, I was not prepared to take any action, believing that the American Government would not be disposed to participate in any arrangement of this kind, even to the point of asking Chinese consent. I informed MacKillop of action suggested by Grew in his 378, June 14, 2 p. m., and of Department's approval thereof communicated in its 382, June 15, 7 p. m., to Shanghai.

With reference to the question of where head office of Salt Administration should be located, I informed MacKillop that I did not believe the American Government would care to express an opinion one way or another to the Chinese.

Repeated to Peiping and Shanghai. Shanghai please repeat to Tokyo.

JOHNSON

693.002/705 : Telegram

The Consul General at Shanghai (Lockhart) to the Secretary of State

SHANGHAI, June 24, 1938—5 p. m.
[Received 7 : 15 p. m.]

899. The Inspectorate General of Customs has just informed this office that orders have been received by it from the Ministry of Finance

to pay from revenues collected in Chinese controlled ports only 44.66 per cent of the loan and indemnity payments secured on the customs revenues and due on June 30. Loans due June 30 include one of United States dollars 788,437 for the quarterly payment on the consolidated note of the United States consignment [*commodity*] loans of 1931 and 1933 and one of United States dollars 157,760 for the American share of the Boxer indemnity. No funds have yet been put at the disposal of the Inspectorate General under the Anglo-Japanese agreement for the loan quotas of the ports under Japanese occupation and these quotas would amount to 55.34 per cent of the total amount due. The Inspectorate General states that in a similar crisis over payments due earlier this month, Japanese authorities were prevailed upon to pay a sufficient amount from the quotas that would be due if the agreement were implemented to prevent a default and in strict confidence said that arrangements had been made with the Ministry of Finance for an overdraft sufficient to prevent a default in case the Japanese did not pay. However, both the Japanese authorities and the Ministry of Finance stated at the time, according to the Inspectorate General, that no such provision would again be made to prevent default. The Inspectorate General states that the Japanese authorities are adamant this time in their demands that the Anglo-Japanese agreement regarding the Chinese Maritime Customs be implemented in full with regard to all items favorable to the Japanese before further contributions will be made toward loan payments. The Inspectorate General states that while every effort is being made to persuade the Chinese Government to prevent a default, no assurance has yet been obtained that an overdraft will be available in case the so-called Japanese share is not provided by the Japanese authorities and confidentially expressed the hope that the interested governments would endeavor to persuade the Japanese authorities to release adequate funds from the customs collections now being withheld to them to enable full June 30 payments to be made.

Repeated to Hankow, Peiping and Tokyo.

LOCKHART

893.51 Salt Funds/192 : Telegram

The Consul General at Shanghai (Lockhart) to the Secretary of State

SHANGHAI, June 28, 1938—4 p. m.
[Received 7:15 p. m.]

919. Reference the Department's 382, June 15, 7 p. m.

1. A summary of a report made to the Minister of Finance by the Associate Director General of the Salt Administration, Dr. Lockhart,

has just been supplied confidentially to me. A brief summary follows. The full report will be sent by mail.[12]

2. The yield of salt duties had increased over the past several years to a total of $213,619,500 in the year ended June 30, 1937. Since that time, as a result of hostilities, the revenue has shrunk in alarming proportions and, despite certain rate increases, is estimated at not over $135,000,000 for the year ending June 30th this year. In consequence the continued service from salt revenue of the foreign loans secured thereon is seriously threatened.

3. The cutting off of practically all revenue from the districts occupied in whole or part by the Japanese military, together with the constant pressure for funds not only for general government purposes but especially for insuring a supply of salt to the Yangtze Valley regions heretofore dependent chiefly on salt from the seacoast, have on the one hand seriously impaired current collections of revenue and on the other greatly increased the demand upon both current collections and accumulated surpluses, so that there is grave doubt indeed whether this service can be continued from salt revenue during the remainder of 1938. The area now occupied normally supplies about 60% of revenue and of loan funds. It is sufficient to point out in this connection that the arrears of loan quota from occupied districts accumulated up to May 31, 1938, amounting to Chinese dollars 2,925,000, would, if remitted to loan service accounts, make possible the full payment of interest and amortization due in 1938 on loans secured upon and hitherto met from salt revenue, of which pounds 514,700 and United States dollars 130,500 remain to be paid.

4. In conformity with the policy of the Ministry of Finance and of the Government as understood here, the Shanghai office of the Directorate General has consistently refrained from any action that could be considered an approach to the Japanese authorities in regard to the question of a resumption of remittances of loan quotas and loan quota surtaxes from those districts temporarily out of control to the National Government, but has given earnest thought to the problems involved and has stood ready to consider the details of any proposals that might be advanced either directly by the Japanese authorities in control at Shanghai or indirectly through officials of a friendly power. Such proposals, if made and having acceptable features, might then be submitted to the Minister of Finance for decision with such recommendations as appeared to be warranted.

5. Dr. Lockhart left last night for Hankow.

6. Repeated to Hankow, Peiping, and Tokyo.

LOCKHART

---

[12] Despatch No. 1535, July 8, not printed.

693.002/706 : Telegram

The Consul General at Shanghai (Lockhart) to the Secretary of State

SHANGHAI, June 29, 1938—1 p. m.
[Received June 29—4 a. m.]

922. Reference my 899, June 24, 5 p. m., Inspector General Maze has just received a telegram from the Minister of Finance authorizing him to create an overdraft with the Central Bank sufficient to provide the difference between the amount he has available to meet the June 30 payments and the amount required to meet these payments in full. This last minute authorization was obtained only as the result of most strenuous appeals by Maze to Finance Minister Kung supported by the British Ambassador and is limited to June 30 payments [13] and no provision is yet made for subsequent payments which matter will be taken up by British Ambassador and Financial Adviser on their arrival in Hankow on July 2.

2. Repeated to Hankow, Peiping and Tokyo.

LOCKHART

693.002/707 : Telegram

The Consul General at Shanghai (Lockhart) to the Secretary of State

SHANGHAI, June 30, 1938—5 p. m.
[Received June 30—11 : 50 a. m.]

933. My 850, June 16, 6 p. m. Inspector General of Customs informs me that pressure for appointment of Japanese Commissioner of Customs at Amoy is being greatly intensified and that the Japanese have flatly refused to yield any ground. The foreign officers of the customs cruiser at Tsingtao have been withdrawn and the Japanese are now insisting that the Chinese crew on the cruiser remain aboard and continue their customary duties. This demand is creating an extremely awkward situation for the customs and Sir Frederick Maze states that the British authorities in London are becoming greatly exercised over the situation. He suggests some consultation with the British Foreign Office with a view to giving publicity to the matter.

Repeated to Hankow and Tokyo. Code text by mail to Peiping.

LOCKHART

693.002/705 : Telegram

The Secretary of State to the Consul General at Shanghai (Lockhart)

WASHINGTON, June 30, 1938—6 p. m.

418. Your 899, June 24, 5 p. m., in regard to Chinese customs. Please ascertain, if practicable, the list of "items favorable to the

---

[13] Payments were met in full June 30.

Japanese" that must "be implemented in full" before contributions
will be made by Japanese-controlled areas toward loan payments, and
inform the Department and Tokyo.

Please repeat to Tokyo.

HULL

793.94112/202

*The Consul at Tsingtao (Gourley) to the Ambassador in China
(Johnson)*[14]

No. 334   TSINGTAO, June 30, 1938.

SIR: With reference to the Consulate's despatch No. 288, of March
17, 1938,[15] subject: "Customs Preventive Ship Reported Given Protection by Japanese Navy against Japanese Army", I have the honor
to report, as of possible interest, that the Chinese Maritime Customs
preventive ship *Hai An* was confiscated by the Japanese naval authorities on June 22, 1938. The vessel was boarded while at anchor in the
inner harbor by a Japanese naval officer and a detachment of marines,
and the officer demanded that the ship be turned over to the Japanese
navy. The Master replied that he had no authority to do so, whereupon the Japanese officer threatened to take the vessel by force.
Being unable to offer any resistance, the Master and Chief officer, both
of whom are British, abandoned the ship. The Chinese officers and
crew are being retained at least for the time being.

Respectfully yours,   L. H. GOURLEY

793.94/13356 : Telegram

The Consul at Chefoo (Roberts) to the Secretary of State

CHEFOO, July 1, 1938—10 a. m.
[Received 8 : 44 p. m.]

Japanese naval forces yesterday boarded Chinese Maritime Customs cruiser *Hai Cheng* in Chefoo harbor and seized vessel ordering
British master and executive officer Theodore W. Joyce, American,
ashore. Chinese officers and crew were ordered to remain on board
under penalty court martial.

Repeated to Embassy at Peiping and Hankow.

ROBERTS

---

[14] Copy transmitted to the Department without covering despatch; received
August 13.
[15] Not printed.

693.002/708 : Telegram

The Consul General at Shanghai (Lockhart) to the Secretary of State

SHANGHAI, July 2, 1938—2 p. m.
[Received July 3—6 a. m.]

943. Department's 418, June 30, 8 [6] p. m.

1. The "items favorable to the Japanese" as the Japanese require shall be implemented in full before contributions will be made by Japanese controlled areas on loan payments are items 5 (*a*) and 5 (*d*) in the Anglo-Japanese arrangement.

2. "5 (*a*)—The arrears on the Japanese portion of the Boxer indemnity held in a suspense account at the Hong Kong and Shanghai Bank since September 1937 shall be paid to the Japanese Government". These arrears, according to the Financial Secretary of the Inspectorate General, on May 2, the date upon which the report was expected to be implemented, totaled £262,598 and 1 penny and today totals £328,247 10 shillings 1 penny, payment of which would cost $5,521,199.27 Chinese currency. With each month the agreement remains unimplemented, the amount in arrears under this item is increased by £32,824 and 15 shillings.

3. "5 (*d*)—The balance of the customs accounts with the Hong Kong and Shanghai Bank in each port under Japanese occupation shall be transferred from the account of the Commissioner of Customs at the branch of the Yokohama Specie Bank in each port at which such a balance exists and utilized for future foreign loan quota payments". The balance of customs accounts referred to under this item, according to the above-named authority, now totals $26,494,418.93. The Commercial Counselor of the British Embassy and the Financial Secretary of the Inspectorate General of Customs inform this office that the total amount to be paid from these balances to the Yokohama Specie Bank is subject to certain fixed payments [by?] the Chinese Government totaling $19,319,648.32 and also state that the Japanese authorities have agreed with the Inspector General of Customs that when they receive the check for the transfer envisaged in the same item they will legitimately redeposit with the Hong Kong and Shanghai Bank in the name of the Yokohama Specie Bank the amount of the balance left over from the transactions (which balance would amount to $7,174,770.61 according to the Financial Secretary's figures), thus avoiding an actual transfer of funds from the Hong Kong and Shanghai Bank to the Yokohama Specie Bank.

Repeated to Hankow and Tokyo by mail to Peiping.

LOCKHART

693.002/710 : Telegram

The Consul General at Shanghai (Lockhart) to the Secretary of State

SHANGHAI, July 3, 1938—1 p. m.
[Received July 3—6 a. m.]

942. My 850, June 16, 6 p. m., second paragraph, and my 933, June 30, 5 p. m.

1. Inspector General of Customs informs me that customs preventive cruiser *Haicheng* at Chefoo has been taken over by the Japanese naval authorities, that the two foreign officers have been forcibly disembarked and that the Chinese officers with one junior Japanese officer and the crew have been compelled to remain on board. Inspector General has instructed Commissioner at Chefoo to launch protest with Japanese quarters.

2. Inspector General cites this as a further impairment of the integrity of the customs service.

Repeated to Hankow and Tokyo, code text by mail to Peiping.

LOCKHART

693.002/727 : Telegram

The Consul General at Shanghai (Lockhart) to the Secretary of State

SHANGHAI, July 21, 1938—10 a. m.
[Received 1:30 p. m.]

1017. Reference my 899, June 24, 5 p. m.; and 922, June 20 [*29*], 1 p. m. The Inspector General of Customs has supplied me with copies of an exchange of telegrams between himself and the Minister of Finance regarding the August 1938 installment of the Reorganization loan due July 18 and amounting to some 124,000 pounds. The Inspector General was directed on July 14 to again negotiate with the Japanese authorities direct for approval of the withdrawal from the Shanghai customs revenue deposited with the Hong Kong and Shanghai Bank of the amount needed to make up the difference between the percentage allotted by the Ministry of Finance for payment from the revenues of the unoccupied ports and the total amount due. It will be recalled that Japanese consent was obtained for such action on the July installment. The Japanese authorities, however, declined to consider the question of advancing loan quotas or to again consent to the payment of loan quotas from the deposits in the Hong Kong and Shanghai Banks unless the Anglo-Japanese customs arrangement was implemented especially with respect to the payment of the Japanese Boxer indemnity and the transfer to the Yokohama Specie Bank of revenue balances now lying in the Hong Kong and Shanghai Bank. Consequently on July 18 the Inspector General paid the August installment of the Reorganization loan in full from funds available from remittances accrued from non-occupied ports. Copies of this exchange of telegrams are being forwarded by mail.

Repeated to Hankow, by mail to Tokyo and Peiping.

LOCKHART

793.94/13614 : Telegram

The Consul General at Hankow (Josselyn) to the Secretary of State

HANKOW [undated].
[Received August 3—11:29 a. m.]

Hankow raided by 18 Japanese bombers this morning. Bombs dropped in the vicinity airfield.

Chinese customs vessel bombed and sunk by Japanese planes yesterday 36 miles below Hankow. Customs river officer J. T. C. Crawley, British, and two members of Chinese crew were killed and several wounded. His Majesty's ship *Gnat* proceeded scene early this morning.

Repeated to Embassy and Peiping.

JOSSELYN

893.156 CH/226 : Telegram

The First Secretary of Embassy in China (Salisbury) to the Secretary of State

PEIPING, September 8, 1938—4 p. m.
[Received September 9—8 a. m.]

551. 1. At the suggestion of the Consul General at Shanghai this office asked Chefoo to investigate reported attempt to place Chefoo Harbor Commission under Provisional Government authority. The following is Chefoo's reply :

"September 3, 2 p. m. Referring to the Embassy's telegram of September 1, I learn quite confidentially from a reliable source the Japanese Consul at Chefoo has been discreetly approaching certain members of the Chefoo Harbor Improvement Commission seeking a means of placing the Harbor Commission under the puppet mayor of Chefoo. Their efforts already dominate the Chefoo Harbor Commission controlling the votes of the Superintendent of Customs, the Acting Commissioner Customs, the representative of the Chinese Chamber of Commerce and the Japanese Consul. The consular body at Chefoo would [not?] oppose the Japanese move to place the Commission under the puppet municipal authorities at Chefoo unless the diplomatic representatives of Norway, Netherlands, Finland and Italy instruct their Consuls to vote against the Japanese."

2. We suggest instructing Chefoo as follows:

"The Chefoo Harbor Commission was created in 1913 by the diplomatic body at Peiping and the Chinese Foreign Office and any proposed change in its status must properly be agreed upon by the powers concerned. Thus the question of placing the Commission under the mayor's office does not fall within the competence of the Commission. The activities of the Japanese Consul, who is the consular representative on the Commission, would seem to be irregular unless undertaken at the instance of the consular body acting under instructions of the interested diplomatic representatives. Please consult your interested colleagues and ascertain what action, if any, they propose taking in the matter."

Please instruct.

SALISBURY

893.156 CH/228 : Telegram

The Consul at Chefoo (Roberts) to the Secretary of State

CHEFOO, September 11, 1938—6 p. m.
[Received September 11—12:55 p. m.]

The Provisional Government authorities and the Japanese Naval authorities at 7:30 last night convened the Chefoo Harbor Improvement Commission and read a proclamation taking over the Harbor Commission and its property for the Provisional Government. The Harbor Commission by a vote of 4 to 1 dissolved itself. The Japanese Consul as representative of the Consular Corps on the Commission cast his vote to dissolve Commission without consulting Consular Corps. At 11 this morning Japanese naval officers called to inform me that the premises now leased by the United States from the Harbor Commission as United States Consulate have been taken over by the Japanese naval authorities.

ROBERTS

893.156 CH/231 : Telegram

The First Secretary of Embassy in China (Salisbury) to the Secretary of State

PEIPING, September 14, 1938—4 p. m.
[Received 4:40 p. m.]

Chefoo's September 11, 6 p. m., regarding Chefoo Harbor Improvement Commission. The following telegram has been received from Shanghai:

"September 13, 5 p. m. My August 30, 4 p. m. Inspector General of Customs has received the following telegram from the Commissioner of Customs at Chefoo:

'Chefoo Mayor demanded 10th September dissolution Chefoo Harbor Improvement Commission and surrender of all works and property in charge of Commission. I called emergency meeting and Mayor's demand complied with under *force majeure* by decision majority. No change intended regarding staff personnel and treatment. Letter follows.'

Please repeat to Department and Chungking this telegram and my August 30, 4 p. m. September 14, 9 a. m."

Shanghai's August 30, 4 p. m., contains the suggestion referred to in Peiping's 551, September 8, 4 p. m.

Repeated to the Ambassador. Tokyo informed.

SALISBURY

893.156 CH/226 : Telegram

The Secretary of State to the First Secretary of Embassy in China (Salisbury), at Peiping

WASHINGTON, September 14, 1938—8 p. m.

245. Your 551, September 8, 4 p. m., and related telegrams in regard to Chefoo Harbor Commission. Department desires that, upon the receipt of the information called for in the last sentence of your telegram under reference, you consult such of your interested colleagues as are available and give the Department your recommendation in regard to procedure having for its purpose the reservation of the position and rights of the various parties of the arrangement under which the Chefoo Harbor Commission was created and under which it operated.

Repeat to Chungking and Tokyo.

HULL

693.002/757

The Consul General of Shanghai (Lockhart) to the Secretary of State

No. 1688   SHANGHAI, September 15, 1938.
                                            [Received October 11.]

SIR: I have the honor to refer to my despatch Number 1639 of September 2, 1938,[16] and to transmit herewith as of probable interest copies of a letter, with its enclosure,[17] addressed to me under date of September 12, 1938, by the Inspector General of Customs with regard to the urgency of an early implementation of the Anglo-Japanese Customs Arrangement.

While the Inspector General has long been known to favor the early implementation of the Customs arrangement this is the first time that he has, to my knowledge, advocated so forcefully its immediate implementation or pointed out so boldly that Japan has already secured

---

[16] Not printed.
[17] Neither printed.

the major advantages she might expect to receive from the arrangement and that financially China has much to gain and little or nothing to lose by its implementation at the present time.

In the face of repeated Japanese warnings that they intend to treat the deposits of Customs revenues now in Japanese banks, after deduction of Customs local expenses, as surplus, the Inspector General calls attention to the danger that Japan will use these deposits as security to obtain immediate cash advances.

While the implementation of the agreement would unquestionably tend to strengthen and regularize the position of the Chinese Maritime Customs staff operating in Japanese controlled areas, this office is not yet convinced that the Chinese Government does not intend to use its failure to receive revenues from the Japanese occupied areas as an excuse for the declaration of a complete or partial moratorium on the payment of amortization and perhaps even of interest on Chinese Government loans. Moreover, under the present conditions the fact that the arrangement envisages the provision of foreign exchange by the Chinese Government to cover all out-payments from loan quota funds received by it in Chinese national currency might be regarded as a disadvantage outweighing any advantages which it could expect to receive from the implementation of the agreement.

Respectfully yours,   FRANK P. LOCKHART

893.156 CH/236 : Telegram

The Ambassador in China (Johnson) to the Secretary of State

CHUNGKING, September 24, 1938—11 a. m.
[Received 3 : 14 p. m.]

464. Reference Department's 245, September 24 [*14*], 8 p. m. to Peiping and my 463, September 24.[18] Following from Peiping:

"September 20, 4 p. m. My September 16, 4 p. m. regarding Chefoo Harbor Commission.

1. Following from Chefoo:

'September 18, 9 a. m. Referring to the Embassy's telegram of September 16, 3 p. m. regarding the Chefoo Harbor Improvement Commission. The Japanese Consul as representative of the consular body on the Chefoo Harbor Improvement Commission in a letter dated September 11 informed the Consular Corps that the Mayor of this city requested the liquidation of the Chefoo Harbor Improvement Commission and the surrender of all its property to the municipality. At the meeting of the Chefoo Harbor Improvement Commission held on September 10 the Japanese Consul, as representative of the consular body, approved the proposal of the Mayor as he believes the Municipal

---

[18] Latter not printed.

Government is capable of administering the harbor works.   The British Consul in answering the letter of the Japanese Consul claimed the action taken is *ultra vires* and reserved all rights.   In my acknowledgment I expressed surprise that action had been taken without consulting the Consular Corps and asked that my vote be recorded against the Japanese Consul's acceptance of Mayor's proposal at the same time informing him that because of the international interests involved, I have referred the matter to the Department and Peiping for appropriate instructions.   The Netherlands Consul will write to Shanghai for instructions.   The Italian Consul will do the same.   The Norwegian Consul and the Finnish Consul reported to the Norwegian Consul General in Shanghai only.   The Swedish Consul and the Belgian Consul is telegraphing the diplomatic representatives of these two countries for instructions.   The honorary Consuls because of business interests are reluctant to take a definite stand against the Japanese.

The funds of the Commission deposited in the Hong Kong [and] Shanghai Bank were held 4 days, then released on the receipt of instructions by telegraph from the British Ambassador.'

2. Following from Shanghai:

'September 19, 3 p. m.   My September 13, 5 p. m.[19]   British Ambassador has informed me that he has today telegraphed to his Foreign Office pointing out that the Chefoo Harbor Improvement Commission as a purely executive body established by virtue of an agreement between the Chinese Government and the diplomatic body has no powers to dissolve itself.   Ambassador has recommended that the Japanese Government be informed that the British, as parties to the creation of the Commission and as interested in its preservation, do not agree to its dissolution.   The British Ambassador states that the French Ambassador is making a similar recommendation to his Government. You may wish to consider making a similar recommendation to the Department.'

3. I have today consulted my British and French colleagues and [suggest?] the American Ambassador at Tokyo make representations to the Japanese Government similar to those suggested for the British and French Governments.

4. As regards last paragraph of Chefoo's telegram quoted above, the July financial statement of Commission shows a cash balance of approximately $100,000 Chinese currency in the Chefoo branch of the Hong Kong and Shanghai Banking Corporation and approximately $425,000 on fixed deposit in the Bank of Communications at Shanghai. Sent to Ambassador only." [20]

Repeated to Shanghai.   Shanghai please repeat to Tokyo.

JOHNSON

---

[19] See telegram of September 14, 4 p. m., from the First Secretary of Embassy in China, p. 739.
[20] After authorization by the Ambassador in China, disapproval of the Japanese action at Chefoo was expressed at Peiping on October 20.

893.156 CH/228 : Telegram

The Secretary of State to the First Secretary of Embassy in China (Salisbury), at Peiping

WASHINGTON, September 28, 1938—6 p. m.

Following for Tokyo:

"338. Reference Chungking's 464, September 24, 11 a. m., and previous telegrams in regard to Chefoo Harbor Commission. Please consult your interested colleagues and, if and when they are prepared to take substantially similar but separate action, approach the Japanese Government, in such manner as you may deem appropriate, along the lines of the telegrams under reference, with such changes or additions as subsequent information or conversations with your colleagues may render appropriate.["]

Repeat to Chungking and Chefoo.

HULL

893.156 CH/240 : Telegram

The Ambassador in Japan (Grew) to the Secretary of State

TOKYO, October 7, 1938—4 p. m.
[Received October 8—7 : 15 a. m.]

650. Department's 338, September 28, 6 p. m.[21] Chefoo Harbor Commission. Formal note was delivered today to the Foreign Office. The British Ambassador has taken similar action.

Repeated to Chungking and Chefoo.

GREW

693.002/761 : Telegram

The Consul General at Shanghai (Gauss) to the Secretary of State

SHANGHAI, October 16, 1938—noon.
[Received October 16—8 : 30 a. m.]

1339. Inspector General of Customs informs me confidentially that he is sending a message to the Minister of Finance through the British Embassy substantially as follows:

"The extension of the occupied areas has automatically increased the financial strain on China in respect of obligations secured on the customs and unless a *modus vivendi* on the lines of the proposals set forth in the so-called Anglo-Japanese understanding is found, the drain on China's reserves will not diminish during hostilities and will probably be increased. The Minister has already instructed the Inspector General to keep informed the interested powers (America, Great Britain

[21] See *supra*.

and France) and while executing these instructions he has been instructed to take no action likely in his judgment to be prejudicial to China's prestige or interest. As Your Excellency is aware, the interested powers are unanimous in advocating the paramount importance of maintaining the integrity of the service, in order to preserve as far as possible the various interests connected with Chinese and foreign trade, shipping and finance. The Inspector General thinks that in endeavoring to conform with this policy, a somewhat wider latitude in giving effect to the suggestions of the powers in connection with the adjustment by the customs of the service of the loans, et cetera, secured on the customs should not be opposed. If the advice of the powers in this connection is followed, the release of the accumulated Shanghai revenue now lying in the Hong Kong Bank would in effect be merely a book transaction, since the quotas due from the occupied areas for loan payments, et cetera, exceed the present balance by about 10 million dollars; and as regards the indemnity balance in commerce (pounds sterling 420,000, that is about 7 million dollars) it has already been suggested that this could possibly be adjusted by a reduction in the sum due from the occupied areas leaving the sterling balance in the Hong Kong Bank, provided, of course, that the Japanese authorities would accept such a plan. If some such arrangement could now be effected locally, the Inspector General considers that the financial interests of the Government would be better preserved for the time being."

2. Inspector General orally expressed to me the hope that we would support his representations to the Minister of Finance. I replied that I would report the matter to the Department and to the Ambassador. At the same time upon reading the text of his message I made the comment that it was not my understanding that the American Government had tendered advice as to the detailed proposals made in the penultimate sentence of his message to the Minister of Finance.

3. As Japanese military operations have now in effect closed the port of Canton and the principal customs revenue ports are now in Japanese hands, the question of the integrity of the customs and the question of foreign loans and indemnities secured from customs are becoming increasingly serious. The Chinese Government having failed to accept the Anglo-Japanese customs arrangement or to authorize the Inspector General of Customs to exercise a discretion which might permit him in effect to implement that authority without formal approval, we find a situation in which all customs revenues are passing into Japanese control and there is no release of any funds for loan and indemnity payments. More serious perhaps is the danger of complete disruption of the present more or less international character of the customs service. I am informed that certain foreign advisers of the Ministry of Finance and certain elements of the Chinese Government favor the withdrawal of the Customs Administration from all Japanese occupied ports. If this should be ordered or if the Japanese should take the position that China having or [now?] failed [to] accept the Anglo-Japanese arrangement, Japan

is under no obligation further to respect the existing Customs Administration, we would soon find a situation similar to that in Manchuria where the customs is under complete Japanese domination and control to the disadvantage of other foreign trade and interests. From the purely selfish standpoint of the interests of our trade it seems to me that we should do whatever we can to guard against such a calamity.

4. As to the proposals made by the Inspector General to the Minister of Finance, I doubt very much whether the Japan [*Japanese?*] would be willing to accept the suggestion concerning the Japanese portion of the Boxer indemnity now deposited in the Hong Kong Bank to the amount of 420,000 pounds. Will insist upon the foreign currency payment and refuse to accept its equivalent in local Chinese dollars.

Repeated to Chungking and Peiping. By mail to Embassy at Tokyo.

GAUSS

693.002/762 : Telegram

The Consul General at Shanghai (Gauss) to the Secretary of State

SHANGHAI, October 19, 1938—6 p. m.
[Received October 19—3 : 26 p. m.]

1350. In a confidential letter received today from the Inspector General of Customs he points out that in view of the imminent fall of Hankow and Canton it is expected that Japan will adopt a still stronger and more aggressive attitude in conjunction with the Chinese Customs Administration and through the medium of the "Reformed Government" may insist upon dominating the policy of Inspectorate General. He argues that should such a situation arise it would be detrimental to Chinese and foreign commercial shipping and financial interests in China. He states that treaties and circumstances have invested the Inspectorate General with an international character and have charged the Customs Administration with various responsibilities not usually undertaken by customs authorities elsewhere. These responsibilities provide for uniformity of tariff rates and equality of fiscal treatment; for the maintenance of the Open Door policy; for the administration of the Lighthouse and Harbor Department; and for the service of domestic and foreign loans. In order to protect these responsibilites, in the opinion of the Inspector General, an essential preliminary is the preservation of the integrity of the service and the continuation of the existing [Inspectorate?] system on broad international lines with equal facilities, without discrimination, for all. He therefore suggests that the interested powers may consider it expedient at the present juncture to issue a further statement to the effect that they expect the integrity of the customs and the existing constitution of the Inspectorate to be maintained. He believes that the general customs position would thus be strengthened.

Repeated to Chungking, to Peiping and Tokyo by confidential despatch.

GAUSS

693.002/763 : Telegram

The Ambassador in China (Johnson) to the Secretary of State

CHUNGKING, October 20, 1938—10 a. m.
[Received October 20—9 a. m.]

504. Shanghai's 1339, October 16, 12 noon. While we have on appropriate occasion expressed to both the Chinese and to the Japanese Governments our concern for the preservation of the Chinese Maritime Customs Administration we have not offered the Chinese Government any advice as to providing for specific method of achieving that end. I for my part perceive no new reason why we should at this time depart from that policy.

Repeated to Shanghai and Peiping.

JOHNSON

693.002/762 : Telegram

The Secretary of State to the Ambassador in Japan (Grew)

WASHINGTON, October 24, 1938—7 p. m.

359. Shanghai's 1350, October 19, 6 p. m., in regard to Chinese Customs, which has been forwarded to you by mail. It is suggested that, bearing in mind our position as set forth during the past year in telegraphic instructions to your office, you avail yourself of a convenient opportunity to discuss this matter with your British and French colleagues and that you inform the Department of the result of your discussions and of your views in the matter.

Sent to Tokyo via Shanghai.

Repeated to Chungking and Peiping.

HULL

693.002/766 : Telegram

The Ambassador in Japan (Grew) to the Secretary of State

TOKYO, October 26, 1938—5 p. m.
[Received October 26—11 a. m.]

686. Department's 359, October 24, 7 p. m. My British and French colleagues and I are in agreement that the position of our respective

Governments with regard to the integrity of the Chinese customs has already been made abundantly clear and that a further statement of our position at this juncture might do more harm than good. We believe that such a statement would be more timely if and when some further step in derogation of the integrity of the customs is taken by the Japanese authorities or by the "Reformed Government."

Repeated to Chungking and Peiping.

GREW

893.156 CH/245 : Telegram

The Ambassador in China (Johnson) to the Secretary of State

CHUNGKING, November 2, 1938—11 a. m.
[Received 11 : 54 a. m.]

532. Tokyo's October 7, 4 p. m., to the Department. Chefoo Harbor Commission. Note dated October 28 from the Chinese Foreign Office quotes communication from the Ministry of Finance reporting transfer of the Commission to the control of the Japanese Navy and asserting that the Commission should not be subject to interference by any party without the agreement of the Chinese Government and of the powers concerned. The Ministry of Foreign Affairs asks that the Department conduct negotiations with the Japanese to stop these activities. Note indicates that similar representations have been made to the British and French Embassies. I have replied that the contents of the note have been reported to my Government.

Repeated to Peiping and Shanghai, Shanghai repeat to Tokyo.

JOHNSON

693.002/766 : Telegram

The Secretary of State to the Ambassador in Japan (Grew)

WASHINGTON, November 3, 1938—7 p. m.

377. Your 686, October 26, 5 p. m., in regard to the Chinese Maritime Customs. The Department has received from the British Embassy at Washington an *aide-mémoire* over date October 29 [22] containing information substantially in accord with that contained in your telegram under reference and saying in addition that the Inspector General of Customs has received information that the Japanese Government intends in the immediate future to demand a considerable increase in the Japanese personnel of the Chinese customs service. The British Embassy suggests that in such event it might be helpful if the interested powers were to make parallel representations to the effect that while increases in the Japanese personnel in the customs

[22] Not printed.

staff is not necessarily undesirable, it is impossible, pending the cessation of hostilities and the restoration of normal conditions, to determine whether such increase is desirable.

The Department has replied that it concurs in the views expressed by you in your telegram under reference but that it would prefer to await further Japanese demands upon the customs before reaching a definite decision in regard to appropriate action to meet such demands. The Department added, however, that it was inclined to agree in principle that parallel representations by the interested governments might be desirable if and when the Japanese authorities or a régime supported by them take steps in derogation of the integrity of the Chinese Maritime Customs.

Repeated to Chungking and Peiping.

HULL

893.156 CH/245 : Telegram

The Secretary of State to the Ambassador in China (Johnson)

WASHINGTON, November 5, 1938—noon.

286. Your 532, November 2, 11 a. m., in regard to Chefoo Harbor Commission. The Department suggests that, unless you perceive objection, you inform the Chinese Foreign Office that prior to the receipt of its note the matter of the Chefoo Harbor Commission was taken up with the appropriate Japanese authorities.

Repeated to Peiping. Peiping, please repeat to Tokyo.

HULL

693.002/777 : Telegram

The Ambassador in Japan (Grew) to the Secretary of State

TOKYO, November 18, 1938—10 p. m.
[Received November 18—1 : 15 p. m.]

739. My British colleague has just sent me the following letter marked "immediate":

"I have received instructions to take an early opportunity of protesting to the Japanese Government against the taking over of the Canton customs by representatives of the Japanese naval and military authorities in the name of the Japanese Government as from 2 p. m., on the 8th November. I am at the same time to make it clear that this is a matter to which my Government attach serious importance.

Since the taking over of the Canton customs constitutes a new act by the Japanese Government in derogation of the integrity of the customs, my Government wish me first to consult you and our French colleague before action on these instructions, in case you should consider that the situation now warrants further and parallel representations by the three of us. My communication will, I think, take the form of an official note."

Please instruct.

Repeated to Shanghai for Chungking.

GREW

693.002/777 : Telegram

The Secretary of State to the Ambassador in Japan (*Grew*)

WASHINGTON, November 18, 1938—8 p. m.

392. Your 739, November 18, 10 p. m.

1. Under date November 9 the American Consul General at Canton telegraphed as follows:

"The Japanese consular and military authorities today went to the Canton Customhouse and informed the Acting Deputy Commissioner in charge that they were taking over the Chinese Maritime Customs as from 2 p. m., today.

For the present the Japanese flag will not be flown nor must any other flag. The present customs staff is asked to continue as before but documents must be shown to the Japanese authorities when asked for. They added that no customs funds now owing or here in banks may be transferred to the Inspector General without their permission. The Deputy Commissioner has asked the Inspector General at Shanghai for instructions."

2. The Department authorizes you, if and when your interested colleagues are prepared to take similar but separate action, to protest to the Japanese Foreign Office in such manner as you may deem appropriate against the taking over of the Chinese Maritime Customshouse at Canton by the Japanese authorities. You should base your representations on the ground that the reported action constitutes an infringement of the integrity of the Chinese Maritime Customs and you should reexpress the broad interest which this Government has in the preservation of the integrity of the customs.[23]

Repeated to Chungking, Peiping, Canton and Shanghai.

HULL

693.002/793 : Telegram

The Consul General at Shanghai (*Gauss*) *to the Secretary of State*

SHANGHAI, December 7, 1938—5 p. m.
[Received December 7—3 : 07 p. m.]

1465. The British Ambassador informs me that as it is clear that unless the pressure for the employment of Japanese in the

---

[23] For Ambassador Grew's note of November 24 and the Japanese reply of December 16, see *Foreign Relations, Japan, 1931–1941,* vol. I, pp. 746 and 747. British and French representations were made also on November 24 at Tokyo and again by the British on December 1.

Chinese Maritime Customs ceases or the recruiting of foreigners is resumed on an international basis the balance of the service will be seriously affected, he has now been instructed to invite the Chinese Government to agree in principle to resumption of the recruiting of the foreign staff for the customs on a broad basis. In this connection see my despatch No. 1809 of November 9th as well as my despatch No. 1813 November 15th [24] which should reach the Department in the near future.

Repeated to Chungking and Peiping.

GAUSS

693.002/794 : Telegram

The Consul General at Canton (Myers) to the Secretary of State

CANTON, December 13, 1938—6 p. m.
[Received December 13—1 : 15 p. m.]

80. Reference my 69, November 24, noon.[25] I have learned that after the return last week of the Japanese Consul General from a brief visit to Tokyo he gave assurances to the Commissioner of Customs that the control over the customs contemplated by the Japanese will be similar to that exercised at other ports in Japanese occupied areas and that the Commissioner has accepted the situation under protest.

It is understood that the Japanese have promised to protect the staff for whom quarters have been procured in the city and the customs is ready to function outside as well as in the customhouse, however, the Japanese have not thus far agreed to the exercise by the customs of control over the harbor or have they returned the customs launches which were seized shortly after the entry of Japanese troops into Canton.

Repeated to Chungking, Peiping, Shanghai. Shanghai please repeat to Tokyo.

MYERS

893.51 Salt Funds/223

The Ambassador in China (Johnson) to the Secretary of State

No. 107

CHUNGKING, December 19, 1938.
[Received March 2, 1939.]

SIR: For the documentation of the Department's files I have the honor to enclose copies of the following documents [26] that have been handed to the Embassy.

---

[24] Neither printed.
[25] Not printed.
[26] None printed.

1. Copy of a Memorandum dated October 13, 1938, from the British Consul General at Chungking to the Minister of Finance transmitting an offer of the British Government, through the British Ambassador, to attempt to obtain the consent of the Japanese Government to a temporary *modus vivendi* whereby salt revenues for loan services and the present administration of the salt revenue would not be intered [*interfered?*] with. The offer was accompanied by an expression of opinion that the Japanese would hardly negotiate on this subject so long as the Anglo-Japanese Customs Agreement had not been brought into force.

2. Copy of a letter from Mr. J. D. Greenway, Secretary of the British Embassy, dated November 23, 1938, asking for a reply to the communication listed above.

3. Copy of letter dated December 7, 1938, from the Minister of Finance to Mr. Greenway expressing the opinion that it would be inopportune to undertake negotiations with the Japanese authorities toward the object proposed while the customs question remained unsettled, but asking that the British Government continue its efforts to prevent measures by the Japanese prejudicial to salt affairs.

Respectfully yours,   For the Ambassador:
                 WILLYS R. PECK

693.002/801

The Department of State to the French Embassy

AIDE-MÉMOIRE

The receipt is acknowledged of the French Embassy's *aide-mémoire* of December 23 [27] on the subject of the Chinese Maritime Customs at Canton. The French Government refers to the Japanese Government's negative replies to the representations made by the French, British and American Ambassadors in Tokyo [28] and inquires with regard to the intentions of the American Government in this matter.

Subsequent to the date upon which representations were made in Tokyo, the American Government received information from the American Consul General at Canton to the effect that the control over the Chinese customs at Canton contemplated by the Japanese authorities is similar to that exercised by the Japanese at other ports under the control of the Japanese military and that the Commissioner of Customs at Canton has accepted the situation under protest. The American Government continues to maintain its interest in the preservation of the integrity of the Chinese Maritime Customs but, in the

---

[27] Not printed.
[28] For the Japanese reply to Ambassador Grew, see *Foreign Relations*, Japan, 1931–1941, vol. I, p. 747.

absence of information indicating that additional action would be advisable, it does not perceive that any beneficial purpose would be served by its making further representations to the Japanese Government in this matter at this time.

WASHINGTON, December 28, 1938.

[Correspondence on the undeclared war between Japan and China is continued in volume IV.]

INDEX

INDEX

Afghanistan, 81, 137
Agreements. *See* Treaties, conventions, etc.
Airplanes. *See* Outer Mongolia: U. S. planes; Undeclared war: Military operations: Bombings, *and under* Japan.
Alaska fisheries question, 28, 162
Anti-Comintern pacts: Berlin–Rome–Tokyo Axis, 296, 308–309, 316, 326, 389, 400, 403–406, 410, 439, 485; Communist view of, 247; German-Japanese agreement (*1936*), 308; German-Italian-Japanese protocol (*1937*), 308
Australia, 579–580
Austria: Influence on Japan of Hitler's action in, 124; military supplies to China, 214, 602
Aviation. *See* Undeclared war: Military operations: Bombings.

Bankers Trust Co., 526, 528–530
Belgium: League of Nations, activity at meeting of, 514, 517; "Manchoukuo," Belgian view of abolition of extraterritoriality in, 446–447; military supplies to China, 214, 592, 593, 602
Berlin–Rome–Tokyo Axis. *See under* Anti-Comintern pacts.
Brussels Conference (*1937*), convened under *art. 7* of Nine Power Treaty of *1922*, 40, 45, 144, 152–153, 374, 520, 521, 611, 702
Burma:
  Chinese National Government banking, etc., headquarters transferred to, 608
  Supply routes to China, 20–21, 115, 165, 214, 320, 364, 386–387, 592, 598, 601, 605, 608, 612; Burma Road, construction of, 530, 553, 598; railroad, 386–387, 552–553, 581
  Tariff on transshipment of war materials, 605

Changkufeng affair. *See* "Manchoukuo": Japanese-Soviet border clashes.
Chase National Bank, 559–560
Chiang Kai-shek: Addresses and policy statements, 12, 174–175, 195–196, 226, 321–322, 349–350, 356, 377–379, 380–382, 384, 389–390; attitude to-

Chiang Kai-shek—Continued
  ward Communists, 388; attitude toward Japan, 177, 263, 267; forcible detention in Sian, and release, 173–175; position in National Government and political situation, 4, 132, 134, 157, 158, 174, 221, 267, 293, 320, 349, 421–422, 427, 435–436, 519; Roosevelt, Franklin D., correspondence with, 36–37, 59–61, 312–313, 321–322, 325, 376–377; war operations, 290, 434–435, 436
Chiang Kai-shek. Madam, 381, 382
China (*see also* League of Nations; Undeclared war; *and under* Japan):
  Boxer Protocol (*1901*), 77–78, 86
  Chiang Kai-shek. *See* Chiang Kai-shek.
  Chou En-lai, 299–300, 313–314, 333–**334**
  Communists, Chinese:
    Chou En-lai, 299–300, 313–314, 333–334
    Chu Teh, 331
    Domestic policy: Economic, 389; general, 274–275
    Foreign policy, 246–247, 253–254, 388–389
    Kidnapping and release of Chiang Kai-shek, 173–175
    "Manchoukuo," activity in, 444, 454–455
    Mao Tse-tung, 274
    National Government, relations with, 115, 130, 154, 165, 313–314, 334, 365, 369, 387–389, 398
    Position in China, 78–80, 178–180, 229, 274–275, 314
    Yenan Conference (*Sept. 28–Oct. 7*), 299–300, 313, 397–398
  Cotton and wheat credits. *See under* Economic and financial matters: U. S. financial aid, *infra*.
  Customs problems, 626–752
    Administration: Inspector General, attitude and actions of, 627–631, 633–636, 640, 642, 644–645, 647–648, 655, 656, 657, 659, 664, 676, 697, 703, 704, 708, 711–712, 717–720, 724, 734, 737–738, 740–741, 743–744, 745; Japanese or Japanese-selected personnel, 633, 635, 661, 669, 703, 718, 724–725, 729, 734, 747–750; launches, 662, 673, 677, 678, 685, 729, 734, 735, 737, 738, 750

755